T0178402

Lecture Notes in Computer Science 14403

Founding Editors

Gerhard Goos
Juris Hartmanis

The series Lecture Notes in Computer Science (LNCS), including its subseries Lecture Notes in Artificial Intelligence (LNAI) and Lecture Notes in Bioinformatics (LNBI), has established itself as a medium for the publication of new developments in computer science and information technology research, teaching, and education.

LNCS enjoys close cooperation with the computer science R & D community, the series counts many renowned academics among its volume editors and paper authors, and collaborates with prestigious societies. Its mission is to serve this international community by providing an invaluable service, mainly focused on the publication of conference and workshop proceedings and postproceedings. LNCS commenced publication in 1973.

Wei Qi Yan · Minh Nguyen · Parma Nand ·
Xuejun Li

Editors

Image and Video Technology

11th Pacific-Rim Symposium, PSIVT 2023
Auckland, New Zealand, November 22–24, 2023
Proceedings

 Springer

Editors
Wei Qi Yan
Auckland University of Technology
Auckland, New Zealand

Minh Nguyen
Auckland University of Technology
Auckland, New Zealand

Parma Nand
Auckland University of Technology
Auckland, New Zealand

Xuejun Li
Auckland University of Technology
Auckland, New Zealand

ISSN 0302-9743   ISSN 1611-3349 (electronic)
Lecture Notes in Computer Science
ISBN 978-981-97-0375-3   ISBN 978-981-97-0376-0 (eBook)
https://doi.org/10.1007/978-981-97-0376-0

This Springer imprint is published by the registered company Springer Nature Singapore Pte Ltd.
The registered company address is: 152 Beach Road, #21-01/04 Gateway East, Singapore 189721, Singapore

Paper in this product is recyclable.

Preface

PSIVT 2023 marks the 11th edition of the Pacific-Rim Symposium on Image and Video Technology, a conference that gathers researchers and practitioners from around the globe to discuss the latest breakthroughs in image and video processing, analysis, and applications. This year's symposium is proudly taking place in Auckland, New Zealand, a city celebrated for its natural beauty, cultural diversity, and welcoming atmosphere. PSIVT 2023 was held both online and onsite on Nov 22–24, 2023, in Auckland, New Zealand at Auckland University of Technology (AUT), City Campus.

The conference PSIVT 2023 was organized by the Department of Computer Science and Software Engineering within the School of Engineering, Computer, and Mathematical Sciences (ECMS) at Auckland University of Technology (AUT). AUT is a leading higher education institution in New Zealand, dedicated to fostering innovation, creativity, and academic excellence. The ECMS school, recognized for its cutting-edge research and teaching, provides an outstanding platform for interdisciplinary collaboration, connecting experts from various fields to develop pioneering solutions in image and video technology.

The PSIVT 2023 conference welcomed submissions on a wide range of topics, including but not limited to:

3D point cloud processing
3D vision and modeling
Adversarial images and anti-attacking
AI-based image/video processing for autonomous vehicles
AI-based image/video processing for dynamic scene understanding
Artificial intelligence in image and video processing
Biomedical image and video analysis
Biometrics and image forensics
Caption and script generation
Computer vision
Computational photography and arts
Deep learning for computer vision
Document processing applications
Fact/claim detection and verification
Human-computer interaction
Image and video analysis applications
Image and video compression
Image and video processing
Image and video retrieval
Image and video synthesis
Image to text and text to image generation
Image/video coding and transmission
Imaging and graphics hardware and visualization

Machine learning for images and videos
Mis/Dis Information detection
Multimedia content analysis and understanding
Object and scene recognition
Pattern recognition
Remote sensing and geospatial image analysis
Robotics and autonomous systems
Video tracking and motion analysis
Virtual and augmented reality
Visual surveillance and security
Other emerging topics in image, video, and text technology

This conference used double-blind review throughout the review process. By the end, we had 75 full papers submitted to the EasyChair conference system. We received 153 reviews in total. On average, each reviewer was assigned approximate three papers to assess. After the double-blind reviewing process, 34 papers were accepted for presentation at the conference. This resulted in a 45% acceptance rate. We, therefore, grouped accepted papers in seven sessions during the three days of the conference. From the selected papers, we chose one paper for the best paper award. Additionally, we successfully invited four renowned keynote speakers:

- Tiejun Huang, Peking University, China
- Mohan Kankanhalli, National University of Singapore, Singapore
- Domingo Mery, Universidad Católica de Chile, Chile
- Richard Green, University of Canterbury, New Zealand

December 2023

Wei Qi Yan
Minh Nguyen
Parma Nand
Xuejun Li

Organization

Organising Committee

Minh Nguyen (General Chair)	New Zealand
Wei Qi Yan (Program Chair)	New Zealand
Parma Nand (Publication Chair)	New Zealand
Xuejun (Jack) Li (Local Arrangement Chair)	New Zealand
Raymond Lutui (Publicity Chair)	New Zealand

Regional Chairs

Bok-Suk Shin	Korea Polytechnic, South Korea
Domingo Mery	Universidad Católica de Chile, Chile
Fawzi Nashashibi	Inria, France
Guilin Yang	NIIT, CAS, China
Nevrez İmamoğlu	AIST, Japan
Jinjian Wu	Xidian University, China
Han Wang	Xiamen University Malaysia, Malaysia
Manoranjan Paul	Charles Sturt University, Australia

Programme Committee Members

Aarij Mahmood Hussaan	Iqra University, Pakistan
Abdul Bais	University of Regina, Canada
Aisha Ajmal	Victoria University of Wellington, New Zealand
Akbar Ghobakhlou	AUT, New Zealand
Ali Ahsan	Torrens University, Australia
Alireza Alaei	Southern Cross University, Australia
Andreas W. Kempa-Liehr	University of Auckland, New Zealand
Atiya Masood	Iqra University, Pakistan
Binh P. Nguyen	Victoria University of Wellington, New Zealand
Boris Bacic	AUT, New Zealand
Brendan McCane	Otago University, New Zealand
Burkhard Claus Wünsche	University of Auckland, New Zealand
Chiou-Shann Fuh	National Taiwan University, Taiwan
Chunhong Yoon	SLAC National Accelerator Laboratory, USA

Daisuke Miyazaki	Hiroshima City University, Japan
Daniel Riccio	University of Naples Federico II, Italy
David Berry	ControlVision, New Zealand
Dharmendra Sharma	University of Canberra, Australia
Domingo Mery	Pontificia Universidad Católica de Chile, Chile
Donald Bailey	Massey University, New Zealand
Du Huynh	University of Western Australia, Australia
Erik Meijering	University of New South Wales, Australia
Fang-Lue Zhang	Victoria University of Wellington, New Zealand
Faranak Tohidi	Charles Sturt University, Australia
Fatih Kurugollu	University of Sharjah, United Arab Emirates
Fay Huang	National Ilan University, Taiwan
Gisela Klette	AUT, New Zealand
Hamid Gholamhosseini	AUT, New Zealand
Harith Al-Sahaf	Victoria University of Wellington, New Zealand
Harvey Ho	University of Auckland, New Zealand
Huy Hoang Nguyen	Hanoi University of Science and Technology, Vietnam
Héctor Allende-Cid	Pontificia Universidad Católica De Valparaaiso, Chile
Ibrahim Rahman	Open Polytechnic, New Zealand
Jaco Fourie	Lincoln Agritech Ltd, New Zealand
Jacques Blanc-Talon	DGA TA, France
Jean-Bernard Hayet	CIMAT, A.C., Mexico
Jeremiah Deng	University of Otago, New Zealand
Jinsheng Xiao	Wuhan University, China
Jules-Raymond Tapamo	University of KwaZulu-Natal, South Africa
Junjie Cao	Dalian University of Technology, China
Kaier Wang	Volpara Health Technologies, New Zealand
Kar-Ann Toh	Yonsei University, South Korea
Kaushik Roy	West Bengal State University, India
Kourosh Neshatian	University of Canterbury, New Zealand
Krishna Raghuwaiya	University of the South Pacific, Suva, Fiji
Lee Streeter	University of Waikato, New Zealand
Li Cheng	University of Alberta, Canada
Lihong Zheng Charles	Sturt University, Australia
Loulin Huang	AUT, New Zealand
Mahdi Setayesh	Microsoft, USA
Manoranjan Paul	Charles Sturt University, Australia
Mansoor Ebrahim	Iqra University, Pakistan
Mariano Rivera Meraz	Gobierno De México, Mexico
Martin Stommel	AUT, New Zealand

Michael Cree	University of Waikato, New Zealand
Minh Nguyen	AUT, New Zealand
Muhammad Rafiqul Islam	Melbourne Institute of Technology, Australia
Mukesh Prasad	University of Technology Sydney, Australia
Mukku Nisanth Karthee	VIT University, India
Parma Nand	AUT, New Zealand
Pascal Peter	Saarland University, Germany
Patrice Delmas	University of Auckland, New Zealand
Peter Chong	AUT, New Zealand
Qurrat Ul Ain	Victoria University of Wellington, New Zealand
Raghavendra Bhalerao	Institute of Infrastructure, Technology, Research and Management, Ahmedabad, India
Ramesh Rayudu	Victoria University of Wellington, New Zealand
Raymond Lutui	AUT, New Zealand
Richard Clare	University of Canterbury, New Zealand
Ryszard Kozera	Warsaw University of Life Sciences, Poland
Sanjoy Pratihar	Indian Institute of Information Technology Kalyani, India
Sarbani Palit	Indian Statistical Institute, India
Shang-Hong Lai	National Tsing Hua University, Taiwan
Shihua Zhou	Dalian University, China
Shilpa Gite	Symbiosis Institute of Technology, Pune, India
Shmuel Peleg	Hebrew University of Jerusalem, Israel
Shuhei Tarashima	NTT Communications Corporation, Japan
Sobhan Kanti Dhara	National Institute of Technology Rourkela, India
Subrata Chakraborty	University of New England, Australia
Thanh Hai Tran	Hanoi University of Science and Technology, Vietnam
Thi-Lan Le	Hanoi University of Science and Technology, Vietnam
Vijay John	RIKEN, Japan
Wang Han	Xiamen University Malaysia, Malaysia
Wei Qi Yan	AUT, New Zealand
Xinyi Gao	AUT, New Zealand
Xiping Fu	PredictHQ, New Zealand
Xuejun Li	AUT, New Zealand
Yalin Zheng	University of Liverpool, UK
Yasushi Yagi	Osaka University, Japan
Ying Bi	Victoria University of Wellington, New Zealand
Yuanyuan (Derek) Zhang	Auckland Transport, New Zealand
Zezhong Xu	Changzhou Institute of Technology, China
Zhixun Su	Dalian University of Technology, China

Sponsors

Department of Computer Science & Software Engineering @ AUT
School of Engineering, Computer & Mathematical Sciences @AUT

Contents

Evaluating Mammogram Image Classification: Impact of Model Architectures, Pretraining, and Finetuning

Kaier Wang$^{(\boxtimes)}$ (ID), Aristarkh Tikhonov (ID), Melissa Hill (ID), and Lester Litchfield (ID)

Volpara Health Technologies, Wellington, New Zealand
{kyle.wang,aristarkh.tikhonov,melissa.hill,
lester.litchfield}@volparahealth.com

Abstract. This study conducts a thorough evaluation of deep learning architectures, pretraining methods, and finetuning approaches for mammogram classification for tissue density. No architecture was distinctly superior. However, models pretrained on ImageNet consistently surpassed those trained on custom mammogram datasets. Finetuning strategies played a crucial role in model performance. In particular, finetuning the entire model yielded better results. Investigation of confusion matrices revealed that most misclassifications occurred within a one-grade difference, but severe misclassifications were observed in certain configurations. While some architectures offered comparable performance, trade-offs between model performance and computational efficiency were observed, with convolutional neural networks showing faster inference times on CPUs compared to vision transformers.

Keywords: Mammogram · Breast density · Classification

1 Introduction

Digital mammography aids in discerning breast tissue density, a crucial risk factor for detecting cancer due to the obscuring effect of dense tissue [16]. Traditionally, radiologists utilised the subjective Breast Imaging-Reporting and Data System (BI-RADS) classification, which is susceptible to inter- and intra-reader variability [1]. This led to the development of automated methods, such as volumetric breast density calculation, using software tools like Quantra and Volpara [21], enhancing standardisation and reliability in clinical practice.

Deep learning methodologies have significantly transformed the landscape of breast density classification, shifting from conventional computer vision techniques to data-centric approaches that deduce hierarchical representations from mammography images. Most advanced models focus on BI-RADS classification [17]. Convolutional Neural Networks (CNNs) exhibit potential in identifying patterns in digital mammograms, with studies highlighting the benefits of combining

W. Q. Yan et al. (Eds.): PSIVT 2023, LNCS 14403, pp. 1–14, 2024.
https://doi.org/10.1007/978-981-97-0376-0_1

AI algorithms with radiologists' expertise [31]. The practice of transfer learning, involving the use of pre-trained models on extensive non-medical image datasets and fine-tuning them on mammographic images, has improved classification performance [3].

Recent deep learning developments have highlighted the use of Vision Transformer (ViT) in mammogram classification, specifically in distinguishing between benign and cancerous cases [2]. ViTs handle image patches as a token sequence, excelling in global feature learning and producing impressive results. A comparison of transformers and CNNs further confirmed ViT's superior performance [6]. Pre-training, particularly on the ImageNet dataset, is crucial in achieving superior performance [24]. Masked autoencoders, a novel pre-training method, learn by predicting missing parts of the input, fostering rich internal data representations. This method, combined with self-supervised pre-training, has emerged as a promising approach for medical imaging [7,15].

This paper provides a comprehensive examination of various architectures, particularly CNNs and ViTs, for categorising breast density from digital mammograms. We also explore different pre-training methods and fine-tuning strategies. A novel aspect of our work is the development and application of a unique image pre-processing approach. We utilise a custom gamma correction to normalise raw mammogram images, a method that notably contributes to the standardisation and consistency of the images processed from various mammography systems. This innovative approach, validated in our previous work [28], has significant potential for enhancing the performance of deep learning models in classifying breast density

The paper is structured as follows: the Data Collection and Annotation section details the datasets used for pre-training and fine-tuning; Experiment Settings discusses the chosen architectures, pre-training methods, and fine-tuning strategies; Results presents the findings, comparing the performance of different methods; and the Discussion section interprets the results, considering potential implications and future research directions.

2   Data Collection and Annotation

This study leverages a substantial dataset of anonymised mammogram images and the FDA-approved Volpara algorithm to train and assess deep learning models, aiming to enhance the accuracy and reliability of machine learning applications in clinical mammography.

2.1   Image Dataset Acquisition

The de-identified image data, collected from multiple health institutions in the United States, comprises a substantial collection of 8,165 raw (for-processing) mammogram images from three X-ray systems: GE, Hologic, and Siemens Inspiration. Each system has a distinct resolution and millimeters per pixel rate, with GE images featuring a resolution of 2,294 × 1,914 and 0.1 mm per pixel, Hologic

Table 1. Reported mammogram datasets (see [22] for a comprehensive overview).

Dataset	No. of Images	Mode of Image Acquisition
DDSM [12]	10,480	digitised film mammograms
MIAS [25]	322	digitised film mammograms
INbreast [20]	410	full-field digital mammography (processed images)
VinDr-Mammo [22]	20,000	full-field digital mammography (processed images)

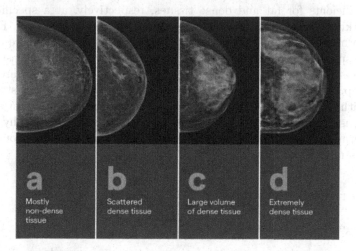

Fig. 1. Representative mammographic images illustrating Volpara Density Grade™, supplied by Volpara Health Technologies.

images offering a resolution of 4,096 × 3,328 and 0.07 mm per pixel, and Siemens Inspiration images providing a resolution of 3,506 × 2,800 and 0.085 mm per pixel. This dataset is potentially one of the more substantial raw mammogram collections initially reported for training and evaluating deep learning models, as compared to other datasets summarized in Table 1. However, it is important to consider the potential existence of larger raw mammogram datasets that might not have been covered in this analysis.

2.2 Annotation

In this study, mammogram image data annotation was conducted using the Volpara® algorithm v3.4.0, an FDA-cleared and widely accepted algorithm for clinical applications that offers automated, objective measures of breast density [27]. The algorithm calculates volumetric breast density by estimating the volume of fibroglandular tissue and the total breast volume. The ratio of these volumes is then utilised to assign a Volpara Density Grade™ (VDG), which correlates with the four categories of BI-RADS (5th edition) density classification as seen in Fig. 1.

The Volpara® algorithm identifies a region of the breast in contact with the compression paddle, consisting entirely of fatty tissue, denoted as P^{fat}. This region serves as a reference level for calculating dense tissue thickness h^{dt} at each pixel location (x, y) using Eq.(1) [16]:

$$h^{dt}(x, y) = \frac{\ln(P(x, y)/P^{fat})}{\mu^{fat} - \mu^{dt}} , \tag{1}$$

where $P(x, y)$ represents the pixel value, linearly correlated to the energy imparted to the x-ray detector. μ^{fat} and μ^{dt} denote the effective linear attenuation coefficients for fat and dense tissues, respectively, at a specified peak potential (kilovoltage peak, or kVp) applied to the x-ray tube [13]. Equation (1) transforms a raw mammographic image into a density map, where the pixel value corresponds to the dense tissue thickness. The volumetric breast density is subsequently computed through integration over the entire breast area in the density map. The VolparaDensity™ algorithm results demonstrate a strong correlation with ground truth readings (magnetic resonance imaging data) [27] and exhibits consistent density measurements across various mammography systems [8]. Furthermore, VolparaDensity™ has been utilised as the density ground truth in several studies [18, 23, 30]

3   Experiment Settings

3.1   Image Pre-processing

Digital mammography generates two image types: *raw* and *processed*. Raw images, acquired with minor technical adjustments like pixel calibration and inhomogeneity correction, are modified into processed images through manufacturer-specific algorithms, enhancing contrast for improved lesion detection by the human eye. However, this processing may cause the same breast to appear differently on two x-ray systems, as illustrated in Fig. 2. As reported by [29], deep learning models trained on processed images from one manufacturer may not transfer well to external datasets, possibly due to image inconsistency. In comparison, raw images preserve the original detector response information, making them ideal for further processing to achieve consistent contrast and visual appearance across various mammography systems.

In this study, we employed custom gamma correction to normalise raw mammogram images. For a given raw image I^{raw}, we applied a logarithm transform, as shown in Eq. (2) [19], to brighten breast object intensities:

$$I^{ln} = \ln(I^{raw} + 1.0). \tag{2}$$

Next, we applied gamma correction Eq. (3) to the log-transformed image:

$$I^{gamma} = [(I^{ln} - I^{ln}_{min})/(I^{ln}_{max} - I^{ln}_{min})]^{1/2} \tag{3}$$

Here, I^{ln}_{min} and I^{ln}_{max} represent the minimum and maximum pixel values in the breast region of I^{ln}. The breast region was identified using a segmentation map (Fig. 3) that labelled the pectoral muscle, fully compressed, and peripheral

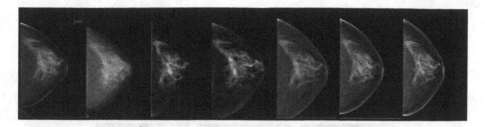

Fig. 2. Mammograms of the same patient over seven consecutive years, presented as processed images from three distinct mammography systems (left to right): Hologic, GE, Hologic, Hologic, Siemens, Siemens, Siemens. The processed images exhibit considerable variation due to the system-specific characteristics and image processing techniques.

Fig. 3. Compressed breast during mammography (left) and its mammographic segmentation in craniocaudal (middle) and mediolateral oblique (right) views. Compressed region (white), pectoral muscle (light gray), periphery (dark gray), and directly exposed x-ray area (black) are colour labelled. (Color figure online)

regions, generated by VolparaDensity™ software. The segmentation accuracy was validated by Branderhorst et al. [4].

Figure 4 illustrates preprocessed images employing our gamma correction technique on raw images from three X-ray systems. Despite identical intensity ranges, the Siemens Inspiration image is distinctly brighter, rendering dense tissues barely discernible. Upon correction, visualisation becomes more uniform, offering enhanced contrast. Our prior work [28] suggested the proposed gamma correction as an efficient, straightforward preprocessing approach for segmenting breast arterial calcifications from raw images.

3.2 Dataset Split

We employed stratified sampling based on three criteria: X-ray system, VDG, and breast volume. Breast volume is calculated using the Volpara® algorithm, which provides physics modelling of the breast shape after compression. Based on the analysis of more than 26 million mammogram images, we empirically determined thresholds for classifying breast volume into three categories: low ($< 565 \, \text{cm}^3$, labelled as 0), average (565–$1315 \, \text{cm}^3$, labelled as 1), and high ($> 1315 \, \text{cm}^3$, labelled as 2). The data were divided into training, validation, and testing sets at an 80%, 10%, and 10% ratio, respectively. Stratified sampling

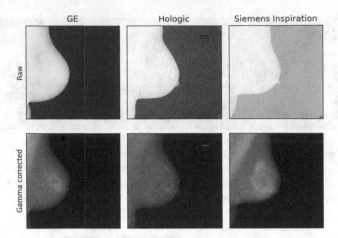

Fig. 4. Examples of normalising raw images from three different xray systems using simple gamma correction. The 16-bit raw images (first row) are displayed in the same range of [50000, 65535] for better visibility, and the gamma corrected images are shown in the full [0, 65535] range.

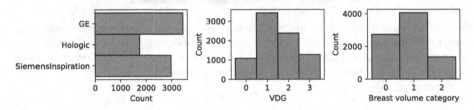

Fig. 5. Data distribution across X-ray systems, VDG, and breast volume categories for the entire dataset.

ensured each subset maintained the same distribution of X-ray system, VDG, and breast volume as the entire dataset. The complete dataset's distribution is displayed in Fig. 5.

3.3 Pretraining Methods

Pretraining is a key strategy in deep learning, serving as an initial phase where a model is trained on a broad, extensive dataset before undergoing fine-tuning on a smaller, task-focused dataset. This study investigates two pretraining methods using weights pretrained on the ImageNet-1K dataset and a third method using a custom mammogram dataset.

The first two methods, which involve weights pretrained on ImageNet-1K, were obtained from PyTorch (ver. 1.12.1) and the original masked autoencoder study [11]. The methods include supervised classification and a masked autoencoder. The supervised classification approach instructs the model to predict class labels of the ImageNet-1K dataset, enabling the model to learn a comprehensive range of features. The masked autoencoder method trains the model to reconstruct original images from partially masked versions, encouraging the learning of structural and content-based features.

The third pretraining method, implemented by us, used a masked autoencoder on a custom mammogram dataset (i.e. the training set in Sect. 3.2). This method enabled learning features that are more specific and potentially more relevant to mammogram image classification.

3.4 Model Architectures

This study utilised three cutting-edge deep learning architectures for classifying mammogram images based on VDG: EfficientNet-B0 [26], MobileNet V3 Large [14], and ViT Large (ViT-L, specifically ViT-L-16) [9]. All architectures were constructed using PyTorch 1.12.1.

EfficientNet-B0, part of the EfficientNet family, is known for its optimal balance between model size and performance. As the baseline model in this series, it offers a good compromise between computational cost and accuracy.

MobileNet V3 Large, from the MobileNet family, is designed for mobile and embedded vision applications. This large variant provides increased accuracy at the cost of higher computational demands compared to other MobileNet models.

ViT Large (ViT-L) is part of the ViT family, a new class of models applying transformer architectures-commonly used in natural language processing-to vision tasks. The Large variant of ViT delivers high performance but requires more computational resources.

Each architecture was tested with different pretraining and fine-tuning approaches to assess their effectiveness in VDG classification for mammogram images.

3.5 Training Settings

The input mammograms are 16-bit, grayscale images. These images underwent contrast normalisation using the method in Sect. 3.1, followed by an 8-bit RGB conversion (by repeating the single channel three times) and an ImageNet-based pixel value redistribution to achieve a mean of $[0.485, 0.456, 0.406]$ and a standard deviation of $[0.229, 0.224, 0.225]$. The images were further downsampled to 224×224 to fit the default setting of ViT.

We also implemented common augmentations, such as blurring the image with a random-sized kernel, random affine transformations, and random brightness and contrast adjustments [5].

During the training process, the validation loss was assessed after each epoch. The learning rate was adjusted by reducing it by a factor of 10 if the validation loss exhibited no improvement for five consecutive epochs. The training was terminated if there was no improvement in validation loss after 10 epochs. The model corresponding to the best validation loss was retained. This optimal model was subsequently evaluated on the test dataset, with the F1 score and confusion matrices calculated for comparative purposes.

4   Results

Table 2 presents a comprehensive summary of the experimental results, which provides insights into the impact of different model architectures, pretraining data sources, pretraining methods, and finetuning approaches on the mammogram image classification task, as evaluated by the F1 score.

Figure 6(a) presents the F1 scores achieved by three distinct architectures: EfficientNet-B0, MobileNet V3 Large, and ViT-L. The average F1 scores for these architectures were approximately 0.773, 0.779, and 0.787, respectively. A one-way ANOVA test was conducted to compare the performance of these architectures, yielding an F-statistic of approximately 0.072 and a p-value of approximately 0.931. These results suggest no statistically significant difference in the performance among the three architectures for this classification task.

The source of pretraining data, however, influenced the model performance (Fig. 6(b)). Models pretrained with ImageNet-1K, a considerably larger dataset, achieved a higher average F1 score (approximately 0.790) compared to those pretrained on the custom mammogram dataset (approximately 0.764) or trained from scratch (approximately 0.757). This suggests that a larger, more diverse pretraining dataset provides a more effective set of initial weights for this classification task. The reduced performance could also be attributed to the size of the custom mammogram dataset, which will be investigated in our future work.

Figure 6(c) illustrates the influence of pretraining methods on model performance. The Masked Autoencoder plus Generative Adversarial Networks (MAE + GAN) approach, proposed by Fei et al. [10], yielded a higher average F1 score (approximately 0.802) compared to the Masked Autoencoder alone. This method entails utilising a generator to produce masked patches and a discriminator to differentiate between synthesized and original patches within a ViT backbone. However, it is important to note that the supervised classification task on ImageNet-1K outperformed both of these methods, achieving the best F1 score among the pretraining methods.

The choice of finetuning approach, whether to finetune the entire model or only the classification head, also impacts model performance, as shown in Fig. 6(d). When finetuning the whole model, MobileNet V3 Large achieved the highest average F1 score (approximately 0.818). However, when only the classification head was finetuned, ViT-L achieved the highest average F1 score (approximately 0.755).

5   Discussion

Despite the insights afforded by the classification F1 score, it does not fully capture the nuances of model misclassifications. For a more granular understanding, we turn to the confusion matrices of each experimental configuration in Fig. 7.

Table 2. Comparison of architectures with different pretraining and finetuning methods on test F1 scores for breast density classification. Model without pretraining step is marked as N/A.

Architecture	Pretrain		Finetune		Test F1
	Data	Method	Full	Head	
EfficientNet-B0	ImageNet-1K	Classification	x		0.8414
EfficientNet-B0	ImageNet-1K	Classification		x	0.6937
EfficientNet-B0	N/A	N/A	x		0.7828
MobileNet V3 Large	ImageNet-1K	Classification	x		0.8361
MobileNet V3 Large	ImageNet-1K	Classification		x	0.7018
MobileNet V3 Large	N/A	N/A	x		0.7999
ViT-L	ImageNet-1K	MAE	x		0.8180
ViT-L	ImageNet-1K	MAE + GAN	x		0.8297
ViT-L	ImageNet-1K	MAE		x	0.7628
ViT-L	ImageNet-1K	MAE + GAN		x	0.7742
ViT-L	Custom	MAE	x		0.7994
ViT-L	Custom	MAE		x	0.7286
ViT-L	ImageNet-1K	Classification	x		0.8493
ViT-L	N/A	N/A	x		0.7310

Examination of the confusion matrices reveals that most misclassifications occur within a one-grade difference, aligning with the relatively high F1 scores. Such misclassifications, while not ideal, may be acceptable in a clinical context as they are unlikely to significantly alter patient management. However, instances of severe misclassifications, denoting a grade difference of more than 2, do occur and pose a potential risk of drastically altering patient management.

A closer look reveals that certain configurations, specifically 'MobileNet V3 Large with ImageNet pretraining, classification pretraining method, and finetuning only the classification head' and 'ViT-L with custom mammogram data pretraining, MAE pretraining method, and finetuning only the classification head' exhibit higher instances of severe misclassifications. This observation suggests that finetuning only the classification head may be less effective for these architectures.

The model's inference speed on the CPU is another crucial factor to consider in real-world clinical applications. In the context of a typical Picture Archiving and Communication System (PACS) in a hospital setting, GPUs are often not available due to higher cost and maintenance requirements. As a result, models must be able to run efficiently on CPUs. Table 3 presents the CPU inference time

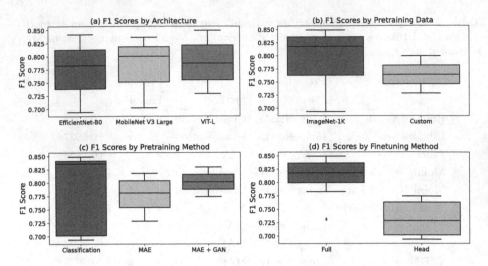

Fig. 6. Box plots showing the distribution of F1 scores for (a) different architectures, (b) pretraining data sources, (c) pretraining methods, and (d) finetuning method.

Table 3. Comparing CPU (AMD EPYC 7V12) inference time across architectures

Architecture	CPU inference time (sec/image)
EfficientNet-B0	0.0218
MobileNet V3 Large	0.0151
ViT-L	0.1642

for each of the architectures examined in our study. Notably, both EfficientNet-B0 and MobileNet V3 Large achieve relatively fast inference times of 0.0218 and 0.0151 s per image, respectively. However, the ViT-L, despite its competitive performance in terms of F1 score, requires significantly more time, with an inference time of 0.1642 s per image. This suggests a trade-off between model performance and computational efficiency. While transformer-based models like ViT-L can achieve high performance, they may not be as practical for deployment in certain resource-constrained settings like PACS. Conversely, CNNs, including EfficientNet-B0 and MobileNet V3 Large, provide a more practical solution due to their accelerated CPU inference times (approximately 7.5 and 10.9 times faster than ViT-L, respectively), despite marginally lower performance compared to ViT-L.

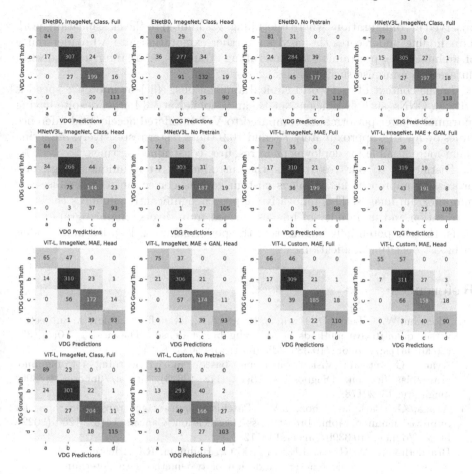

Fig. 7. Confusion matrices for different model configurations corresponding to Table 2. Each sub-figure corresponds to a specific combination of model architecture, pretraining data, pretraining method, and finetuning method.

6 Conclusion

This study provides an extensive evaluation of various architectures, pretraining methods, and finetuning approaches in the context of mammogram image classification. The F1 scores obtained indicate that ImageNet-1K, as a source of pretraining data, has the potential to offer beneficial initial model weights, even when the target task significantly deviates from the original pretraining task. Although no architecture was found to be unequivocally superior, the interplay of pretraining data, pretraining method, and the extent of finetuning can result in varying performance outcomes.

The examination of confusion matrices indicated that most misclassifications were restricted to a one-grade difference. However, a noteworthy occurrence of severe misclassifications, with a grade difference exceeding 2, was predominantly observed in configurations where finetuning was limited to the classification head. This finding underscores the need for further exploration into a broader range of architectures, pretraining and finetuning strategies, and larger, more diverse datasets to minimise such misclassifications.

In the context of real-world clinical applications, efficient inference speed is critical. CNNs, such as EfficientNet-B0 and MobileNet V3 Large, despite having marginally lower performance compared to ViT-L, offered accelerated inference times on a CPU, approximately 7.5 and 10.9 times faster respectively, rendering them more feasible for deployment in resource-constrained settings.

Distinctive to our research is the introduction of a unique image pre-processing approach that employs custom gamma correction to normalise raw mammogram images. This innovative approach significantly enhances the standardisation and uniformity of images derived from diverse mammography systems, thereby potentially augmenting the performance of deep learning models in breast density classification.

References

1. Alomaim, W., O'Leary, D., Ryan, J., Rainford, L., Evanoff, M., Foley, S.: Subjective versus quantitative methods of assessing breast density. Diagnostics **10**(5), 331 (2020). https://doi.org/10.3390/diagnostics10050331
2. Ayana, G., et al.: Vision-transformer-based transfer learning for mammogram classification. Diagnostics **13**(2), 178 (2023). https://doi.org/10.3390/diagnostics13020178
3. Ayana, G., Park, J., Choe, S.W.: Patchless multi-stage transfer learning for improved mammographic breast mass classification. Cancers **14**(5), 1280 (2022). https://doi.org/10.3390/cancers14051280
4. Branderhorst, W., Groot, J.E., Lier, M.G., Highnam, R.P., Heeten, G.J., Grimbergen, C.A.: Technical note: Validation of two methods to determine contact area between breast and compression paddle in mammography. Med. Phys. **44**(8), 4040–4044 (2017). https://doi.org/10.1002/mp.12392
5. Buslaev, A., Iglovikov, V.I., Khvedchenya, E., Parinov, A., Druzhinin, M., Kalinin, A.A.: Albumentations: fast and flexible image augmentations. Information **11**(2), 125 (2020). https://doi.org/10.3390/info11020125
6. Cantone, M., Marrocco, C., Tortorella, F., Bria, A.: Convolutional networks and transformers for mammography classification: an experimental study. Sensors (Basel, Switzerland) **23**(3), 1229 (2023). https://doi.org/10.3390/s23031229
7. Chen, Z., et al.: Multi-modal masked autoencoders for medical vision-and-language pre-training. In: Wang, L., Dou, Q., Fletcher, P.T., Speidel, S., Li, S., (Eds.), Medical image computing and computer assisted intervention - MICCAI 2022, pp. 679–689. Lecture Notes in Computer Science. Springer Nature Switzerland (2022). https://doi.org/10.1007/978-3-031-16443-9_65
8. Damases, C.N., Brennan, P.C., McEntee, M.F.: Mammographic density measurements are not affected by mammography system. J. Med. Imaging **2**(1), 015501 (2015). https://doi.org/10.1117/1.JMI.2.1.015501
9. Dosovitskiy, A., et al.: An image is worth 16 × 16 words: transformers for image recognition at scale. In: Proceedings of the International Conference on Learning Representations (2020)

10. Fei, Z., Fan, M., Zhu, L., Huang, J., Wei, X., Wei, X.: Masked auto-encoders meet generative adversarial networks and beyond. In: Proceedings of the IEEE/CVF Conference on Computer Vision and Pattern Recognition, pp. 24449–24459 (2023)
11. He, K., Chen, X., Xie, S., Li, Y., Dollar, P., Girshick, R.: Masked autoencoders are scalable vision learners. In: Proceedings of the IEEE/CVF Conference on Computer Vision and Pattern Recognition (CVPR), pp. 15979–15988. IEEE (2022). https://doi.org/10.1109/CVPR52688.2022.01553
12. Heath, M., Bowyer, K., Kopans, D., Moore, R., Jr, P.K. The digital database for screening mammography. In: Proceedings of the Fifth International Workshop on Digital Mammography, pp. 212–218. Medical Physics Publishing (2001)
13. Highnam, R., Brady, J.M.: Mammographic Image Analysis. Computational Imaging and Vision, Springer, Netherlands (1999). https://doi.org/10.1007/978-94-011-4613-5
14. Howard, A., et al.: Searching for MobileNetV3. In: Proceedings of the IEEE/CVF International Conference on Computer Vision (ICCV), pp. 1314–1324. IEEE Computer Society (2019). https://doi.org/10.1109/ICCV.2019.00140
15. Huang, S.C., Pareek, A., Jensen, M., Lungren, M.P., Yeung, S., Chaudhari, A.S.: Self-supervised learning for medical image classification: a systematic review and implementation guidelines. NPJ Digital Med. **6**(1), 1–16 (2023). https://doi.org/10.1038/s41746-023-00811-0
16. Khan, N., Wang, K., Chan, A., Highnam, R.: Automatic BI-RADS classification of mammograms. In: Bräunl, T., McCane, B., Rivera, M., Yu, X. (eds.) PSIVT 2015. LNCS, vol. 9431, pp. 475–487. Springer, Cham (2016). https://doi.org/10.1007/978-3-319-29451-3_38
17. Kumar, I., et al.: Dense tissue pattern characterization using deep neural network. Cogn. Comput. **14**(5), 1728–1751 (2022). https://doi.org/10.1007/s12559-021-09970-2
18. Lau, S., Ng, K.H., Abdul Aziz, Y.F.: Volumetric breast density measurement: sensitivity analysis of a relative physics approach. The British J. Radiol. **89**(1066), 20160258 (2016). https://doi.org/10.1259/bjr.20160258
19. Marchesi, A., et al.: The effect of mammogram preprocessing on microcalcification detection with convolutional neural networks. In: Proceedings of the IEEE 30th International Symposium on Computer-Based Medical Systems (CBMS), pp. 207–212. IEEE (2017). https://doi.org/10.1109/CBMS.2017.29
20. Moreira, I.C., Amaral, I., Domingues, I., Cardoso, A., Cardoso, M.J., Cardoso, J.S.: INbreast: toward a full-field digital mammographic database. Acad. Radiol. **19**(2), 236–248 (2012). https://doi.org/10.1016/j.acra.2011.09.014
21. Morrish, O.W.E., Tucker, L., Black, R., Willsher, P., Duffy, S.W., Gilbert, F.J.: Mammographic breast density: comparison of methods for quantitative evaluation. Radiology **275**(2), 356–365 (2015). https://doi.org/10.1148/radiol.14141508
22. Pham, H.H., Nguyen Trung, H., Nguyen, H.Q.: VinDr-Mammo: a large-scale benchmark dataset for computer-aided detection and diagnosis in full-field digital mammography (2023). https://doi.org/10.13026/BR2V-7517
23. Solís, N., Fedon, C., Hill, M.L., Sechopoulos, I.: Validation of a breast density quantization software with 3D printed breast phantoms. In: Proceedings of the Medical Imaging 2022: Physics of Medical Imaging, vol. 12031, pp. 222–230. SPIE (2022). https://doi.org/10.1117/12.2611534
24. Steiner, A., Kolesnikov, A., Zhai, X., Wightman, R., Uszkoreit, J., Beyer, L.: How to train your ViT? Data, augmentation, and regularization in vision transformers (2022). https://doi.org/10.48550/arXiv.2106.10270

25. Suckling, J., et al.: Mammographic image analysis society (MIAS) database v1.21 (2015)
26. Tan, M., Le, Q.V.: EfficientNet: rethinking model scaling for convolutional neural networks (2020). https://doi.org/10.48550/arXiv.1905.11946
27. Wang, J., et al.: Agreement of mammographic measures of volumetric breast density to MRI. PLoS ONE 8(12), e81653 (2013). https://doi.org/10.1371/journal.pone.0081653
28. Wang, K., Hill, M., Knowles-Barley, S., Tikhonov, A., Litchfield, L., Bare, J.C.: Improving segmentation of breast arterial calcifications from digital mammography: good annotation is all you need. In: Zheng, Y., Keleş, H.Y., Koniusz, P., (Eds.), Computer vision - ACCV 2022 workshops, vol. 13848, pp. 134–150. Springer Nature Switzerland (2023). https://doi.org/10.1007/978-3-031-27066-6_10
29. Wang, X., Liang, G., Zhang, Y., Blanton, H., Bessinger, Z., Jacobs, N.: Inconsistent performance of deep learning models on mammogram classification. J. Am. Coll. Radiol. 17(6), 796–803 (2020). https://doi.org/10.1016/j.jacr.2020.01.006
30. Warren, L.M., et al.: Deep learning to calculate breast density from processed mammography images. In: Proceedings of the 15th International Workshop on Breast Imaging (IWBI2020), vol. 11513, pp. 352–358. SPIE (2020). https://doi.org/10.1117/12.2561278
31. Yoon, J.H., Kim, E.K.: Deep learning-based artificial intelligence for mammography. Korean J. Radiol. 22(8), 1225–1239 (2021). https://doi.org/10.3348/kjr.2020.1210

Cluster-Based Video Summarization with Temporal Context Awareness

Hai-Dang Huynh-Lam[1,2], Ngoc-Phuong Ho-Thi[1,2]([✉]), Minh-Triet Tran[1,2][ID], and Trung-Nghia Le[1,2][ID]

[1] University of Science, VNU-HCM, Vietnam
htnphuong19@apcs.fitus.edu.vn
[2] Vietnam National University, Ho Chi Minh, Vietnam

Abstract. In this paper, we present TAC-SUM, a novel and efficient training-free approach for video summarization that addresses the limitations of existing cluster-based models by incorporating temporal context. Our method partitions the input video into temporally consecutive segments with clustering information, enabling the injection of temporal awareness into the clustering process, setting it apart from prior cluster-based summarization methods. The resulting temporal-aware clusters are then utilized to compute the final summary, using simple rules for keyframe selection and frame importance scoring. Experimental results on the SumMe dataset demonstrate the effectiveness of our proposed approach, outperforming existing unsupervised methods and achieving comparable performance to state-of-the-art supervised summarization techniques. Our source code is available for reference at https://github.com/hcmus-thesis-gulu/TAC-SUM.

Keywords: video summarization · clustering · unsupervised learning

1 Introduction

Video summarization is a crucial research area that aims to generate concise and informative summaries of videos, capturing their temporal and semantic aspects while preserving essential content. This task poses several challenges, including identifying important frames or shots, detecting significant events, and maintaining overall coherence. Video summarization finds applications in diverse fields, enhancing video browsing, retrieval, and user experience [4].

The current state-of-the-art methods in summarizing videos are SMN [24] and PGL-SUM [5]. SMN stacks LSTM and memory layers hierarchically to capture long-term temporal context and estimate frame importance based on this information. Its training, however, relies on LSTMs and is not fully parallelizable. PGL-SUM uses self-attention mechanisms to estimate the importance and

---

H.-D. Huynh-Lam and N.-P. Ho-Thi—Both authors contributed equally to this research.

dependencies of video frames. It combines global and local multi-head attention with positional encoding to create concise and representative video summaries. Both SMN and PGL-SUM heavily rely on human-generated summaries as ground truth, introducing biases and inconsistencies during training.

To eliminate the need for labeled data required by supervised approaches, unsupervised algorithms have been explored, such as Generative Adversarial Networks [3] and Reinforcement Learning [30]. While achieving remarkable results without annotations, their performance gains have been minor compared to supervised methods, and the computational requirements can be high with GPU usage.

A line of research focusing on the use of clustering algorithms for video summarization has been pioneered by De *et al.* [9] and followed by Mahmoud *et al.* [18] to create interpretable summaries without labels and training. Such methods demonstrate acceptable performance in low-resource environments, but their effectiveness has yet to be competitive with learnable approaches.

In this paper, we propose a training-free approach called Temporal-Aware Cluster-based SUMmarization (TAC-SUM) to address the challenges encountered by previous studies. This method leverages temporal relations between frames inside a video to convert clusters of frames into temporally aware segments. Specifically, frame similarities available from these clusters are used to divide the video into non-overlapping and consecutive segments. The proposed algorithm then applies simple and naive rules to select keyframes from these segments as well as assign importance scores to each frame based on its segment's information. Our approach is expected to outperform existing cluster-based methods by injecting temporal awareness after the clustering step. It eliminates the need for expensive annotation, increases efficiency, and offers high interpretability due to its visualizability and transparent rules. An important distinction from some previous unsupervised studies is that TAC-SUM currently relies on naive rules, leaving ample room for future improvement, including the integration of learnable components, which have been successful in learning-free algorithms [18].

We conduct quantitative and qualitative experiments on the SumMe dataset [11] to evaluate our method's performance in video summarization. The quantitative experiment shows that our approach significantly outperforms existing unsupervised methods and is comparable to current state-of-the-art supervised algorithms. The qualitative study demonstrates that our approach produces effective visual summaries and exhibits high interpretability with the use of naive rules.

The main contributions presented in the paper are as follows:

- We introduce the integration of temporal context into the clustering mechanism for video summarization, addressing the shortcomings of traditional cluster-based methods.
- We propose a novel architecture that effectively embeds temporal context into the clustering step, leading to improved video summarization results.
- Our approach demonstrates superior performance compared to existing cluster-based methods and remains competitive with state-of-the-art deep learning summarization approaches.

2   Related Work

Video summarization techniques can be broadly classified into two categories: supervised methods and unsupervised methods. While supervised methods demonstrate superior performance in domain-specific applications, they rely heavily on labeled data, making them less practical for general video summarization tasks where labeled data may be scarce or costly to obtain. As a result, unsupervised methods remain popular for their versatility and ability to generate summaries without the need for labeled data. Within unsupervised approaches, clustering algorithms have emerged as a popular choice.

Cluster-based video summarization methods utilize the concept of grouping similar frames or shots into clusters and selecting representative keyframes from each cluster to form the final summary. These approaches have shown promise in generating meaningful summaries, as they can capture content diversity and reduce redundancy effectively. Prior works have explored various clustering techniques for video summarization. Mundu et al. [20] employed Delaunay triangulation clustering using color feature space, but high computational overhead limited its practicality. De et al. [9] utilized K-means clustering with hue histogram representation for keyframe extraction. Shroff et al. [23] introduced a modified version of K-means that considers inter-cluster center variance and intra-cluster distance for improved representativeness and diversity. Asadi et al. [6] applied fuzzy C-means clustering with color component histograms. Mahmoud et al. [19] used DBSCAN clustering with Bhattacharya distance as a similarity metric within the VSCAN algorithm. Cluster-based methods offer simplicity and interpretability, often relying on distance metrics like Euclidean or cosine similarity to group similar frames. Their computational efficiency allows for scalability to large video datasets. However, traditional cluster-based approaches have limitations. Notably, they may overlook temporal coherence, leading to fragmented and incoherent summaries. Additionally, handling complex video content with multiple events or dynamic scenes can pose challenges, as these methods primarily rely on visual similarity for clustering.

With the rise of deep learning, video summarization has seen significant advancements. In supervised approaches, temporal coherence is addressed by modeling variable-range temporal dependencies among frames and learning their importance based on ground-truth annotations. This has been achieved using various architectures, such as LSTM-based key-frame selectors [25, 27–29], Fully Convolutional Sequence Networks [22], and attention-based architectures [10, 15, 16].

However, achieving temporal coherence in unsupervised learning poses challenges. One promising direction is the utilization of Generative Adversarial Networks (GANs). Mahasseni et al. [17] combined an LSTM-based key-frame selector, a Variational Auto-Encoder (VAE), and a trainable Discriminator in an adversarial learning framework to reconstruct the original video from the summary. Other works extended this core VAE-GAN architecture with tailored attention mechanisms to capture frame dependencies at various temporal granularities during keyframe selection [12–14]. These methods focus on important

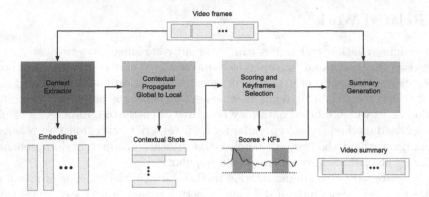

Fig. 1. Pipeline of the proposed approach showcasing four modules and information flow across main stages.

temporal regions and model long-range dependencies in the video sequence. Although GAN-based models have shown promise in generating coherent summaries, they face challenges of unstable training and limited evaluation criteria.

The proposed method leverages cluster-based models by utilizing visual representations generated by unsupervised deep learning approaches such as DINO [7]. Addressing the problem of temporal coherence, our developed TAC-SUM introduces the temporal context into the process. This integration of temporal context enhances the summarization performance, as demonstrated by experimental results.

3   Proposed Approach

Our approach selects an ordered subset $S = \{I_{t_1}, I_{t_2}, \ldots, I_{t_L}\}$ of L frames from a video $I = \{I_1, I_2, \ldots, I_T\}$, where T is the total number of frames and the summarized subset S is obtained by selecting frames indexed at t_i positions. The timestamp vector t comprises such positions $\{t_1, t_2, \ldots, t_L\}$. In Fig. 1, we illustrate the four stages of our method as distinct modules. Each stage comprises several steps tailored to the specific role and algorithm implemented. We provide a detailed explanation of each stage in the remaining text of this section. In addition, Sect. 3.4 is dedicated to clarifying several technical details related to the implementation of our approach.

3.1   Generating Contextual Embeddings

This stage extracts the context of an input video I from its frames I_t. It involves two steps: sampling the video and constructing embeddings for each sampled frame.

Sampling Step. To reduce computational complexity, we employ a sampling technique to extract frames from I into a sequence of samples $\hat{I}$. The frame rate of $\hat{\mathbf{I}}$ is matched to a pre-specified frame rate R. This method ensures representativeness and serves as normalization for different inputs. The sampling process involves dividing the original frames within a one-second period into equal-length snippets and selecting the middle frame of each snippet as the final sample.

Embedding Step. For each sampled frame $\hat{I}_i$, we utilize a pre-trained model to extract its visual embedding $\mathbf{e}_i$. The pre-trained model is denoted as a function $g : \mathbb{R}^{W \times H \times C} \longrightarrow \mathbb{R}^D$ that converts $\hat{I}_i$ into an embedding vector of size D. All embeddings are concatenated to form the contextual embedding of the sampled video $\mathbf{E} = \{\mathbf{e}_1, \mathbf{e}_2, \ldots, \mathbf{e}_{\hat{T}}\}$. Figure 2 gives two examples of contextual embeddings.

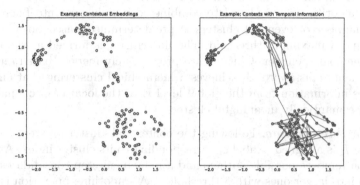

Fig. 2. Visual illustration of contextual information.

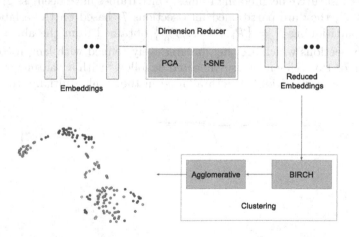

Fig. 3. Overall pipeline for the Contextual Clustering step.

3.2   From Global Context to Local Semantics

This stage distills global information from the contextual embedding $\mathbf{E}$ into finer, local levels. Our method comprises two steps: using traditional clustering to propagate contextual information into partition-level clusters, and further distilling partition-level information into sample-level.

Contextual Clustering. Clustering the contextual embeddings $\mathbf{E}$ captures global and local relationships between visual elements in the video. We first reduce the dimension of $\mathbf{E}$ to a reduced embedding $\hat{\mathbf{E}}$. A coarse-to-fine clustering approach is then applied to divide the sampled frames into K clusters, creating a label vector $\mathbf{c} \in \mathbf{N}^{\hat{T}}$. More details can be found in Fig. 3. Starting with the contextual embedding $\mathbf{E} \in \mathbb{R}^{\hat{T} \times D}$, a reduced embedding $\hat{\mathbf{E}} \in \mathbb{R}^{\hat{T} \times \hat{D}}$ is computed using PCA and t-SNE. A traditional clustering method called BIRCH algorithm [26] is applied to compute coarse clusters of sampled frames, creating a sample-level notation for coarse clusters $\hat{\mathbf{c}} = \{\hat{c}_1, \hat{c}_2, \dots, \hat{c}_{\hat{T}}\}$. Then, a hierarchical clustering algorithm is employed to combine coarse clusters into finer clusters with the number of eventual clusters is pre-determined based on a sigmoidal function and a maximum threshold. The fine cluster is formed as the union of at least one coarse cluster. Clusters are progressively merged based on affinity between them. This approach achieves a hierarchical clustering that effectively propagates information from the global level $\hat{\mathbf{E}}$ to the local level $\mathbf{c}$, enabling us to extract semantically meaningful clusters.

Semantic Partitioning. Following the contextual clustering step, each sampled frame $\hat{I}_i$ is assigned a label c_i corresponding to its cluster index. An outlier elimination removes possible outliers and a refinement step consolidates smaller partitions into larger ones with a threshold ϵ. A smoothing operation is applied to labels by assigning the final label $\hat{c}_i$ of each frame by taking a majority vote among its consecutive neighboring frames. Once frames have been assigned their final labels $\mathcal{C}$, they are partitioned into sections $\mathcal{P}$ based on these labels. The semantic partitioning $\mathcal{P} = \{\mathcal{P}_1, \mathcal{P}_2, \dots, \mathcal{P}_{\hat{N}}\}$ obtained from the above process contains $\hat{N}$ sections which are then progressively refined with length condition. Algorithm for this refinement is delineated as follows with a parameter ϵ denoting the minimum partition's length allowed in the result. Initially, the number

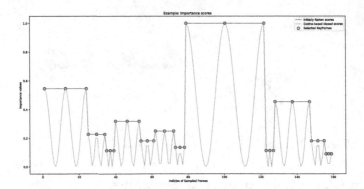

Fig. 4. Comparison between cosine-interpolated scores and flat scores are demonstrated for two examples.

of partitions N is set to $\hat{N}$. Subsequently, while the minimum length of the partitions is less than ϵ, the index of the shortest partition $\hat{i}$ is determined. The left and right sides of partition $\hat{i}$ are merged with their respective neighboring partitions and their lengths are updated accordingly. The indexes of $\mathcal{P}$ are then updated and the number of partitions N is reduced by 1. This process continues until all partitions have a length of at least ϵ. This partitioning result allows us to focus on individual semantic parts within the video and analyze their characteristics independently, enabling more detailed analysis and summary generation in subsequent stages.

3.3   Keyframes and Importance Scores

After the partitioning step, the resulted partitions $\mathcal{P}$ are used to generate keyframes $\mathbf{k}$ which carry important information of the original input. An importance score v_i is calculated for every sampled frame $\hat{I}_i$.

Keyframes Selection. The set of keyframes $\mathbf{k}$ is a subset of the indexes of sampled frames $\mathbf{k} \subset \mathbf{t}$, and is a union of partition-wise keyframes $\mathbf{k}^{(i)}$, that is $\mathbf{k} = \bigcup_{i=1}^{N} \mathbf{k}^{(i)}$. There are three options for extracting the partition-wise keyframes $\mathbf{k}^{(i)}$ from its associated partition $\mathcal{P}_i$ which are respectively *Mean*, *Middle*, and *Ends*. These options can be further combined into more advanced settings such as the rule *Middle + Ends* demonstrated in Fig. 4.

Importance Scores. The individual importance scores v_i of all sampled frames $\hat{I}_i$ form a vector of importances $\mathbf{v} \in \mathbb{R}^{\hat{T}}$. We initialize the importance score $\hat{\mathbf{v}}$ to be the length of the section it belongs to. The final importance score of each sample v_i is computed by scaling the initialized value $\hat{v}_i$ using a keyframe-biasing method. Several biasing options are given to either increase the importance of frames closer to keyframes or decrease the scores of others. Different interpolating methods are used to fill the importance scores of samples between key positions. Two options for interpolation are `cosine` and `linear`. An example illustrating the difference between cosine-interpolated importances and flat scores is given in Fig. 4. By determining the importance scores of frames, we can prioritize and select the most significant frames for inclusion in the video summary.

3.4   Implementation Details

Before the feature extraction step, the video is sampled with a target frame rate of $R = 4$ frames per second. We experiment with 2 pre-trained models to generate embeddings for each frame: DINO [7] and CLIP [21]. The input frame is processed using the pre-trained image processor associated with the pre-trained model. The output is an image, which is fed into the pre-trained model to obtain embeddings. For DINO, we select the first vector (cls token) in its output embedding as the semantic embedding of the sample. We concatenate the vector from all frames in to obtain the contextual embedding.

For dimension reduction, we utilize models from `scikit-learn`, including PCA and t-SNE. The number of clusters K in contextual clustering is then computed by the equation provided in Sect. 3.2. In the semantic partition step, we set the window size W for mode convolution to 5, and the minimum length ϵ for each segment to 4. For keyframe selection, we employ the setting *Middle + End*. In the importance scoring step, we use `cosine` interpolation and set keyframe biasing scheme to *Increase the importances of keyframes* with $B = 0.5$.

4 Experiments

4.1 Dataset

For evaluating the performance of our TAC-SUM model, we utilize the SumMe dataset [11]. This benchmarking dataset consists of 25 videos ranging from 1 to 6 min in duration, covering various events captured from both first-person and third-person perspectives. Each video is annotated with multiple (15–18) key-fragments representing important segments. Additionally, a ground-truth summary in the form of frame-level importance scores (computed by averaging the key-fragment user summaries per frame) is provided for each video to support supervised training.

4.2 Evaluation Measures

The summary selected by our summarizer is then compared with those generated by humans to determine its correctness, in other words, whether that summary is good or not depends on its similarity with regard to the annotated ones. A widely established metric for this comparison is f-measure, which is adopted in prior works [1,5,8]. This metric requires an automatic summarizer to generate a proxy summary $\hat{S}$ from pre-computed consecutive segmentations S associated with each video in the dataset. The f-measure metric is computed as f1-score between the segments chosen by automatic method against ground-truth selected by human evaluators. Previous studies [5,25] have formulated the conversion from importances to choice of segments as a Knapsack problem so that a simple dynamic programming method can be implemented to recover the proxy summary from outputted scores. The formulation includes lengths of segments as weighting condition while individual segment's value is computed using importance scores. More detailed information can be found in prior research [25].

4.3 Comparison with State-of-the-art Methods

The performance of our proposed TAC-SUM approach is compared with various summarization methods from the literature in Table 1. These referenced approaches include both supervised and unsupervised algorithms that have been previously published, and the evaluation metric used is established under Sect. 4.2. As a general baseline, we include a random summarizer, which assigns

Table 1. Comparison of performance in f-measure (%) among previous approaches and our method together with rankings on unsupervised only as well as in general.

Methods		F-Score	Rank (Unsupervised)	Rank (General)
Random summary		40.2	7	13
Supervised	SMN [24]	**58.3**	-	1
	VASNet [10]	49.7	-	10
	PGL-SUM [5]	57.1	-	2
	H-MAN [16]	51.8	-	5
	SUM-GDA [15]	52.8	-	4
	SUM-DeepLab [22]	48.8	-	12
Unsupervised	CSNet [13]	51.3	2	6
	AC-SUM-GAN [1]	50.8	3	7
	CSNet+GL+RPE [14]	50.2	4	8
	SUM-GAN-AAE [3]	48.9	6	11
	SUM-GDA$_{unsup}$ [15]	50.0	5	9
	TAC-SUM (ours)	**54.48**	1	3

importance scores to each frame based on a uniform distribution. The final performance is averaged over 100 sampling runs for each video [2].

The results in Table 1 highlight the effectiveness of our training-free approach, which achieves remarkable performance without any learning aspect. It outperforms existing unsupervised models by at least 3.18%, demonstrating its ability to generate high-quality summaries. Moreover, our model ranks third when compared to state-of-the-art supervised methods, showing competitive performance and even surpassing several existing approaches.

It is worth noting that the SMN method has been evaluated using only one randomly created split of the used data [24]. Apostolidis *et al.* [2] suggest that these random data splits show significantly varying levels of difficulty that affect the evaluation outcomes.

We acknowledge that the pre-trained models used in our architecture were originally trained on general image datasets, which may not perfectly align with the distribution of the specific dataset used in this evaluation. Despite this potential distribution mismatch, our proposed method exhibits strong performance on the evaluated dataset, showcasing the generalizability and adaptability of this training-free framework.

4.4 Ablation Study

To assess the contribution of each core component in our model, we conduct an ablation study, evaluating the following variants of the proposed architecture: variant **TAC-SUM w/o TC**: which is not aware of temporal context by skipping the semantic partitioning stage (Sect. 3.2), and the full algorithm

Table 2. Ablation study based on the performance (F-Score(%)) of two variants of the proposed approach on SumMe

Settings	F-Score
TAC-SUM w/o TC	46.00
TAC-SUM (ours)	**54.48**

Table 3. Comparison of performance (F-Score(%)) with different embedding pre-trained models

Setting		F-Score
Embedding Model	Best Config	
dino-b16	Euclidean PCA (34) + t-SNE (2)	**54.48**
clip-base-16	Euclidean PCA (44) + t-SNE (3)	52.33

TAC-SUM (ours). The results presented in Table 2 demonstrate that removing the temporal context significantly impacts the summarization performance, thus confirming the effectiveness of our proposed techniques. The inclusion of temporal context enhances the quality of the generated summaries, supporting the superiority of our proposed TAC-SUM model.

As mentioned in Sect. 3.4, we conducted experiments using different pre-trained models for visual embedding extraction. Table 3 compares the result of the framework using different pre-trained models: dino-b16 and clip-base-16. Both models are base models with a patch size of 16. The "Best Config" column shows the configuration that achieved the best result, including the distance used in the clustering step (Euclidean), the algorithms used for embedding size reduction (PCA and t-SNE), and the dimension of the reduced embeddings represented by the number next to the reducer. The results presented in Table 3 demonstrate that our proposed framework performs relatively well with various pre-trained models, showcasing its flexibility and efficiency. The ability to work effectively with different pre-trained models indicates that our approach can leverage a wide range of visual embeddings, making it adaptable to various video summarization scenarios. This flexibility allows practitioners to choose the most suitable pre-trained model based on their specific requirements and available resources.

4.5 Qualitative Assessment

To evaluate the interpretability of the proposed approach, we compared the automatically generated importance scores with those assigned by human annotators. Figure 5 displays the importance scores obtained through averaging human annotations as well as the scores generated by the proposed method. The flat result shows that each computed partition may be associated with one or several peaks in the user summaries, located at different positions within the partition.

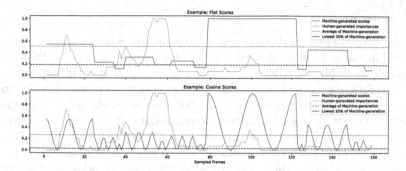

Fig. 5. Comparison of importance scores between user-annotated scores and scores generated by the proposed method under the unbiased `flat` rule as well as the biased `cosine` rule.

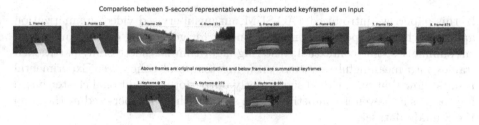

Fig. 6. Comparison between the representatives sampled from the original video with its summarization as a set of keyframes.

Longer partitions, which have higher flat scores according to the definition, tend to provide a more stable estimation of users' peaks. The experimental result also provides insights into the keyframe-biasing method employed in the proposed method, wherein higher importance is assigned to frames that are closer to keyframes. This figure reveals that the majority of the peaks in the `cosine` scores align with the peaks of the annotated importance. However, there are some peaks in the users' scores that are not captured by the `cosine` interpolation.

A visual inspection of our method's summarization results is conducted in which a reference video is analyzed against its summary generated through the approach. We present the inspection's result in Fig. 6 with the original frames of the reference video and selected keyframes. The original frames are sampled every 5 s from the video, which shows a man playing a game of sliding down a slope and jumping into a pool of water. The keyframes are selected based on their importance scores, which are higher than the average on the video level. Our method preserves the main content and events of the video and selects diverse and representative keyframes that show different aspects of the video. Our method generates informative and expressive keyframes that convey the main theme, message, or story of the video.

4.6 Limitations

While the proposed method offers several advantages which have been already illustrated in the experimental results, it also has certain limitations that should be acknowledged. **Naive rules** for scoring and selection of keyframes are being used. Therefore, our current approach may not always accurately predict frame importance. Incorporating more sophisticated scoring mechanisms can enhance the summarization process. **Limited learnability** is demonstrated by our method as it lacks the ability to improve in a data-driven way due to its current reliance on predefined rules. Future research could explore integrating data-driven approaches like machine learning algorithms or attention mechanisms to enhance adaptability.

5 Conclusion

In this paper, we introduced TAC-SUM, an unsupervised video summarization approach that incorporates temporal context for generating concise and coherent summaries. The contextual clustering algorithm has successfully partitioned frames into meaningful segments, ensuring temporal coherence. Experimental results show that our method significantly outperforms traditional cluster-based approaches and even is competitive with state-of-the-art supervised methods on the SumMe dataset.

Despite its success, TAC-SUM has limitations related to pre-trained models and data-driven improvement. To address these limitations, future work will focus on integrating learnable components into the model to enhance the summarization process and improve adaptability to various video domains. This includes replacing the current algorithm for contextual clustering with a deep neural network having trainable parameters, enabling the model to capture more complex patterns and adapt to diverse video datasets. Additionally, various architectures and training techniques will be explored to transform the naive rules of importance into a data-driven scoring process, allowing complicated scores to be predicted.

Acknowledgement. This research is supported by research funding from Faculty of Information Technology, University of Science, Vietnam National University - Ho Chi Minh City.

References

1. Apostolidis, E., Adamantidou, E., Metsai, A.I., Mezaris, V., Patras, I.: AC-SUM-GAN: connecting actor-critic and generative adversarial networks for unsupervised video summarization. IEEE Trans. Circuits Syst. Video Technol. **31**(8), 3278–3292 (2020)
2. Apostolidis, E., Adamantidou, E., Metsai, A.I., Mezaris, V., Patras, I.: Performance over random: a robust evaluation protocol for video summarization methods. In: Proceedings of the 28th ACM International Conference on Multimedia, pp. 1056–1064 (2020)

3. Apostolidis, E., Adamantidou, E., Metsai, A.I., Mezaris, V., Patras, I.: Unsupervised video summarization via attention-driven adversarial learning. In: Ro, Y.M., et al. (eds.) MMM 2020. LNCS, vol. 11961, pp. 492–504. Springer, Cham (2020). https://doi.org/10.1007/978-3-030-37731-1_40
4. Apostolidis, E., Adamantidou, E., Metsai, A.I., Mezaris, V., Patras, I.: Video summarization using deep neural networks: a survey. IEEE Trans. Pattern Anal. Mach. Intell. (2021)
5. Apostolidis, E., Balaouras, G., Mezaris, V., Patras, I.: Combining global and local attention with positional encoding for video summarization. In: 2021 IEEE International Symposium on Multimedia (ISM), pp. 226–234 (2021)
6. Asadi, E., Charkari, N.M.: Video summarization using fuzzy C-means clustering. In: 20th Iranian Conference on Electrical Engineering (ICEE2012), pp. 690–694. IEEE (2012)
7. Caron, M., et al.: Emerging properties in self-supervised vision transformers. In: Proceedings of the International Conference on Computer Vision (ICCV) (2021)
8. Chu, W.T., Liu, Y.H.: Spatiotemporal modeling and label distribution learning for video summarization. In: 2019 IEEE 21st International Workshop on Multimedia Signal Processing (MMSP), pp. 1–6. IEEE (2019)
9. De Avila, S.E.F., Lopes, A.P.B., da Luz Jr, A., de Albuquerque Araújo, A.: VSUMM: a mechanism designed to produce static video summaries and a novel evaluation method. Pattern Recogn. Lett. 32(1), 56–68 (2011)
10. Fajtl, J., Sokeh, H.S., Argyriou, V., Monekosso, D., Remagnino, P.: Summarizing videos with attention. In: Carneiro, G., You, S. (eds.) ACCV 2018. LNCS, vol. 11367, pp. 39–54. Springer, Cham (2019). https://doi.org/10.1007/978-3-030-21074-8_4
11. Gygli, M., Grabner, H., Riemenschneider, H., Van Gool, L.: Creating summaries from user videos. In: ECCV (2014)
12. He, X., et al.: Unsupervised video summarization with attentive conditional generative adversarial networks. In: Proceedings of the 27th ACM International Conference on multimedia, pp. 2296–2304 (2019)
13. Jung, Y., Cho, D., Kim, D., Woo, S., Kweon, I.S.: Discriminative feature learning for unsupervised video summarization. In: Proceedings of the AAAI Conference on artificial intelligence, vol. 33, pp. 8537–8544 (2019)
14. Jung, Y., Cho, D., Woo, S., Kweon, I.S.: Global-and-Local relative position embedding for unsupervised video summarization. In: Vedaldi, A., Bischof, H., Brox, T., Frahm, J.-M. (eds.) ECCV 2020. LNCS, vol. 12370, pp. 167–183. Springer, Cham (2020). https://doi.org/10.1007/978-3-030-58595-2_11
15. Li, P., Ye, Q., Zhang, L., Yuan, L., Xu, X., Shao, L.: Exploring global diverse attention via pairwise temporal relation for video summarization. Pattern Recogn. 111, 107677 (2021)
16. Liu, Y.T., Li, Y.J., Yang, F.E., Chen, S.F., Wang, Y.C.F.: Learning hierarchical self-attention for video summarization. In: 2019 IEEE International Conference on Image Processing (ICIP), pp. 3377–3381. IEEE (2019)
17. Mahasseni, B., Lam, M., Todorovic, S.: Unsupervised video summarization with adversarial LSTM networks. In: CVPR (2017)
18. Mahmoud, K.M., Ghanem, N.M., Ismail, M.A.: Unsupervised video summarization via dynamic modeling-based hierarchical clustering. In: Proceedings of the 12th International Conference on Machine Learning and Applications, vol. 2, pp. 303–308 (2013)

19. Mahmoud, K.M., Ismail, M.A., Ghanem, N.M.: VSCAN: an enhanced video summarization using density-based spatial clustering. In: Petrosino, A. (ed.) ICIAP 2013. LNCS, vol. 8156, pp. 733–742. Springer, Heidelberg (2013). https://doi.org/10.1007/978-3-642-41181-6_74
20. Mundur, P., Rao, Y., Yesha, Y.: Keyframe-based video summarization using Delaunay clustering. Int. J. Digit. Libr. **6**, 219–232 (2006)
21. Radford, A., et al.: Learning transferable visual models from natural language supervision. In: International Conference on Machine Learning, pp. 8748–8763. PMLR (2021)
22. Rochan, M., Ye, L., Wang, Y.: Video summarization using fully convolutional sequence networks. In: Proceedings of the European Conference on Computer Vision (ECCV), pp. 347–363 (2018)
23. Shroff, N., Turaga, P., Chellappa, R.: Video précis: highlighting diverse aspects of videos. IEEE Trans. Multimedia **12**(8), 853–868 (2010)
24. Wang, J., Wang, W., Wang, Z., Wang, L., Feng, D., Tan, T.: Stacked memory network for video summarization. In: Proceedings of the 27th ACM International Conference on Multimedia, pp. 836–844 (2019)
25. Zhang, K., Chao, W.-L., Sha, F., Grauman, K.: Video summarization with long short-term memory. In: Leibe, B., Matas, J., Sebe, N., Welling, M. (eds.) ECCV 2016. LNCS, vol. 9911, pp. 766–782. Springer, Cham (2016). https://doi.org/10.1007/978-3-319-46478-7_47
26. Zhang, T., Ramakrishnan, R., Livny, M.: BIRCH: an efficient data clustering method for very large databases. SIGMOD Rec. **25**(2), 103–114 (1996). https://doi.org/10.1145/235968.233324
27. Zhao, B., Li, X., Lu, X.: Hierarchical recurrent neural network for video summarization. In: Proceedings of the 25th ACM International Conference on Multimedia, pp. 863–871 (2017)
28. Zhao, B., Li, X., Lu, X.: HSA-RNN: hierarchical structure-adaptive RNN for video summarization. In: Proceedings of the IEEE Conference on Computer Vision and Pattern Recognition, pp. 7405–7414 (2018)
29. Zhao, B., Li, X., Lu, X.: TTH-RNN: tensor-train hierarchical recurrent neural network for video summarization. IEEE Trans. Industr. Electron. **68**(4), 3629–3637 (2020)
30. Zhou, K., Qiao, Y., Xiang, T.: Deep reinforcement learning for unsupervised video summarization with diversity-representativeness reward. In: AAAI (2018)

Image Recognition and Threat Detection in Bags Arriving at the Airport

Ivan Koptev$^{(\boxtimes)}$ (iD), Cameron Walker (iD), and Andreas W. Kempa-Liehr (iD)

Department of Engineering Science and Biomedical Engineering,
The University of Auckland, Auckland 1010, New Zealand
ikop695@aucklanduni.ac.nz

Abstract. International transport security policy requires the baggage screening. In airports and railway stations, these operations are processed manually with the help of X-ray or computed tomography machines. There is a need for an automatic system which could reduce the time of the screening process and possibly, increase the accuracy of the detections. More than that, there is a demand for developing and evaluating methodologies for learning on 3D image-like data, which has been addressed only recently, mostly in the field of medical imaging. The main objective of this research is to develop a framework for object detection in 3D computed tomography scans for high-throughput security applications. In this paper, a literature review on the topic of 3D image recognition is presented, and a transfer learning approach is evaluated on the security risk detection task in X-ray images.

Keywords: Object detection · Security · X-ray images

1 Introduction

Baggage screening is a crucial part of maintaining security. Rapid threat detection can be performed by X-ray or computed tomography (CT) machines. Traditionally, baggage inspection is done by human operators and sniffer dogs. Different factors (for example, emotional exhaustion [3]) might affect the quality of screening and the decision time of human operators [28,33].

Computer vision techniques have been rapidly developing in the last decade. However, the demand for learning on 3D image-like data has occurred only recently. Therefore, current methodologies for 3D image recognition have not been tested on a lot of applications. The majority of the research occurred in medical imaging.

Recently, computer vision techniques have been widely-applied in computer-aided baggage screening for threat detection in X-ray security imaging [2,35]. Nowadays, the most advanced and widely-used algorithms in computer vision are based on convolutional neural networks. Typically, these models contain millions of adaptable parameters which complicates the training process. Models with a large number of parameters tend to overfit [21], and they require a lot of data

© The Author(s), under exclusive license to Springer Nature Singapore Pte Ltd. 2024
W. Q. Yan et al. (Eds.): PSIVT 2023, LNCS 14403, pp. 29–42, 2024.
https://doi.org/10.1007/978-981-97-0376-0_3

to train on. One of the ways to mitigate these problems is to apply transfer learning [36]. In transfer learning, the knowledge of the model is transferred from one domain to another.

The current solutions for the automatic baggage security systems are implemented for 2D images. However, the new generation scanners are able to yield 3D image-like data. More than that, current applications of computer-aided threat detections focus on explosives and weapons while other categories are left out of the scope. Object detection and classification in 3D images have been addressed only recently, and the methodologies for these tasks are not as developed as for 2D cases. Another problem is the application of transfer learning to these tasks, as the state-of-the-art models and the most extensive datasets were initially developed for 2D images.

In this paper, the methodology for 2D representation of 3D images based on projections is presented. Also, object detection model based on *You Only Look Once* architecture is validated on threat detection from X-ray images of baggage scanned in an international airport.

2   Related Work

The computer vision research field is vast and includes such areas as image and video segmentation, classification, object detection etc. In this research, the primary domain is object detection in 3D image-like data. Therefore, a systematic literature review which covers existing solutions for this narrow research area was conducted. This section covers both the basics of convolutional neural networks and the systematic literature review.

2.1   Convolutional Neural Networks

Nowadays, the most widely-used algorithms in the computer vision field are convolutional neural networks (CNNs). Historically, the inspiration for the architectural design of CNNs was the primate's visual cortex [10].

CNNs are able to learn the most informative representations of image data themselves instead of manual feature engineering used in classical machine learning models [9]. The structure of CNNs helps the network to extract the features hierarchically.

Transfer learning is a technique used in machine learning where the model performance is improved by transferring knowledge from another model trained on the task from the same domain [36]. The need for transfer learning often occurs when there is a limited collection of target training data [9,36].

CNNs are applied in various tasks in image recognition. Object detection is essentially the combination of image classification and object localization. Given the image, the model should be able to output the coordinates of the detected object and one of the pre-defined classes. In [24], a novel method for object detection called *You Only Look Once* was introduced. Instead of proposing regions of interest, the whole image is split into a grid, and the network predicts

Table 1. The comparison of approaches on modelling 3D images in deep learning. Table adapted from [38].

Approach	Pros	Cons
2D convolutions	– Extensive variety of pretrained models – Large 2D datasets – Developed methodology	– Natively 2D representations – Transformation from 3D to 2D adds another level of complexity
3D convolutions	– Natively 3D representations – No information loss	Lack of training data

the bounding boxes and confidence for each of the grid cells. This method was then improved in [25], where the prediction of bounding boxes is upgraded, and [26] where object detection on different scales is introduced.

2.2 Processing of 3D Images

The state-of-the-art deep learning algorithms require a lot of data to train on. Recently, relatively large datasets of 3D images have become accessible [29,30]; these datasets include thousands of annotations. Notably, these datasets are not large compared to 2D datasets [5,18], which contain millions of annotations. Also, 3D datasets suffer from imperfect annotations [32]. The problem of a lack of training data might be resolved with the usage of transfer learning. However, the transfer of models from 2D to 3D is non-trivial, and recently, there have been considerable debates over 2D and 3D representation learning on 3D images. The main advantages and disadvantages of 2D and 3D representations of 3D images are described in Table 1, which was adapted from [38]. Generally, the main advantages of 2D approaches are the well-developed methodology of training 2D CNNs, and a sizeable number of large-scale 2D datasets for performing transfer learning. Also, there are a lot of pretrained models validated on many tasks. On the other hand, 2D approaches utilize 2D representations of 3D data which leads to an information loss. The advantages of 3D approaches are the native 3D representations and, therefore, low information loss. The main disadvantage is a lack of large-scale 3D datasets.

Existing methods for 3D image recognition found in the literature are shown in Table 2. The papers are divided into three groups depending on the type of the representation of 3D data (2D, 3D or hybrid). Also, the table represents the models which were used in each of the articles. Altogether, purely 2D representation was used in 11 articles, 3D representation was used in two, and hybrid representation was used in six.

Table 2. The existing methods and models used for 3D image recognition found in the literature.

Approach	Paper	Models AlexNet	VGG	ResNet	LSTM	3D CNN	Other
2D	[39]	✓					
	[12]		✓				
	[22]	✓	✓				
	[13]	✓	✓				
	[8]			✓			
	[15]		✓				
	[27]			✓			
	[1]				✓		
	[7]	✓			✓		
	[34]				✓		
	[4]			✓			
3D	[11]					✓	
	[6]			✓		✓	
Hybrid	[17]			✓		✓	
	[23]			✓		✓	
	[37]						✓
	[40]						✓
	[16]					✓	✓
	[38]			✓			

2.3 2D Approaches

In 2D approaches found in the literature, either multi-planar or multi-slice representation of 3D images are used. However, the choice of the slices for the input of the 2D model is not straightforward. In most of the works, especially in medical imaging, expert knowledge guides the slice selection. For instance, Jakubicek et al. [13] used the slices in middle-sagittal view to localize the spinal canal.

Some works proposed to use all the slices in one or several views [13,27,34,39]. In some works, the choice was random [8,22]. Generally, this approach does not guarantee that the most informative parts of 3D images will not be discarded. Some works used more sophisticated methods: in [12], the entropy-based sorting mechanism was implemented to take the most informative slices from each of the scans, and [19] proposed a nonorthogonal decomposition method.

Such CNNs as AlexNet, VGG and ResNet models were used as backbones in eight papers. The type of usage of these models depended on the task and on the methodology. In classification problems, these models were used purely as pre-trained networks [12,13,22,27]. In object detection problems, the networks served as the feature extractors. R-CNN [13] and Mask R-CNN [4,8] models were built upon these architectures. Moreover, different types of transfer learning might be combined. For example, Jakubicek et al. [13] applied AlexNet for the preprocessing step in their method. The slices in middle-sagittal views were classified into several categories. Then, they used R-CNN with VGG-16 as a backbone to localize the spinal canal. In the work devoted to the segmentation problem [15], the model was based on U-Net architecture with the VGG-16 model as a backbone.

Some studies treat 3D volumes as a sequence of 2D slices [1,7,34]. This approach allows that each slice (or a selected range of slices) is processed with a 2D architecture network, while the 3D contextual information is captured in the sequences of these slices. One of the most sophisticated algorithms to process the sequences of the objects of the same nature (speech, text, video etc.) are called recurrent neural networks (RNN). In [1], multi-view 2D CNN and long short-term memory (LSTM) network were combined for the problem of lung cancer nodule identification. LSTM is a kind of recurrent neural network (RNN). This approach allowed the network to exploit the 3D context. A similar methodology was followed in [7] for the problem of glaucoma detection in optical coherence tomography scans. Several 2D CNN architectures were experimented with. The model based on VGG16 feature extractor showed better performance. In [34], recurrent neural networks were made use of for the problem of acute intracranial haemorrhages in head CT scans. First, the 2D CNN detects the objects of interest in each of the slices, then, the sequences of predictions are passed to a RNN with a gated recurrent unit. The outputs of these two models and the meta-information about the slice thickness are passed as a feature vector to the second RNN. For the interpretation of results, the saliency maps of slices were produced. These maps are able to highlight the regions most relevant to the model prediction in a given image.

2.4   3D Approaches

In 3D approaches, the original 3D volumes are used as an input to a model. In such cases, the general idea is to utilize 3D CNNs. Normally, 3D CNNs contain a much larger number of parameters than 2D counterparts. Therefore, they are less robust to overfitting and less memory-efficient. Transfer learning on bigger datasets can be used to mitigate these problems.

In [11], 3D CNN was pre-trained on a video dataset comprising one million videos with 487 classes. Then, the network was used to detect lung nodules on 3D CT scans.

In [6], the methodology to transfer weights from 2D pre-trained CNNs to 3D CNNs was introduced. The pre-trained weights of the ResNet-18 model were copied along the third dimension. Of course, the number of parameters for 3D CNN was larger than for 2D CNN; therefore, the Taguchi method [31] was utilized to reduce the number of experiments with hyperparameters. The 3D model was trained to predict Alzheimer's disease from MRI scans.

2.5 Hybrid Approaches

Hybrid approaches attempt to combine the advantages of 2D and 3D approaches. In some works, the images were processed via 2D and 3D architectures successively: In [16], 3D CNN was used for the slice of interest detection in 3D head MRI scans, then a 2D CNN was predicting the location of the target. In [37], the 2D architecture was utilized to create the predictions for each of the slices along three axes. Then, these predictions were concatenated with the original volume resulting in four channels as an input to the 3D network. Similarly, in [17], the 2D UNet architecture was combined with a 3D counterpart for a tumour segmentation task. The feature extractor for 2D UNet was a ResNet-like network. First, the 2D slices of 3D scans were processed via the 2D architecture. Then, the 3D counterpart distilled the 3D visual features by concatenating the original volumes with the contextual information from the 2D network. Finally, the results of the 2D and the 3D pipelines were fused. A similar methodology was applied in [23] to 13 segmentation tasks in medical images.

In [40], ensemble learning was used for a segmentation task. There were four base learners used: the DenseVoxNet architecture for the predictions on 3D volumes and a fully-convolutional network for the predictions on the slices along three axes. Therefore, the 2D and 3D architectures were used in parallel.

In [38], axial-coronal-sagittal (ACS) convolutions were proposed to perform learning on 3D volumes. The main idea was that 2D convolution kernels are split by channel into three parts, and convoluted separately on the three views (axial, coronal and sagittal). This allowed the model to both exploit the 3D context and use the pre-trained weights from 2D CNNs. The ResNet-18 weights were transformed to ACS convolutions, and the methodology was evaluated on medical image segmentation and classifications tasks.

3 Threat Detection

3.1 Criteria for Dataset Selection

As discussed in the literature review, 2D representations of 3D data were exploited in the majority of works on image recognition in 3D images. As stated earlier, the clear benefit of 2D approaches is the ability to use a variety of pre-trained models for transfer learning. On the other hand, 2D representations might lead to spatial information loss. In the literature, different slicing approaches are described. However, 17 of 19 articles are on applications in the medical field. Medical datasets contain homogeneous images, while in the case of real-world baggage images, the content might be manifold. In an object detection task, a random slice from 3D images might lead to the object of interest disappearing entirely. In baggage threat detection task, the location of the target is unknown. In contrast, in medical imaging, the location of objects of interest are approximately known. Therefore, the proposed methodology for 2D representation is the projection of 3D data onto a plane. Given 3D images as 3D matrices of intensity values, some statistical measures (mean, median, standard deviation, etc.) of these values can be taken along one of the cartesian axes. Later on, several different projections could be used to augment the dataset and prevent overfitting. The following formula represents the projection method using an average of values along one of the axis:

$$F(i,j) = \frac{\sum\limits_{k} I(i,j,k)}{N},\tag{1}$$

where $F(i,j)$ is the element of the 2D matrix $F \in \mathbb{R}^{L \times M}$, $I(i,j,k)$ is the element of the initial 3D matrix $I \in \mathbb{R}^{L \times M \times N}$ representing a 3D image, and L, M and N are height, width and depth of the 3D image.

Different materials have different attenuation coefficients for X-rays [20]. Therefore, one can assume that objects of interest (weapons, metal objects, explosives, biomatter) would interact with X-rays differently than the normal content of the passengers' bags. Also, normal threats (for example, cutting items) have well-limited and defined shapes. In comparison, objects of interest in medical imaging (for instance, tumours) often have irregular borders.

Thus, the criteria for the choice of the dataset were:

1. The objects of interest should have sharp edges.
2. The background and objects of interest should consist of different materials.

In this paper, the results of the application of transfer learning for the object detection task in X-ray images are presented.

3.2   The Occluded Prohibited Items X-Ray Dataset

In order to evaluate transfer learning approaches for threat detection applications on X-ray images, we have chosen the Occluded Prohibited Items X-ray (OPIXray) dataset [35]. The dataset contains computed tomography images of the baggage scanned by a security inspection machine and annotated manually by professional inspectors from an international airport. The objects of interest are cutting items such as knives, scissors, etc. The standard of annotating is based on the standard of training security inspectors.

The disadvantage of the dataset is the absence of non-threat images. Therefore, this dataset is appropriate for training a classification-of-threats model but not for training a threat-non-threat discriminator. Also, in terms of the objectives of this research, the drawback of the OPIXray dataset is that it consists of 2D, not 3D images. However, this dataset is still appropriate for the initial motivation: to validate object detection models and machine learning pipeline.

The OPIXray dataset contains 8885 X-ray images (7019 for training, 1776 for testing). Five categories of cutting items are represented, such as folding knives, straight knives, scissors, utility knives, and multi-tool knives. The class-wise distribution of the dataset is presented in Table 3. As one can see, the straight knife class is underrepresented, and other classes are relatively balanced. Each sample in the dataset is an RGB image of size 1225×954. The annotations for

Table 3. The class-wise distribution of the samples in the OPIXray dataset [35].

Category	Training	Testing	Total
Folding knife	1589	404	1993
Straight knife	809	235	1044
Scissors	1494	369	1863
Utility knife	1635	343	1978
Multi-tool knife	1612	430	2042
Total	7109	1776	8885

each image were documented in a text file in the following format: image file name, class, coordinates x_1 and y_1 of the top-left corner of the bounding box of a prohibited item, and coordinates x_2 and y_2 of the bottom-right corner.

3.3 Architecture of the Model

In [24], a novel approach to object detection was presented. This was one of the first single-stage architectures, uniting object localization and object classification blocks helped reduce the inference time. As mentioned earlier, the model was successively improved to [25, 26]. In this research, YOLOv3 [26] was used.

The feature extractor of YOLOv3 is called Darknet-53. It contains three prediction heads for three different spatial compressions. For example, if the original input image is of size 416×416, three prediction stages would occur for the processed image of sizes 13×13, 26×26 and 52×52. This helps the model to detect objects on different scales. Each of the prediction stages implements the following strategy: the image is divided into a grid of cells, and for each of these cells, the model predicts the objectness score, the class, and the coordinates relative to the cell. After the model has been trained, the model outputs the classes and bounding boxes of those detections which exceeded the objectness score threshold.

The implementation of the YOLOv3 architecture for the OPIXray dataset uses the `pytorch`[1] package. It is inspired by the implementations of Redmon's original articles [24–26], which are published on his website[2]. The initial weights of the model pre-trained on the MS-COCO dataset were also downloaded from this website.

3.4 The Preprocessing Pipeline

Each image of the OPIXray dataset was resized to the size of 256×256. As the original images did not have square shapes but rectangle ones, the borders were zero-padded to keep the aspect ratio. Then, the pixel intensities were rescaled

---

[1] https://pytorch.org/.
[2] https://pjreddie.com/darknet/yolo/.

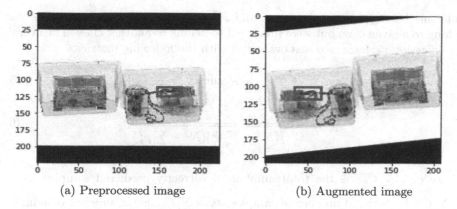

(a) Preprocessed image   (b) Augmented image

Fig. 1. Example showing the preprocessed and one of the augmented versions of an image from the OPIXray dataset. The image's ID is 016424.

to be in the range $[0, 1]$. Next, images were normalized with the statistics from the MS-COCO dataset (channel-wise means and standard deviations) as the Darknet-53 model was pre-trained on this dataset. As for data augmentation techniques, horizontal flipping and random-angle rotation were applied. During the training phase, each image in the training dataset was horizontally flipped with a probability of 50% and rotated by a random angle between $-20°$ and $20°$. These augmentation techniques were applied to increase the generalizability of the model. An example of a preprocessed and augmented image is presented in Fig. 1.

The loss function consisted of three components: the cross-entropy loss for class predictions, the mean squared error function for coordinates' predictions, and the binary cross-entropy loss for objectness prediction. The coordinates' loss was multiplied by a factor of 1000 to keep the magnitudes of the values of these components similar. The Adam optimizer was used with a learning rate of 0.0001. The model was trained for 100 epochs.

4   Model Performance

The following performance metrics were used for the evaluation of the model's performance on each of the classes:

$$\text{Precision} = \frac{TP_k}{TP_k + FP_k}, \tag{2}$$

$$\text{Recall} = \frac{TP_k}{TP_k + FN_k}, \tag{3}$$

$$F_1 = 2 \times \frac{Precision \times Recall}{Precision + Recall}, \tag{4}$$

where TP_k is the number of samples predicted correctly for a given class k, FP_k is the number of the samples that were predicted to belong to a given class but truly belonged to another class, and FN_k is the number of the samples that belong to a given class but were predicted to belong to another class. The overall classification performance was evaluated with the following metrics:

$$\text{Accuracy} = \frac{c}{N} \text{ and} \tag{5}$$

$$\text{MCC} = \frac{c \times N - \sum_k t_k \times p_k}{\sqrt{(N^2 - \sum_k t_k^2)(N^2 - \sum_k p_k^2)}}, \tag{6}$$

where $c = \sum_k C_{kk}$ is the total number of correctly predicted samples, $N = \sum_i \sum_j C_{ij}$ is the total number of samples, $t_k = \sum_i C_{ik}$ is the number of samples belonging to class k and $p_k = \sum_i C_{ki}$ is the number of samples predicted to belong to class k, C_{ij} being the element of the confusion matrix. The abbreviation MCC stands for Matthews-Correlation Coefficient. Here, the generalized form is given. The MCC is especially well suited to quantify the classification performance on imbalanced datasets.

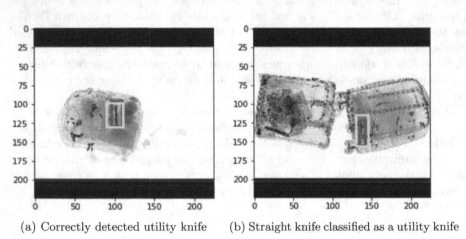

(a) Correctly detected utility knife   (b) Straight knife classified as a utility knife

Fig. 2. The examples of the output of the model on the testing data. The red rectangles represent the true bounding boxes, and yellow represent the predicted ones. (Color figure online)

All the experiments were computed on a workstation with two Nvidia RTX A6000 GPUs. The average time of training for one epoch was 92 s.

The performance metrics are presented in Table 4. The overall performance of our model is good as total accuracy and MCC are high on both the training and testing datasets. Speaking of class performance, the model shows excellent

Table 4. The performance metrics for the YOLOv3 object detection model for the training and testing datasets.

	Train set			Test set		
Category	Precision	Recall	F_1-score	Precision	Recall	F_1-score
Folding knife	0.95	0.92	0.93	0.95	0.91	0.93
Multi-tool knife	0.96	0.97	0.96	0.99	0.95	0.97
Scissors	0.95	0.98	0.96	0.97	0.98	0.97
Straight knife	0.88	0.71	0.79	0.84	0.60	0.70
Utility knife	0.86	0.94	0.90	0.75	0.96	0.84
Total Accuracy	0.92			0.90		
MCC	0.90			0.88		

results on three out of five classes. There is a relatively high amount of false negatives for the straight knife class. According to other metrics, this class is often misclassified for the utility knife class (the utility knife class has a relatively high number of false positives). The reason for that might be the fact that this class is underrepresented (see Table 3). At the same time, the results for MCC show that the performance is quite balanced. Two examples of the output of the model are presented in Fig. 2.

5   Conclusion

In this paper, we propose a methodology for object detection in 3D CT scans via transfer learning. The projection technique is proposed as a method for 2D representation of 3D data. Different models can be applied to 2D images via transfer learning. The YOLOv3 object detection model is validated on the trial dataset consisting of CT scans. The results show that the accuracy of the model is 0.90 on the test set.

In future research, the proposed methodology will be applied to a biomatter dataset consisting of 3D images showing biomatter like fruits and meat within passengers' bags. This dataset only recently has become available to us. The biosecurity policy of some states [14] (Australia, New Zealand, Hawaii) requires the screening of items coming from abroad. Unwanted pests and organisms might be harmful to the environment, economy and people's health. The future research might lead to benefits for the rapid biomatter detection.

Acknowledgement. Supported by the New Zealand Ministry for Primary Industries.

References

1. Abid, M.M.N., Zia, T., Ghafoor, M., Windridge, D.: Multi-view convolutional recurrent neural networks for lung cancer nodule identification. Neurocomputing **453**, 299–311 (2021)
2. Akcay, S., Kundegorski, M.E., Willcocks, C.G., Breckon, T.P.: Using deep convolutional neural network architectures for object classification and detection within X-ray baggage security imagery. IEEE Trans. Inf. Forensics Secur. **13**(9), 2203–2215 (2018)
3. Chavaillaz, A., Schwaninger, A., Michel, S., Sauer, J.: Expertise, automation and trust in X-ray screening of cabin baggage. Front. Psychol. **10**, 256 (2019)
4. De Silva, T., Jayakar, G., Grisso, P., Hotaling, N., Chew, E.Y., Cukras, C.A.: Deep learning-based automatic detection of ellipsoid zone loss in spectral-domain OCT for hydroxychloroquine retinal toxicity screening. Ophthalmol. Sci. **1**(4), 100060 (2021)
5. Deng, J., Dong, W., Socher, R., Li, L.J., Li, K., Fei-Fei, L.: ImageNet: a large-scale hierarchical image database. In: 2009 IEEE Conference on Computer Vision and Pattern Recognition, pp. 248–255. IEEE (2009)
6. Ebrahimi, A., Luo, S., Chiong, R.: Introducing transfer learning to 3D ResNet-18 for Alzheimer's disease detection on MRI images. In: 2020 35th International Conference on Image and Vision Computing New Zealand (IVCNZ), pp. 1–6. IEEE (2020)
7. García, G., Colomer, A., Naranjo, V.: Glaucoma detection from raw SD-OCT volumes: a novel approach focused on spatial dependencies. Comput. Methods Programs Biomed. **200**, 105855 (2021)
8. Gené-Mola, J., et al.: Fruit detection and 3D location using instance segmentation neural networks and structure-from-motion photogrammetry. Comput. Electron. Agric. **169**, 105165 (2020)
9. Géron, A.: Hands-on machine learning with Scikit-Learn, Keras, and TensorFlow: concepts, tools, and techniques to build intelligent systems. O'Reilly Media, Inc. (2019)
10. Hubel, D.H., Wiesel, T.N.: Receptive fields, binocular interaction and functional architecture in the cat's visual cortex. J. Physiol. **160**(1), 106 (1962)
11. Hussein, S., Cao, K., Song, Q., Bagci, U.: Risk stratification of lung nodules using 3D CNN-Based multi-task learning. In: Niethammer, M., et al. (eds.) IPMI 2017. LNCS, vol. 10265, pp. 249–260. Springer, Cham (2017). https://doi.org/10.1007/978-3-319-59050-9_20
12. Jain, R., Jain, N., Aggarwal, A., Hemanth, D.J.: Convolutional neural network based Alzheimer's disease classification from magnetic resonance brain images. Cogn. Syst. Res. **57**, 147–159 (2019)
13. Jakubicek, R., Chmelik, J., Jan, J., Ourednicek, P., Lambert, L., Gavelli, G.: Learning-based vertebra localization and labeling in 3D CT data of possibly incomplete and pathological spines. Comput. Methods Programs Biomed. **183**, 105081 (2020)
14. Jay, M., Morad, M., Bell, A.: Biosecurity, a policy dilemma for New Zealand. Land Use Policy **20**(2), 121–129 (2003)
15. Kaur, A., Kaur, L., Singh, A.: GA-UNet: UNet-based framework for segmentation of 2D and 3D medical images applicable on heterogeneous datasets. Neural Comput. Appl. **33**(21), 14991–15025 (2021)

16. Li, S., et al.: Automatic location scheme of anatomical landmarks in 3D head MRI based on the scale attention hourglass network. Comput. Methods Programs Biomed. **214**, 106564 (2022)
17. Li, X., Chen, H., Qi, X., Dou, Q., Fu, C.W., Heng, P.A.: H-DenseUNet: hybrid densely connected UNet for liver and tumor segmentation from CT volumes. IEEE Trans. Med. Imaging **37**(12), 2663–2674 (2018)
18. Lin, T.-Y., et al.: Microsoft COCO: common objects in context. In: Fleet, D., Pajdla, T., Schiele, B., Tuytelaars, T. (eds.) ECCV 2014. LNCS, vol. 8693, pp. 740–755. Springer, Cham (2014). https://doi.org/10.1007/978-3-319-10602-1_48
19. Meng, X., Peng, Y., Guo, Y.: An adaptive multi-scale network with nonorthogonal multi-union input for reducing false positive of lymph nodes. Biocybern. Biomed. Eng. **41**(1), 265–277 (2021)
20. Mery, D.: Computer Vision for X-Ray Testing. Springer, Cham (2015). https://doi.org/10.1007/978-3-319-20747-6
21. Mitchell, T.M.: Machine Learning, vol. 1. McGraw-hill New York (1997)
22. Nigri, E., Ziviani, N., Cappabianco, F., Antunes, A., Veloso, A.: Explainable deep CNNs for MRI-based diagnosis of Alzheimer's disease. In: 2020 International Joint Conference on Neural Networks (IJCNN), pp. 1–8. IEEE (2020)
23. Perslev, M., Dam, E.B., Pai, A., Igel, C.: One network to segment them all: a general, lightweight system for accurate 3D medical image segmentation. In: Shen, D., et al. (eds.) MICCAI 2019. LNCS, vol. 11765, pp. 30–38. Springer, Cham (2019). https://doi.org/10.1007/978-3-030-32245-8_4
24. Redmon, J., Divvala, S., Girshick, R., Farhadi, A.: You only look once: unified, real-time object detection. In: Proceedings of the IEEE Conference on Computer Vision and Pattern Recognition, pp. 779–788 (2016)
25. Redmon, J., Farhadi, A.: YOLO9000: better, faster, stronger. In: Proceedings of the IEEE Conference on Computer Vision and Pattern Recognition, pp. 7263–7271 (2017)
26. Redmon, J., Farhadi, A.: YOLOv3: an incremental improvement. arXiv preprint arXiv:1804.02767 (2018)
27. Rohila, V.S., Gupta, N., Kaul, A., Sharma, D.K.: Deep learning assisted COVID-19 detection using full CT-scans. Internet of Things **14**, 100377 (2021)
28. Schwaninger, A., Bolfing, A., Halbherr, T., Helman, S., Belyavin, A., Hay, L.: The impact of image based factors and training on threat detection performance in X-ray screening (2008)
29. Setio, A.A.A., et al.: Validation, comparison, and combination of algorithms for automatic detection of pulmonary nodules in computed tomography images: the LUNA16 challenge. Med. Image Anal. **42**, 1–13 (2017)
30. Simpson, A.L., et al.: A large annotated medical image dataset for the development and evaluation of segmentation algorithms. arXiv preprint arXiv:1902.09063 (2019)
31. Taguchi, G.: Introduction to quality engineering: designing quality into products and processes (1986)
32. Tajbakhsh, N., Jeyaseelan, L., Li, Q., Chiang, J.N., Wu, Z., Ding, X.: Embracing imperfect datasets: A review of deep learning solutions for medical image segmentation. Med. Image Anal. **63**, 101693 (2020)
33. Wales, A., Halbherr, T., Schwaninger, A.: Using speed measures to predict performance in X-ray luggage screening tasks. In: 43rd Annual 2009 International Carnahan Conference on Security Technology, pp. 212–215. IEEE (2009)
34. Wang, X., et al.: A deep learning algorithm for automatic detection and classification of acute intracranial hemorrhages in head CT scans. NeuroImage: Clin. **32**, 102785 (2021)

35. Wei, Y., Tao, R., Wu, Z., Ma, Y., Zhang, L., Liu, X.: Occluded prohibited items detection: an X-ray security inspection benchmark and de-occlusion attention module. In: Proceedings of the 28th ACM International Conference on Multimedia, pp. 138–146 (2020)
36. Weiss, K., Khoshgoftaar, T.M., Wang, D.: A survey of transfer learning. J. Big data 3(1), 1–40 (2016)
37. Xia, Y., Xie, L., Liu, F., Zhu, Z., Fishman, E.K., Yuille, A.L.: Bridging the gap between 2D and 3D organ segmentation with volumetric fusion net. In: Frangi, A.F., Schnabel, J.A., Davatzikos, C., Alberola-López, C., Fichtinger, G. (eds.) MICCAI 2018. LNCS, vol. 11073, pp. 445–453. Springer, Cham (2018). https://doi.org/10.1007/978-3-030-00937-3_51
38. Yang, J., et al.: Reinventing 2D convolutions for 3D images. IEEE J. Biomed. Health Inform. 25(8), 3009–3018 (2021)
39. Zhang, Q., Wang, X., Jiang, J., Ma, L.: Deep learning features inspired saliency detection of 3D images. In: Chen, E., Gong, Y., Tie, Y. (eds.) PCM 2016. LNCS, vol. 9917, pp. 580–589. Springer, Cham (2016). https://doi.org/10.1007/978-3-319-48896-7_57
40. Zheng, H., et al.: A new ensemble learning framework for 3D biomedical image segmentation. In: Proceedings of the AAAI Conference on Artificial Intelligence, vol. 33, pp. 5909–5916 (2019)

AUAAC: Area Under Accuracy-Accuracy Curve for Evaluating Out-of-Distribution Detection

Wonjik Kim[1]([envelope]) [ID], Masayuki Tanaka[1,2] [ID], and Masatoshi Okutomi[2] [ID]

[1] Artificial Intelligence Research Center,
National Institute of Advanced Industrial Science and Technology,
Umezono, Tsukuba 305-8560, Japan
kim-wonjik@aist.go.jp
[2] Department of Systems and Control Engineering, School of Engineering,
Tokyo Institute of Technology, Meguro-ku, Tokyo 152-8550, Japan
{mtanaka,mxo}@sc.e.titech.ac.jp

Abstract. Determining whether input data are out-of-distribution (OOD) is important for real-world applications of machine learning. Various approaches to OOD detection have been proposed, and there is a growing interest in evaluating their performance. A commonly employed approach for OOD detection is training the network model using an in-distribution (IND) task and then applying a threshold to the probability estimated of unknown data. However, current evaluation metrics only assess the OOD detection performance while neglecting the IND task performance. To address this issue, we propose new evaluation metrics for OOD detection. Our novel metric, the area under the accuracy-accuracy curve (AUAAC), is designed to simultaneously evaluate both the IND task and OOD detection performances. Specifically, it calculates the area under the accuracy-accuracy curve after estimating the accuracy of the IND task and OOD detection for all thresholds. Flaws within the training dataset, such as contaminated labels or inaccurate annotations, disturb the network in properly performing the IND task. Nevertheless, the network may distinguish whether new input data are in IND because it was priorly exposed to IND data and trained by their features. The proposed AUAAC can asses such malfunction while existing evaluation metrics overlook the performance of the IND task and cannot identify such issues.

Keywords: Deep learning · Out-of-distribution detection · Evaluation metric

1 Introduction

Learning-based deep neural network methods have demonstrated high performance with controlled data in various tasks. Those methods implicitly assume that training and test data distributions are the same. However, the test data

© The Author(s), under exclusive license to Springer Nature Singapore Pte Ltd. 2024
W. Q. Yan et al. (Eds.): PSIVT 2023, LNCS 14403, pp. 43–55, 2024.
https://doi.org/10.1007/978-981-97-0376-0_4

distribution is often different from that of training data. That mismatch significantly degrades the performance. Then, in practice, it is important to detect unexpected data before using it. This detection task is known as the out-of-distribution (OOD) detection task [5]. The main task is called as in-distribution (IND) task. In this paper, we focus on the classification task for the IND task.

Various OOD detection algorithms have been proposed after the OOD detection task was well formulated [5]. One of these approaches is to feed OOD data to the network during the IND task training phase, so that the network can learn differences between IND and OOD data [2,6,8,13,16,25]. However, those approaches require IND and OOD data to train the network model. Then, OOD detection algorithms only require IND datasets have been proposed [1,3,14,15,19,20]. The OOD detection performance of the network model is usually evaluated after training the network model for the IND task, implicitly assuming that the IND task performance of the network model is good enough. The OOD detection performance of the network model is usually evaluated after training the network model for the IND task, implicitly assuming that the IND task performance of the network model is good enough. However, we can easily improve the OOD detection performance if we allow the degradation of the IND task performance. For this reason, it is very important to evaluate simultaneously the IND task performance and the OOD detection performance.

The true negative rate (TNR) at 95% true positive rate (TPR) is a widely used metric to evaluate the OOD detection performance. The TPR is defined by TP/(TP+FN) and the TNR is defined by TN/(TN+FP), where TP, TN, FP, and FN are the numbers of true positive, true negative, false positive, and false negative, respectively. IND and OOD data are considered as positive and negative samples. The metric of the TNR at 95% TPR indicates the probability of correctly detecting OOD data when the network model can detect the IND data with 95% accuracy. Scherreik *et al.* [18] used maximum Youden's index [23] as a metric to evaluate the OOD detection performance. Youden's index is defined by the sum of TPR and TNR and is usually used to determine the proper parameter based on Receiver Operating Characteristic (ROC) curve. The area under the receiver operating characteristic curve (AUROC) has become a popular metric, as it summarizes TPR performance for all possible thresholds and is insensitive to threshold selection. The ROC curve for calculating AUROC depicts the relationship between true and false positive rates. An open-set F-score [10] is recently proposed for a metric to evaluate the OOD detection performance. Note that those three metrics can evaluate the OOD performance, while they commonly neglect the classification accuracy of the IND data.

However, in practice, OOD detection is not the final goal of the classification task. In this sense, we need to evaluate both IND classification accuracy and OOD detection performance. For example, if the network model has high IND classification accuracy with low OOD detection performance, that network model cannot work well in the practical situation because the input data includes both IND and OOD data. To address this issue, a concise pairwise formulation called OpenAUC [21] has been proposed for simultaneously evaluating both the IND task and OOD detection performance. OpenAUC is a concise pairwise formulation where each pair consists of IND and OOD data. First, the metric checks whether the IND data are correctly classified into known IND classes, then confirms whether the OOD data are detected. This approach allows for a more comprehensive evaluation of OOD detection methods.

We introduce a new metric called the area under the accuracy-accuracy curve (AUAAC) which is designed to simultaneously evaluate both the IND task and OOD detection performance. We first estimate the accuracy of the IND task and OOD detection for all thresholds. Next, we draw the accuracy-accuracy curve (AAC), with the OOD detection accuracy on the horizontal axis and the IND task accuracy on the vertical axis. Finally, we calculate the area under the AAC (AUAAC) to comprehensively evaluate OOD detection performance.

In order to validate the proposed metrics, we conducted experiments on two different network models using three IND datasets and five OOD datasets. We evaluated the OOD detection performance using three metrics: TNR at TPR 95%, AUROC, and AUAAC. Our analysis confirmed the importance of incorporating AUAAC to account for IND task performance. The dataset used for the IND task can potentially contain flaws, such as contaminated labels or incorrect annotations. When trained with such flawed data, the network may fail to perform correctly on the IND task. However, the network might still demonstrate an ability to detect OOD data. This is because the network previously encountered IND data and was trained by their features, enabling it to recognize characteristics that observe data as different from the IND. In other words, the network exposed to IND data allows it to distinguish whether the brand new data are in IND. Since existing evaluation metrics do not consider the performance of the IND task, they cannot catch out such malfunctioning networks. This highlights the importance of considering IND task performance even in OOD detection, and AUAAC can operate as an evaluation metric for this purpose. Additionally, we investigated the behavior of AUAAC during the training phase to gain further insights into its characteristics. Based on the experimental results, we concluded that the proposed metrics serve as valuable tools for evaluating network models in terms of both OOD detection and IND task performance.

2   Proposed Metric

Let $\mathbf{f} : \mathcal{X} \to \mathbb{R}^K$ be a network model which infers the class from an input image, where $\mathcal{X}$ is the input image space and K is the number of classes. The network model $\mathbf{f}$ has parameters to be trained with the training data.

We consider the problem of distinguishing IND and OOD data with a trained network model. For an input image $\mathbf{x}$, the network model estimates a probability $\mathbf{f}(\mathbf{x})$, and compare with the OOD threshold τ. An input image $\mathbf{x}$ is classified as IND if the maximum probability is greater than the threshold τ as follows:

$$\mathbf{x} \text{ is classified as } \begin{cases} \text{IND} & (\max \mathbf{f}(\mathbf{x}) \geq \tau) \\ \text{OOD} & (else) \end{cases}. \tag{1}$$

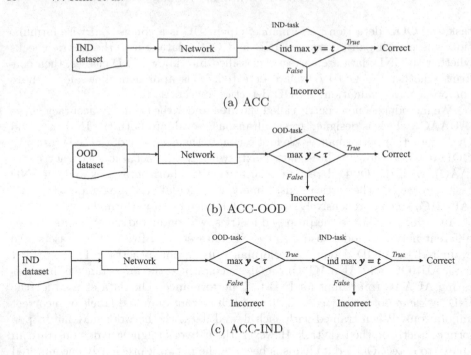

(a) ACC

(b) ACC-OOD

(c) ACC-IND

Fig. 1. Calculation flowchart of three metrics.

2.1 Three Accuracy Metrics

First, we review the performance evaluations of the IND classification and the OOD detection tasks. Here, we consider three accuracies related to the IND classification and the OOD detection tasks; ACC, ACC-IND, and ACC-OOD. ACC represents the classical accuracy focusing on the IND classification task only. ACC-IND is the accuracy of the IND classification task considering the OOD detection, which is newly introduced in this paper. ACC-OOD is the accuracy of the OOD detection task. The accuracy can be generally defined by

$$\text{Accuracy} = E_{(x,t)\sim\Omega}[g(f(x), t)], \tag{2}$$

where Ω represents a dataset of the images and the labels, x represents the image, t is associated ground truth label index, and the function g is refer to the correctness function which specifies the property of the accuracy. Here, we consider ground truth label index has a positive integer value for the IND sample and a negative value for the OOD sample. We will show three different correctness functions with the dataset are associated to three accuracies of ACC, ACC-IND, and ACC-OOD.

For ACC which is the accuracy of the classical IND classification task, the correctness function g_{ACC} can be defined by

$$g_{\text{ACC}}(y, t) = \begin{cases} 1 & (\text{ind} \max y = t) \\ 0 & (else) \end{cases}, \tag{3}$$

where $\operatorname{ind} \max \boldsymbol{y}$ represents the index of maximum element of $\boldsymbol{y}$. The correctness function g_{ACC} returns one if the IND classification inference by the network model is correct. Then, ACC of the classical IND classification accuracy can be evaluated by Eq. 2 with the correctness function g_{ACC} in Eq. 3 and the IND dataset of Ω_{IND}. The flowchart for calculating ACC can be illustrated in Fig. 1a.

For ACC-OOD which is the OOD detection task, the function g_{OOD} can be defined by

$$g_{\mathrm{OOD}}(\boldsymbol{y}, t; \tau) = \begin{cases} 1 \ (t \times (\max \boldsymbol{y} - \tau) > 0) \\ 0 \qquad (else) \end{cases}. \tag{4}$$

If the maximum value of inference $\boldsymbol{y}$ is greater than the threshold τ, the associated sample is estimated as an IND sample. We set the positive integer value for the label of the IND sample and the negative value for the label of the OOD sample. Then, the function g_{OOD} in Eq. 4 returns one if the OOD detection inference is correct. ACC-OOD of the OOD detection accuracy can be evaluated by Eq. 2 with the function g_{OOD} in Eq. 4 and the OOD dataset of Ω_{OOD}, as shown in Fig. 1b. Based on the equations, it is obvious that the calculation of ACC-OOD solely relies on the OOD dataset and does not take into account the IND data.

For the practical classification task, we need to evaluate the classification accuracy considering the OOD detection. Here, we introduce the new accuracy of ACC-IND (Fig. 1c), which can evaluate the IND classification accuracy after the OOD detection. If both the IND classification inference and the OOD detection inference are correct, we consider it to be correct for the ACC-IND. The associated correctness function of g_{IND} can be defined by

$$g_{\mathrm{IND}}(\boldsymbol{y}, t; \tau) = g_{\mathrm{ACC}}(\boldsymbol{y}, t) \times g_{\mathrm{OOD}}(\boldsymbol{y}, t; \tau). \tag{5}$$

For the IND dataset, the function g_{OOD} should be one for the correct inference. In addition, the IND classification inference should also be correct, or the function g_{ACC} should be one for the correct inference. The function g_{IND} returns ones if the inference is correct. Then, ACC-IND of the IND classification accuracy considering the OOD detection can be evaluated by Eq. 2 with the function g_{IND} in Eq. 5 and the IND dataset of Ω_{IND}. Note that ACC-IND is evaluated based on the IND dataset Ω_{IND}.

2.2 AUAAC: Area Under Accuracy-Accuracy Curve

We propose a metric to evaluate both the IND classification accuracy and the OOD detection accuracy, which we call the area under the accuracy-accuracy curve (AUAAC). The AUAAC is defined based on ACC-IND and ACC-OOD, which were introduced in the previous section. As mentioned above, ACC-IND and ACC-OOD have the parameter of threshold τ. Then, we can draw the accuracy-accuracy curve whose horizontal and vertical axes are ACC-OOD and ACC-IND, changing the threshold parameter τ. Figure 2b shows an example of the accuracy-accuracy curve. Following the idea of area under the ROC curve, we propose a metric of the AUAAC as the area under the accuracy-accuracy. The

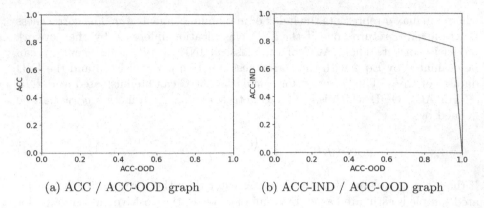

(a) ACC / ACC-OOD graph   (b) ACC-IND / ACC-OOD graph

Fig. 2. Example of the accuracy-accuracy curve.

maximum value of the AUAAC is one. It is worth noting that employing ACC instead of the proposed ACC-IND on the Y-axis, as depicted in Fig. 2a, restricts the examination of IND task performance through threshold value changes.

Recall that ACC-IND is evaluated only with the IND dataset and that ACC-OOD is evaluated only with the OOD dataset. Assuming the network model infers posterior probabilities, when the thresholding parameter τ is 0, ACC-OOD is zero because all data of the OOD dataset is wrongly classified as IND data. In addition, ACC-OOD is one for $\tau = 1$ because all data of the OOD dataset is correctly classified as OOD data. When the thresholding parameter τ increases, the ACC-OOD also increases. ACC-IND of $\tau = 0$ is identical to the classical ACC. In other words, ACC-IND at zero ACC-OOD equals the classical ACC. By definition of Eq. 5, when the thresholding parameter τ increases, the ACC-IND decreases. Then, the accuracy-accuracy curve is non-increase property.

Let's consider the real-world application. In the real-world application, input data includes the IND and the OOD data. Assuming we have a trained network model, we need to determine the suitable threshold parameter τ, because here is a trade-off relationship between ACC-IND and ACC-OOD as shown in Fig. 2b.

Recent deep neural networks often overfit the training data, which leads to improved performance on the IND task during continued training. However, the network model can become overconfident, resulting in high confidence estimates even for OOD data and a decrease in OOD detection accuracy. Deciding when to stop training becomes a complex multi-objective optimization problem when considering both IND task performance and OOD detection accuracy. The proposed AUAAC metric evaluates both performance metrics simultaneously and can be used as a simple criterion for stopping network training.

3   Experiments

First, we evaluated the OOD detection performance of two network models, ResNet-34 and DenseNet-VC-100, trained with three different IND datasets. We employed three evaluation metrics: TNR at TPR 95%, AUROC, and proposed AUAAC, to evaluate the OOD detection performance. Subsequently, we examined the behavior of ACC, ACC-IND, ACC-OOD, and proposed AUAAC of ResNet-34 during the training phase to gain insights into the characteristics of the proposed AUAAC.

3.1 Experimental Setup

We conducted comparative experiments under the following conditions to confirm the behavior of the proposed AUAAC metric compared to other evaluation metrics for OOD detection. For the IND datasets, we used the standard split of CIFAR-100 [11], CIFAR-10 [11], and SVHN [17]. These datasets contain RGB images with 32×32 pixels. For the OOD test dataset, we used iSUN [22], LSUN [24], and TinyImageNet [12]. As same as in [14], we used two variants of TinyImageNet, and LSUN sets: '(C)' stands for using a 32×32 image crop, and '(R)' stands for using resized images to 32×32 pixels. We also used CIFAR-100, CIFAR-10, and SVHN as OOD if a model was not trained with them. We employed ResNet-34 [4] and DenseNet-BC-100 [7] to train the image classification models. The networks were trained by categorical cross-entropy loss function using Adam [9] with a 0.001 learning rate in 400 epochs, and the batch size is 128.

Additionally, we investigated the behavior of ACC, ACC-IND, ACC-OOD, and AUAAC of ResNet-34 during the training phase. In calculating ACC-IND and ACC-OOD, a threshold was set so that 95% of IND data were correctly determined as IND. For a dataset that represents known classes, we used the standard split of CIFAR-10 [11]. For the OOD performance evaluation, we use TinyImageNet [12] with 32×32 image crop. The network was trained by categorical cross-entropy loss function using Adam [9] with a 0.001 learning rate in 1000 epochs. The batch size is 128.

3.2 Results

Table 1 presents the results of OOD detection using DenseNet-BC-100. TNR at TPR 95% shows a similar tendency as AUROC since both metrics only evaluate OOD detection accuracy. Since AUAAC does not directly evaluate OOD detection performance, it may exhibit less sensitivity toward OOD detection compared to other metrics. This trend is evident in Tables 1 and 2, where the values of AUAAC show a similar trend to AUROC but exhibit smaller changes compared to TNR at TPR 95% and AUROC.

By incorporating AUAAC alongside other metrics, we can better understand the network's performance. For instance, AUROC helps determine the network's ability to effectively distinguish between IND and OOD data. On the other hand, AUAAC allows us to assess not only OOD detection performance but also the network's performance in the IND task. While a high AUROC suggests good

Table 1. OOD detection performance of DenseNet-BC-100 in three metrics. Results reported in percentage.

IND	OOD	Metrics		
		TNR at TPR 95%	AUROC	AUAAC
CIFAR-100	iSUN	3.3	37.2	37.8
	LSUN (C)	13.8	70.7	54.8
	LSUN (R)	2.8	34.9	37.8
	ImageNet (C)	6.9	50.6	44.4
	ImageNet (R)	4.0	39.5	39.6
	SVHN	11.2	70.0	54.1
CIFAR-10	iSUN	31.0	87.4	81.9
	LSUN (C)	42.2	91.3	84.7
	LSUN (R)	32.5	88.5	83.0
	ImageNet (C)	30.1	87.7	82.2
	ImageNet (R)	28.6	86.7	81.7
	SVHN	46.2	92.8	85.0
SVHN	iSUN	60.4	93.7	89.2
	LSUN (C)	55.4	91.3	86.1
	LSUN (R)	57.5	92.9	88.5
	ImageNet (C)	60.6	93.6	88.8
	ImageNet (R)	61.7	93.6	89.3
	CIFAR-10	53.6	91.6	86.1
	CIFAR-100	52.8	91.4	86.1

OOD detection capability, it does not guarantee strong performance in the IND task. Conversely, a high AUAAC indicates potential competence in both the IND task and OOD detection. Table 3 presents the OOD detection results for ResNet34, which was trained on Cifar10 as an IND dataset but had a Top-1 accuracy of 6.2% due to incorrect class labels. The results indicate that even when trained with the wrong labels, the metrics TNR at TPR 95% and AUROC, which only evaluate OOD detection performance, exhibit acceptable values. However, it is meaningful that the AUAAC, which also assesses the performance of the IND task, demonstrates significantly lower values. In other words, the existing evaluation metrics cannot identify if the network does not perform adequately in IND tasks for some reason. It highlights the advantage of utilizing the proposed AUAAC metric, which can simultaneously assess the IND task and OOD detection performance.

Figure 3 shows the change in ACC, ACC-IND, AUAAC, and ACC-OOD for a thousand epochs of network training. Figure 3a shows that the classification

Table 2. OOD detection performance of ResNet-34 in three metrics. Results reported in percentage.

IND	OOD	Metrics		
		TNR at TPR 95%	AUROC	AUAAC
CIFAR-100	iSUN	14.0	75.4	58.6
	LSUN (C)	15.5	75.6	58.5
	LSUN (R)	15.7	77.6	59.9
	ImageNet (C)	17.4	78.5	60.3
	ImageNet (R)	14.3	76.4	59.2
	SVHN	12.2	72.9	57.2
CIFAR-10	iSUN	39.2	89.4	84.9
	LSUN (C)	46.7	91.9	86.9
	LSUN (R)	40.2	89.7	85.1
	ImageNet (C)	39.5	88.2	83.8
	ImageNet (R)	34.4	86.5	82.4
	SVHN	38.8	91.4	86.3
SVHN	iSUN	67.8	94.2	90.4
	LSUN (C)	67.4	94.1	90.2
	LSUN (R)	67.0	93.9	90.1
	ImageNet (C)	70.4	94.9	91.0
	ImageNet (R)	70.0	94.6	90.7
	CIFAR-10	62.2	92.6	88.9
	CIFAR-100	61.5	92.3	88.6

accuracy stably improves as the number of epochs increases. Figure 3b shows that the ACC-OOD achieves a peak at 572 epochs and then gradually falls off. The moving average graph more explicitly confirms the trend of accuracy decay. The graphs of AUAAC in Fig. 3a and the accuracy of OOD detection in Fig. 3b show similar tendencies in peaks and valleys. This is because the ACC-OOD is also taken into account when calculating AUAAC. However, we can see that the range of variation in AUAAC is smaller than that of OOD detection accuracy.

Table 4 summarizes four metrics of ACC, ACC-IND, ACC-OOD, and AUAAC at several epochs. For example, early stopping is an important technique to avoid overfitting. But, it is not an easy task to determine when we should stop the training. If we want to maximize the classical ACC, Table 1 shows that we need to continue the training until 990 epochs. On the other hand, if we focus on ACC-OOD, which represents the OOD detection accuracy, it might be good to stop at 572 epochs. However, ACC-OOD does not reflect any information about ACC and/or ACC-IND. So, there is no guarantee that the network model has sufficient good accuracy in terms of the IND classification accuracy. The proposed AUAAC can evaluate both the IND classification

Table 3. OOD detection performance of ResNet-34 trained with wrong label (Top-1 accuracy of 6.2%) in three metrics. Results reported in percentage.

IND	OOD	Metrics		
		TNR at TPR 95%	AUROC	AUAAC
CIFAR-10	iSUN	51.2	92.5	4.3
	LSUN (C)	46.9	92.4	4.2
	LSUN (R)	53.7	93.5	4.4
	ImageNet (C)	47.7	92.3	4.1
	ImageNet (R)	48.5	92.4	4.2
	SVHN	40.9	90.7	3.8

Table 4. ACC, ACC-IND, ACC-OOD, and AUAAC of different training epochs.

Epoch	ACC	ACC-IND	ACC-OOD	AUAAC
572	0.935	0.910	**0.520**	0.879
612	0.939	0.914	0.486	**0.882**
796	0.943	**0.918**	0.450	0.872
884	**0.944**	0.915	0.418	0.851

accuracy and the OOD detection performance. Therefore, we can use AUAAC for the stopping criteria. If we train the network to maximize the AUAAC, the network model is expected to have reasonably good IND classification accuracy and OOD detection accuracy.

We also show the Accuracy-Accuracy Curves (AACs) and the proposed metric of AUAAC at several epochs in Fig. 4. As shown in Fig. 4, the AAC varies as the training progresses and the area changes. Therefore, it is also possible to check at what epoch and at what threshold the desired IND classification accuracy and OOD detection accuracy are achieved. For instance, when comparing the AACs at 700 epochs and 1000 epochs, the AUAAC of the 700 epoch is larger, suggesting superior performance. Nevertheless, if an OOD detection rate of 0.8 is sufficient, then training for 1000 epochs is the preferred choice since it yields greater accuracy for IND classification at the OOD detection rate of 0.8. On the other hand, if a desired OOD detection rate of 95% is targeted, training for 700 epochs would be more suitable. Thus, the proposed method can facilitate the selection of networks and thresholds based on more intricate decision criteria.

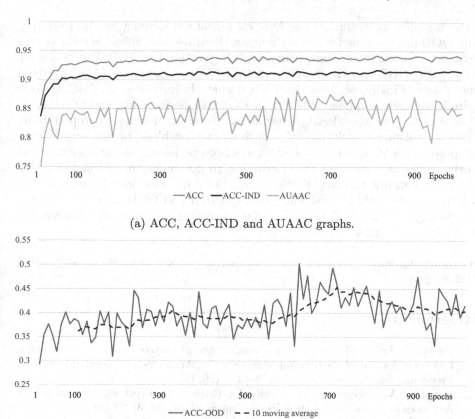

(a) ACC, ACC-IND and AUAAC graphs.

(b) ACC-OOD and 10 moving average graphs.

Fig. 3. Training graphs of four-different metrics. The threshold τ is selected that 95% of IND data are determined as IND data.

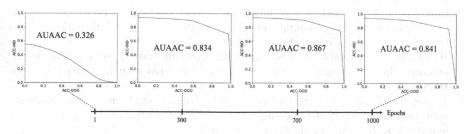

Fig. 4. AUAACs of different training epochs.

4   Conclusions

We have proposed a new metric named the area under the accuracy-accuracy curve (AUAAC) to simultaneously evaluate IND task and OOD detection accuracy. Initially, we evaluated the IND classification accuracy of the IND task and OOD detection performance changing the threshold. Subsequently, we constructed an accuracy-accuracy curve (AAC), plotting the OOD detection accuracy (ACC-OOD) on the X-axis and the IND task accuracy (ACC-IND) on the Y-axis. Finally, we have determined that the proposed AUAAC is good criteria for early stopping. When both IND task performance and OOD detection accuracy are considered, determining the optimal point to stop training becomes a complex multi-objective optimization problem. In this context, the proposed AUAAC metric, which evaluates both performance metrics simultaneously, serves as a straightforward criterion to determine the optimal stopping point for network training. Furthermore, the AAC can provide guidance for selecting a threshold to distinguish between IND and OOD data. By choosing the desired accuracy of IND task or OOD detection, we can readily confirm the accuracy of the other metric.

Acknowledgment. This work was supported by JSPS KAKENHI Grant Number JP23K19985.

References

1. Bibas, K., Feder, M., Hassner, T.: Single layer predictive normalized maximum likelihood for out-of-distribution detection. In: Advances in Neural Information Processing Systems, vol. 34, pp. 1179–1191 (2021)
2. Dhamija, A.R., Günther, M., Boult, T.: Reducing network agnostophobia. In: Advances in Neural Information Processing Systems, vol. 31 (2018)
3. Dong, X., Guo, J., Li, A., Ting, W.T., Liu, C., Kung, H.: Neural mean discrepancy for efficient out-of-distribution detection. In: Proceedings of the IEEE/CVF Conference on Computer Vision and Pattern Recognition, pp. 19217–19227 (2022)
4. He, K., Zhang, X., Ren, S., Sun, J.: Deep residual learning for image recognition. In: Proceedings of the IEEE conference on computer vision and pattern recognition, pp. 770–778 (2016)
5. Hendrycks, D., Gimpel, K.: A baseline for detecting misclassified and out-of-distribution examples in neural networks. In: Proceedings of International Conference on Learning Representations (2017)
6. Hendrycks, D., Mazeika, M., Dietterich, T.: Deep anomaly detection with outlier exposure. In: Proceedings of the International Conference on Learning Representations (2019)
7. Huang, G., Liu, Z., Van Der Maaten, L., Weinberger, K.Q.: Densely connected convolutional networks. In: Proceedings of the IEEE Conference on Computer Vision and Pattern Recognition, pp. 4700–4708 (2017)
8. Katz-Samuels, J., Nakhleh, J.B., Nowak, R., Li, Y.: Training OOD detectors in their natural habitats. In: International Conference on Machine Learning, pp. 10848–10865. PMLR (2022)
9. Kingma, D.P., Ba, J.: Adam: a method for stochastic optimization. arXiv preprint arXiv:1412.6980 (2014)
10. Kong, S., Ramanan, D.: OpenGAN: open-set recognition via open data generation. In: Proceedings of the IEEE/CVF International Conference on Computer Vision, pp. 813–822 (2021)

11. Krizhevsky, A., Hinton, G., et al.: Learning multiple layers of features from tiny images (2009)
12. Le, Y., Yang, X.: Tiny imagenet visual recognition challenge. CS 231N **7**(7), 3 (2015)
13. Lee, K., Lee, H., Lee, K., Shin, J.: Training confidence-calibrated classifiers for detecting out-of-distribution samples. arXiv preprint arXiv:1711.09325 (2017)
14. Liang, S., Li, Y., Srikant, R.: Enhancing the reliability of out-of-distribution image detection in neural networks. arXiv preprint arXiv:1706.02690 (2017)
15. Liu, W., Wang, X., Owens, J., Li, Y.: Energy-based out-of-distribution detection. In: Advances in Neural Information Processing Systems, vol. 33, pp. 21464–21475 (2020)
16. Moller, F., Botache, D., Huseljic, D., Heidecker, F., Bieshaar, M., Sick, B.: Out-of-distribution detection and generation using soft Brownian offset sampling and autoencoders. In: Proceedings of the IEEE/CVF Conference on Computer Vision and Pattern Recognition, pp. 46–55 (2021)
17. Netzer, Y., Wang, T., Coates, A., Bissacco, A., Wu, B., Ng, A.Y.: Reading digits in natural images with unsupervised feature learning. In: NIPS Workshop on Deep Learning and Unsupervised Feature Learning 2011 (2011)
18. Scherreik, M.D., Rigling, B.D.: Open set recognition for automatic target classification with rejection. IEEE Trans. Aerosp. Electron. Syst. **52**(2), 632–642 (2016)
19. Sun, Y., Guo, C., Li, Y.: React: Out-of-distribution detection with rectified activations. In: Advances in Neural Information Processing Systems, vol. 34, pp. 144–157 (2021)
20. Sun, Y., Li, Y.: Dice: Leveraging sparsification for out-of-distribution detection. In: Avidan, S., Brostow, G., Cissé, M., Farinella, G.M., Hassner, T. (eds.) ECCV 2022. LNCS, vol. 13684, pp. 691–708. Springer, Cham (2022). https://doi.org/10.1007/978-3-031-20053-3_40
21. Wang, Z., Xu, Q., Yang, Z., He, Y., Cao, X., Huang, Q.: OpenAUC: towards AUC-oriented open-set recognition. In: Advances in Neural Information Processing Systems, vol. 35, pp. 25033–25045 (2022)
22. Xu, P., Ehinger, K.A., Zhang, Y., Finkelstein, A., Kulkarni, S.R., Xiao, J.: Turkergaze: crowdsourcing saliency with webcam based eye tracking. arXiv preprint arXiv:1504.06755 (2015)
23. Youden, W.J.: Index for rating diagnostic tests. Cancer **3**(1), 32–35 (1950)
24. Yu, F., Seff, A., Zhang, Y., Song, S., Funkhouser, T., Xiao, J.: LSUN: construction of a large-scale image dataset using deep learning with humans in the loop. arXiv preprint arXiv:1506.03365 (2015)
25. Yu, Q., Aizawa, K.: Unsupervised out-of-distribution detection by maximum classifier discrepancy. In: Proceedings of the IEEE/CVF International Conference on Computer Vision, pp. 9518–9526 (2019)

Local Brightness Normalization for Image Classification and Object Detection Robust to Illumination Changes

Yanshuo Lu$^{(\boxtimes)}$, Masayuki Tanaka, Rei Kawakami, and Masatoshi Okutomi

Tokyo Institute of Technology, Tokyo, Japan
ylu@ok.sc.e.titech.ac.jp,
{mtanaka,reikawa,mxo}@sc.e.titech.ac.jp

Abstract. Deep neural networks are typically trained on images taken under controlled illumination. Those networks work well on such images, but not on images that contain severe illumination changes which often occur in practice. To improve the robustness of networks to illumination changes, we propose to use local brightness normalization (LBN) as pre-processing of the input images and to train the network on those normalized images. The LBN can convert images to have similar appearances from various types of illumination changes. Then, we assume that input images of training and testing are more aligned by the LBN. Experimental comparisons of the image classification task and the object detection task show that the proposed LBN-based approach can improve the accuracy with images of uniform and non-uniform illumination changes.

Keywords: Image classification · Object detection · Deep neural network · Image normalization · Local brightness normalization

1 Introduction

A data-driven approach such as deep learning has been a success in many applications of computer vision. In this paper, we focus on image classification and object detection tasks.

The distribution of test images is often different from that of training images in a practical situation. Then, one of the challenges in a data-driven approach is to improve generalization performance. Several corruptions such as noise, blur, compression and adversarial attacks have been introduced to verify the robustness of deep networks [1–6]. Classification networks that are robust to degradation by JPEG distortion, noise, and blur have also been proposed [7–11]. In this paper, we focus on the robustness of the networks against drastic illumination change.

Almost all researchers apply brightness normalization with mean and standard deviation based on statistics of ImageNet dataset [12] as a pre-processing before feeding the images to the networks, assuming that ImageNet dataet represents statistics of natural images. We refer to this normalization as ImageNet

W. Q. Yan et al. (Eds.): PSIVT 2023, LNCS 14403, pp. 56–68, 2024.
https://doi.org/10.1007/978-981-97-0376-0_5

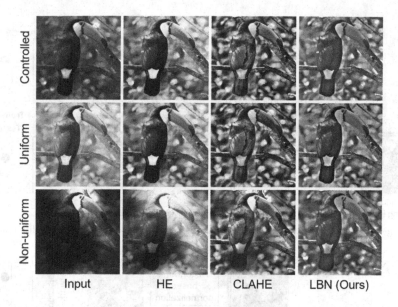

Fig. 1. Appearance restorations of images with controlled illumination, uniform and non-uniform illumination change by histogram equalization (HE) [13], contrast limited adaptive histogram equalization (CLAHE) [14], and local brightness normalization (LBN) [15].

normalization. Many images in ImageNet, however, are a representative image of an object, and therefore they were captured under controlled or appropriate illumination. Therefor, the ImageNet normalization may not work well for images captured under severe illumination changes such as low-light images or images that have very bright and dark regions.

We specifically consider two types of illumination changes: spatially uniform and non-uniform changes. Figure 1 shows examples of appearance restoration for images with controlled illumination, uniform and non-uniform illumination change by histogram equalization (HE) [13], contrast limited adaptive histogram equalization (CLAHE) [14], and local brightness normalization (LBN) [15]. In this paper, we refer to HE and CLAHE as histogram-based normalization. HE and CLAHE can restore the appearance of images with uniform illumination change, while they fail to restore the appearance of images with non-uniform change. On the other hand, LBN can restore the appearance of images with both changes. This is the key observation of this paper.

People may simply think that appearance restoration is good enough for pre-processing; therefore, a combination of histogram-based normalization and ImageNet normalization is often used as shown in Fig. 2-(a). However, that naive approach does not work well because the statistics of the restored images are different from those of natural or training images, even though they appear to

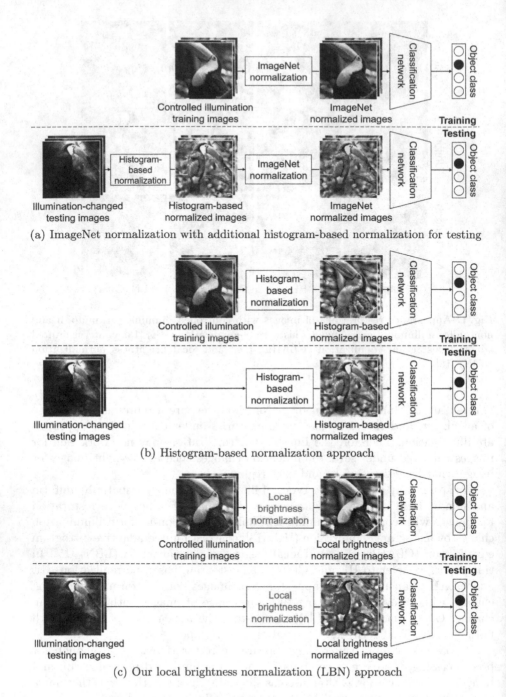

(a) ImageNet normalization with additional histogram-based normalization for testing

(b) Histogram-based normalization approach

(c) Our local brightness normalization (LBN) approach

Fig. 2. Three normalization approaches.

be restored without problems to human eyes[1]. It is important to apply identical pre-processing in training and test phases as shown in Fig. 2-(b) and (c). Based on the above observation, we propose an LBN-based image classification app-roach to improve robustness against illumination changes. The use of LBN is inspired by the finding that the spatial local normalization is a necessary mod-ule in neural computation, while LBN is more simplified compared to the retinal normalization model [16].

Experimental comparisons demonstrate that our LBN-based approach out-performs existing ImageNet normalization approaches and histogram-based nor-malization approaches.

2   Proposed Method

In our LBN-based approach, we apply LBN as pre-processing in both the train-ing and test phases as shown in Fig. 2-(c). LBN normalizes images by subtract-ing the local mean and by dividing the local standard deviation (std.) [15]. For color images, we can consider two variations of LBNs: channel-wise and channel-common LBNs. The channel-wise LBN normalizes each channel image independently. It means that the local mean and the local standard deviation are estimated channel-by-channel. In the channel-common LBN, we calculate the common local mean and the common local standard deviation by averag-ing. Then, the channel-common LBN normalizes images based on the estimated common local mean and standard deviation.

As demonstrated in the experiment section, the channel-common LBN has better performance than the channel-wise LBN. Therefore, here, we describe the channel-common LBN. We estimate the local mean and the local standard deviation by simply applying Gaussian blur. The local mean $I_m(x, y)$, the local variance $I_v(x, y)$, and the normalized image $\tilde{I}(x, y)$ can be expressed as

$$I_m(x, y) = \frac{1}{3} \sum_{c \in \{R, G, B\}} G_\sigma(I_c(x, y)), \tag{1}$$

$$I_v(x, y) = \frac{1}{3} \sum_{c \in \{R, G, B\}} G_\sigma(|I_c(x, y) - I_m(x, y)|^2), \tag{2}$$

$$\tilde{I}_c(x, y) = \frac{I_c(x, y) - I_m(x, y)}{\sqrt{I_v(x, y) + \varepsilon}}, \ c \in \{R, G, B\}, \tag{3}$$

where (x, y) represents image coordinate, $c \in \{R, G, B\}$ represents channels, $I_c(x, y)$ is the pixel intensity of c-channel at (x, y), $G_\sigma(\cdot)$ represents blur opera-tion with Gaussian kernel whose standard deviation is σ, and ε is a small positive value to avoid divided-by-zero, respectively. We set $\varepsilon = 10^{-3}$ in our experiments. After applying the channel-common LBN, we feed normalized images into the network model in both the training and test phases.

---

[1] Such failure of the combination of histogram-based normalization and ImageNet normalization is experimentally validated in Table 1 and Table 4.

Here, we compare three approaches in Fig. 2. The baseline approach is the ImageNet normalization approach without histogram-based normalization. This baseline approach is widely used in the image classification task. However, this baseline approach works well only when the statistics of the training and test images are similar. Then, Fig. 2-(a) represents a simple extension of that baseline approach. Applying adequate brightness adjustment itself is not an easy task. As we have already discussed, even if we can restore the appearance of images with illumination change, statistics of restored images are often different from statistics of images captured under controlled illumination. In other words, there is a mismatch between the training inputs and the test inputs, which degrades the test performance. In order to avoid such a mismatch, we consider applying exactly the same normalization as pre-processing before feeding into networks. The histogram-based normalization like HE [13] and CLAHE [14] can only restore appearances of images with uniform illumination change, while LBN [15] can restore appearances of images with both uniform and non-uniform illumination change as shown in Fig. 1.

3 Illumination Change Dataset Generation

3.1 Image Classification Dataset: ImageNet-SIC

To comprehensively evaluate the robustness of classification approach against illumination changes, we built a dataset with simulated illumination changes (SIC) dataset based on ImageNet dataset [12] by ourselves. It consists of three subsets based on different illumination conditions: controlled illumination, uniform, and non-uniform illumination changes. Figure 3 shows examples from those three subsets. We used the original ImageNet validation set, which contains 50K validation images, as it is as the controlled illumination subset. The ImageNet validation set is also used for creating the other two subsets.

To simulate uniform illumination changes, we simply applied change of exposure values (EVs) to the images to have both brighter and darker images. We used Adobe Lightroom to synthesize those changes and EV values applied are $-2, -1, +1,$ and $+2$.

To simulate non-uniform illumination changes, we used a two-dimensional diamond-square algorithm which is used to generate fractal-based height maps in computer graphics [17]. The generated height maps are used as maps of multiplication factor. More concretely, we synthesized an image with non-uniform illumination changes by multiplying the controlled-illumination image and the multiplication factor map pixel-by-pixel, where the multiplication map is normalized so that the range is from 0.0 to 2.0. Larger multiplication factor leads to brighter images and vice versa.

We evaluated the robustness of image classification approaches against illumination changes with the ImageNet-SIC dataset where the networks are trained on images with different normalization methods. Note that we only build the validation dataset. For training of the network, we use the original ImageNet training dataset. The evaluation metric is based on the accuracies on three subsets of

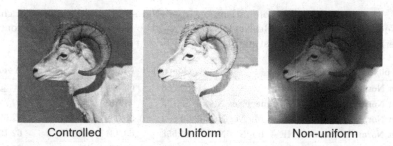

| Controlled | Uniform | Non-uniform |

Fig. 3. Samples of our simulated illumination change (SIC) dataset: (a) Controlled illumination, (b) Uniform illumination change (including under- and over-exposure), (c) Non-uniform illumination change.

images with controlled illumination, and images with uniform and non-uniform illumination changes. The average accuracy over the three subsets is reported.

3.2 Object Detection Dataset: COCO-SIC

We built a COCO-SIC dataset for evaluating the robustness of the object detection approach to illumination changes using a method similar to building the ImageNet-SIC dataset in Sect. 3.1. The controlled illumination subset is the original COCO validation set [18], which contains 5K validation images. To make the uniform illumination changed subset, we used the relative EVs -3, -2, -1, $+1$, $+2$, and $+3$ to render images of the controlled illumination subset. For the non-uniform illumination changed subset, we still used the random height maps generated by the two-diamond-square algorithm [17] to multiply the controlled illumination images pixel-by-pixel. Note that we only build the validation dataset. For training of the network, we use the original COCO training dataset. The evaluation metric is based on the AP metrics on three subsets of COCO-SIC. AP represents the average precision rate, which is computed over ten different IoU thresholds (*i.e.* , $0.5 : 0.05 : 0.95$) and all categories. If not specified, we report AP as bbox AP.

4 Experiments: Image Classification

4.1 Implementation Details

Our code is based on PyTorch framework. We trained classifiers on ImageNet [12] from scratch using $4 \times$ P100 GPUs and emploied the same training parameters as the PyTorch official pre-trained model.

The details are as follows. The input image was randomly resized and cropped to 224×224, and we also applied the random horizontal flip. We used an SGD optimizer with a mini-batch size of 256. The initial learning rate was set to 0.1 for ResNet [19], DenseNet [20], and 0.01 for AlexNet [21] and VGG [22]. Each network was trained for 90 epochs. The learning rate was divided by 10 every 30

Table 1. Top-1 accuracy (%) comparison on ImageNet simulated illumination change (ImageNet-SIC) dataset using ResNet18 [19], where the numbers in the bold font and the underlined represent the best and the second best, respectively.

Training phase	Testing phase	Controlled	Uniform	Non-uniform	**Average**
ImageNet Norm	ImageNet Norm	<u>69.758</u>	66.598	<u>62.610</u>	<u>66.322</u>
ImageNet Norm	CLAHE [14] + ImageNet Norm	42.190	41.513	36.068	39.924
ImageNet Norm	Chan-wise HE + ImgNet Norm	59.692	58.069	54.812	57.524
ImageNet Norm	Chan-com HE + ImgNet Norm	64.558	63.431	58.588	62.192
CLAHE [14]	CLAHE [14]	68.350	67.056	60.382	65.263
Channel-wise HE	Channel-wise HE	67.950	66.934	60.684	65.189
Channel-com HE	Channel-com HE	68.769	**67.975**	62.098	66.281
LBN (Ours)	LBN (Ours)	**69.870**	<u>67.339</u>	**63.916**	**67.042**

epochs. We used a weight decay of 0.0001 and a momentum of 0.9. We applied different normalization methods to training images of the SIC dataset to verify the effectiveness of LBN approach. Official models are commonly normalized by global normalization *i.e.*, ImageNet normalization whose detail is given in Sect. 4.2. Our models are normalized by the LBN. In the test, we resized the input image to 256×256 and applied center crop of the size to 224×224. Then, we applied the corresponding normalization method to them.

For the LBN, we chose the "channel-common" version and set 10.0 for the sigma of the Gaussian kernel according to the experimental results in Sect. 4.4.

4.2 ImageNet Normalization

When training a classification network with ImageNet dataset [12], many researchers apply normalization based on mean and standard deviation to input images. We refer to this normalization as ImageNet normalization. The ImageNet normalization can be expressed by

$$\hat{I}_c(x,y) = \frac{I_c(x,y) - \mu_c}{\sigma_c}, \quad c \in \{R, G, B\}, \tag{4}$$

where (x, y) represents image coordinate, c represents the channel, μ_c and σ_c are the mean intensity and the standard deviation of images in ImageNet dataset, $I_c(x, y)$ is the input image, and $\hat{I}_c(x, y)$ is the normalized image, respectively. Actual values of means and standard deviations for each channel are (0.485, 0.456, 0.406) and (0.229, 0.224, 0.225), where the intensity range of the input image is from 0 to 1.

4.3 Comparison with Existing Methods

We trained the ResNet18 [19] classifiers with different normalization methods and evaluated them on our ImageNet-SIC dataset. The top-1 accuracies are summarized in Table 1. Our LBN-based approach shows the best accuracy on average. In two cases of the controlled illumination and the non-uniform illumination

Table 2. ImageNet Top-1 Acc. (%) comparison of different standard deviation values of blurring in channel-wise/common LBN on ResNet18 [19], where the numbers in the bold font and the underlined represent the best of channel-common and channel-wise, respectively.

	Channel-wise LBN					
Std σ of blur	3	5	7	10	15	20
Controlled	69.304	69.442	69.642	69.520	69.554	<u>69.644</u>
Uniform	66.873	66.973	<u>67.096</u>	66.890	66.949	67.050
Non-uniform	62.430	62.826	63.296	63.610	<u>63.654</u>	63.492
Average	66.202	66.407	66.678	66.673	66.719	<u>66.729</u>
	Channel-common LBN					
Std σ of blur	3	5	7	10	15	20
Controlled	69.434	69.730	69.822	**69.870**	69.868	69.730
Uniform	67.455	**67.495**	67.291	67.339	67.314	67.245
Non-uniform	62.926	63.892	63.868	**63.916**	63.826	63.848
Average	66.605	67.039	66.994	**67.042**	67.003	66.941

change, the best and the second-best accuracies are our LBN-based approach and the baseline approach of ImageNet normalization. It shows that all histogram-based normalization approach has a negative impact on both the controlled illumination and the non-uniform illumination change. Although our LBN-based approach has the second-best accuracy in uniform illumination change, only our LBN-based approach can improve the accuracy compared with the baseline approach in every case.

4.4 Ablation Study

LBN has two variations of normalization: channel-wise and channel-common. LBN also has a parameter of a standard deviation of blur Gaussian kernel, where we used the same parameter for two Gaussian blur operations in the LBN. Here, we evaluate two variations of LBN with different standard deviations. Table 2 shows the top-1 accuracies. In general, we can see the channel-common LBN has better accuracy than the channel-wise LBN. If we compare the average accuracy, the channel-common LBN with a standard deviation of 10 performs the best. Based on the comparison, we used the parameters that work best in this study for our LBN approach in Tables 1 and 3.

We also evaluate the effectiveness of the LBN for five network architectures: AlexNet [21], VGG11 [22], ResNet18 [19], ResNet50 [19], and Dense121 [20]. Table 3 shows the top-1 accuracies of five different network architectures of the baseline approach and our LBN approach. Those results demonstrate that our LBN approach can improve the accuracy in three different illumination conditions, controlled illumination and illumination with uniform and non-uniform changes for every network architecture.

Table 3. Comparison of the top-1 accuracy(%) of different backbones on ImageNet simulated illumination-change (ImageNet-SIC) dataset. "+LBN" represents the network is trained by our local-brightness-normalization approach.

Network	Controlled	Uniform	Non-uniform	Ave.
AlexNet [21]	56.522	49.718	49.774	52.005
+ LBN	**56.638**	**52.216**	**51.212**	**53.355**
VGG11 [22]	70.370	67.264	62.268	66.634
+ LBN	**70.572**	**68.882**	**62.810**	**67.205**
ResNet18 [19]	69.758	66.598	62.610	66.322
+ LBN	**69.870**	**67.339**	**63.916**	**67.042**
ResNet50 [19]	76.130	73.519	69.280	72.976
+ LBN	**76.506**	**74.671**	**70.338**	**73.838**
Dense121 [20]	74.434	72.213	68.210	71.619
+ LBN	**75.006**	**73.129**	**69.240**	**72.458**

5   Experiments: Object Detection

5.1   Implementation Details

The code is based on PyTorch framework. We trained detectors on COCO dataset [18]. We used ImageNet-pretrained ResNet50 [19] models trained in Sect. 4.1 with frozen batch-norm layers as the feature extractor of detectors. We selected a two-stage detector Faster-RCNN-fpn [23] and a one-stage detector DETR [24] to conduct the object detection experiments. We trained these detectors on $4 \times$ P100 GPUs. The details are as follow.

When training Faster-RCNN-fpn [23], we did not change the size of input images, and we applied the random horizontal flip on input images. We used an SGD optimizer with a mini-batch size 4 for each GPU. The initial learning rate was set to 0.01. The network was trained for 26 epochs. The learning rate was divided by 10 when the 16th epoch and the 22nd epoch. We used a weight decay of 0.0001 and a momentum of 0.9. When training DETR [24], we followed the original paper's settings with a smaller epochs. We used training schedule of 150 epochs with a learning rate drop by a factor of 10 after 100 epochs.

5.2   Comparison with Existing Methods

We trained the Faster-RCNN-fpn [23] with different normalization methods and evaluated them on our COCO-SIC dataset. If not specified, we apply the same normalization method for the detector and its own backbone. For the LBN, we chose the "channel-common" version and set 10.0 for the sigma of the Gaussian kernel according to Table 2. The AP results are summarized in Table 4. Our LBN-based approach shows the best performance on average. Meanwhile, all histogram-based normalization approach will harm the detectors' performance

Table 4. AP (%) comparison on COCO simulated illumination change (COCO-SIC) dataset using Faster-RCNN-fpn [11] as the detector and ResNet50 [8] as its backbone, where the numbers in the bold font are the best.

Training phase	Testing phase	Controlled	Uniform	Non-uniform	**Ave.**
ImageNet Norm	ImageNet Norm	36.9	33.7	34.2	35.0
ImageNet Norm	CLAHE [14] + ImageNet Norm	29.6	29.4	30.2	29.7
ImageNet Norm	Chan-wise HE + ImgNet Norm	33.2	32.1	32.5	32.6
ImageNet Norm	Chan-com HE + ImgNet Norm	34.9	33.9	33.5	34.1
CLAHE [14]	CLAHE [14]	36.2	34.9	34.6	35.2
Channel-wise HE	Channel-wise HE	36.7	34.6	35.1	35.5
Channel-com HE	Channel-com HE	36.7	**35.0**	35.3	35.7
LBN (Ours)	LBN (Ours)	**37.2**	34.8	**35.9**	**36.0**

Table 5. Comparison of the AP (%) of different detectors on COCO simulated illumination-change (COCO-SIC) dataset. "+LBN" represents the network is trained by the local-brightness-normalization approach.

Network	Controlled	Uniform	Non-uniform	Ave.
Faster-RCNN-fpn [23]	36.9	33.7	34.2	35.0
+ LBN	**37.2**	**34.8**	**35.9**	**36.0**
DETR [24]	**39.5**	36.7	37.4	37.9
+ LBN	**39.5**	**37.1**	**38.2**	**38.3**

on the controlled illumination condition, which is the most common situation in reality. Only our LBN-based approach can improve the performance compared with the baseline approach in every case.

The visual comparison between the baseline approach and our LBN-based approach shows in Fig. 4. In the controlled illumination situation, the baseline approach and the proposed LBN approach show comparable performances, 5 persons, 3 motorbikes and 1 bike were detected. But on both the uniform illumination changes and the non-uniform illumination changes, the baseline approach can not detect all objects, for example the motorbike in the left dark area. But in all three illumination conditions, our proposed LBN-based approach successfully detected all 9 objects.

5.3 Ablation Study

We evaluate the effectiveness of the LBN for two different network architectures: two-stage detector Faster-RCNN-fpn [23] and one-stage detector DETR [24]. Table 5 shows the AP of two detectors of the baseline approach and our LBN approach. Those results demonstrate that our LBN approach can improve the accuracy in three different illumination conditions, controlled illumination and illumination with uniform and non-uniform changes for every network architecture.

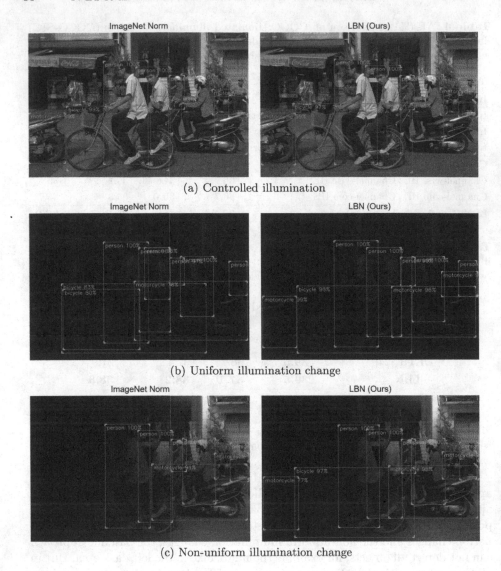

(a) Controlled illumination

(b) Uniform illumination change

(c) Non-uniform illumination change

Fig. 4. Visual comparison of object detection.

We also compared different normalization combinations of the backbone and the detector. The results are summarized in Table 6. It shows that if we apply LBN on the backbone, it can sightly improve the performance in the controlled illumination condition; if we apply LBN on the training phase of the detectors, it can improve the performance in uniform and non-uniform illumination change conditions; if we apply LBN on both backbone and detector, we can improve the performance for all three illumination conditions and get the best average accuracy.

Table 6. AP (%) comparison on COCO simulated illumination change (COCO-SIC) dataset using Faster-RCNN-fpn [23] as the detector and ResNet50 [19] as its backbone, where the numbers in the bold font and the underlined represent the best and the second best, respectively.

Backbone Training	Detector Training	Controlled	Uniform	Non-uniform	Average
ImageNet Norm	ImageNet Norm	36.9	33.7	34.2	35.0
ImageNet Norm	LBN	36.9	<u>34.5</u>	<u>35.7</u>	<u>35.7</u>
LBN	ImageNet Norm	**37.2**	33.0	34.2	34.8
LBN (Ours)	LBN (Ours)	**37.2**	**34.8**	**35.9**	**36.0**

6   Conclusion

We have pointed out the limitation of widely used ImageNet normalization that it only works for images under controlled illumination. We have also shown that classical histogram-based normalization approaches can create visually pleasing images but cannot improve robustness of the networks against illumination changes. We have proposed a local brightness normalization (LBN) approach, which applies the LBN to input images in both training and testing phases to improve such robustness. Experimental comparisons and ablation studies have validated our hypothesis while the LBN approach can also keep the good performance for images under controlled illumination.

References

1. Hendrycks, D., Dietterich, T.: Benchmarking neural network robustness to common corruptions and perturbations. In: Proceedings of the International Conference on Learning Representations (2019)
2. Michaelis, C., et al.: Benchmarking robustness in object detection: autonomous driving when winter is coming. arXiv preprint arXiv:1907.07484 (2019)
3. Croce, F., et al.: RobustBench: a standardized adversarial robustness benchmark. arXiv preprint arXiv:2010.09670 (2020)
4. Goodfellow, I., Shlens, J., Szegedy, C.: Explaining and harnessing adversarial examples. In: Proceedings of the International Conference on Learning Representations (2015)
5. Hendrycks, D., Gimpel, K.: A baseline for detecting misclassified and out-of-distribution examples in neural networks. In: Proceedings of International Conference on Learning Representations (2017)
6. Steinhardt, J., Koh, P.W.W., Liang, P.S.: Certified defenses for data poisoning attacks. In: Advances in Neural Information Processing Systems, vol. 30 (2017)
7. Endo, K., Tanaka, M., Okutomi, M.: CNN-based classification of degraded images with awareness of degradation levels. IEEE Trans. Circuits Syst. Video Technol. **31**(10), 4046–4057 (2020)
8. Endo, K., Tanaka, M., Okutomi, M.: Cnn-based classification of degraded images without sacrificing clean images. IEEE Access **9**, 116094–116104 (2021)
9. Dodge, S.F., Karam, L.J.: Quality robust mixtures of deep neural networks. IEEE Trans. Image Process. **27**(11), 5553–5562 (2018)

10. Zheng, S., Song, Y., Leung, T., Goodfellow, I.: Improving the robustness of deep neural networks via stability training. In: Proceedings of the IEEE Conference on Computer Vision and Pattern Recognition (2016)
11. Borkar, T.S., Karam, L.J.: Deepcorrect: correcting DNN models against image distortions. IEEE Trans. Image Process. **28**(12), 6022–6034 (2019)
12. Deng, J., Dong, W., Socher, R., Li, L.J., Li, K., Fei-Fei, L.: Imagenet: a large-scale hierarchical image database. In: 2009 IEEE Conference on Computer Vision and Pattern Recognition. IEEE (2009)
13. Gonzalez, R.C.: Digital Image Processing. Pearson Education India, Bangalore (2009)
14. Pizer, S.M., et al.: Adaptive histogram equalization and its variations. Comput. Vision Graph. Image Process. **39**(3), 355–368 (1987)
15. Jarrett, K., Kavukcuoglu, K., Ranzato, M., LeCun, Y.: What is the best multi-stage architecture for object recognition? In: 2009 IEEE 12th International Conference on Computer Vision. IEEE (2009)
16. Carandini, M., Heeger, D.J.: Normalization as a canonical neural computation. Nat. Rev. Neurosci. **13**, 51–62 (2012)
17. Fournier, A., Fussell, D., Carpenter, L.: Computer rendering of stochastic models. Commun. ACM **25**(6), 371–384 (1982)
18. Lin, T.-Y., et al.: Microsoft COCO: common objects in context. In: Fleet, D., Pajdla, T., Schiele, B., Tuytelaars, T. (eds.) ECCV 2014. LNCS, vol. 8693, pp. 740–755. Springer, Cham (2014). https://doi.org/10.1007/978-3-319-10602-1_48
19. He, K., Zhang, X., Ren, S., Sun, J.: Deep residual learning for image recognition. In: Proceedings of the IEEE Conference on Computer Vision and Pattern Recognition (2016)
20. Huang, G., Liu, Z., Van Der Maaten, L., Weinberger, K.Q.: Densely connected convolutional networks. In: Proceedings of the IEEE Conference on Computer Vision and Pattern Recognition (2017)
21. Krizhevsky, A., Sutskever, I., Hinton, G.E.: Imagenet classification with deep convolutional neural networks. Commun. ACM **60**(6), 84–90 (2017)
22. Simonyan, K., Zisserman, A.: Very deep convolutional networks for large-scale image recognition. In: International Conference on Learning Representations (2015)
23. Ren, S., He, K., Girshick, R., Sun, J.: Faster R-CNN: towards real-time object detection with region proposal networks. In: Advances in Neural Information Processing Systems, vol. 28 (2015)
24. Carion, N., Massa, F., Synnaeve, G., Usunier, N., Kirillov, A., Zagoruyko, S.: End-to-end object detection with transformers. In: Vedaldi, A., Bischof, H., Brox, T., Frahm, J.-M. (eds.) ECCV 2020. LNCS, vol. 12346, pp. 213–229. Springer, Cham (2020). https://doi.org/10.1007/978-3-030-58452-8_13

Computational Analysis of Table Tennis Matches from Real-Time Videos Using Deep Learning

Hong Zhou, Minh Nguyen, and Wei Qi Yan[✉]

Auckland University of Technology, Auckland, New Zealand
wyan@aut.ac.nz

Abstract. In this paper, utilizing a multiscale training dataset, YOLOv8 demonstrates rapid inference capabilities and exceptional accuracy in detecting visual objects, particularly smaller ones. This outperforms transformer-based deep learning models, makes it a leading algorithm in its domain. Typically, the efficacy of visual object detection is gauged by using pre-trained models based on augmented datasets. Yet, for specific situations like table tennis matches and coaching sessions, fine-tuning is essential. Challenges in these scenarios include the rapid ball movement, color, light conditions, and bright reflections caused by intense illumination. In this paper, we introduce a motion-centric algorithm to the YOLOv8 model, aiming to boost the accuracy in predicting ball trajectories, landing spots, and ball velocity within the context of table tennis. Our adapted model not only enhances the real-time applications in sports coaching but also showcases potential for applications in other fast-paced environments. The experimental results indicate an improvement in detection rates and reduced false positives.

Keyword: YOLOv8 · Moving balls · DETR · Image pre-process · Image post-process · Background subtraction · Deep learning

1 Introduction

Deep learning has gained applications in sports competitions, particularly in tasks such as determining the placement of balls in table tennis. This shows inherent challenges in table tennis, such as the diminutive size and subtle texture patterns of table tennis balls. Compared to other sports, table tennis balls can be hard to distinguish from background textures, complicating the process of determining the landing points and velocities.

In addressing the complexities associated with detecting and identifying visual objects in fast-moving environments such as table tennis, the selection of the most optimal model emerges as an indispensable step. Currently, deep learning predominantly features in two mainstream ways: YOLOv8 algorithm [1] and transformer-based algorithms [2] for computer vision tasks [13–16]. While the solutions for the dynamic and real-time requirements of table tennis training and actual competitions, the speed of real-time object detection becomes paramount. This elevates inference time to a critical determinant in algorithm selection process.

© The Author(s), under exclusive license to Springer Nature Singapore Pte Ltd. 2024
W. Q. Yan et al. (Eds.): PSIVT 2023, LNCS 14403, pp. 69–81, 2024.
https://doi.org/10.1007/978-981-97-0376-0_6

Among the contenders, YOLOv8 distinctively stands out. Not only is it more stream-lined, but it also boasts a markedly rapid inference time, making it a preferable choice over many transformer-based algorithms. To provide a holistic understanding of YOLOv8 efficacy, this paper embarks on a comparative analysis with DETR (End-to-End Object Detection with Transformers), a flagship representation of transformer-based algorithms. This comparison underscores the relative advantages of YOLOv8 model, particularly spotlighting its superior performance in inference speed and proficiency in detecting small objects. Beyond just its speed, the YOLOv8 model is underpinned by a cutting-edge architectural design coupled with avant-garde training methodologies. These compo-nents synergize to achieve heightened precision in localizing and recognizing diminutive objects within images, even in the most challenging scenarios. This positions YOLOv8 as not just an alternative, but potentially the future standard in object detection for real-time applications.

The solid color of table tennis balls can cause them to be mistaken for light sources. We observed many instances where background items were misidentified as balls, nega-tively impacting detection rates. To address this, we've integrated a module that focuses on motion patterns in constancy of the balls. This module employs background sub-traction to differentiate between static background and moving foreground elements, based on the parameters detailed in this paper. This approach enhances density estima-tion, clustering similar data together. Once the background is removed from the video sequence, the ball path is evident through aiding the YOLOv8 model in extracting visual cues and predicting outcomes.

High-speed cameras can potentially mitigate motion blur challenges faced when capturing swift moving balls in table tennis. Still, the inference time of YOLOv8 model struggles to match the speed of digital cameras. To ensure proper detection, the training dataset must accommodate various ball shapes, including the distortions from motion blur. Adjusting the camera speed in frame per second can provide a more diverse training dataset for the model.

Measuring the actual velocity of a table tennis ball in the entails determining its three-dimensional path, emphasizing on the importance of object distance. While Lidar can detect small and reflective objects like the table tennis balls, inaccuracies can arise due to the laser interaction with such surfaces. Camera calibration presents a more reliable method for determining the ball depth across successive frames.

Properly pinpointing where the ball lands on the table mandates precise detection, especially on the table surface. Traditional evaluation methods, such as comparing pre-dicted bounding boxes with ground truth boxes, may not be sufficient. Thus, we propose a novel evaluation method focusing on the landing point of the balls on the table.

This paper systematically delves into literature reviews, methodologies, outcomes, discussions, and conclusions. It comprehensively covers model structures, experimental strategies, and algorithm deployment.

2 Literature Review

The velocity that a flying ball in table tennis games is the specific feature. This fast-moving object which generated by the players' explosive power of swinging the bat and hitting a ball is a challenge in computer vision. By considering the speed factors, the landing spot where a player hits the ball on the table is also an evaluation of playing skills.

A prior study highlighted the formidable challenge of ball detection within the realm of computer vision, attributed to diminutive size and swift motion of the balls [3], even YOLOv8 model struggles with a variation of aspect ratio and accurately detects balls due to fast motion. While an anchor-free approach was proposed to counter this issue during the evolution of YOLO models. This challenge in detecting such balls is still difficult as the state-of-the-art algorithm. Nonetheless, the limitations may not only stem from false positives by using anchor-free algorithms, but the small size of sports balls could also cause to a significant influence.

A valuable reference was dedicated to track moving or airborne objects [17–20]. In 2022, a method employing LSTM in deep learning and simple physical motion models corrected deviations, through establishing a binocular vision-based trajectory extraction system for table tennis that relies on digital cameras [4]. The visual feature extraction was completed by using MobileNet and SSD models, a compromise between resource-constrained environments and accuracy. Nevertheless, it falls compared to the pyramid feature network in YOLOv8 architecture, particularly for challenging datasets and small visual objects.

After reviewed the video footages of 2017 Summer Universiade Men's Singles Final, persisting in achieving precise recognition and positioning of high-speed, small balls was considered a challenge [5]. The TrackNet model, built upon deep learning, can identify balls from single frames with blurred images and lingering trails, even unable to be seen from a visual perspective. However, the performance of TrackNet model heavily hinges on training data it encounters, potentially faltering if exposed to visual objects or environments deviating significantly from the training data.

VAR (i.e., Video Assistant Referee) was available in the 2018 FIFA World Cup, volleyball matches, and fencing competitions. Conversely, it has not been applicable in table tennis competitions due to the exceptional speeds of balls up to 112.5 km per h [6]. As a widely participated sport with 800 million table tennis players globally, it laid the foundation for popularity ranking at the Olympics. Tracking and detecting table tennis are anything but routine. Employing VAR introduces the risk of misjudgment constrained by the ball's incredible speed.

Apart from overcoming the challenges associated with tracking and detecting table tennis, we have to face the problems related to the relationship between training datasets and accuracy enhancement. A group of models struggle to achieve the officially announced accuracy, with actual detection results falling short of expectations. Fast or erratic object motion causes motion blur [7], making it difficult to comprehensively cover training datasets and assess detection outcomes.

An end-to-end BFAN (i.e., Blur-aid Feature Aggregation Network) for visual object detection has been proposed [8]. However, the application of this approach seems unsuitable for table tennis due to its requirement for multiscale feature training datasets [21]. Deblurring may restore clarity to the balls in consecutive frames, yet distinguishing blurred foreground from background poses a significant challenge.

Optimizing the predicted bounding box scale might offer a solution. This entails learning scale features from a few samples, as demonstrated by using MSNN (i.e.,

MultiScale Meta-relational Network) [9]. MSNN enhanced the generalization capability of the proposed model for measurements and improving classification accuracy without necessitating model-independent meta-learning algorithms. While the dataset yielded positive results, further research work was required to fine-tune meta-learning methods for improving the performance on other datasets.

In order to calculate the ball speed of a table tennis using computer vision, it is necessary to find the depth of scenes of table tennis in digital images. The movement of balls of table tennis may be perpendicular to camera lens, which requires at least two fixed cameras to synchronously record from different angles so as to avoid the ball in table tennis being considered as not moving during two consecutive frames. A few of camera APIs provide timestamp information for captured video frames satisfying stereo vision. The frames from different cameras can be aligned using these timestamps. This approach might require prudently handling of the timestamps and proper synchronization logic.

A stereo camera installed on a robot has been studied for tracking table tennis balls after being synchronized [9]. It explores a method that captures and processes stereo images of the ball motion and analyses the disparities between corresponding points in the stereo images, they determine the ball 3D position in space. This method focuses on image synthesis after asynchronous cameras captured images, even if only one camera's frame rate is known. However, this method increases the processing interval time for each frame, which seems to significantly increase the detection time of motion-based YOLOv8 algorithm.

In this experiment, replacing the image information captured by using camera with the image information obtained by using auxiliary cameras only occurs when the table tennis ball captured in two consecutive frames in the main camera are in the same position. In other words, this calculation method only changes the data source from the main camera to an auxiliary camera, without increasing the computational workload under limited computing resources.

In summary, diversifying training dataset scales, deblurring table tennis affected by motion blur, and employing the multiscale meta-relational network appear as viable avenues for investigation. The focus of this paper is on dataset scale diversity while deblurring methods will be explored in subsequent research endeavors.

3 Methodology

3.1 Customed Training Dataset

The scene of table tennis is specific with a moving small ball that is different from the released training datasets. Thus, a customed training dataset needs to be tailored resulting in better performance. However, it requires effort in terms of data collection, annotation, and quality control. Fortunately, a huge number of parameters can be utilized from pre-trained models through transfer learning. A great number of factors will affect establishing a customed training dataset. The approach how to collect enough data samples is the first challenge.

According to real scene of table tennis competitions and training, the table occupying the entire width of the video frame seems to be the dieal position with the appropriate angle, which can maximize the size of table as the target detected in the frame without missing any landing spots on the table. This is also conducive for prediction using YOLOv8 models. The real-time video footages captured under these conditions can serve as the main source of images in the training dataset. In addition, the scale of data needs to be enriched through methods based on computer vision to improve data diversity, such as random resizing. The shape of balls in table tennis is simulated at different depths using the frames by setting random scale factors.

On the other hand, the fast-moving object leads to motion blur after captured by a camera, even if the camera has 120 Hz plus the fastest inference time [15]. It is easier to obtain the ball shape under this deformation by using a low-speed camera to capture images. Meanwhile, this type of images with motion blur also requires a randomly resizing. Finally, the balls in table tennis games with various textures and colors need to be used for sampling and recording.

3.2 Modelling

Swin transformer [2, 10, 11] is a hybrid architecture which is good at large-scale image classification tasks that are efficient by using hierarchical windows and local self-attention mechanisms. In contrast, regarding Swing transformers, DETR [2, 10] is much versatile and efficient, the primary focus of DETR is on visual object detection. A bipartite matching loss is deployed for a set of prediction tasks for visual object detection. As a result of eliminating the need for anchor-based methods, object classes and locations are directly predicted in a single forward pass. Thus, DETR is selected to determine which one is much suitable for this experiment that will be conducted in a Google Collab virtual environment equipped with a V100 GPU (graphics processing unit) to satisfy the basic requirements of real-time object detection.

After a real-time video was processed and ball position is predicted by using YOLOv8 model, it is obvious to see that two textured regions in the background are recognized as balls in Fig. 1. In this situation, it is almost impossible to calculate the ball speed and landing spots of a ball. The detection results with these errors cannot be filtered by using shapes and colors, even texture. The correct detection rate of a real ball has become the key to visual object detection.

Fig. 1. Original video with the prediction results by using YOLOv8s model

Real-time recordings from table tennis training and gaming contain abundant light spots and reflective patches in the background. MoG (Mixture of Gaussians) is employed for background subtraction to remove light spots and reflective patches in the pre-processing stage before the video as input to be predicted by using YOLOv8 model.

Based on precise location of balls in table tennis games detected by YOLOv8 algorithm from video frames, the velocity of balls can be calculated through the variation of location between two consecutive frames corresponding to the frame rate. A camera with 120 Hz can effectively prevent the disappearance of the table tennis ball in each frame and ensure the surface of table completely exists in the screen, whilst maintaining an angle that allows for landing spot on the table. An auxiliary camera is fixed at a 90-degree angle to the main camera. Once a ball of table tennis moves perpendicular to the main camera lens in two consecutive frames, which will be replaced by the image information captured by the auxiliary camera in two consecutive frames. The velocity of a ball in each two-dimensional space needs to be mapped to real-world 3D coordinates by using camera calibration which depends on the perspective transformation of a black and white chessboard as a reference that was put in the scene on the table. The intrinsic and extrinsic parameters including focal length principal point, position and orientation obtained lead to depth information added into the coordinates of bounding boxes. The instantaneous velocity with spatial direction can be calculated through the mapped spatial displacement and frame rate.

In order to detect the landing spots, we detect the surface of table as shown in Fig. 2. Each side of the table is split into nine regions respectively. One table has left side or right side from the camera viewpoint. The landing spots of the table tennis ball on both sides of the table will be continuously recorded and displayed to the players in percentage form based on the number of times the region of table has been hit. The probability of each region hit by the ball can be analyzed for understanding the players' skills in the aftermath of a match.

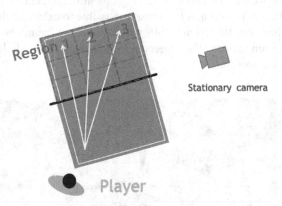

Fig. 2. The sketch of a table division in table tennis

3.3 Methods

The light spots and reflective patches are immovable in a video while using a static camera for ball detection in table tennis games, which provides feasibility for addressing
these influencing factors. MoG (Mixture of Gaussians) can subtract background in video
sequences based on the pixel intensities in the background. Generally, the initialized approach requires a trade-off between subtle differences in background and computational
efficiency. If the pixels represented as Gaussian distribution mixtures are considered as
background by using one or more components, it is most possible to be evaluated as
background by using MoG.

$$N(\mu, cov) = \frac{1}{\sqrt{2\pi \ det(cov)}} e^{-0.5(\chi-\mu)'(\chi-\mu)inv(cov)} \tag{1}$$

$$P = \sum [weight_\rangle \cdot N(\mu_\rangle, cov_\rangle)] \tag{2}$$

The probabilities assigned to each Gaussian component represent a potential class
of a Gaussian distribution, such as background. The higher the likelihood, the greater
the probability that it belongs to the background. By setting and adjusting the threshold,
the accuracy of this classification method can be controlled. Figure 3 displays the frame
of a real-time video that a mask is added to cover the background, the static objects
including the light spots and reflective patches are removed after pre-processing. In this
experiment, the background subtraction approach does not seem to reduce the accuracy
of table tennis ball detection though the color and texture of the ball in each frame is
replaced by a white mask.

The results of YOLOv8 prediction involve a 2D tensor of bounding box coordinates.
The center point of a table-tennis ball that occurs on the screen is signed as the current
box time and coordinates which need to be transferred to real-world coordinates using the
perspective transformation with an initialized z-coordinate added as a 2D homogeneous
point $(x, y, 1)$. The camera projection matrix combines intrinsic and extrinsic parameters,
the inverse matrix is employed to transform points from image coordinates to normalized
camera coordinates f_x and f_y are the focal lengths along x-axis and y-axes; c_x and c_y are
the optical center coordinates. (X, Y, Z) is the center point coordinates of the ball in the
real world.

$$(X, Y, Z) = \begin{bmatrix} 1/f_x & 0-c_x/f_x & 0 \\ 0 & 1/f_y-c_y/f_y & 0 \\ 0 & 01 & 0 \end{bmatrix} \cdot (x, y, 1) \tag{3}$$

The displacement of a ball between the consecutive frames can be calculated based
on coordinate transformation by using Eq. (3), the instantaneous velocity will be acquired
depending on this time interval, which is the frame rate.

In the grayscale image, corners are at where there are rapid changes in intensity in
both the horizontal and vertical directions. Harris corner detection algorithm discovers
local intensity variations in the image that are characteristic of corners. Figure 4 displays
the findings of the internal corner on the chessboard placed on the table for camera
calibration. The surface of the chessboard is considered perpendicular to z-axis in world

Fig. 3. Separating the moving object from background in an image sequence.

coordinates and coincident with the plane enclosed by using x-axis and y-axis. The intrinsic, distortion coefficients, rotation vectors and translation vectors can be computed through the mapping points of the internal corners in the real-world due to the known number of rows and columns in the chessboard and the size of each square in the real world [12].

$$Matrix = \begin{bmatrix} Sum(G_x^2) & Sum(G_x \cdot G_y) \\ Sum(G_x \cdot G_y) & Sum(G_y^2) \end{bmatrix} = \begin{bmatrix} A & C \\ C & B \end{bmatrix} \tag{4}$$

$$\lambda = \frac{(A+B) \pm \sqrt{(A+B)^2 - 4(AB - C^2)}}{2} \tag{5}$$

On the table surface, the most significant manifestation of a table tennis ball bouncing after hitting the surface of the table is the change in velocity direction in y-axis when the camera and the table are pointing in the same plane. That means, y-coordinates for the center point of the table tennis ball change in the vertical axis in consecutive three frames. The function $sign\,(y_m - y_f)$ represents the sign of position difference in y-axis between the previous two frames consecutively, $sign\,(y_c - y_m)$ shows the sign of change of ball positions in y-axis between the current frame and the previous one. In Eq. (6), if $LS = -1$, the ball hits on the table and then bounces back; or else, the ball of table tennis is considered flying without hitting the table. The bottom of the bounding box for the table tennis ball in the previous frame is compared with the regions to determine where it lands.

$$LS = \begin{cases} not\ hit, & if\ sign(y_m - y_f) \cdot sign(y_c - y_m) = 1 \\ hit, & if\ sign(y_m - y_f) \cdot sign(y_c - y_m) = -1 \end{cases} \tag{6}$$

Fig. 4. Finding of the corners of a chessboard in an image for camera calibration

3.4 Results and Discussions

Figure 5 is an example after an original image is resized, different resized images will be obtained with 10 random scale factors set as variables for the balls in table tennis games. Figure 6 demonstrates the resized images with motion blur as an example. This deformation exhibits a variety of forms due to a diversity of directions and velocities of motions, such as rectangles, arches, and shapes approximate to the letter 'v'.

Fig. 5. The example after an original image is resized.

Fig. 6. The example after an original image with motion blur is resized.

The balls for table tennis games with different colors and textures can be detected, Fig. 7 displays five types of colors detected by using YOLOv8 algorithm before the motion-based algorithm is added.

Fig. 7. Five types of colors for the balls in table tennis games are detected by using YOLOv8 model.

The weights and parameters of the pretrained COCO dataset through YOLOv8 model are employed to start with the original 1,774 images captured by 30 Hz and 60 Hz cameras in table tennis training and competition. Accompanied by increasing the amount of random scale factor of resizing to trade-off the influence of the incremental size of the training dataset and the testing dataset on the improvement of AP (Average Precision) based on the prediction of new data, the effectiveness of background subtraction, class matching and circular evaluation, then exploring the optimal solution to terminate the excessive expansion of the training dataset in the case. As a result of illumination, shadows may be generated when the ball approaches the table, and it can be recognized as a ball. In the experiment, although it is not the optimal solution, shadows considered as balls were removed through position-based determination.

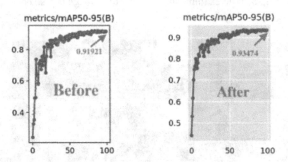

Fig. 8. Comparison of mAP50-95 in 100-th epoch before and after resizing by random scale factor.

The mAP50-95 (i.e., mean Average Precision at 50 and 95 recall) shown in Fig. 8 increases from 0.91921 to 0.93474 after 100th epoch training of motion-based YOLOv8s model that means the model is now better at accurately detecting and localizing objects across a variety of recall levels, 90% of 17,740 images were employed as training datasets, and the remaining images are left for the validation dataset and testing dataset.

The inference time and the detection accuracy of table tennis balls are significant evaluations. Table 1 illustrates that the inference time of the YOLOv8 algorithm with a shorter inference time compared with the DETR algorithm in the experiment under Google Colab environment equipped with V100 GPU.

Table 1. Comparisons between DETR and YOLOv8

Name	Size (pixel)	Backbone	Inf_time (ms) V100 GPU
DETR	640	ResNet-50	75
YOLOv8m	640	CSPDarknet53	7.2

Figure 9 displays the table which is automatically divided into nine regions on each side for visual object detection through region segmentation. The bounding boxes of balls touch these regions on the table surface are the landing spots.

(a)   (b)

Fig. 9. In the scene, the table surface is automatically segmented into nine regions on each side. (a) color images with 9 regions on each side (b) Binary images of the table.

Figure 10 demonstrates the real-time analysis system of table tennis matches. On the left side, it is the video footage of ongoing competition captured by using a 120 Hz stationary camera. The statistics and analysis listed on the right side consist of the instantaneous flying speed of the ball and the percentages of the regions that are hit by the ball on the table. Through this system, both the player and coach can accurately grasp the player's actions that can set training plan for further improvement. Compared with table tennis robot machine which was used as ground truth to serve 50 times at speeds of 20 km per h, 40 km per h, and 60 km per h; The real-time analysis system of table tennis matches was applied for speed measurement, the average accuracy can reach 95%. By manually counting 100 times landing spots of a table tennis ball in a competition, the accuracy of the statistics reaches 99%.

Fig. 10. The interface of real-time analysis of table tennis matches

3.5 Conclusion and Future Work

In this comprehensive study, we delve deep into the fusion of motion-based features and the formidable capabilities of the YOLOv8 model to precisely detect balls in table tennis matches. Our objective extends beyond mere detection by targeting the precise estimation of landing spots and ball velocity. To achieve a detailed, nuanced understanding, we harnessed the capabilities of high-resolution cameras operating at both 30 Hz and 60 Hz. These feeds were then enriched through the adoption of multiscale variation techniques, designed explicitly for data augmentation. This methodological enhancement not only amplified the AP (i. e., Average Precision) but also dramatically curtailed the instances of false positives often instigated by intrusive light reflective interferences.

An innovative inclusion in our research methodology was the deployment of stereoscopic cameras. These cameras are often deployed to capture depth and dimension, which presented a unique advantage. They facilitated the extraction of multiple perspectives and depth information, all while circumventing the typical computational overheads associated with such depth extraction. This strategic utilization paves the way for a precise computation of both the landing spot and ball velocity, leveraging deep learning to decode and interpret real-world video data from table tennis tournaments.

In order to revolutionize table tennis competitions and training regimes by seamlessly integrating motion-centric algorithms, one conspicuous hurdle we encountered was the erroneous recognition of ball shadows as tangible objects, an artifact of the ground subtraction. Although one could potentially discriminate between the actual object and its shadow based on their respective positions during landing spot calculations, we opine that a more holistic solution might lie in the preliminary stages. By refining our pre-processing approaches to systematically eliminate shadows from video frames,

References

1. Xiao, B., Nguyen, M., Yan, W.Q.: Fruit ripeness identification using YOLOv8 model. Multimedia Tools Appl. 1–18 (2023)
2. Yan, W.: Computational methods for Deep Learning: Theory, Algorithms, and Implementations. Springer, Singapore (2023). https://doi.org/10.1007/978-981-99-4823-9
3. Tian, B., Zhang, D., Zhang, C.: High-speed tiny tennis ball detection based on deep convolutional neural networks. In International Conference on Anti-counterfeiting, Security, and Identification (ASID), pp. 30–33 (2020)
4. Cai, G.L.: A method for prediction the trajectory of table tennis in multirotation state based on binocular vision. Comput. Intell. Neurosci. (2022)
5. Huang, Y., Liao, I., Chen, C., İk, T., Peng, W.: TrackNet: a deep learning network for tracking high-speed and tiny objects in sports applications. In: IEEE International Conference on Advanced Video and Signal Based Surveillance (AVSS), pp. 1–8 (2019)
6. Moshayedi, A.J., Chen, Z., Liao, L., Li, S.: Kinect based virtual referee for table tennis game: TTV (Table Tennis Var System). In: International Conference on Information Science and Control Engineering (ICISCE), pp. 354–359 (2019)
7. Shi, J., Xu, L., Jia, J.: Discriminative blur detection features. In: IEEE Conference on Computer Vision and Pattern Recognition (CVPR), pp. 2965–2972 (2014)
8. Wu, Y., Zhang, H., Li, Y., Yang, Y., Yuan, D.: Video object detection guided by object blur evaluation. IEEE Access **8**, 208554–208565 (2020)
9. Zheng, W., Liu, X., Yin, L.: Research on image classification method based on improved multi-scale relational network. J. Comput. Sci. **7**, 613 (2012)
10. Yan, W.: Introduction to Intelligent Surveillance: Surveillance Data Capture, Transmission, and Analytics. Springer, Cham (2019). https://doi.org/10.1007/978-3-030-10713-0
11. Xiao, B., Nguyen, M., Yan, W.Q.: Apple ripeness identification from digital images using transformers. Multimedia Tools Appl. 1–15 (2023)
12. Liu, Y., Liu, L.: Accurate real-time ball trajectory estimation with onboard stereo camera system for humanoid ping-pong robot. Robot. Auton. Syst. **101**, 34–44 (2018)
13. Mehtab, S., Yan, W.: Flexible neural network for fast and accurate road scene perception. Multimedia Tools Appl. (2022)
14. Mehtab, S., Yan, W.: FlexiNet: fast and accurate vehicle detection for autonomous vehicles-2D vehicle detection using deep neural network. In: International Conference on Control and Computer Vision (2021)
15. Xiang, Y., Yan, W.: Fast-moving coin recognition using deep learning. Multimedia Tools Appl. (2021)
16. Qi, J., Nguyen, M., Yan, W.: Small visual object detection in smart waste classification using transformers with deep learning. In: IVCNZ (2022)
17. Liu, J., Pan, C., Yan, W.: Litter Detection From Digital Images Using Deep Learning. Springer, Cham (2022). https://doi.org/10.1007/s42979-022-01568-1
18. Pan, C., Yan, W.: Object detection based on saturation of visual perception. Multimedia Tools Appl. **79**(27–28), 19925–19944 (2020)
19. Pan, C., Yan, W.: A learning-based positive feedback in salient object detection. In: IVCNZ (2018)
20. Pan, C., Liu, J., Yan, W., Zhou, Y.: Salient object detection based on visual perceptual saturation and two-stream hybrid networks. IEEE Trans. Image Process. (2021)
21. Qi, J., Nguyen, M., Yan, W.: CISO: co-iteration semi-supervised learning for visual object detection. Multimedia Tools Appl. (2023)

Multiscale Kiwifruit Detection from Digital Images

Yi Xia[(✉)], Minh Nguyen, Raymond Lutui, and Wei Qi Yan

Auckland University of Technology, 1010 Auckland, New Zealand
xiayi.shawn.001@gmail.com

Abstract. In this paper, we propose an improved YOLOv8-based Kiwifruit detection method using Swin Transformer, aiming to address challenges posed by significant scale variation and inaccuracies in multiscale object detection. Specifically, our approach embeds the encoder from Swin Transformer, based on its sliding-window design, into the YOLOv8 architecture to capture contextual information and global dependencies of the detected objects at multiple scales, facilitating the learning of semantic features. Through comparative experiments with the state-of-the-art object detection algorithms on our collected dataset, our proposed method demonstrates efficient detection of objects at different scales, significantly reducing false negatives while im-proving precision. Moreover, the method proves to be versatile in detecting objects of various sizes in different environmental settings, fulfilling the real-time requirements in complex and unknown Kiwifruit cultivation scenarios. The results highlight the potential practical applications of the pro-posed approach in Kiwifruit industry, showcasing its suitability for addressing real-world challenges and complexities.

Keyword: Object detection · Transformer · Multiscale object detection · YOLOv8

1 Introduction

The detection of visual objects from digital images is a fundamental and challenging problem in computer vision, with numerous applications ranging from autonomous driving to precision agriculture [18]. In particular, accurate and efficient detection of Kiwifruits from multiscale images is of utmost value for Kiwifruit industry, enabling better monitoring, assessment, and management of Kiwifruit cultivation processes [15]. However, this task poses salient challenges, including significant scale variation, occlusion, and the presence of complex backgrounds, which can lead to inaccuracies and increased computational requirements in traditional object detection methods [3].

To overcome these challenges, in this paper we propose an advanced Kiwifruit detection method that combines the strengths of Swin Transformer and YOLOv8 frameworks together. Swin Transformer has demonstrated the state-of-the-art performance in various computer vision tasks, particularly in capturing long-range dependencies and contextual information within given images [12]. Meanwhile, YOLOv8, an evolution of the

© The Author(s), under exclusive license to Springer Nature Singapore Pte Ltd. 2024
W. Q. Yan et al. (Eds.): PSIVT 2023, LNCS 14403, pp. 82–95, 2024.
https://doi.org/10.1007/978-981-97-0376-0_7

popular YOLO (You Only Look Once) architecture, is renowned for its capabilities and versatility of visual object detection in real time [19]. By integrating Swin Transformer into YOLOv8, we aim to enhance the model ability to accurately and efficiently detect Kiwifruits across a variety of scales and complex environments. The main contributions of this research are:

- Enhanced multiscale detection. Swin Transformer augmented YOLOv8 effectively handles the challenge of multiscale Kiwifruit detection. By leveraging the hierarchical transformer architecture, the model efficiently captures context and dependencies across various image scales, enabling it to detect Kiwifruits accurately regardless of their size.
- Improved precision and recall. The proposed method reduces false negatives and false positives, achieving a more balanced precision-recall trade-off. The integration of Swin Transformer enhances the model's understanding of complex scenes, leading to more reliable and precise Kiwifruit detection results.
- Versatility in real world settings. Our approach demonstrates strong adaptability to diverse environmental conditions, making it well-suited for real-time Kiwifruit detection in complex and unknown cultivation scenarios. This feature is crucial for practical applications in Kiwifruit industry, where unpredictable conditions are prevalent.

To evaluate the effectiveness of our proposed method, we have collected a comprehensive dataset of multiscale Kiwifruit images from geographical locations and cultivation setups. We conduct extensive experiments and compare the performance of our approach against the state-of-the-art object detection methods, including traditional YOLOv8 and other transformer-based models.

The rest of this paper is organized as follows: We provide a detailed review of related work in object detection, transformer-based models, and their applications in agricultural contexts in Sect. 2. In Sect. 3, we present the methodology, explaining the integration of Swin Transformer and YOLOv8 for multiscale Kiwifruit detection. In Sect. 4, we describe experimental setup, dataset, and evaluation metrics to assess the proposed method and the results of the experimental outcomes, demonstrating the superiority of our approach over existing methods. Finally, in Sect. 5, we conclude the paper and discuss the contributions, limitations, and future directions for research in this area.

2   Literature Review

Fruit detection is a crucial task in precision agriculture and automated harvesting systems [22, 23]. Accurate and efficient fruit detection is essential for yield estimation, crop monitoring, and fruit quality assessment. In recent years, with the advent of deep learning, a number of approaches have been proposed for fruit detection using Convolutional Neural Networks (CNNs), YOLO model, and transformer-based models [11, 24, 25]. Fruit detection using deep learning methods has shown promising results. CNNs have been widely employed for visual object detection tasks, including fruit detection. The YOLO model, known for its real-time object detection capabilities, has been adapted for fruit detection tasks. YOLO models have been extended to improve its accuracy and handle multiscale fruit detection. Transformer-based models, originally developed for natural language processing, have also been explored for fruit detection [4].

2.1 Traditional CNN Models

Traditional CNN models have served as the backbone for a slew of deep learning-based object detection tasks, including fruit detection [11, 13]. AlexNet, VGG, and ResNet are among the most influential CNN architectures that have significantly contributed to advancements in computer vision [4, 5].

AlexNet was one of the pioneering CNN architectures that achieved a breakthrough in the ImageNet competition. It comprises multiple convolutional and pooling layers, followed by fully connected layers. AlexNet's success motivated the widespread adoption of CNNs in various vision tasks, including fruit detection [8].

VGG employs a deep network with small (3 × 3) convolutional filters. The use of smaller filters enables a deeper exploration of spatial information, leading to improve feature representation. VGG has been broadly applied to fruit detection tasks, achieved high accuracy in identifying various fruit categories.

ResNet introduced the concept of residual connections to address the vanishing gradient problem in very deep networks [7]. By introducing skip connections that enable the direct flow of gradients, ResNet allowed training significantly deeper networks. In fruit detection applications, ResNet as a feature extractor has achieved competitive performance.

2.2 YOLO Model

The initial version of YOLO models, YOLOv1, provided real-time object detection but faced limitations in detecting small objects, such as tiny fruits, due to its single scale approach. Subsequent versions (YOLOv2 and YOLOv3) addressed these limitations by introducing improvements such as anchor boxes, multiscale detection, and feature extraction across different network layers [19]. Since then, a series of versions of YOLO have been proposed, including YOLOv2, YOLOv5, YOLOX, YOLOv7 and YOLOv8, through the modifications in network architecture and the addition of data augmentation modules. Currently, YOLO has been successfully applied to fruit detection tasks, achieved real-time and accurate fruit detection results in various agricultural settings [27]. The versatility and real-time capabilities of YOLO models in handling multiscale objects have made it a popular choice for fruit detection in automated agricultural systems [16, 20].

2.3 Transformer-Based Models

The overall framework of Transformer-based image detection consists of three main components. Firstly, the input image undergoes visual feature extraction using a CNN backbone network, such as VGG, ResNet, or others. Subsequently, visual features are encoded and decoded by using Transformer architecture, which includes multi-head self-attention and encoder-decoder attention mechanisms. Finally, the object classes and bounding boxes are predicted using a feed-forward network [1].

DEtection Transformer (DETR) is a pioneering object detection method that adopts the Transformer architecture. It incorporates a CNN backbone network, Transformer encoder-decoder structure, and a feedforward network (FFN). The CNN backbone extracts image features, which are then transformed into one-dimensional feature maps and processed by Transformer encoder. However, DETR has limitations in terms of slow training convergence, high computational complexity, and relatively poor performance in detecting small objects. In response, Deformable DETR was proposed by utilizing the deformable attention module to improve small object detection and training efficiency [21].

YOLOS is another series of widely applied object detection models based on Vision Transformer (ViT) architecture [2]. YOLO replaces the image classifier in ViT with a bipartite matching loss, enabling it to handle arbitrary-sized object detection tasks without requiring precise spatial or geometric structures [10]. YOLO stands for its adaptability to different Transformer structures, offering flexibility in object detection tasks.

Swin Transformer is a novel approach that leverages the Transformer architecture for computer vision tasks. It has gained attention in image segmentation and visual object detection domains. Swin Transformer takes use of shifted window-based self-attention effectively reduces computational complexity while maintaining desirable performance and making it advantageous for dense prediction tasks downstream. However, further enhance of the object detection is due to the occluded objects.

3 Methodology

Swin Transformer model exhibits the capability to interact between local and global information across different network layers, thereby extracting hierarchical features. However, this model comes with a drawback of having a large number of parameters and high sensitivity, leading to high computational demands and training complexity. On the other hand, YOLOv8 model offers the advantage of having a smaller number of model parameters, resulting in faster training speed. However, its feature extraction ability is relatively weaker compared to Swin Transformer model.

In light of these considerations, we propose a novel approach that combines the feature extraction strengths of Swin Transformer with the practicality of YOLOv8, aiming to enhance the feature extraction capability of YOLOv8 and improve the accuracy and speed of multiscale object detection. By leveraging the advantages of both models, we aim to address the challenges posed by real-world scenarios involving multiscale targets, particularly in the context of Kiwifruit detection. This model is tailored to meet the demands of diverse target scales encountered in real-world settings, striking a balance between feature extraction efficiency and detection performance.

3.1 Swin Transformer

In Swin Transformer, Microsoft proposes Transformer as a versatile backbone for computer vision tasks, attracting significant attention in various domains such as image segmentation and object detection. The overall structure of Swin Transformer is depicted in

Fig. 1 [13]. Similar to the hierarchical structure of the feature pyramid, Swin-Transformer model [21] is a multiscale fusion-based Transformer model that extracts features at different scales using a design with non-overlapping movable windows, enabling cross-window connections for information interaction between local and global features. As shown in Fig. 1(a), Swin-Transformer encoder comprises a patch partition module and four consecutive stages. Each stage includes two types of attention modules: Window Multi-Head Self-Attention (W-MSA) module and Shifted Window Multi-Head Self-Attention (SW-MSA) module. The W-MSA module divides the feature map into non-overlapping windows and employs multi-head self-attention mechanism (MSA) to compute attention scores for each individual window.

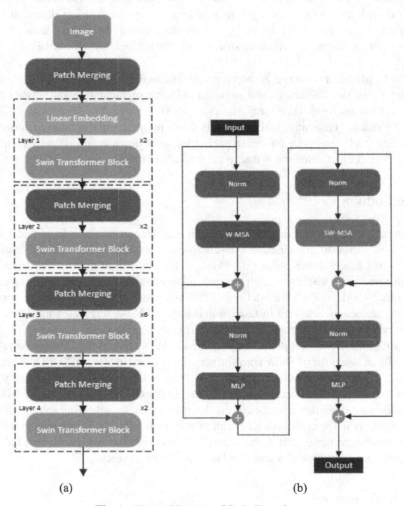

Fig. 1. The architecture of Swin Transformer

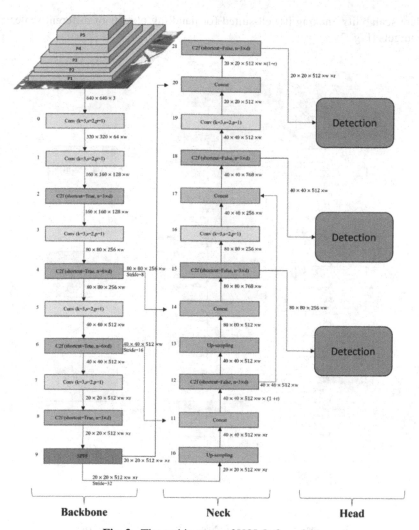

Fig. 2. The architecture of YOLOv8 model

However, the W-MSA module lacks global correlation among windows. To address this, the SW-MSA module modifies the window partitioning by cyclically shifting windows through Shift Window, thus fusing features from multiple windows while preserving the relative positional relationship using a Mask mechanism to incorporate context information at different scales. In Fig. 1(b), alternating use of W-MSA and SW-MSA modules in each stage combines hierarchical local attention with global self-attention mechanism, resulting in features at different levels. Stage 1 contains a Linear Embedding layer that linearly transforms the channel dimension of each pixel, mapping it to C dimensions. The remaining stages utilize the patch merging layer for downsampling and merging information from multiple windows. As a result, Swin Transformer exhibits excellent scalability, making it well-suited for handling objects of different scales and dense targets (Fig. 2).

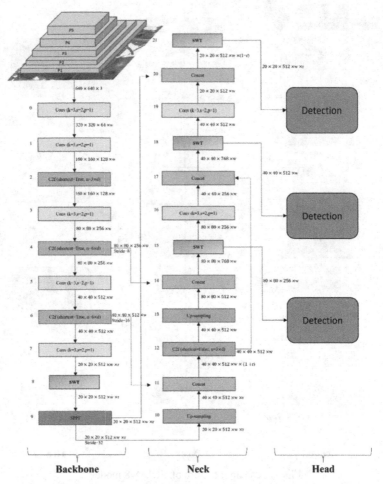

Fig. 3. The architecture of enhanced Kiwifruit detection model

3.2 YOLOv8

YOLOv8 architecture is composed of four main components, as illustrated in Fig. 1, including Input, Backbone, Neck, and Detection Head [20]. The input images undergo a series of data augmentation processes such as cropping, adaptive scaling, and Mosaic, before being fed into the Backbone. The Backbone is responsible for extracting features from the preprocessed images and generates three sets of feature maps at different scales, which are then forwarded to the Neck for further processing. In contrast to YOLOv5, the Neck of YOLOv8 replaces the CSP module with the C2f module and directly incorporates the feature outputs from different stages of the Backbone through upsampling operations. The prediction section decouples the tasks of object classification and bounding box regression, conducting separate predictions. The three detection heads are designed to handle objects of different sizes, thus accelerating model convergence speed and improving detection accuracy.

The classification loss adopts the VFL Loss, characterized by asymmetric positive-negative sample weighting to emphasize on positive samples as primary instances, effectively addressing the issue of class imbalance. For regression loss, the DFL module is introduced to enable the network to quickly focus on the distribution of positions close to the target locations. Notably, YOLOv8 demonstrates exceptional performance in terms of speed and accuracy, surpassing current state-of-the-art object detectors. The ability of this model achieved a balance between computational efficiency and detection precision positions as a promising solution for various practical applications in the field of object detection.

3.3 Enhanced Kiwifruit Detection Model

As illustrated in Fig. 3, to address the issue of imprecise multiscale object detection caused by the semantic information of Convolutional Neural Networks (CNNs) in real-world Kiwifruit images, we have integrated Swin Transformer model into the YOLOv8 backbone network, specifically replacing the top-level C2f module with the Swin-Transformer module. This modification allows us to perform global pixel-level operations on the low-resolution feature maps extracted by C2f. Thus, we can leverage the advantages of the self-attention mechanism while effectively reducing computational complexity and conserving memory space [22].

Furthermore, we have incorporated Swin Transformer module into the Neck structure to capture correlations and importance across different regions. This enhancement contributes to improve the adaptability of this model to various object sizes, enhance visual object detection accuracy, and achieve a better balance between speed and precision under parallel computation. The backbone network of this improved Kiwifruit detection model demonstrates robust modeling capabilities for capturing context information related to target backgrounds, edge shapes, and other contextual factors. These capabilities effectively guide downstream tasks of classification and localization based on semantic information. Moreover, the enhanced model exhibits superior scalability and practical applicability.

By adopting Swin Transformer model and integrating it into the YOLOv8 backbone network, our enhanced Kiwifruit detection model achieves much precise and efficient multiscale object detection [14]. The effective combination of self-attention mechanisms and computational optimizations results in a robust and efficient detection framework. The ability of this model to leverage semantic information for downstream tasks makes it well-suited for real-world Kiwifruit detection scenarios. The integration of Swin Transformer into YOLOv8 framework represents a novel and promising approach for achieving better detection performance and maintaining a balance between speed and accuracy, thus advancing the state-of-the-art in Kiwifruit detection [6].

4 Results

4.1 Dataset and Evaluation Metrics

We collected a comprehensive dataset of Kiwifruit images to conduct our experiments. The dataset was obtained by downloading Kiwifruit orchard videos from the internet and segmenting them into individual frames. Additionally, we sourced Kiwifruit images from various online platforms to enhance the dataset's robustness. The dataset comprises of 3,000 original Kiwifruit images, gathered from diverse sources, including videos from different orchards, images at different ripeness stages, and images with varying sizes due to different camera distances. Our aim was to cover a wide range of Kiwifruit object scales to meet the requirements of multiscale Kiwifruit detection in real-world scenarios. To ensure data quality and consistency, the dataset underwent rigorous data cleaning procedures. We employed the Roboflow tool for efficient data labeling and ensure accurate object detection annotations for each image. Augmentation techniques, including mirror flipping and horizontal/vertical axis flipping, were applied to augment the dataset and enhance the generalization capability of this model. The final dataset consisted of 3,700 training images, 1,057 testing images, and 530 validation images. The diversity of this training set enabled the model to learn robust features across various scenarios, while the testing and validation sets served as critical benchmarks to evaluate the generalization performance on previously unseen data effectively (Fig. 4).

Fig. 4. Dataset of Kiwifruit images at multiple scales

In this paper, the evaluation criterion of this model is the mean Average Precision (mAP). For a specific class of objects, its detection accuracy can be obtained from the Precision-Recall (PR) curve, where Precision (P) represents the probability of a positive prediction being correct, and Recall (R) shows the probability of correctly identifying positive samples [17]. The calculations are defined as follows:

$$Precision = \frac{TP}{TP+FP} = \frac{TP}{Total\ Positive\ Results} \tag{1}$$

$$Recall = \frac{TP}{TP+FN} = \frac{TP}{Total\ Ground\ Truths} \tag{2}$$

$$AP_i = \int_0^1 p(r)dr \tag{3}$$

$$mAP = \frac{1}{N} \sum_{i=1}^{N} AP_i \tag{4}$$

where TP denotes the number of true positives (actual positive samples correctly predicted as positive), FP shows the number of false positives (actual negative samples incorrectly predicted as positive), and FN indicates the number of false negatives (actual positive samples incorrectly predicted as negative).

Since Precision and Recall are measured on different dimensions, Average Precision (AP) is introduced, which represents the average precision values at different recall levels. A higher AP indicates fewer detection errors. The mAP is obtained by taking the average of AP values across all class categories, providing an overall measure of the model's detection performance.

Fig. 5. Visual results of multiscale Kiwifruit detection model

4.2 Experimental Parameter Configuration

The experiments in this paper were conducted on a system running Windows 11 Operating System, equipped with a Geforce RTX 3060 GPU, an AMD R7–5800 CPU, and 16 GB of RAM. The CUDA version used was 12.0. The experiment was conducted using Python 3.8 and PyTorch 2.0, a deep learning framework, to build the model.

The training process involved setting the number of epochs to 150, indicating the number of complete iterations over the entire training dataset. The batch size was configured to 16, defining the number of samples processed in each iteration. The stochastic gradient descent (SGD) optimization algorithm was adopted for weight updates during training, with a weight decay of 0.0005 applied to regulate the magnitude of weight updates and prevent overfitting.

4.3 Analysis of Experimental Results

In Fig. 5, we present visual representation of the prediction results obtained from our proposed multiscale Kiwifruit detection model, which was trained on the custom dataset specifically created for this study. The displayed images vividly demonstrate the robust and accurate detection capabilities of our model, as it successfully identifies Kiwifruits having a diversity of colors, sizes, and shapes. The model exhibits a remarkable ability to discern Kiwifruits from cluttered backgrounds and handle variations in appearance, enabling it to effectively adapt to real-world scenarios. The obtained results highlight the efficacy of our novel model in addressing the challenges posed by multiscale Kiwifruit detection, thereby reaffirming the practical relevance of our model for applications in automated agricultural systems and other computer vision tasks.

Table 1. The comparison of various object detection models on our dataset

Model	Epoch	Size	Precision	Recall	mAP@0.5	mAP@0.5:0.95
YOLOv4	150	640	0.861	0.813	0.854	0.513
YOLOv5	150	640	0.892	0.833	0.873	0.585
YOLOv6	150	640	0.904	0.876	0.906	0.609
YOLOv7	150	640	0.917	0.897	0.917	0.649
YOLOv8	150	640	0.921	0.905	0.921	0.658
CornerNet	150	640	0.772	0.694	0.764	0.462
DETR	150	640	0.671	0.625	0.619	0.415
Swin Transformer	150	640	0.836	0.794	0.809	0.511
Our proposed (SWT + YOLOv8)	150	640	0.951	0.932	0.947	0.712

The comparison of visual object detection models on our dataset is presented in Table 1. We evaluated the state-of-the-art models, including YOLOv4, YOLOv5, YOLOv6, YOLOv7, YOLOv8, CornerNet, DETR, and Swin Transformer, along with our proposed model (SWT + YOLOv8) [9]. Among all models, our proposed model demonstrates the best overall performance, achieving an impressive precision of 0.951, recall of 0.932, mAP@0.5 of 0.947, and mAP@[.5:.95] of 0.712. Furthermore, compared with the performance of our proposed model with other models, it is evident that fusion of Swin Transformer with YOLOv8 results in a substantial enhancement in both precision and recall. The mAP scores also show a significant boost, indicating the effectiveness of our proposed approach in handling multiscale object detection tasks.

To further demonstrate the effectiveness of Swin Transformer in our proposed Kiwifruit detection model, we conducted a series of ablation experiments. In these experiments, we investigated the impact of integrating SWT at a scale of components of the model: 1) Adding SWT to the backbone; 2) Adding SWT to the neck; 3) Adding SWT to both the backbone and neck. We set the YOLOv8 model as the baseline model for conducting ablation experiments as shown in Table 2.

For the first ablation experiment (1), we incorporated SWT into the backbone of the YOLOv8 model. The results show that the addition of SWT to the backbone significantly improved the model's performance. Specifically, the precision, recall, mAP@0.5, and mAP@[.5:.95] scores all demonstrated notable enhancements, validating the effectiveness of SWT in enhancing the feature extraction capability at the backbone level.

In ablation experiment, we introduced SWT to the neck component of YOLOv8 model. Similar to the first experiment, this integration also led to remarkable improvements in the detection results. The precision, recall, mAP@0.5, and mAP@[.5:.95] scores all exhibited substantial increases, which affirm the positive impact of SWT in refining the feature fusion process at the neck level.

Lastly, in the third ablation experiment, we simultaneously added SWT to both the backbone and neck of the YOLOv8 model. This comprehensive integration of SWT at both levels further boosted the model's performance, resulting in the highest precision, recall, mAP@0.5, and mAP@0.5:0.95 scores among all the ablation settings. The combined effect of SWT in both Backbone and Neck demonstrated its complementary nature, which led to superior detection results.

Table 2. The ablation experiments of Kiwifruit detection models based on our dataset

Model	Epoch	Size	Precision	Recall	mAP@0.5	mAP@0.5:0.95
Baseline	150	640	0.921	0.905	0.921	0.658
(1)	150	640	0.928	0.911	0.924	0.673
(2)	150	640	0.939	0.916	0.940	0.689
(3)	150	640	0.951	0.932	0.947	0.712

From the ablation experiments presented in Table 2, it can be observed that inserting Swin Transformer modules at different locations within the YOLOv8 model has varying degrees of impact on its performance. After Swin-Transformer modules are inserted in the Backbone, there is a slight improvement in the performance of our proposed model. However, if Swin Transformer modules are inserted in the Neck, the mAP shows a significant improvement compared to the baseline. Notably, if Swin Transformer modules are inserted at multiple positions, such as in both the Backbone and Neck, the model exhibits further improvement in all evaluated metrics.

4.4 Discussion

In this paper, we presented a novel approach for multiscale Kiwifruit detection by combining the strengths of Swin Transformer and YOLOv8 models. The integration of Swin Transformer and YOLOv8 model is proved to be a powerful strategy for multiscale object detection. The hierarchical and multiscale feature extraction capabilities of Swin Transformer effectively captured contextual information, resulting in robust performance in real-world Kiwifruit detection scenarios. Leveraging YOLOv8 as the baseline model provided a strong foundation to showcase the advantages of our proposed method. The ablation experiments further confirmed the significance of incorporating Swin Transformer modules at different positions within the YOLOv8 architecture. Notably, the improvements in model performance were most notable after inserting Swin Transformer modules in the Neck, underscoring the importance of utilizing Swin Transformer's capabilities in feature fusion and enhancing the representation of different scales. The achieved results of our proposed (SWT + YOLOv8) model, surpassing the state-of-the-art models in terms of precision, recall, and mAP, highlight the effectiveness of our approach in tackling multiscale object detection challenges. The substantial gains in detection accuracy demonstrate the potential applicability of our method not only in Kiwifruit detection but also in other object detection tasks.

5 Conclusion

In this paper, we address limitations of the existing models in achieving accurate multiscale Kiwifruit object detection. To overcome these limitations, we propose a novel approach that combines the hierarchical and multiscale feature extraction capabilities of Swin Transformer with the practicality of YOLOv8, which has demonstrated excellent performance in handling multiscale object detection tasks. By enhancing the feature extraction capabilities of the model, our approach improves the accuracy of multiscale object detection. Specifically, our model effectively captures contextual information and demonstrates robustness in real-world Kiwifruit detection scenarios. The experimental results validate the effectiveness of our proposed method and achieve the state-of-the-art performance on our Kiwifruit dataset. Through comprehensive evaluation metrics, we measure the precision, recall, and mAP of the model, confirming its superior detection accuracy [5].

To sum up, the achievements of this research project is the advancement of Transformer-based object detection models and demonstrate the potential in addressing the challenges of multiscale object detection in real-world scenarios. The proposed method shows promise in various computer vision tasks, further will drive the development of research work related to visual object detection.

References

1. Carion, Nicolas, Massa, Francisco, Synnaeve, Gabriel, Usunier, Nicolas, Kirillov, Alexander, Zagoruyko, Sergey: End-to-end object detection with Transformers. In: Vedaldi, Andrea, Bischof, Horst, Brox, Thomas, Frahm, Jan-Michael. (eds.) ECCV 2020. LNCS, vol. 12346, pp. 213–229. Springer, Cham (2020). https://doi.org/10.1007/978-3-030-58452-8_13
2. Fang, Y., et al.: You only look at one sequence: rethinking Transformer in vision through object detection. https://arxiv.org/abs/2106.00666
3. Ferguson, A.: 1904—the year that Kiwifruit (Actinidia deliciosa) came to New Zealand. N. Z. J. Crop. Hortic. Sci. **32**, 3–27 (2004)
4. Fu, Y., Nguyen, M., Yan, W.Q.: Grading methods for fruit freshness based on deep learning. SN Comput. Sci. **3** (2022)

5. Girshick, R., Donahue, J., Darrell, T., Malik, J.: Rich feature hierarchies for accurate object detection and semantic segmentation. In: IEEE Conference on Computer Vision and Pattern Recognition, pp. 580–587 (2014)

6. Gong, H., et al.: Swin-transformer-enabled YOLOv5 with attention mechanism for small object detection on satellite images. Remote Sens. **14**, 2861 (2022)

7. He, K., Zhang, X., Ren, S., Sun, J.: Identity mappings in deep residual networks. In: Leibe, B., Matas, J., Sebe, N., Welling, M. (eds.) ECCV 2016. LNCS, vol. 9908, pp. 630–645. Springer, Cham (2016). https://doi.org/10.1007/978-3-319-46493-0_38

8. Krizhevsky, A., Sutskever, I., Hinton, G.E.: ImageNet classification with deep convolutional Neural Networks. Commun. ACM **60**, 84–90 (2012)

9. Law, H., Deng, J.: CornerNet: detecting objects as paired keypoints. Int. J. Comput. Vision **128**, 642–656 (2019)

10. Liu, Y., Nand, P., Hossain, M.A., Nguyen, M., Yan, W.Q.: Sign language recognition from digital videos using feature pyramid network with detection transformer. Multimedia Tools Appl. **82**, 21673–21685 (2023)

11. Liu, Y., Yang, G., Huang, Y., Yin, Y.: SE-Mask R-CNN: an improved Mask R-CNN for apple detection and segmentation. J. Intell. Fuzzy Syst. **41**, 6715–6725 (2021)

12. Liu, Z., et al.: Swin transformer: hierarchical vision transformer using shifted windows. In: IEEE/CVF International Conference on Computer Vision (ICCV). (2021)

13. Liu, Z., Yan, W., Yang, B.: Image denoising based on a CNN model. IEEE ICCAR (2018)

14. Luo, Z., Yan, W.Q., Nguyen, M.: Kayak and sailboat detection based on the improved YOLO with transformer. In: International Conference on Control and Computer Vision (2022)

15. Massah, J., AsefpourVakilian, K., Shabanian, M., Shariatmadari, S.: Design, development, and performance evaluation of a robot for yield estimation of Kiwifruit. Comput. Electron. Agric. **185**, 106132 (2021)

16. Pan, C., Liu, J., Yan, W., et al.: Salient object detection based on visual perceptual saturation and two-stream hybrid networks. IEEE Trans. Image Process. (2021)

17. Pan, C., Yan, W.: A learning-based positive feedback in salient object detection. In: IEEE IVCNZ (2018)

18. Pan, C., Yan, W.: Object detection based on saturation of visual perception. Multimedia Tools Appl. **79**(27–28), 19925–19944 (2020)

19. Redmon, J., Divvala, S., Girshick, R., Farhadi, A.: You only look once: Unified, real-time object detection. In: IEEE CVPR, pp. 779–788 (2016)

20. Shen, D., Xin, C., Nguyen, M., Yan, W.: Flame detection using deep learning. In: IEEE ICCAR (2018)

21. Vaswani, A., et al.: Attention is all you need. In: Advances in Neural Information Processing Systems, vol. 30 (2017)

22. Wang, L., Yan, W.Q.: Tree leaves detection based on deep learning. In: International Symposium on Geometry and Vision, pp. 25–38 (2021)

23. Xia, Y., Nguyen, M., Yan, W.Q.: A real-time Kiwifruit detection based on improved YOLOv7. In: Image and Vision Computing, pp. 48–61 (2023)

24. Yan, W.Q.: Computational Methods for Deep Learning – Theory, Algorithms, and Implementations, 2nd edn. Springer, Singapore (2023). https://doi.org/10.1007/978-981-99-4823-9

25. Zhao, K., Yan, W.Q.: Fruit detection from digital images using CenterNet. In: Nguyen, M., Yan, W.Q., Ho, H. (eds.) ISGV 2021. CCIS, vol. 1386, pp. 313–326. Springer, Cham (2021). https://doi.org/10.1007/978-3-030-72073-5_24

26. Yan, W.Q.: Introduction to Intelligent Surveillance, 3rd edn. Springer, Cham (2019). https://doi.org/10.1007/978-3-030-10713-0

27. Xia, Y.: Kiwifruit Detection and Tracking from A Deep Learning Perspective Using Digital Videos. Master's thesis, Auckland University of Technology, New Zealand (2023)

A High-Accuracy Deformable Model
for Human Face Mask Detection

Xinyi Gao$^{(\boxtimes)}$, Minh Nguyen, and Wei Qi Yan

Auckland University of Technology, Auckland 1010, New Zealand
xinyi.gao@autuni.ac.nz

Abstract. Human face mask detection leverages computer vision technology to discern whether individuals in images or videos are wearing masks. Ensuring proper mask usage is crucial in settings such as hospital operating rooms and flu clinics. As deep learning advances, face mask detection has emerged as a significant research area within the computer vision field. In this paper, we propose a deformable state-of-the-art (DSOTA) model based on Deformable ConvNets v2 (DCNv2) and YOLOv8 (i.e., You Only Look Once). We use this new model to improve the accuracy of face mask detection. Our experimental results show that the integration of DCNv2 and YOLOv8 significantly improves the accuracy of face mask detection. The average highest accuracy rate of the YOLOv8n model is 91.7%, and the average highest accuracy rate of the DSOTAn model is 94.4%. The average highest accuracy rate of the YOLOv8s model is 97.0%, and the average highest accuracy rate of the DSOTAs model is 97.4%. These promising results underscore the potential of our approach for practical applications and further exploration in the computer vision domain.

Keywords: Human Face Mask Detection · Deformable ConvNets · YOLOv8 · Deep Learning

1 Introduction

Hospitals encounter diverse patients daily, many of whom may carry various viruses. A significant number of these viruses, such as the flu virus, are airborne and can spread quickly. Wearing a mask effectively reduces the risk of contracting infectious diseases. In high-risk environments like operating rooms, medical staff wearing masks can substantially decrease the risk of infection for patients during surgical procedures. Additionally, wearing masks can prevent the cross-infection of pathogens among hospital patients. Consequently, proper mask usage has become mandatory in numerous hospitals and medical institutions. Wearing a mask correctly not only offers self-protection against viruses but also helps mitigate the spread.

In a hospital setting, wearing a mask can significantly reduce the risk of contracting the flu. To ensure patients comply with this requirement, a number of hospitals employ professionals to remind individuals to wear masks at their entrances. However, this approach can lead to the inefficient use and waste of human resources. Deep learning-based face mask detection can assist hospitals in determining whether patients entering the facility are wearing masks correctly [8, 34], offering a more efficient and cost-effective solution for maintaining public health and safety.

Face mask detection, as a detection task, has emerged as a main research direction in the field of computer vision in recent years [12]. With the rapid advancement of deep learning algorithms [9], various neural networks have found widespread application in face mask detection tasks. YOLO, a popular algorithm for visual object detection [20], has become a benchmark in single-stage target detection due to its exceptional performance in both recognition accuracy and inference speed.

As a classic single-stage target detection algorithm, YOLO has been extensively utilized in a range of object recognition and detection research endeavours. In recent years, the YOLO series of algorithms have undergone continuous updates and iterations, resulting in significant improvements to the performance of the YOLO model in recognition accuracy and reasoning speed. These advancements have solidified YOLO's position as a leading algorithm for face mask detection and other computer vision tasks.

In this paper, we adopt the Face Mask Detection dataset as the training and testing datasets. YOLOv8 [2] is trained on the Face Mask Detection dataset and will eventually be used for human face mask detection tasks. The contribution of this paper is to propose a new model based on Deformable ConvNets v2 [36] and YOLOv8 [30], and apply it to the face mask detection task. By analyzing and comparing the prediction results of the model, it is proved that the improved DSOTA model has achieved better detection accuracy.

2 Related Work

2.1 YOLO

YOLO is a state-of-the-art deep learning model for real-time object detection that can detect visual objects from images and videos with high accuracy and speed. Due to its excellent performance, YOLO has been widely employed in various fields.

YOLO model has undergone a number of evolutions since its initial release. The YOLOv1 model took use of GoogLeNet to extract feature maps, with the output by putting the extracted feature map directly on the fully connected layer. This dramatically improves the inference speed of the model. YOLOv2 further enhances the ability to detect small objects by adding Darknet19 as the backbone network [22]. YOLOv3 improved the backbone network and proposed a Darknet53 backbone network framework [23]. It also integrates Feature Pyramid Networks (FPN) into the network. On the basis of YOLOv3, YOLOv4 added Cross Stage Partial (CSP) to the backbone network so that the model can obtain richer gradient information. In addition, YOLOv4 also added modules such as Spatial Pyramid Pooling (SPP) and Path Aggregation Network (PAN) to fuse features and reduce the amount of calculation [3]. YOLOv5 improves SPP and proposes Spatial Pyramid Pooling-Fast (SPPF) [31]. YOLOvX joins SimOTA label assignment strategy and takes advantage of decoupling operations in the head. YOLOv6 makes use of the EfficientRep backbone. Rep-PAN was also designed additionally [14]. The concept of an Extended Efficient Layer Aggregation Network (E-ELAN) [25] was proposed in YOLOv7 model. YOLOv8 has been improved on the basis of YOLOv5. In the backbone of the network, the C3 module is replaced with C2f. In the Head, decoupling operations are also used. As the latest YOLO model, YOLOv8 outperforms other YOLO models. At the same time, YOLOv8 is also the basic model in this paper, the specific structure will be explained in the methodology [13]. In summary, YOLO is a state-of-the-art object detection model, which remains the most popular choice for object detection tasks.

2.2 Deformable ConvNets

Traditional convolution does not work very well while facing visual objects with complex deformations. In response to this, Deformable ConvNets (DCN) were proposed [4]. DCN is an improvement over traditional convolution operations. By including a learnable offset in the receptive field, the receptive field is more flexible. The improved receptive field is closer to the actual shape of the object and has better performance on the object detection task. After using DCN, the characteristics of the network will be more easily affected by irrelevant image content, which in turn will affect the performance.

To improve this problem Deformable ConvNets v2 (DCNv2) is proposed. Improving the shortcomings of DCN requires the new DCN to have stronger training and modeling capabilities [27]. Therefore, DCNv2 introduces deformable convolution structure with more layers of the feature extraction network. The modulation is also introduced in deformable convolution. Modulation is simply weight and more accurate feature extraction are achieved by assigning different weights. This makes the feature extraction process more focused on the effective information area. These improvements effectively improve the performance of DCNv2, making DCNv2 perform better than DCN in object detection.

2.3 Face Mask Detection

In recent years, YOLO was employed in the field of face mask detection. Liu et al. adopted the YOLO model to replace the Mask R-CNN with ResNet as the backbone [18, 21]. By using the YOLO model to reduce the computational cost of the automatic face mask detection with RNN, the processing speed is increased without reducing the accuracy. In addition, they also utilized simple CNAPs to improve classification performance. Yu et al. achieved a mAP of 98.3% by using a YOLOv4-based model for face mask detection on a dataset of 10,855 images [35]. Abbasi et al. adopted YOLOv4+CNN to perform face mask detection tasks [1]. Among them, YOLOv4 is employed as a target detector for face mask detection, and a fast and efficient CNN model for classification. An accuracy rate of 99.5% was obtained through this model.

Wu et al. proposed a FMD-YOLO by using Im-Res2Net-101 as the feature extractor of the network [29]. In the end, FMD-YOLO got mAP50 values of 92.0% and 88.4% on the dataset. Wang et al. created a PP-YOLO-Mask model using PP-YOLO based on YOLOv3 [10]. The final experimental results show that the model has obtained a mAP value of 86.69% and has faster accuracy and detection speed than YOLOv3. Degadwala et al. took use of a pre-programmed YOLOv4 model to detect medical mask models [5]. After extensive testing, the model achieved an accuracy of 98.90%. The YOLO model used in most of the work is based on YOLOv3 or YOLOv4, and there are few tasks for face mask detection using YOLOv8.

3 Methodology

In this paper, YOLOv8 is employed for face mask detection, a DSOTA model based on the YOLOv8 for object detection is proposed. The YOLOv8 model is the latest object detection algorithm based on YOLOv5. The specific structure of the model includes: Backbone, Neck and Head. We describe each structure of YOLOv8 in the following sections. We also detail the difference between our proposed model and YOLOv8.

3.1 Backbone

Backbone is the backbone network of YOLOv8 for extracting image features. The network structure of Backbone still uses the Cross Stage Partial (CSP) DarkNet structure [26]. A simple model diagram of the network is shown in Fig. 1.

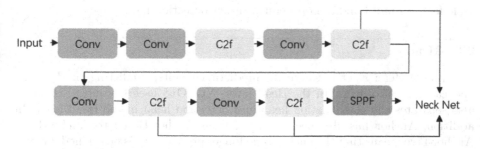

Fig. 1. Structure of Backbone network of YOLOv8

We see that the network is composed of Conv+BN+SiLU (CBS) layer, C2f layer and SPPF layer in terms of specific structure. Compared with YOLOv5, YOLOv8 changes C3 in the backbone to C2f. In terms of design, the design of the

C2f module refers to the C3 module of YOLOv5 [15] and the E-ELAN module of YOLOv7 [25]. This design not only ensures the lightweight of YOLOv8, but also helps the model to obtain richer gradient flow information. The C2f module consists of two convolutional layers and Bottlenecks. Bottleneck is a residual module that also consists of two convolutions. The C2f module divides multiple tensors of the channel dimension through Split [24]. The C2f module stitches together multiple tensors of the channel dimension through Concat.

The SPPF layer improved by SPP is applied to improve the detection speed of the model. There is one CBS convolutional layer and three maxpooling layers in SPPF [32]. It concatenates the feature map without max pooling and the feature map obtained after each increase of max pooling to achieve feature fusion. As shown in Fig. 2.

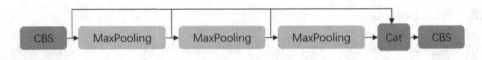

Fig. 2. SPPF module

3.2 Neck

Neck is placed between the backbone and the head in the overall network structure. Neck structurally takes use of the PAN framework and the FPN framework for multi-scale feature fusion. As the depth of the network gradually deepens, there are more and more convolution operations. The increase in convolution operations may cause information loss. Using multi-scale feature fusion can help the network reduce this information loss and make better use of the features extracted by the backbone. The structure of Neck is shown in Fig. 3. In YOLOv8, the C2f module is widely used in backbone and neck to extract and fuse multi-scale features and build a more refined target detection model.

3.3 Head

The role of Head layer is to output prediction results, predicting the location and category of objects. In the Head layer, YOLOv8 uses Decoupled-Head. It also separates the classification head and detection head in the Head layer. In addition, Anchor has also been changed from Anchor-Based to Anchor-Free. Anchor-Free means that the anchor is no longer present, but is positioned directly through the center of the object and detected or identified.

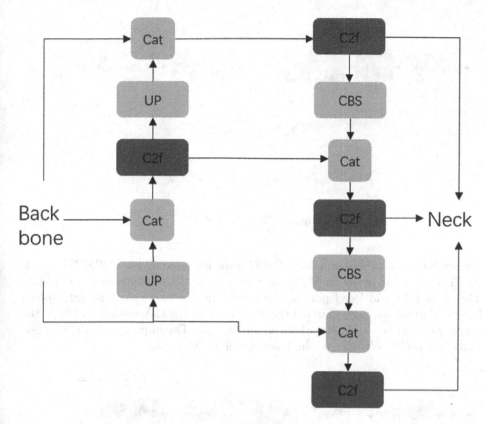

Fig. 3. Structural of the Neck part

3.4   C2fDCNv2

To improve the detection accuracy, we propose the DSOTA model. We combine DCNv2 with C2f in the network and implement a new module called C2fDCNv2. The structure diagram of this module is shown in Fig. 4.

The C2fDCNv2 module includes two convolutional layers, a series of Bottle-neckDCNv2 modules for extracting and fusing features of different scales. In the first half of the C2fDCNv2 module, the input features are extracted through the first convolutional layer to extract high-level features, and then divided into two parts. The two parts of features are sent to multiple BottleneckDCNv2 modules for further processing of different scales and feature fusion. In the second half of the C2fDCNv2 module, the processed features are stitched together by con-cat, and then sent to the cv2 convolutional layer for final feature extraction and output. The BottleneckDCNv2 module is improved based on the standard bot-tleneck module. The standard bottleneck module consists of two convolutional layers. We replace these two convolutional layers with DCNv2 to implement the deformable convolution function. This module is harnessed to perform depth expansion and feature transformation on the input features to extract richer

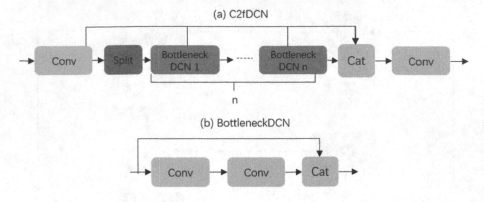

Fig. 4. C2fDCN module

feature information. We propose a DSOTA model based on the C2fDCNv2 module. The structure of the backbone part of the DSOTA model is shown in Fig. 5. The Neck part and Head part of the model are the same as those introduced before. Furthermore, we doubled the width of the DSOTA model, and kept the number of channels and network layers unchanged. The improved model is called DSOTAs model. We refer to the base model as DSOTAn.

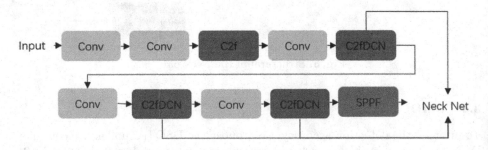

Fig. 5. The Backbone structure of DSOTA model

3.5   Loss Function

Before calculating the loss function, positive and negative samples need to be determined. We use Task Aligned Assigner as the positive and negative sample assignment strategy for the model. Task Aligned Assigner is a sample assigner in the Training Objectives for Object Detection (TOOD) framework [6]. The purpose is to assign each anchor to the closest ground-truth object in order to better match the features between the object and the anchor. Specifically, Task Aligned Assigner will match each anchor point with the corresponding real target [17]. Anchor points whose matching degree is higher than a certain threshold is marked as positive samples and other anchor points will be marked as negative samples. The specific formula is as follows,

$$t = s^{\alpha} \times u^{\beta} \tag{1}$$

where s are classification scores, u is the IoU value, α and β are weight hyper-parameters, t implements Task Alignment Assigner by optimizing s and u. By using this allocation strategy, our model can better learn the key features in the object detection task, focusing on high-quality anchors.

Intersection over Union (IoU) is a measure of the degree of overlap between two collections [11]. In computer vision, IoU is often used to evaluate the performance of object detection algorithms. Specifically, the intersection ratio measures the degree of overlap of two sets by calculating the ratio between their intersection and union. Let the intersection of sets A and B be C, and their union be D, then the intersection-union ratio can be expressed as,

$$IoU(A, B) = \frac{|C|}{|D|} \tag{2}$$

where $|C|$ represents the number of elements in set C, and $|D|$ represents the number of elements in set D. If the IoU value is larger, it means that the degree of overlap between the two sets is higher, and the performance of the target detection algorithm is better.

On the loss function, YOLOv8 divides the loss function into classification loss and regression loss and discards the objectness loss. The classification loss uses Binary Cross-Entropy Loss (BCE Loss) [28]. The BCE loss measures the specific performance of the model by calculating the cross-entropy between the output of the model and the real label.

$$BCE_{loss} = -wy\Delta log p + (1 - y)\Delta log(1 - p) \tag{3}$$

where y is the labeled true value, and p is the predicted value of the model output and w is the weight. The regression loss is composed of two parts: CIoU loss [7] and Distribute Focal Loss (DFL) [16]. CIoU loss can more accurately evaluate the distance between the predicted box and the real object. This is because the CIoU loss takes more account of the distance between the center of the predicted frame and the center of the real object, the difference between the aspect ratio and the influence of the overlapping area. The specific formula is as follows,

$$CIoU_{loss} = 1 - [IoU - \frac{d^2}{c^2} - \alpha \frac{v}{(1 - IoU) + v}] \tag{4}$$

where d^2 represents the Euclidean distance between the center points, c^2 represents the diagonal length of the predicted frame and the real target, v represents the aspect ratio difference between the predicted frame and the real target, α is an adjustable parameter, the general value is 0.5.

DFL is a loss function used to alleviate the class imbalance problem and sample imbalance problem in object detection tasks. It can make the model pay more attention to rare class samples. The DFL loss function Helps the model to better learn the distribution of the data set. This can help improve the performance of object detection. The specific formula is as follows,

$$DFL(S_i, S_{i+1}) = -((y_{i+1})log(S_i) + (y - y_i)log(S_{i+1})) \tag{5}$$

where S_i is the sigmoid output of the network, y_i and y_{i+1} are the predicted probabilities, and y is the label value.

In the next experimental part, we will make use of the model to conduct experiments and analyze the obtained experimental results.

4   Experimental Results and Analysis

4.1   Dataset and Environment

In this paper, we utilize the Face Mask Detection dataset [19] as our primary data source. The dataset comes from Kaggle and contains a total of 853 images. The dataset is divided into three different categories: mask wearing, mask not wearing, and mask wearing incorrectly.

We randomly partition the Face Mask Detection dataset into training, validation, and test sets. The training set accounts for 80% of the total dataset, the validation set for 5%, and the test set for 15%.

Throughout our experiments, we employ a Tesla T4 GPU for training, validation, and testing of the models [33]. During the training process for all models used in this paper, we set the number of epochs to 100 and the batch size to 8. Ultimately, we obtain all the necessary experimental results for our analysis.

4.2   Experimental Results and Analysis

Experimental Results. In order to better evaluate the performance of the model, we sequentially trained YOLOV8n, DSOTAn, YOLOv8s and DSOTAs on the dataset. YOLOv8n and YOLOv8s are two models of different sizes based on YOLOv8. The two models have the same number of convolutional layers and channels, and the network width of YOLOv8s is twice that of YOLOv8n. The DSOTAs model is also obtained by doubling the network width on the basis of DSOTAn. The parameters of the four groups of models are shown in Table 1.

According to the above picture, we see that after 100 epochs of training, all the models get a smooth curve. This means that the model has finally converged. In addition, after observing the precision graphs of the four models, we found that each model had different degrees of overfitting in the initial stage of training. This may be because the model learned too much noise early in the training phase. The overfitting phenomenon of the model without DCNv2 is more obvious than

Table 1. The parameters of YOLOV8n, DSOTAn, YOLOv8s and DSOTAs

Model	Layers	Parameters	FLOPs	Gradients
YOLOv8n	225	3011433	8.2	3011417
DSOTAn	225	3167863	7.7	3167847
YOLOv8s	225	11136761	28.7	11136745
DSOTAs	225	11449351	25.2	11449335

that of the model with DCNv2. This is because the model using DCNv2 is better able to extract the really useful features in the data than the unused model.

Table 2. The training results for YOLOv8n, DSOTAn, YOLOv8s, DSOTAs

Model Name	Precision	Recall	mAP50	mAP50-95	Training Time (Hour)
YOLOv8n	0.917	0.823	0.903	0.663	2.341
DSOTAn	0.944	0.824	0.909	0.668	2.478
YOLOv8s	0.970	0.893	0.957	0.732	2.305
DSOTAs	0.974	0.899	0.961	0.773	2.368

In terms of specific training results, the precision of face mask detection using YOLOv8n is 91.7%, recall is 0.823, mAP50 is 0.903, mAP50-95 is 0.663, and the training time is 2.341 h. The precision of face mask detection using DSOTAn model is 94.4%, recall is 0.843, mAP50 is 0.909, mAP50-95 is 0.668, and the training time is 2.478 h. The precision of face mask detection using YOLOv8s is 97%, recall is 0.893, mAP50 is 0.957, mAP50-95 is 0.732, and the training time is 2.305 h. The precision of face mask detection using DSOTAs model is 97.4%, recall is 0.899, mAP50 is 0.961, mAP50-95 is 0.773, and the training time is 2.368 h. We obtained Table 2 according to the training results of each model.

Error Analysis. The best model in our evaluation makes an average of 21 mistakes out of 4072 instances. In the test results, "red" means that the mask is not worn, "orange" unfolds that the mask is not worn correctly, and "pink" refers to that the mask is worn correctly. Two-thirds of the 21 errors were model mispredictions that the masks were correctly worn on the faces. For example, the second person at the top of the picture from left to right in Fig. 6 just covers her mouth and nose with a scarf and does not wear a mask. However, the test results showed that the mask was worn incorrectly. Other errors were identifying people who were not wearing a mask as wearing one. For example, in the case of the bottom pink box in Fig. 6, the person in the picture uses a scarf to cover his face completely, but the detection result we get is that he is wearing a mask.

Fig. 6. An example of a misclassified human face mask image

Overall Analysis. As shown in Fig. 6, we see that the training speed of the two models based on YOLOv8n is relatively slow. Specifically, the training time of YOLOv8n is 0.036 h slower than YOLOv8s. The training time of DSOTAn is 0.172 h than the hours of DSOTAs. The detection precision of the two models based on YOLOv8s is higher. Specifically, the accuracy of YOLOv8n is 5.3% lower than that of YOLOv8s. The precision of DSOTAn is 3% lower than the precision of DSOTAs. In addition, the model with DCNv2 performs better than the model without DCNv2. Although the training time of the model using DCNv2 is higher than that of the model without DCNv2, the precision of the model using DCNv2 is higher. Specifically, the training time of YOLOv8n is 0.37 h faster than that of DSOTAn. The training time of YOLOv8s is 0.063 h faster than DSOTAs. The precision of YOLOv8n is 2.7% lower than that of DSOTAn. The precision of YOLOv8s is lower than that of DSOTAs.

From the value of mAP, the mAP value of the model using DCNv2 is higher than that of the model without DCNv2. Specifically, YOLOv8n's mAP50 is 0.006 lower than DSOTAn, and mAP50-95 is 0.004 lower. The mAP50 of YOLOv8s is 0.004 lower than that of DSOTAs, and the mAP50-95 is 0.041 lower.

To provide a more intuitive assessment of the performance disparities and mAP values among the four models, we generated the PR curves for each model, as depicted in Fig. 7. The illustration reveals that the overall curve for the model incorporating DCNv2 encompasses a larger area. These experimental findings demonstrate that the integration of DCNv2 into YOLOv8 has a favourable influence on the model's performance.

From the comprehensive experimental results and data presented, it is evident that the incorporation of the DCNv2 module into the YOLOv8 framework substantially enhances the model's performance. Among the four models evaluated in our study, the DSOTAs model emerged as the most effective, attaining an exceptional 97.7% precision and a 0.961 mAP50 score.

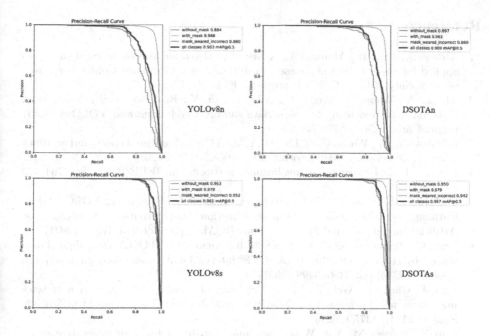

Fig. 7. The PR Curves of the YOLOv8n, DSOTAn, YOLOv8s, DSOTAs

5   Conclusion

In this paper, we highlight the remarkable potential of combining the YOLOv8 model with DCNv2 in human face mask detection. Our systematic comparative analysis and rigorous experimentation prove that integrating the DCNv2 module within YOLOv8 markedly improves face mask detection performance. The DSOTAn model delivered an impressive accuracy of 94.4 while the DSOTAs model exceeded expectations, achieving an extraordinary precision of 97.4% in face mask detection tasks.

These results have far-reaching real-world implications, particularly in the current global context, where precise and efficient face mask detection systems are paramount for public health and safety. The innovations presented in this research have the potential to transform face mask detection technology, laying the foundation for more secure and protected environments.

Moving forward, our research efforts should concentrate on developing lightweight models, aiming to strike the optimal balance between a streamlined model and preserving the exceptional accuracy of face mask detection demonstrated in this paper. The creation of such lightweight models would enable swifter and more efficient deployment across a range of applications, further underscoring the significance of our discoveries in enhancing public health and safety on a global scale.

References

1. Abbasi, S., Abdi, H., Ahmadi, A.: A face-mask detection approach based on YOLO applied for a new collected dataset. In: International Computer Conference, Computer Society of Iran (CSICC), pp. 1–6. IEEE (2021)
2. Aboah, A., Wang, B., Bagci, U., Adu-Gyamfi, Y.: Real-time multi-class helmet violation detection using few-shot data sampling technique and YOLOv8. arXiv preprint arXiv:2304.08256 (2023)
3. Bochkovskiy, A., Wang, C.Y., Liao, H.Y.M.: YOLOv4: optimal speed and accuracy of object detection. arXiv preprint arXiv:2004.10934 (2020)
4. Dai, J., et al.: Deformable convolutional networks. In: IEEE ICCV, pp. 764–773 (2017)
5. Degadwala, S., Vyas, D., Chakraborty, U., Dider, A.R., Biswas, H.: YOLO-v4 deep learning model for medical face mask detection. In: International Conference on Artificial Intelligence and Smart Systems (ICAIS), pp. 209–213. IEEE (2021)
6. Feng, C., Zhong, Y., Gao, Y., Scott, M.R., Huang, W.: TOOD: task-aligned one-stage object detection. In: IEEE/CVF International Conference on Computer Vision (ICCV), pp. 3490–3499 (2021)
7. Gao, J., Chen, Y., Wei, Y., Li, J.: Detection of specific building in remote sensing images using a novel YOLO-S-CIOU model. Case: Gas station identification. Sensors **21**(4), 1375 (2021)
8. Gao, X., Nguyen, M., Yan, W.Q.: Face image inpainting based on generative adversarial network. In: International Conference on Image and Vision Computing New Zealand (IVCNZ), pp. 1–6. IEEE (2021)
9. Gao, X., Nguyen, M., Yan, W.Q.: A method for face image inpainting based on autoencoder and generative adversarial network. In: Wang, H., et al. (eds.) PSIVT 2022. LNCS, vol. 13763, pp. 24–36. Springer, Cham (2022). https://doi.org/10.1007/978-3-031-26431-3_3
10. Jian, W., Lang, L.: Face mask detection based on Transfer learning and PP-YOLO. In: IEEE ICBAIE, pp. 106–109. IEEE (2021)
11. Jiang, P., Ergu, D., Liu, F., Cai, Y., Ma, B.: A review of YOLO algorithm developments. Procedia Comput. Sci. **199**, 1066–1073 (2022)
12. Jindal, N., Singh, H., Rana, P.S.: Face mask detection in COVID-19: a strategic review. Multimedia Tools Appl. **81**(28), 40013–40042 (2022)
13. Ju, R.Y., Cai, W.: Fracture detection in pediatric wrist trauma X-ray images using YOLOv8 algorithm. arXiv preprint arXiv:2304.05071 (2023)
14. Li, C., et al.: YOLOv6: a single-stage object detection framework for industrial applications. arXiv preprint arXiv:2209.02976 (2022)
15. Li, J., Liu, C., Lu, X., Wu, B.: CME-YOLOv5: an efficient object detection network for densely spaced fish and small targets. Water **14**(15), 2412 (2022)
16. Li, X., Wang, W., Wu, L., Chen, S., Hu, X., Li, J., Tang, J., Yang, J.: Generalized focal loss: learning qualified and distributed bounding boxes for dense object detection. Adv. Neural. Inf. Process. Syst. **33**, 21002–21012 (2020)
17. Liu, F., Chen, R., Zhang, J., Xing, K., Liu, H., Qin, J.: R2YOLOX: a lightweight refined anchor-free rotated detector for object detection in aerial images. IEEE Trans. Geosci. Remote Sens. **60**, 1–15 (2022)
18. Liu, R., Ren, Z.: Application of YOLO on mask detection task. In: IEEE ICCRD, pp. 130–136. IEEE (2021)
19. Pooja, S., Preeti, S.: Face mask detection using AI. Predictive and Preventive Measures for COVID-19 Pandemic, pp. 293–305 (2021)

20. Qi, J., Nguyen, M., Yan, W.Q.: Small visual object detection in smart waste classification using transformers with deep learning. In: Yan, W.Q., Nguyen, M., Stommel, M. (eds.) IVCNZ 2022. LNCS, vol. 13836, pp. 301–314. Springer, Cham (2022). https://doi.org/10.1007/978-3-031-25825-1_22

21. Qi, J., Nguyen, M., Yan, W.Q.: Waste classification from digital images using ConvNeXt. In: Wang, H., et al. (eds.) PSIVT 2022. LNCS, vol. 13763, pp. 1–13. Springer, Cham (2022)

22. Redmon, J., Farhadi, A.: YOLO9000: Better, faster, stronger. In: IEEE CVPR, pp. 7263–7271 (2017)

23. Redmon, J., Farhadi, A.: YOLOv3: An incremental improvement. arXiv preprint arXiv:1804.02767 (2018)

24. Sun, Z., Li, P., Meng, Q., Sun, Y., Bi, Y.: An improved YOLOv5 method to detect tailings ponds from high-resolution remote sensing images. Remote Sensing **15**(7), 1796 (2023)

25. Wang, C.Y., Bochkovskiy, A., Liao, H.Y.M.: YOLOv7: trainable bag-of-freebies sets new state-of-the-art for real-time object detectors. arXiv preprint arXiv:2207.02696 (2022)

26. Wang, C.Y., et al.: CSPNet: a new backbone that can enhance learning capability of CNN. In: IEEE/CVF CVPR Workshops, pp. 390–391 (2020)

27. Wang, R., Shivanna, R., Cheng, D., Jain, S., Lin, D., Hong, L., Chi, E.: DCN v2: Improved deep & cross network and practical lessons for web-scale learning to rank systems. In: The Web Conference. pp. 1785–1797 (2021)

28. Wang, Y., Yan, G., Meng, Q., Yao, T., Han, J., Zhang, B.: DSE-YOLO: detail semantics enhancement YOLO for multi-stage strawberry detection. Comput. Electron. Agric. **198**, 107057 (2022)

29. Wu, P., Li, H., Zeng, N., Li, F.: FMD-YOLO: an efficient face mask detection method for COVID-19 prevention and control in public. Image Vis. Comput. **117**, 104341 (2022)

30. Xiao, B., Nguyen, M., Yan, W.Q.: Fruit ripeness identification using YOLOv8 model. Multimedia Tools and Applications, pp. 1–18 (2023)

31. Xue, Z., Lin, H., Wang, F.: A small target forest fire detection model based on YOLOv5 improvement. Forests **13**(8), 1332 (2022)

32. Xue, Z., Xu, R., Bai, D., Lin, H.: YOLO-Tea: a tea disease detection model improved by YOLOv5. Forests **14**(2), 415 (2023)

33. Yan, W.Q.: Introduction to Intelligent Surveillance: Surveillance Data Capture, Transmission, and Analytics. Springer, Cham (2019). https://doi.org/10.1007/978-3-030-10713-0

34. Yan, W.Q.: Computational Methods for Deep Learning: Theory, Algorithms, and Implementations. Springer, Singapore (2023). https://doi.org/10.1007/978-981-99-4823-9

35. Yu, J., Zhang, W.: Face mask wearing detection algorithm based on improved YOLO-v4. Sensors **21**(9), 3263 (2021)

36. Zhu, X., Hu, H., Lin, S., Dai, J.: Deformable ConvNets v2: more deformable, better results. In: IEEE/CVF CVPR, pp. 9308–9316 (2019)

MobileNet-SA: Lightweight CNN with Self Attention for Sketch Classification

Viet-Tham Huynh[1,2]([✉]) [ID], Trong-Thuan Nguyen[1,2] [ID], Tam V. Nguyen[3] [ID], and Minh-Triet Tran[1,2] [ID]

[1] Software Engineering Laboratory and Faculty of Information Technology, University of Science, VNU-HCM, Ho Chi Minh City, Vietnam
[2] Vietnam National University, Ho Chi Minh City, Vietnam
`hvtham@selab.hcmus.edu.vn`
[3] Department of Computer Science, University of Dayton, Dayton, USA

Abstract. Sketch classification plays a crucial role across diverse domains, including image retrieval, artistic style analysis, and content-based image retrieval. While CNNs have demonstrated remarkable success in various image-related tasks, the computational complexity of large models poses challenges in resource-constrained environments. To address this concern, we propose MobileNet-SA, a novel lightweight model that seamlessly integrates a self-attention module into the MobileNet architecture, with a specific focus on enhancing sketch classification performance. The MobileNet-SA model leverages the inherent efficiency of lightweight CNN while harnessing the power of self-attention mechanisms to effectively capture spatial dependencies and enrich feature representations within sketch data. In our experiments, MobileNet-SA achieves state-of-the-art results, demonstrating an impressive accuracy of 93.5% on the challenging SketchyCOCO dataset and 96.7% on the GM-Sketch dataset. We thoroughly evaluate the model's performance across diverse sketch classes, confirming its robustness and generalization capabilities, which make it well-suited for real-world applications where input sketches may exhibit significant variations. Our research indicates that MobileNet-SA not only outperforms existing methods but also offers an efficient and interpretable solution for sketch classification tasks.

Keywords: Sketch Classification · Convolutional Neural Network · Self-Attention

1   Introduction

Sketch classification is a vital and challenging task in the field of computer vision, with numerous applications spanning various domains, including image retrieval [7,8], artistic style analysis [18], and content-based image retrieval [6,9]. Despite their simplicity, free-hand sketches present a unique set of challenges for computer vision models due to their abstract nature and sparse representation compared to traditional full-color images. Nonetheless, humans exhibit remarkable proficiency in recognizing sketches almost as effectively as with highly detailed photographs. This exceptional human capability has increased interest in harnessing the potential of sketch analysis for practical applications, particularly with the proliferation of touchscreen devices, which have fostered sketch-based image retrieval and sketch-to-photo synthesis.

Meanwhile, Convolutional Neural Networks (CNNs) [12] have achieved substantial success in various image-related tasks, fueling hopes for similar performance in sketch classification. However, the computational complexity of large CNN models poses significant challenges, especially in resource-constrained environments such as mobile devices and embedded systems. Addressing this concern and finding the right balance between efficiency and accuracy is crucial to unleashing the full potential of sketch classification in real-world scenarios.

In this paper, we introduce our proposed method dubbed MobileNet-SA, a novel and lightweight model tailored explicitly for enhancing sketch classification performance. The cornerstone of MobileNet-SA's architecture is the seamless integration of a self-attention module into the MobileNet framework. MobileNet, known for its computational efficiency, serves as the foundation, while self-attention mechanisms allow the model to capture spatial dependencies and enrich feature representations effectively. This fusion of lightweight architecture and attention-based mechanisms empowers MobileNet-SA to achieve state-of-the-art results in sketch classification while operating efficiently even in resource-constrained settings. Our main contributions in this research are two-fold:

– Firstly, we introduce MobileNet-SA, which provides a compelling solution to the challenges posed by sketch classification. By leveraging the inherent advantages of lightweight CNNs and harnessing the power of self-attention mechanisms, the model successfully overcomes computational complexity issues while improving classification accuracy significantly.
– Secondly, we conduct extensive experiments to evaluate the performance of MobileNet-SA thoroughly. We employ challenging benchmark datasets, including the SketchyCOCO and GM-Sketch datasets to validate their effectiveness. The results demonstrate an impressive accuracy of 93.5% on the SketchyCOCO dataset and 96.7% on the GM-Sketch dataset, surpassing the performance of existing state-of-the-art methods in sketch classification tasks.

Furthermore, we analyze MobileNet-SA's robustness and generalization capabilities, ensuring that it can adapt to diverse sketch classes and handle variations commonly encountered in real-world applications. Additionally, the model's interpretability is a key aspect, allowing users to gain insight into its decision-making process, thereby building trust in its output.

The remainder of this paper is organized as follows. Section 2 provides an overview of related works in sketch classification, highlighting the state-of-the-art approaches and the challenges they address. Section 3 details the architecture and implementation of MobileNet-SA, elucidating the design choices made to enhance its efficiency and classification performance. Section 4 presents the experimental results and performance analysis of MobileNet-SA on benchmark datasets, demonstrating its superiority over existing methods. Section 5 discusses the implications of our findings, potential applications, and future research directions in sketch analysis and classification.

2   Related Work

In computer vision, sketch-based representations have garnered significant interest and research due to their unique challenges. Yang et al. [19] have extensively studied the abstract nature of free-hand sketches, composed of only a few coarse strokes, yet remarkably recognizable by humans almost as well as full-color photos. This intrinsic human ability has led to the exploration of practical applications, particularly in sketch-based image retrieval and sketch-to-photo synthesis, propelling the development of purpose-made sketch representations that can accommodate their abstract characteristics for various downstream tasks in computer vision.

In the field of fine-grained sketch-based image retrieval (FG-SBIR), Sain et al. [14] have made noteworthy advancements by addressing critical issues faced by the FG-SBIR community. They propose a robust baseline that outperforms existing methods by approximately 11%, achieved through a simple modification to the standard triplet loss. This modification enforces the separation of photo and sketch instances, ensuring a holistic latent space geometry. At the same time, a novel knowledge distillation module leverages photo data during training to overcome the scarcity of sketch data. The proposed approach demonstrates promising results, enhancing the potential of sketches in image retrieval tasks. Chowdhury et al. [2] emphasize the expressive power of human sketches, historically used to convey and record ideas. They introduce a sketch-enabled object detection framework that identifies objects based on corresponding sketches, a novel approach to the fundamental vision task of object detection. Bhunia et al. [1] explore using sketches to detect salient objects in images. Their novel method generates sequential sketch coordinates through a 2D attention mechanism, harnessing attention information inherently embedded in sketches to learn image saliency. Both studies extend the applications of sketches beyond traditional image retrieval and classification, showcasing their versatility in computer vision.

Innovative efforts to transform sketch representations have been made by Lin et al. [10] and Ribeiro et al. [13]. Lin et al. propose the Sketch Gestalt task, considering sketches as sequential data rather than traditional 2D images, aiming to recover masked parts of sketches and complete their shapes. They introduce Sketch-BERT, a generalized version of BERT [3] for the sketch domain. It is trained using self-supervised learning [11] of sketch gestalt, contributing to improved performance in various downstream tasks. Ribeiro et al. introduce Sketchformer, the first-ever Transformer-based network designed to learn deep representations for free-hand sketches, evaluating its efficacy across everyday sketch interpretation tasks, including Sketch Classification, Generative Sketch Model, and Sketch-based Image Retrieval (SBIR).

Furthermore, Tripathi et al. [16] present the intriguing problem of sketch-guided object localization, where hand-drawn sketches serve as queries to locate instances of objects in natural images. They propose a cross-modal attention scheme, guiding the region proposal network to generate object proposals relevant to the sketch query. The proposed method demonstrates effectiveness with as little as a single sketch query. It generalizes well to object categories not seen during training, showcasing the potential of sketch-guided object localization in practical applications.

In literature, the related work in sketch-based representations illustrates the diverse efforts to explore and utilize sketches in various computer vision applications. The studies discussed above contribute valuable insights, techniques, and methodologies, propelling sketch-based representations to the forefront of computer vision research and opening new avenues for future advancements and practical applications. We present our proposed method in Sect. 3.

3 Proposed Method

In this paper, we introduce a novel approach termed MobileNet-SA, specifically tailored for the classification of sketches, as exemplified in Fig. 1. This approach involves integrating attention modules into the *MobileNetV2* architecture to enhance feature representation and object recognition. These *Self-Attention* modules are deliberately inserted at specific layers to strategically capture both local and global dependencies within feature maps. This coordinated attention enables the model to effectively discern intricate details and overarching spatial relationships. By dynamically modulating the significance of spatial positions based on contextual relevance, the attention mechanism enhances feature representation, reduces noise, and amplifies visual cues.

3.1 Base Architecture

MobileNetV2 [15] leverages depthwise separable convolutions and inverted residual blocks, offering computational efficiency without compromising accuracy. We briefly introduce its components as below.

Depthwise Separable Convolution consist of a depthwise convolution followed by a pointwise convolution. This factorized convolution significantly reduces the computational cost by decoupling spatial filtering and channel mixing.

Inverted Residual Blocks consist of three main layers: an expansion convolution to increase the number of channels, a depthwise separable convolution to capture spatial features, and a projection convolution to reduce the number of channels back to the original size. The residual connection is used to aid gradient flow during training.

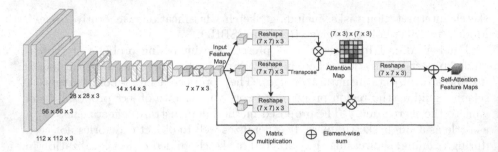

Fig. 1. Overview of the proposed system: attention modules integrated into MobileNetV2 and the self-attention mechanism.

Global Average Pooling spatially downsampled feature maps, resulting in a fixed-size feature vector regardless of the input image size. This pooling operation further reduces the model's computational complexity.

3.2   Self-Attention Module

Self-Attention mechanism draws inspiration from the Transformer's [17] attention mechanism, widely used in natural language processing tasks. The module comprises three essential components: query convolution, key convolution, and value convolution. These components are formulated as follows:

Query, Key, and Value Feature Maps Generation: The F_{in} is passed through three separate convolutional layers: Query Convolution (Q_{conv}), Key Convolution (K_{conv}), and Value Convolution (V_{conv}). The Query Convolution reduces the number of channels to obtain query feature maps Q, the Key Convolution produces key feature maps K with the same reduced channel size, and the Value Convolution retains the original number of channels to obtain value feature maps V.

$$Q = Conv(F_{in}) \in R^{C_q \times H \times W} \tag{1}$$

$$K = Conv(F_{in}) \in R^{C_k \times H \times W} \tag{2}$$

$$V = Conv(F_{in}) \in R^{C_v \times H \times W} \tag{3}$$

Here, C_q, C_k, and C_v represent the reduced number of channels for the query, key, and value feature maps, respectively.

Attention Score Calculation: The attention scores are calculated by performing a matrix multiplication between the query and key feature maps. The resulting matrix contains attention weights that represent the importance of each spatial position in F_{in} with respect to the queries. Additionally, the attention scores are scaled by the square root of the reduced dimension C_q to counteract vanishing gradient issues. Mathematically, the attention scores (A) are calculated as follows:

$$F_{att} = softmax(\frac{QK^T}{\sqrt{C_q}}) \in R^{H \times W \times H \times W} \qquad (4)$$

Attention Application: The attention scores (A) are used to perform element-wise multiplication with the value feature maps (V), resulting in attended feature maps F_{att}. This process allows the model to focus on salient spatial regions in the feature maps.

$$F_{att} = A \odot V \in R^{C_v \times H \times W} \qquad (5)$$

Residual Connection: The attended feature maps F_{att} are combined with the original input feature maps F_{in} using a residual connection. The residual connection facilitates gradient flow during training and helps retain essential information from the original feature maps. Mathematically, the output feature maps after applying the self-attention module can be represented as follows:

$$F_{out} = F_{in} + F_{att} \in R^{C_{in} \times H \times W} \qquad (6)$$

3.3   Attention Module Insertion Strategy

We effectively harness the benefits of the self-attention mechanism and attention modules are inserted after specific layers within the MobileNetV2 architecture as illustrated in Fig. 1. The choice of layers for integrating the attention modules is critical and depends on two main considerations:

1. *Desired Level of Spatial Granularity*: Different layers in the MobileNetV2 architecture capture features at varying scales and levels of abstraction. Lower layers tend to capture local details and fine-grained information, while higher layers capture more abstract and global features. By inserting attention modules at different depths in the network, MobileNet-SA can selectively emphasize both local and global spatial relationships within the feature maps.
2. *Computational Budget*: The computational cost of the self-attention module should be taken into account to ensure that the overall model remains efficient and suitable for resource-constrained environments. Placing attention modules after layers that have a manageable number of channels and spatial dimensions helps strike a balance between accuracy and computational efficiency.

In MobileNet-SA, attention modules are thoughtfully positioned to effectively capture both local and global dependencies within the feature maps. Lower-level attention modules are integrated after early layers in the network, concentrating on fine-grained spatial relationships and local contextual information. This strategic placement enables the model to recognize intricate object details and their distinctive features with greater precision. Conversely, higher-level attention modules are inserted after deeper layers in the network to capture more global dependencies and contextual relationships. These attention modules empower the model to comprehend the overall spatial layout and interactions among different objects in the scene, thus enhancing object recognition within their contextual context. The strategic combination of local and global attention mechanisms results in MobileNet-SA achieving a more comprehensive and robust representation of visual information, leading to improved object recognition performance compared to the baseline MobileNetV2 model.

We strategically leverage attention modules to selectively focus on relevant regions while suppressing noise, which leads to improved feature representation with accentuated visual cues and reduced distractions. The self-attention mechanism dynamically adjusts the importance of spatial positions within the feature maps based on their contextual relevance, allowing the model to learn discriminative features that are highly informative for object recognition. This adaptability enhances the model's robustness to variations in object appearance and background clutter, resulting in higher recognition accuracy. Consequently, MobileNet-SA exhibits promising potential as an architecture for various computer vision tasks, offering an effective solution for tasks that demand enhanced feature representation and improved object recognition performance.

4   Experiments

4.1   Benchmark Datasets

Regarding the evaluation, we employed the SketchyCOCO dataset [4] and GM-Sketch dataset [5] to evaluate and validate our proposed method, MobileNet-SA. The SketchyCOCO dataset and GM-Sketch dataset serve as the foundation for testing the effectiveness and performance of our approach in automatic image generation from freehand sketches.

SketchyCOCO Dataset. To conduct the experiments, we used the MobileNet-SA architecture, which incorporates the Self-Attention Module strategically integrated into the MobileNetV2 architecture. This attention module enables the model to selectively focus on relevant regions and capture both local and global dependencies within the feature maps, leading to improved feature representation and enhanced object recognition performance (Table 1).

By leveraging the SketchyCOCO dataset in combination with our proposed MobileNet-SA method, we aimed to demonstrate its ability to generate high-quality images in response to specific requirements from freehand sketches. The dataset's unique composition of sketch and photo pairs allows us to assess the model's capability to generate visually appealing images based on the user's intuitive freehand sketches.

In this work, in order to effectively learn sketch features, we focused solely on utilizing the data present in the "Sketch" directory for both training and testing purposes. We did not use any data from the "gt" and "edge" directories. Our approach solely relied on the information contained in the "Object" directory,

Table 1. Statistics of subsets used in SketchyCOCO dataset.

Name	dog	giraffe	plane	sheep	motobike	car	cat
Train set	2,902	2,065	1,848	1,095	1,145	1,094	3,917
Test set	80	232	168	111	21	55	7
Name	trafficLights	elephants	bicycle	cow	zebra	horse	fireHydrant
Train set	481	1,395	249	1,694	2,091	1,851	892
Test set	27	104	15	156	189	143	32

including object-specific details and background information, while excluding other data or information not utilized in this research. By concentrating on the "Sketch" directory and the pertinent object-related information, we aimed to develop a robust model for sketch feature learning.

By using the SketchyCOCO dataset alongside our proposed method, we sought to establish the practical applicability and superiority of MobileNet-SA for automatic image generation tasks. The combination of the dataset and the proposed method aimed to contribute significantly to the advancement of image generation techniques, particularly in the context of freehand sketches (Fig. 2).

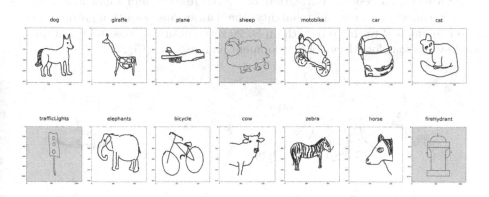

Fig. 2. Samples for each category in the training set of SketchyCOCO dataset.

GM-Sketch Dataset. In addition to testing on SketchyCOCO dataset, we also test our method on GM-Sketch dataset. GM-Sketch dataset is a comprehensive and diverse collection of sketch images carefully curated for artificial intelligence applications. Developed through a meticulous process, this dataset encompasses a wide array of objects sourced from various platforms, including Google, to ensure a rich variety of angles and shapes. The primary focus of GM-Sketch dataset lies in household items, furniture, animals, and vehicles, making it suitable for a multitude of use cases (Table 2).

Table 2. Statistics of subsets used in GM-Sketch dataset.

Name	dog	laptop	banana	clock	bed	car
Train set	150	150	150	150	150	150
Test set	150	150	150	150	150	150
Name	cat	cup	sofa	bicycle	book	bottle
Train set	150	150	150	150	150	150
Test set	150	150	150	150	150	150

To maintain the dataset's high quality, rigorous filtering was applied, eliminating low-quality images and ensuring only the finest representations were included. Additionally, GM-Sketch dataset has been enriched using MidJourney, an advanced AI image generator. Leveraging deep learning, MidJourney empowers users to create unique and captivating images, making it an invaluable resource for designers and creatives seeking visually engaging content.

GM-Sketch dataset comprises 1800 sketch images, thoughtfully organized into 12 categories, each containing 150 images. These categories have been further grouped into Furniture, Personal Belongings, Animals, Vehicles, and Others, facilitating easy access and navigation for various research and application needs.

For utmost accuracy and reliability, the dataset has been thoughtfully split into training and testing sets with an 80:20 ratio, ensuring consistent and unbiased evaluations for AI model development and analysis (Fig. 3).

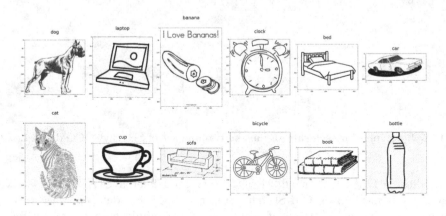

Fig. 3. Samples for each category in trainset of GM-Sketch dataset.

4.2   Implementation Details

We utilize the `PyTorch` library, along with `torchvision`, to build and train the model. `AdamW` and `CrossEntropyLoss` are employed as the optimizer and loss function for model training. During training, the script logs the training loss to `TensorBoard` for visualization and periodically saves checkpoints of the model to track its progress. We also leverage the best-performing model based on the lowest achieved loss on the validation set.

4.3   Evaluation Metrics

Accuracy is a classification performance metric that quantifies a model's capability to correctly predict instances in a dataset. *Precision*, a performance measure, assesses the model's accuracy in identifying positive instances among all instances predicted as positive. *Recall*, also known as sensitivity, evaluates the model's ability to identify all positive instances from the total actual positive instances in the dataset. *F1-score*, a composite metric, takes into consideration both precision and recall, providing a balanced evaluation of the model's effectiveness, especially in datasets with imbalanced class distributions.

4.4   Experimental Results

We dedicate to exploring the utilization of lightweight CNN models, namely ShuffleNetv2, MobileNetV2, ResNet50, and EfficientB0, in conjunction with self-attention mechanisms to enhance the performance of sketch classification. The integration of self-attention is particularly advantageous with lightweight CNN models owing to their inherent parameter efficiency, ability to effectively capture spatial information, and improvements in feature representation. This combination is sought to achieve an optimal equilibrium between model complexity and classification performance.

Table 3. Comparison of lightweight CNN models with Self-Attention (SA) on *Sketchy-COCO dataset*. The best result is highlighted .

Method	Accuracy	Precision	Recall	F1-score
MobileNet-SA (Ours)	93.5%	91.9%	94.0%	92.1%
EfficientNetB0-SA (Ours)	92.0%	91.5%	94.2%	92.3%
ResNet50-SA (Ours)	91.3%	91.0%	92.1%	90.9%
MobileNetv2 [15]	89.7%	89.2%	92.0%	89.5%
ShuffleNetv2 [20]	90.4%	94.4%	89.2%	90.2%

Our empirical study in Table 3 demonstrates the MobileNet-SA model's superiority over other models in terms of accuracy. This enhanced performance is primarily attributed to the integration of self-attention within the MobileNetv2 architecture. By incorporating self-attention, the model effectively captures spatial dependencies inherent in sketches, allowing for the identification of intricate patterns and relationships among different sketch elements. This capability proves essential for achieving accurate sketch classification and generating corresponding images. Notably, the parameter efficiency characteristic of the MobileNet architecture remains unaffected despite the inclusion of self-attention, ensuring efficient sketch processing while leveraging the benefits of enhanced feature representation.

MobileNet-SA achieves a notable Accuracy of 93.5%, which signifies a well-balanced trade-off between precision and recall. This balance holds significant importance for tasks like automatic image generation, as it enables the model to accurately identify positive instances with high precision while avoiding the exclusion of critical sketch details with high recall.

Additionally, MobileNet-SA exhibits robustness and generalization capabilities across the 14 diverse sketch classes found in the SketchyCOCO dataset. Its ability to accommodate various sketching styles and object categories is of considerable value for real-world applications, where input sketches may exhibit substantial variations. Moreover, the attention mechanism employed in MobileNet-SA contributes to the model's interpretability and explainability, rendering it highly suitable for tasks that demand transparent decision-making processes.

Similarly, the EfficientNetB0 architecture with self-attention achieves competitive performance, attaining an Accuracy of 92.0%. Notably, it demonstrates high Precision (91.5%) and Recall (94.2%), leading to an impressive F1-score of 92.3%. These results indicate its ability to effectively minimize both false positives and false negatives. Furthermore, the ResNet50-SA model delivers robust classification performance with an accuracy of 91.3%. Although it slightly trails behind MobileNet-SA and EfficientNetB0-SA in terms of accuracy, it consistently exhibits favorable outcomes across various evaluation metrics.

Table 4. Comparison of MobileNet-SA and MobileNetv2 on the *GM-Sketch dataset*. The best result is highlighted .

Method	Accuracy	Precision	Recall	F1-score
MobileNet-SA (Ours)	96.7%	96.7%	96.7%	96.7%
MobileNetV2[5]	96.1%	96.1%	96.1%	96.1%

In our comparative analysis, we evaluate the MobileNet-SA model with two baseline architectures, MobileNetv2 and ShuffleNetv2. The standard MobileNetv2 architecture achieves an accuracy of 89.7%, displaying stable and commendable results across all evaluation metrics. However, its lack of self-attention may limit its capacity to capture complex spatial dependencies in sketches. On the other hand, the standard ShuffleNetv2 architecture achieves an accuracy of 90.4%, demonstrating notable performance, especially in precision (94.4%), indicating its effectiveness in reducing false positive classifications.

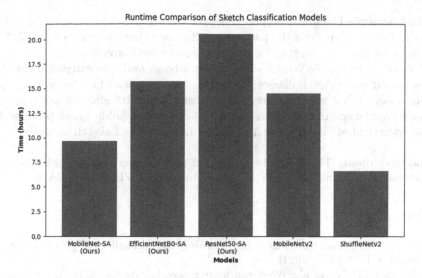

Fig. 4. Runtime Comparison of Sketch Classification Models

From the runtime results, it can be observed that our proposed method - MobileNet-SA, achieves faster execution time compared to the standard MobileNetV2, with a reduction of approximately 33.7%. Specifically, the runtime of MobileNet-SA is 9.635 h compared to 14.54 h for MobileNetV2 (Fig. 4). Despite the significant reduction in runtime, the accuracy of MobileNet-SA is not only unaffected but also shows a notable increase. Specifically, the accuracy improves by 3.8% (Table 3).

Furthermore, MobileNet-SA achieves 96.7% in terms of accuracy on the GM-Sketch dataset, with congruent values for precision, recall, and F1-score (Figure 4). This consistent performance across all evaluation metrics indicates the model's proficiency in accurately classifying sketch images while maintaining a harmonious trade-off between precision (the capacity to correctly identify positive instances) and recall (the capability to avoid overlooking significant instances).

5   Conclusion

In this paper, we have presented MobileNet-SA, a novel lightweight model that seamlessly integrates a self-attention module into the MobileNet architecture to enhance sketch classification performance. Through extensive experiments on challenging benchmark datasets, we have demonstrated the superiority of MobileNet-SA over other models, achieving state-of-the-art results with an impressive accuracy of 93.5% on the SketchyCOCO dataset and 96.7% on the GM-Sketch dataset. The integration of self-attention within the MobileNetv2 architecture has proven crucial in capturing spatial dependencies within sketches, enabling accurate classification and generating corresponding images. Additionally, MobileNet-SA retains the parameter efficiency characteristic of MobileNet, making it an efficient solution for resource-constrained environments.

Furthermore, MobileNet-SA exhibits robustness and generalization capabilities across diverse sketch classes, showcasing its potential for real-world applications where input sketches may vary substantially. Its efficient yet powerful architecture, leveraging the benefits of self-attention, holds great promise for various practical applications and advances in the field of sketch analysis.

Acknowledgment. This research was funded by Vingroup and supported by Vingroup Innovation Foundation (VINIF) under project code VINIF.2019.DA19.

References

1. Bhunia, A.K., et al.: Sketch2Saliency: learning to detect salient objects from human drawings. In: CVPR (2023)
2. Chowdhury, P.N., et al.: What can human sketches do for object detection? In: CVPR (2023)
3. Devlin, J., Chang, M.-W., Lee, K., Toutanova, K.: BERT: pre-training of deep bidirectional transformers for language understanding. In: Proceedings of the 2019 Conference of the North American Chapter of the Association for Computational Linguistics: Human Language Technologies, Volume 1 (Long and Short Papers). Minneapolis, Minnesota: Association for Computational Linguistics, June 2019, pp. 4171–4186 (2019). https://doi.org/10.18653/v1/N19-1423. https://aclanthology.org/N19-1423
4. Gao, C., et al.: SketchyCOCO: image generation from freehand scene sketches (2020). arXiv: 2003.02683 [cs.CV]
5. Huynh, V.-T., Nguyen, and T.V., Tran, M.-T.: Light-weight sketch recognition with knowledge distillation. In: International Conference on Multimedia Analysis and Pattern Recognition (2023)
6. Kim, H., Yeo, C., Cha, M., Mun, D.: A method of generating depth images for view-based shape retrieval of 3D CAD models from partial point clouds. Multimedia Tools Appl. **80**, 10859–10880 (2021)
7. Le, T.-N., et al.: SketchANIMAR: sketch-based 3D animal fine- grained retrieval. Comput. Graphics (2023)
8. Le, T.-N., et al.: TextANIMAR: text-based 3D animal fine-grained retrieval. Comput. Graph. (2023)
9. Li, Z., Junyu, X., Zhao, Y., Li, W., Nie, W.: MPAN: multipart attention network for point cloud based 3D shape retrieval. IEEE Access **8**, 157322–157332 (2020)
10. Lin, H., Fu, Y., Jiang, Y.-G., Xue, X.: Sketch- BERT: learning sketch bidirectional encoder representation from transformers by self-supervised learning of sketch gestalt (2020). arXiv: 2005.09159 [cs.CV]
11. Liu, X., et al.: Self-supervised learning: generative or contrastive. en. In: arXiv:2006.08218 [cs, stat] (July 2020). arXiv:2006.08218. http://arxiv.org/abs/2006.08218 (visited on 10/30/2020)
12. O'Shea, K., Nash, R.: An introduction to convolutional neural networks (2015). arXiv: 1511.08458 [cs.NE]
13. Ribeiro, L.S.F., Bui, T., Collomosse, J., Ponti, M.: Sketchformer: transformer-based Representation for Sketched Structure. In: Proceedings of the CVPR (2020)

14. Sain, A., et al.: Exploiting Unlabelled Photos for Stronger Fine-Grained SBIR (2023). arXiv: 2303.13779 [cs.CV]
15. Sandler, M., Howard, A., Zhu, M., Zhmoginov, A., Chen, L.-C.: MobileNetV2: inverted residuals and linear bottlenecks (2019). arXiv: 1801.04381 [cs.CV]
16. Tripathi, A., Dani, R.R., Mishra, A., Chakraborty, A.: Sketch-guided object localization in natural images. In: Vedaldi, A., Bischof, H., Brox, T., Frahm, J.-M. (eds.) ECCV 2020. LNCS, vol. 12351, pp. 532–547. Springer, Cham (2020). https://doi.org/10.1007/978-3-030-58539-6_32
17. Vaswani, A., et al.: Attention is all you need. In: Advances in Neural Information Processing Systems, vol. 30 (2017)
18. Xie, X., et al.: Artistic style discovery with independent components. In: Proceedings of the IEEE/CVF Conference on Computer Vision and Pattern Recognition, pp. 19870–19879 (2022)
19. Yang, L., Pang, K., Zhang, H., Song, Y.-Z.: SketchAA: abstract representation for abstract sketches. In: 2021 IEEE/CVF International Conference on Computer Vision (ICCV), pp. 10077–10086 (2021). https://doi.org/10.1109/ICCV48922.2021.00994
20. Zhang, X., Zhou, X., Lin, M., Sun, J.: Shufflenet: an extremely efficient convolutional neural network for mobile devices. In: Proceedings of the IEEE Conference on Computer Vision and Pattern Recognition, pp. 6848–6856 (2018)

Enhancement of Human Face Mask Detection Performance by Using Ensemble Learning Models

Xinyi Gao[✉], Minh Nguyen, and Wei Qi Yan

Auckland University of Technology, Auckland 1010, New Zealand
xinyi.gao@autuni.ac.nz

Abstract. Given the prevalence of worldwide pandemics, the need of adhering to appropriate mask use becomes more paramount. Therefore, the importance of developing a human face mask detection model that is both efficient and accurate cannot be overstated. Nevertheless, there is a need for additional enhancement in the accuracy and efficiency of face mask detection algorithms, particularly in dealing with increasingly complex scenarios. In this paper, we make a valuable contribution to the current literature by utilizing Swin Transformer model to address face mask detection challenges. The Swin Transformer, an innovative deep learning architecture, has shown remarkable effectiveness in computer vision applications. The main aim of our research work is to assess the efficacy of the Swin Transformer in improving precision and efficiency of face mask detection. Our methodology includes the careful selection of datasets, design of model architecture, and implementation of experimental settings. The test results show that our suggested model, Swin+YOLOv8, surpassed the baseline models in terms of accuracy and mean average precision (mAP). The research outcomes of this paper will facilitate the advancement of general object detection and make a valuable contribution to the improvement of public health and safety.

Keywords: Human Face Mask Detection · Swin Transformer · YOLOv8 · Deep Learning

1 Introduction

In current worldwide pandemic, the use of masks has become imperative in public settings, serving a crucial function in safeguarding people's well-being. The development of accurate and efficient face mask detection is a significant problem, particularly in diverse contexts such as surveillance recordings in crowded public areas, individual or group photographs, and social media platforms. Given the context, the primary objective of this paper is to construct a proficient face mask detection model using deep learning [24].

Currently, there exists a number of conventional machine learning methods as well as deep learning approaches for the purpose of face mask detection [5]. These

© The Author(s), under exclusive license to Springer Nature Singapore Pte Ltd. 2024
W. Q. Yan et al. (Eds.): PSIVT 2023, LNCS 14403, pp. 124–137, 2024.
https://doi.org/10.1007/978-981-97-0376-0_10

include feature-based methods, convolutional neural networks (CNN) [9], and recurrent neural networks (RNN) [1]. Nevertheless, there is a need for enhancing the accuracy and efficiency of face mask detection algorithms. Recently, there has been a notable surge in the interest of academics towards Transformer models, particularly Swin Transformer [13], owing to its exceptional efficacy in a diversity of computer vision applications. The advent of Swin Transformer presents a novel approach to address visual problems, including image classification and object recognition. In contrast to conventional convolutional neural networks, it exhibits notable benefits in resolving long-range problems.

The primary contribution of this paper is in the use of Swin Transformer model for the purpose of conducting face mask detection, leveraging its window partitioning and self-attention mechanism. The objective of this paper is to assess the effectiveness of the model in enhancing the accuracy and efficiency of face mask detection. Additionally, this research project aims to provide a novel solution for the practical application of face mask recognition. The outcomes of our study will facilitate the progress of face mask detection technology and make a valuable contribution to enhancing public health safety.

The following sections provide a comprehensive account of our study methodologies and the detailed findings obtained from our experiments. In this paper, we will commence by conducting a comprehensive examination of pertinent studies on face mask detection and the fundamental principles underlying the Swin Transformer. Subsequently, we will present our approach, encompassing the selection of datasets, model architecture, and experimental configurations. Following this, we will meticulously discuss our experimental findings, including a detailed comparison and analysis of model performance. Ultimately, we will summarise our contributions and deliberate on potential avenues for future research.

2   Related Work

Deep learning algorithms [25] have been the dominant approaches in contemporary face mask detection challenges. There are two often adopted deep learning methods [6]. The two-stage target detection paradigm encompasses two distinct stages: feature extraction and feature classification, effectively partitioning the target detection process, such as Faster R-CNN [14]. Another approach is a single-stage object detection model. This model has the capability to immediately derive classification outcomes using the regression approach, hence enabling real-time detection, such as You Only Look Once (YOLO) [3].

Ren et al. reviewed the identification of mask-wearing using the YOLOv3 algorithm [16]. The work proposed an enhanced Face_Mask Net identification approach based on a convolutional neural network (CNN) to address the labor-intensive task of manually finding masks. In the work, enhancements were made to the non-maximum Suppression (NMS) module of YOLOv3 [10]. The Distance-IoU (DIoU) metric is proposed as a replacement for the popular Intersection over Union (IoU) metric in Non-Maximum Suppression (NMS) algorithms. The use of the K-Means algorithm aims to optimize anchor boxes and enhance the accuracy of object identification. The training and testing procedures are conducted by using the self-collected Face_Mask dataset. The experimental findings of the Face_Mask Net model demonstrate its efficacy in detecting the presence of masks on individuals, with a great level of accuracy compared to the pre-trained networks.

Ye et al. discussed a mask-wearing detection algorithm based on an improved YOLOv4 network [26]. The improved algorithm integrates the CBAM attention mechanism and depthwise over-parameterized convolution (DO-Conv) to enhance accuracy and reduce the number of parameters. The experimental results using a dataset of approximately 4000 images show that the improved algorithm achieves significantly higher recognition accuracy than the original algorithm and algorithm outperforms current mainstream algorithms in terms of recognition accuracy.

Yu et al. utilized YOLOv4 model to accurately identify and classify face masks, as well as determine if they are being worn correctly according to established guidelines [28]. The study focuses on the challenges posed by intricate surroundings, including poor precision, real-time performance, and resilience. The experimental findings indicate that the algorithm attains a mean average accuracy (mAP) of 98.3% and exhibits a notable frame rate of 54.57 FPS.

The YOLOv5+CBD method was built on an enhanced iteration of the YOLOv5 model [8]. This approach aims to tackle several issues encountered in computer vision, including occlusion, dense targets, and small-scale objects. The proposed approach integrates many techniques to enhance the accuracy of object recognition. These techniques include the use of the Coordinate Attention mechanism, the incorporation of a weighted bidirectional feature pyramid network, and the implementation of Distance Intersection over Union with Non-Maximum Suppression. The experimental findings demonstrated that the YOLOv5+CBD model attains a detection accuracy of 96.7%, exhibiting a notable enhancement of 2.1% in comparison to the baseline model.

Wang et al. proposed a face mask-wearing detection model based on a loss function and attention mechanism [20]. An attention mechanism was integrated in the feature fusion process to improve feature utilization and explore different attention mechanisms to enhance deep network models. The impact of different bounding box loss functions was investigated on mask-wearing recognition. The model achieved a mean average precision (mAP) of 90.96% on a dataset of mask-wearing images, outperforming traditional deep learning methods.

Wang et al. introduced a new mask-wearing detection model called YOLOv7-CPCSDSA [19]. This model combined YOLOv7 base model with the CPC structure, SD structure, and SA mechanism. The CPC structure reduces computational redundancy and improves memory access, while the SD structure enhances the detection of small targets. The SA mechanism focuses on important local information, further improving accuracy. Comparative and ablation experiments using a mask dataset validate the effectiveness of the YOLOv7-CPCSDSA model.

The results show that the model achieves higher mean average precision compared to YOLOv7 and meets real-time detection requirements [21].

Deng et al. proposed an enhanced mask-wearing inspection algorithm based on the single shot multibox detector (SSD) algorithm [2]. The algorithm incorporated with inverse convolution, feature fusion, and attention mechanisms to improve the accuracy of mask-wearing detection. A dataset with 3,656 manually labeled images was created for training the network. The experimental results demonstrate that the algorithm has good accuracy for mask-wearing inspection, with an average accuracy of 91.7%.

Jesús et al. examined the identification of improper face mask use via the utilization of convolutional neural networks (CNNs) with transfer learning. The machine learning methods, namely convolutional neural networks [17] were employed. A comprehensive analysis of the difficulties encountered in constructing a training dataset for the given task was conducted, while also providing a thorough examination of the existing literature pertaining to artificial intelligence (AI) technological approaches. A comprehensive overview of initiatives that have devised AI-enabled systems for the purpose of mask identification was taken, exhibiting diverse degrees of precision and efficacy.

Xue et al. presented an intelligent detection and recognition system for mask-wearing based on an improved RetinaFace algorithm [23]. It consists of a face mask detection algorithm, a mask standard wearing detection algorithm, and a face recognition algorithm. The system utilizes the improved RetinaFace algorithm for real-time detection of mask-wearing and identification of proper mask usage. It also incorporates a voice prompt module to assist in the functionality of the system. The system has been tested and proven effective in achieving its purpose of face mask detection and recognition.

Ullah et al. described a novel algorithm for face mask detection and recognizing human actions during the COVID-19 pandemic [18]. The proposed method for detecting face masks uses the Mask R-CNN ROI wrapping with the Resnet-152 algorithm and evaluates the model using Apache MXNet. The article also emphasizes the need for developing AI, IoT, big data, and machine learning technologies.

Swin Transformer was introduced as a general-purpose backbone for computer vision in 2021 [13], which addresses the challenges of adapting the Transformer from language to vision by proposing a hierarchical Transformer with Shifted windows. The Swin Transformer outperforms previous state-of-the-art models in ImageNet 1K image classification, visual object detection, and semantic segmentation tasks. Due to the superiority of Swin transformer in the field of vision, more and more researchers apply Swin transformer to vision tasks. Ye et al. proposed to solve the difficulty of simultaneously completing masked face detection and recognition tasks by enhancing the performance of Swin Transformer in the field of face feature extraction [27].

Zeng et al. successfully proposed a novel framework called Swin+CasUNet based on Swin Transformer for the restoration of masked faces [30]. Previous studies have acknowledged pain expression recognition by considering the whole face, and Yuan et al. used the Swin Transformer model to recognize pain intensity by recognizing the whole face [29]. It is becoming more and more common to use Swin Transformer for vision tasks.

3 Methodology

In this paper, we present a novel deep learning model for human face mask detection, which is built on the integration of YOLOv8 [22] and Swin Transformer. The objective of our paper is to identify face features in photographs and ascertain the presence or absence of masks on individuals. The model structure of the Swin Transformer [15] is adopted in our approach. The recognition step use the detection module of YOLOv8. The network architecture in our paper has two main components: A backbone network responsible for extracting features, and a head network dedicated to making predictions.

3.1 Backbone

The backbone component is employed for the purpose of feature extraction. It is comprised of many PatchEmbed, SwinStage, and PatchMerging modules [13]. The first step is the use of the PatchEmbed module to partition the input picture into patches with dimensions of 4×4. Subsequently, these patches are encoded. Subsequently, the SwinStage module proceeds to extract the characteristics of these compact units by using the self-attention process. The PatchMerging module is responsible for the consolidation of neighbouring tiny blocks, therefore reducing the computational complexity of future computations and enhancing the model's capacity to accurately identify bigger items. As shown in Fig. 1, the aforementioned procedure undergoes numerous iterations inside the SwinStage and PatchMerging modules.

3.2 Head

The primary function of the head network is to convert the extracted characteristics obtained from the backbone network into the ultimate prediction outcome. Initially, by using a sequence of upsampling and connecting procedures, we integrate characteristics of varying sizes. The integration of these fusion operations allows our model to effectively process objects of varying sizes concurrently. Next, the Conv module is applied to do a convolution operation in order to extract more features. Ultimately, by use of the Detect module, the model generates the predicted outcomes for each category, along with the matching bounding box. The comprehensive network architecture is shown in Fig. 1.

The YOLOv8 model was included in our methodology for the purpose of face mask detection. Initially, the input picture undergoes a preprocessing stage. The input picture is transformed into a PyTorch tensor and the pixel values are normalised from the range of $0 \sim 255$ to the range of $0.0 \sim 1.0$. Subsequently, the YOLO model is proffered to provide predictions on the preprocessed images.

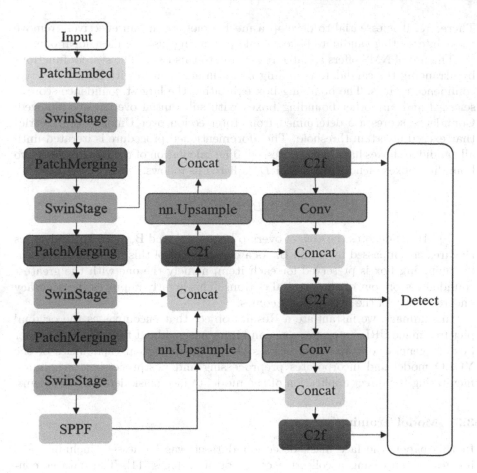

Fig. 1. Structure of Swin+YOLO model

The outcome of the prediction is a collection of object candidate boxes, with each box carrying the associated category and a measure of confidence.

Following the acquisition of the predicted outcomes, postprocessing was conducted based on the obtained findings. The Non-Maximum Suppression (NMS) method is propounded to eliminate object candidate boxes that overlap and to maintain the box with the greatest confidence [7]. Subsequently, the coordinates of the remaining object recommendations are converted from the scale of the input picture to the scale of the original image.

NMS is a populat post-processing approach in the field of object detection. The primary objective of NMS is to address the problem of redundant detection boxes that arise from the prediction of numerous bounding boxes for the same item, frequently exhibiting substantial overlap. If left unattended, there is a possibility that the same item might be identified many times, which would subsequently lead to a decline in the quality of the detection results.

Therefore, it is essential to develop a methodology that can effectively remove these intersecting candidate boxes, while preserving just the most ideal one.

The use of NMS offers a viable resolution to this issue. The system functions by arranging the candidate bounding boxes in accordance with their respective confidence ratings. The bounding box exhibiting the largest confidence score is selected and any other bounding boxes with substantial overlap are removed. Confidence scores are determined from Intersection over Union (IoU) metrics that exceed a certain threshold. The aforementioned procedure is iterated until all candidate boxes have been processed. The calculation of the IoU between two bounding boxes, denoted as A and B, is listed as follows.

$$IoU(A, B) = \frac{|A \cap B|}{|A \cup B|} \tag{1}$$

where $|A \cap B|$ denotes the area of overlap between A and B, and $|A \cup B|$ denotes the area encompassed by A and B. As a consequence of this procedure, a singular bounding box is preserved for each item, namely the one with the greatest confidence score out of all potential options. This greatly improves the accuracy and reliability of the detection outcomes.

In summary, we instantiate a Results object that encompasses the original picture, image URL, category name, and information about the object contender box. In general, our approach utilises the robust detection capabilities of the YOLO model and incorporates preprocessing and postprocessing techniques, facilitating the direct application of the model to face mask detection problems.

3.3   Model Training

In this paper, the face mask detection dataset was harnessed, including 853 images encompassing a collective count of 4072 faces [11]. The dataset contains face images that have been labelled with one of three distinct labels: "with_mask", "without_mask", or "mask_weared_incorrect". The dataset presented below offers an extensive collection of instances suitable for training our models, including a wide range of scenarios that depict the many ways in which masks are either worn or not worn.

The face mask detection dataset was partitioned into training, validation, and test sets by using a random splitting method. The training set comprises 80% of the whole dataset, while the validation set is 5% and the test set represents 15%. During the training process, it is essential to continuously check the loss and accuracy metrics on the validation set in order to mitigate the risk of overfitting. Overfitting is a phenomenon that arises when a model exhibits high performance on the training dataset, but fails to generalise well to unknown data. This discrepancy suggests that the model has excessively focused on memorising the training data, rather than acquiring the ability to generalise from it.

During the course of the studies, the models are trained, validated, and tested on Google Colab using Tesla T4 GPU. The model under consideration has been trained for a total of 100 epochs using the dataset specifically designed for face mask detection. The training process was conducted using a batch size of 8. An epoch signifies a whole iteration throughout the entirety of the dataset. Every epoch is comprised of a forwards pass and a backwards pass. After the training was completed, we evaluated the model's performance on a separate test set that the model had not seen during training. This allowed us to assess the model's ability to generalize to unseen data, which is crucial for its practical application.

During the process of training the model, the cross-entropy loss function was created. The cross-entropy loss function is widely employed as a means of measuring the predictive performance of classification issues [4]. The metric quantifies the disparity between the probability distribution projected by the model and the observed probability distribution. The mathematical formulation for classification issues may be expressed as follows.

$$Loss_{CEL} = -\frac{1}{N} \sum_{i=1}^{N} y_i \log(p_i) + (1 - y_i) \log(1 - p_i) \qquad (2)$$

where N represents the total number of samples, y_i is the actual label of the i sample (either 0 or 1), and p_i represents the probability assigned by the model to the i sample belonging to the positive class.

The cross-entropy loss function is adopted in our face mask detection job to optimise the predictive performance of the model. The model provides a probability value for each picture, indicating the likelihood of the individual in the image wearing a mask. The projected probability value is compared to the actual label, which indicates whether the individual is wearing a mask, in order to compute the cross-entropy loss. During the training phase, the objective is to minimise the aforementioned loss.

In order to enhance the performance of the model, we take use of the Adam optimizer, which is a kind of adaptive learning rate optimisation technique specifically developed to mitigate the issues of gradient sparsity and noise that may arise during the training phase. Furthermore, we implemented an early stopping technique, whereby the training process is halted when the loss on the validation dataset fails to exhibit a drop across a consecutive number of epochs. Upon the completion of the training process, we proceeded to save the model that exhibited the highest performance on the validation set.

By using this approach, our model demonstrates proficiency in accurately detecting the presence of individuals in the picture and determining if they are wearing face masks. The performance of our model on the test set demonstrates its superiority over other current face mask detection methods.

4   Experimental Results and Analysis

4.1   Evaluation Index

Mean Average Precision. Mean Average Precision (mAP) [12] is a metric to determine the performance of an object detection algorithm. mAP is the average of multiple class average precision (AP), where the AP for each class is calculated from the detection results of that class. The specific formula is as follows,

$$mAP = \frac{1}{C} \sum_{i=1}^{N} AP_i \qquad (3)$$

where C represents the total number of classes. Where mAP is one of the most popular indicators in object detection, and it is usually utilized to evaluate the accuracy and reliability of object detection algorithms. In order to better evaluate the performance, we use mAP50 and mAP50-95 for evaluation. mAP50 indicates the mAP value when IoU is 0.5. $mAP50-95$ indicates the mAP value when IoU is 0.5~ 0.95.

Precision-Recall Curve. The precision-recall curve (PR-cure) is the curve of the model for the confidence score threshold element. The horizontal axis is the recall rate, indicating the proportion of detected positive samples to all positive samples. The recall formula is,

$$Precision = \frac{TruePositives}{TruePositives + FalsePositives} \qquad (4)$$

The vertical axis is precision, which represents the proportion of the true correct number of detected positive samples to the total number of detected samples. The exact formula is,

$$Recall = \frac{TruePositives}{TruePositives + FalseNegatives} \qquad (5)$$

In visual object detection, mAP is precisely determined by calculating the area under the precision-recall curve. That is to say, the larger the area under PR-cure, the larger the mAP value, and the better the performance of the model.

4.2   Experimental Results and Analysis

Experimental Results. To accurately assess the variation in detection speed across various models, we conducted a comparative analysis by subjecting two baseline models, namely YOLOv7 and YOLOv8, to identical data set conditions for detection purposes. The results are shown in Table 1.

Table 1. Comparison of detection speed between YOLOv7 and YOLOv8

Model	Total time	Average time	Number of detected images	GPU
YOLOv8n	464.2ms	42.2ms	11	Tesla T4
YOLOv7	12060ms	1096ms	11	Tesla T4

Based on the facts shown in Table 1, it is evident that the experimental conditions and inference dataset remain consistent. The YOLOv8n model exhibits much quicker reasoning speed compared to the YOLOv7 model. The inference speed of YOLOv8n is 11596ms greater than that of YOLOv7. On average, there is a speed improvement of 1053 milliseconds per image.

While it has been shown that the model using YOLOv7 is comparatively less efficient than the model employing YOLOv8, for the purpose of enhancing the reliability of the experimental findings, we have opted to choose a model based on YOLOv7 for the comparative experiment. To enhance the assessment of the model's performance, we conducted sequential training on the dataset using YOLOv7+CBAM, YOLOV8n, YOLOV8n+DCNv2, and Swin+YOLOv8. Table 2 displays the parameters pertaining to the four sets of models.

Table 2. Comparison of four models

Model	Layers	Parameters	FLOPs	Gradients
YOLOv7+CBAM	415	37207344	105.1	37207344
YOLOv8n	225	3011433	8.2	3011417
YOLOV8n+DCNv2	225	3167863	7.7	3167847
Swin+YOLOv8	348	51382394	455.5	51382378

Based on the data presented in Table 2, it is evident that there are significant variations in several parameters across different models. In terms of the network layer count, YOLOv8 exhibits a smaller number of network layers compared to YOLOv7. The YOLOv8 model using SwinTransformer exhibits a greater number of layers compared to the YOLOv8 model without SwinTransformer. From a parameterization standpoint, it can be seen that the SwinTransformer model has a greater overall parameter count compared to other models. Based on the number of parameters, it can be initially deduced that the training duration of the SwinTransformer model is expected to be the longest.

Based on the obtained training outcomes, the face mask detection accuracy achieved using the YOLOv7+CBAM model is 92%. The recall rate, which measures the proportion of true positive instances correctly identified, is 0.84. The mean average precision at a threshold of 50% (mAP50) is 0.90, while the mean average precision throughout a range of thresholds from 50% to 95% (mAP50-95) is 0.609. The total duration of the training process amounts to 2.260 h. The face mask detection accuracy achieved by using the YOLOv8n model is 91.7% in terms of precision. The recall rate is measured at 0.823, while the mean Average Precision at mAP50 stands at 0.903. Furthermore, the mean Average Precision throughout the range of mAP50-95 is calculated to be 0.663. Lastly, the training process for this model requires 2.341 h. The YOLOV8n+DCNv2 model achieves a precision of 94.4% in detecting face masks. The recall rate is 0.843, indicating the model's ability to accurately identify positive instances. The mean Average Precision at mAP50 is 0.909, reflecting the model's performance in object identification. The mAP50-95, which measures the average accuracy across different overlap thresholds, is 0.668. The training process for this model is 2.478 h. The Swin+YOLOv8 model achieved a face mask detection accuracy of 96.1%. The recall rate is measured at 0.906, while the mAP50 and mAP50-95 scores are reported as 0.962 and 0.727, respectively. The training process for this model takes around 3.999 h. Table 3 is derived from the training outcomes of each model.

Table 3. The training results for YOLOv8n, YOLOV8n+DCNv2, YOLOv8s, DSOTAs

Model Name	Precision	Recall	mAP50	mAP50-95	Training Time (Hour)
YOLOv7+CBAM	0.920	0.840	0.903	0.609	2.260
YOLOV8n	0.917	0.823	0.903	0.663	2.341
YOLOV8n+DCNv2	0.944	0.824	0.909	0.668	2.478
Swin+YOLOv8	0.961	0.906	0.962	0.727	3.999

The disparity in accuracy often elicits an intuitive perception of the variance in model performance. The data illustrates that the training speed of the three models using YOLOv8n is comparatively slower in comparison to YOLOv7. Nevertheless, the detection accuracy of the three models using YOLOv8 is consistently high. In particular, the YOLOV8n+DCNv2 model demonstrates a 2.4% increase in accuracy compared to the YOLOv7+CBAM model. The precision of Swin+YOLOv8 surpassed that of YOLOv7+CBAM by 4.1%. Moreover, it has been seen that models using Swin+YOLOv8 or YOLOV8n+DCNv2 exhibit superior performance compared to models that do not use the Transformer architecture. The model's accuracy, while using YOLOV8n+DCNv2, achieves a level of 94.4%. The Swin+YOLOv8 model achieves a model accuracy of 96.1%, surpassing the other three models and attaining the greatest accuracy.

The duration required for training a model using a Swin Transformer architecture exceeds that of a model without Swin Transformer. However, the performance of this model in terms of accuracy is superior when utilizing a Transformer. The training duration of YOLOv8n is 1.5 h shorter compared to Swin+YOLOv8. The precision of YOLOv8n is observed to be 1.7% inferior in comparison to Swin+YOLOv8. The model using Transformer exhibits higher accuracy compared to YOLOv8n. The mean Average Precision (mAP) value of Swin+YOLOv8 is seen to be greater compared to the model that does not include other models. Frequently, a higher mAP number is indicative of a more pronounced impact of the model. In contrast to the model without Swin Transformer, Swin+YOLOv8 has the highest mAP value of 0.961.

Error Analysis. Our model produces erroneous results on real face mask detection. For example, in the detection results of Fig. 2, the person at the top of the image wears the mask correctly. But the reality is that the person at the top of the image is wearing a mask incorrectly. We found multiple similar errors in our detection results. Through the analysis of the error results, it is found that errors are prone to occur when detecting people wearing masks on the side face. Inspection of the dataset shows that the dataset has only a small number of images of people wearing masks in profile. We will collect more profiles of people wearing masks in future work.

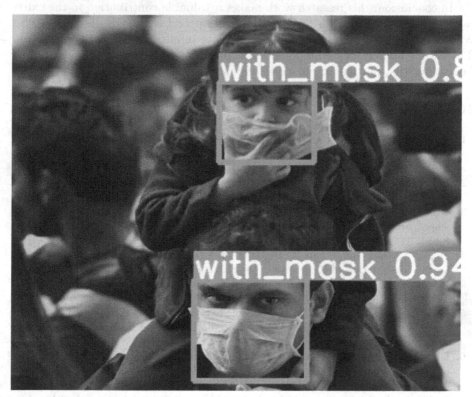

Fig. 2. One instance of a human face mask image that has been erroneously categorised.

5   Conclusion

In this paper, we introduce a fresh use of Swin Transformer model in the context of face mask detection challenges. The proposed model, referred to as Swin+YOLOv8, combines Swin Transformer with the detection module YOLOv8. This integration showcases the enhanced performance compared to the existing face mask detection models. The findings indicated that Swin+YOLOv8 model exhibited a face mask detection accuracy 96.1% and a mean average precision (mAP) of 0.962, therefore exceeding the performance of traditional models. The use of Swin Transformer inside our model enabled the management of complicated situations and complex data, demonstrated its efficacy in augmenting the precision and efficiency of face mask detection jobs.

Nevertheless, the research outcomes also revealed that the Swin+YOLOv8 model required a lengthier training period compared to the other models. This observation underscores the possibility of a compromise between the performance of the model and its computing efficiency. Subsequent investigations may prioritize the refinement of the training procedure for Swin Transformer-based models, with the aim of achieving an optimal equilibrium between computational expenditure and performance outcomes.

In conclusion, this research work makes a valuable contribution to the existing body of knowledge on face mask detection technology by showcasing the considerable potential of the Swin Transformer in effectively identifying masks. The Swin+YOLOv8 has the potential in practical scenarios to augment public health security, particularly in times of pandemics.

References

1. Addagarla, S.K., Chakravarthi, G.K., Anitha, P.: Real time multi-scale facial mask detection and classification using deep transfer learning techniques. Int. J. **9**(4), 4402–4408 (2020)
2. Deng, H., Zhang, J., Chen, L., Cai, M.: Improved mask wearing detection algorithm for SSD. J. Phys. Conf. Ser. **1757**, 012140 (2021)
3. Diwan, T., Anirudh, G., Tembhurne, J.V.: Object detection using YOLO: challenges, architectural successors, datasets and applications. Multimedia Tools Appl. **82**(6), 9243–9275 (2023)
4. Du, Z., Su, J., Ding, J., Liu, Z.: Research on YOLO-v3 road target detection based on the combination of K-means++ algorithm and cross-entropy loss function. In: International Conference on Electronic Information Technology (EIT 2022), vol. 12254, pp. 756–760. SPIE (2022)
5. Gao, X., Nguyen, M., Yan, W.Q.: Face image inpainting based on generative adversarial network. In: International Conference on Image and Vision Computing New Zealand (IVCNZ), pp. 1–6. IEEE (2021)
6. Gao, X., Nguyen, M., Yan, W.Q.: A method for face image inpainting based on autoencoder and generative adversarial network. In: Wang, H., et al. Image and Video Technology. PSIVT 2022. Lecture Notes in Computer Science, vol. 13763, pp. 24–36. Springer, Cham (2022). https://doi.org/10.1007/978-3-031-26431-3_3
7. Gong, M., Wang, D., Zhao, X., Guo, H., Luo, D., Song, M.: A review of non-maximum suppression algorithms for deep learning target detection. In: The Symposium on Novel Photoelectronic Detection Technology and Applications, vol. 11763, pp. 821–828. SPIE (2021)
8. Guo, S., Li, L., Guo, T., Cao, Y., Li, Y.: Research on mask-wearing detection algorithm based on improved YOLOv5. Sensors **22**(13), 4933 (2022)
9. Kattenborn, T., Leitloff, J., Schiefer, F., Hinz, S.: Review on convolutional neural networks (CNN) in vegetation remote sensing. ISPRS J. Photogramm. Remote. Sens. **173**, 24–49 (2021)
10. Le, H., Nguyen, M., Yan, W.Q., Nguyen, H.: Augmented reality and machine learning incorporation using YOLOv3 and ARKit. Appl. Sci. **11**(13), 6006 (2021)
11. Li, X., et al.: Mask dataset (2022). https://makeml.app/datasets/mask
12. Li, Y., Li, S., Du, H., Chen, L., Zhang, D., Li, Y.: YOLO-ACN: focusing on small target and occluded object detection. IEEE Access **8**, 227288–227303 (2020)
13. Liu, Z., et al.: Swin transformer: Hierarchical vision transformer using shifted windows. In: IEEE/CVF International Conference on Computer Vision, pp. 10012–10022 (2021)

14. Maity, M., Banerjee, S., Chaudhuri, S.S.: Faster R-CNN and YOLO based vehicle detection: a survey. In: International Conference on Computing Methodologies and Communication (ICCMC), pp. 1442–1447. IEEE (2021)

15. Qi, J., Nguyen, M., Yan, W.Q.: Small visual object detection in smart waste classification using transformers with deep learning. In: Yan, W.Q., Nguyen, M., Stommel, M. (eds.) Image and Vision Computing. IVCNZ 2022. Lecture Notes in Computer Science, vol. 13836, pp. 301–314. Springer, Cham (2022). https://doi.org/10.1007/978-3-031-25825-1_22

16. Ren, X., Liu, X.: Mask wearing detection based on YOLOv3. J. Phys. Conf. Ser. **1678**, 012089 (2020)

17. Tomás, J., Rego, A., Viciano-Tudela, S., Lloret, J.: Incorrect facemask-wearing detection using convolutional neural networks with transfer learning. Healthcare **9**, 1050 (2021)

18. Ullah, N., Javed, A., Ghazanfar, M.A., Alsufyani, A., Bourouis, S.: A novel Deep-MaskNet model for face mask detection and masked facial recognition. J. King Saud Univ. Comput. Inf. Sci. **34**(10), 9905–9914 (2022)

19. Wang, J., Wang, J., Zhang, X., Yu, N.: A mask-wearing detection model in complex scenarios based on YOLOv7-CPCSDSA. Electronics **12**(14), 3128 (2023)

20. Wang, Z., Sun, W., Zhu, Q., Shi, P.: Face mask-wearing detection model based on loss function and attention mechanism. Comput. Intell. Neurosci. **2022**, 2452291 (2022)

21. Xia, Y., Nguyen, M., Yan, W.Q.: A real-time kiwifruit detection based on improved YOLOv7. In: Yan, W.Q., Nguyen, M., Stommel, M. (eds.) Image and Vision Computing. IVCNZ 2022. Lecture Notes in Computer Science, vol. 13836, pp. 48–61. Springer (2022). https://doi.org/10.1007/978-3-031-25825-1_4

22. Xiao, B., Nguyen, M., Yan, W.Q.: Fruit ripeness identification using YOLOv8 model. Multimedia Tools Appl. 1–18 (2023)

23. Xue, B., Hu, J., Zhang, P.: Intelligent detection and recognition system for mask wearing based on improved retinaface algorithm. In: International Conference on Machine Learning, Big Data and Business Intelligence (MLBDBI), pp. 474–479. IEEE (2020)

24. Yan, Wei Qi: Introduction to Intelligent Surveillance. TCS, Springer, Cham (2019). https://doi.org/10.1007/978-3-030-10713-0

25. Yan, W.Q.: Computational Methods for Deep Learning: Theory, Algorithms, and Implementations. Springer Nature (2023). https://doi.org/10.1007/978-981-99-4823-9

26. Ye, Q., Zhao, Y.: Mask wearing detection algorithm based on improved YOLOv4. J. Phys. Conf. Ser. **2258**, 012013 (2022)

27. Ye, Z., Zhang, H., Liu, Q.: Swtface: a multi-branch network for masked face detection and recognition. In: International Conference on Pattern Recognition and Artificial Intelligence (PRAI), pp. 381–387. IEEE (2022)

28. Yu, J., Zhang, W.: Face mask wearing detection algorithm based on improved YOLO-v4. Sensors **21**(9), 3263 (2021)

29. Yuan, X., Zhang, S., Zhao, C., He, X., Ouyang, B., Yang, S.: Pain intensity recognition from masked facial expressions using swin-transformer. In: IEEE International Conference on Robotics and Biomimetics (ROBIO), pp. 723–728. IEEE (2022)

30. Zeng, C., Liu, Y., Song, C.: Swin-CasUNet: cascaded U-Net with Swin Transformer for masked face restoration. In: International Conference on Pattern Recognition (ICPR), pp. 386–392. IEEE (2022)

Efficient 3D Brain Tumor Segmentation with Axial-Coronal-Sagittal Embedding

Tuan-Luc Huynh[1,2], Thanh-Danh Le[1,2], Tam V. Nguyen[3],
Trung-Nghia Le[1,2], and Minh-Triet Tran[1,2(✉)]

[1] University of Science, VNU-HCM, Ho Chi Minh City, Vietnam
htluc@selab.hcmus.edu.vn
[2] Vietnam National University, Ho Chi Minh City, Vietnam
[3] University of Dayton, Dayton, USA

Abstract. In this paper, we address the crucial task of brain tumor segmentation in medical imaging and propose innovative approaches to enhance its performance. The current state-of-the-art nnU-Net has shown promising results but suffers from extensive training requirements and underutilization of pre-trained weights. To overcome these limitations, we integrate Axial-Coronal-Sagittal convolutions and pre-trained weights from ImageNet into the nnU-Net framework, resulting in reduced training epochs, reduced trainable parameters, and improved efficiency. Two strategies for transferring 2D pre-trained weights to the 3D domain are presented, ensuring the preservation of learned relationships and feature representations critical for effective information propagation. Furthermore, we explore a joint classification and segmentation model that leverages pre-trained encoders from a brain glioma grade classification proxy task, leading to enhanced segmentation performance, especially for challenging tumor labels. Experimental results demonstrate that our proposed methods in the fast training settings achieve comparable or even outperform the ensemble of cross-validation models, a common practice in the brain tumor segmentation literature.

Keywords: Brain Tumor Segmentation · ACS Convolutions · Joint Classification and Segmentation

1 Introduction

Brain tumor segmentation in medical imaging is a critical task with significant applications in diagnosis and treatment planning. nnU-Net [11], the winning solution in BraTS2020 [2,3,16], has shown promising performance by incorporating heuristic rules for pre-processing and network architectures. However, it encounters limitations, including the need for extensive training and the lack of utilization of pre-trained weights. Leveraging pre-trained weights from large-scale image datasets, such as ImageNet [5], has been proven to be valuable in terms of achieving competitive results in various computer vision tasks; Therefore, using these pre-trained weights on downstream tasks to leverage learned

W. Q. Yan et al. (Eds.): PSIVT 2023, LNCS 14403, pp. 138–152, 2024.
https://doi.org/10.1007/978-981-97-0376-0_11

representations as a good initialization is desirable instead of random initialization. To address these limitations in brain tumor segmentation, we propose novel approaches based on transfer learning with pre-trained weights and proxy task training to enhance both efficiency and performance of nnU-Net [10,11].

Our inspiration for this work stems from a presentation at the Brainlesion workshop during MICCAI2023, where the successful use of Axial-Coronal-Sagittal (ACS) convolutions [23] in the GanDLF framework [19] led to superior performance on the BraTS2020 dataset with fewer epochs, in contrast to claims by Isensee *et al.* [17]. Additionally, upon careful examination, we observe striking similarities between the nnU-Net generated network and ResNet18 [8], providing an opportunity to leverage the valuable pre-trained weights of ResNet18 while preserving the integrity of the nnU-Net framework. To this end, we propose an innovative integration approach incorporating ACS convolutions into the nnU-Net framework [10]. We introduce two distinct methods for transferring pre-trained 2D weights to the 3D domain, focusing on preserving nnU-Net's network topology during initialization while retaining critical learned relationships and feature representations essential for effective information propagation.

Furthermore, we explore a joint classification and segmentation model for enhanced performance. This approach leverages a pre-trained encoder on a brain gliomas grade classification proxy task, guiding the segmentation task and leading to improved overall performance. Through these comprehensive contributions, we aim to push the boundaries of brain tumor segmentation, opening up new possibilities for efficient and accurate medical image analysis. Our contributions are summarized as follows:

- Explore nnU-Net's efficacy in fast training settings, reducing required training epochs for brain tumor segmentation.
- Introduce Axial-Coronal-Sagittal (ACS) convolutions and propose two integration strategies to seamlessly transfer 2D pre-trained weights (e.g., ImageNet) to the 3D domain within nnU-Net's network topology, enhancing training efficiency, and preserving crucial learned relationships and feature representations for effective information propagation.
- Propose a joint classification and segmentation nnU-Net model leveraging pre-trained proxy tasks for distinguishing high-grade and low-grade gliomas, enhancing segmentation for the challenging enhancing tumor labels.
- Achieve competitive or better performance than baseline models while maintaining efficiency through reduced training epochs and trainable parameters.

2   Related Work

Since its inception, U-Net [20] has become the *de facto* standard for medical image segmentation with its iconic encoder and decoder architecture. Recent BraTS challenge solutions [1,3,16] have prominently relied on CNNs using the U-shaped encoder-decoder design [11,14,15,18,24]. Notably, Isensee *et al.* secured victory in the BraTS2020 challenge with the nnU-Net framework [10], which features an automated configuration mechanism. The winning solution of the subsequent year [15] further built upon nnU-Net's achievements. Despite transformer-based methods like TransBTS [21] and SwinUNetR [6] showing comparable performance, CNNs continue to dominate in medical image segmentation.

In the existing literature, a common strategy involves laborious cross-validation, assembly, and training of multiple models from scratch. To address the efficiency challenge, transfer learning has garnered attention. One notable attempt in this direction is Med3D [4], which offers 3D pre-trained weights. However, it is crucial to acknowledge that the scale of its pre-trained data remains incomparable to the vast 2D natural image datasets commonly utilized in transfer learning.

Another approach, Model Genesis [25], leverages self-supervised methods on 3D medical images. Although innovative, these methods have yet to surpass the performance of widely explored fully-supervised approaches, which span over a decade of research in the field.

Our work posits that the full potential of efficient training and fine-tuning in the brain tumor segmentation problem is yet to be fully realized, particularly concerning large-scale 3D pre-trained models.

3   Proposed Methods

3.1   ACS nnU-Net

Our work builds on Sarthak Pati's insights [19] and aims to explore the benefits of using pre-trained weights in the nnU-Net framework for 3D medical image segmentation. nnU-Net has shown strength in semantic segmentation but lacks specialized pre-trained weights for 3D medical images. To overcome this, we propose integrating 2D pre-trained ACS convolutions into nnU-Net. This integration seeks to demonstrate significant performance improvements in demanding biomedical image segmentation tasks. However, a major challenge is transferring these pre-trained weights while preserving nnU-Net's core design principle of adapting the network topology for each dataset. Maintaining the integrity of the generated network is essential to address this issue. For further details of ACS convolutions, we refer readers to [23].

ACS-ResNet18 nnU-Net. We integrate ACS convolutions into nnU-Net by leveraging similarities with ResNet18 [8]. This allows us to use ResNet18 as pre-trained weights for the encoder, as shown in Fig. 1. We replace 3D convolutions in the decoder with ACS convolutions, reducing parameters and ensuring symmetry with the encoder, leading to optimized performance.

Our approach uses partial transfer learning, seamlessly integrating 2D domain pre-trained weights with ACS convolutions in nnU-Net. Careful selection and initialization of the corresponding layers preserve critical learned relationships and feature representations, facilitating the effective propagation of information. We prioritize connected pre-trained layers, initializing nnU-Net's specific convolutions with corresponding layers in ResNet18 to enhance integration.

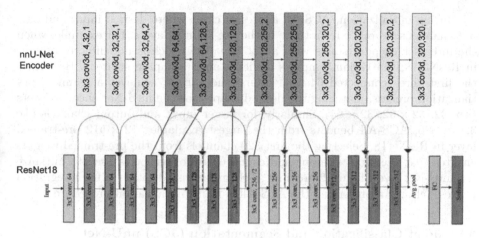

Fig. 1. Schematic design of our ACS nnU-Net encoder. Convention: "kernel-size, input channels, output channels, stride" in each block.

We follow nnU-Net's default Kaiming normal initialization for non-initialized layers [7]. Our comprehensive approach, encompassing encoder and decoder, exploits pre-trained weights, ACS convolutions, and connected CNN pre-trained layers to boost nnU-Net's performance.

ACS-All-ResNet18 nnU-Net. To increase the availability of pre-trained weights, we introduce a second variant called ACS-All for the nnU-Net. Unlike the previous variant, which only transferred pre-trained weights for convolutional layers with matching properties, ACS-All utilizes sets of connected pre-trained layers in ResNet18 to initialize corresponding layers in the nnU-Net encoder.

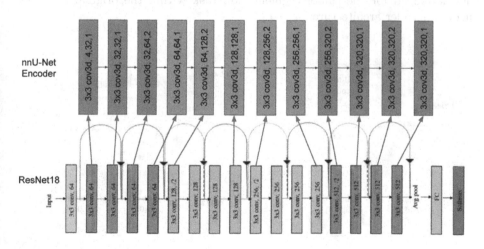

Fig. 2. Schematic design of our ACS-All nnU-Net encoder.

During initialization, ACS-All addresses cases where desired input and output channel sizes differ from those in the pre-trained layers. For example, when the nnU-Net encoder starts with a 4×32 layer, which is not directly present in ResNet18, the variant employs a slicing and reshaping strategy. By slicing the first three connected 64×64 layers, the variant achieves a seamless initialization process, matching the desired shapes for the nnU-Net encoder layers (4×32, 32×32, 32×64). Similarly, for larger input and output channels like 320×320, ACS-All benefits from the largest available 512×512 pre-trained layer in ResNet18. Selecting the first 320 channels from the pre-trained weights ensures that the most relevant and connected information is used to initialize the nnU-Net layer. Figure 2 provides a schematic visualization of the integration process, clearly representing the ACS-All variant initialization procedure.

3.2   Joint Classification and Segmentation (JCS) nnU-Net

To preserve performance with limited training epochs, we leverage pre-training the nnU-Net encoder with a glioma grade classification proxy task using HGG/LGG metadata. This equips the encoder with a comprehensive understanding of brain MRI characteristics, enhancing segmentation performance even in cases with minimal enhancing tumor or none. This pre-training approach shares the same motivation as the ACS-based nnU-Net variants, optimizing integration and leveraging pre-trained knowledge for improved performance in challenging biomedical image segmentation tasks like the BraTS dataset [2,3,16].

To perform the proxy task pre-training, the encoder is detached from the nnU-Net architecture, and a classifier head is added (Fig. 3). Spatial CNN features are aggregated using global average pooling, followed by fully connected layers with LeakyReLU activation. Dropout layers are incorporated for regularization during training. The learned representations from the proxy task are then leveraged for the tumor segmentation task within the original nnU-Net encoder-decoder architecture.

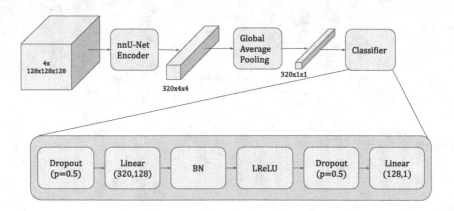

Fig. 3. HGG-LGG nnU-Net classifier.

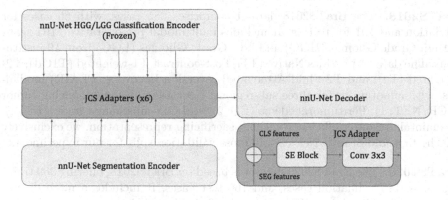

Fig. 4. Schematic view of the JCS nnU-Net.

Directly substituting the nnU-Net's encoder with the HGG-LGG encoder's classification component does not significantly improve performance compared to the baseline due to the inherent task gap between classification and segmentation. Instead, we propose a strategic adaptation by incorporating the HGG-LGG nnU-Net encoder's classification capabilities as a frozen component within the Joint Classification and Segmentation (JCS) model, inspired by Wu *et al.* [22]. This unified framework combines classification and segmentation strengths, improving tumor segmentation results' accuracy and robustness.

The decision to freeze the classification branch is partly due to limited training resources and overall efficiency. In the JCS framework, we achieve a powerful and balanced approach by combining classification features from the glioma grade classification task to enhance the segmentation task performance.

Figure 4 illustrates the schematic view of our proposed Joint Classification and Segmentation (JCS) nnU-Net architecture. JCS Adapter, inspired by Wu *et al.* [22], is used to seamlessly integrate classification and segmentation while bridging the gap between the two tasks. Given that the nnU-Net encoder consists of six stages, we employed six adapters, each tailored to a specific stage, with variations in input and output channels. The JCS Adapter takes two inputs, classification features (CLS) and segmentation features (SEG), which are concatenated before being passed through a subsequent SE block [9] and a 3×3 convolution layer.

4   Experimental Setup

4.1   Dataset

We focus on the BraTS2018 dataset [2,3,16] due to its relevance in evaluating our research. Additionally, we assess the transferability and robustness of our methods on the more recent BraTS2020 data set [2,3,16]. Utilizing both datasets allows us to explore performance in different contexts, advancing brain tumor segmentation in medical image analysis.

BraTS2018. The BraTS2018 dataset comprises 285 cases, with 66 cases for validation and 191 for testing. It includes multimodal pre-operative MRI scans of High-Grade Gliomas (HGG) and Low-Grade Gliomas (LGG) from 19 institutions. The dataset provides Native (T1), Post-contrast T1-weighted (T1Gd), T2-Weighted (T2), and T2 Fluid Attenuated Inversion Recovery (FLAIR) modalities, with annotations for three sub-regions: Necrotic and non-enhancing tumor (NCR/NET, 1), Peritumoral edema (ED, 2), and GD-enhancing tumors (ET, 4). To maintain resource efficiency without sacrificing representation, we exclusively use the first fold of nnU-Net's 5-fold cross-validation split for our experiments.

BraTS2020. The BraTS2020 dataset is based on BraTS2018, offering 369 training cases, 125 validation cases, and 166 test cases. It includes a more diverse collection of multimodal MRI scans and refines the naming convention. Similar to BraTS2018, our experiments solely focus on the first fold of nnU-Net's 5-fold cross-validation split for BraTS2020, ensuring consistent and representative evaluations of proposed methods.

4.2 Evaluation Metrics

Dice score (Sørensen-Dice coefficient), also known as Dice similarity coefficient (DSC), or simply Dice score, quantifies the agreement between segmented regions and actual regions of interest. It is computed by comparing true positives to the sum of pixels in both the predicted and ground-truth masks. The Dice coefficient is defined as follows:

$$DSC = \frac{2TP}{2TP + FP + FN} \tag{1}$$

Hausdorff distance 95% (HD95) calculates the maximum distance of a set to the nearest point in another set. 95% Hausdorff distance is based on calculating the 95th percentile of the distances between the boundary points in X and Y. The formula for Hausdorff distance is given by:

$$d_H(X,Y) = \max d_{XY}, d_{YX} = \max \max_{x \in X} \min_{y \in Y} d(x,y), \max_{y \in Y} \min_{x \in X} d(x,y). \tag{2}$$

4.3 Implementation Details

All segmentation experiments are conducted using the nnU-Net framework [10] with provided planning files. We use a batch size of 4 and train for 50 epochs on a single Nvidia Quadro RTX 5000 GPU with 16GB VRAM. The JCS models are trained on an Nvidia RTX A5000 GPU with 24GB VRAM. HGG/LGG classifiers undergo 100 epochs of training with a batch size of 5, learning rate of 0.001, stratified sampling strategy, and PyTorch's BCEWithLogitsLoss with a pos_weight parameter set to the LGG-to-HGG ratio.

4.4   Implementation Variants

We represent our models, with region-based training [11,13] by default, using different variants:

- **BN**: Batch normalization instead of instance normalization.
- **DA**: BraTS-specific intensive data augmentation [11].
- **Post**: apply a post-processing strategy using empirical thresholds of 200 voxels for BraTS2018 and 1000 voxels for BraTS2020.
- **CV**: 5-fold cross-validation and default post-processing as nnU-Net's training scheme. The final result is an ensemble of these five models.

5   Experimental Results

5.1   Quantitative Results

BraTS2018.

Baselines: Table 1 presents the baselines examined in our fast training setup. We exclusively train and evaluate our model on the first fold of the 5-fold cross-validation split file. This approach yields a mean Dice score of 0.85394 and a mean HD95 of 5.70207, establishing it as our baseline evaluation (in bold). Replacing instance normalization with batch normalization marginally reduces the Mean Dice score in the Baseline+BN variant, but significantly improves the mean HD95, achieving a value of 5.17258 with relatively low standard deviation.

Table 1. Baselines comparison on the BraTS2018 validation set.

Methods	Mean Dice ↑	SD Dice ↓	Mean HD95 ↓	SD HD95 ↓
CV [12]	0.85600	–	5.25667	–
Baseline+BN+DA	0.85568	0.00415	5.32355	0.51249
Baseline	**0.85394**	**0.00341**	**5.70207**	**0.22982**
Baseline+BN	0.85338	0.00320	5.17258	0.13719
CV (run once)	0.85089	–	5.91061	–

We include the result of Isensee *et al.* on the BraTS2018 validation set in row four of Table 2 [12], as it closely aligns with our settings. Their approach demonstrates superior performance due to a 500-epoch training ensemble and 5-fold cross-validation with an ensemble of five models. Adapting the nnU-Net framework's default training scheme [10] with a modification of the training epochs to 50 yields a modest mean Dice score of 0.85089 and a mean HD95 of 5.91061. The Baseline+BN+DA variant with intensive data augmentation slightly lags behind Isensee *et al.*'s approach.

ACS nnU-Net variants: Table 2 presents the performance of our proposed ACS nnU-Net variants. Both ACS-ResNet18 variants leverage pre-trained weights, achieving comparable performance while significantly reducing the number of parameters. ACS-ResNet18 attains a mean Dice score of 0.85312, while ACS-ResNet18-All outperforms the baseline with a mean Dice score of 0.85444 and a low standard deviation of 0.00130. Pre-trained weights prove vital in leveraging knowledge from natural image datasets, enhancing medical segmentation performance. However, we note that in terms of HD95, we slightly lag behind baseline.

Table 2. ACS nnU-Net variants performance on BraTS2018 validation set.

Methods	Mean Dice ↑	SD Dice ↓	Mean HD95 ↓	SD Dice ↓
ACS-ResNet18-All	**0.85444**	**0.00130**	5.88153	0.34028
Baseline	0.85394	0.00341	**5.70207**	**0.22982**
ACS-ResNet18	0.85312	0.00493	5.80819	0.23196

Table 3. ACS nnU-Net variants with batch normalization and intensive data augmentation performance on BraTS2018 validation set.

Methods	Mean Dice ↑	SD Dice ↓	Mean HD95 ↓	SD Dice ↓
ACS-ResNet18-All+BN+DA	**0.85665**	**0.00194**	**4.87734**	0.24654
CV [12]	0.85600	–	5.25667	–
Baseline+BN+DA	0.85568	0.00415	5.32355	0.51249
ACS-ResNet18+BN+DA	0.85389	0.00324	5.42373	0.65147
Baseline+BN	0.85338	0.00320	5.17258	**0.13719**
ACS-ResNet18+BN	0.84999	0.00233	5.22337	0.13054

In the competitive context of the BraTS challenge, we evaluate our ACS nnU-Net variants with batch normalization (BN) and intensive data augmentation (DA) in Table 3, following a similar approach as Isensee *et al.* [11]. Remarkably, the top-performing model, ACS-ResNet18-All+BN+DA, achieves an impressive mean Dice score of 0.85665 with a low standard deviation of 0.00194, and excels in the mean HD95 with a score of 4.87734. Notably, in both metrics, this variant outperforms the Baseline+BN+DA model and Isensee*et al.*'s ensemble attempt in the BraTS2018 challenge [12]. The results further validate that BN significantly improves mean HD95 while slightly reducing the mean Dice score, as demonstrated by ACS-ResNet18+BN.

JCS nnU-Net: Table 4 presents a detailed performance comparison of the proposed JCS nnU-Net and HGG-LGG nnU-Net against the baseline. The HGG-LGG nnU-Net achieves an impressive mean Dice score of 0.8071 in the enhancing tumor region, aligning with its classification proxy task of distinguishing high-grade gliomas (HGG) from low-grade gliomas (LGG). However, there is an unexpected degradation in the tumor core region, indicating limitations in capturing complex features specific to TC segmentation, resulting in lower overall performance compared to the Baseline in terms of mean Dice score.

In contrast, the JCS nnU-Net improves over the baseline, achieving a mean Dice score of 0.8557 compared to the baseline's 0.8539. Notably, the JCS nnU-Net outperforms the HGG-LGG nnU-Net in most sub-regions, except for the enhancing tumor (ET) region where the HGG-LGG nnU-Net excels, leveraging the strengths of both classification and segmentation tasks. The JCS approach proves to be a powerful and balanced strategy, effectively combining pre-existing knowledge from classification with fine-tuned segmentation to achieve superior performance.

Table 4. Performance of JCS nnU-Net and HGG-LGG nnU-Net. Abbreviations: whole tumor (WT), tumor core (TC), and enhancing tumor (ET). Four floating point precision is used for clarity to avoid crowding the table with numbers.

Methods	Mean Dice ↑				Mean HD95 ↓			
	WT	TC	ET	All	WT	TC	ET	All
JCS	**0.9110**	**0.8546**	0.8016	**0.8557**	4.7712	**7.055**	5.2610	**5.6958**
Baseline	0.9105	0.8508	0.8005	0.8539	4.5199	7.4927	**5.0937**	5.7021
HGG-LGG nnU-Net	**0.9110**	0.8429	**0.8071**	0.8537	**4.4473**	8.1035	5.1186	5.8898

Table 5. Results on BraTS2018 validation set.

Methods	Mean Dice ↑	SD Dice ↓	Mean HD95 ↓	SD HD95 ↓
ACS-ResNet18+BN+DA+Post	**0.86231**	0.00062	4.95997	0.20410
ACS-ResNet18-All+BN+DA+Post	0.86170	0.00194	**4.87734**	0.24654
JCS+Post	0.86098	0.00203	5.43545	0.23385
ACS-ResNet18+BN+Post	0.86009	0.00233	4.88076	**0.13614**
Baseline+Post	0.85993	**0.00045**	5.47518	0.20718
Baseline+BN+DA+Post	0.85899	0.00163	4.93538	0.28096
CV [12]	0.85600	–	5.25667	–
Baseline+CV (run once)	0.85089	–	5.91061	–

Post-processing results: We evaluate our proposed methods with post-processing techniques, as shown in Table 5. The ACS-ResNet18+BN+DA+Post and ACS-ResNet18-All+BN+DA+Post variants achieve the highest mean Dice scores of 0.86231 and 0.86170, respectively, along with impressive segmentation performance in terms of mean HD95. Interestingly, the ACS-ResNet18+BN+Post variant outperforms Baseline+BN+DA+Post, indicating that using BN and post-processing alone already achieves competitive performance, considering the significant increase in training time associated with DA. Notably, all post-processed methods surpass the default nnU-Net training baseline with an ensemble of 5 models in cross-validation, as well as Isensee *et al.*'s previous attempt [12], in terms of Mean Dice score.

BraTS2020: We validate the relevance and adaptability of our methods on the BraTS2020 dataset [3,16] and compare them with the winning solution by Isensee *et al.* [11] in BraTS2020, which shares similar training settings. Table 6 presents the results, highlighting the performance of our approaches.

Table 6. Results on BraTS2020 validation set.

Methods	Mean Dice ↑	Mean HD95 ↓
CV [11]	**0.85580**	11.93000
ACS-ResNet18+BN+DA+Post	0.85546	**11.44526**
JCS+Post	0.84291	17.05532
JCS	0.83009	17.31020
ACS-ResNet18+BN+DA	0.82553	19.71874

Our ACS-ResNet18+BN+DA+Post model achieves a mean Dice score of 0.85546, closely approaching the best-performing CV model with a Dice score of 0.85580. Additionally, our model performs competitively in terms of the mean 95% Hausdorff distance, with a value of 11.44526, compared to the winning solution's 11.93. The JCS nnU-Net model does not show significant improvement with post-processing, with a mean Dice score of 0.84291 and a marginal increase in the mean HD95 (17.31020). In contrast, after applying post-processing, our ACS nnU-Net variants demonstrate substantial improvements in both metrics.

5.2 Qualitative Results

BraTS2018. Figure 5 provides a qualitative overview of the segmentation performance of our top 3 models, along with the baseline, after pre-processing. The first row demonstrates the effectiveness of post-processing in removing insignificant enhancing tumor voxels, resulting in the display of only whole tumor (WT) and necrosis (NCR) labels. As ground truth masks are unavailable for direct comparison, we highlight that the ACS-based nnU-Net variants, despite having fewer parameters, exhibit competitive segmentation performance compared to the baseline nnU-Net.

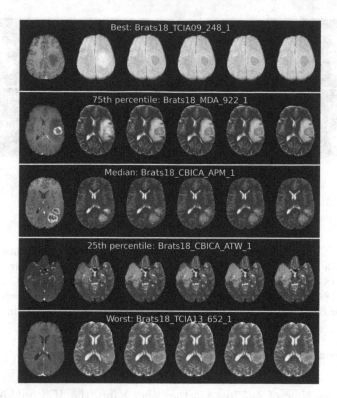

Fig. 5. Qualitative results on the BraTS2018 validation set: Rows show the best, 75th percentile, median, 25th percentile, and worst predictions of our best model ACS-ResNet18+BN+DA+Post. Columns display raw T1ce, raw T2, Baseline+BN+DA+Post, JCS+Post, ACS-ResNet18-All+BN+DA+Post, and ACS-ResNet18+BN+DA+Post predictions. Yellow, green, and red highlight the whole tumor, tumor core, and enhancing tumor, respectively. (Color figure online)

BraTS2020: Figure 6 presents qualitative results of our proposed methods on the updated BraTS2020 dataset. The 25th percentile case indicates the successful removal of negligible ET voxels through post-processing. Additionally, the ACS-based approach outperforms JCS in the TC region significantly.

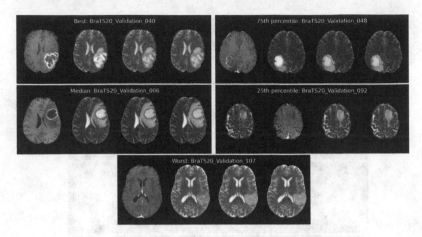

Fig. 6. Qualitative results on the BraTS2020 validation set: Rows show the best, 75th percentile, median, 25th percentile, and worst predictions of our best model ACS-ResNet18+BN+DA+Post. Columns display raw T1ce, raw T2, JCS+Post, and ACS-ResNet18+BN+DA+Post predictions. Yellow, green, and red highlight the whole tumor, tumor core, and enhancing tumor, respectively. (Color figure online)

5.3 Space and Time Complexity Analysis

The baseline nnU-Net, with 88.629 million parameters, achieves a relatively quick inference time of 4.7776 s. On the other hand, the JCS nnU-Net model, incorporating additional adapters in each stage, has 125.158 million parameters and requires 7.4381 s for inference. The ACS-based nnU-Net stands out with only 18.601 million parameters, which is approximately 21% of the baseline's parameter count; however, the inference time is 6.4320 s. While ACS convolutions offer efficiency benefits, their current PyTorch implementation lacks native support, indicating a need for more efficient implementations to achieve competitive results in terms of runtime [23] (Table 7).

Table 7. Trainable parameters and inference time comparison.

Methods	Trainable parameters ↓	Inference time (s) ↓
ACS nnU-Net	**18.601M**	6.4320
Baseline	88.629M	**4.7776**
JCS nnU-Net	125.158M	7.4381

6   Conclusion

In this paper, we present two efficient brain tumor segmentation approaches within the fast training settings of the nnU-Net framework. By seamlessly integrating 2D pre-trained weights using ACS convolutions into the 3D domain, we reduce trainable parameters, enhance resource efficiency, and maintain robust segmentation performance. The Joint Classification and Segmentation (JCS) model shows promise, despite its current underperformance, as it combines classification and segmentation tasks. Our methods are evaluated on the BraTS2018 and BraTS2020 datasets. The extensive experiments show the competitive performance of our proposed work.

Future work involves exploring the generalization of ACS convolutions' pretrained weights to nnU-Net architectures and optimizing the JCS approach. We also aim to evaluate our proposed method on the later BraTS datasets in the future.

Acknowledgment. This research is funded by Vietnam National University Ho Chi Minh City (VNU-HCM) under grant number DS2020-42-01.

References

1. Baid, U., et al.: The RSNA-ASNR-MICCAI brats 2021 benchmark on brain tumor segmentation and radiogenomic classification. arXiv preprint arXiv:2107.02314 (2021)
2. Bakas, S., et al.: Advancing the cancer genome atlas glioma MRI collections with expert segmentation labels and radiomic features. Sci. Data **4**(1), 1–13 (2017)
3. Bakas, S., et al.: Identifying the best machine learning algorithms for brain tumor segmentation, progression assessment, and overall survival prediction in the brats challenge. arXiv preprint arXiv:1811.02629 (2018)
4. Chen, S., Ma, K., Zheng, Y.: Med3D: transfer learning for 3D medical image analysis. arXiv preprint arXiv:1904.00625 (2019)
5. Deng, J., Dong, W., Socher, R., Li, L.J., Li, K., Fei-Fei, L.: ImageNet: a large-scale hierarchical image database. In: 2009 IEEE CVPR, pp. 248–255. IEEE (2009)
6. Hatamizadeh, A., Nath, V., Tang, Y., Yang, D., Roth, H.R., Xu, D.: Swin UNETR: swin transformers for semantic segmentation of brain tumors in MRI images. In: Crimi, A., Bakas, S. (eds.) Brainlesion: Glioma, Multiple Sclerosis, Stroke and Traumatic Brain Injuries. BrainLes 2021. Lecture Notes in Computer Science, vol. 12962, pp. 272–284. Springer, Cham (2021). https://doi.org/10.1007/978-3-031-08999-2_22
7. He, K., Zhang, X., Ren, S., Sun, J.: Delving deep into rectifiers: surpassing human-level performance on ImageNet classification. In: Proceedings of the IEEE ICCV, pp. 1026–1034 (2015)
8. He, K., Zhang, X., Ren, S., Sun, J.: Deep residual learning for image recognition. In: Proceedings of the IEEE CVPR, pp. 770–778 (2016)
9. Hu, J., Shen, L., Sun, G.: Squeeze-and-excitation networks. In: Proceedings of the IEEE CVPR, pp. 7132–7141 (2018)
10. Isensee, F., Jaeger, P.F., Kohl, S.A., Petersen, J., Maier-Hein, K.H.: nnU-Net: a self-configuring method for deep learning-based biomedical image segmentation. Nat. Methods **18**(2), 203–211 (2021)
11. Isensee, F., Jäger, P.F., Full, P.M., Vollmuth, P., Maier-Hein, K.H.: nnU-Net for brain tumor segmentation. In: Crimi, A., Bakas, S. (eds.) BrainLes 2020. LNCS, vol. 12659, pp. 118–132. Springer, Cham (2021). https://doi.org/10.1007/978-3-030-72087-2_11

12. Isensee, F., Kickingereder, P., Wick, W., Bendszus, M., Maier-Hein, K.H.: Brain tumor segmentation and radiomics survival prediction: contribution to the BRATS 2017 challenge. In: Crimi, A., Bakas, S., Kuijf, H., Menze, B., Reyes, M. (eds.) BrainLes 2017. LNCS, vol. 10670, pp. 287–297. Springer, Cham (2018). https://doi.org/10.1007/978-3-319-75238-9_25

13. Isensee, F., Kickingereder, P., Wick, W., Bendszus, M., Maier-Hein, K.H.: No New-Net. In: Crimi, A., Bakas, S., Kuijf, H., Keyvan, F., Reyes, M., van Walsum, T. (eds.) BrainLes 2018. LNCS, vol. 11384, pp. 234–244. Springer, Cham (2019). https://doi.org/10.1007/978-3-030-11726-9_21

14. Jiang, Z., Ding, C., Liu, M., Tao, D.: Two-stage cascaded U-Net: 1st place solution to BraTS Challenge 2019 segmentation task. In: Crimi, A., Bakas, S. (eds.) BrainLes 2019. LNCS, vol. 11992, pp. 231–241. Springer, Cham (2020). https://doi.org/10.1007/978-3-030-46640-4_22

15. Luu, H.M., Park, S.H.: Extending nn-UNet for brain tumor segmentation. In: Crimi, A., Bakas, S. (eds.) Brainlesion: Glioma, Multiple Sclerosis, Stroke and Traumatic Brain Injuries. BrainLes 2021. Lecture Notes in Computer Science, vol. 12963, pp. 173–186. Springer, Cham (2021). https://doi.org/10.1007/978-3-031-09002-8_16

16. Menze, B.H., et al.: The multimodal brain tumor image segmentation benchmark (BRATS). IEEE TMI **34**(10), 1993–2024 (2015)

17. MIC-DKFZ: nnUNet. https://github.com/MIC-DKFZ/nnUNet (2023)

18. Myronenko, A.: 3D MRI Brain Tumor Segmentation Using Autoencoder Regularization. In: Crimi, A., Bakas, S., Kuijf, H., Keyvan, F., Reyes, M., van Walsum, T. (eds.) BrainLes 2018. LNCS, vol. 11384, pp. 311–320. Springer, Cham (2019). https://doi.org/10.1007/978-3-030-11726-9_28

19. Pati, S., et al.: GaNDLF: the generally nuanced deep learning framework for scalable end-to-end clinical workflows. Commun. Eng. **2**(1), 23 (2023)

20. Ronneberger, O., Fischer, P., Brox, T.: U-Net: convolutional networks for biomedical image segmentation. In: Navab, N., Hornegger, J., Wells, W.M., Frangi, A.F. (eds.) MICCAI 2015. LNCS, vol. 9351, pp. 234–241. Springer, Cham (2015). https://doi.org/10.1007/978-3-319-24574-4_28

21. Wang, W., Chen, C., Ding, M., Yu, H., Zha, S., Li, J.: TransBTS: multimodal brain tumor segmentation using transformer. In: de Bruijne, M., et al. (eds.) MICCAI 2021. LNCS, vol. 12901, pp. 109–119. Springer, Cham (2021). https://doi.org/10.1007/978-3-030-87193-2_11

22. Wu, Y.H., et al.: JCS: an explainable COVID-19 diagnosis system by joint classification and segmentation. IEEE Tip **30**, 3113–3126 (2021)

23. Yang, J., et al.: Reinventing 2D convolutions for 3D images. IEEE JBHI **25**(8), 3009–3018 (2021)

24. Zeineldin, R.A., Karar, M.E., Burgert, O., Mathis-Ullrich, F.: Multimodal CNN networks for brain tumor segmentation in MRI: a brats 2022 challenge solution. arXiv preprint arXiv:2212.09310 (2022)

25. Zhou, Z., Sodha, V., Pang, J., Gotway, M.B., Liang, J.: Models genesis. Med. Image Anal. **67**, 101840 (2021)

Spatial Variation Sequences for Remote Sensing Applications with Small Sample Sizes

Hayden Jeune, Niklas Pechan, Sharn-Konet Reitsma, and Andreas W. Kempa-Liehr[✉][iD]

Department of Engineering Science and Biomedical Engineering, The University of Auckland, Auckland 1010, New Zealand
a.kempa-liehr@auckland.ac.nz

Abstract. Machine learning applications in remote sensing often require a labour-intensive feature engineering step, if only a small number of samples is available and transfer learning is not applicable. Here, we are introducing the concept of Spatial Variation Sequences, which allows to apply methodologies from automated time-series feature engineering to remote sensing applications of static images. The presented example application detects swimming pools from four-channel satellite images with an F_1-score of 0.95, by generating spatial variation sequences from a modified swimming pool index. The automated feature engineering approach reduced the dimensionality of the classification problem by 99.7%. A more traditional approach using transfer learning on pre-trained Convolutional Neural Networks (CNN) was evaluated in parallel for comparison. The CNN approach boasted a higher performance of F_1-score of 0.98 but required the use of pre-trained weights. The comparable performance of the FE and CNN approach demonstrates that time-series feature extraction is a valuable alternative to traditional remote sensing methods in the presence of data scarcity or the need of significant dimensionality reduction.

Keywords: Pattern recognition · Swimming pool detection · Feature engineering · Explainable machine learning

1 Introduction

The best-performing remote sensing methods for general-purpose classification commonly use Convolutional Neural Networks (CNNs) [4,8]. Most high-performing networks leverage existing architectures that are trained from millions of images by fine-tuning them to a new purpose [10]. However, in applications with no suitable pre-trained CNN architectures and small sample sizes, data scarcity limits the effectiveness of traditional CNN architectures. This paper proposes

J. Jeune, N. Pechan, Sh.-K. Reitsma—Work was performed while the author was with the Department.

an approach to remote sensing that uses interpretable machine learning features while demonstrating high performance under data scarcity. The approach requires images to be transformed into a one-dimensional signal, termed a Spatial Variation Sequence (SVS), which allows for features to be extracted using a library of established feature calculation algorithms [1]. This paper demonstrates the effectiveness of the approach by using it to detect pools from 4-channel satellite images, which are combined into a Modified Pool Index (MPI), and comparing the results to that of pre-trained CNN architectures.

This case study was motivated by an amendment made in 2016 to New Zealand's Building Act [11] requiring councils to inspect all swimming pools in their jurisdiction on a three-yearly basis. This new requirement highlighted to the Gisborne District Council (GDC) that their records of swimming pools in the district were incomplete [12]. Previously, the GDC hired staff to classify pools manually using aerial images. By developing an automated machine learning solution, the GDC could reduce ongoing costs and the time needed to scope out how many pools exist. Recent developments in remote sensing approaches, such as the implementation of convolutional neural networks (CNNs) [4,8] and the effectiveness of ensemble models [3], have led to marked improvements in accuracy, suggesting that such a machine learning model is plausible.

CNNs have become the go-to model for learning and extracting features from images for image classification. In practice, the state-of-the-art performance of these models is known to require large amounts of training data and require transfer learning in situations of data scarcity [9]. Because of this, a CNN classifier would serve as a suitable benchmark to compare against the proposed systematic feature engineering approach. The research aimed to produce two accurate classifiers:

1. A CNN that leverages the large amount of data encoded into existing architectures.
2. A novel signal processing approach based on Automated Feature Engineering (AFE) from Spatial Variation Sequences (SVS), which is trained only on the data given.

As a part of this research, the shortcomings of both classifiers will be discussed. The analysis of failure modes allows for a more practical discussion surrounding the suitability of the new classification approach.

2   Machine Learning Pipelines

The dataset provided by the GDC was a complete copy of the GDC's Geographic Information System (GIS) database. The dataset included:

- Four-channel (colour and infrared) satellite images with 30cm resolution for the entire district.
- Geographic Information System (GIS) databases describing around 36,000 land parcels, including the location and shape of 1083 swimming pools.

(a)   (b)   (c)

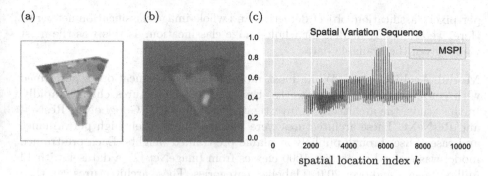

Fig. 1. Transformations of remote sensing images. (a) Masked aerial images of a specific lot. (b) Modified Swimming Pool Index (MSPI)$_{i,j}$ of (a) downscaled to 100×100 pixels in false colour representation. The pool is visible as bright yellow spot. (c) Spatial variation sequence of the MSPI shown in (b). The pool is represented by a sequence of peaks between $k = 5000$ and $k = 6200$.

In order to create a suitable dataset for training and evaluating our machine learning pipelines, we combined the information from the GIS databases and the orthorectified satellite images to extract 28,895 images, which were centred on a specific parcel. The orthorectification corrects any distortion in photos where the images were not taken directly above the target area. Each extracted property-centered image had a resolution of 256×256 pixels. Of the known properties containing pools, a total of 622 properties were manually selected for which the pool was located within the $77 \times 77\text{m}^2$ rectangle of the property-centred images. To generate the negative set, we randomly selected property-centred images which were not showing a pool. This process generated a dataset of 1301 labelled images. This dataset was randomly split into a training set (70%), a validation set (15%), and a test set (15%).

2.1 Preprocessing

Another concern is capturing pools or other features from neighbouring properties within the sub-images, particularly for urban properties where housing is denser than rural areas. If included, these features from neighbouring properties would influence the classification of an unrelated property and creating misleading results. Therefore, neighbouring properties are masked from the property-centred images using the provided parcel coordinates. Figure 1a shows an example of a masked image. The masked images were either used as input for the convolutional neural networks (Sect. 2.2) or for the automated feature engineering approach (Sect. 2.3).

2.2 Convolutional Neural Network Approach

For a machine learning pipeline using a Convolutional Neural Network (CNN), different kinds of classification tasks can be performed. These tasks often include per-pixel classification, object detection and whole-image classification networks. Here, we are fitting models for whole-image classification, as this was the most viable given the available data.

Model Architecture. While most modern image classification is performed with convolutional neural networks, the specific architectures change rapidly. In this study, the architectures investigated include VGG, GoogLeNet, ResNet, and ResNeXt. These architectures were selected due to their high performance and ease of use through publicly available pre-trained weights. Each pre-trained model was trained to predict 1000 classes from ImageNet [2], a dataset with 14 million images and over 20,000 labelled categories. These architectures can then be fine-tuned to the GDC dataset, capitalising on the generic features learned from the larger dataset.

By default, each of these architectures takes an input of standard three-channel (RGB) images and outputs a probability-like distribution over 1000 classes. These architectures can be modified to handle four-channel images as well as have a binary output for pool classification.

Transfer Learning leverages an existing model by freezing earlier layers, useful for extracting generic image classification features and tuning the remaining parameters for a new task. As layers earlier in the network are complex and take longer to train [5], utilising pre-trained weights is particularly beneficial in learning fundamental convolutional features which would otherwise require significant amounts of data to learn [13]. In this approach, the first layer is replaced with a 2-D convolutional layer that operates on four-channel images rather than the three-channel images used in ImageNet. The parameters relevant to the first three channels are then set back to the values from the pre-trained model, leaving the weights for the infrared channel randomly initialised. The final fully connected layer was then replaced with a fully connected layer that performs binary classification instead of 1000 class classification. This final output is then passed through the sigmoid function, which scales it between 0 and 1.

Regularisation. With a relatively small training dataset, it is crucial to avoid over-fitting. Several techniques are used to avoid this. Firstly, the tested architectures implement dropout [6]. This layer randomly disconnects a proportion of the connections to the next layer in the network for each batch during training, limiting the network's ability to depend on any specific pathway. Secondly, data augmentation was used to apply label-preserving transformations to input images [6,7]. This effectively increases the variation in the dataset used in training, encouraging more robust features to be learned. Finally, the parameters are updated based on randomly sampled mini-batches, which helps to ensure that parameters do not converge to a solution that fits all training data optimally to reduce overfitting and increase the generalisability of the classifier.

Training. The model architectures were trained and tested on the available aerial images to determine which architecture generalises the best to the given problem. The available data were randomly split into a training set, a validation set, and a test set based on a 0.7/0.15/0.15 split for this comparison. The training set is fed into the model in random mini-batches of 32 images each, and the loss function used for training is the binary cross-entropy loss function.

After each epoch, the accuracy of the validation set is calculated. The model is stored if the validation accuracy is the highest seen so far. After 50 epochs or 15 epochs with no improvement in validation accuracy, training terminates, and the model that achieved the highest validation accuracy is returned. This model is evaluated against the test set with the accuracy metrics detailed in Sect. 2.4.

This process has been implemented with the tensor computation and automatic differentiation package PyTorch [14]. A stochastic gradient descent routine is used for initial model training with a learning rate of 0.1 and momentum of 0.9. These parameters were later revised, as discussed in Sect. 3.3.

2.3 Automated Feature Engineering

The Automated Feature Engineering (AFE) approach comprises four core steps: simplification, sequence construction, automated feature extraction, and classification. The purpose of this process is the conversion of a 2D image into an interpretable set of features for use in a generic classification model such as XGBoost.

Simplification involves any transformations that reduces the problem's dimensionality before constructing the spatial variation sequences. This dimensionality reduction could be done by down-sampling the image to reduce the number of pixels or by combining layers of the image. Simplifying the problem in these ways reduces the overall training time, allowing for more experimentation in model development and reducing the tendency of complex models to overfit.

In this analysis, simplification is performed by two subsequent transformations, namely the computation of the Modified Swimming Pool Index (MSPI) and the downscaling of the resulting image to 100×100 pixels: The Modified Swimming Pool Index (MSPI) simplifies the four-channel images (red, green, blue, near-infrared) to a single channel by taking into account that a swimming pool, in general, is cooler than its environment and reflects blue light. In particular, the MSPI decreases proportional to the intensity of the near-infrared (NIR) channel and increases proportional to the intensity of the blue channel, while the intensities of the red and green channels are ignored:

$$(\text{MSPI})_{i,j} = \begin{cases} \frac{(\text{BLUE})_{i,j} + (255 - (\text{NIR})_{i,j})}{2} & : \text{if } (i,j) \in \mathcal{L}, \\ \text{median}_{(i,j) \in \mathcal{L}} (\text{MSPI})_{i,j} & : \text{if } (i,j) \notin \mathcal{L}. \end{cases} \quad (1)$$

Here, set $\mathcal{L}$ comprises all pixels, which correspond to the respective plot of land. The MSPI consolidates the four-channel image into a single channel effectively highlighting pools (Fig. 1b). The MSPI was inspired by two existing indices, the Normalized Difference Vegetation Index (NDVI) and the Normalised Difference Swimming Pool Index (NDSPI) [15].

Sequence Construction involves a contrast adjustment of the MSPI image followed by concatenating the rows of the adjusted image to a vector. The contrast adjustment increases the separation between light and dark portions of the MSPI and makes pools stand out more in the signal.

Once the contrast is adjusted, each MSPI is transformed into a 1D signal by concatenating the image rows into a vector with row-major order. Given that the input MSPI has N rows and M columns, the kth element s_k of the constructed Spatial Variation Sequence $\vec{s} = (s_0, \ldots, s_{M \times N - 1})$ is given by

$$s_k = s_{M \times i + j} = (\text{MSPI})_{M \times i, j} \text{ with } i = 0, \ldots, N - 1 \text{ and } j = 0, \ldots M - 1. \quad (2)$$

The SVS unravels the two-dimensional structure of an image into a one-dimensional signal, which shows prominent features of the image as a sequence of pulses (Fig. 1c). The construction of the SVS is a topological transformation, similar to glue the left and right vertical edges of an image together such that the end of the first pixel row connects to the start of the second pixel row. The resulting cylinder sees the SVC as a helix with a pitch of one row running continuously from the first pixel of the first row to the last pixel of the last row.

Automated Feature Extraction takes advantage of the fact that an SVS is ordered with respect to their spatial location index k. This ordering is comparable to a time series but, of course, has a different ordering dimension. Therefore, libraries of established time-series feature calculators can be used to project an SVS into a well-defined feature space. This process is called automated feature extraction and is implemented, e.g. in the Python module tsfresh [1].

While in naïve feature engineering, the SVS vector $\vec{s}$ would be used as the row of a feature matrix directly, in automated feature engineering, the SVS vector $\vec{s}$ is used as input to a collection of feature calculator functions $\phi_1(\vec{s}), \ldots, \phi_F(\vec{s})$. These feature calculators typically comprise statistical measures of random variables (e.g. mean, median), approximations from time-series forecasting (e.g. autocorrelation), signal processing (Fourier coefficients), financial time-series analysis (e.g. change of linear trend), information content (e.g. entropy), or nonlinear time-series analysis (e.g. Friedrich coefficients). Projecting the SVS $\vec{s}$ into the F-dimensional feature space takes advantage of the numerous machine learning projects on time series, which have identified a multitude of different feature extractors for signals of any kind. In the following experiments, we selected the *efficient* set of feature calculators and extracted 787 features for each SVS. The automated feature extraction finalises a significant dimensionality reduction of 99.7% from the originating ($256 \times 256 \times 4$)-dimensional input images.

For an overview of the extracted features, refer to the documentation of tsfresh[1]. Two examples of features extracted from the SVSs are visualised in Fig. 2 as histograms. Figure 2a shows a feature which could have been chosen by manual feature engineering, too. The feature calculator returns the maximum

---

[1] https://tsfresh.readthedocs.io/en/v0.11.1/text/list_of_features.html has the same features as tsfresh v0.11.2, which is used for this study.

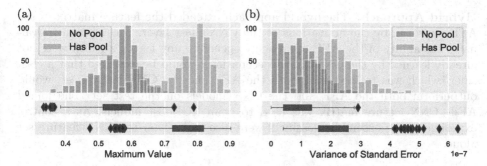

Fig. 2. Histograms of features extracted from SVS characterising aerial images with and without pools. (a) Maximum value of SPS. (b) Aggregated Linear Trend of SVSs summarised as variance of standard errors for piecewise linear models of length 10. Both features show a distinct separation between aerial images with and without pools.

value of the respective SVS. As expected from the exploratory analysis (Fig. 1), large values of this feature indicate properties with pools.

A more complex but still intuitive feature is shown in Fig. 2b. It captures that MSPIs exhibit characteristic pulse trains representing swimming pools (Fig. 1c). This characteristic can be captured by breaking each SVS into chunks and fitting piecewise linear models to each of the chunk. For each linear regression model, the standard error can be calculated, which becomes a random variable characterising the originating SVS. If the distribution of the standard error for a specific SVS has a large variance, it is more likely that the respective SVS represents a property with a pool (Fig. 2b). For this feature, each SVS has been broken into $\nu = 1, \ldots, 1000$ chunks of length 10. The aforementioned feature $\phi(\vec{s})$ is a variance calculated as

$$\phi(\vec{s}) = \sum_{\nu=1}^{1000} \frac{(\sigma_\nu - \overline{\sigma})^2}{999}, \tag{3}$$

$$\sigma_\nu = \sqrt{\sum_{k=10(\nu-1)}^{10\nu-1} \frac{(s_k - (\hat{\alpha}_\nu + \hat{\beta}_\nu k))^2}{8}}, \tag{4}$$

$$\hat{\alpha}_\nu, \hat{\beta}_\nu = \arg\min_{\alpha_\nu, \beta_\nu} \sum_{k=10(\nu-1)}^{10\nu-1} (s_k - (\alpha_\nu + \beta_\nu k))^2. \tag{5}$$

Here, σ_ν is the standard error of the νth piecewise linear model fitted to the SVS window $(s_{10(\nu-1)}, \ldots, s_{10\nu-1})$. Symbol $\overline{\sigma}$ represents the mean of $\{\sigma_1, \ldots, \sigma_{1000}\}$.

Classification. The 787 features extracted from the SVS are then used to train a classification model. Because of its historically high performance in classification problems in various contexts, XGBoost is investigated in this paper.

Hybrid Approach. The hybrid approach extended the feature matrix of the AFE approach by the activations of the CNN's last layer. This approach evaluates the ability of the AFE approach to generate any features which were not already learned by the CNN. In this scenario, it would be expected that a classifier, which was trained with both the AFE and the CNN feature set, would outperform both the AFE and the CNN models on the test set. The joined AFE+CNN feature matrix was used to train XGBoost models. As a control experiment, the ensemble classifiers were also trained on the CNN feature set alone.

2.4   Performance Metrics

In existing literature for pool detection, accuracy was the most common metric used to evaluate a classifier's effectiveness. However, datasets used in these studies commonly exhibit significant class imbalance, and unfortunately, accuracy can oversell the classifier's performance in these cases.

For this study, F_1-score will be used to evaluate all classifiers. This metric heavily penalises small values of either precision or recall, allowing for a fair measure of performance that is robust to class imbalance.

In addition to the F_1 score, the Area Under Receiver Operator Curve (AUROC) and the Area Under Precision-Recall Curve (AUPRC) are used to evaluate performance between different CNN architectures. The metrics were chosen due to being threshold agnostic, which allows for meaningful comparisons between the different models.

3   Model Selection

Hyperparameter tuning allowed for additional performance gains in both the AFE and CNN approaches of classification. Selection of these hyperparameters is computationally expensive and must often be done through a grid search of the parameter space, choosing the set of parameters that best minimises the cross-validated error. In the following sections, our approach is discussed, and the findings are presented for reproducibility and inference.

In order to achieve direct comparability with the results obtained between the AFE and CNN approach, an identical test/train split was used between both approaches. As the AFE approach does not require a validation split, this portion of the data is removed from the training split.

3.1   Hyperparameter Optimisation for the Ensemble Model

A Sequential Model-Based Optimisation (SMBO) strategy was used to determine appropriate hyperparameters for the AFE approach. SMBO has been proven to increase the performance of ensemble models in studies such as [17] and is openly available in packages such as `scikit-optimize`, which generalises SMBO to any optimisation problem and model type.

Table 1. Optimal hyperparameters for the contrast adjustment transformation and XGBoost models fitted to different feature sets.

Features	CA	Depth	Rounds	Min Weight	η	γ	SR	CSR	α	λ
AFE only	0	10	5000	1	0.05	0.5	0.95	0.95	0.842	0
CNN only	N/A	6	4846	7	0.321	0.234	0.510	0.626	0.289	0.353
AFE+CNN	20	9	4774	1	0.382	0.475	0.554	0.524	0.057	0.454

CA – Contrast Adjustment   SR–Subsample Ratio   CSR–Column Subsample Ratio

The implementation used in this study used the number of random restarts and the number of improvement iterations to control the search. These parameters tune the amount of exploration and exploitation in the search, respectively. In the search, 32 improvement iterations were used, and 20 random restarts were used for each model to determine the best choice of hyperparameters, with an objective to minimise the 10-fold cross-validated F_1 score. The results of the hyperparameter optimisation are shown in Table 1. It is interesting to observe that contrast adjustment was effective for XGBoost models using the AFE+CNN feature set but not for models using the AFE feature set alone.

3.2   Convolutional Neural Network Architecture

As discussed in Sect. 2.2, four different CNN architectures are considered for transfer learning: VGG13, ResNet50, ResNeXT50, and GoogLeNet. Each architecture is trained using similar hyperparameters, which allows for a meaningful comparison between each of the architectures. Table 2 shows that the ResNeXt50 architecture has the best performance on the threshold agnostic metrics AUROC and AUPRC. However, the difference in performance between VGG13, ResNet50 and ResNeXt50 is marginal.

Thresholds for the decision model were selected such that each architecture achieves the optimal F_1 score on the validation set, with the reported F_1 score evaluated on an entirely unseen test set. Table 2 shows that the ResNet50 architecture has a significantly higher F_1 score on the test set, so this architecture will be adopted for the final model.

3.3   Hyperparameter Optimisation for the CNN Model

Once the ResNet50 architecture was chosen, hyperparameters were optimised using a grid search that minimised the classification error on the validation set. Due to hardware limitations, the model took 20 min to train, which constrained how well these hyperparameters could be optimised. The chosen hyperparameters which maximised the F_1 score were a learning rate of 0.02 and a momentum of 0.8.

In addition to learning rate and momentum, another important hyperparameter is the selection of layers to be frozen during training. Each frozen layer retains its pre-trained weights throughout the training process, and freezing early layers ensures that basic features are not significantly altered from the pre-trained model. For the ResNet50 model, the best performance was achieved by freezing the first six layers after the input layer.

4   Results and Discussion

4.1   Performance

In order to compare the performance of AFE and CNN models for the pool detection problem, all models were evaluated on identical test/train splits. Images were split into groups of 1172 for training and 129 for testing. Each split has a balanced proportion of positive and negative examples. The results shown in Table 3. indicate that the CNN model learned features that are overall more discriminative compared to the AFE approach. Notably, the combination of CNN and AFE features did not show any performance improvements. This observation indicates that AFE was not able to generate any features from the Spatial Variation Sequences (SVS) that completed the pattern recognition of the CNN.

Using the AFE features alone, the XGBoost model still performed well on the test set with an F_1-score of 0.951 compared to the top performance of $F_1 = 0.977$ achieved by the CNN. This observation is notable because the ensemble model was only trained on 1172 images, while the CNN had been pre-trained on millions of images. This demonstrates the AFE approach as a valid and valuable alternative when faced with limited data and unique features which are not captured well by traditional architectures.

4.2   Modified Swimming Pool Index and Failure Modes

Through the development of the AFE classifier, the MSPI was proven to be a reliable indicator of swimming pools within satellite images. It retains important information from multiple channels of images while simplifying the data to a distinct signal. Notably, there were images for which the index would indirectly lead to misleading classifications. In particular, insulated homes would lead to large values of MSPI, as shown in Fig. 3. The larger values can make it hard to determine the presence of a pool, mainly if the roof is also blue. MSPI would also fail for properties with empty or filthy pools and ones with blue, circular, or rectangular objects on the property.

Table 2. Classification performance of CNN architectures for the validation set.

Architecture	AUROC	AUPRC	Optimal Threshold	Optimal F_1
			validation set	test set
VGG13	0.992	0.994	0.48	0.94
ResNet50	0.994	0.995	0.31	**0.96**
ResNeXT50	**0.996**	**0.996**	0.33	0.94
GoogLeNet	0.984	0.989	0.09	0.93

Table 3. Comparison of pool detection models on the basis of mean F_1 scores. Models using CNN features outperform the XGBoost model relying on AFE alone.

Model	Features	Training Set	Test Set
XGBoost	AFE only	0.916	0.951
	CNN only	**0.988**	0.946
	AFE and CNN	**0.988**	0.961
ResNet50	CNN only	0.957	**0.977**

Original Image   MSPI Transformation

Fig. 3. Effects of good insulation on MSPI. In this example the swimming pool nearly vanishes compared to the well-insulated roof, which is painted in a bluish-grey colour. (Color figure online)

4.3 Convolutional Neural Network Performance

In order to understand what features of satellite images had been learned by the CNN, generative techniques are applied so that the model morphs the input image to generate pool-like features that did not originally exist in the image. For this purpose, the following steps are applied:

1. Load the model which has already been trained.
2. Load an image that does not contain a pool.
3. Calculate the loss of that image when passed into the network as if the image should contain a pool.
4. Optimise the pixel values of the image such that the loss is minimised.

As shown in Fig. 4a,b, the CNN model has developed an interpretable understanding of pools. By using gradients of the model to modify the image, pool-shaped objects begin to appear in the image as green-blue splodges, following intuition. Interestingly, the model also places the pools in plausible locations, suggesting that it has learnt additional spatial features from the available data.

In addition, saliency maps can be generated by mapping the gradient of the loss function to each pixel in the input image [16]. By displaying a transparent heat map of these gradients overlain onto the original image, areas of the image which are important for classification can be identified. The automatic differentiation functionality of PyTorch has been used to calculate the gradient of

(a) Original   (b) Mutated   (c) Original   (d) Saliency map

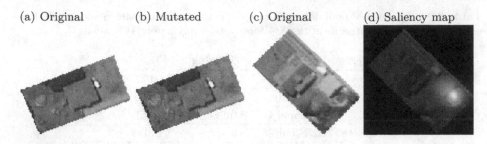

Fig. 4. Visual analysis of the adapted ResNet50 model. (a), (b) Generative approach imputing pool-like features. The CNN has learned the shape and location of pools. (c), (d) Saliency map indicating that the pixels depicting a pool have the largest contribution to the overall activation.

each pixel in the input image with respect to the loss function. Then a Gaussian blur is applied to the resulting saliency maps to make the most important areas more apparent. In practice, the classifier correctly identifies the region of the image that contains a pool. This verification provides confidence that the classifier is classifying based on the presence of a pool and not some other feature of the image that happens to be highly correlated. An example of this mapping is shown in Fig. 4c,d.

Saliency maps also give a way to investigate the misclassifications of the CNN. This helps to validate the network output and investigate potential areas of improvement. Figure 4c,d shows the only false positive classified within the test set. The saliency map clearly points towards a rectangular object with an adjacent circular structure. False negatives can also be investigated using saliency maps, showing if the network has identified a pool at all in its classification. Saliency maps showed that the model often receives a signal from the pool but that the final activation is not strong enough for the final classification to be positive.

4.4   Combined Approach Performance

The potential benefits of combining features for use in classification have been investigated. As shown in Table 3, it is apparent that the additional features from the CNN increase the classifier's performance but never beyond the performance of the CNN itself. From this observation, it is concluded that the AFE approach did not generate any features that amend the pattern recognition of the CNN, otherwise, the hybrid approach had been expected to outperform all other models.

5   Conclusions

Models for the classification of swimming pools have been successfully created using both a novel automated feature engineering approach from spatial variation sequences of the introduced modified swimming pool index and a more traditional convolution neural network approach. The two classification approaches both achieve F_1-scores of 0.95 or greater, with the CNN outperforming the automated feature engineering approach by 3.2%.

Applying generic automated feature engineering techniques from time-series classification to image classification is surprisingly practical, with excellent performance on the test data. At the same time, this approach generated interpretable features in a significantly reduced feature space (781 features compared to 262,144 pixels). Feature extraction from a spatial variation sequence requires much less training data than state-of-the-art CNNs, with only marginally worse performance using ensemble classifiers such as XGBoost. As a result, this approach may serve as a competitive alternative for niche problems where datasets are small and pre-trained models are unavailable.

The combination of CNN and signal features showed a classification performance equal to that of a classifier using only the CNN features. Thus, while the automated feature engineering approach could extract useful features from the images, it could not identify information that the CNN could not extract. Still, the combination of spatial variation sequences and an automated feature engineering approach can be considered a valuable alternative for remote sensing applications with small sample sizes or the need for a significantly reduced memory footprint.

Acknowledgements. This research is indebted to the Gisborne District Council. Without their willingness to provide aerial photography and land parcel data, this research would not have been possible.

The Machine Learning team at Xero is also acknowledged for providing a wealth of knowledge and advice around the training and interpretation of convolutional neural networks.

References

1. Christ, M., Braun, N., Neuffer, J., Kempa-Liehr, A.W.: Time series FeatuRe extraction on basis of scalable hypothesis tests (tsfresh - a Python package). Neurocomputing **307**, 72–77 (2018). https://doi.org/10.1016/j.neucom.2018.03.067
2. Deng, J., Dong, W., Socher, R., Li, L.-J., Li, K., Fei-Fei, L.: ImageNet: a large-scale hierarchical image database. In: 2009 IEEE Conference on Computer Vision and Pattern Recognition, pp. 248–255 (2009). https://doi.org/10.1109/CVPR.2009.5206848
3. Dietterichl, T.G.: Ensemble learning. In: Arbib, M. (ed.) The Handbook of Brain Theory and Neural Networks, pp. 405–408. MIT Press (2002)
4. Dimitrovski, I., Kitanovski, I., Kocev, D., Simidjievski, N.: Current trends in deep learning for earth observation: an open-source benchmark arena for image classification. ISPRS J. Photogramm. Remote. Sens. **197**, 18–35 (2023). https://doi.org/10.1016/j.isprsjprs.2023.01.014
5. He, K., Zhang, X., Ren, S., Sun, J.: Deep residual learning for image recognition. In: 2016 IEEE Conference on Computer Vision and Pattern Recognition (CVPR), pp. 770–778 (2016). https://doi.org/10.1109/CVPR.2016.90

6. Hinton, G.E., Srivastava, N., Krizhevsky, A., Sutskever, I., Alakhutdinov, R.: Improving neural networks by preventing co-adaptation of feature detectors. cs.NE 1207.0580v1, arXiv https://arxiv.org/abs/1207.0580v1 (2012)

7. Krizhevsky, A., Sutskever, I., Hinton, G.E.: ImageNet classification with deep convolutional neural networks. In: Pereira, F., Burges, C.J.C., Bottou, L., Weinberger, K.Q. (eds.) Advances in Neural Information Processing Systems, vol. 25, pp. 1097–1105. Curran Associates, Inc. (2012)

8. Krizhevsky, A., Sutskever, I., Hinton, G.E.: ImageNet classification with deep convolutional neural networks. Commun. ACM **60**(6), 84–90 (2017). https://doi.org/10.1145/3065386

9. Li, W., et al.: Classification of high-spatial-resolution remote sensing scenes method using transfer learning and deep convolutional neural network. IEEE J. Sel. Top. Appl. Earth Observations Remote Sens. **13**, 1986–1995 (2020). https://doi.org/10.1109/JSTARS.2020.2988477

10. Lu, D., Weng, Q.: A survey of image classification methods and techniques for improving classification performance. Int. J. Remote Sens. **28**(5), 823–870 (2007). https://doi.org/10.1080/01431160600746456

11. Ministry of Business Innovation and Employment, N.Z.: Building (Pools) Amendment Act 2016 (2016). https://www.legislation.govt.nz/act/public/2016/0071/latest/DLM6581358.html

12. Morrison, L., Chalmers, D.J., Langley, J.D., Alsop, J.C., McBean, C.: Achieving compliance with pool fencing legislation in New Zealand: a survey of regulatory authorities. Inj. Prev. **5**(2), 114–118 (1999). https://doi.org/10.1136/ip.5.2.114

13. Oquab, M., Bottou, L., Laptev, I., Sivic, J.: Learning and transferring mid-level image representations using convolutional neural networks. In: 2014 IEEE Conference on Computer Vision and Pattern Recognition, pp. 1717–1724 (2014). https://doi.org/10.1109/CVPR.2014.222

14. Paszke, A., et al.: PyTorch: an imperative style, high-performance deep learning library. cs.LG 1912.01703, arXiv https://arxiv.org/abs/1912.01703 (2019)

15. Rodríguez-Cuenca, B., Alonso, M.: Semi-automatic detection of swimming pools from aerial high-resolution images and LIDAR data. Remote Sens. **6**(4), 2628–2646 (2014). https://doi.org/10.3390/rs6042628

16. Simonyan, K., Vedaldi, A., Zisserman, A.: Deep inside convolutional networks: visualising image classification models and saliency maps. In: Bengio, Y., LeCun, Y. (eds.) 2nd International Conference on Learning Representations, ICLR 2014, Banff, AB, Canada, April 14–16, 2014, Workshop Track Proceedings, pp. 1–8 (2014). http://arxiv.org/abs/1312.6034

17. Sobel, I.: An isotropic 3×3 image gradient operator. In: Machine Vision for Three-Dimensional Scenes, pp. 376–379 (1990)

Exploring the Potential of High-Resolution Drone Imagery for Improved 3D Human Avatar Reconstruction: A Comparative Study with Mobile Images

Ali Salim Rasheed[1,2(✉)], Marwa Jabberi[2,3], Tarak M. Hamdani[2,4], and Adel M. Alimi[2,5]

[1] Department of Media Technology and Communications Engineering, College of Engineering, University of Information Technology and Communications, Baghdad, Iraq
alisalim.tv@gmail.com

[2] Research Groups in, Intelligent Machines, (REGIM Lab), University of Sfax, National Engineering, School of Sfax (ENIS), BP 1173, 3038 Sfax, Tunisia

[3] University of Sousse, ISITCom, 4011 Sousse, Tunisia

[4] Higher Institute of Computer Science Mahdia (ISIMa), University of Monastir, 5147 Monastir, Tunisia

[5] Department of Electrical and Electronic Engineering Science, Faculty of Engineering and the Built Environment, University of Johannesburg, Johannesburg, South Africa

Abstract. Reconstructing a 3D avatar of a human body from 2D images is not an easy task since it depends on several processing steps to enhance 3D acquisition devices input. Using camera-equipped drones with computer vision algorithms and photogrammetry tools to capture high-quality imagery data for 3D models reconstruction has become widespread recently. In this paper, a comparative study between 3D human avatars reconstruction based on 2D images captured from two different photography sources is conducted. Each acquisition device with an integrated lens has the same resolution parameters: a DJI Mavic Mini2 drone with a 12-megapixel camera lens and an iPhone 8 Plus with a 12-megapixel camera lens. To collect 2D images of a group of volunteers simulating a crowded human scene in both instances, the lens is approximately 5 m away from the human model. We used BUFF dataset to train our model and produce a high-quality 3D reconstructed human avatar. To validate our work, we employed the following evaluation metrics: PSNR, MSE, and SSIM. The obtained results showed that reconstructing 3D avatars from 2D images captured by a drone is more sophisticated in terms of quality and clarity. In contrast, images captured by a smartphone suffers from noise and distortions.

Keywords: Computer graphic · 3D reconstruction · Unmanned aerial vehicles · 3D virtual scene · 3D avatar · Virtual reality

© The Author(s), under exclusive license to Springer Nature Singapore Pte Ltd. 2024
W. Q. Yan et al. (Eds.): PSIVT 2023, LNCS 14403, pp. 167–181, 2024.
https://doi.org/10.1007/978-981-97-0376-0_13

1   Introduction

Commercial drones, called also Unmanned Aerial Vehicles (UAVs), are widely used to record photos and videos of interesting scenes at high altitudes that are non accessible to typical cameras [1]. Indeed, the ability to control and monitor a drone in the wild in real time is a critical feature of a mobile drone application. In addition, drones equipped with portable cameras can capture distant scenes and target objects in overcrowded environments that are inaccessible to targets using smartphones or traditional photography methods [2].

The quality of captures produced by the drone are discriminant and sophisticated with salient details [3] which provide better results in 3D object reconstruction compared with images of low quality with blurring or pixel distortions [4]. This largely depends drone features and its capacity to capture images with high-resolution [5]. Also, the lighting variation has a significant impact in terms of clarity and precision of captured images. Consequently, recovering 3D objects yields poorer results for dark or ambiguous details [6].

Moreover, due to the raise development of digital equipment in the electronic industry, signals received from UAVs are of High Definition (HD) or even of 4K quality (ultra HD). Thus, UAVs have remarkable graphics, animation, and simulation of virtual environments (VEs) capabilities [7].
Yet, sources of 2D images production vary based on the used acquisition device and to the quality ratio of 2D images generated by lenses [8].

In this paper, our approach consists in 3D reconstruction of human bodies based on 2D images generated by two different sources: the first is a DJI Mavic mini combo drone (12-megapixel camera) [9], and the second is an iPhone 8 Plus (12-megapixel camera) [10]. These two acquisition devices have the same engineering efficiency in RGB rendering during capturing or video recording.

The identical capture settings and acquisition methodology were used for these two capture sources. Then, two simulations are considered: an outdoor environment in the first simulating and an indoor environment in the second simulating for the same purpose (Volunteers).

We used PIFuHD [11] which is a deep neural network for producing 3D models with high resolution from 2D images. PIFuHD can be used in 3D geometry reconstruction, complete 3D shapes prediction, and 3D features extraction under challenging scenarios such as occlusions and complex poses. Indeed, 3D reconstruction is employed in the construction of virtual scenes that simulate reality and improve the quality of electronic games [15,16], also in security such as face alignment, missing facial parts generation, etc. such as detailed in [38–40].
Our approach aims to reconstruct 3D avatars of human bodies using 2D images generated from two distinct sources: a drone and a mobile device to emphasize how the reconstruction rendering is impacted by the quality, resolution, and capture of the input images.

2   Related Works

Reconstruction in three dimensions is a rapidly expanding discipline of study. The reconstruction of 3D objects from 2D images is particularly valuable because it generates more realistic representations that can be viewed from any angle. This allows for detailed analysis and application in various settings. An ideal 3D reconstruction necessarily requires high-quality input images.

2.1   Image Capture Based on Drone

Christos et al. [17] proposed a neural architecture for binary semantic segmentation of RGB images. This method enables drones to extract semantic segmentation maps during flight, thereby defining no-fly zones and improving UAV flight safety. The proposed method outperforms previous aerial crowd detection methods without post-processing.

In [18], authors introduced a 3D human-drone system for indoor and outdoor scene capture and supported a reconstruction algorithm to recover full-body motion from high-quality video. The approach is evaluated on DroCap dataset and demonstrated its applicability using an end-user drone with full performance.

Another work in the same context presented by Dawood et al. [19], which consists on software development for selfie drones. It eliminates manual manoeuvring using 2D image capture from DJI Phantom 4 video. The drone is controlled by an RC transmitter, and users can choose an appropriate template. Also, a software is used to manipulate the drone with regard to users position. An accuracy rate of 80% in real-world situations is used to qualitatively assess the method's effectiveness on mobile platforms.

2.2   Image Capture Based on Smartphone

Tong He et al. [20], used RGB images captured by a standard cell phone camera and SLAM technology to estimate 3D transformations for layout generation. Then, Google ARcore library is introduced to estimate camera pose during image capture. Actually, the objective is to let people use standard pictures to create layouts. The proposed system called "GRIHA" outperforms other methodologies and has superior outcomes.

In [21], authors presented a smartphone photogrammetry to determine particle size and shape. So, Digital Elevation Models (DEMs) were generated using motion photogrammetry to estimate the morphological properties. Size and shape of 110 subjects were compared using sieving, hand measurement, and 2D image analysis methods. Results show that the strategy is extremely applicable and acceptable by users, having $-2.7\% \pm 6.3\%$, $-1.8\% \pm 9.9\%$, respectively.

Alberto J. Ruiz et al. [22] introduced a smartphone-based fluorescence imaging system to optimise PDT treatment by mapping PpIX concentration onto a 2D image. They used a custom iPhone 6s application and a 3D-printed measurement base with a miniaturised light source, electronics, and a filter system.

Experimentation demonstrated the prototype's ability to detect clinically relevant concentrations of PpIX within 20–30 min of incubation in mice which is very challenging.

2.3   3D Avatars of Human Reconstruction from 2D Image Based on Deep Learning Methods

Marko Mihajlovic et al. [23] consider the spatial information obtained from RGB pixels to recreate 3D avatars since analyzing spatial encoding challenges leads to develop high-resolution 2D human images. This strategy successfully integrated temporal information and produced advanced results for 3D object reconstruction. ECON system presented by Yuliang Xiu et al. [24], employs implicit presentation and explicit body regularisation to create detailed 2D normal maps for clothed individuals. Then rendering recovers 2.5D front and back surfaces, called d-BiNI, and registers them using an SMPL-X body mesh. ECON "paints" the geometry of d-BiNI surfaces and can replace noisy faces and hands with SMPL-X alternatives. This method infers high-fidelity 3D human models, even in lax clothing and difficult poses. According to quantitative evaluations on CAPE and Renderpeople datasets, ECON overcomes previous methods and has significantly superior perceived realism.

In [25], a novel adversarial generative model for creating 3D people from 2D images is introduced. A holistic 3D generator and a flexible articulation module are combined to depict body shape and deformations. To enhance realism, the model trains with multiple discriminators and incorporates geometric cues such as predicted 2D normal maps. This technique outperforms previous 3D and articulation-aware techniques in terms of geometry and appearance.

Celong Liu et al. [26] proposed the InferGAN network, which reconstructs 3D human geometry body maps from a single 2D image. It separates human body parts, fits them to a generic model, and infers the back texture from the frontal image using silhouette-based dense correspondence. Experimental results demonstrated that this strategy is robust and successful on both public and private datasets. Human avatars can be easily rigged and animated using MoCap data.

According to Shunsuke Saito et al. research work presented in [27], ARCH++ is an image-based method for 3D avatars reconstruction with flexible clothing designs. It is an animation-ready and highly realistic in both visible and occluded regions. A point-based geometry encoder is often added to address occupancy ambiguity caused by topological modifications. Also, a deep networks is used for image-to-image translation which the purpose is to improve the detailed topology and surface of the reconstructed object. Based on public benchmarks and user assessments, the trials illustrate advances in reconstruction quality and realism compared with other methods in the same field.

3   Proposed Method

Our method, presented in Fig. 1, introduces the final rendering of 3D avatar reconstruction for human models from 2D images generated from two different sources: a drone and a mobile device with the same geometry specifications for their lenses. We perform data collection by capturing 2D images of a group of volunteers with varying actions of the body in a scene that simulates crowding of people standing at a distance of about 5 m from the photography lens.

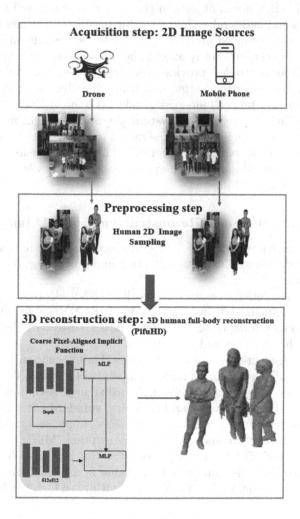

Fig. 1. Overall pipeline

3.1   Image Acquisition

The first stage of our approach involves collecting 2D images using two distinct sources, each of which has an integrated lens with the same resolution and focal length engineering specifications for image capability. One of them is a DJI Mavic Mini2 drone with a 12-megapixel camera and 1920 1080 HD resolution. The additional source was an iPhone 8 Plus with a 12-megapixel camera and an HD resolution of 1920 1080 pixels. The lens is approximately 5 m from the subject in both instances.

Due to the interference of objects in the target scenes as well as the appearance of obstacles and undesirable shapes during photography when using a handheld mobile phone, distorted and blurry 2D images are generated. Capturing pictures in the wild can negatively affects the 3D reconstruction [28]. So, simultaneously, the drone controllers provide (auto tracking system) stable automated movement along various fixed paths, which may be circular or spiral, without trembling due to crowding or human stampede as done in [29].

The Drone Gimbal Stabilization System [30] and top-flight mode enable an integrated scan from all dimensions of the model to be captured without obstructions or barriers. This allows a two-dimensional images producing with high resolution and sharp details and can achieve advanced results when reconstructing 3D avatars from single 2D images.

3.2   3D Avatars of Human Reconstruction from 2D Images

The goal of our work is not actually 3D reconstruction, but rather to demonstrate how acquisition device used for data collecting and processing steps might affect the final outcome.

We used Convolutional neural network (CNN) algorithm in particular PIFuHD for 3D human body reconstruction. PIFuHD enables high-resolution (HR) outputs as shown in [31,32]. The network is trained on BUFF dataset [34] to estimate the human pose and body in 3D.

The 3D reconstruction stage incorporates high-resolution image features (512×512) from higher-resolution input images (1024×1024). The second module predicts an occupancy probability field using high-resolution embeddings. To improve reconstruction quality and accuracy, standard patterns for both the front and rear sides were projected and given as supplementary input using a neural network architecture and multi-layer perception (MLP).

The main goal of 3D human body reconstruction and pose estimation from 512×512 cropped image is to predict F(X) value in a virtual environment(VE) for any 3D point position $X = X_1, X_2, X_3 in R^3$, with I is a high-resolution 2D grey image.

F(X, I)= 1 if X is inside the mesh surface
F(X, I)= 0 otherwise

F is then trained using a neural network, and image feature embedding is extracted from the projected 2D position at $\varphi(X) = x \in R^2$ which we denote by φ (x, I). Perpendicular projection is used for π, and thus $x = \pi(X) = (X1, X2)$ [33]. Then, it estimates 3D point X, and thus:

$$f(\mathbf{X}, \mathbf{I}) = g(\Phi(\mathbf{x}, \mathbf{I}), Z) \tag{1}$$

where $Z = Xz$ is the depth specified by the 2D projection x along the ray.

$$f^H(\mathbf{X}) = g^H\left(\Phi^H\left(\mathbf{x}_H, \mathbf{I}_H, \mathbf{F}_H, \mathbf{B}_H,\right), \Omega(\mathbf{X})\right) \tag{2}$$

where $I_{(H)}, F_{(H)}, B_{(H)}$ are the input image maps in the frontal and backside. $\Omega(X)$ denotes a 3D human model reconstructed and rendered in a blender virtual environment to display the 3D human reconstruction.

4   Experimental Results

In this study, we used the following environment to conduct material experimentation:
Device name: Microsoft Service3
Processor: Intel(R) Core(TM) i5-6300U CPU @ 2.40GHz 2.50 GHz
Installed RAM: 8.00 GB
System type: 64-bit operating system, x64-based processor
Code environment: Colab
Programming Language: Python
Graphic Software: Blender
Mobile Device: Iphone 8 Plus

Apple iPhone 8 Plus: comes with dual rear camera and 5.5-inch LED-backlit IPS LCD capacitive (1080 × 1920 HD) touchscreen display. It is powered by a Hexa-core (2x Monsoon + 4x Mistral) processor along with 3 GB of RAM. The device runs on iOS 11-OS with 64/256GB internal storage and no expandable memory. It packs a 2691-mAh non-removable Li-ion battery. The smartphone offers a 12-megapixel dual rear camera and 7-megapixel selfie camera. On the connectivity front, it offers 4G LTE, 3G, Bluetooth v5.0, NFC, micro USB v2.0, and Wi-Fi 802.11 a/b/g/n/ac options.

DJI Mavic Mini 2: Weight: 0.55 lbs/249 g, dimensions unfolded: 245× 289×56 mm, dimensions folded: 138×81×58 mm, max. Speed: 35 mph/57 kph, Transmission Distance: 6.2 mi/10 km, Transmission: OcuSynch 2.0, battery capacity: 2250 mAh, Flighttime: 31 min., Wind Resistance: Level 5 up to 10.5 m/s, Sensor: 12 MP 1/2.3″ (CMOS), Video Resolution: 4 K - max. 30 fps 2.7 K - max. 30 fps 1080p - max. 60 fps, HDR Video: no, Lens: FOV 83° aperture f/2.8, Bitrate: max. 40 Mbps H.264,. mp4, max. Photo Resolution: 12 MP 1080 1920 HD.

4.1   Quantitative Evaluation

In this paper, we provide a comparison study of two sources of captures. Our goal is to highlight that 2D image quality and resolution have an impact in 3D analysis and reconstruction. To obtain a 3D realistic renders, it is necessary to choose a good capture source and also a sophisticated processing techniques.

To compare and measure the quality of 3D reconstructed models, it is necessary to conduct an evaluation of the 2D images captured from the drone and mobile phone. This evaluation involves the calculation of image resolution. We used peak signal-to-noise ratio (PSNR) according to Eq. 3, mean squared error (MSE) according to Eq. 4, and structural similarity (SSIM) to validate this experimentation. If the PSNR value is high, the maximum pixel value (MAXi) is greater than the MSE, indicating that the 2D image quality is superior. When I is the monochrome image and K is the noise approximation in dB scale, the image is monochrome.

$$PSNR = 10 \cdot \log_{10}\left(\frac{MAX_I^2}{MSE}\right)$$
$$= 20 \cdot \log_{10}(MAX_I) - 10 \cdot \log_{10}(MSE)$$

(3)

$$MSE = \frac{1}{mn}\sum_{i=0}^{m-1}\sum_{j=0}^{n-1}[I(i,j) - K(i,j)]^2$$

(4)

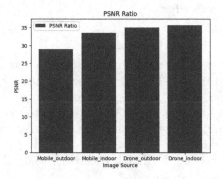

Fig. 2. PSNR to image source ratio.

The quantitative evaluation, as shown in Table 1 using the PSNR metric yielded superior results for the indoor scene, with a resolution of 4.55 MP, compared with the outdoor scene, with a resolution of 2.68 MP, because the percentage of illumination on the volunteers is greater and more directed in the indoor scene. Also, the PSNR values, as shown in Fig. 2 obtained using the DJI Mavic Mini2 drone in the indoor scene were 35.7 dB, which is higher than the value provided by the iPhone 8 Plus, where it was 33.5 dB, while the results of MSE in the indoor scenes were less in error than in the outdoor scenes. As shown in

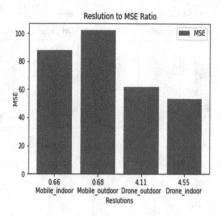

Fig. 3. Image resolution to the MSE ratio.

Fig. 3 the 2D images taken using the DJI Mavic Mini 2 Drone achieved MSE results of 53.1 achieved a lower error rate compared to the results provided by the iPhone 8 Plus 87,7.

SSIM results of 2D images captured by the drone is 0.97 is better than the image captured by mobile-phone is 0.96. These results validate our approach to adopt drones in data collection in crowded or densely populated scenes, as they provide accurate results and high-quality images devoid of blurring, fusion of features, or overlapping of objects that adversely impact the 3D reconstruction methods.

Table 1. 2D images quality evaluation

Acquisition device	Drone		Mobile Phone	
Region	Indoor	outdoor	Indoor	outdoor
Dimensions	2844×1600	2702×1520	1127×588	1095×621
Resolution (MP)	4.55	4.11	2.68	2.42
PSNR (db)	35.7	35.0	33.5	29.0
MSE	53.1	61.5	87.7	102.0
SSIM	0.97	0.95	0.96	0.90

4.2 Visual Evaluation and Graphical Results

We used three human models (A, B, C) in the 3D reconstruction derived from the 2D images captured by the drone and mobile phone.

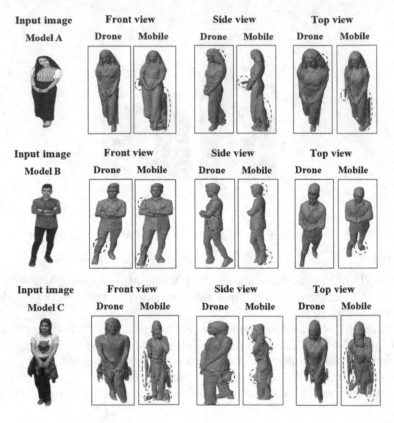

Fig. 4. Visual evaluation and details comparison between 3D reconstructed avatars captured from two different acquisition devices: drone and smartphone

As shown in Fig. 4, the objective is to conduct a visual evaluation of the graphical results and a comparison between the 3D human avatar results from images captured by the drone and the 3D human avatar results from images captured by the mobile device.

3D reconstructed avatars provided high-resolution results for those based on 2D images acquired by the drone, as they are free of distortions and fusion in the body details. Compared with the 2D images captured by a mobile phone, the 2D images had less quality and more distortion.

The clear results of the 3D human full-body avatar 3D reconstruction from 2D images of two different sources, one of which is a drone and the other is a mobile device, indicate that the technical capabilities available in the drone in terms of the high-resolution images provided by its lens and the stability of movement during the scene capture play a major role in providing high-resolution 3D results. So, graphical results reveals that the quality of the mobile device images is inferior to that of the drone.

The 3D full-body reconstruction of a human displays 2D images from two separate sources: the front footage of the drone and the mobile device. The drone has engineering features that make it vastly superior to other imaging sources, including high precision and stability during the imaging process as well as a wide and comprehensive view of the subject being photographed. Thus, sophisticated, high-quality results are possible during 3D reconstruction. During the visual evaluation of the 3D model.

5   Rendering of 3D Cinematic Virtual Scene

Fig. 5. 3D avatars of humans are rendering in Blender virtual environment.

As shown in Fig. 5, Virtual Production in Computer Graphics is an emergent trend that includes a variety of computer-aided film maker techniques designed to promote innovation and save time using real-time software such as Blender [35, 36]. There are numerous 3D computer graphic approaches in virtual system environments. Some studies concentrate on various virtualisation algorithms, whereas others explore new methods for enhancing the application's realism while maintaining its fluidity. The subsequent related work concentrates solely on new approaches to 3D computer graphics and their comparison [37]. The results of this study demonstrate that avatars can be reconstructed from high-quality images with sharp surfaces, which are generated by devising sources to obtain or capture them under integrated lighting, lens quality, and vibration-free conditions.

6   Conclusion

In this paper we introduced a consensus mechanism between the capabilities of advanced drones for image capturing and acquisition. We used a deep learning networks with applications to 3D human avatars reconstruction from 2D images. This technique is widely used in a virtual cinematic scene. In fact, the selection of acquisition tools and devices and 2D images processing produced a convincing 3D reconstruction with geometric high-fidelity. In the future, we will recommend 3D reconstruction for objects captured by drones in real-time broadcasts since drones can be directed to detect human bodies through 3D human pose estimation networks.

Acknowledgment. This study was supported by the Tunisian Ministry of Higher Education and Scientific Research under grant agreement number LR11ES48.

References

1. Ebeid, E., Skriver, M., Jin, J.: A survey on open-source flight control platforms of unmanned aerial vehicle. In: Proceedings of - 20th Euromicro Conference on Digital System Design (DSD 2017), no. August, pp. 396–402 (2017). https://doi.org/10.1109/DSD.2017.30
2. Bangkui, F., Yun, L., Ruiyu, Z., Qiqi, F.: Review on the technological development and application of UAV systems. Chinese J. Electron. **29**(2), 199–207 (2020). https://doi.org/10.1049/cje.2019.12.006
3. Elharrouss, O., Almaadeed, N., Al-Maadeed, S.: A review of video surveillance systems. J. Vis. Commun. Image Represent. **77**, 103116 (2021). https://doi.org/10.1016/j.jvcir.2021.103116
4. Zhang, H., Yao, Y., Xie, K., Fu, C.W., Zhang, H., Huang, H.: Continuous aerial path planning for 3D urban scene reconstruction. ACM Trans. Graph. **40**(6), 1–15 (2021). https://doi.org/10.1145/3478513.3480483
5. Delavarpour, N., Koparan, C., Nowatzki, J., Bajwa, S., Sun, X.: A technical study on UAV characteristics for precision agriculture applications and associated practical challenges. Remote Sens. **13**(6), 1204 (2021). https://doi.org/10.3390/rs13061204
6. Jia, B., et al.: Essential processing methods of hyperspectral images of agricultural and food products. Chemom. Intell. Lab. Syst. **198**, 103936 (2020). https://doi.org/10.1016/j.chemolab.2020.103936
7. Garcia, M.G., Wahl, S., Pusti, D., Artal, P., Ohlendorf, A.: Peripheral 2D image quality metrics of different types of multifocal contact lens. Investig. Ophthalmol. Vis. Sci. **60**(9), 3718 (2019)
8. Wei, X.K., Chai, J.: Modeling 3D human poses from uncalibrated monocular images. In: Proceedings of IEEE International Conference on Computer Vision, pp. 1873–1880 (2009). https://doi.org/10.1109/ICCV.2009.5459415
9. Myburgh, A., Botha, H., Downs, C.T., Woodborne, S.M.: The Application and Limitations of a Low-Cost UAV platform and open-source software combination for ecological mapping and monitoring. African J. Wildl. Res. **51**(1) (2021). https://doi.org/10.3957/056.051.0166
10. Zhang, P., et al.: Enhancing the performance of optical camera communication via accumulative sampling. Opt. Express **29**(12), 19015 (2021). https://doi.org/10.1364/oe.430503
11. Saito, S., Simon, T., Saragih, J., Joo, H.: PIFuHD: multi-level pixel-aligned implicit function for high-resolution 3D human digitization. In: Proceedings of IEEE Conference on Computer Vision and Pattern Recognition, pp. 81–90 (2020). https://doi.org/10.1109/CVPR42600.2020.00016

12. Wang, G., Li, L., Li, Q., Gu, K., Lu, Z., Qian, J.: Perceptual evaluation of single-image super-resolution reconstruction. In: Proceedings of International Conference on Image Processing (ICIP), vol. 2017-Septe, pp. 3145–3149 (2018). https://doi.org/10.1109/ICIP.2017.8296862

13. de Leon, J.A., et al.: Deep learning approach to 2D capacitive resistivity imaging inversion. In: Vasant, P., Weber, GW., Marmolejo–Saucedo, J.A., Munapo, E., Thomas, J.J. (eds.) Intelligent Computing & Optimization. ICO 2022. LNNS, vol. 569. Springer, Cham (2023). https://doi.org/10.1007/978-3-031-19958-5_43

14. Wang, X., et al.: ESRGAN: enhanced super-resolution generative adversarial networks. In: Leal-Taixé, L., Roth, S. (eds.) ECCV 2018. LNCS, vol. 11133, pp. 63–79. Springer, Cham (2019). https://doi.org/10.1007/978-3-030-11021-5_5

15. Lugrin, J.L., et al.: Any body there? Avatar visibility effects in a virtual reality game. In: 25th IEEE Conference on Virtual Reality and 3D User Interfaces, VR 2018, pp. 17–24 (2018). https://doi.org/10.1109/VR.2018.8446229

16. Bartl, A., Wenninger, S., Wolf, E., Botsch, M., Latoschik, M.E.: Affordable but not cheap: a case study of the effects of two 3D-reconstruction methods of virtual humans. Front. Virtual Real. 2, 694617 (2021). https://doi.org/10.3389/frvir.2021.694617

17. Papaioannidis, C., Mademlis, I., Pitas, I.: Autonomous UAV safety by visual human crowd detection using multi-task deep neural networks. In: Proceedings of IEEE International Conference on Robotics and Automation, pp. 11074–11080 (2021). https://doi.org/10.1109/ICRA48506.2021.9560830

18. Zhou, X., Liu, S., Pavlakos, G., Kumar, V., Daniilidis, K.: Human motion capture using a drone. In: Proceedings of IEEE International Conference on Robotics and Automation, pp. 2027–2033 (2018). https://doi.org/10.1109/ICRA.2018.8462830

19. Ahmed, D., Shahid Qureshi, W., Arsalan Aijaz, S., Muhammad Imran, B., Manshoor Ali Naqvi, S., Lin, C.Y.: Towards selfie drone: spatial localization and navigation of drone using human pose estimation. In: 2021 International Conference on Robotics and Automation in Industry (ICRAI 2021) (2021). https://doi.org/10.1109/ICRAI54018.2021.9651330

20. Goyal, S., Khan, N., Chattopadhyay, C., Bhatnagar, G.: GRIHA: synthesizing 2-dimensional building layouts from images captured using a smartphone. Multimed. Tools Appl. 81(10), 14589–14612 (2022). https://doi.org/10.1007/s11042-022-11918-z

21. An, P., Tang, H., Li, C., Fang, K., Lu, S., Zhang, J.: A fast and practical method for determining particle size and shape by using smartphone photogrammetry. Meas. J. Int. Meas. Confed. 193, 110943 (2022). https://doi.org/10.1016/j.measurement.2022.110943

22. Ruiz, A.J., LaRochelle, E.P.M., Shapman, M.S., Hasan, T., Pogue, B.W.: Smartphone-based fluorescence imager for PpIX-based PDT treatment planning: system design and initial results, p. 26 (2019). https://doi.org/10.1117/12.2510403

23. Mihajlovic, M., Bansal, A., Zollhöfer, M., Tang, S., Saito, S.: KeypointNeRF: generalizing image-based volumetric avatars using relative spatial encoding of keypoints. In: Avidan, S., Brostow, G., Cissé, M., Farinella, G.M., Hassner, T. (eds.) Computer Vision – ECCV 2022. ECCV 2022. LNCS, vol. 13675. Springer, Cham (2022). https://doi.org/10.1007/978-3-031-19784-0_11

24. Xiu, Y., Yang, J., Cao, X., Tzionas, D., Black, M.J.: ECON: Explicit Clothed humans Optimized via Normal integration (2022). http://arxiv.org/abs/2212.07422

25. Dong, Z., Chen, X., Yang, J., Black, M.J., Hilliges, O., Geiger, A.: AG3D: Learning to Generate 3D Avatars from 2D Image Collections (2023). http://arxiv.org/abs/2305.02312

26. Li, Z., et al.: Animated 3D human avatars from a single image with GAN-based texture inference. Comput. Graph. **95**, 81–91 (2021). https://doi.org/10.1016/j.cag.2021.01.002

27. He, T., Xu, Y., Saito, S., Soatto, S., Tung, T.: ARCH++: animation-ready clothed human reconstruction revisited. In: Proceedings of IEEE International Conference on Computer Vision, pp. 11026–11036 (2021). https://doi.org/10.1109/ICCV48922.2021.01086

28. Niu, Y., Zhong, Y., Guo, W., Shi, Y., Chen, P.: 2D and 3D image quality assessment: a survey of metrics and challenges. IEEE Access **7**, 782–801 (2019). https://doi.org/10.1109/ACCESS.2018.2885818

29. Hernandez, A., Copot, C., De Keyser, R., Vlas, T., Nascu, I.: Identification and path following control of an AR. Drone quadrotor. In: 2013 17th International Conference on System Theory, Control and Computing (ICSTCC 2013); Jt. Conference on SINTES 2013, SACCS 2013, SIMSIS 2013, pp. 583–588 (2013). https://doi.org/10.1109/ICSTCC.2013.6689022

30. Mansur, V., Reddy, S., Sujatha, R.: Deploying complementary filter to avert gimbal lock in drones using quaternion angles. In: 2020 IEEE International Conference on Computing, Power and Communication Technologies (GUCON 2020), pp. 751–756 (2020). https://doi.org/10.1109/GUCON48875.2020.9231126

31. Shao, R., et al.: DoubleField: bridging the neural surface and radiance fields for high-fidelity human reconstruction and rendering. In: Conference on Computer Vision and Pattern Recognition, vol. 2022-June, pp. 15851–15861 (2022). https://doi.org/10.1109/CVPR52688.2022.01541

32. Yu, T., Zheng, Z., Guo, K., Liu, P., Dai, Q., Liu, Y.: Function4D: real-time human volumetric capture from very sparse consumer RGBD sensors. In: Conference on Computer Vision and Pattern Recognition, pp. 5742–5752 (2021). https://doi.org/10.1109/CVPR46437.2021.00569

33. Zhang, C., Pujades, S., Black, M., Pons-Moll, G.: Detailed, accurate, human shape estimation from clothed 3D scan sequences. In: Proceedings of 30th IEEE Conference on Computer Vision and Pattern Recognition (CVPR 2017), vol. 2017-Janua, pp. 5484–5493 (2017). https://doi.org/10.1109/CVPR.2017.582

34. Sobota, B., Mattova, M.: 3D Computer Graphics and Virtual Reality. 'Comput. Game Dev. (2022). https://doi.org/10.5772/intechopen.102744

35. Ilmaranta, K.: Cinematic space in virtual production. In: De Paolis, L.T., Bourdot, P. (eds.) AVR 2020. LNCS, vol. 12243, pp. 321–332. Springer, Cham (2020). https://doi.org/10.1007/978-3-030-58468-9_23

36. Reitmann, S., Neumann, L., Jung, B.: BLAINDER-a blender AI add-on for generation of semantically labeled depth-sensing data. Sensors **21**(6), 1–28 (2021). https://doi.org/10.3390/s21062144

37. Li, Z., Oskarsson, M., Heyden, A.: Detailed 3D human body reconstruction from multi-view images combining voxel super-resolution and learned implicit representation. Appl. Intell. **52**(6), 6739–6759 (2022). https://doi.org/10.1007/s10489-021-02783-8

38. Jabberi, M., Wali, A., Chaudhuri, B.B., Alimi, A.M.: 68 landmarks are efficient for 3D face alignment: what about more?. Multimedia Tools Appl. **82**(27), 1–35 (2023)

39. Jabberi, M., Wali, A., Alimi, A.M.: Generative data augmentation applied to face recognition. In: Proceedings of International Conference on Information Networking (ICOIN), pp. 242–247 (2023)
40. Jabberi, M., Wali, A., Neji, B., Beyrouthy, T., Alimi, A.M.: Face ShapeNets for 3D Face Recognition. IEEE Access (2023)

Point Cloud Novelty Detection Based on Latent Representations of a General Feature Extractor

Shizuka Akahori[1](✉), Satoshi Iizuka[2,3] (ID), Ken Mawatari[4,5] (ID),
and Kazuhiro Fukui[2,3] (ID)

[1] Graduate School of Science and Technology, University of Tsukuba,
1-1-1 Tennodai, Tsukuba, Ibaraki 305-8571, Japan
`akahori.shizuka@image.iit.tsukuba.ac.jp`
[2] Institute of Systems and Information Engineering, University of Tsukuba,
1-1-1 Tennodai, Tsukuba, Ibaraki 305-8571, Japan
`{iizuka,kfukui}@cs.tsukuba.ac.jp`
[3] Center for Artificial Intelligence Research, University of Tsukuba, 1-1-1 Tennodai,
Tsukuba, Ibaraki 305-8571, Japan
[4] Division of Physics, Faculty of Pure and Applied Sciences, University of Tsukuba,
1-1-1 Tennodai, Tsukuba, Ibaraki 305-8571, Japan
`mawatari.ken.ka@u.tsukuba.ac.jp`
[5] Tomonaga Center for the History of the Universe (TCHoU),
Faculty of Pure and Applied Sciences, University of Tsukuba, 1-1-1 Tennodai,
Tsukuba, Ibaraki 305-8571, Japan

Abstract. We propose an effective unsupervised 3D point cloud novelty detection approach, leveraging a general point cloud feature extractor and a one-class classifier. The general feature extractor consists of a graph-based autoencoder and is trained once on a point cloud dataset such as a mathematically generated fractal 3D point cloud dataset that is independent of normal/abnormal categories. The input point clouds are first converted into latent vectors by the general feature extractor, and then one-class classification is performed on the latent vectors. Compared to existing methods measuring the reconstruction error in 3D coordinate space, our approach utilizes latent representations where the shape information is condensed, which allows more direct and effective novelty detection. We confirm that our general feature extractor can extract shape features of unseen categories, eliminating the need for autoencoder re-training and reducing the computational burden. We validate the performance of our method through experiments on several subsets of the ShapeNet dataset and demonstrate that our latent-based approach outperforms the existing methods.

Keywords: 3D point cloud · Novelty detection · Anomaly detection

1 Introduction

Novelty detection, also known as out-of-distribution detection or unsupervised anomaly detection, is a critical classification task to identify anomalous patterns that differ from trained data distribution [1,2]. Although deep neural networks have improved recognition tasks in recent years, their performance is susceptible to novel data not included in the training set. In particular, given data that does not belong to any training classes, the trained classifier network will force the given data to be classified into one of the predefined classes, causing serious classification errors. In this situation, novelty detection can be applied as a preprocessing step to eliminate such anomalous data, thereby enhancing the reliability of the classification results. While various methods have been proposed for novelty detection in 2D images, limited research has focused on novelty detection in 3D point clouds, which is essential to improve 3D classification performance in industrial systems.

Recently, Masuda et al. [3] proposed a novelty detection method using a variational autoencoder [4] by measuring the reconstruction loss of 3D point clouds as the anomaly score. While it is the first method to tackle unsupervised anomaly detection in 3D point clouds, the detection performance depends on the quality of the decoder network, and the anomaly score measured in 3D coordinate space tends to be sensitive to detailed object geometry, sampling, and data noise as mentioned in [5]. Moreover, different distribution or classes of normal data requires the encoder network re-training process, which results in high computational costs.

To address these issues, we propose an unsupervised 3D point novelty detection approach comprising a general point cloud feature extractor and a one-class classifier. As the general feature extractor, we first train an autoencoder (AE) [6] on the dataset of which the data is agnostic to the normal and anomaly class categories. Next, by the feature extractor, the training data of only normal classes are converted into latent vectors to extract condensed shape information. Then, one-class classification such as One-Class Support Vector Machine (OC-SVM) [7] and Kernel PCA-based Novelty Detection (KPCA-ND) [8] is trained on the latent vectors of the training data. For testing, an input point cloud is also transformed into a latent vector and measured its abnormality by the one-class classification. We confirm that our general feature extractor has the ability to extract the shape information of even unseen classes, which is beneficial for effective novelty detection and lower computational expenses. We validate our approach on three types of point cloud datasets and compare it with the state-of-the-art method. The results demonstrate that our latent-based OC-SVM and KPCA-ND exhibit significant improvements in point cloud novelty detection. In addition, we compared the performance of general feature extractors trained on different datasets while visualizing latent variables.

2   Related Work

There have been various approaches for novelty detection of 2D images [9–14]. Although these methods show high performance, they focus only on image data and do not handle 3D point cloud data. Unlike 2D image data, where each pixel has color information, 3D point cloud data has position information. In this work, we propose an effective framework for novelty detection of point cloud data.

2.1   Novelty Detection of 3D Point Clouds

Recently, Masuda et al. [3] proposed a reconstruction-based method measuring the anomaly score between the input and the reconstructed point cloud using a Variational AutoEncoder (VAE) [4]. Qin et al. [15] introduced a teacher-student network that minimizes a multi-scale loss between the feature vectors generated by the teacher and student networks. While the student network can be trained on a few training data, the performance is sensitive to the selection of the training samples especially in cases where the dataset contains many sparse point clouds like ShapeNet [16].

Feature Learning of 3D Point Clouds. In order to extract 3D shape features from point clouds, deep feature learning approaches are proposed, including supervised-based [17–19], self-supervised-based [20–22], and unsupervised-based [23,24]. While the recent image anomaly detection tasks often utilize the general feature extractor such as ResNet [38] trained on ImageNet [39], it is less common to use such trained feature extractors in point cloud anomaly detection tasks. One factor behind this is the lack of publically available large-scale point cloud datasets. Recently, a novel method for generating training data with natural 3D structures using fractal geometries has been proposed [25].

2.2   One-Class Classification

Various one-class classification methods [7,8,26–30] have been developed for image analysis, sensors, and signal monitoring. OC-SVM is the method to maximize the margin of the discriminative hyperplane from the origin, where the data points located outside the hyperplane are considered anomalies or novelties. The use of kernel functions can improve discrimination by projecting data into a higher dimensional space. Deep Support Vector Data Description (DeepSVDD) [29] is the deep learning-based extension of the SVDD [28] technique that identifies a hypersphere enclosing the training data with a minimum possible radius. It trains a neural network to map the input data close to the center of the hypersphere. Generalised One-class Discriminative Subspaces (GODS) [32] learns a set of discriminative hyperplanes to bound normal data, where each hyperplane consists of an orthogonal subspace. GODS can combine the linearity of OC-SVM with the nonlinear boundary properties of SVDD. KPCA-ND [8] is a nonlinear classification method that utilizes Kernel PCA [31]. Training data is mapped into an infinite-dimensional feature space using the kernel function such as Gaussian kernel, and PCA is performed on the mapped training data to compute eigenvectors. The cosine similarity between the eigenvectors and the test data that is mapped into the same feature space is measured.

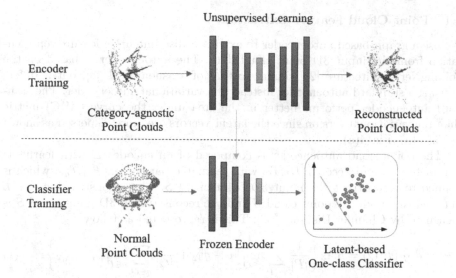

Fig. 1. Our latent-based one-class classification approach. Composed of a general point cloud feature extractor and a one-class classifier. As the general feature extractor, an autoencoder is trained on the dataset that is independent of detection categories. Input point clouds are converted into latent vectors by the trained frozen autoencoder. A one-class classifier trained on the latent vectors of normal classes classifies input as normal or anomaly.

3   Proposed Framework

Our framework comprises two main components: a general point cloud feature extractor and a one-class classifier. First, the autoencoder is trained on a dataset that is independent of normal and abnormal categories (Fig. 1). This training process is performed only once, and the trained autoencoder functions as a general feature extractor that can be used independently of specific test classes and distributions. Second, both training and test data are fed into the trained autoencoder, and the latent vectors are extracted at the bottleneck of the autoencoder. Third, the one-class classifier is trained on the extracted latent vectors of training data consisting only of normal data, then is used to classify whether the test data is normal or anomaly via a trained one-class classifier. In contrast to existing reconstruction-based approaches that measure anomalies in 3D coordinate space, our method operates in latent space where geometric features are compressed, allowing for more effective and robust novelty detection. In addition, once the autoencoder is trained, the weights are fixed, and the frozen autoencoder can be used as the general feature extractor, which eliminates the need for the encoder re-training and is effective in reducing computational costs. The training of both the encoder and classifier is performed in unsupervised learning.

3.1 Point Cloud Feature Extractor

We use a graph-based autoencoder to extract a discriminative feature representation from the input 3D point cloud data. The autoencoder is based on the FoldingNet architecture [23] similar to that of Masuda et al. [3], but it differs in using a standard autoencoder instead of a variational autoencoder. The standard autoencoder performs better in the area under the curve (AUC) metric than the variational version since the latent vectors are more dispersed as shown in Fig. 3(a), Fig. 4(a).

The point cloud autoencoder is composed of an encoder E with learnable parameters θ_e and decoder D_1, D_2 with learnable parameters θ_{d1}, θ_{d2}, which is trained to reconstruct the input 3D point cloud S. The reconstruction loss L between the input 3D point cloud S and the reconstructed 3D point cloud $\hat{S}$ is measured by Chamfer Distance [33]. This is represented as follows:

$$d_{CD}(P,Q) = \max\left\{ \frac{1}{|P|} \sum_{p \in P} \min_{q \in Q} \|p - q\|_2 + \frac{1}{|Q|} \sum_{q \in Q} \min_{p \in P} \|q - p\|_2 \right\}. \tag{1}$$

$$L = d_{CD}(S, \bar{S}_1) + d_{CD}(S, \bar{S}_2). \tag{2}$$

$$\hat{S} = D_2(D_1(E(S; \theta_e); \theta_{d1}); \theta_{d2}). \tag{3}$$

We use the trained encoder E to extract the latent vector z, i.e., $z = E(S; \theta_e)$. This latent vector is a more discriminative representation than the form of a 3D point cloud, and we found it can be efficiently classified using one-class classifiers.

Training for the General Feature Extractor. The point cloud autoencoder is trained on a dataset that is independent of normal and anomaly class distributions and is used as a general feature extractor. By training the autoencoder to reconstruct various shapes of the input data, it can extract shape features of unseen classes. We observed that both CAD models [37] and mathematically generated fractal 3D structures [25] (Fig. 2) serve as effective encoder training datasets.

Fig. 2. Auto-generated 3D fractal point clouds based on the formula of [25].

3.2 Latent-Based One-Class Classifiers

The trained general feature extractor transforms the input 3D point cloud into a 512-dimensional latent vector z at the bottleneck of the feature extractor where the local and global shape features condense. The extracted latent vectors of training data is used to train an unsupervised one-class classification approach. Note that, only normal data is available during training of the classifier.

We compare several one-class classification techniques, including OC-SVM [7], GODS [32], DeepSVDD [29], KPCA-ND [8] in order to validate which classifier is appropriate for identifying the point cloud latent vectors.

In OC-SVM, kernel OC-SVM with RBF kernel is used to enhance discrimination. The Gaussian kernel is used for KPCA-ND to map the features to an infinite-dimensional feature. For DeepSVDD, we replaced the convolution layers with several connected layers to handle 512-dimensional latent vectors as the network input. For GODS, we used the higher number of subspace hyperplanes to increase the discrimination power in the latent space where the shape features are nonlinearly expressed.

4 Experiments

4.1 Training of the General Feature Extractor

In our point cloud autoencoder, the input and output sizes of 3D point clouds are set to 2048. We set the learning rate to 0.0001, the training epochs to 300, and Chamfer distance as the reconstruction loss, following the work of [3]. Once the autoencoder is trained, the weights are fixed and the frozen autoencoder is commonly used in testing all the datasets.

Encoder-Training Datasets. We compare the performance of the encoder training datasets - ModelNet10, ModelNet40 [37], Fractal400 and Fractal1000 as Fractal 3D point clouds [25] (Table 1). The fractal point clouds are generated by the 3D fractal models and mixed with fractal noise following [25] with the variance threshold 0.05 and the noise ratio 0.2 (Fig. 2). From each point cloud, 2048 points are randomly sampled.

Table 1. Encoder-training datasets.

Encoder-training Dataset	Description	Number of classes	Sample size
ModelNet10	3D CAD object models	10	3991
ModelNet40	3D CAD object models	40	9843
Fractal400	Fractal point clouds	400	4000
Fractal1000	Fractal point clouds	1000	10000

4.2 Novelty Detection Datasets

Following the work of [3], we perform novelty detection on the subsets of the point cloud dataset [16] by defining one class as an anomaly and the rest classes of the subset as normal. The training data contains only a normal class, while test data includes both normal and anomaly classes. While the previous work [3] uses only one subset of the ShapeNet dataset [16] with seven classes, we prepare three different subsets to deeply evaluate the performances of each method.

1) ShapeNet-7 is composed of seven classes in the ShapeNet dataset used in the previous work [3]: Lamp, Chair, Table, Car, Sofa, Rifle, and Airplane.

2) ShapeNet-small includes seven classes with smaller sample sizes than the ShapeNet-7: Bookshelf, Laptop, Knife, Train, Motorbike, Guitar, and Faucet.

3) ShapeNet-14 is the combined dataset of ShapNet-7 and ShapeNet-small with 14 classes: Lamp, Chair, Table, Car, Sofa, Rifle, Airplane, Bookshelf, Laptop, Knife, Train, Motorbike, Guitar, and Faucet.

Each class contains hundreds of samples, and each sample has 2048 3D points that are randomly selected from the original point cloud. If the number of 3D points is smaller than 2048, they are randomly duplicated to reach 2048. The samples within each class are randomly divided into a training, validation, and test set at a ratio of 7:1:2. The training data is used to train the one-class classifier.

4.3   Training and Inference of One-Class Classifiers

The extracted latent vectors of training data from the frozen autoencoder are utilized to train the one-class classifier. The test data is also transformed into latent vectors and then classified by the trained classifiers. OC-SVM and GODS compute the anomaly score by the normalized signed distance between the input latent vector and the learned hyperplane. KPCA-ND calculates the anomaly score by cosine similarity between the eigenvectors and the mapped latent vector. DeepSVDD defines the anomaly score directly using the anomaly class probabilities output by the classifier network. The hyperparameters of each one-class classifier are determined through a grid search using the validation data, with a predefined range of each hyperparameter. A single set of selected hyperparameters is then used to evaluate each novelty detection (Table 2).

Evaluation. We evaluate each method by calculating AUC while varying the threshold value of the anomaly score according to the proposed methods [34,35].

Table 2. Parameters for the grid search.

Method	Parameter
OC-SVM	an upper bound on the fraction of training errors ν, kernel coefficient γ
GODS	the weight of controlling how far the predictions is from the hyperplanes η, step size λ, the number of subspaces
DeepSVDD	an upper bound on the fraction of training data ν, radius r, network, epoch
KPCA-ND	kernel width σ, the number of eigenvectors

Table 3. Comparison of novelty detection performance on ShapeNet-7. Each row represents the result where one class is defined as an anomaly class, and the rest classes are defined as normal. "Baseline" detects anomalies by the autoencoder reconstruction loss.

Anomaly class	Masuda et al. [3]	Baseline	Latent-based Method (Ours)			
			OC-SVM	KPCA-ND	DeepSVDD	GODS
lamp	0.716	0.715	**0.936**	0.880	0.866	0.868
chair	0.689	0.643	0.789	0.721	**0.831**	0.658
table	0.787	0.723	0.774	**0.920**	0.898	0.712
car	0.409	0.399	0.798	**0.923**	0.841	0.362
sofa	0.716	0.764	0.717	**0.769**	0.765	0.702
rifle	0.587	0.689	**0.941**	0.916	0.915	0.720
airplane	0.674	0.410	0.936	**0.947**	0.913	0.733
average	0.654	0.620	0.841	**0.868**	0.861	0.679

Table 4. Comparison of novelty detection performance on ShapeNet-small.

Anomaly class	Masuda et al. [3]	Baseline	Latent-based Method (Ours)			
			OC-SVM	KPCA-ND	DeepSVDD	GODS
bookshelf	0.886	0.903	0.911	**0.926**	0.857	0.855
laptop	0.930	0.904	0.964	**0.982**	0.956	0.984
knife	0.731	0.730	**0.863**	0.801	0.614	0.769
train	0.512	0.724	**0.837**	0.778	0.778	0.800
motorcycle	0.373	0.450	0.890	0.932	**0.941**	0.826
guitar	0.561	0.735	**0.919**	0.874	0.885	0.810
faucet	0.881	0.843	0.954	**0.982**	0.927	0.950
average	0.696	0.756	**0.905**	0.896	0.851	0.856

4.4 Comparison

We experiment with our latent-based approach with several one-class classifiers, where the autoencoder is trained on ModelNet10. Additionally, we compare our method against two different reconstruction-based methods, one using a variational autoencoder (Masuda et al. [3]), and the other using a standard autoencoder that we set as the baseline. For [3] and baseline methods, we train the networks with the normal classes of each Shepenet subset, and use the chamfer distance as the anomaly score, since it showed better AUC than the other types of anomaly scores of [3]. The measured AUC on Shapnent-7, ShapeNet-small, and ShapeNet-14 are shown in Table 3, Table 4, and Table 5. These results show that our latent-based methods outperform the reconstruction-based approaches across all the datasets, demonstrating the efficiency of one-class classification on latent vectors of 3D point clouds. Among the one-class classifiers, OC-SVM and KPCA-ND exhibit higher performance on average in all the datasets.

Table 5. Comparison of novelty detection performance on ShapeNet-14 with Different classifiers.

Anomaly class	Masuda et al. [3]	Baseline	Latent-based Method (Ours)			
			OC-SVM	KPCA-ND	DeepSVDD	GODS
lamp	0.553	0.578	**0.861**	0.819	0.753	0.794
chair	0.605	0.636	0.660	0.747	**0.773**	0.526
table	0.616	0.750	0.703	**0.868**	0.858	0.593
car	0.309	0.527	0.783	**0.931**	0.848	0.677
sofa	0.771	0.723	**0.818**	0.760	0.793	0.702
rifle	0.521	0.636	**0.929**	0.836	0.855	0.729
airplane	0.421	0.621	0.907	0.914	**0.920**	0.799
bookshelf	0.566	0.566	0.855	0.860	**0.904**	0.463
laptop	0.771	0.903	0.939	0.943	**0.955**	0.927
knife	0.631	0.669	**0.828**	0.672	0.685	0.659
train	0.579	0.703	**0.863**	0.661	0.577	0.611
motorcycle	0.357	0.501	0.900	**0.951**	0.891	0.455
guitar	0.583	0.555	**0.904**	0.840	0.892	0.804
faucet	0.786	0.695	**0.914**	0.841	0.800	0.858
average	0.572	0.647	**0.847**	0.832	0.822	0.686

Table 6. Comparison of novelty detection performance on different encoder-training datasets.

	Encoder-training Dataset							
	ModelNet10		ModelNet40		Fractal400		Fractal1000	
	OC-SVM	KPCA-ND	OC-SVM	KPCA-ND	OC-SVM	KPCA-ND	OC-SVM	KPCA-ND
ShapeNet-7	0.841	**0.868**	0.813	0.851	0.784	0.846	0.820	0.865
ShapeNet-small	0.905	0.896	0.885	0.888	0.881	0.876	**0.915**	0.908
ShapeNet-14	0.847	0.832	0.827	0.844	0.811	0.839	0.831	**0.853**
average	0.865	0.865	0.842	0.861	0.825	0.854	0.855	**0.875**

Comparison of Encoder-Training Datasets. We compare the performance of the general feature extractor with different encoder-training datasets, ModelNet10, ModelNet40, Fractal400, and Fractal1000. As shown in Table 6, Fractal1000 and ModelNet10 exhibited the highest AUC among the datasets.

4.5   Discussion

The results demonstrate that our latent-based one-class classification using the general feature extractor outperforms existing reconstruction-based methods for point cloud novelty detection.

Effects of General Feature Extractor. Figure 3 (a) illustrates the latent vectors of ShapeNet-7 that are extracted from the autoencoder trained on ModelNet10. The latent vectors show good separation within classes, suggesting the

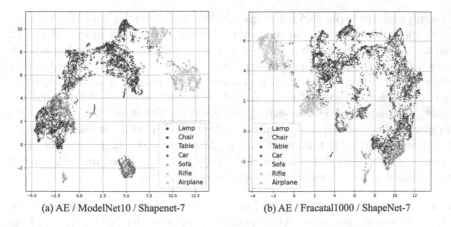

(a) AE / ModelNet10 / Shapenet-7   (b) AE / Fracatal1000 / ShapeNet-7

Fig. 3. Latent vectors of ShapeNet-7 visualized using Umap [36]. (a) The latent vectors are extracted by the autoencoder trained on ModelNet10. (b) The latent vectors are extracted by the autoencoder trained on Fractal1000.

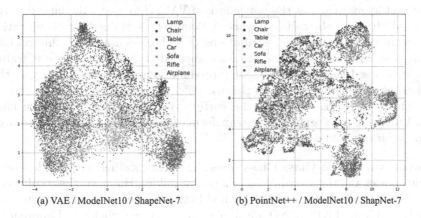

(a) VAE / ModelNet10 / ShapeNet-7   (b) PointNet++ / ModelNet10 / ShapNet-7

Fig. 4. Latent vectors of ShapeNet-7 visualized using Umap [36]. (a) The VAE [3] trained on ModelNet10. (b) The PointNet++ [18] trained on ModelNet10. Each color represents each class.

successful shape feature extraction in the latent space. This leads to effective one-class classification in the latent representations.

Comparison of Encoder-Training Datasets. When comparing the encoder-training datasets, Fractal1000 and ModelNet10 exhibited greater AUC scores. While ModelNet10 has some similar shapes in ShapeNet, fractal geometric structures generated from formulas do not have any similar categories in ShapeNet, yet showed superior performance to the existing methods. Figure 3 (b) illustrates the latent vector distributions of ShapeNet-7. This shows that each class remains distinguishable even when utilizing Fractal geometric shapes for the encoder training, indicating the various shapes in fractal geometries allow for the training of the autoencoder to capture shape features from even unseen data. This characteristic can be beneficial to apply it to a wide range of novelty detection tasks with low computational burden. The second row of Table 8 shows the performance when the autoencoder is trained on the normal data of ShapeNet-7, that is, the feature extractor is trained each time by using the normal categories. The performance is measured by OC-SVM. The result demonstrates that the general feature extractor exhibits higher AUC, indicating the effectiveness of utilizing the general feature extractor. This result also highlights the advantage of our latent-based method over the reconstruction-based method when the same dataset is used between methods Table 3, Table 8.

Importance of using AE. Table 7 presents the performance of different feature extractors: our autoencoder (AE), variational autoencoder (VAE) [3], and Point-Net++ [18]. All the feature extractors are trained on ModelNet10, and the classification performance is measured by OC-SVM. The results demonstrate that our autoencoder outperforms the other feature extractors. Figure 4 (a) illustrates the latent vectors extracted at the bottleneck of VAE, (b) depicts the latent vectors extracted after the abstraction layers in PointNet++ trained for classification. Both figures reveal that the distributions of each class are closely intertwined, making the one-class classification task complicated. As PointNet++ is trained using supervised learning, the latent representations are learned in a way that emphasizes the separation of seen classes, which may not be suitable for extracting features of unseen classes if the feature is extracted in the middle layer. Also, VAE employs a probabilistic transformation, which can hinder clear latent vector separation among classes.

Comparison of One-Class Classifiers. The best classifier can vary depending on the dataset and the distribution of latent variables. However, the results show that OC-SVM and KPCA-ND performed better than other one-class classifiers. Both OC-SVM and KPCA-ND are simple but effective kernel-based approaches, which we assume are effective to classify novelties from normal samples in the non-linear latent space. While Deep SVDD showed also good performance, it is relatively sensitive to the training epoch, which may make it challenging to opt for parameters in practical applications. Further improvement of the network architecture for this task could improve the detection performance.

Limitation of the Proposal Framework. Among the classes of the datasets, the anomaly classes 'chair' and 'sofa' showed the lower performance. Figure 3 illustrates that the latent vector distribution of the 'chair' class is closer to that of the 'sofa' class compared to the other classes. This suggests that detection becomes challenging when there are minor shape differences and the latent vectors have similar features.

Table 7. Comparison of novelty detection performance on ShapeNet-7 with different feature extractors. The average AUC is measured.

Network	Dimension	Encoder-training Dataset	AUC
Our AE	512×1	ModelNet10	**0.841**
VAE [3]	512×1	ModelNet10	0.643
PointNet++ [18]	1024×1	ModelNet10	0.749

Table 8. Comparison of novelty detection performance on ShapeNet-7 with different encoder-training datasets. The average AUC is measured.

Network	Encoder-training Dataset	AUC
Our AE	ModelNet10	**0.841**
Our AE	Normal Classes of ShapeNet-7	0.817

5   Conclusion

This paper has proposed the point cloud novelty detection approach consisting of the general feature extractor and the one-class classifier. The autoencoder trained on a synthetic dataset can be used as the general feature extractor agnostic to the normal and anomaly categories and converts the input data into the latent vectors that represent shape features. The one-class classifier is trained on the latent vectors and classifies inputs as normal or anomalous. We conduct experiments on the subsets of ShapeNet dataset and our approach achieves higher performance than the existing reconstruction-based novelty detection methods. Also, the experiments showed the effectiveness of using the general feature extractor and OC-SVM and KPCA-ND as the one-class classifier. In the future, we will expand our methods for 3D point cloud novelty detection in real scenes.

Acknowledgment. This work is partly supported by the Japan Society for the Promotion of Science (JSPS) through KAKENHI Grant Number 20K14516. The computation of this work was in part carried out on the Multi-wavelength Data Analysis System operated by the Astronomy Data Center (ADC), National Astronomical Observatory of Japan.

References

1. Pimentel, M.A.F., Clifton, D.A., Clifton, L., Tarassenko, L.: A review of novelty detection. Signal Process. **99**, 215–249 (2014). https://doi.org/10.1016/j.sigpro.2013.12.026
2. Yang, J., Zhou, Z., Li, Y., Liu, Z.: Generalized Out-of-Distribution Detection: A Survey. Preprint at arXiv2110.11334 (2021)
3. Masuda, M., Hachiuma, R., Fujii, R., Saito, H., Sekikawa, Y.: Toward Unsupervised 3D Point Cloud Anomaly Detection Using Variational Autoencoder. In: 2021 IEEE International Conference on Image Processing (ICIP), pp. 3118–3122, Anchorage, AK, USA (2021). https://doi.org/10.1109/ICIP42928.2021.9506795

4. An, J., Cho, S.: Variational autoencoder based anomaly detection using reconstruction probability. Special Lecture on IE (2015)
5. Urbach, D., Ben-Shabat, Y., Lindenbaum, M.: DPDist: comparing point clouds using deep point cloud distance. In: Computer Vision - ECCV 2020: 16th European Conference, pp. 545–560, Glasgow, UK (2020). https://doi.org/10.1007/978-3-030-58621-8_32
6. Chen, Z., Yeo, C.K., Lee, B.S., Lau, C.T.: Autoencoder based network anomaly detection. In: Wireless Telecommunications Symposium (WTS), pp. 1–5 (2018). https://doi.org/10.1109/WTS.2018.8363930
7. Schölkopf, B., Platt, J.C., Shawe-Taylor, J.C., Smola, A.J., Williamson, R.C.: Estimating the support of a high-dimentional distribution. Neural Comput. **13**(7), 1443–1471 (2001). https://doi.org/10.1162/089976601750264965
8. Hoffmann, H.: Kernel PCA for novelty detection. Pattern Recogn. **40**(3), 863–874 (2007). https://doi.org/10.1016/j.patcog.2006.07.009
9. Sabokrou, M., Khalooei, M., Fathy, M., Adeli, E.: Adversarially learned one-class classifier for novelty detection. In: 2018 IEEE/CVF Conference on Computer Vision and Pattern Recognition, pp. 3379–3388, Salt Lake City, UT, USA (2018). https://doi.org/10.1109/CVPR.2018.00356
10. Sastry, C.S., Oore, S.: Detecting out-of-distribution examples with gram matrices. In: Proceedings of the 37th International Conference on Machine Learning (ICML 2020), vol. 119, pp. 8491–8501 (2020)
11. Tack, J., Mo, S., Jeong, J., Shin, J.: CSI: novelty detection via contrastive learning on distributionally shifted instances. In: Advances in Neural Information Processing Systems, vol. 33, pp. 11839–11852 (2020)
12. Huang, R., Geng, A., Li, Y.: On the importance of gradients for detecting distributional shifts in the wild. In: Advances in Neural Information Processing Systems (2021)
13. Xuefeng, D., Wang, Z., Cai, M., Li, Y.: VOS: learning what you don't know by virtual outlier synthesis. In: Proceedings of the International Conference on Learning Representations (2022)
14. Sun, Y., Guo, C., Li, Y.: ReAct: out-of-distribution detection with rectified activations. In: Advances in Neural Information Processing Systems (2021)
15. Qin, J., Gu, C., Yu, J., Zhang, C.: Teacher-student network for 3D point cloud anomaly detection with few normal samples. Expert Syst. Appl. **228**, 120371 (2023). https://doi.org/10.1016/j.eswa.2023.120371
16. Chang, A.X., et al.: ShapeNet: An Information-Rich 3D Model Repository. Preprint at arXiv1512.03012 (2015)
17. Charles, R., Su, H., Kaichun, M., Guibas, L.: PointNet: deep learning on point sets for 3d classification and segmentation. In: 2017 IEEE Conference on Computer Vision and Pattern Recognition (CVPR), pp. 77–85, Honolulu, HI, USA (2017). https://doi.org/10.1109/CVPR.2017.16
18. Qi, C.R., Yi, L., Su, H., Guibas, L.J.: PointNet++: deep hierarchical feature learning on point sets in a metric space (2017). Preprint at arXiv:1706.02413
19. Li, J., Chen, B.M., Lee, G.H.: SO-Net: Self-Organizing Network for Point Cloud Analysis (2018). Preprint at arXiv:1803.04249
20. Xie, S., Gu, J., Guo, D., Qi, C.R., Guibas, L., Litany, O.: PointContrast: unsupervised pre-training for 3D point cloud understanding. In: Vedaldi, A., Bischof, H., Brox, T., Frahm, J.-M. (eds.) ECCV 2020. LNCS, vol. 12348, pp. 574–591. Springer, Cham (2020). https://doi.org/10.1007/978-3-030-58580-8_34

21. Achituve, I., Maron, H., Chechik, G.: Self-supervised learning for domain adaptation on point clouds. In: 2021 IEEE Winter Conference on Applications of Computer Vision (WACV), pp. 123–133, Waikoloa, HI, USA (2021). https://doi.org/10.1109/WACV48630.2021.00017

22. Liu, X., Liu, X., Liu, Y.-S., Han, Z.: SPU-Net: self-supervised point cloud up sampling by coarse-to-fine reconstruction with self-projection optimization. In: IEEE Transactions on Image Processing, vol. 31, pp. 4213–4226 (2022). https://doi.org/10.1109/TIP.2022.3182266

23. Yang, Y., Feng, C., Shen, Y., Tian, D.: FoldingNet: point cloud auto-encoder via deep grid deformation. In: 2018 IEEE/CVF Conference on Computer Vision and Pattern Recognition, pp. 205–215, Salt Lake City, UT, USA (2018). https://doi.org/10.1109/CVPR.2018.00029

24. Han, Z., Wang, X., Liu, Y-S., Zwicker, M.: Multi-angle point cloud-VAE: unsupervised feature learning for 3D point clouds from multiple angles by joint self-reconstruction and half-to-half prediction (2019). Preprint at arXiv:1907.12704

25. Yamada, R., Kataoka, H., Chiba, N., Domae, Y., Ogata, T.: Point cloud pre-training with natural 3D structures. In: 2022 IEEE/CVF Conference on Computer Vision and Pattern Recognition (CVPR), pp. 21251–21261, New Orleans, LA, USA (2022). https://doi.org/10.1109/CVPR52688.2022.02060

26. Pokrajac, D., Lazarevic, A., Latecki, L.: Incremental local outlier detection for data streams. In: 2007 IEEE Symposium on Computational Intelligence and Data Mining, pp. 504–515, Honolulu, HI, USA (2007). https://doi.org/10.1109/CIDM.2007.368917

27. Syed, Z., Saeed, M., Rubinfeld, I.: Identifying high-risk patients without labeled training data: anomaly detection methodologies to predict adverse outcomes. In: AMIA Annual Symposium Proceedings, pp. 772–776 (2010)

28. Tax, D., Duin, R.: Support vector data description. Mach. Learn. **54**, 45–66 (2004). https://doi.org/10.1016/S0167-8655(99)00087-2

29. Ruff, L., et al.: Deep one-class classification. In: Dy, J., Krause, A. (eds.) Proceedings of the 35th International Conference on Machine Learning, vol. 80, pp. 4393–4402 (2018)

30. Jolliffe, I.T.: Principal Component Analysis. Springer Series in Statistics, 2nd edn. Springer, New York, NY (2002). https://doi.org/10.1007/b98835

31. Schölkopf, B., Smola, A., Müller, K.-R.: Nonlinear component analysis as a kernel eigenvalue problem. Neural Comput. **10**(5), 1299–1319 (1998). https://doi.org/10.1162/089976698300017467

32. Wang, J., Cherian, A.: GODS: Generalized One-class Discriminative Subspaces for Anomaly Detection. Preprint at arXiv1908.05884 (2019)

33. Fan, H., Su, H., Guibas, L. J.: A point set generation network for 3D object reconstruction from a single image. In: 2017 IEEE Conference on Computer Vision and Pattern Recognition (CVPR), pp. 2463–2471, Honolulu, HI, USA (2017). https://doi.org/10.1109/CVPR.2017.264

34. Akcay, S., Atapour-Abarghouei, A., Breckon, T.P.: GANomaly: semi-supervised anomaly detection via adversarial training. In: Jawahar, C.V., Li, H., Mori, G., Schindler, K. (eds.) ACCV 2018. LNCS, vol. 11363, pp. 622–637. Springer, Cham (2019). https://doi.org/10.1007/978-3-030-20893-6_39

35. Kimura, D., Chaudhury, S., Narita, M., Munawar, A., Tachibana, R.: Adversarial discriminative attention for robust anomaly detection. In: Proceedings of the 2020 IEEE/CVF Winter Conference on Applications of Computer Vision (WACV), pp. 2172–2181 (2020). https://doi.org/10.1109/WACV45572.2020.9093428

36. McInnes, L., Healy, J., Melville, J.: UMAP: Uniform Manifold Approximation and Projection for Dimension Reduction. Preprint at arXiv1802.03426 (2018)
37. Wu, Z., Song, S., Khosla, A., Yu, F., Zhang, L., Tang, X., Xiao, J.: 3D ShapeNets: a deep representation for volumetric shapes. In: 2015 IEEE Conference on Computer Vision and Pattern Recognition (CVPR), pp. 1912–1920, Boston, MA, USA (2015). https://doi.org/10.1109/CVPR.2015.7298801
38. He, K., Zhang, X., Ren, S., Sun, J.: Deep residual learning for image recognition. In: 2016 IEEE Conference on Computer Vision and Pattern Recognition (CVPR), pp. 770–778, Las Vegas, NV, USA (2016). https://doi.org/10.1109/CVPR.2016.90
39. Deng, J., Dong, W., Socher, R., Li, L.-J., Li, K., Fei-Fei, L.: ImageNet: a large-scale hierarchical image database. In: 2009 IEEE Conference on Computer Vision and Pattern Recognition, pp. 248–255, Miami, FL, USA (2009). https://doi.org/10.1109/CVPR.2009.5206848

Efficient 3Dconv Fusion of RGB and Optical Flow for Dynamic Hand Gesture Recognition and Localization

Gibran Benitez-Garcia[1]([⊠])(ID) and Hiroki Takahashi[1,2]

[1] Graduate School of Informatics and Engineering, The University of Electro-Communications, Tokyo, Japan
gibran@ieee.org, rocky@inf.uec.ac.jp
[2] Artificial Intelligence eXploration Research Center (AIX), Meta-Networking Research Center (MEET), The University of Electro-Communications, Tokyo, Japan

Abstract. Hand Gesture Recognition (HGR) has been significantly advanced through multimodal approaches utilizing RGB and Optical Flow (OF). Yet, two main challenges often remain (i) The computational burden triggered by advanced techniques which rely on intricate multi-level fusion blocks distributed across the architecture, and (ii) the limited exploration into the impact of OF estimators on multimodal fusion. To address these, this paper introduces an efficient RGB+OF fusion relying on just a few 3DConv layers applied early in the architecture. Concurrently, we explore the impact of five state-of-the-art OF methods on this fusion. Advancing beyond traditional HGR, we prioritize recognizing and precisely localizing the hand gesture, which is critical for a wide range of computer vision applications. Thus transitioning the focus to Hand Gesture Recognition and Localization (HGRL). Accordingly, we employ a YOLO-based architecture renowned for its real-time efficacy and precision in object localization, aligning with the demands of dynamic gestures often seen in HGRL. We evaluate our approach with the IPN-Hand dataset, augmenting its scope for HGRL evaluation by manually annotating 82,769 frames. Our experiments show significant results of 10% enhancement in mAP against the RGB-only method and a 7% gain over 2DConv-based fusion.

Keywords: Hand Gesture Recognition and Localization · RGB+Optical Flow Fusion · YOLO-based Architecture

1 Introduction

Automatic Hand Gesture Recognition (HGR) is critical in developing intuitive human-computer interfaces since it focuses on interpreting user hand movements as instructions or commands [1,6]. However, when the crucial aspect of spatial localization is included in the process, we transition to the more comprehensive

Supported by a Research Grant (S) at Tateisi Science and Technology Foundation.

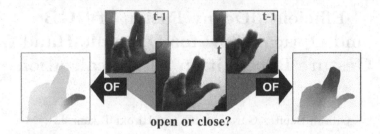

Fig. 1. Illustration of the limitations of relying only on the current frame (t) for classifying dynamic gestures. Temporal information from previous frames must be considered to discern if the fingers are opening (right) or closing (left). Dense Optical Flow (OF) can effectively capture and depict the crucial temporal features for HGRL.

challenge of Hand Gesture Recognition and Localization (HGRL). In HGRL, the gesture and precise hand location play an essential role in a wide range of applications in the automotive sector, virtual reality, industrial electronics, and others [6,23,25]. For instance, touchless screen manipulation is a technology that has become increasingly relevant in a world focused on hygiene and reduced physical contact [1,16]. For such interfaces, while simple commands might be captured through static hand gestures relying solely on spatial cues, interpreting more complex, dynamic gestures need motion interpretation. As depicted in Fig. 1, dynamic gestures are ambiguous when viewed as a single frame, underscoring the importance of temporal cues for HGRL.

Dense Optical Flow (OF) has traditionally been a standard method to extract temporal features for HGR. Several deep learning approaches in the literature have fused the complementary nature of RGB and OF data to create robust multimodal features [7,12,13,17,20]. However, two critical challenges often remain under-addressed in most RGB+OF approaches. Firstly, the computational cost of multimodal architectures frequently goes overlooked. So, the necessity to compute dense OF as a preprocessing step significantly limits their application. Secondly, the accuracy and inference speed performance of OF estimators become crucial to the success of the entire system. Therefore, these challenges must be carefully addressed to design efficient and reliable multimodal HGRL fusion approaches.

The fusion of RGB and OF data is commonly achieved through different techniques, with middle multi-level fusion standing out as it effectively captures low-level and high-level correlations between modalities through the whole Convolutional Neural Network (CNN) [7,12,19]. However, traditional fusion methods rely on fusion blocks to merge modal-specific features, often increasing computational costs. In contrast, in this paper, we introduce an efficient RGB+OF fusion purely based on a couple of 3DConv layers from the early stages of the architecture. This allows the network to holistically learn the complementary multimodal characteristics in an integrated manner rather than generating isolated features that need subsequent fusion. To further optimize our approach, we adopt a YOLO-based single-stage architecture chosen for its real-time processing and exceptional accuracy in spatially localizing objects, aligning perfectly with the demands of dynamic HGRL tasks. This configuration ensures end-to-end learning while maintaining a mix of initial 3D and subsequent 2D convolutions for computational efficiency. On the other hand, the contribution of different OF methods for multimodal HGR has been barely investigated. Therefore, we explore the impact of five state-of-the-art (SOTA) OF methods, specifically in early RGB+OF fusion.

We evaluate our proposed approach using 11 distinct gesture classes of the IPN-Hand dataset [2], known for its challenging dynamic gestures tailored for interactions with touchless devices. While this dataset offers temporal annotation of the gestures, hand location is not provided. Therefore, we manually annotate 82,769 frames, adding another dimension to the dataset, enabling it to evaluate HGRL approaches. Through comprehensive experiments and an in-depth ablation study, we validate the effectiveness of our proposed RGB+OF approach. The results show a notable 10% boost in mAP compared to the RGB-only strategy and a significant 7% increase over a 2Dconv-based fusion. Note that this performance is achieved with a marginal increase in the computational cost of about 1 GFLOP to the baseline architecture. Testing code, pre-trained models, and extended annotations of the IPN-Hand dataset will be publicly available at https://github.com/GibranBenitez/IPN-hand/.

In resume, the main contributions of this paper include:

- Introduction of an efficient 3Dconv fusion of RGB+OF data employing a YOLO-based single-stage architecture for dynamic hand gesture recognition and localization (HGRL).
- Comprehensive analysis and evaluation of five SOTA OF methods: RAFT [22], GMA [10], KPA [15], SKF [21], and FlowFormer [9] for HGRL based on RGB+OF.
- Extension of the IPN-Hand dataset annotations of about 82K frames resulting in 83,613 annotated hands.

2   Related Work

The explosion of deep learning in the last decade urged several solutions for HGR, capitalizing on the advancements of CNNs [1,13,26] and their 3D counterparts, 3D-CNNs [7,12,17]. Preliminary techniques for RGB+OF HGR predominantly adopted the two-stream-based framework [20]. In this architecture, a spatial stream processes individual RGB frames via a CNN, while a temporal stream captures motion information by stacking and processing optical flow images with another CNN. Finally, the classification scores of each stream are combined by a late fusion block. Contemporary methods, such as those proposed by the works of Molchanov et al. [17] and Kopuklu et al. [13], have adeptly integrated both RGB and OF data, resulting in significant improvements in recognition accuracy and a richer representation of hand gestures. However, despite the HGR advancements, a notable gap in the existing literature is the limited attention to spatial localization of hands, which is crucial when distinguishing multiple hands in a scene or determining the precise location of a gesture.

An important issue for the RGB+OF fusion is determining the optimal level within CNN models for information integration. Numerous efforts have fused multimodal information at different levels, namely early, late, and middle fusion [1,7,19]. Early fusion combines features at the data level or the early stages of the HGR architecture, while late fusion merges predictions from individual models as the last step of the architecture. Moreover, some methods have shown that mid-fusion is more effective because it captures intricate correlations between modalities throughout the entire network [7,12,19]. The middle multi-level fusion strategy has notable contributions, such as those by Joze et al. [12] and recently Hampiholi et al. [7], emphasizing the potential of middle fusion when integrating RGB and OF data. However, many existing approaches often neglect challenges like architectural complexity, inefficiencies from traditional fusion blocks, and the computational costs introduced by OF estimators. This highlights the urgency for methodologies that seamlessly balance performance and computational efficiency, the core objective of this work.

3   Proposed Method

In this section, we detail our YOLO-based single-stage architecture that leverages the benefits of both RGB and OF data to achieve robust and efficient Dynamic Hand Gesture Recognition and Localization (HGRL). Figure 2 presents a block diagram detailing the entire architecture, capturing the flow from the multimodal RGB+OF input to the precise HGRL output. The diagram offers a holistic perspective of our architecture. However, for a more detailed understanding, we'll dissect it into its core segments: the Backbone, the RGB+OF fusion, the Neck, and the Head. These elements are crucial, each contributing uniquely to the balance between speed and accuracy in our method.

Backbone. The backbone serves as the foundational structure of the architecture, responsible for initial feature extraction. Our design adopts the CSP-Darknet53 structure, a modification of the renowned Darknet architecture [18] based on the CSP (Cross Stage Partial) principle [24]. This structure efficiently enhances learning by decomposing the feature map from the previous stage into two parts and then merging them with a convolution layer after a series of bottlenecks, as illustrated in the CSP_N-2D diagram of Fig. 2. Note that the output size of feature maps is specified in each block of the diagram. The core of the backbone is constructed by stacking multiple 2DConv-CSP modules, with each 2DConv layer comprising a 3×3 Convolution, followed by Batch Normalization, and then activated by the SiLU (Sigmoid Linear Unit) function [4]. In summary, the backbone effectively captures both low-level and high-level features, setting a robust foundation for the subsequent processing stages.

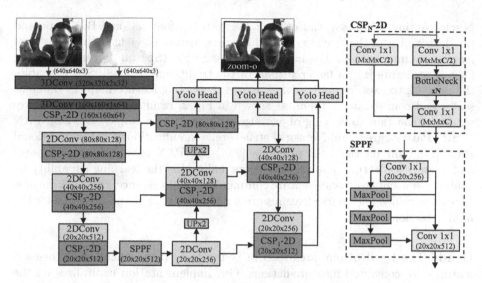

Fig. 2. Block diagram of our YOLO-based architecture with efficient 3Dconv fusion of RGB and OF for HGRL.

RGB+OF Fusion. Crucial to our architecture is the fusion of RGB and OF data. These modalities, when combined, offer a comprehensive view of dynamic hand gestures comprising appearance (RGB) and motion dynamics (OF). Our chosen methodology for fusion leverages 3Dconv layers, designed to extract spatiotemporal features by processing depth-wise spatial information across consecutive time steps. This is particularly advantageous for our input, which consists of two consecutive images (RGB and OF) of size 640×640×3, as depicted in Fig. 2. Thus, the input is initially shaped as 640×640×2×3. It then undergoes two 3Dconv layers as follows:

- The data first passes through a 3Dconv layer with 32 filters and a spatial stride of 2. This step processes the RGB and OF frames together, yielding an output shape of 320×320×2×32.
- It then traverses another 3Dconv layer with 64 filters and spatial and temporal strides of 2. This operation condenses the temporal dimension by effectively merging the RGB and OF data, resulting in a 160×160×1×64 feature map shape.
- The rest of the 2DCNN-based architecture processes this fused data by simply reshaping the feature maps to 160×160×64.

In this way, our fusion strategy doesn't just append one modality to another. Instead, it learns and retains the spatial and temporal intricacies of both modalities, setting the stage for subsequent processing stages to work with a richer feature representation.

Neck. Acting as an essential conduit between the foundational Backbone and the decisive Head, the Neck in our architecture ensures efficient high-to-low level feature communication. We incorporate the SPPF (Spatial Pyramid Pooling Faster) structure [11], a faster variant of the traditional SPP [8]. SPPF enables the network to capture multi-scale features by pooling feature maps at different scales and concatenating them, as shown in Fig. 2, resulting in a robust representation resistant to varying object sizes. Alongside, we employ the CSP-PAN (CSP - Path Aggregation Network) structure, a modification of the conventional PAN [14] built on the CSP principle [24]. CSP-PAN effectively redistributes and aggregates feature maps across layers, enhancing the learning capability by enabling efficient cross-scale feature communication. In essence, the Neck ensures that fine-grained and coarse features are seamlessly bridged and prepared for the final detection phase.

Head. The Head of our architecture is the last stage, where the processed features are converted into predictions. Our implementation capitalizes on the YOLOv3 Head [18], known for its high efficiency in real-time object detection tasks. YOLOv3 introduces three sizes of anchor boxes at three different scales, catering to varying object sizes. Each of these scales uses its set of anchor boxes to predict both the bounding box coordinates and the objectness score. Additionally, each bounding box prediction predicts the confidence score, which signifies the probability of an object being present and how well the bounding box fits the object. As illustrated in Fig. 2, the Head also benefits from a three-tier detection mechanism, allowing detections at three different resolutions, thereby enhancing accuracy across a range of object sizes. This meticulous design ensures precise localization of hand gestures while optimizing computational overhead, making it particularly apt for our purpose.

In summary, our single-stage architecture begins with the robust CSP-Darknet53 backbone for feature extraction, then integrates RGB+OF inputs through a simple yet effective 3Dconv fusion process. This harmonized information then traverses the efficient SPPF and the adaptable CSP-PAN in the Neck, culminating in the precise and real-time detection capabilities of the YOLOv3 Head. As illustrated in Fig. 2, our design prioritizes both accuracy and computational efficiency, presenting a significant contribution to HGRL.

4   State-of-the-art Optical Flow Methods

Dense Optical Flow (OF) consists of estimating pixel motion between consecutive frames in a video sequence, making it an invaluable asset, particularly for HGRL applications. As the movement of hands and fingers becomes intricate and fast-paced, reliable OF estimation becomes essential to distinguishing gestures accurately. Despite several OF methods existing in the literature, we focus our selection on approaches that have demonstrated state-of-the-art (SOTA) performance on conventional benchmarks, such as Sintel [3] and KITTI [5]. This section explores five leading methods, highlighting their contributions and evaluating their computational and performance capabilities.

RAFT: Recurrent All-Pairs Field Transforms [22]. Deviating from conventional approaches that compute per-pixel displacements, RAFT employs recurrent neural networks and constructs a 4D cost volume to analyze all possible pixel pairs, ensuring a more cohesive motion estimate across frames. Utilizing ConvGRU, it iteratively updates a dense flow field, beginning with a coarse level and progressively refining it. This guarantees exceptional precision even in complex dynamic scenes. This methodology not only contributes to its superior accuracy but also results in visually coherent and smooth flow fields. RAFT has been validated extensively, being the backbone of several incremental improvements, underscoring its efficacy and relevance in the field of optical flow estimation.

GMA: Global Motion Aggregation [10]. GMA is a novel approach that specifically targets the intricate issues presented by occlusions when estimating OF. The authors introduce a transformer-based methodology that leverages an attention mechanism to identify long-range interdependencies between individual pixels in the reference frame. This attention mechanism, often referred to as the GMA block, enables the model to give varying importance to different pixels, ensuring a more accurate and nuanced estimation, especially in occluded regions. Instead of solely relying on local evidence, the method aggregates the motion characteristics of these pixels on a global scale. This holistic approach results in a more accurate and detailed representation of motion, particularly in regions with prevalent occlusions. By incorporating GMA features into the RAFT framework [22], a new SOTA performance has been established.

KPA: Kernel Patch Attention [15]. Despite the considerable advancements made by deep learning-based OF methods, their primary emphasis lies in learning and measuring feature similarities, often neglecting the spatial relations that reveal motion affinities. KPA addresses this by introducing kernel patch attention, which operates on each local patch to determine context affinities for better flow field inference. Traditional optical flow algorithms emphasized both feature similarities and spatial smoothness. In contrast, KPA effectively blends both aspects, focusing on local relations based on context and spatial affinities. The proposed KPA operator employs a patch-based sliding window strategy, offering a comprehensive solution for reliable motion understanding. Once more, the KPA method builds upon the RAFT framework [22] to achieve a new SOTA performance on standard benchmarks.

SKF: Super Kernel Flow Network [21]. Similar to GMA, the SKF method is proposed to mitigate the impacts of occlusions in OF estimation. This approach benefits from super kernels (SK), which provide enlarged receptive fields to complement absent matching information and recover occluded motions. SKF introduces an efficient architecture utilizing a conical design with residual connections, which splits the convolution operation into depth-wise convolutions, consisting of a large depth-wise kernel and an auxiliary smaller depth-wise kernel. SKF introduces an efficient architecture with a conical design complemented by residual connections. This design aims to split the convolution operation into depth-wise convolutions, using both a large depth-wise kernel and an auxiliary smaller depth-wise kernel. Despite the architecture reminiscence of GMA, especially in using the GMA module, SKF distinguishes itself through the innovative application of SK modules. It also differs from the RAFT framework by utilizing the SK block as an updater instead of ConvGRU.

FlowFormer: Transformer Architecture for OF [9]. FlowFormer presents a novel approach representing a fusion of transformer architectures with established OF estimation techniques. It takes inspiration from the rising popularity of transformers, known for modeling long-range relations. Unlike directly operating on image pixels that demand a large number of parameters and training samples, FlowFormer incorporates the advantages of the cost volume from previous techniques. It employs an encoder-decoder architecture that transforms the 4D cost volume into compact, globally aware latent cost tokens. The proposed cost decoder also adopts a recurrent attention layer inspired by RAFT [22]. This decoder treats cost decoding as a recurrent query process with dynamic positional cost queries, delivering state-of-the-art performance.

Comparative Analysis. Table 1 presents a detailed comparison of the performance and computational costs of the five OF methods. On evaluating the benchmarks, the most recent addition to the field (FlowFormer, ECCV'22) exhibits superior accuracy on the Sintel dataset, registering the lowest error rate of 2.09. However, the KPA establishes superiority on the KITTI dataset with an error rate of 4.60. Regarding computational efficiency, RAFT stands out for both input resolutions, demanding 242.8 and 60.7 GFLOPs for 640×480 and 320×240 resolutions, respectively. FlowFormer, despite its leading performance, demands a computational burden nearly three times heavier than that of RAFT. Nonetheless, GMA and SKF present a good trade-off of performance and efficiency. In the next section, we delve deeper, evaluating the significance of these findings in the RGB+OF context for HGRL.

Table 1. Computational cost and performance on standard benchmarking of the five analyzed OF methods.

Method	Params	GFLOPs (640×480)	(320×240)	Results Sintel	KITTI
RAFT (ECCV'20)	5.26M	242.8	60.7	2.86	5.10
GMA (ICCV'21)	5.88M	272.3	68.1	2.47	4.93
KPA (CVPR'22)	5.99M	327.6	82.2	2.36	**4.60**
SKF (NeurIPS'22)	6.27M	295.2	73.8	2.27	4.84
FlowFormer (ECCV'22)	16.17M	756.5	173.5	**2.09**	4.68

Point	Click	Th-up	Th-down	Th-left	Th-right	Open-2	2click	Zoom-in	Zoom-o	Grab

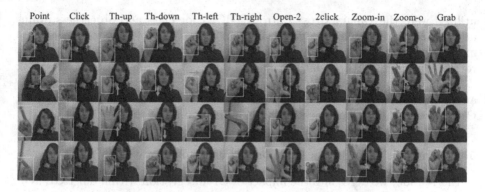

Fig. 3. Dynamic gestures with hand annotations from the IPN Hand dataset used in the HGRL Evaluation.

5   Experimental Results

5.1   Dataset

In this paper, we utilize the IPN Hand dataset [2], a comprehensive collection of dynamic gestures tailored for touchless screen interaction. The dataset comprises RGB videos recorded at 640×480 resolution and 30fps using PC or laptop cameras. The videos originate from 28 distinct scenes involving 50 participants, including challenges such as cluttered backgrounds and varying illumination conditions.

For our evaluation, we assess the performance of HGRL on 11 specific gestures, illustrated in Fig. 3, which account for a total of 3,457 gesture instances. Given the absence of hand location data in the dataset, we manually annotate 82,769 keyframes from all instances. To facilitate this, we trained a YOLOv5 [11] model on a smaller dataset to produce candidate hand locations. Subsequently, we manually refine the hand annotations for each instance at an approximate rate of 9 fps. The training set consists of 2,531 gesture instances from 37 subjects, translating to 64,768 annotated frames. Conversely, the test set includes 926 instances from 13 subjects, generating 18,001 annotated frames.

5.2   Implementation Details

We use Python 3.7.16 and PyTorch 1.10.2 with CUDA 12.0 on an Intel Core i7-9700K desktop with a single Nvidia GTX 2080Ti GPU for all experiments. To train the proposed YOLO-based architecture with RGB+OF 3Dconv fusion, we set 30 epochs using a batch size of 32 and cropped regions of size 640×640. We initialized the CSP-Darknet53 backbone with pre-trained weights from ImageNet, specifically for the 2DConv layers, while training all other layers from scratch. The optimization approach was Stochastic Gradient Descent, with a momentum of 0.937, a learning rate of 0.01, and a weight decay of 0.0005. The loss functions utilized were the Binary Cross Entropy (BCE) for class and objectness evaluations, and the Complete Intersection over Union (CIoU) for location loss, as in [11]. Furthermore, we incorporated Mosaic Augmentation alongside random rotation, scaling, and translation as part of our data augmentation strategy.

For OF approaches, we leveraged the official open-source implementations and pre-trained models released by the authors of each method. We obtained OF representations from the 82,769 annotated frames of the IPN hand dataset.

5.3   Analysis of of in the Proposed Fusion Framework

In this section, we delve into the impact of OF integration within our RGB+OF framework. A comprehensive analysis was performed to objectively assess each OF method's contribution to our fusion scheme. Our evaluation is based on standard metrics, such as Precision, Recall, and the mean Average Precision (mAP) at varying Intersection over Union (IoU) thresholds.

Table 2 presents the results for our RGB+OF fusion model with different SOTA Optical Flow methods, benchmarked against the "RGB only" results. As expected, the fusion models consistently surpass the RGB-only metrics. In particular, the RGB+SKF combination achieves the highest scores in all categories, yielding an average 10% improvement over the baseline. This emphasizes SKF's ability to represent motion nuances, enhancing gesture recognition when combined with RGB. These findings reinforce that integrating OF can significantly augment gesture recognition performance, primarily when implemented with the right OF methodology.

Table 2. Evaluation of the proposed RGB+OF fusion model with SOTA OF methods.

Method	Precision	Recall	mAP@0.5	mAP@0.5:0.95
RGB-only	*54.24*	*61.23*	*57.85*	*46.15*
RGB+RAFT	56.59	69.95	64.66	57.47
RGB+GMA	56.11	70.07	64.84	57.88
RGB+KPA	56.88	68.27	65.25	58.45
RGB+SKF	**58.04**	**71.61**	**66.98**	**59.47**
RGB+FlowFormer	56.98	68.07	64.40	57.77

For a more detailed analysis of the impact of OF integration, we present class-specific Average Precision (AP) results. As illustrated in Fig. 4, the RGB+SKF combination outperforms the RGB-only approach for most gesture classes. For example, the "Point" gesture, one of the fundamental human-computer interactions, witnesses a 5% increase in AP when augmented with SKF. Similarly, more complex gestures like "2click" and "Zoom-in" observe substantial improvements of more than 10% and 15%, respectively. However, for a couple of classes, such as "Th-down" and "Open-2", the RGB+SKF does not achieve top results.

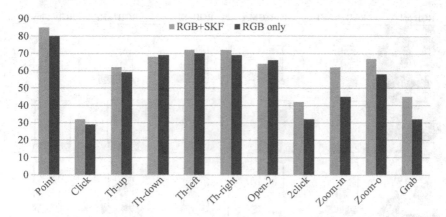

Fig. 4. Class-AP comparison between RGB+SKF and RGB-only methods.

Still, these differences are minimal, suggesting the overall positive impact of the RGB+OF fusion. This detailed analysis reinforces the importance of blending motion information, particularly when recognizing gestures with complex motions.

Figure 5 presents qualitative results of gesture recognition capabilities across different methods. The static nature of RGB-only makes it challenging to discern the gestures in the first three examples, making the integration of RGB+OF vital. Most RGB+OF approaches converge in their predictions, particularly for 'Zoom-o' and 'Zoom-in' gestures. Nevertheless, discrepancies arise in the third and fourth examples, highlighted by RGB-only's 'Grab' misclassification and the spurious gestures detected by GMA and FlowFormer due to the user's head movements. Interestingly, FlowFormer's representation in the occluded-hand scenario of the first example leans towards image appearance rather than actual motion. This figure highlights the importance of accurately detecting motion to improve gesture recognition in RGB+OF methods.

5.4   Ablation Study

Finally, we conducted an ablation study to explore the effectiveness of different fusion methods in our RGB+OF framework. Table 3 presents the comparative results, where the baseline RGB-only model serves as a reference. The initial attempt to integrate OF using 2DConvs exhibited a drop in precision but an increase in the remaining metrics. However, the transition to 3DConvs displayed evident advantages. A single layer of 3DConv brought significant improvements in mAP over the RGB-only baseline, with negligible computational overhead. Our proposed method, which incorporates two layers of 3DConvs ($3Dconv_{2layers}$), achieves the highest recall and nearly the best mAP@0.5 with just a marginal increase in parameters and GFLOPs. Further, adding a CSP-3D block increased the precision but also added considerable computational burden, increasing the GFLOPs by 11.3 compared to our proposed

RGB only   RGB+RAFT   RGB+GMA   RGB+KPA   RGB+SKF   RGB+FlowForm

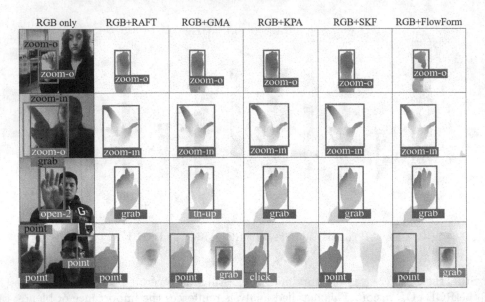

Fig. 5. Qualitative results of HGRL and the corresponding optical flow representations.eps

model. Notably, the increase in GFLOPs for our models is negligible when considering the computational requirements of optical flow estimators. This accentuates that most of the computation lies in the OF estimation and not in the fusion technique itself, making our choices in model design effective and efficient.

Table 3. Ablation study of different fusion approaches.

Method	Params	GFLOPs	Precision	Recall	mAP@0.5
RGB-only	*7.05*M	*16.1*	*54.24*	*61.23*	*57.85*
2Dconv	7.06M (+0.01)	16.8 (+0.7)	47.78	68.99	60.42
3Dconv$_{1layer}$	7.06M (+0.01)	16.8 (+0.7)	57.11	69.83	65.49
3Dconv$_{2layers}$	7.10M (+0.05)	17.2 (+1.1)	58.04	**71.61**	66.98
3D$_{2layers+CSP-3D}$	7.24M (+0.19)	27.4 (+11.3)	**58.36**	71.36	**67.02**

6 Conclusion

In this paper, we explored the integration of Optical Flow (OF) into RGB-based hand gesture recognition and localization. We found that our YOLO-based architecture with RGB+OF 3DConv fusion consistently surpassed the RGB-only baseline, especially when fused with SKF. Our ablation study highlighted the minimal computational overhead added by our fusion technique, emphasizing that the core computational cost lies in OF estimation. Qualitative results further illustrated challenges and potential areas for improvement. For future work, we aim to investigate loss functions that can penalize the RGB+OF contribution. Additionally, we intend to enrich temporal information by incorporating multiple Optical Flow representations.

References

1. Asadi-Aghbolaghi, M., et al.: A survey on deep learning based approaches for action and gesture recognition in image sequences. In: 2017 12th IEEE International Conference on Automatic Face & Gesture Recognition (FG 2017), pp. 476–483. IEEE (2017)
2. Benitez-Garcia, G., Olivares-Mercado, J., Sanchez-Perez, G., Yanai, K.: IPN hand: a video dataset and benchmark for real-time continuous hand gesture recognition. In: 2020 25th International Conference on Pattern Recognition (ICPR), pp. 4340–4347. IEEE (2021)
3. Butler, D.J., Wulff, J., Stanley, G.B., Black, M.J.: A naturalistic open source movie for optical flow evaluation. In: Fitzgibbon, A., Lazebnik, S., Perona, P., Sato, Y., Schmid, C. (eds.) ECCV 2012. LNCS, vol. 7577, pp. 611–625. Springer, Heidelberg (2012). https://doi.org/10.1007/978-3-642-33783-3_44
4. Elfwing, S., Uchibe, E., Doya, K.: Sigmoid-weighted linear units for neural network function approximation in reinforcement learning. Neural Netw. **107**, 3–11 (2018)
5. Geiger, A., Lenz, P., Urtasun, R.: Are we ready for autonomous driving? The kitti vision benchmark suite. In: 2012 IEEE Conference on Computer Vision and Pattern Recognition, pp. 3354–3361. IEEE (2012)
6. Guo, L., Lu, Z., Yao, L.: Human-machine interaction sensing technology based on hand gesture recognition: a review. IEEE Trans. Hum.-Mach. Syst. **51**(4), 300–309 (2021)
7. Hampiholi, B., Jarvers, C., Mader, W., Neumann, H.: Convolutional transformer fusion blocks for multi-modal gesture recognition. IEEE Access **11**, 34094–34103 (2023)
8. He, K., Zhang, X., Ren, S., Sun, J.: Spatial pyramid pooling in deep convolutional networks for visual recognition. IEEE Trans. Pattern Anal. Mach. Intell. **37**(9), 1904–1916 (2015)
9. Huang, Z., et al.: FlowFormer: a transformer architecture for optical flow. In: Avidan, S., Brostow, G., Cissé, M., Farinella, G.M., Hassner, T. (eds.) Computer Vision – ECCV 2022. ECCV 2022. LNCS, vol. 13677. Springer, Cham (2022). https://doi.org/10.1007/978-3-031-19790-1_40
10. Jiang, S., Campbell, D., Lu, Y., Li, H., Hartley, R.: Learning to estimate hidden motions with global motion aggregation. In: Proceedings of the IEEE/CVF International Conference on Computer Vision, pp. 9772–9781 (2021)
11. Jocher, G., et al.: ultralytics/yolov5: v3.0. https://github.com/ultralytics/yolov5/. Accessed 15 Feb 2023
12. Joze, H.R.V., Shaban, A., Iuzzolino, M.L., Koishida, K.: MMTM: multimodal transfer module for CNN fusion. In: Proceedings of the IEEE/CVF Conference on Computer Vision and Pattern Recognition, pp. 13289–13299 (2020)
13. Kopuklu, O., Kose, N., Rigoll, G.: Motion fused frames: data level fusion strategy for hand gesture recognition. In: Proceedings of the IEEE Conference on Computer Vision and Pattern Recognition Workshops, pp. 2103–2111 (2018)

14. Liu, S., Qi, L., Qin, H., Shi, J., Jia, J.: Path aggregation network for instance segmentation. In: Proceedings of the IEEE Conference on Computer Vision and Pattern Recognition, pp. 8759–8768 (2018)
15. Luo, A., Yang, F., Li, X., Liu, S.: Learning optical flow with kernel patch attention. In: Proceedings of the IEEE/CVF Conference on Computer Vision and Pattern Recognition, pp. 8906–8915 (2022)
16. Molchanov, P., Gupta, S., Kim, K., Kautz, J.: Hand gesture recognition with 3D convolutional neural networks. In: Proceedings of the IEEE Conference on Computer Vision and Pattern Recognition Workshops, pp. 1–7 (2015)
17. Molchanov, P., Yang, X., Gupta, S., Kim, K., Tyree, S., Kautz, J.: Online detection and classification of dynamic hand gestures with recurrent 3D convolutional neural network. In: Proceedings of the IEEE Conference on Computer Vision and Pattern Recognition, pp. 4207–4215 (2016)
18. Redmon, J., Farhadi, A.: YOLOv3: An incremental improvement. arXiv preprint arXiv:1804.02767 (2018)
19. Roitberg, A., Pollert, T., Haurilet, M., Martin, M., Stiefelhagen, R.: Analysis of deep fusion strategies for multi-modal gesture recognition. In: Proceedings of the IEEE/CVF Conference on Computer Vision and Pattern Recognition Workshops (2019)
20. Simonyan, K., Zisserman, A.: Two-stream convolutional networks for action recognition in videos. In: Advances in Neural Information Processing Systems, vol. 27 (2014)
21. Sun, S., Chen, Y., Zhu, Y., Guo, G., Li, G.: SKFlow: learning optical flow with super kernels. Adv. Neural. Inf. Process. Syst. **35**, 11313–11326 (2022)
22. Teed, Z., Deng, J.: RAFT: recurrent all-pairs field transforms for optical flow. In: Vedaldi, A., Bischof, H., Brox, T., Frahm, J.-M. (eds.) ECCV 2020. LNCS, vol. 12347, pp. 402–419. Springer, Cham (2020). https://doi.org/10.1007/978-3-030-58536-5_24
23. Wachs, J.P., Kölsch, M., Stern, H., Edan, Y.: Vision-based hand-gesture applications. Commun. ACM **54**(2), 60–71 (2011)
24. Wang, C.Y., Liao, H.Y.M., Wu, Y.H., Chen, P.Y., Hsieh, J.W., Yeh, I.H.: CSPNet: a new backbone that can enhance learning capability of CNN. In: Proceedings of the IEEE/CVF Conference on Computer Vision and Pattern Recognition Workshops, pp. 390–391 (2020)
25. Zengeler, N., Kopinski, T., Handmann, U.: Hand gesture recognition in automotive human-machine interaction using depth cameras. Sensors **19**(1), 59 (2019)
26. Zhang, W., Wang, J., Lan, F.: Dynamic hand gesture recognition based on short-term sampling neural networks. IEEE/CAA J. Automatica Sin. **8**(1), 110–120 (2020)

An Investigation of Video Vision Transformers for Depression Severity Estimation from Facial Video Data

Ghazal Bargshady(✉)[iD] and Roland Goecke[iD]

Human-Centred Technology Research Centre, Faculty of Science and Technology
University of Canberra, Canberra, Australia
{ghazal.bargshady,roland.goecke}@ieee.org

Abstract. Recognising depression from facial expressions and movements in video data using machine learning models has gained considerable attention in recent years. Researchers have explored various approaches and techniques to develop models capable of detecting
depression-related patterns in facial video data. Recently, *Video Vision
Transformers* have emerged as a powerful deep learning architecture for
analysing sequential data, such as video data. While vision transformers have primarily gained attention in computer vision tasks involving
images, their application to video analysis tasks, such as the recognition of depression or the estimation of depression severity from facial
video data, is an active area of research. In this paper, two different
architectures of vision transformers are used to capture spatio-temporal,
facial information relevant to estimating the severity of depression and,
thus, to provide valuable insights for depression analysis. The models are
trained and evaluated on the AVEC2013 and AVEC2014 datasets. The
results indicate that the fine-tuned vision transformers can outperform
earlier deep learning models in visual depression analysis, achieving a
Root Mean Square Error (RMSE) of 5.73 for the vision transformer and
5.39 for the video vision transformers, respectively.

Keywords: Facial Expressions · Depression Recognition · Video
Vision Transformers

1 Introduction

Clinical depression, also known as major depressive disorder (MDD), is a mental
health condition characterised by persistent feelings of sadness, lack of interest
or enjoyment in activities, and a variety of physical and emotional symptoms.
It is a prevalent and severe illness that influences a person's thoughts, emotions,
actions, and overall well-being. In addition to the impact on those who suffer
from depression and their families and friends, there is also a strong economic

This research is partially funded by the Australian Government through the Australian
Research Council's Discovery Projects funding scheme (project DP190101294).

impact due to reduced functioning in the workplace, absenteeism and healthcare costs. Timely identification and regular monitoring of individuals experiencing depression are crucial for receiving effective treatment. The diagnosis of clinical depression typically involves self-report interviews and evaluations conducted by trained professionals. However, these diagnostic approaches carry the risk of subjective biases since there are no definitive laboratory tests available. This limitation may have an impact on the accuracy of diagnosis and subsequent treatment.

Creating a reliable diagnostic aid for clinicians to objectively and precisely assess the severity of depression based on biomarkers, such as facial expressions, has been a benchmark task in affective computing. The use of deep learning techniques for recognising depression has gathered significant attention in recent times. Convolutional neural networks (CNN) and recurrent neural networks (RNN) are examples of deep learning models that have shown promise in analysing various forms of audio-vision data. Vision Transformers (ViT) as sequence-to-sequence deep learning models have achieved remarkable results in various computer vision tasks recently. However, research on the performance of vision transformers in depression analysis is still in its infancy at the time this paper was written.

Therefore, in this study, the performance of ViTs [6] and Video Vision Transformers (ViViTs) [3] for estimating the severity of depression from facial videos has been investigated. Vision transformer adapts the transformer architecture in [18] to process 2D images with minimal changes. In particular, ViT extracts N non-overlapping image patches, $x_i \in R^{h \times w}$, performs a linear projection and then rasterises them into 1D tokens $z_i \in R^d$. The sequence of tokens input to the following transformer encoder is $z = [z_c ls, Ex_1 Ex_2, \ldots, Ex_N] + p$ where the projection by E is equivalent to a 2D convolution. ViViT considers two simple methods for mapping a video $V \in R^{T \times H \times W \times C}$ to a sequence of tokens $z \in R^{n_t \times n_h \times n_w \times d}$. It adds the positional embedding and reshape into $R^{N \times d}$ to obtain z, the input to the transformer [3]. As shown in Fig. 1, a straightforward method of tokenising the input video is to uniformly sample n_t frames from the input video clip, embed each 2D frame independently using the same method as ViT, and concatenate all these tokens together.

Training has been carried out on the AVEC2013 and AVEC2014 datasets. The ViViT [3] model modifies and fine-tunes as ViViT-MDD trained and evaluated on two depression datasets to estimate the severity of depression for each subject. We achieve state-of-the-art performance for the RMSE and MAE metrics, demonstrating the potential of transformer models for automated depression analysis and laying the foundation for further research in this direction.

The contributions of this paper are:

1. We propose the first ViViT pipeline as ViViT-MDD for automated depression severity estimation.
2. We propose the first video vision transformer pipeline as ViViT-MDD for regression analysis.

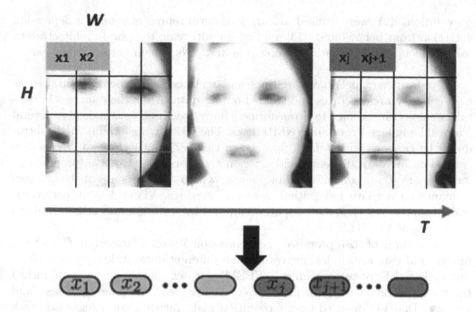

Fig. 1. ViViT samples n_t frames with embedding 2D frame following ViT.

3. We demonstrate competitive performance of both compared to prior work in depression recognition with ViViT-MDD achieving state-of-the-art performance for vision-based approaches.

2 Related Work

Currently, depression is the most prevalent mental health disorder worldwide. An effective depression recognition system is especially crucial for the early detection of depression and, thus, treatment. Different classic methods such as Partial Least-squares Regression [14], Motion History Histogram [15], Space-Time Interest Points (STIP) [5,11], Pyramid of Histogram of Gradients (PHOG) [4], and Local Gabor Binary Patterns from Three Orthogonal Planes (LGBP-TOP) [2] have been applied for depression analysis. The AVEC2013 baseline models were obtained using Local Phase Quantisation (LPQ) visual features and Support Vector Regression (SVR).

Several deep learning approaches have been developed to recognise depression severity levels from facial expressions. CNN-based methods are the most common. For example, Jan *et al.* [10] used a pre-trained VGG network to explore spatial information and feature dynamic history histograms (FDHH) to explore temporal information. [1] proposed to employ a 3DCNN (C3D) method to produce spatio-temporal features from facial videos at two different scales and a Recurrent Neural Network (RNN) to model transitions. [9] employed a Causal Convolutional Neural Network (C-CNN) to analyse 3D videos of facial landmarks. In [7], a Temporal Convolutional Network (TCN) and authors (dilated) convolutions [21] were utilised to learn long-term representations for depression detection from behaviours. [13] applied a multi-scale temporal architecture to solve the long-range variations problem in 3DCNNs, which outperformed earlier models.

Transformer models have been particularly successful when instantiated as high-capacity architectures and trained on big data. After their success in neural machine translation [18], transformers have been used as standard in several Natural Language Processing (NLP) tasks. The vision transformers model introduced by Dostovitskiy *etal.* [6] has shown that ViT outperforms CNN models trained on big data. Recently, video vision transformers have been proposed to model spatio-temporal information and shown to achieve state-of-the-art performance on activity recognition in several settings. ViViT has outperformed earlier approaches that model spatio-temporal information and other temporal extensions of ViT [3,8].

The authors of [20] proposed the Depression Vision Transformer (Dep-ViT) model to investigate clinical depression in a different dataset, known as the Voluntary Facial Expression Mimicry (VFEM) dataset containing seven mimicked facial expressions, namely neutral, anger, disgust, fear, happiness, sadness, and surprise. Dep-ViT focused on a recognition task, rather than a regression task as is described in this paper for estimating the depression severity.

3   Methods

In model design We follow the original Video Vision Transformers (ViViT) architecture of [3] as closely as possible and fine-tuned it on the depression data as ViViT-MDD.

3.1   Video Vision Transformer (ViViT)

The ViViT model extracts spatio-temporal tokens from the input video, which are then encoded by a series of transformer layers. The architecture of ViViT is illustrated in Fig. 2. This model is a straightforward extension of ViT [6] to capture the interaction between all spatio-temporal tokens and then develop more efficient variants, which factorise the spatial and temporal dimensions of the input video at various levels of the transformer architecture. It is a multiple transformer based model and Multi-Headed Self Attention (MSA) has quadratic complexity with respect to the number of tokens. This complexity is pertinent for video, as the number of tokens increases linearly with the number of input frames, and motivates the development of more efficient architectures next. In the proposed ViViT self-attention, the queries $Q = XW_q$, keys $K = XW_k$, and values $V = XW_v$ are linear projections of input X with $X, Q, K, V \in R^{N \times d}$.

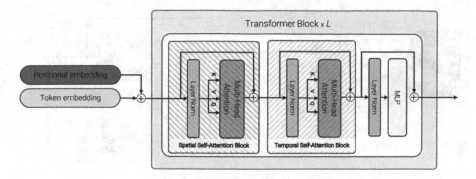

Fig. 2. Self-attention and transformer block of Video Vision Transformer introduced in [3].

3.2   Fine-Tuning and Resolution Changing

We fine-tuned ViViT [3] to ViViT-MDD as the follows:

We designed a depression detection pipeline utilising the ViT regression model as ViT-MDD to compare against the results of ViViT-MDD. The ViT-MDD model includes a patch encoder layer, positional embedding, transformer encoder, multi-headed self-attention (MSA), and multi-layer perceptron blocks [6]. ViTs' self-attention layer enables it to integrate information globally throughout the full picture. To recreate the visual structure from the training data, ViT-MDD learns to encode the relative placement of the patches. Self-attention has a quadratic cost as each pixel in the image is given as input, self-attention requires each pixel to pay attention to every other pixel. The input images resized to $128 \times 128 \times 3$, patch size $= 16$, 128 attention heads applied for a total of 3.903 million parameters. We applied attention block with heads $=8$ and dim-head$=32$ and dropout$=0.5$. In transformer block two attention block with a feedforward including two fully connected (FC) layers applies. we keep the patch size the same, which results in a larger effective sequence length and for number of class we applied one due to regression problem investigations. The Layer Norm is used before each block, which assists in reducing the training time and improving the generalisation performance. The proposed ViViT block model for depression recognition is shown in Fig. 3.

3.3   Datasets

Over the last decade, there has been a growing interest in automated depression analysis from facial expressions and movements. The Audio-Visual Emotion Challenge and Workshop in the years of 2013 [17] (AVEC2013) and 2014 [16] (AVEC2014) included a sub-challenge for estimating depression severity. In the following, a brief explanation of both databases is provided.

1. **AVEC2013 Depression Database**   [17]: The AVEC2013 Depression Database is a subset of the audio-visual depressive language corpus (AViD)

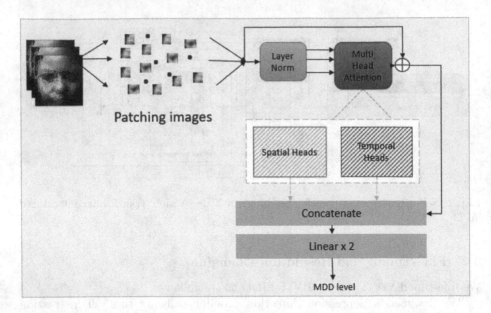

Patching images

Fig. 3. The proposed ViViT block model used for depression recognition

Corpus, comprising 150 videos from 82 German-speaking subjects. Data was collected by a webcam and a microphone between one and four times per subject over a period of two weeks. The subjects' average age is 31.5 years old at the time of recording. The video duration varies from 20 to 50 min, with an average of about 25 min. Video is recorded at 30 frames per second and with a spatial resolution of 640×480 pixels (RGB, 24 bits per pixel). The depression dataset was split into three predefined subsets (training, development, and test). Each subset contains 50 videos with a label to correspond to the subject's depression severity level.

2. **AVEC2014 Depression Database** [16]: The database used for the Audio-Visual Emotion Challenge 2014 consisted of a further subset of the AViD Corpus for the depression sub-challenge. The same subjects as in the AVEC2013 data appear, but data of two additional tasks known as *Freeform* and *Northwind* were provided. We used the *Freeform* subset for training and validation. In the first, the subjects respond to prompts such as discussing a sad childhood memory. In the second one, subjects read audibly an excerpt from a fable. In both tasks, the recordings are segmented into three partitions: training, development and test set. Each partition contains 50 videos that have a ground truth label. In total, there are 300 videos ranging in duration between 6 and 248 s. In line with the baseline paper of AVEC2014 [16], the *Northwind* data was ignored for the depression recognition as it was found that using only the *Freeform* data attained superior performance. Therefore, we perform experiments employing the training and development sets from the *Freeform* task as training data and the test sets are used to measure the performance

of the model. The data used in AVEC2014 again has three predefined subsets (training, development, and test), each consisting of 50 videos.

3.4 Experiments

The proposed deep learning regression models were implemented using the Python programming language (Version 3.9) and its popular PyTorch library. The ViT-MDD and ViViT-MDD models were trained, validated, and tested from scratch on a GPU with the CUDA version of PyTorch (1.10). The Adam opti-miser with an initial learning rate of 0.000001 is used for training the model. We extract video frames from the sequences by using the *CV2* module and then apply the *dlib* module for face detection and face cropping from the whole frames. We apply the Albumentations Python library for data pre-processing (e.g., resiz-ing, normalising). The performance of the models is measured by the Root Mean Squared Error (RMSE) and Mean Absolute Error (MAE) performance metrics for the regression loss calculation.

4 Results and Discussion

The obtained results of the ViViT-MDD proposed regression models for depres-sion recognition from facial expressions are presented in Table 1. Tables 2 and 3 show the depression severity estimation results of our proposed ViViT-MDD model pipeline compared to previous studies using standard deep learning mod-els and ViT [6] model.

Table 1. Performance of the ViViT-MDD models for depression severity estimation.

Models	Dataset	RMSE	MAE
ViT [6]	AVEC2013	7.53	6.95
ViT [6]	AVEC2014	5.73	5.2
ViViT-MDD	AVEC2013	7.34	6.64
ViViT-MDD	AVEC2014	5.39	4.8

Studies have shown that the regular analysis of patients' biomarkers would be useful for clinicians as a means to estimate the depression severity level to check on an individual's mental health wellbeing and to follow up on treatment progress if clinical depression was diagnosed and treated. Although there are several cues, which could be helpful in depression recognition (e.g., facial expression, vocal characteristics, heart rate variation), in this research project, we focused on facial expression vision cues in video format as an informative cue in clinical depression analysis. Earlier research studies in this domain focused on traditional models of feature extraction and the (binary) classification of depression levels. Recently, deep learning models, such as Convolutional Neural Networks and Recurrent

Table 2. Comparison of the results of the proposed ViViT-MDD models with previous deep learning models for video analysis on AVEC2013.

Models	Ref	RMSE	MAE
Baseline	[17]	13.61	10.88
LPQ-Top +SVR	[19]	10.27	8.22
Appearance-DCNN and Dynamics-DCNN	[23]	9.82	7.58
DepressNet	[13]	8.28	6.20
DRR-DepressionNet	[12]	8.08	6.18
MSN	[22]	7.90	5.98
ViT	[6]	7.53	6.95
ViViT-MDD	–	7.34	6.64

Table 3. Comparison of the results of the ViViT-MDD models with previous models on AVEC2014.

Models	Ref	RMSE	MAE
Baseline	[16]	10.86	8.86
Appearance-DCNN and Dynamics-DCNN	[23]	9.55	7.47
DepressNet	[22]	8.39	6.21
DRR-DepressionNet	[12]	8.01	6.14
MSN	[13]	7.61	5.82
ViT	[6]	5.73	5.2
ViViT-MDD	–	5.39	4.8

Neural Networks, have been successful in various video analysis tasks, but still, deep neural networks require improvements for an effective analysis of visual cues such as facial expressions and movements. Recently, vision transformers including video vision transformers, were introduced for video sequences analysis and outperformed standard deep learning models in video sequences analysis.

The results of the algorithms in our study, trained on the AVEC2013 and AVEC2014 datasets, indicate that both ViT-MDD and ViViT-MDD outperform the previous models. Moreover, the results show that ViViT-MDD's performance was better than ViT [6] for both datasets. While the differences in the performance metrics for ViT and ViViT-MDD are not high, ViViT-MDD was significantly faster in the computation than ViT introduced in [6]. Therefore, we could conclude that ViViT-MDD is more efficient than ViT and requires fewer computational resources than ViT.

In this study, we proposed a new pipeline for estimating the depression sever-ity from facial video data based on ViViT [10] as ViViT-MDD. To the best of our knowledge, this is the first time that such models have been used for depression severity estimation from facial expression video data to find relevant information in spatio-temporal scales of depression face video data.

5 Conclusion

In this research study, we trained and evaluated vision transformer algorithms, including ViT [6] and ViViT-MDD, on the task of depression severity esti-mation from facial video data. The results show the trained vision transformer models outperform earlier models on the AVEC2013 and AVEC2014 datasets. Future work will focus on the generalisation of the models to other depression, emotion, and pain datasets. A limitation of the study is the limited availability of depression video data, ideally clinically validated, which is generally a chal-lenge in the field of affective computing. This includes limited multimodal (i.e., audio, video, text, physiological signals) data to learn comprehensive depression representations for improved analysis.

References

1. Al Jazaery, M., Guo, G.: Video-based depression level analysis by encoding deep spatiotemporal features. IEEE Trans. Affect. Comput. **12**(1), 262–268 (2018)
2. Almaev, T.R., Valstar, M.F.: Local gabor binary patterns from three orthogonal planes for automatic facial expression recognition. In: 2013 Humaine Association Conference on Affective Computing and Intelligent Interaction, pp. 356–361. IEEE (2013)
3. Arnab, A., Dehghani, M., Heigold, G., Sun, C., Lučić, M., Schmid, C.: Vivit: a video vision transformer. In: Proceedings of the IEEE/CVF International Conference on Computer Vision, pp. 6836–6846 (2021)
4. Bosch, A., Zisserman, A., Munoz, X.: Representing shape with a spatial pyramid kernel. In: Proceedings of the 6th ACM International Conference on Image and Video Retrieval, pp. 401–408 (2007)
5. Cummins, N., Joshi, J., Dhall, A., Sethu, V., Goecke, R., Epps, J.: Diagnosis of depression by behavioural signals: a multimodal approach. In: Proceedings of the 3rd ACM International Workshop on Audio/Visual Emotion Challenge, pp. 11–20 (2013)
6. Dosovitskiy, A., et al.: An image is worth 16x16 words: transformers for image recognition at scale. In: Proceedings of the International Conference on Learning Representations (ICLR) (2021)
7. Du, Z., Li, W., Huang, D., Wang, Y.: Encoding visual behaviors with attentive temporal convolution for depression prediction. In: 2019 14th IEEE International Conference on Automatic Face & Gesture Recognition (FG 2019), pp. 1–7. IEEE (2019)
8. Fiorentini, G., Ertugrul, I.O., Salah, A.A.: Fully-attentive and interpretable: vision and video vision transformers for pain detection. arXiv preprint arXiv:2210.15769 (2022)

9. Haque, A., Guo, M., Miner, A.S., Fei-Fei, L.: Measuring depression symptom severity from spoken language and 3d facial expressions. arXiv preprint arXiv:1811.08592 (2018)

10. Jan, A., Meng, H., Gaus, Y.F.B.A., Zhang, F.: Artificial intelligent system for automatic depression level analysis through visual and vocal expressions. IEEE Trans. Cogn. Dev. Syst. **10**(3), 668–680 (2017)

11. Laptev, I., Marszalek, M., Schmid, C., Rozenfeld, B.: Learning realistic human actions from movies. In: 2008 IEEE Conference on Computer Vision and Pattern Recognition, pp. 1–8. IEEE (2008)

12. Li, X., Guo, W., Yang, H.: Depression severity prediction from facial expression based on the drr_depressionnet network. In: 2020 IEEE International Conference on Bioinformatics and Biomedicine (BIBM), pp. 2757–2764. IEEE (2020)

13. de Melo, W.C., Granger, E., Hadid, A.: A deep multiscale spatiotemporal network for assessing depression from facial dynamics. IEEE Trans. Affect. Comput. **13**(3), 1581–1592 (2020)

14. Meng, H., Huang, D., Wang, H., Yang, H., Ai-Shuraifi, M., Wang, Y.: Depression recognition based on dynamic facial and vocal expression features using partial least square regression. In: Proceedings of the 3rd ACM International Workshop on Audio/visual Emotion Challenge, pp. 21–30 (2013)

15. Meng, H., Pears, N.: Descriptive temporal template features for visual motion recognition. Pattern Recogn. Lett. **30**(12), 1049–1058 (2009)

16. Valstar, M., et al.: Avec 2014: 3d dimensional affect and depression recognition challenge. In: Proceedings of the 4th International Workshop on Audio/Visual Emotion Challenge, pp. 3–10 (2014)

17. Valstar, M., et al.: Avec 2013: the continuous audio/visual emotion and depression recognition challenge. In: Proceedings of the 3rd ACM International Workshop on Audio/Visual Emotion Challenge, pp. 3–10 (2013)

18. Vaswani, A., et al.: Attention is all you need. In: Advances in Neural Information Processing Systems, vol. 30 (2017)

19. Wen, L., Li, X., Guo, G., Zhu, Y.: Automated depression diagnosis based on facial dynamic analysis and sparse coding. IEEE Trans. Inf. Forensics Secur. **10**(7), 1432–1441 (2015)

20. Ye, J., Fu, G., Liu, Y., Cheng, G., Wang, Q.: Dep-ViT: uncertainty suppression model based on facial expression recognition in depression patients. In: Pimenidis, E., Angelov, P., Jayne, C., Papaleonidas, A., Aydin, M. (eds.) Artificial Neural Networks and Machine Learning - ICANN 2022. ICANN 2022. LNCS, Part III, vol. 13531, pp. 113–124 Springer, Cham (2022). https://doi.org/10.1007/978-3-031-15934-3_10

21. Yu, F., Koltun, V.: Multi-scale context aggregation by dilated convolutions. In: 2016 Proceedings of International Conference on Learning Representations, pp. 1–13 (2016)

22. Zhou, X., Jin, K., Shang, Y., Guo, G.: Visually interpretable representation learning for depression recognition from facial images. IEEE Trans. Affect. Comput. **11**(3), 542–552 (2018)

23. Zhu, Y., Shang, Y., Shao, Z., Guo, G.: Automated depression diagnosis based on deep networks to encode facial appearance and dynamics. IEEE Trans. Affect. Comput. **9**(4), 578–584 (2017)

Real-Time Automated Body Condition Scoring of Dairy Cows

Jia-Hong Lai[1], Fay Huang[1]([✉])(iD), Yi-Hsin Yeh[2], Kuo-Hua Lee[2],
Kuo-Kai Cheng[3], and Chao-Chien Chen[3]

[1] Department of Computer Science and Information Engineering,
National Ilan University, Yilan, Taiwan
`fay@niu.edu.tw`
[2] Livestock Research Institute, Council of Agriculture, Executive Yuan, Taipei,
Taiwan
[3] Smartagri Integration Service Co., Ltd., Taipei, Taiwan

Abstract. Traditional management and farming of dairy cows have
relied primarily on human labor and experience. However, this approach
has limitations such as the lack of real-time monitoring and predictive
capabilities. With the emergence of technologies such as artificial intelligence and internet of things, new solutions have been provided for these
challenges. To enhance dairy cow productivity, this paper proposes a
deep learning approach for real-time automated body condition scoring
of dairy cows. Two convolutional neural network models were proposed.
By analyzing each frame of video footage captured by a remote monitoring system, the first model determines whether the image contains
the characteristic features of the cow's hindquarters. The second model
evaluating the extracted hindquarter features to estimate the body condition score of the cow. The experimental results demonstrate that the
proposed approach can detect cows in the video footage in real time and
provide the corresponding body condition scores with an accuracy above
90% satisfactory for practical applications.

Keywords: Body Condition Score · Smart Agriculture · Dairy
Farming · Deep Learning

1 Introduction

The world is currently facing a loss of agricultural labor force. According to the
Food and Agriculture Organization of the United Nations (FAO), the global agricultural workforce in year 2020 decreased by 166 million people (i.e., 13% of the
global employment population) compared to year 2000 [5]. While facing the con-
tinuing labor shortages, traditional agriculture and especially animal husbandry
must incorporate technology from various fields to undergo transformation and

This project was mainly supported by Smartagri Integration Service, Taipei, Taiwan.
Additionally, it was partially supported by Ministry of Science and Technology Program, Taiwan, with grant number MOST 111-2221-E-197-022-MY2.

upgrading. Smart agriculture has emerged as the epitome of this transformation, utilizing robotics for harvesting, drones for pesticide spraying, and incorporating sensing, identification, Internet of Things (IoT), and blockchain technologies to automate farm management. This kind of transformation and upgrading replaces labor-intensive work towards intelligence and efficiency.

Dairy products, or milk-based food, are among the most consumed products globally, leading to a significant demand for milk production. This places pressure on dairy farmers to increase milk yield and optimize milk quality to meet commercial demands. Therefore, maintaining the physiological health of dairy cows becomes a critical task to achieve optimal milk production. The physical appearance of cows reflects their physiological condition, and experts can assess their current state by examining specific characteristics in the hindquarter region of the cows. This assessment helps determine whether a cow needs to be removed from the milk production, thereby maintaining the cow's health and milk quality. Traditionally, farmers relied on manual observation and identification of livestock's physiological conditions, which incurred substantial labor costs and time, especially on large-scale farms. Recently, in the awareness of smart livestock farming, farmers can use various sensing devices to monitor the physiological conditions of livestock. It greatly increases the production capacity of large farms without increasing the need for more manpower.

Body Condition Score (BCS) is a scoring system based on the physical condition of dairy cows. It is closely related to their productivive performace [10]. If cows do not reach the desired score, they may face calving difficulties, postpartum metabolic diseases, and low milk production [3]. The BCS serves as a rapid indicator of a cow's physical health and assists farmers in making decisions regarding livestock management [6]. The scoring criteria may vary among countries, but generally, lower values indicate thinness while higher values indicate obesity [11]. The BCS ranges from 1 to 5, with a 0.25 interval, and experts assess it by observing the back, loin, tailhead region, and pelvic area of the cows [4]. However, the subjective nature of BCS assessment often requires multiple experts to discuss their obervations in order to reach a consensus, making it a time-consuming process. Hence, there is a need to develop a system to achieve high accuracy, automatic, real-time, and low cost BCS determination.

The objective of this paper is to design a real-time automated system for evaluating the BCS of dairy cows to replace the traditional expert-based manual assessment approach. By installing cameras along the pathway from resting area to the milking parlor in the farm, cow's hindquarters images can be captured, and the BCS can be obtained based on image features appeared in cow's hip region such as characteristics of pin bone and hook bone. The develped BCS system must be able to achieve a recognition accuracy rate higher than 90% in order to meet the practical applications. This preliminary assessment will help farmers determining the cows' health status. An immediate alert can be triggered to prevent them from entering the milking parlor, becasue milk from unhealthy cows is not suitable for consumption and must be discarded. Mixing such milk with the milk from healthy cows would require the disposal of the entire batch, leading to more significant economic losses. One of the main purposes of this study is to prevent such scenarios from occurring.

2 Related Work

Zin et al. [12] introduced a method using geometric image features for automate BCS assessment utilizing dataset provided by Azzaro et al. [2]. The method achieved accurate BCS evaluation by measuring the similarity between the extracted geometric features of input images and those in a dataset. The method was tested on ten images, and all of them obtained correct BCS values. This study shows that using geometric features to estimate BCS is an effective appraoch. Most of the BCS assessment researches before year 2018 emphasising the use of image processing and machine learning techniques. Starting from this point, some scholars have started to explore the application of artificial neural network models to address the issue of BCS assessment.

Alvarez et al. [1] proposed a BCS system taking into account the depth information of cows captured by Microsoft's Kinect V2 device, edge features of the input images by Canny algorithm, and spatial frequency features of the images by Fourier Transformation. Then, the SqueezeNet [7] model was trained and used for predicting the BCS value. The accuracy of the system reached 40% when no score error was allowed. However, when score errors of ± 0.25 and ± 0.50 were permitted, the accuracy increased to 78% and 94% , respectively, indicating the system's good performance compared to other existing systems at that time. This study demonstrates that convolutional neural networks (CNN) have good potential for solving the BCS assessment task.

Çevik et al. [3] proposed an image segmentation and BCS assessment method using deep learning techniques. The method utilized existing models including AlexNet [8], VGG16, and VGG19 [9] through transfer learning and segmenting the desired image regions for BCS evaluation. The accuracy of the models ranged from 60% to 67.39%, with VGG19 achieving the highest accuracy. Although the accuracy did not reach the desired standard for practical use, the results demonstrated the presence of useful hidden characteristics in the images for BCS determination without accompanying any additional inforamaiton, such as depth. In other words, normal cameras is enough to complete this task, no other special imaging equipment is needed.

3 Body Condition Scoring Approach

The main focus of this paper is to develop a real-time automated method for determining the BCS of dairy cows from the farm's surveillance camera system. While designing a single model and training it to make BCS estimation for camera images appears to be an intuitive approach. However, due to the complexity of real-world scenarios, including variations in on-site lighting conditions, workers, livestock species, and non-targeted parts of cows, such as the head, abdomen,

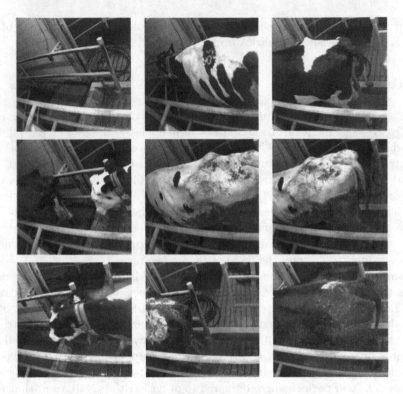

Fig. 1. Training image examples of hip region detection model. The first and the second columns are examples of negative images, which includes background, head, incomplete hindquarters, etc. The third column are examples of positive images.

or incomplete hindquarters, achieving sufficient accuracy in practical applications with a single model requires an extensive training dataset. Unfortunately, academic institutions often face resource constraints, making it challenging to obtain a sufficiently large and well-annotated training dataset. As a result, this paper sugested splitting the BCS scoring task into two steps. The proposed system is composed of two recognition models: the hip region detection model and the body condition scoring model. The reason for dividing the system into two parts is to simplify the objectives of each model in order to increase the accuracy of the overall task.

3.1   Hip Region Detection Model

The goal of hip region detection model is to determine if the input image contains a complete hindquarters of a cow. This would be a binary classification problem. Some labled training images are shown in Fig. 1. A novel hip region detection model has been designed based on the essence of AlexNet and VGG structure. A great effort was made to maintaining the model's recognition accuracy while

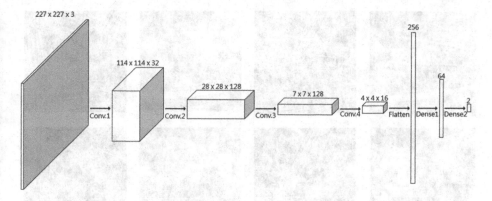

Fig. 2. Structure of the hip region detection model.

reducing the total number of model parameters. Eventually, the final model, as shown in Fig. 2, includes four convolutional layers and two fully connected layers. The detailed architecture of the proposed hip region detection model is described below.

The input images for the model are three-channel 227 × 227 color images. Therefore, input size of the model is 227 × 227 × 3. Convolutional layer 1 (conv2d) uses 32 convolutional kernels of size 5 × 5, resulting in a feature map size of 114 × 114 × 32. The ReLU activation function is applied, followed by a pooling layer (MaxPooling2D) with size of 3 × 3 and strides of 2 to compress the image and preserve important features. Convolutional layer 2 (conv2d_1) uses 128 convolutional kernels of size 5 × 5, resulting in a feature map size of 28 × 28 × 128. Similar to the previous layer, ReLU activation and pooling are applied. Convolutional layer 3 (conv2d_2) uses128 convolutional kernels of size 3 × 3 resulting in a feature map size of 7 × 7 × 32. Unlike the previous layer, only the ReLU activation is applied without pooling. Convolutional layer 4 (conv2d_3) uses 16 convolutional kernels of size 3 × 3, resulting in a feature map size of 4 × 4 × 16. Similar to the previous layer, only the ReLU activation is applied. The output is flattened and used for the transition from convolutional layers to fully connected layers. Fully connected layer 1 (dense) uses 64 neurons, applying the ReLU activation function, and using Dropout for regularization. Dropout is a regularization method that randomly drops hidden layer neurons during training to avoid over-reliance on specific neurons and prevent overfitting. Fully connected layer 2 (dense_1) uses 2 neurons, applying the Softmax activation function to output the probabilities of the two classes.

The objective of this model is to achieve a recognition accuracy of over 90% with the minimum number of parameters. As a result, the propsoed model has approximately 280,000 parameters, which is much less compared to the original AlexNet and VGG models with over few million parameters. The hip region detection model was trained using a dataset consisting of approximately 1,400 images. The dataset includes 460 positive images and 920 negative images. A

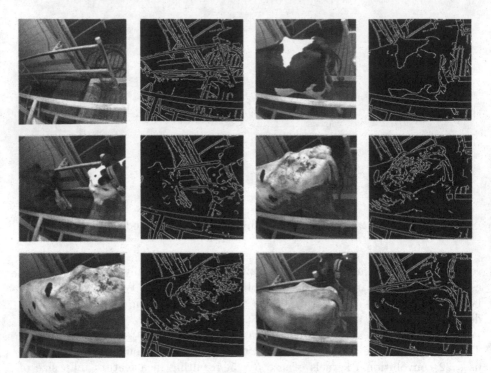

Fig. 3. Examples of the training images. First column illustrates three cases of negative images, they are either background only, head region of cow, or incomplete hindquarter region. Second column shows the corresponding edge images after applying Canny edge detection. Third column illustrates various positive images of hindquarter region of dairy cows. Last column are their corresponding edge images.

separate test set of 50 images were used to evaluate the recognition accuracy. During training, the model achieved an average recognition accuracy of around 90% on the validation image set. However, when testing on the 50 unseen test images, the accuracy was only around 65% on average. This accuracy does not meet the requirement for the real-world application.

The low accuracy of the model may be attributed to the limited number of color images in the dataset. Additionally, the cows' skin color is diverse, ranging from black and white to completely yellow. Even among black and white cows, each individual has unique patterns on their skin. Furthermore, some cows in the farm may have dirt on their bodies, which can pose challenges for the model's learning process. These factors limit the availability of representative samples for the model to learn the distinctive features for hip region recognition.

To mitigate the impact of variations in cattle coat color and stains on image recognition, grayscale conversion and Canny edge detection were employed. The original images were converted to grayscale, and the Canny algorithm was applied to extract edge features (Fig. 3). This approach emphasizes edge information while excluding color variations and background complexities that may affect the recognition task. The Canny edge detection algorithm is a comprehensive method for edge detection. It utilizes a Gaussian filter to suppress noise, calculates image gradients using Sobel filters to identify edges, performs non-maximum suppression to select the maximum gradient values and corresponding edge directions, and applies double thresholding to detect edges. The thresholds can be adjusted based on image characteristics and requirements, providing flexibility in the process.

When the input images were substituted by grayscale edge images, the input layer of the abovementioned model (Fig. 2) has been adjusted accordingly, and the rest of the network structure remained unchanged. The total parameter count for the modified model is reduced by approximately 1,000 compared to the previous color-image version. More experimental results will be reported in Sect. 4.

3.2 Dairy Cow Body Condition Scoring Model

In the second stage, the task of body condition scoring model is to assess the cow's hindquarter region in the input image and give an estimated BCS for the cow accoring to its pin and hook bone features. The hindquarter of the cow is assumed clearly presented in each of the input images at this stage. The values of BCS fall within the range of 1 to 5 points, with intervals of 0.25 points. Consequently, values such as 1.15 points or 3.05 points are not possible. The avaiable labled training images are shown in Table 1. Currently, there is no image data of scores lower than 1.75 and higher than 4.25, due to the fact that these are rare extreme situations. Therefore, our BCS model focuses on estimating score within range [1.75, 4.25]. The purpose of scoring is to determine the current physical condition of the cows, assist farmers in maintaining the health of cows on the farm, and ensure the quality of milk production.

The body condition scoring task differs from the binary classification of hip region detection as it belongs to multi-class classification. (Note taht since the traditional BCS visual inspection evaluation method is based on decision trees, the scoring results have an interval of 0.25, and there is no intermediate value, so our method adopts a classification method.) Therefore, more distinguishing features are required for accurate classification. Therefore three-channel color images are used in this body condition scoring model. Currently, some BCS categories are lack of training data, therefore the cow's body condition scores are divided into 11 categories. The number of images for each category is reported in Table 1. Image augmentation technique has been applied to increase the training dataset. Here, five-degree image clockwise and counter-clockwise rotations are employed to augment the training images. Small numbers of images were deleted after rotation if the hindquarter region of the cow was no longer clearly presented.

The design of body condition scoring model for dairy cows is based on the hip region detection model with only a few modifications, as shown in Fig. 4. The modifications include the input, output, and the removal of one convolutional layer. The proposed body condition scoring model consists of three convolutional

Table 1. Dataset for BCS model training.

BCS	Number of Images before Augmentation	Number of Images after Augmentation
1.75	39	81
2.00	49	144
2.25	36	108
2.50	48	144
2.75	58	164
3.00	66	192
3.25	64	190
3.50	56	110
3.75	36	108
4.00	55	161
4.25	47	138
Sum	554	1,540

layers and two fully connected layers. The detailed network architecture of the model isdescribed below.

Input image size is $227 \times 227 \times 3$ for color images. Convolutional Layer 1 (conv2d) employs 32 convolutional kernels of size 5×5, resulting in a feature map size of $114 \times 114 \times 32$. It applies the ReLU activation function to discard negative values and includes a pooling layer to compress the image and retain features. The size of the max pooling layers is consistently set to 3×3 with a stride of 2. Convolutional Layer 2 (conv2d_1) uses 128 convolutional kernels of size 5×5, generating a feature map size of $28 \times 28 \times 128$. Similar to conv2d_1, it includes the ReLU activation function and pooling layer to discard negative values and compress the image. Convolutional Layer 3 (conv2d_2) utilizes 128 convolutional kernels of size3×3, producing a feature map size of $7 \times 7 \times 32$. Unlike the previous layer, it only applies the ReLU activation function to discard negative values. The output is flattened into a vector for transitioning from convolutional layers to fully connected layers. Fully Connected Layer 1 (dense) consists of 64 neurons for fully connected connections. The ReLU activation function is applied, and Dropout regularization is utilized. Fully Connected Layer 2 (dense_1) comprises 11 neurons for fully connected connections. The Softmax activation function is applied to output the probabilities of the 11 categories. The total parameter count is 654,731, which is significantly higher compared to the hip region detection model. The increase in parameter count is due to the difference in classification objectives between the two models.

4   Experimental Results

Currently, there are approximately 20 dairy cows in the experimental field. The number of dairy cows fluctuates slightly due to the replacement of cows during the start or end of the lactation period. The images in the training dataset were

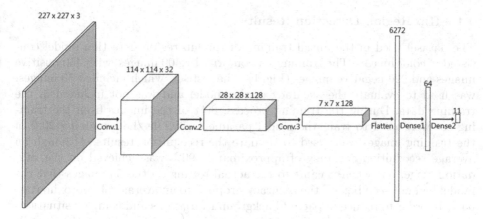

Fig. 4. Structure of the body condition scoring model.

collected in various months of the year 2022. Besides the black and white spotted cows, there are also cows with a uniform yellow-brown color.

During the experiment, three issues were observed. Firstly, there were variations in brightness and darkness when cows entered the scene. Secondly, fast movement of the cows resulted in blurry images. Lastly, there was a high level of data redundancy in the surveillance footages.

The variation in image brightness is caused by the white balance function of the camera itself. White balance corrects the color tone of photos taken under various lightings such as different sunlight conditions of a day. As a result, there was a significant color difference between the training images. Therefore, a fixed overhead light source was added to reduce color differences between images in the surveillance footages.

The blurriness in the images was caused by the fast movement of cows after entering the camera field of view. The camera captures 30 frames per second and does not have the capability to capture high frame rate videos. Cameras with normal frame rates do not capture as much detailed information per second as high frame rate cameras, making fast-moving objects appear blurry. Two possible solutions were considered for this issue. One option was to replace the camera with a high frame rate camera. The other option was to slow down the movement of cows. Eventually, the latter approach was chosen, and a gate was installed at the end of the milking pathway. When cows reached the gate, they would pause briefly, allowing the camera to capture clearer images.

The high level of data redundancy was due to videos consisting of a sequence of continuous images. Therefore, images captured within the same second often had high similarity or were nearly identical. High data redundancy in deep learning can have adverse effects on model training. To maintain the quality of training dataset, manual selection was employed to filter out highly similar images.

4.1 Hip Region Detection Results

The dataset used in the initial training of the hip region detection model consisted of color images. The training set comprised 1,400 images, with 460 positive images and 920 negative images (Fig. 1). The test set, which included 50 images, was used to evaluate the accuracy of the model and was not included in the training data. During the training process, 80% of the images from the training set were used to train the model parameters, while the remaining 20% of the training images were used to validate the recognition results. Although an average recognition accuracy of approximately 90% was achieved on the validation stage, but when it came to the actual testing on the 50 images that the model had not seen before, the accuracy dropped to an average of approximately 65%. In order to reduce impact of background variations and complex situations present in the original color images during training and to enhance the model's ability to extract relevant image features, an attempt was made to apply Canny algorithm to extract edge features. Consequently, edge images were used to train the hip region detection model (Fig. 3). During the training process, an average recognition accuracy of approximately 90% was achieved on the validation image set. Furthermore, when tested on the 50 images in the test set, the accuracy also reached an average of over 90%, as shown in Table 2. Those are the average accuracy over ten trials.

Table 2. Accuracy of hip region detection.

Training Data	Validation Accuracy	Testing Accuracy
Color Images	89.57%	64.2%
Edge Images	88.33%	90.2%

Besides the training and the testing image sets, the hip region detection model was also tested on actual surveillance videos. For a one-minute video with a frame rate of 30 frames per second, the model performed detection on each frame, resulting in a total of 1,786 frames being detected. The proposed model accurately captured the hip regions of every cow in the video, achieving a cow-hindquarter detection accuracy of almost 100%. This is because each cow produces more than 20 images of the hip region as it passes through the camera. So even though the hip region detection rate per frame is about 90%, we can almost 100% certain that each cow's hip region can be detected at least once. The average processing time of the program was 51.3 s, which is approximately 1.17 times faster than the length of the video. When performing detection while displaying image frames on the computer screen at the same time, the average processing time was slightly increased to 53.0 s, still 1.13 times faster than the length of the video. Therefore, the developed program can achieve the goal of real-time processing.

4.2   Body Condition Scoring Results

For the training of body condition scoring model, the training set consists of totally 1540 color images without any image enhancement (Table 1). 80% of the images from the training set were used to train the model parameters, while the remaining 20% of the training images were used to validate the recognition results. An additional 50 color images were used for testing. The validation image set achieved an average recognition accuracy of approximately 70%, as shown in Table 3. Testing yielded an average accuracy of approximately 70%. Since the scores assigned by experts are relatively subjective, there are often discrepancies among different experts. Therefore, during scoring, multiple experts typically engage in discussions, considering slight score variations as reasonable errors. In the body condition scoring model, scores falling within the range of ± 0.25 of the ground truth scores are considered correct judgments. If we consider the model's body condition score judgments to be correct if they fall within a range of positive or negative 0.25 compared to the ground truth provided by experts, then the accuracy increased to 95% in average.

Table 3. Accuracy of body condition scoring.

Training Accuracy	Testing Accuracy	Testing Accuracy(± 0.25)
71.95%	68.20%	95.40%

Two models were integrated to form a complete system for assessing the body condition of dairy cows in real-life surveillance videos. For an one-minute video, the processing speed of the program is slightly slower compared to solely detecting the hindquarter regions. Without displaying the real-time image frames, the average processing time is 54.9 s, which can still achieve the real-time processing standard. If image frames are simultaneously displayed on computer screen, the program achieves an average processing time of 60.0 s, approaching near-zero latency.

An issue was identified when testing the model on real-life surveillance video that the scores of a cow may vary between consecutive frames due to body movements or deviations in the viewing angle. Ideally, the body condition scores for the same cow should be consistent. To solve this issue, mode of the scores of the same cow was calculated. So far, there is no ground truth scores available for the testing videos, the purpose was to evaluate the real-time capability of the program instead of its recognition accuracy. A screenshot of the developed system is illustrated in Fig. 5. The hip region has been identified in this image frame and enclosed by red rectangle. The estimated BCS is shown on the top-left corner of the screen.

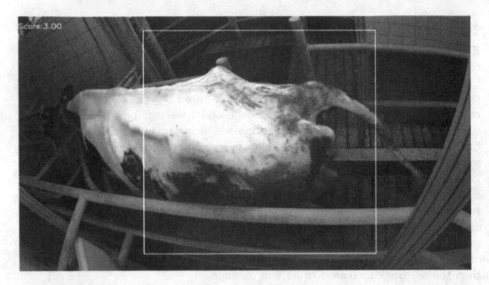

Fig. 5. A screenshot of the integrated system. The hip region has been identified in this image frame and enclosed by red rectangle. The estimated BCS is shown on the top-left corner of the screen. (Color figure online)

5   Conclusions and Future Work

Body condition scoring of dairy cows is an important and effective indicator for assessing their physical condition and health status. By monitoring real-time changes in cow body condition, farmers can make appropriate nutritional adjustments and implement health management measures to ensure milk production and productivity. In this paper, a real-time automated system for assessing the BCS of dairy cows was presented. By utilizing convolutional neural network learning technique, two novel recognition models were proposed. The first model detects the hip region of cows in each frame of the input video footage, and the second model provides estimation of their body condition scores.

Experimental results demonstrated that the hip region detection accuracy for an image is over 90%, and the recognition rate for each cow's hip region is almost 100%. The accuracy of body condition scoring is above 95% in average if resonable tolerance such as ±0.25 is allowed. Integrating the two aforementioned models into a real-time automated system for assessing the body condition of dairy cows, practical testing on on-site videos demonstrates the system's ability to achieve real-time recognition. Moreover, the recognition performance meets the accuracy requirement for practical applications.

Although the current method has reached practical application standards, there are still areas for improvement in the future. For example, the current body condition scoring method was tested using a single camera. In the future, integrating multiple camera angles and comparing scoring results could provide a more comprehensive assessment of cow body condition and enhance the reliability of the scoring evaluation. Moreover, regression approaches can be considered instead of classification methods for the BCS estimation.

References

1. Alvarez, J.R., et al.: Body condition estimation on cows from depth images using convolutional neural networks. Comput. Electron. Agric. **155**, 12–22 (2018)
2. Azzaro, G., et al.: Modeling cow body shape for objective estimation of body condition score from digital images. In: Proceedings of Joint Meeting of ADSA, CSAS and ASAS, Québec, Canada, July 2009
3. Çevik, K.K., Boğa, M.: Body condition score (BCS) segmentation and classification in dairy cows using R-CNN deep learning architecture. Eur. J. Sci. Technol. **17**, 1248–1255 (2019)
4. Ferguson, J.D., Galligan, D.T., Thomsen, N.: Principal descriptors of body condition score in holstein cows. J. Dairy Sci. **77**, 2695–2703 (1994)
5. Food, of the United Nations, A.O.: World Food and Agriculture - Statistical Yearbook 2020. Food and Agriculture Organization of the United Nations (FAO), Rome (2020)
6. Garnsworthy, P.: Body condition score in dairy cows: targets for production and fertility. Recent Adv. Anim. Nutr. **2006**(1), 61–86 (2006)
7. Iandola, F.N., Han, S., Moskewicz, M.W., Ashraf, K., Dally, W.J., Keutzer, K.: Squeezenet: alexnet-level accuracy with 50x fewer parameters and <0.5 mb model size (2016), https://arxiv.org/abs/1602.07360, cite arxiv:1602.07360Comment. In ICLR Format
8. Krizhevsky, A., Sutskever, I., Hinton, G.E.: Imagenet classification with deep convolutional neural networks. In: Pereira, F., Burges, C., Bottou, L., Weinberger, K. (eds.) Advances in Neural Information Processing Systems, vol. 25. Curran Associates, Inc. (2012)
9. Liu, S., Deng, W.: Very deep convolutional neural network based image classification using small training sample size. In: 2015 3rd IAPR Asian Conference on Pattern Recognition (ACPR), pp. 730–734 (2015). https://doi.org/10.1109/ACPR. 2015.7486599
10. Pryce, J.E., Coffey, M.P., Simm, G.: The relationship between body condition score and reproductive performance. J. Dairy Sci. **84**, 1508–1515 (2001)
11. Roche, J.R., Friggens, N.C., Kay, J.K., Fisher, M.W., Stafford, K.J., Berry, D.P.: Invited review: body condition score and its association with dairy cow productivity, health, and welfare. J. Dairy Sci. **92**, 5769–5801 (2009)
12. Zin, T.T., Tin, P., Kobayashi, I., Horii, Y.: An automatic estimation of dairy cow body condition score using analytic geometric image features. In: Proc. IEEE 7th Global Conference on Consumer Electronics (GCCE), pp. 775–776. Nara, Japan, October 2018

Logo-SSL: Self-supervised Learning with Self-attention for Efficient Logo Detection

Yilin Li$^{(\boxtimes)}$ ⓘ, Junke Xu$^{(\boxtimes)}$ ⓘ, and Alireza Dehghani$^{(\boxtimes)}$ ⓘ

CeADAR, Ireland's Centre for AI, University College Dublin, Dublin, Ireland
`yilin.li@ucd.ie`

Abstract. Logo detection is pivotal in various real-world applications, such as trademark protection, advertising analysis, image search, and copyright enforcement, enabling companies to protect their brand identity, gauge market influence, and enhance search and recommendation systems. However, traditional methods are constrained by their heavy reliance on manually annotated large-scale logo datasets, a labour-intensive, time-consuming process, and prone to variability. This paper introduces Logo-SSL, an innovative approach integrating self-supervised learning and self-attention mechanisms to advance logo detection. By leveraging unsupervised data for pre-training and incorporating self-attention, Logo-SSL transcends the limitations of traditional methods, achieving comparable logo detection accuracy and efficiency without the need for manual annotation. Experimental results, benchmarked against several other SSL pre-trained models, validate the hypotheses that SSL can attain performance similar to supervised learning and that training on logo-specific datasets outperforms general object datasets like ImageNet. Logo-SSL reduces labour costs and time and offers a practical, cost-effective, and scalable logo detection approach to more extensive and diverse real-world logo detection applications.

Keywords: Logo detection · Self-supervised learning · Self-attention mechanisms

1 Introduction

In recent years, with the ubiquity of logos in modern media, logo detection has become increasingly important. Automated detection and recognition of logos, with many applications, including trademark protection, advertising analysis, image search, and copyright enforcement, have enormous potential to provide valuable insights into consumer behaviour, brand perception, and advertising effectiveness [1]. Traditional methods for logo detection have relied on hand-crafted visual features, such as SIFT [7] and HOG [8], and traditional classification models, such as BoW [9]. However, these methods face limitations due to the small size of the dataset and the limited number of logo images and categories [2].

W. Q. Yan et al. (Eds.): PSIVT 2023, LNCS 14403, pp. 234–245, 2024.
https://doi.org/10.1007/978-981-97-0376-0_18

In the realm of computer vision, multiple tasks, including detection, localisation, classification, and identification, present distinctive challenges. Detection concerns itself with the task of identifying if an object (in this context, a logo) exists within an image. At the same time, localisation seeks to pinpoint the exact position of the detected object by typically providing bounding boxes. Classification, on the other hand, determines the category or class an object belongs to, distinguishing, for instance, between various logo brands. Identification goes a step further by not only classifying the object but also determining its individual identity within that class, akin to differentiating between specific versions or iterations of a logo. The problem of logo detection, which is our primary focus, combines elements of detection and localisation: it not only determines the presence of a logo in an image but also its exact location. This poses unique challenges, especially given the wide variety of logos, their potential for overlap with other graphical elements, and the myriad ways they can be presented in different media.

Deep learning-based approaches using convolutional neural networks have emerged as a promising solution for logo detection. Various methods, including the popular Faster R-CNN [10], have significantly improved logo detection performance. However, these methods require a large amount of labelled training data, which is time-consuming and expensive to obtain [2]. Despite their state-of-the-art results, existing methods like R-CNN have inherent limitations that make object detection a complex and computationally inefficient task [27]. Some methods are also overly reliant on hand-designed priors, which can limit their effectiveness and adaptability.

Self-supervised learning (SSL), one of the most promising ways to build background knowledge and approximate a form of common sense in AI systems[1], has successfully cut the requirement to expensive time and labour cost of labelling datasets. SSL has emerged as a promising approach in response to object detection challenges. It enables models to learn from unlabeled data by formulating pre-text tasks that exploit inherent patterns and structures within the data [3]. Pre-text tasks, such as jigsaw puzzles [11], colouring [12], instance recognition [13], and clustering [14], facilitate the capture of useful features and the learning of generic representations from unlabeled data. This approach reduces the dependency on extensive human-labelled annotations while still achieving performance outcomes comparable to or surpassing those attained by conventional supervised learning methods relying on large labelled datasets [4].

Moreover, attention mechanisms inspired by human visual attention have been widely employed in deep neural networks [5]. Self-attention mechanism, a specific attention mechanism, allows models to selectively focus on relevant parts of the input data and capture dependencies between features [6]. In the object detection context, the self-attention mechanism can guide the model to focus on the crucial features of objects, thereby enhancing the model's ability to detect and classify them [15] accurately.

---

[1] Yann LeCun, Chief AI Scientist at Meta.

Recent research has shown promising results by leveraging SSL and attention mechanisms in various computer vision tasks. For instance, the Self-Supervised Equivariant Attention Mechanism (SEAM) has been proposed to discover additional supervision and narrow the gap between full and weak supervision [16]. Moreover, the effectiveness of self-supervised learning as a pre-training strategy for medical image classification has been studied, introducing a novel Multi-Instance Contrastive Learning (MICLe) method that uses multiple images of the underlying pathology per patient case [26]. The integration of SSL with attention mechanisms, which is still an under-explored area in computer vision, is hypothesised to improve the logo detection approach performance.

Despite the advancements in logo detection, mostly through supervised learning approaches, its performance heavily depends on the size of the labelled dataset, making efficient logo detection systems not only resource-intensive but also not easily adaptable to new logo detection scenarios. Advancements in SSL and attention mechanisms motivate us to integrate them to overcome the limitations of traditional logo detection methods and improve the efficiency and accuracy of logo detection tasks.

Accordingly, our proposed Logo-SSL integrates self-supervised learning and self-attention mechanisms for logo detection, leveraging unlabeled data to learn meaningful representations without the need for human-labeled annotations. In our proposed approach, the model is initially SSL pre-trained on extensive logo unlabelled datasets to learn the general features of logos. Subsequently, the SSL pre-trained model is fine-tuned using other smaller, separate, annotated logo datasets. By incorporating the self-attention mechanism, the model can selectively focus on important parts of logo images, thereby improving the accuracy and robustness of logo detection. The use of a large unlabelled logo dataset rather than just general image datasets such as ImageNet is a key factor that sets this approach apart from others, as it provides the integration of SSL and self-attention to efficiently get a good grasp of logo images in our proposed Logo-SSL approach.

This paper aims to contribute to the field by demonstrating the potential of integrating SSL and self-attention mechanisms in logo detection tasks, particularly when applied to large datasets. The rest of this paper is outlined as follows: Sect. 2 presents the proposed algorithm. Evaluation and conclusions are discussed in Sects. 3 and 4, respectively.

2   Logo-SSL

The proposed Logo-SSL logo detection approach begins with the SSL pre-text task, i.e., pre-training the model, from scratch, on an extensive unlabelled logo dataset. This model is then fine-tuned using smaller, annotated datasets curated for logo detection. Integrating the self-attention mechanism allows the model to focus on crucial logo image parts, enhancing detection accuracy and robustness. Figure 1. shows the block diagram of our proposed Logo-SSL approach. In the following section, we will discuss the Logo-SSL stages in detail.

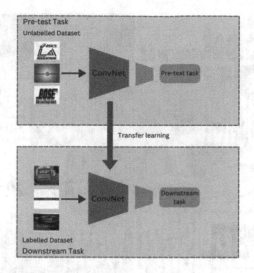

Fig. 1. The block diagram of our proposed Logo-SSL approach.

2.1 Pre-text and Downstream Tasks Dataset Preparation

To initiate the pre-training process of our SSL model from scratch, as outlined above, it's necessary to first compile a substantial dataset of unlabelled logo images with a high level of coverage and diverse logo categories. Instead of training the SSL model on general image datasets like ImageNet or utilising a pre-trained network, we create our own unlabelled logo dataset. The LogoDet-3K [17] dataset is a fully annotated collection of logo images comprising 158,652 manually annotated images from 3,000 unique logo categories. This dataset presents the most challenging benchmark for logo detection than other existing datasets due to its higher coverage of logo categories and annotated objects and greater diversity. Figure 2. provides a sample of the different classes of images from LogoDet-3K.

To clarify the process and address potential concerns: while the LogoDet-3K dataset provides annotations that allow us to identify and crop the logos, once these logos are extracted, the resulting dataset does not retain the original annotations. In this context, the labels used to identify bounding boxes are not employed to provide a direct supervised signal during the training of the SSL model. Instead, the bounding boxes are simply a preprocessing tool to extract regions of interest. Hence, the resulting dataset used for pre-training is "unlabelled" because it does not carry the original categorical annotations from LogoDet-3K.

To develop our unlabeled logo dataset for Logo-SSL pre-training and to improve the accuracy of the model's extracted features, we preprocess the LogoDet-3K images by cropping the logo patches based on their annotated bounding boxes, followed by resizing all the images to 224 × 224, as illustrated in Fig. 3. We generate this unlabelled logo dataset rather than training the SSL

Fig. 2. Image samples from LogoDet-3K

model on general image datasets such as ImageNet or even using a pre-trained network. This key factor sets the SSL-Logo approach apart from others, as it integrates SSL and self-attention to get a good grasp of logo images efficiently.

For the fine-tuning and testing stages, we select the FlickrLogos-32 [18], another prominent logo detection dataset, to comply with the idea that separate pre-training and fine-tuning datasets can benefit the result. FlickrLogos-32 comprises a carefully curated collection of images encompassing 32 logo classes spanning various industries and brands. Despite its smaller scale compared to LogoDet-3K, it still offers a rich and diverse set of images that can be effectively utilised for fine-tuning and testing the Logo-SSL approach.

2.2   Pre-text Task

The inspiration for Logo-SSL comes from two key needs in the field of deep learning: the ability to harness the power of vast amounts of unlabeled data and the capacity to model long-range dependencies within data. In the context of logo detection, these needs become particularly pronounced. There exists a plethora of images containing logos, yet these often lack specific labels at scale, indicating the logos' presence or location. Moreover, the critical features of a logo can be scattered across the image, necessitating a model that can discern relationships between distant but interconnected parts of the logo. Logo-SSL tackles these obstacles by enhancing the model's ability to identify logos under diverse conditions. This is achieved by learning robust features from vast unlabeled data, which we prepared from the LogoDet-3k dataset during the initial model training in the pre-text task.

Fig. 3. Examples of cropping annotated images as the pre-training dataset.

Logo-SSL employs a strategy known as contrastive clustering [14]. It leverages the foundation of SwAV, a prominent self-supervised learning technique, as its pre-text task. SwAV involves training the ResNet50 encoder [19] using multiple augmented views of the same image, treating them as different data views. Its primary objective is to maximise agreement between feature representations of these views while minimising agreement with representations of other random images in the dataset. This encourages the model to learn semantically meaningful features, effectively grouping similar images together in the learned feature space. To provide SwAV with augmented distinct views of the images, a series of pre-processing steps, including a diverse range of transformations, such as cropping, flipping, and colour jittering, are applied to the input cropped images prepared from the LogoDet-3k dataset.

To further enhance the performance of Logo-SSL, an additional self-attention mechanism is integrated into the pre-text task, which dynamically assigns weights to the embedding elements, emphasising the most relevant ones for accurate logo detection. This mechanism allows the model to concentrate on pertinent regions of the image, regardless of their location, while encoding visual data. This could potentially enhance the quality of the learned representations and result in more precise logo detection.

Overall, the Logo-SSL framework combines contrastive clustering with the self-attention mechanism and mutual prediction to learn invariant representations for logo detection. Logo-SSL effectively encodes and predicts representations across different views by clustering similar features and utilising the prototype matrix, leading to robust and accurate logo detection. Figure 4. illustrates the architecture of Logo-SSL.

Figure 4. illustrates the Logo-SSL training process, which starts with an input image undergoing various augmentations to prepare the model for diverse logo detection scenarios. The augmented images are transformed into embeddings

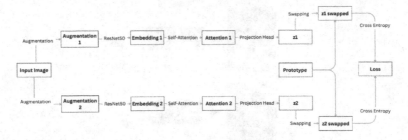

Fig. 4. The Logo-SSL approach's main architecture.

by an encoder, capturing essential visual information. Logo-SSL then applies a self-attention mechanism to these embeddings, dynamically weighting the most relevant elements for logo detection and focusing on significant logo features. These attended embeddings are processed through a projection head, mapping them onto a latent space to bring similar images closer. The model then employs a view-swapping strategy, which is represented as 'z1 swapped' and 'z2 swapped', enhancing generalisation and ensuring consistency across different logo perspectives. Minimising cross-entropy loss is involved between the view swaps and clustering assignments, facilitating class-based clustering and consistent logo detection. Thus, the comprehensive pipeline of Logo-SSL, incorporating attention-based processing and view swapping, provides a robust mechanism for capturing distinctive logo characteristics and enables highly reliable logo detection in various downstream tasks.

2.3   Downstream Task

The training process for the Logo-SSL model commenced with the SSL pre-training phase, utilising a ResNet-50 backbone for its exceptional ability to extract general visual features. Following this, the model enters the fine-tuning phase, where the network architecture is tweaked to enable the pre-trained model to better suit the logo detection task, thereby enhancing its effectiveness. These include the additional fully connected and convolutional layers, which aim to capture global information and learn spatial hierarchies of features respectively. In addition, Logo-SSL employs the Faster R-CNN framework implemented in Detectron2 [20], an efficient and modular implementation of Faster R-CNN. This widely used object detection model combines a region proposal network (RPN) and a region-based convolutional neural network (R-CNN). The architecture of Faster R-CNN is illustrated in Fig. 5.

By combining the strengths of the FlickrLogos-32 dataset, which provided labelled instances of logos for fine-tuning and evaluation, with the Faster R-CNN framework implemented in Detectron2, Logo-SSL is able to assess the effectiveness of our self-supervised learning approach in the context of logo detection. The dataset served as a valuable resource for training, evaluation, and benchmarking. At the same time, the Detectron2 framework facilitated the fine-tuning

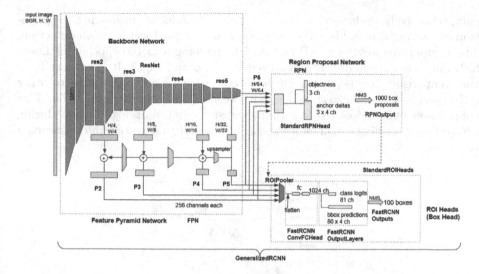

Fig. 5. A Faster R-CNN with Feature Pyramid Network. (Figure courtesy of Hiroto Honda. https://medium.com/@hirotoschwert/digging-into-detectron-2-47b2e794f abd.)

and testing processes, enabling us to analyse the performance and compare our results with other state-of-the-art methods in the field.

3   Evaluation

To assess the effectiveness of our proposed Logo-SSL approach, we employ the remaining 30% of the FlickrLogos-32 dataset, with the other 70% having been utilised during the fine-tuning phase. This subset is equally divided for validation and testing purposes. We use the fine-tuned model to carry out object detection on the test images, measuring its performance based on the accuracy of logo detection and the precision of localisation.

To evaluate the performance of our proposed Logo-SSL approach, we benchmarked it against several other SSL pre-trained models, such as Sela, deepCluster v2, SWaV, SimCLR v2, MoCo v1, and MoCo v2 [21]. These models, which are publicly accessible, were initially trained on the extensive ImageNet dataset using contrastive learning methods for SWaV, SimCLR v2, and MoCo v1/v2, and clustering-based techniques for Sela and deepCluster v2. We adapted these SSL models to our logo detection challenge by fine-tuning them with the identical 70% of the FlickrLogos-32 dataset we allocated for Logo-SSL fine-tuning. The objective was to capitalise on the inherent strengths of these SSL models, tailoring their pre-existing knowledge toward the task of logo detection.

In assessing the performance of object detection models, Average Precision (AP) and AP50 metrics are commonly used, and we have applied them to compare our approach with other SSL models mentioned earlier. Using AP and AP50 comprehensively evaluates an object detection model by measuring its precision at varying thresholds and effectiveness in general object location detection. The comparative results of AP and AP50, spanning 0 to 100 epochs, for Logo-SSL and other methods, are illustrated in Fig. 6 and Fig. 7. It is evident from the comparison that Logo-SSL outperforms in logo detection relative to other self-supervised learning techniques, with respect to both AP and AP50. This comparison underscores the fact that exclusive reliance on logo images during pre-test task training can enhance the accuracy of logo detection in downstream tasks.

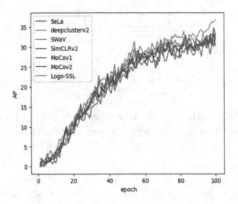

Fig. 6. AP Comparison of Self-Supervised Models.

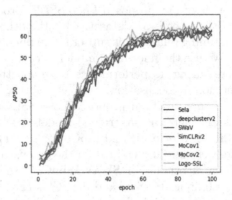

Fig. 7. AP50 Comparison of Self-Supervised Models.

To assess the ability of self-supervised learning to compete with the performance of supervised learning without relying on an extensive labelled dataset, we compare the performance of Logo-SSL with a supervised trained Faster-R-CNN model on the Logo-Det3K dataset. The AP and AP50 outcomes, as presented in Table 1, indicate that Logo-SSL can attain results comparable to supervised learning. Moreover, it surpasses the performance of SSL models trained on extensive but specific logo datasets, such as the ImageNet dataset.

Table 1. Comparison of different methods

Methods	Dataset	AP	AP50
Sela [22]	ImageNet	32.69	64.01
deepclusterv2 [14]	ImageNet	33.51	62.57
SWaV [14]	ImageNet	34.30	63.61
SimCLRv2 [23]	ImageNet	33.33	62.76
MoCov1 [24]	ImageNet	32.17	61.98
MoCov2 [25]	ImageNet	34.75	63.92
Logo-SSL(Ours)	Logo-Det3k	36.74	66.47
Faster R-CNN(Supervised)	Logo-Det3k	36.82	66.81

4   Conclusion

In this paper, we introduced Logo-SSL, a novel approach that combines self-supervised learning and self-attention mechanisms to improve logo detection. Two central hypotheses guided our work: 1) An SSL approach can achieve performance on par with supervised learning methods for logo detection, eliminating the need for labelled data and the costly labelling process and facilitating easy adaptation to new logo detection scenarios without creating labelled logo datasets. 2) SSL training on logo-specific datasets would surpass the use of pretrained SSL networks on general object datasets like ImageNet, even if they are comprehensive.

The experimental findings from this study justify our hypotheses, demonstrating that SSL, coupled with fine-tuning through a transfer learning approach, can attain reasonable performance, enhance adaptability, and reduce the need for extensive logo dataset creation. Logo-SSL achieves comparable logo detection accuracy and efficiency on large-scale logo datasets by learning rich and meaningful representations from unlabeled data coupled with a self-attention mechanism. Moreover, it significantly diminishes the labour and time associated with manual annotation. This makes it a practical and cost-effective solution for real-world applications.

Future research could explore more self-supervised learning techniques, integrate complex attention mechanisms, and investigate the transferability of learned representations to other visual recognition tasks. Examining the scalability of Logo-SSL to more extensive and diverse logo datasets could further substantiate its efficacy and potential for real-world implementation.

References

1. Li, K.W., Chen, S.Y., Su, S., Duh, D.J., Zhang, H., Li, S.: Logo detection with extendibility and discrimination. Multimedia Tools Appl. **72**(2), 1285–1310 (2014)
2. Bishop, C.M., Nasrabadi, N.M.: Pattern recognition and machine learning (Vol. 4, No. 4, p. 738). Springer, New York (2006)
3. Kolesnikov, A., Zhai, X., Beyer, L.: Revisiting self-supervised visual representation learning. In: Proceedings of the IEEE/CVF Conference on Computer Vision and Pattern Recognition, pp. 1920–1929 (2019)
4. Goyal, P., Mahajan, D., Gupta, A., Misra, I.: Scaling and benchmarking self-supervised visual representation learning. In: Proceedings of the IEEE/CVF International Conference on Computer Vision, pp. 6391–6400 (2019)
5. Rensink, R.A.: The dynamic representation of scenes. Vis. Cogn. **7**(1–3), 17–42 (2000)
6. Niu, Z., Zhong, G., Yu, H.: A review on the attention mechanism of deep learning. Neurocomputing **452**, 48–62 (2021)
7. Ng, P.C., Henikoff, S.: SIFT: predicting amino acid changes that affect protein function. Nucleic Acids Res. **31**(13), 3812–3814 (2003)
8. Wang, X., Han, T.X., Yan, S.: An HOG-LBP human detector with partial occlusion handling. In: 2009 IEEE 12th International Conference on Computer Vision, pp. 32–39. IEEE (2009)
9. Wu, X., Sahoo, D., Hoi, S.C.: Recent advances in deep learning for object detection. Neurocomputing **396**, 39–64 (2020)
10. Ren, S., He, K., Girshick, R., Sun, J.: Faster r-cnn: towards real-time object detection with region proposal networks. In: Advances in Neural Information Processing Systems, vol. 28 (2015)
11. Noroozi, M., Favaro, P.: Unsupervised learning of visual representations by solving jigsaw puzzles. In: Leibe, B., Matas, J., Sebe, N., Welling, M. (eds.) ECCV 2016, Part VI. LNCS, vol. 9910, pp. 69–84. Springer, Cham (2016). https://doi.org/10.1007/978-3-319-46466-4_5
12. Zhang, R., Isola, P., Efros, A.A.: Colorful image colorization. In: Leibe, B., Matas, J., Sebe, N., Welling, M. (eds.) ECCV 2016, Part III. LNCS, vol. 9907, pp. 649–666. Springer, Cham (2016). https://doi.org/10.1007/978-3-319-46487-9_40
13. Wu, Z., Xiong, Y., Yu, S.X., Lin, D.: Unsupervised feature learning via non-parametric instance discrimination. In: Proceedings of the IEEE Conference on Computer Vision and Pattern Recognition, pp. 3733–3742 (2018)
14. Caron, M., Misra, I., Mairal, J., Goyal, P., Bojanowski, P., Joulin, A.: Unsupervised learning of visual features by contrasting cluster assignments. Adv. Neural. Inf. Process. Syst. **33**, 9912–9924 (2020)
15. Liu, Ze, et al.: Swin transformer: hierarchical vision transformer using shifted windows. In: Proceedings of the IEEE/CVF International Conference on Computer Vision (2021)
16. Wang, Yude, et al.: Self-supervised equivariant attention mechanism for weakly supervised semantic segmentation. In: Proceedings of the IEEE/CVF Conference on Computer Vision and Pattern Recognition (2020)
17. Wang, J., Min, W., Hou, S., Ma, S., Zheng, Y., Jiang, S.: Logodet-3k: a large-scale image dataset for logo detection. ACM Trans. Multimedia Comput. Commun. Appl. (TOMM) **18**(1), 1–19 (2022)
18. Romberg, S., Pueyo, L.G., Lienhart, R., Van Zwol, R.: Scalable logo recognition in real-world images. In: Proceedings of the 1st ACM International Conference on Multimedia Retrieval, pp. 1–8, April 2011

19. He, K., Zhang, X., Ren, S., Sun, J.: Deep residual learning for image recognition. In: Proceedings of the IEEE Conference on Computer Vision and Pattern Recognition, pp. 770–778 (2016)
20. Sathe, P., Rao, A., Singh, A., Nair, R., Poojary, A.: Helmet detection and number plate recognition using deep learning. In: 2022 IEEE Region 10 Symposium (TENSYMP), pp. 1–6. IEEE, July 2022
21. Ericsson, L., Gouk, H., Hospedales, T.M.: How well do self-supervised models transfer?. In: Proceedings of the IEEE/CVF Conference on Computer Vision and Pattern Recognition, pp. 5414–5423 (2021)
22. Asano, Y.M., Rupprecht, C., Vedaldi, A.: Self-labelling via simultaneous clustering and representation learning. arXiv preprint arXiv:1911.05371 (2019)
23. Chen, T., Kornblith, S., Swersky, K., Norouzi, M., Hinton, G.E.: Big self-supervised models are strong semi-supervised learners. Adv. Neural. Inf. Process. Syst. **33**, 22243–22255 (2020)
24. He, K., Fan, H., Wu, Y., Xie, S., Girshick, R.: Momentum contrast for unsupervised visual representation learning. In: Proceedings of the IEEE/CVF Conference on Computer Vision and Pattern Recognition, pp. 9729–9738 (2020)
25. Chen, X., Fan, H., Girshick, R., He, K.: Improved baselines with momentum contrastive learning. arXiv preprint arXiv:2003.04297 (2020)
26. Azizi, Shekoofeh, et al.: Big self-supervised models advance medical image classification. In: Proceedings of the IEEE/CVF International Conference on Computer Vision (2021)
27. Diego, A., et al.: Logo detection with no priors. IEEE Access **9**, 106998–107011 (2021)

HAHANet: Towards Accurate Image Classifiers with Less Parameters

Arren Matthew C. Antioquia[1,2]([✉]) [iD] and Macario O. Cordel II[2] [iD]

[1] Center for Computational Imaging and Visual Innovations, De La Salle University, Manila, Philippines
[2] Dr. Andrew L. Tan Data Science Institute, De La Salle University, Manila, Philippines
{arren.antioquia,macario.cordel}@dlsu.edu.ph

Abstract. Utilizing classical convolutional networks results in lackluster performance in certain classification tasks. To address this problem, recent solutions add extra layers or sub-networks to increase the classification performance of existing networks. More recent methods employ multiple networks coupled with varying learning strategies. However, these approaches demand larger memory and computational requirement due to additional layers, prohibiting usage in devices with limited computing power. In this paper, we propose an efficient convolutional block which minimizes the computational requirements of a network while maintaining information flow through concatenation and element-wise addition. We design a classification architecture, called Half-Append Half-Add Network (HAHANet), built using our efficient convolutional block. Our approach achieves state-of-the-art accuracy on several challenging fine-grained classification tasks. More importantly, HAHANet outperforms top networks while reducing parameter count by at most 54 times. Our code and trained models are publicly available at https://github.com/dlsucivi/HAHANet-PyTorch.

Keywords: Image Classification · Convolutional Neural Networks · Deep Learning

1 Introduction

Classification is a still a difficult task in computer vision. Due to challenges such as intra-class variations and inter-class similarities, some classification tasks usually require manual inspection by trained experts, which is expensive and time consuming. For example, some insects can only be identified by closely examining their body patterns. Thus, it is beneficial to integrate an automated approach using classifiers to lessen the cost and time requirement for prediction. Moreover, existing classifiers [4,9,14,24,26] show excellent potential in recognizing objects in images and are now being used in different applications, such as in identifying food [1,12], insects [6,33], logos [29], aircrafts [25], cars [16,23], and diseases [2,3,18,20], among others.

W. Q. Yan et al. (Eds.): PSIVT 2023, LNCS 14403, pp. 246–258, 2024.
https://doi.org/10.1007/978-981-97-0376-0_19

Several approaches present solutions to increase accuracy on challenging classification datasets. One method [21] adds more layers to the structure of existing networks, while other approaches [5,15] employ ensemble learning to achieve state-of-the-art accuracy on benchmark datasets. More recent methods [25,32] utilize multiple sub-networks to first locate informative regions of the image and then perform pre-processing before producing the final classification output. Other approaches [8,17,25] employ two individual classifiers which are updated using novel training strategies. These works are insightful in increasing accuracy in classification tasks. However, these techniques entail more computations due to increased model size.

In this paper, we propose an efficient convolutional block, called Half-Append Half-Add (HAHA) block, to reduce the computational requirements of networks used in classification. More specifically, our proposed HAHA block maintains strong information flow by incorporating computationally efficient connections through a combination of concatenation and element-wise addition operations, as discussed in Sect. 3. To showcase the capabilities of our proposed block, we design a classification architecture called Half-Append Half-Add Network (HAHANet). Experiments on different fine-grained datasets [13,25,29,30] from various domains reveal that HAHANet exhibits superior performance over current state-of-the-art classifiers in terms of accuracy. More importantly, our model achieves the highest accuracy even with a smaller model size.

In summary, our main contributions are as follows:

1. We design a classification architecture called Half-Append Half-Add Network (HAHANet) which incorporates our novel HAHA block. Compared to other approaches, our method maintains strong information flow efficiently via concatenation and element-wise addition resulting in reduced computations.
2. We show that HAHANet exceedingly surpasses the classification accuracy of state-of-the-art networks, even those with larger models, ensembles, and novel training strategies. Contrary to existing classifiers, our network produces better predictions on various fine-grained classification datasets while reducing parameter count.

2   Related Work

Classification tasks are challenging especially due to intra-class variations (*i.e.*, same class but many forms) and inter-class similarities (*i.e.*, different classes but similar forms). Recent works improve accuracy using various methods.

2.1   Improvements Through Network Modifications

In [21], ResNets are redesigned to introduce feature reuse through dense connections inside residual blocks. Their method reuses input maps from previous convolutional layers by concatenating them to the output, before performing element-wise addition similar to residual blocks. Their FR-ResNet-34 and FR-ResNet-50 show increased classification accuracy on fine-grained tasks versus their corresponding ResNet variants. Their method improves classification accuracy but requires more computations due to additional convolutions inserted inside residual blocks.

2.2 Improvements Through Ensemble Learning

In [5], ensembles are used to increase performance in classification. Various classifiers [7,22,27] are utilized to form two ensembles. The Sum-of-Maximum-Probabilities Ensemble (SMP-Ensemble) only retains the highest class probability for a given image and zeroes-out the probabilities of other classes for each network. These probabilities from all networks are then summed to determine the class of a given image. On the other hand, GA-Ensemble employs a genetic algorithm to determine the optimum weight of each network in the outcome of the ensemble.

In [15], Bilinear-CNN (B-CNN) utilizes two CNN streams to extract features from input images. The final set of predictions is represented as a bilinear vector, which is obtained by getting the outer product of the outputs of the two sub-networks. This formulation captures pairwise correlations between different features extracted from the two CNN streams.

These ensembles attain higher classification accuracy on various datasets. However, ensembles inherently require more computing power due to the use of multiple networks.

2.3 Improvements Through Training Strategies

Different training strategies are also proposed to improve classification performance. In [17], two classifiers are trained simultaneously but are only updated when their predictions are different. This technique, called Decoupling, assumes that datasets usually contain noisy labels. Thus, updates should not be solely based on the ground-truth labels but should also be based on the agreement between networks.

Similar to decoupling, Co-Teaching [8] also trains two networks simultaneously. This method assumes that each network learns a distinct set of features. Thus, both networks should cross-update based on the useful information learned by each other. This is contrary to decoupling which updates each network individually.

In [25], Peer-Learning integrates both Decoupling and Co-Teaching. Similar to Decoupling, this method learns based on disagreements between networks. As in Co-Teaching, networks are trained through cross-updating.

Empirical results show that these learning strategies improve accuracy. However, using multiple networks, like in ensemble learning, results in larger model size.

2.4 Improvements Through Multi-agent Cooperation

The Navigator-Teacher-Scrutinizer Network (NTS-Net) [32] involves multi-agent cooperation. The *navigator* agent selects the most informative regions in the

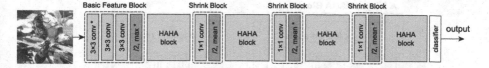

Fig. 1. Half-Append Half-Add Network (HAHANet). The first four layers constitute the *basic feature block* which captures rudimentary features essential for classification tasks. Our novel Half-Append Half-Add (HAHA) block enforces strong information flow through efficient connections by concatenation and element-wise addition operations. Spatial resolution of the input image is reduced by shrink blocks placed between HAHA blocks. * means the stride is 2.

image, while the *teacher* agent evaluates the probability of each selected region belonging to the ground-truth class. Features from the final set of selected regions are fused with the features of the whole image and are processed by the *scrutinizer*, which produces the final classification result. In [29], Discriminative Region Navigation and Augmentation Network (DRNA-Net) adds another agent before the *scrutinizer* to perform data augmentation on the selected regions, which empirically improves accuracy on classification tasks.

Contrary to these, our proposed network is composed of computationally efficient densely-connected convolutional blocks. We achieve state-of-the-art accuracy with less parameters and without additional layers, ensemble learning, nor multi-agent cooperation.

3 Half-Append Half-Add Network

Half-Append Half-Add Network (HAHANet) is a lightweight convolutional classifier composed of a basic feature block, followed by a series of alternating HAHA blocks and shrink blocks. Figure 1 displays the overall detailed structure of our classification network. We propose two variations of HAHANet with different number of layers, as shown in Table 1.

3.1 Basic Feature Block

Most modern CNN architectures [9,11] usually decrease the spatial dimension of the input image by a factor of 4 at the first convolution and pooling operations of the network. We argue that downsampling at the shallow layers negatively affects the classification performance of the network, especially in some classification problems where differences between classes are usually found in the smaller details of the image.

In our proposed network, the basic feature block is designed to extract simple features, *i.e.,* lines and shapes, from the input image, but with delay in downsampling to obtain better features. As illustrated in Fig. 1, we only decrease the spatial dimension by a factor of 2 at the first convolution of the network. This is followed by two 3×3 convolutions which maintain the resolution of the input

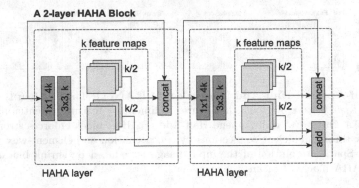

Fig. 2. Half-Append Half-Add (HAHA) Block. Each HAHA layer produces k feature maps. The first $k/2$ output feature maps produced from the HAHA layer are concatenated with the first $k/2$ feature maps from the output of previous HAHA layers. The second $k/2$ output feature maps produced from the HAHA layer are added element-wise to the second $k/2$ feature maps from the output of previous HAHA layers.

image. Then, a max pooling layer reduces the size by a factor of 2. After these operations, the spatial dimension of the input image is reduced by a factor of 4.

3.2 Half-Append Half-Add Block

Half-Append Half-Add (HAHA) block implements efficient connections by appending half of the output as input to succeeding layers and propagates the rest through the network via element-wise addition, as illustrated in Fig. 2. HAHA block maintains strong information flow within the network while reducing its parameter count.

Suppose that we have an input image x_0 and a HAHA block with L layers. Each layer is composed of a 1×1 convolution and a 3×3 convolution. Each layer in the block produces k feature maps. Specifically, the 1×1 convolution functions as a bottleneck layer which outputs $4k$ feature maps from a larger input size. The 3×3 convolution then produces k feature maps from the output of the bottleneck layer. Both of these convolutions are preceded by a batch normalization layer and a ReLU activation, which comprise the composite function $H_\ell(\cdot)$.

Our proposed method implements efficient connections by concatenating the first $k/2$ feature maps from the output of each layer in the HAHA block, which are eventually used as input to succeeding layers. Thus, the output of the ℓth layer in the HAHA block, denoted as x_ℓ, is:

$$x_\ell = H_\ell([x_0, x_1^{(1)}, x_2^{(1)}, ..., x_{\ell-1}^{(1)}]) \tag{1}$$

where $x_\ell^{(1)}$ represents the first $k/2$ feature maps in the output of the ℓth layer in the HAHA block and $[x_0, x_1^{(1)}, x_2^{(1)}, ..., x_{\ell-1}^{(1)}]$ is the concatenation of the input feature maps to the first $k/2$ feature maps from the output of layers $1, 2, ..., \ell-1$, respectively.

Table 1. HAHANet architectures. Details about the layers of each network configuration are shown together with the corresponding output size. Each network is trained
with an input size of 224×224.

Layers	Output Size	HAHANet-83		HAHANet-123	
Basic Feature Block	112 × 112	3 × 3 conv, stride 2			
		3 × 3 conv			
		3 × 3 conv			
Pooling	56 × 56	3 × 3 max pool, stride 2			
HAHA Block (1)	56 × 56	$\begin{bmatrix} 1 \times 1 \text{ Conv} \\ 3 \times 3 \text{ Conv} \end{bmatrix}$	×6	$\begin{bmatrix} 1 \times 1 \text{ Conv} \\ 3 \times 3 \text{ Conv} \end{bmatrix}$	×6
Shrink Block (1)	56 × 56	1 × 1 conv			
	28 × 28	2 × 2 average pool, stride 2			
HAHA Block (2)	28 × 28	$\begin{bmatrix} 1 \times 1 \text{ Conv} \\ 3 \times 3 \text{ Conv} \end{bmatrix}$	×12	$\begin{bmatrix} 1 \times 1 \text{ Conv} \\ 3 \times 3 \text{ Conv} \end{bmatrix}$	×12
Shrink Block (2)	28 × 28	1 × 1 conv			
	14 × 14	2 × 2 average pool, stride 2			
HAHA Block (3)	14 × 14	$\begin{bmatrix} 1 \times 1 \text{ Conv} \\ 3 \times 3 \text{ Conv} \end{bmatrix}$	×12	$\begin{bmatrix} 1 \times 1 \text{ Conv} \\ 3 \times 3 \text{ Conv} \end{bmatrix}$	×24
Shrink Block (3)	14 × 14	1 × 1 conv			
	7 × 7	2 × 2 average pool, stride 2			
HAHA Block (4)	7 × 7	$\begin{bmatrix} 1 \times 1 \text{ Conv} \\ 3 \times 3 \text{ Conv} \end{bmatrix}$	×8	$\begin{bmatrix} 1 \times 1 \text{ Conv} \\ 3 \times 3 \text{ Conv} \end{bmatrix}$	×16
Classification Layer	1 × 1	7 × 7 global average pool			
		fully connected, softmax			

The remaining feature maps, *i.e.*, the second half, of all L layers in the HAHA
block are propagated through element-wise addition. This operation assures that
the information from these feature maps are also transmitted throughout the
network. The result of this operation, denoted as a_L, is computed as:

$$a_L = x_1^{(2)} + x_2^{(2)} + ... + x_L^{(2)} \tag{2}$$

where $x_\ell^{(2)}$ represents the other $k/2$ feature maps in the output of the ℓth layer,
i.e., feature maps $k/2 + 1$ to k.

We concatenate the input feature maps, *i.e.*, x_0, with the first half output
of all L layers, *i.e.*, x_L, and a_L to produce the final output of the whole HAHA
block, denoted as y. Mathematically, we can express that as:

$$y = [x_0, x_1^{(1)}, x_2^{(1)}, ..., x_L^{(1)}, a_L] \tag{3}$$

The output y of the HAHA block is then passed through the succeeding shrink
block. By utilizing half of the output of each convolution as input to succeeding
layers in a HAHA block, we greatly improve the computational efficiency of the

network while preserving strong information flow through concatenation and element-wise addition.

3.3   Shrink Block

Shrink blocks are placed after a HAHA block to minimize the spatial dimension of the input image. Each block contains a 1×1 convolution which reduces the number of input feature maps m to $\lfloor Sm \rfloor$, where $0 < S \leq 1$. This is followed by a 2×2 average pooling layer which downscales the spatial resolution by half. The convolution operation is preceded by a batch normalization layer and a ReLU activation function. In our network, we use $S = 0.5$.

4   Experimental Results

4.1   Implementation Details

We train our classification architecture using an input size of 224×224. We use standard data augmentation techniques, *e.g.*, random change in noise, saturation, hue, contrast, and brightness, coupled with random flip and random crop. We fine-tune the proposed network using a Stochastic Gradient Descent (SGD) optimizer with learning rate 0.01 and batch size 64. We train our model for 80 epochs, and decrease the learning rate by a factor of 10 on epochs 40 and 60. HAHANet models are all implemented using PyTorch 1.7 and are trained using a machine with 16 GB memory and Nvidia GTX 2070 GPU. Several fine-grained classification datasets are used to showcase the performance of our model, as summarized in Table 2.

4.2   Results on Foodx-251 Dataset

The Foodx-251 [13] dataset includes *158k* images of 251 food categories collected from the web. There are *118k*, *12k*, and *28k* images in the train, validation, and test sets, respectively.

Our proposed model attains better classification accuracy compared to methods that employ retraining strategies such as in [31,34]. Without using similar schemes, the larger variant of our proposed model improves the classification score by 3.47% while using 3.91× fewer parameters compared to the current best approach, *i.e.*, a DenseNet-201 model trained using the fast retraining method as described in [34].

4.3   Results on IP102 Dataset

The IP102 [30] dataset includes *75k* images of 102 common crop insect pest species, where 60%, 10%, and 30% of these samples are for the train, validation, and test sets, respectively. To date, this is the largest dataset on insect pests.

Table 2. Classification results. Our HAHANet models outperform current state-of-the-art CNN architectures, both single models and ensembles, on different datasets from various domains while significantly reducing parameter count.

Dataset	Method	Parameters	Ratio to HAHANet-83	Ratio to HAHANet-123	Accuracy
Foodx-251 [13]	VGGNet-16+R [31]	135.29M	51.64×	28.48×	56.90%
	ResNet-50+R [31]	24.02M	9.17×	5.06×	61.80%
	Inception-v3+R [31]	27.16M	10.37×	5.72×	60.80%
	DenseNet-201+R [31]	18.58M	7.09×	3.91×	62.40%
	VGGNet-16+FR [34]	135.29M	51.64×	28.48×	57.40%
	ResNet-50+FR [34]	24.02M	9.17×	5.06×	61.80%
	Inception-v3+FR [34]	27.16M	10.37×	5.72×	61.80%
	DenseNet-201+FR [34]	18.58M	7.09×	3.91×	62.80%
	HAHANet-83 (Ours)	**2.62M**	**1.00×**	**0.55×**	**64.89%**
	HAHANet-123 (Ours)	**4.75M**	**1.81×**	**1.00×**	**66.27%**
IP102 [30]	AlexNet [14]	57.40M	22.33×	12.29×	41.80%
	GoogleNet [26]	12.00M	4.67×	2.57×	43.50%
	VGGNet-16 [24]	134.60M	52.37×	28.82×	48.20%
	ResNet-50 [9]	23.70M	9.22×	5.07×	49.40%
	FR-ResNet-34 [21]	20.67M	8.04×	4.43×	54.73%
	FR-ResNet-50 [21]	30.78M	11.98×	6.59×	55.24%
	SMP-Ensemble [5]	48.80M	18.99×	10.45×	66.21%
	GA-Ensemble [5]	48.80M	18.99×	10.45×	67.13%
	HAHANet-83 (Ours)	**2.57M**	**1.00×**	**0.55×**	**69.64%**
	HAHANet-123 (Ours)	**4.67M**	**1.82×**	**1.00×**	**70.55%**
Logo2k+ [29]	AlexNet [14]	66.59M	20.18×	11.29×	48.80%
	GoogleNet [26]	14.38M	4.36×	2.44×	62.36%
	VGGNet-16 [24]	143.85M	43.59×	24.38×	62.83%
	ResNet-50 [9]	28.30M	8.58×	4.80×	66.34%
	ResNet-152 [9]	62.94M	19.07×	10.67×	67.65%
	VGGNet-16+Efficient+LS [10]	143.85M	43.59×	24.38×	65.45%
	ResNet-50+Efficient+LS [10]	28.30M	8.58×	4.80×	66.94%
	ResNet-152+Efficient+LS [10]	62.94M	19.07×	10.67×	67.99%
	NTS-Net [32]	59.73M	18.10×	10.12×	69.41%
	DRNA-Net (ResNet-50) [29]	45.35M	13.74×	7.69×	71.12%
	DRNA-Net (ResNet-152) [29]	79.99M	24.24×	13.56×	72.09%
	HAHANet-83 (Ours)	**3.30M**	**1.00×**	**0.56×**	**78.33%**
	HAHANet-123 (Ours)	**5.90M**	**1.79×**	**1.00×**	**79.41%**
Web-Aircraft [25]	VGGNet-16 [24]	134.67M	52.40×	28.84×	68.38%
	VGGNet-19 [24]	139.98M	54.47×	29.97×	70.99%
	ResNet-50 [9]	23.71M	9.23×	5.08×	60.79%
	ResNet-101 [9]	42.71M	16.62×	9.15×	63.46%
	GoogleNet [26]	12.08M	4.70×	2.59×	66.02%
	B-CNN (VGGNet-16) [15]	40.93M	15.93×	8.76×	64.33%
	Decoupling (B-CNN) [17]	40.93M	15.93×	8.76×	75.97%
	Co-Teaching (B-CNN) [8]	40.93M	15.93×	8.76×	72.76%
	Peer-Learning (B-CNN) [25]	40.93M	15.93×	8.76×	74.38%
	HAHANet-83 (Ours)	**2.57M**	**1.00×**	**0.55×**	**78.10%**
	HAHANet-123 (Ours)	**4.67M**	**1.82×**	**1.00×**	**79.72%**
Web-Car [25]	VGGNet-16 [24]	135.06M	51.95×	28.61×	61.62%
	VGGNet-19 [24]	140.37M	53.99×	29.74×	67.21%
	ResNet-50 [9]	23.91M	9.20×	5.07×	60.64%
	ResNet-101 [9]	42.90M	16.50×	9.09×	65.51%
	GoogleNet [26]	12.18M	4.68×	2.58×	65.87%
	B-CNN (VGGNet-16) [15]	66.10M	25.42×	14.00×	67.42%
	Decoupling (B-CNN) [17]	66.10M	25.42×	14.00×	75.00%
	Co-Teaching (B-CNN) [8]	66.10M	25.42×	14.00×	73.10%
	Peer-Learning (B-CNN) [25]	66.10M	25.42×	14.00×	78.52%
	HAHANet-83 (Ours)	**2.60M**	**1.00×**	**0.55×**	**80.04%**
	HAHANet-123 (Ours)	**4.72M**	**1.82×**	**1.00×**	**81.72%**

Our models outperform current state-of-the-art classifiers, both single models [9,14,19,21,24,26] and ensembles [5]. Compared to the best performing single model, *i.e.*, FR-ResNet-50 [21], HAHANet-123 raises the classification accuracy by 15.31%, while reducing the parameter count by 6.59×. Contrary to GA-Ensemble [5], our model manages to increase accuracy by 3.42% even without ensemble learning. More importantly, our model uses 10.45× fewer parameters compared to both ensembles.

4.4   Results on Logo2k+ Dataset

The Logo2k+ [29] dataset includes *167k* images of 2,341 real-world logos. There are *117k* and *50k* images in the train and test sets, respectively.

Aside from outperforming single models [9,14,24,26], our network exhibits higher classification performance compared to models trained with efficient training tricks and label smoothing, *i.e.*, models tagged with Efficient+LS [10]. More specifically, HAHANet-123 improves classification score by 11.42% while reducing parameter count by 10.67× compared to the best single model, *i.e.*, ResNet-152 with efficient training and label smoothing. Moreover, our method attains higher scores compared to multi-agent approaches, such as NTS-Net [32] and DRNA-Net [25]. Our model increases classification accuracy by 7.32% while requiring 13.56× less parameters compared to the previous best performing method.

4.5   Results on Web-Aircraft Dataset

The Web-Aircraft [25] dataset includes *16k* images of 100 aircrafts collected from the web. There are *13k* and *3k* images in the train and test sets, respectively.

Our HAHANet-123 outperforms the top single model, *i.e.*, VGGNet-19, by 8.73% while minimizing computational costs by 29.97×. Aside from vanilla classifiers [9,24,26], our models also surpass the accuracy of B-CNN [15] and its varieties trained through novel strategies, such as Decoupling [17], Co-Teaching [8], and Peer-Learning [25]. More specifically, our best performing model raises the classification score on the dataset by 5.34% while reducing parameter count by 8.76× compared to the previous best approach.

4.6   Results on Web-Car Dataset

The Web-Car [25] dataset includes *29k* images of 196 cars collected from the web. There are *21k* and *8k* images in the train and test sets, respectively.

Similar to the results in the Web-Aircraft dataset, HAHANet remarkably surpasses the classification performance of other methods. Our HAHANet-123 obtains a 14.51% increase in accuracy while reducing parameter count by 29.74× compared to the best performing single model, *i.e.*, VGGNet-19. Moreover, our proposed method is 3.20% more accurate than the previous best approach while having 14.00× fewer parameters.

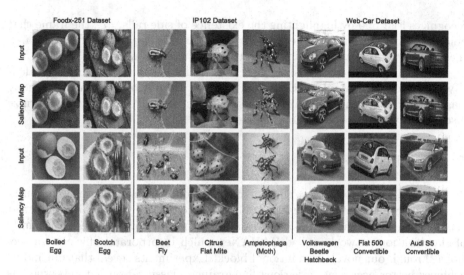

Fig. 3. Saliency maps produced by HAHANet on various images from different datasets. *Left:* Saliency maps show that the color of the outer portion of the egg is important in differentiating between a boiled egg from a scotch egg (columns 1-2). *Middle:* Body patterns are important in identifying insects, as seen in the saliency maps for beet flies (column 3), citrus flat mite (column 4), and ampelophaga (column 5). *Right:* The shape of the hood in Volkswagen Beetle Hatchback is one of its notable features (column 6), while the top of the windshield is a prominent feature in convertible cars like the Fiat 500 and Audi S5 (columns 7-8). Best viewed in color. (Color figure online)

4.7   Saliency Maps

Figure 3 shows saliency maps produced by our HAHANet-123 model using Score-CAM [28] on various images from different domains. As shown in columns 1 and 2, our model can correctly distinguish different dishes with the same main ingredient. For example, the model can differentiate between a boiled egg and a scotch egg by examining its outer portion.

Body patterns are crucial in correctly identifying insect pests. Although several insects share some characteristics, *e.g.*, beet fly, citrus flat mite, and ampelophaga are round in shape, our model manages to recognize them through body patterns, as highlighted in columns 3 to 5. Moreover, HAHANet is capable of locating the salient patterns in images with multiple instances of the same insect, as shown in row 4.

Certain parts are critical in correctly determining the model of a given car. For example, the shape of the hood is one of the salient characteristic of the Volkswagen Beetle Hatchback, as shown in column 6. On the other hand, our model focuses on the upper part of convertible cars, *e.g.*, Fiat 500 and Audi S5, as displayed in columns 7 and 8. Although certain characteristics are shared between Fiat 500 and Audi S5, HAHANet can identify the correct class by looking for certain distinct parts. More specifically, our proposed method correctly recognizes Fiat 500 by highlighting the existence of side rails, *i.e.*, the frame that holds the car roof. On the other hand, the model relies on the front header, *i.e.*, the frame on top of the windshield, to correctly classify an Audi S5.

These qualitative results show that our model is capable of correctly identifying the class of a given image even if there are obvious similarities among classes. Moreover, this visualization also reveals that HAHANet can recognize discriminative features of various classes.

5 Conclusion

In this work, we propose an efficient convolutional block to reduce computational requirements of networks used in image recognition while exhibiting better classification performance through strong information flow. We design a family of classification networks called HAHANet which incorporates efficient connections through our novel convolutional block. Experiments reveal that our model achieves better accuracy on various fine-grained classification datasets, such as Foodx-251 [13], IP102 [30], Logo2k+ [29], Web-Aircraft [25], and Web-Car [25]. Finally, our network surpasses the performance of current top classification architectures with larger network size, both single models and ensemble networks, while significantly reducing parameter count. Our code and trained models are available online for research reproducibility and for utilization in applications.

References

1. Aguilar, E., Radeva, P.: Uncertainty-aware integration of local and flat classifiers for food recognition. Pattern Recogn. Lett. **136**, 237–243 (2020)
2. Antioquia, A.M.C.: Accurate thoracic disease classification via ensemble networks. In: Proceedings of the 2022 5th International Conference on Image and Graphics Processing, ICIGP 2022, New York, NY, USA, pp. 196–201. Association for Computing Machinery (2022). https://doi.org/10.1145/3512388.3512417
3. Antioquia, A.M.C.: Effsemble: faster, smaller and more accurate ensemble networks for thoracic disease classification. Int. J. Comput. Appl. Technol. **71**(4), 332–339 (2023). https://doi.org/10.1504/IJCAT.2023.132406
4. Antioquia, A.M.C., Stanley Tan, D., Azcarraga, A., Cheng, W.H., Hua, K.L.: Zip-Net: ZFNet-level accuracy with 48× fewer parameters. In: 2018 IEEE Visual Communications and Image Processing (VCIP), pp. 1–4 (2018)
5. Ayan, E., Erbay, H., Varçın, F.: Crop pest classification with a genetic algorithm-based weighted ensemble of deep convolutional neural networks. Comput. Electron. Agric. **179**, 105809 (2020)
6. Cao, X., Guo, S., Lin, J., Zhang, W., Liao, M.: Online tracking of ants based on deep association metrics: method, dataset and evaluation. Pattern Recogn. **103**, 107233 (2020)
7. Chollet, F.: Xception: deep learning with depthwise separable convolutions. In: 2017 IEEE Conference on Computer Vision and Pattern Recognition (CVPR), Los Alamitos, CA, USA, pp. 1800–1807. IEEE Computer Society, July 2017

8. Han, B., et al.: Co-teaching: robust training of deep neural networks with extremely noisy labels. In: Bengio, S., Wallach, H., Larochelle, H., Grauman, K., Cesa-Bianchi, N., Garnett, R. (eds.) Advances in Neural Information Processing Systems, vol. 31. Curran Associates, Inc. (2018)

9. He, K., Zhang, X., Ren, S., Sun, J.: Deep residual learning for image recognition. In: 2016 IEEE Conference on Computer Vision and Pattern Recognition (CVPR), Los Alamitos, CA, USA, pp. 770–778. IEEE Computer Society, June 2016

10. He, T., Zhang, Z., Zhang, H., Zhang, Z., Xie, J., Li, M.: Bag of tricks for image classification with convolutional neural networks. In: 2019 IEEE/CVF Conference on Computer Vision and Pattern Recognition (CVPR), Los Alamitos, CA, USA, pp. 558–567. IEEE Computer Society, June 2019

11. Huang, G., Liu, Z., Maaten, L.V.D., Weinberger, K.Q.: Densely connected convolutional networks. In: 2017 IEEE Conference on Computer Vision and Pattern Recognition (CVPR), Los Alamitos, CA, USA, pp. 2261–2269. IEEE Computer Society, July 2017

12. Jahani Heravi, E., Habibi Aghdam, H., Puig, D.: An optimized convolutional neural network with bottleneck and spatial pyramid pooling layers for classification of foods. Pattern Recognit. Lett. **105**, 50–58 (2018). Machine Learning and Applications in Artificial Intelligence

13. Kaur, P., Sikka, K., Wang, W., Belongie, S.J., Divakaran, A.: FoodX-251: a dataset for fine-grained food classification. CoRR abs/1907.06167 (2019)

14. Krizhevsky, A., Sutskever, I., Hinton, G.E.: ImageNet classification with deep convolutional neural networks. Commun. ACM **60**(6), 84–90 (2017)

15. Lin, T., RoyChowdhury, A., Maji, S.: Bilinear CNN models for fine-grained visual recognition. In: 2015 IEEE International Conference on Computer Vision (ICCV), Los Alamitos, CA, USA, pp. 1449–1457. IEEE Computer Society, December 2015

16. Lu, L., Wang, P., Cao, Y.: A novel part-level feature extraction method for fine-grained vehicle recognition. Pattern Recogn. **131**, 108869 (2022)

17. Malach, E., Shalev-Shwartz, S.: Decoupling "when to update" from "how to update". In: Guyon, I., et al. (eds.) Advances in Neural Information Processing Systems, vol. 30. Curran Associates, Inc. (2017)

18. Mery, D., et al.: On skin lesion recognition using deep learning: 50 ways to choose your model. In: Wang, H., et al. (eds.) Image and Video Technology. LNCS, vol. 13763, pp. 103–116. Springer, Cham (2023). https://doi.org/10.1007/978-3-031-26431-3_9

19. Nanni, L., Maguolo, G., Pancino, F.: Insect pest image detection and recognition based on bio-inspired methods. Eco. Inform. **57**, 101089 (2020)

20. Norouzifard, M., Nemati, A., Abdul-Rahman, A., GholamHosseini, H., Klette, R.: A fused pattern recognition model to detect glaucoma using retinal nerve fiber layer thickness measurements. In: Lee, C., Su, Z., Sugimoto, A. (eds.) PSIVT 2019. LNCS, vol. 11854, pp. 1–12. Springer, Cham (2019). https://doi.org/10.1007/978-3-030-34879-3_1

21. Ren, F., Liu, W., Wu, G.: Feature reuse residual networks for insect pest recognition. IEEE Access **7**, 122758–122768 (2019)

22. Sandler, M., Howard, A., Zhu, M., Zhmoginov, A., Chen, L.: MobileNetV 2: inverted residuals and linear bottlenecks. In: 2018 IEEE/CVF Conference on Computer Vision and Pattern Recognition (CVPR), Los Alamitos, CA, USA, pp. 4510–4520. IEEE Computer Society, June 2018

23. Satyanarayana, G., Deshmukh, P., Das, S.K.: Vehicle detection and classification with spatio-temporal information obtained from CNN. Displays **75**, 102294 (2022)

24. Simonyan, K., Zisserman, A.: Very deep convolutional networks for large-scale image recognition. arXiv preprint arXiv:1409.1556 (2014)
25. Sun, Z., et al.: Webly supervised fine-grained recognition: benchmark datasets and an approach. In: Proceedings of the IEEE/CVF International Conference on Computer Vision (ICCV), pp. 10602–10611, October 2021
26. Szegedy, C., et al.: Going deeper with convolutions. In: 2015 IEEE Conference on Computer Vision and Pattern Recognition (CVPR), Los Alamitos, CA, USA, pp. 1–9. IEEE Computer Society, June 2015
27. Szegedy, C., Ioffe, S., Vanhoucke, V., Alemi, A.A.: Inception-v4, inception-ResNet and the impact of residual connections on learning. In: Proceedings of the Thirty-First AAAI Conference on Artificial Intelligence, AAAI 2017, pp. 4278–4284. AAAI Press (2017)
28. Wang, H., et al.: Score-CAM: score-weighted visual explanations for convolutional neural networks. In: Proceedings of the IEEE/CVF Conference on Computer Vision and Pattern Recognition (CVPR) Workshops, June 2020
29. Wang, J., et al.: Logo-2k+: a large-scale logo dataset for scalable logo classification. In: Proceedings of the AAAI Conference on Artificial Intelligence, vol. 34, no. 04, pp. 6194–6201 (2020)
30. Wu, X., Zhan, C., Lai, Y., Cheng, M., Yang, J.: IP102: a large-scale benchmark dataset for insect pest recognition. In: 2019 IEEE/CVF Conference on Computer Vision and Pattern Recognition (CVPR), Los Alamitos, CA, USA, pp. 8779–8788. IEEE Computer Society, June 2019
31. Yang, Y., Wu, Q., Feng, X., Akilan, T.: Recomputation of the dense layers for performance improvement of DCNN. IEEE Trans. Pattern Anal. Mach. Intell. **42**(11), 2912–2925 (2020)
32. Yang, Z., Luo, T., Wang, D., Hu, Z., Gao, J., Wang, L.: Learning to navigate for fine-grained classification. In: Ferrari, V., Hebert, M., Sminchisescu, C., Weiss, Y. (eds.) Computer Vision – ECCV 2018. LNCS, vol. 11218, pp. 438–454. Springer, Cham (2018). https://doi.org/10.1007/978-3-030-01264-9_26
33. Yu, X., Zhao, Y., Gao, Y., Xiong, S.: MaskCOV: a random mask covariance network for ultra-fine-grained visual categorization. Pattern Recogn. **119**, 108067 (2021)
34. Zhang, W., Yang, Y., Wu, J.: Deep networks with fast retraining (2021)

Melanoma Classification Using Deep Learning

Yehia Mousa[1]([✉]), Radwa Taha[1]([✉]), Ranpreet Kaur[2]([✉]), and Shereen Afifi[1]([✉])

[1] Media Engineering and Technology, German University in Cairo, Cairo, Egypt
yehia.mousa@student.guc.edu.eg, radwataha1999@gmail.com,
shereen.moataz@guc.edu.eg
[2] Media Design School, Auckland University for Technology, Auckland, New Zealand
ranpreet.kaur@mediadesignschool.com

Abstract. The prevalence of skin cancer, specifically melanoma, constitutes a significant global health concern, thus giving rise to intricate detection challenges that demand immediate attention and comprehensive solutions. In this study, we investigate the application of deep learning models for melanoma detection. Five pre-trained models, including VGG-16, ResNet50, InceptionV3, DenseNet-121, and Xception, are evaluated through a series of experiments. The models undergo the same training process with transfer learning, freezing all layers and modifying the classification layer. The experiments reveal that ResNet50 consistently outperforms the other models, demonstrating superior accuracy, precision, recall, and F1 score. Notably, ResNet50 exhibits exceptional accuracy and F1 score, achieving around 93% in both. This study sheds light on the potential use of deep learning in enhancing melanoma diagnosis and underscores the need for robust and accurate classification systems for early detection and effective treatment of skin cancer.

Keywords: Pre-trained models · Transfer Learning · Skin Cancer · Deep Learning

1 Introduction

Melanoma, recognized as the most perilous type of skin cancer worldwide, exhibits its highest incidence rates in New Zealand and Australia. Timely detection of melanoma holds the potential to significantly diminish mortality rates and curtail treatment expenses [1]. Melanoma, which arises from malignant growth in melanocyte cells, is one of the four major types of skin cancer. Despite being the least common, it is the most deadly. Therefore, early detection of melanoma is critical for successful treatment. However, due to its infrequency, diagnosing this disease accurately can be challenging and time consuming [2]. Dermoscopic analysis, biopsy, and histopathology examination are required for a definitive diagnosis. However, to address these challenges and improve diagnostic accuracy, computer-aided systems have emerged using Deep Learning as a promising approach. These systems have the potential to reduce the time and cost associated with melanoma diagnosis while increasing its accuracy.

W. Q. Yan et al. (Eds.): PSIVT 2023, LNCS 14403, pp. 259–272, 2024.
https://doi.org/10.1007/978-981-97-0376-0_20

Numerous studies have delved into the realm of Computer-Aided Diagnosis (CAD) devices for the classification of melanoma, shedding light on the potential of these sophisticated tools in the realm of dermatological diagnostics. Researchers across the globe have contributed to this growing body of knowledge, with investigations spanning a wide array of CAD systems, machine learning algorithms, and image processing techniques [3,4]. These studies collectively emphasize the significant strides being made in harnessing technology to assist in the early and accurate identification of melanoma, ultimately aiming to enhance clinical decision-making and patient outcomes in the field of dermatology [5–9].

This research addresses a significant gap in the field of melanoma detection using Deep Learing, which pertains to the lack of comprehensive evaluations comparing different implementations and approaches. While several classification techniques have been proposed for melanoma detection, a comprehensive comparison among them is lacking. The objective of this research is to bridge this gap by conducting a thorough and systematic evaluation of various models for melanoma classification. By evaluating the performance of different models, this research aims to provide valuable insights and guidance to researchers and practitioners in the field of melanoma detection. The findings of this comprehensive comparison will serve as a valuable resource.

2   Literature Review

Advances in deep learning techniques have revolutionized the field of dermatology, enabling more accurate and efficient skin image classification [10–12]. In this literature review, we explore three prominent studies that employ different deep learning models and methodologies to address the challenges of melanoma detection.

Mahbod et al. employed three pre-trained deep models: AlexNet, VGG16, and ResNet-18. The extracted features are then used to train support vector machine classifiers [13]. In the final step, the outputs of the classifier are combined to create a classification. When tested on the 150 validation images from the ISIC 2017 classification challenge, With an area under the curve of the receiver operating characteristic of 83.83 % for melanoma classification and 97.55 % for seborrheic keratosis classification, the proposed method is demonstrated to have very good classification performance.

In [14] proposed a two-stage framework is utilized for implementing melanoma detection, segmentation of skin lesions, and identification of melanoma lesions. Two FCNs, based on VGG-16 and GoogLeNet, are integrated to improve segmentation accuracy. A hybrid framework is utilized to incorporate these FCNs. Feature extraction from the segmented lesion is performed using a deep residual network and a hand-crafted feature for classification, which is done by a support vector machine. The performance analysis of the framework shows promising accuracy of 88.92% for classification in the ISBI 2016 dataset and 85.3% for the ISIC 2017 dataset.

The performance of the proposed DCNN model, which combines VGG 16 and LSTM, was evaluated using the International Skin Imaging Collaboration datastores (ISIC) [15]. In comparison to other learning models, this integration led to remarkable results, achieving a training accuracy of 90.89% and a testing accuracy of 94.39%. These findings underscore the effectiveness of the DCNN model in accurately classifying skin images and demonstrate its potential for various applications in the field of dermatology.

3 Methodology

From the literature review, it has been observed that there is high impact of hyper-parameters on the performance of pre-trained deep learning models for skin image classification. Thus, in this work, four experiments are conducted by selecting appropriate hyper-parameters on five different models, including AlexNet, VGG16, ResNet-18, VGG-16 and DenseNet-121. The study aims to optimize these models' capabilities and provide valuable insights for dermatological applications, which underwent the same training process. All models utilized transfer learning, with all layers, including the top layer frozen. In the classification layer, we employed the Rectified Linear Unit (ReLU) activation function for the first dense layer. ReLU is a popular activation function known for its ability to introduce non-linearity in the network, allowing the model to learn complex patterns and representations. While the last layer utilized the Sigmoid activation function. The Adam optimizer and categorical cross-entropy loss function were applied to all models. Random shuffling of the data during each epoch was performed to enhance training efficiency. The utilization of transfer learning allowed for the modification of pre-trained models for different classification tasks, offering advantages such as reduced labeled data requirement and leveraging learned features. In this case, the last layer of the pre-trained models was adjusted from Softmax to Sigmoid for the binary classification task of distinguishing between benign moles and malignant melanoma cases. This approach ensured that the models could leverage earlier learned features while adapting to the new classification task. This expedited training, improved model performance, and yielded high accurate results.

Table 1 provides a comprehensive overview of the hyper-parameters settings used in each experiment to evaluate the performance of various deep learning models for melanoma classification. By systematically varying these hyper-parameters, we aimed to identify the optimal configuration that maximizes accuracy and F1 score while mitigating overfitting and enhancing generalization. The results in this table offer valuable insights into the influence of different hyper-parameters choices on the models' efficacy, aiding in the refinement and optimization of deep learning techniques for melanoma detection and diagnosis.

In the proposed system Fig. 1, various performance metrics were utilized to evaluate the effectiveness of the models, including accuracy, precision, recall, F1 score, and Area Under the Curve (AUC). Accuracy measures the proportion of correctly classified samples, while precision quantifies the proportion of true positive predictions out of all positive predictions. Recall assesses the proportion of true positive predictions out of all actual positive samples. Additionally, the F1 score provides a balanced measure of precision and recall. The AUC

Table 1. Hyper-parameters configurations

Layers & hyper-parameters	First Experiment	Second Experiment	Third Experiment	Fourth Experiment
First Layer	Flatten			Global Average Pooling
Second Layer	Dense Layer 256 neurons (ReLU)			
Third Layer	–	–	Dropout Layer(0.2)	–
Fourth Layer	Dense Layer 2 neurons (Sigmoid)			
Learning Rate	10^{-2}	10^{-7}	5×10^{-6}	5×10^{-6}
Batch Size	64			
Number of Epochs	10	70	10	Early Stopping Callback

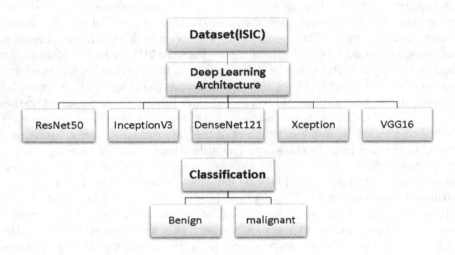

Fig. 1. Proposed system

metric measures the overall performance of the model across different classification thresholds. These performance metrics offer a comprehensive evaluation of the model's classification performance, enabling a thorough assessment of its effectiveness in distinguishing between benign and malignant cases.

Accuracy:

$$Accuracy = \frac{TP + TN}{TP + TN + FP + FN} \tag{1}$$

Precision:

$$Precision = \frac{TP}{TP + FP} \tag{2}$$

Recall:

$$Recall = \frac{TP}{TP + FN} \tag{3}$$

F1 Score:

$$F1Score = \frac{2 \cdot Precision \cdot Recall}{Precision + Recall} \tag{4}$$

Where TP represents True Positive, TN represents True Negative, FP represents False Positive, and FN represents False Negative. FPR and TPR represent False Positive Rate and True Positive Rate, respectively. These equations provide a mathematical representation of the performance metrics used to assess the models' classification performance in the proposed system.

3.1 Data Set

The dataset used in this study was sourced from the International Skin Imaging Collaboration (ISIC) [16] and consisted of approximately 10,600 images. These images were carefully categorized into two distinct classes: malignant melanoma and benign moles. Figure 2 provides a visual representation of some samples from the dataset, showcasing the variations in skin lesions. To ensure unbiased evaluation and reliable model performance assessment, the dataset was divided into three subsets: 60% for training, 10% validation, and 30% test, 6360 images for train, 3180 for the test, 1060 for validation.

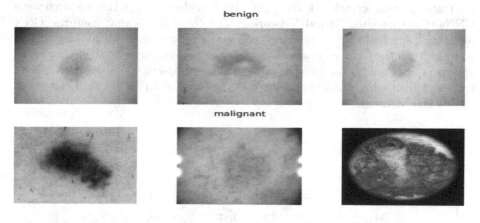

Fig. 2. Data samples [27]

3.2 Transfer Learning

Transfer learning in deep learning is a technique where a pre-trained neural network model, initially trained on a large dataset for a specific task, is adapted for a related task. This approach saves computational resources and training time by leveraging the knowledge the model has acquired during its original training. The process involves fine-tuning the model on the new task by using its learned features as a basis for a new classifier. Transfer learning is particularly beneficial when dealing with limited data for the target task, as it can significantly improve model performance and generalization [17].

The transfer learning process typically involves freezing the pre-trained model's layers to preserve the learned representations and preventing them from being modified during training. Only the top layers, including the classification layer, are trainable and adjusted to fit the new task. This approach ensures that the pre-trained model's valuable knowledge is retained while enabling the model to specialize and optimize its predictions for the specific classification problem at hand.

3.3   Pre-trained Models Architecture

A pretrained model refers to a deep learning model that has undergone training on extensive datasets to perform a particular task. This model embodies a neural algorithm inspired by the workings of the human brain, enabling it to identify patterns and make predictions based on data. Pretrained models offer the advantage of being readily applicable as they are, or they can be further fine-tuned to align with the specific requirements of an application. By leveraging the knowledge gained from extensive training on diverse data, pretrained models serve as powerful tools for various tasks, providing a head start and reducing the need for training from scratch. All the pre-trained models used in this research were CNNs (Convolutional Neural Networks). The three layers that comprise CNN are a convolutional layer, a pooling layer, and a fully connected (FC) layer. The complexity of the CNN increases from the convolutional layer to the FC layer, as shown in Fig. 3. This progression of increasing complexity enables the CNN to recognize increasingly larger and intricate features of an image until the entire object is recognized.

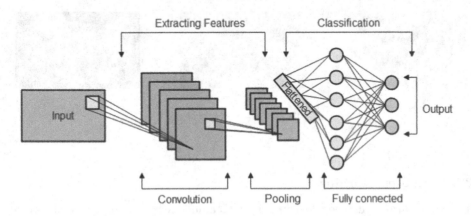

Fig. 3. Basic CNN architecture [28]

VGG16. The VGG-16 architecture with 16 layers takes an initial image input of size 224 * 244 * 3 [18,19]. It undergoes 5 iterations, with each iteration having

2 convolution layers and max pooling. The size, filter size, and stride of each layer vary according to the layer number. The output of each layer serves as the input for the next layer and ranges from 64 to 512. The network utilizes the ReLU activation function along with a SoftMax classifier. The stride varies as 1 and 2 for the consecutive convolutional and max pooling layers used to filter the input volume. The filter/kernel size of each layer is 3 * 3. The final three fully connected input layers, have sizes of 25,088 and 4096 with ReLU activation. The output with a size of 4096. As shown in Fig. 4.

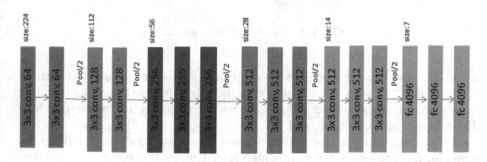

Fig. 4. VGG-16 architecture [19]

RESNET-50. The Resnet50 model comprises five stages and employs two types of layers known as convolutional and identity blocks. The first stage of the model takes the skin cancer input image and passes it to the initial layer, which consists of 64 different filtering layers of 7 * 7 size, with a stride of two [20]. In the second stage, the feature region is selected using a max pooling layer with a stride of two. The second stage convolution layer has nine layers. Stages 3, 4, and 5 of the model include 12, 18, and 9 layers, respectively, comprising filtering and activation layers. The model concludes with an average pooling connected to 1000 nodes, and finally, the output is given by a SoftMax function. The output is classified into either benign or malignant as shown in Fig. 5.

INCEPTIONV3. The Inception V3 architecture takes an input image dataset with a size ratio of 299 * 299 * 3, and the final output is a size of 8 * 8 * 2048. [21,23] The model is composed of 42 layers, which include many convolutions with a patch stride size of 33. The architecture consists of three modules, with module 1 having 3 inception with an input size of 35 * 35 * 288. Module 2 contains 5 inception with an input size of 17 * 17 * 768, while module 3 has 2 inception with an input size of 8 * 8 * 1280. The pooling layer has a patch size of 8 * 8, and the SoftMax classifier is used to classify the output as benign or malignant.

DenseNet-121. The DenseNet-121 architecture has an input image size of 224 * 224 * 3. The network has four dense blocks and three transition layers. Each dense block consists of several convolutional layers, which are densely connected

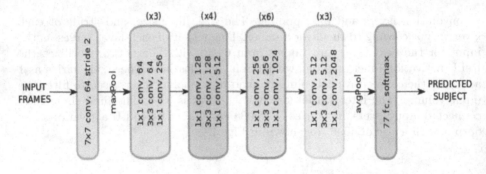

Fig. 5. ResNet-50 architecture [20]

with each other. In the first dense block, the input image is convolved with 64 filters of size 7 * 7 with a stride of 2. [22,24] This is followed by a max pooling layer with a stride of 2, which reduces the feature map size. The remaining three dense blocks have 128, 256, and 512 filters, respectively. Each dense block is connected to a transition layer, which consists of a convolutional layer followed by a pooling layer to reduce the feature map size. The last dense block is connected to a global average pooling layer, which averages the features for each channel across the entire feature map. The output of the global average pooling layer is then fed into a fully connected layer with a SoftMax activation function to produce the final classification output, as shown in Fig. 6.

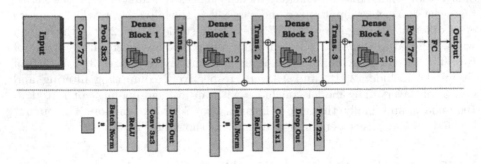

Fig. 6. DenseNet-121 architecture [22]

Xception. The Xception architecture has an input image dataset with a size of $299 \times 299 \times 3$, and the output is obtained with a size of $1 * 1 * 2048$. The model consists of 36 convolutional layers and 2 fully connected layers [25]. There are 14 modules present in the model, each with a varying number of depthwise separable convolutions. The first module has 8 depthwise separable convolutions with a 3×3 kernel size and input size of $299 * 299 * 3$. The second module has 16 depthwise separable convolutions with a 3×3 kernel size and input size of $149 * 149 * 32$. The last module has 3 depthwise separable convolutions with a

3×3 kernel size and input size of $19 * 19 * 728$. The average pooling is performed on the output of the last module, and the classifier used is SoftMax. The resulting output is classified as either benign or malignant. As shown in Fig. 7.

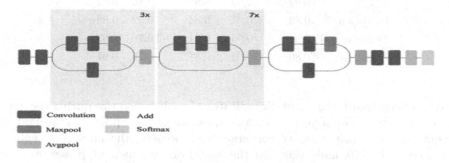

Fig. 7. Xception architecture [25]

4 Results

As outlined in the methodology, this research will carry out four distinct experiments, each employing varied hyper-parameters configurations and making modifications to the layers. The main purpose of these experiments is to examine and contrast the effects of different hyper-parameters on the performance and accuracy of the models. This comparative analysis will allow us to discern the most influential hyper-parameters settings for enhancing model performance in our particular research domain.

4.1 First Experiment

In this Experiment, only three additional layers were introduced for classification purposes. Firstly, a flatten layer was added to reshape the output from the previous layers into a one-dimensional vector. This allows for compatibility with the subsequent fully connected layers. Following the flatten layer, two dense layers were included. The first dense layer had 256 neurons and utilized the Rectified Linear Unit (ReLU) activation function. The second dense layer consisted of 2 neurons and used the Sigmoid activation function. The number of epochs was set to 10, the batch size used was 64. Additionally, the learning rate was set to 0.001. The learning rate is a hyper-parameters that controls the step size during optimization, determining how quickly the model adapts its parameters based on the computed gradients. The results are shown in Table 2.

4.2 Second Experiment

In this experiment, the classification layer from the first experiment was retained, while several modifications were made to the hyper-parameters. The learning

Table 2. Performance metrics for experiment 1

Model	Accuracy	Recall	precision	AUC	F1-Score
RESNET-50	0.92	0.92	0.92	0.94	0.92
VGG-16	0.92	0.92	0.92	0.85	0.92
InceptionV3	0.82	0.82	0.84	0.92	0.82
DenseNet121	0.92	0.94	0.91	0.70	0.93
Xception	0.89	0.93	0.87	0.75	0.91

rate was decreased to 10^{-7}, which indicates a smaller step size during the optimization process. This adjustment allows for more precise updates to the model's weights and can help improve convergence. Moreover, the number of epochs was increased to 70, indicating that the model underwent more passes over the entire training dataset. This increase in epochs provides the model with additional opportunities to learn complex patterns and improve its performance. By adjusting these parameters, we aimed to explore the impact of smaller learning rates, and longer training durations on the models' accuracy and convergence. The results are shown in Table 3.

Table 3. Performance metrics for experiment 2

Model	Accuracy	Recall	precision	AUC	F1-Score
RESNET-50	0.90	0.90	0.90	0.92	0.90
VGG-16	0.78	0.78	0.78	0.73	0.78
InceptionV3	0.78	0.78	0.78	0.85	0.78
DenseNet121	0.88	0.87	0.86	0.85	0.87
Xception	0.70	0.74	0.75	0.60	0.78

4.3 Third Experiment

During this particular experiment, a slight modification was made to the classification layer used in the previous experiments. In addition to the flatten layer and the two dense layers, a dropout layer was introduced with a dropout rate of 0.2. The purpose of the dropout layer is to prevent overfitting by randomly deactivating a portion of the neurons during training, encouraging the model to rely on different sets of features and promoting better generalization. Furthermore, the batch size was increased to 64. Moreover, the learning rate was increased to 0.000005, allowing for larger updates to the model's weights during optimization. In this experiment, a fixed number of 10 epochs was used for all models, providing a sufficient number of training iterations to observe the effects of the modified classification layer, batch size, and learning rate on the models' performance and convergence patterns. By incorporating the dropout layer and adjusting the batch size and learning rate. The results are shown in Table 4.

Table 4. Performance metrics for experiment 3

Model	Accuracy	Recall	precision	AUC	F1-Score
RESNET-50	0.93	0.93	0.93	0.94	0.93
VGG-16	0.88	0.88	0.88	0.91	0.88
InceptionV3	0.83	0.83	0.83	0.75	0.83
DenseNet121	0.88	0.88	0.88	0.88	0.88
Xception	0.84	0.84	0.84	0.70	0.84

4.4 Fourth Experiment

During this Experiments, a learning rate of 0.000005 was utilized. The inclusion of a global averaging layer and the implementation of the Early Stopping callback were intended to address overfitting and improve convergence. The global averaging layer aids in reducing overfitting by providing a more compact and generalized representation of the input features. Additionally, the Early Stopping callback is set with a patience level of 4, ensures that the training process is halted if the model's performance on the validation set does not improve for 4 consecutive epochs. This approach allows the model to take its time to converge, preventing it from becoming trapped in suboptimal solutions and potentially enhancing its overall performance. By incorporating these techniques, the fourth experiment aimed to enhance the model's ability to generalize and achieve better convergence. The results are shown in Table 5.

Table 5. Performance metrics for experiment 4

Model	Accuracy	Recall	precision	AUC	F1-Score
RESNET-50	0.90	0.90	0.90	0.96	0.90
VGG-16	0.87	0.87	0.87	0.91	0.87
InceptionV3	0.80	0.80	0.80	0.65	0.80
DenseNet121	0.84	0.84	0.84	0.75	0.84
Xception	0.79	0.79	0.80	0.65	0.80

5 Discussion

In each experiment, ResNet-50 emerged as the best-performing model. In Experiment 1, where all models had their layers frozen and a simple classification layer was added, ResNet-50 demonstrated superior accuracy, precision, recall, and F1 score compared to the other models. Similarly, in Experiment 2, when the learning rate was decreased and the number of epochs increased, ResNet-50 outperformed the other models, achieving the highest accuracy and F1 score. In Experiment 3, with the inclusion of a dropout layer, increased batch size, and higher learning rate, ResNet-50 once again showcased its prowess, achieving remarkable accuracy and F1 score. Finally, in Experiment 4, where the flatten layer was replaced with a global averaging layer and early stopping was applied, ResNet-50 continued to shine, achieving the best accuracy and F1 score.

The consistent superior performance of ResNet-50 throughout all experiments highlights its robustness and suitability for the task of melanoma classification. Its deep architecture, skip connections, and residual learning framework enable it to effectively capture complex patterns in the data, leading to accurate and reliable predictions. These findings underscore the significance of ResNet-50 as a powerful and versatile deep learning model for melanoma classification, with the potential to serve as a valuable tool for early detection and diagnosis of skin cancer.

When comparing our best model to the related work with our best model, it exhibits exceptional performance across various evaluation metrics. It achieves high accuracy, capturing the correct predictions with remarkable precision. Additionally, it demonstrated excellent recall, effectively identifying relevant instances within the dataset. The model also showcases impressive precision, minimizing false positives and accurately classifying the data. Moreover, its F1 score, which considers both precision and recall, attains a commendable balance between these measures. Lastly, the model's Area Under the Curve (AUC) metric highlights its ability to discriminate between positive and negative instances, further validating its predictive power. Overall, our model excels in accuracy, recall, precision, F1 score, and AUC, showcasing its robust performance across a comprehensive range of evaluation criteria as shown in Table 6.

Table 6. Comparison with previous work

Paper	Accuracy	Precision	Recall	AUC	F1-Score
[15]	90.4%	90.4%	90.3%	–	–
[26]	83.7%	56%	–	81.6%	–
[13]	–	–	–	90.69%	–
[14]	88.9%	–	–	–	–
ResNet-50 in 3rd Exp	93%	93%	93%	94%	93%

6 Conclusion

This research underscores the crucial role of deep learning models in the detection and classification of melanoma, a highly dangerous form of skin cancer. ResNet-50 consistently demonstrating exceptional accuracy across most of the experiments. Specifically, in experiment Three, ResNet-50 achieved an impressive accuracy rate of around 93% and an F1 score of 93%, indicating its effectiveness in accurately classifying the dataset. The consistent superiority of ResNet-50 over other models, as observed through various evaluation metrics such as accuracy, precision, recall, and F1 score, can be attributed to its deep architecture that incorporates skip connections and residual learning. These architectural features empower the model to effectively capture intricate patterns within the dataset, resulting in robustness, adaptability, and suitability for complex classification tasks like melanoma detection. The findings of this research shed light on the significant potential of deep learning in revolutionizing melanoma diagnosis, ultimately leading to improved patient outcomes, enhanced early detection, and targeted treatment strategies.

References

1. Afifi, S., GholamHosseini, H., Sinha, R.: SVM classifier on chip for melanoma detection. In: 2017 39th Annual International Conference of the IEEE Engineering in Medicine and Biology Society (EMBC), pp. 270–274. IEEE, July 2017
2. Cancer.net medical blog. https://www.cancer.net/cancer-types/melanoma/ screening
3. Afifi, S., GholamHosseini, H., Sinha, R.: FPGA implementations of SVM classifiers: a review. SN Comput. Sci. **1**, 1–17 (2020)
4. Afifi, S., GholamHosseini, H., Sinha, R.: A system on chip for melanoma detection using FPGA-based SVM classifier. Microprocess. Microsyst. **65**, 57–68 (2019)
5. Afifi, S., Gholamhosseini, H., Sinha, R., Lindén, M.: A novel medical device for early detection of melanoma. In: pHealth, pp. 122–127, January 2019
6. Afifi, S., GholamHosseini, H., Sinha, R.: Dynamic hardware system for cascade SVM classification of melanoma. Neural Comput. Appl. **32**(6), 1777–1788 (2020)
7. Afifi, S.: An optimized hardware system on chip for a support vector machine classifier: a case study on melanoma detection (Doctoral dissertation, Auckland University of Technology) (2018)
8. Afifi, S., GholamHosseini, H., Sinha, R.: A low-cost FPGA-based SVM classifier for melanoma detection. In: 2016 IEEE EMBS Conference on Biomedical Engineering and Sciences (IECBES), pp. 631–636. IEEE, December 2016
9. Afifi, S., GholamHosseini, H., Sinha, R.: Hardware acceleration of SVM-based classifier for melanoma images. In: Huang, F., Sugimoto, A. (eds.) PSIVT 2015. LNCS, vol. 9555, pp. 235–245. Springer, Cham (2016). https://doi.org/10.1007/978-3-319-30285-0_19
10. Kaur, R., GholamHosseini, H., Sinha, R., et al.: Automatic lesion segmentation using atrous convolutional deep neural networks in dermoscopic skin cancer images. BMC Med. Imaging **22**(103) (2022). https://doi.org/10.1186/s12880-022-00829-y
11. Kaur, R., GholamHosseini, H., Sinha, R.: Deep convolutional neural network for melanoma detection using dermoscopy images. In: 2020 42nd Annual International Conference of the IEEE Engineering in Medicine & Biology Society (EMBC), pp. 1524–1527 (2020). https://doi.org/10.1109/EMBC44109.2020.9175391
12. Kaur, R., GholamHosseini, H., Sinha, R., Lindén, M.: Melanoma classification using a novel deep convolutional neural network with dermoscopic images. Sensors **22**(3), 1134 (2022)

13. Mahbod, A., Schaefer, G., Wang, C., Ecker, R., Ellinger, I.: Skin lesion classification using hybrid deep neural networks, pp. 1229–1233, May 2019
14. Jayapriya, K., Jacob, I.J.: Hybrid fully convolutional networks-based skin lesion segmentation and melanoma detection using deep feature. Int. J. Imaging Syst. Technol. **30**(2), 348–357 (2020)
15. Kaur, R., GholamHosseini, H., Sinha, R., Lind en, M.: Melanoma classification using a novel deep convolutional neural network with dermoscopic images. Sensors **22**(3), 1134 (2022)
16. Rotemberg, V., et al.: A patient-centric dataset of images and metadata for identifying melanomas using clinical context. Sci Data **8**, 34 (2021). https://doi.org/10.1038/s41597-021-00815-z
17. Tsiakmaki, M., Kostopoulos, G., Kotsiantis, S., Ragos, O.: Transfer learning from deep neural networks for predicting student performance. Appl. Sci. **10**(6), 2145 (2020). https://doi.org/10.3390/app10062145
18. Hasan, M., Fatemi, M., Khan, M., Kaur, M., Zaguia, A.: Comparative analysis of skin cancer (benign vs. malignant) detection using convolutional neural networks. J. Healthc. Eng. **2021**, 1–17 (2021). https://doi.org/10.1155/2021/5895156
19. Simonyan, K., Zisserman, A.: Very deep convolutional networks for large-scale image recognition, arXiv:1409.1556 [cs.CV] (2015)
20. He, K., Zhang, X., Ren, S., Sun, J.: Deep residual learning for image recognition, arXiv:1512.03385 [cs.CV] (2015)
21. Demir, A., Yılmaz, F., Kose, O.: Early detection of skin cancer using deep learning architectures: Resnet-101 and Inception-V3, pp. 1–4, October 2019. https://doi.org/10.1109/TIPTEKNO47231.2019.8972045
22. Huang, G., Liu, Z., van der Maaten, L., Weinberger, K.Q.: Densely Connected Convolutional Networks, arXiv:1608.06993 [cs.CV] (2018)
23. Szegedy, C., Vanhoucke, V., Ioffe, S., Shlens, J., Wojna, Z.: Rethinking the inception architecture for computer vision, arXiv:1512.00567 [cs.CV] (2015)
24. Srinivasan, K., et al.: Performance Comparison of Deep CNN Models for Detecting Driver's Distraction. CMC -Tech Science Press, vol. 68, pp. 4109–4124 (2021). https://doi.org/10.32604/cmc.2021.016736
25. Chollet, F.: Xception: deep learning with depthwise separable convolutions, arXiv:1610.02357 [cs.CV] (2017)
26. Thao, L.T., Quang, N.H.: Automatic skin lesion analysis towards melanoma detection. In: 2017 21st Asia Pacific Symposium on Intelligent and Evolutionary Systems (IES), pp. 106–111 (2017). https://doi.org/10.1109/IESYS.2017.8233570
27. DiSanto, N.: ISIC Melanoma Dataset, IEEE Dataport, 26 May 2023. https://dx.doi.org/10.21227/9p2y-yq09
28. Phung, Rhee: A high-accuracy model average ensemble of convolutional neural networks for classification of cloud image patches on small datasets. Appl. Sci. **9**, 4500 (2019). https://doi.org/10.3390/app9214500

3D Formation Control of Multiple Cooperating Autonomous Agents via Leader-Follower Strategy

Roneel Chand[1]([✉]), Jai Raj[2], Krishna Raghuwaiya[2], and Jito Vanualailai[2]

[1] Fiji National University, Suva, Fiji
roneel.chand@fnu.ac.fj
[2] The University of the South Pacific, Suva, Fiji
{jai.raj,krishna.raghuwaiya,jito.vanualailai}@usp.ac.fj

Abstract. The work done in this paper provides solutions to the collision avoidance of multiple point-mass robots in the presence of multiple spherical and cylindrical obstacles in three-dimensional space. A set of autonomous controllers is derived using the architecture of the Lyapunov-based Control Scheme (LbCS) to achieve this task. We implement the leader-follower strategy via the split-rejoin method here, where we choose a leader and the rest of the flock or agents behave with respect to the leader to achieve its predetermined task. In addition, in the presence of fixed obstacles, the whole formation will split to avoid obstacles present in its path using the Minimum Distance Technique and rejoin at a safer place, regaining its pre-defined formation with respect to the leader. The Minimum Distance Technique allows a point-mass agent to avoid the walls of obstacles by approaching them from the closest possible distance in each unit of time. The formation will also avoid inter-collision, which is defined as moving obstacles in this case. Using the Lyapunov-based control scheme, a set of non-linear acceleration-based controllers will be derived such that the desired task is easily completed. The controllers will ensure that the formation travels in a well-planned manner and successfully converges on its targets while avoiding obstacles. To prove the efficiency and simplicity of the nonlinear acceleration-based controllers derived, computer simulations of virtual scenarios have been performed and given in the simulation results and discussion section. The paper concludes with a conclusion and recommendations for future work in this field.

Keywords: Lyapunov · autonomous · controllers · obstacles

1 Introduction

The significance of robotics and autonomous systems (RAS) is rising across a wide range of fields. In a number of locations, such as hospitals, restaurants, airports, military bases, and private homes, robots are becoming more prevalent. In reality, as more and more components of our environment integrate autonomy and smart systems, this rise will amplify over the coming years [3,16,23].

© The Author(s), under exclusive license to Springer Nature Singapore Pte Ltd. 2024
W. Q. Yan et al. (Eds.): PSIVT 2023, LNCS 14403, pp. 273–286, 2024.
https://doi.org/10.1007/978-981-97-0376-0_21

A variety of significant advantages that may be gained from these systems served as inspiration for the creation of RAS. They provide possibilities that are not possible for humans to achieve on their own, are generally efficient machines capable of operating at high speeds, can perform repeated complex actions without becoming tired, can be used to replace humans in dangerous situations, and in some cases are a cost-effective solution to problems [12,14,16,23]. According to the most recent research, the amount of work performed by robotic and autonomous systems increases to increase daily. As a result, businesses and nations are deploying several robot systems simultaneously to carry out many jobs at once [8,9,11,16,20,23]. According to the literature, several robots are preferable since they can work together to provide faster, more effective results [16,23]. Multi-agent operations are also always desired in other sectors [8,9,16,20,23].

Researchers have placed a lot of focus on the formation type and control of RAS because to the rising demand for robotic and autonomous systems. The literature has previously suggested a number of applications, such as cooperative mapping, mapping and planning, flocking and schooling, search and rescue operations, target locating, and so forth to solve this [1,2,6,7,15]. Although the upgraded robotic system has been successful in many activities across the globe, formation control has a big challenge when it comes to avoiding undesirable objects or obstacles in the workspace. Recent research has suggested a number of control techniques for robotic control that aid in the formation control of RAS and enable them to successfully complete the required task. Generic approaches from the literature include leader-follower strategy, generalized coordinates, behavior-based, virtual structures, and social potential fields. [1,2,4,6,15,23].

With all these upgraded techniques, Sharma, on the other hand, in [17] created a novel method known as the artificial potential field (APF), which is based on the architecture of the Lyapunov-based control scheme (LbCS) approach to address the issue of formation control. With the help of this strategy, robotic formations can be controlled and directed to successfully converge on their target by generating attracting and repulsive potential functions. The robots will be able to move closer to the target with the help of the attracting potential field function and avoid obstacles with the help of the repulsive potential field function. In this paper, we use this strategy to control the RAS [17–19].

For the case of this paper, we adopt leader-follower formation control via split-rejoin maneuvers to govern the movement of the entire flock described in [12]. Using the Lyapunov-based control scheme, we design a motion planner for the system as it travels and navigates in the workspace. This will ensure the flock carefully follows its trajectory and successfully achieves its target while avoiding obstacles in its path [5,10,21,22]. In case of obstacles, the formation will split and rejoin at safer distance regaining the predetermined shape.The obstacles in our scenario will be stationary, spherical, and cylindrical barriers, and each moving point mass in the swarm will act as an obstacles for every other member.The Direct Method of Lyapunov will then be used to create continuous acceleration-based controllers that stabilize our system by utilizing artificial potential fields. The research given in this paper is an extension of that found in [3,13], where we introduce leader-follower formation control via the split-rejoin method from multiple agents. We extend the work and look at the formation and control of multiple agents, adopting leader-follower strategy, where we define a leader and followers behave as per the leader's decisions in their predefined formations.

The remaining work in this paper is organized as follows: in Sect. 2, we define the robot model; in Sect. 3, we examine the artificial potential field functions while taking kinodynamic restrictions into account; in Sect. 4, we define the acceleration-based control laws; Sect. 5 explains the stability analysis of the given robotic system; computer simulations of a virtual scenario is given in Sect. 6 which also shows the effectiveness of the designed controllers and finally Sect. 7 brings the paper to a close by outlining potential directions for further research in the field.

2   Point-Mass Model

In this section, we provide an extremely simple kinematic model as in [13] for the formation control of a moving point-mass robot using the leader-follower method. We consider point-mass robots in the Euclidean plane, n, and $n \in \mathbb{N}$, where ρ_1 is the robot leader and ρ_i for $i = 2, \ldots, n$, are the follower robots. Figure 1 displays a two-dimensional schematic of a point-mass robot with and without obstacle avoidance.

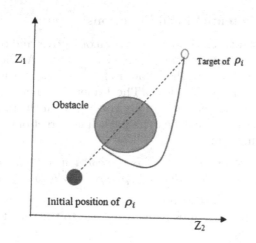

Fig. 1. Kinematic model of ρ_i with obstacles in $Z_1 - Z_2$ plane.

Next, We shall define the model proper using the definition as in [13].

Definition 1. *A point mass, ρ_i, is a sphere of radius rp_i and centered at $(x_i(t),$ $y_i(t), z_i(t)) \in \mathbb{R}^3$ for $t \geq 0$. It then leads to:*

$$\rho_i = \{(Z_1, Z_2, Z_3) \in \mathbb{R}^3 : (Z_1 - x_i)^2 + (Z_1 - y_i)^2 + (Z_1 - z_i)^2 \leq rp_i^2\} \qquad (1)$$

Next, we define the instantaneous velocity of the point mass, ρ_i, as $(v_i(t), \omega_i(t), \mu_i(t) = ((\dot{x}_i(t), \dot{y}_i(t), \dot{z}_i(t))$ at time $t \geq 0$.

Now assuming all the initial conditions, we adopt the kinematics of the system from [16], and model the ODEs of our system for $i \in \{1, \ldots, n\}$, as presented below.

$$\dot{x}_i = v_i(t), \dot{y}_i = \omega_i(t), \dot{z}_i = \mu_i(t),$$
$$\dot{x}_{i0} := x_i(t_0), \dot{y}_{i0} := y_i(t_0), \dot{z}_{i0} := z_i(t_0), \qquad (2)$$

for $i = 1, \ldots n$. Let $x_i := (x_i, y_i, z_i) \in \mathbb{R}^3$ and $x := (x_1, \ldots x_n) \in \mathbb{R}^3$. The system's kinematic model (2) now is a description of the instantaneous speeds and accelerations of ρ_i.

Next, we now define the elements of the Lyapunov function, which are essentially the attractive and repulsive potential field functions in the following section.

3 Artificial Potential Field Function

Here, we derive collision-free trajectories for the point mass, ρ_i, robot under kinodynamic constraints in a predefined workspace. The artificial potential field of the system will be constructed by combining these functions, which will be developed in the sections that follow.

3.1 Attractive Potential Field Functions

Attraction to Target. The leader is given an objective, and the aircraft system is allowed to proceed generally under the leader's control. As the formation moves toward the intended objective, the followers follow the leader in step with it and split in case of danger and obstacles. The leader, ρ_1, must go from a starting point to its pre-defined target, successfully converging at the target's center while avoiding any obstacles that may be in its path. The target of the leader is defined in the following definition:

Definition 2. *The leader robot, ρ_1, is assigned a stationary target which is assumed to be a sphere with center (p_{11}, p_{12}, p_{13}) with radius rt.*

Next, as in [17], the attractive function for the leader ρ_1 to its target is constructed as follows and measures its convergence to the target.

$$V_1(\mathbf{x}) = \frac{1}{2} \left[(x_1 - p_{11})^2 + (y_1 - p_{12})^2 + (z_1 - p_{13})^2 \right]. \qquad (3)$$

Furthermore, we introduce the following function to guarantee that the follower vehicles, ρ_i, for $i = 2, \ldots, n$, keep their desired position in relation to the leader, ρ_1.

$$V_i(\mathbf{x}) = \frac{1}{2} \left[(x_i - p_{i1})^2 + (y_i - p_{i2})^2 + (z_i - p_{i3})^2 \right], \qquad (4)$$

where $(p_{i1}, p_{i2}, p_{i3}) = (x_{11} - a_i, y_{11} - b_i, z_{11} - c_i)$ where a_i, b_i and c_i are relative x, y, z distance of the followers from the leader.

Auxiliary Function. Here, we design an auxiliary function that makes sure the leader successfully converges to its target. After reaching the target, the ρ_i, $i = 1, \ldots, n$, must stop at the target configuration because it has effectively completed the work that was assigned to it. It follows naturally from this that the energy of the robotic system must be zero in the desired configuration. To achieve this, we design the following function:

$$G_1(\mathbf{x}) = V_1(x) \tag{5}$$

and

$$G_i(\mathbf{x}) = V_i(x) \tag{6}$$

for follower vehicles for $i = 2, \ldots, n$. By using the provided auxiliary functions, the controllers are guaranteed to get zero at the leader's objective. The specified potential field functions are multiplied by both the auxiliary function and the final result.

3.2   Repulsive Potential Field Functions

In most cases, our environment contains unknown agents, like obstacles. The ρ_i must successfully avoid this in order to converge on their objectives. We develop an appropriate obstacle avoidance function that determines the Euclidean distances between the robots and obstacles in our workspace in order for this to happen. These repulsive potential fields function, in accordance with [17], is an inverse function that converts an avoidance function into the denominator and a control parameter into the numerator.

Fixed Obstacles. Here, we define two types of obstacles: spheres and cylindrical obstacles.

Spherical Obstacles. The lth obstacle is assumed to be a sphere with a radius of ro_l and a center of (o_{l1}, o_{l2}, o_{l3}). We formulate the avoidance function as follows so that ρ_i can avoid these obstacles. This is done using Minimum Distance Technique adopted from [17]. Also, we fix solid obstacles inside the workspace's confines using $q \in \mathbb{N}$.

$$FO_{il}(\mathbf{x}) = \frac{1}{2} \left[(x_i - o_{l1})^2 + (y_i - o_{l2})^2 + (z_i - o_{l3})^2 - (ro_l + r_{pi})^2 \right]. \tag{7}$$

where $i = 1, \ldots, n$, and $l = 1, \ldots, q$.

Cylindrical Obstacles. The cylinder's surface walls are categorized as fixed obstacles. Therefore, in order to escape the obstacles, mass-mobile robots, ρ_i, must stay away from these walls. We begin by complying with the definition as in [13].

Definition 3. *The kth surface-wall is collapsed into a cylinder in the $Z_1 Z_2 Z_3$ plane with initial coordinates (a_k, b_k, c_{k1}) and the final coordinates (a_k, b_k, c_{k2}) with radius rc_k. The parametric representation of the kth cylinder of the height $(c_{k2} - c_{k1})$ can be given as $Cx_k = a_k \pm rc_k cos\chi_k$, $Cy_k = b_k \pm rc_k sin\chi_k$, and $Cz_k = c_{k1} + \lambda_k(c_{k2} - c_{k1})$ where: $\mathbb{R} \to (-\frac{\pi}{2}, \frac{\pi}{2})$ and $\lambda_k : \mathbb{R}^2 \to [0, 1]$.*

Next, we again use MDT, [17], and compute the avoidance of the resultant point of the surface of the kth cylinder. This can be expressed as $Cx_{ik} = a_k \pm rc_k cos\chi_{ik}$, $Cy_{ik} = b_k \pm rc_{ik} sin\chi_k$, and $Cz_{ik} = c_{k1} + \lambda_{ik}(c_{k2} - c_{k1})$, where

$$\chi_{ik} = tan^{-1}\Big(\frac{y_i - b_k}{x_i - a_k}\Big)$$

and

$$\lambda_{ik} = (z_i - c_{ik})\Big(\frac{1}{c_{k2} - c_{k1}}\Big)$$

and the saturation functions are given by

$$\lambda ik = \begin{cases} 0, & \text{if } \lambda ik < 0 \\ \lambda ik, & \text{if } 0 \le \lambda ik \le 1 \\ 1, & \text{if } \lambda ik > 0 \end{cases}$$

and

$$\chi_{ik} = \Big(-\frac{\pi}{2}, \frac{\pi}{2}\Big)$$

With respect to above functions adopted from [16], for the robot ρ_i to avoid and past the closet point on the wall of the kth cylinder, the following function is introduced.

$$CO_{ik}(\mathbf{x}) = \frac{1}{2}\left[(x_i - Cx_{ik})^2 + (y_i - Cy_{ik})^2 + (z_i - Cz_{ik})^2 - (rp_i)^2\right]. \quad (8)$$

where $k = 1, ...m$ and $i = 1, ...n$.

Moving Obstacles. A multi-robot system with many agents that, by virtue of their presence, turn into moving obstacles for the system's other agents. To avoid collisions, which are represented as moving obstacles in this situation, all agents in the workplace must move away from one another. We design the next avoidance function for ρ_i to avoid ρ_j.

$$MO_{ij}(\mathbf{x}) = \frac{1}{2}\left[(x_i - x_j)^2 + (y_i - y_j)^2 + (z_i - z_j)^2 - (r_{pi} + r_{pj})^2\right]. \quad (9)$$

for $i, j = 1, ..., n, j \ne i$.

Workspace Limitations. For the workspace of our robots, ρ_i, we create a particular 3D framework with the dimensions η_1 by η_2 by η_3. These boundaries are referred to as *fixed obstacles* in our LbCS. We formulate a potential function, as given below, so that the robots, ρ_i, clear these boundaries.

$$
\begin{aligned}
W_{i1}(\mathbf{x}) &= (x_i - r_{pi}), \\
W_{i2}(\mathbf{x}) &= (\eta_2 - (y_i + r_{pi})), \\
W_{i3}(\mathbf{x}) &= (\eta_1 - (x_i + r_{pi})), \\
W_{i4}(\mathbf{x}) &= (y_i - r_{pi}), \\
W_{i5}(\mathbf{x}) &= (z_i - r_{pi}), \\
W_{i6}(\mathbf{x}) &= (\eta_3 - (z_i + r_{pi})),
\end{aligned}
\tag{10}
$$

for $i = 1, ..., n$.

Once combined with the appropriate tuning parameters, these avoidance functions will provide repulsive potential field functions that will be later added to the control rules to ensure that the movement of the ρ_i stays inside the specified workspace boundaries.

4 Design of the Acceleration-Based Controllers

4.1 Lyapunov Function

A Lyapunov function, also referred to as the total potential, needs to be built next. The *control parameters* for $i = 1, \ldots, n$, which will be employed in the repulsive potential function, must be determined in order to do this. The details are as follows:

(i) $\alpha_{il} > 0$, $l = 1, \ldots, q$, for the collision avoidance of q spherical-shaped obstacles.

(ii) $\beta_{ik} > 0$, $s = 1, \ldots, m$, for the avoidance of m cylindrical shape obstacles.

(iii) $\eta_{ij} > 0$, $j = 1, \ldots, n$, $i \neq j$, for the collision avoidance between any two agents, ρ_i.

(iv) $\kappa_{ip} > 0$, $p = 1, \ldots, 6$, for the avoidance of the lane boundaries.

Next, using the above *control parameters*, we design the Lypunov function with two components, namely the attractive and repulsive field functions:

$$
L(\mathbf{x}) = \sum_{i=1}^{n} \left[V_i(\mathbf{x}) + G_i(\mathbf{x}) \left(\sum_{l=1}^{q} \frac{\alpha_{il}}{FO_{il}(\mathbf{x})} + \sum_{k=1}^{m} \frac{\beta_{ik}}{CO_{ik}(\mathbf{x})} + \sum_{p=1}^{6} \frac{\kappa_{ip}}{W_{ip}(\mathbf{x})} \right) \right]
$$
$$
+ \sum_{i=1}^{n} G_i(\mathbf{x}) \left(\sum_{\substack{j=1 \\ j \neq i}}^{n} \frac{\eta_{ij}}{MO_{ij}(\mathbf{x})} \right).
$$

$$\tag{11}$$

4.2   Nonlinear Acceleration Controllers

Here, we extract the control laws for the mobile robots, ρ_i by finding the derivatives of the different components of $L(x)$. Setting the convergence parameters $\alpha_{i1}, \alpha_{i2}, \alpha_{i3} >$, $i = 1, ..., n$, the control outputs are as follows:

$$f_{11} = \left[1 + \sum_{l=1}^{q} \frac{\alpha_{1l}}{FO_{1l}} + \sum_{k=1}^{m} \frac{\beta_{1s}}{CO_{1k}} + \sum_{p=1}^{6} \frac{\kappa_{1p}}{W_{1p}} + \sum_{\substack{j=1 \\ j \neq i}}^{n} \frac{\eta_{1j}}{MO_{1j}}\right](x_1 - p_{11})$$

$$-G_1\left[\sum_{l=1}^{q} \frac{\alpha_{1l}}{FO_{1l}^2}(x_1 - o_{l1}) - 2\sum_{\substack{j=1 \\ j \neq i}}^{n} \frac{\eta_{1j}}{MO_{1j}^2}(x_1 - x_j)\right] - \frac{G_1\kappa_{11}}{(W_{11})^2} + \frac{G_1\kappa_{13}}{(W_{13})^2}$$

$$-G_1\sum_{k=1}^{m} \frac{\beta_{1s}}{CO_{1k}}\left((x_1 - Cx_{1k})\left(1 \pm r_k sin\chi_{1k}\frac{(y_1 - b_k)}{(x_1 - a_k)^2 + (y_1 - b_k)^2}\right)\right.$$

$$\left.\pm(y_1 - Cy_{1k})\left(1 \pm r_k cos\chi_{1k}\frac{(y_1 - b_k)}{(x_1 - a_k)^2 + (y_1 - b_k)^2}\right)\right),$$

$$f_{12} = \left[1 + \sum_{l=1}^{q} \frac{\alpha_{1l}}{FO_{1l}} + \sum_{k=1}^{m} \frac{\beta_{1k}}{CO_{1k}} + \sum_{p=1}^{?} \frac{\kappa_{1p}}{W_{1p}} + \sum_{\substack{j=1 \\ j \neq i}}^{n} \frac{\eta_{1j}}{MO_{1j}}\right](y_1 - p_{12})$$

$$-G_1\left[\sum_{l=1}^{q} \frac{\alpha_{1l}}{FO_{1l}^2}(y_1 - o_{l2}) - 2\sum_{\substack{j=1 \\ j \neq i}}^{n} \frac{\eta_{1j}}{MO_{1j}^2}(y_1 - y_j)\right] - \frac{G_1\kappa_{12}}{(W_{12})^2} + \frac{G_1\kappa_{14}}{(W_{14})^2}$$

$$-G_1\sum_{k=1}^{m} \frac{\beta_{1s}}{CO_{1k}}\left((x_1 - Cx_{1k})\left(1 \pm r_k sin\chi_{1k}\frac{(y_1 - b_k)}{(x_1 - a_k)^2 + (y_1 - b_k)^2}\right)\right.$$

$$\left.\pm(y_1 - Cy_{1k})\left(1 \pm r_k cos\chi_{1k}\frac{(y_1 - b_k)}{(x_1 - a_k)^2 + (y_1 - b_k)^2}\right)\right),$$

$$f_{13} = \left[1 + \sum_{l=1}^{q} \frac{\alpha_{1l}}{FO_{1l}} + \sum_{k=1}^{m} \frac{\beta_{1k}}{CO_{1k}} + \sum_{p=1}^{6} \frac{\kappa_{1p}}{W_{1p}} + \sum_{\substack{j=1 \\ j \neq i}}^{n} \frac{\eta_{1j}}{MO_{1j}}\right](z_1 - p_{13})$$

$$-G_1\left[\sum_{l=1}^{q} \frac{\alpha_{1l}}{FO_{1l}^2}(z_1 - o_{l3}) - 2\sum_{\substack{j=1 \\ j \neq i}}^{n} \frac{\eta_{1j}}{MO_{1j}^2}(z_1 - z_j)\right] - \frac{G_1\kappa_{15}}{(W_{15})^2} + \frac{G_1\kappa_{16}}{(W_{16})^2},$$

and for $i = 2, \ldots, n$.

$$
f_{i1} = \left[1 + \sum_{l=1}^{q} \frac{\alpha_{il}}{FO_{il}} + \sum_{k=1}^{m} \frac{\beta_{ik}}{CO_{ik}} + \sum_{p=1}^{6} \frac{\kappa_{ip}}{W_{ip}} + \sum_{\substack{j=1 \\ j \neq i}}^{n} \frac{\eta_{ij}}{MO_{ij}} \right] (x_i - p_{i1})
$$

$$
- G_i \left[\sum_{l=1}^{q} \frac{\alpha_{il}}{FO_{il}^2} (x_i - o_{l1}) - 2 \sum_{\substack{j=1 \\ j \neq i}}^{n} \frac{\eta_{ij}}{MO_{ij}^2} (x_i - x_j) \right] - \frac{G_i \kappa_{i1}}{(W_{i1})^2} + \frac{G_1 \kappa_{i3}}{(W_{i3})^2}
$$

$$
- G_i \sum_{k=1}^{6} \frac{\beta_{is}}{CO_{ik}} \left((x_i - Cx_{ik}) \left(1 \pm r_k \sin\chi_{ik} \frac{(y_i - b_k)}{(x_i - a_k)^2 + (y_i - b_k)^2} \right) \right.
$$

$$
\left. \pm (y_i - Cy_{ik}) \left(1 \pm r_k \cos\chi_{ik} \frac{(y_i - b_k)}{(x_i - a_k)^2 + (y_i - b_k)^2} \right) \right),
$$

$$
f_{i2} = \left[1 + \sum_{l=1}^{q} \frac{\alpha_{il}}{FO_{il}} + \sum_{k=1}^{m} \frac{\beta_{ik}}{CO_{ik}} + \sum_{p=1}^{6} \frac{\kappa_{ip}}{W_{ip}} + \sum_{\substack{j=1 \\ j \neq i}}^{n} \frac{\eta_{ij}}{MO_{ij}} \right] (y_i - p_{i2})
$$

$$
- G_i \left[\sum_{l=1}^{q} \frac{\alpha_{il}}{FO_{il}^2} (y_i - o_{i2}) - 2 \sum_{\substack{j=1 \\ j \neq i}}^{n} \frac{\eta_{ij}}{MO_{ij}^2} (y_i - y_j) \right] - \frac{G_i \kappa_{i2}}{(W_{i2})^2} + \frac{G_i \kappa_{i4}}{(W_{i4})^2}
$$

$$
- G_i \sum_{k=1}^{6} \frac{\beta_{is}}{CO_{ik}} \left((x_i - Cx_{ik}) \left(1 \pm r_k \sin\chi_{ik} \frac{(y_i - b_k)}{(x_i - a_k)^2 + (y_i - b_k)^2} \right) \right.
$$

$$
\left. \pm (y_i - Cy_{ik}) \left(1 \pm r_k \cos\chi_{ik} \frac{(y_i - b_k)}{(x_i - a_k)^2 + (y_i - b_k)^2} \right) \right),
$$

$$
f_{i3} = \left[1 + \sum_{l=1}^{q} \frac{\alpha_{il}}{FO_{il}} + \sum_{k=1}^{m} \frac{\beta_{ik}}{CO_{ik}} + \sum_{p=1}^{6} \frac{\kappa_{ip}}{W_{ip}} + \sum_{\substack{j=1 \\ j \neq i}}^{n} \frac{\eta_{ij}}{MO_{ij}} \right] (z_i - p_{i3})
$$

$$
- G_i \left[\sum_{l=1}^{q} \frac{\alpha_{il}}{FO_{il}^2} (z_i - o_{l3}) - 2 \sum_{\substack{j=1 \\ j \neq i}}^{n} \frac{\eta_{ij}}{MO_{ij}^2} (z_i - z_j) \right] - \frac{G_i \kappa_{i5}}{(W_{i5})^2} + \frac{G_i \kappa_{i6}}{(W_{i6})^2},
$$

Next, we state the theorem below, extended from [16].

Theorem 1. *Let the ODEs in system (2) govern the movement of the mobile robot's, ρ_i. The main goal is to guide the robot to its final configuration in a dynamic workspace. Convergence to predetermined targets, avoiding fixed spherical and cylindrical objects, avoiding boundary walls, and avoiding other moving-point mass robots are all included in this subtask. We take into consideration the following velocity control laws in order to ensure the stability of system (2) in the Lyapunov sense.*

$$
v_i = -\frac{1}{\alpha_{i1}} f_{i1}, \quad \omega_i = -\frac{1}{\alpha_{i2}} f_{i2}, \quad \mu_i = -\frac{1}{\alpha_{i3}} f_{i3}, \tag{12}
$$

5   Stability Analysis

Next, we use the Direct Method of Lypunov and show and provide the mathematical stability of the system (2). We begin with the following theorem:

Theorem 2. *Let (p_{i1}, p_{i2}, p_{i3}) be the position of the target of the point mass mobile robot, ρ_i. Given that $x_{ei} = (p_{i1}, p_{i2}, p_{i3}, 0, 0, 0) \in \mathbb{R}^6$ is an equilibrium point for (2), then $x_{ei} \in D(L(x))$ is a stable equilibrium point of system (2).*

Proof. Next, we verify the following for $i \in \{1, \dots, n\}$:

1. $L(\mathbf{x})$ is defined, continuous and positive over the domain $D(L(\mathbf{x})) = \{\mathbf{x} \in \mathbb{R}^{6n} : \quad FO_{il}(\mathbf{x}) > 0, l = 1, \dots, q; \quad MO_{ij}(\mathbf{x}) > 0, j = 1, \dots, n, j \neq i; \quad W_{ip}(\mathbf{x}) > 0, p = 1, \dots, 6; \quad CO_{ik}(\mathbf{x}) > 0, k = 1, \dots, m\};$
2. $L(\mathbf{x}_e) = 0, \dot{L}_{(2)}(\mathbf{x}_e) = 0;$
3. $L(\mathbf{x}) > 0 \ \forall \mathbf{x} \in D(L(\mathbf{x}))/\mathbf{x}_e,$
4. $\dot{L}_{(2)}(\mathbf{x}) = -\sum_{i=1}^{n} \left(\delta_{i1} v_i^2 + \delta_{i2} \omega_i^2 + + \delta_{i3} \mu_i^2\right) \leq 0, \forall \mathbf{x} \in D(L(\mathbf{x})),$
5. $L(\mathbf{x}) \in C^1 \left(D(L(\mathbf{x}))\right).$

Hence, $L(\mathbf{x})$ is classified as a Lyapunov function for system (2) and we conclude that $\mathbf{x}_e$ is a stable equilibrium point in the Lyapunov sense.   □

6   Simulation Results and Discussion

Here, we present our results from computer simulations. We have a virtual scenario where four point-mass robots move in *arrowhead formation* in the presence of spherical and cylindrical obstacles. Figure 2 shows how the whole formation moves from its initial position to its final destination. Here, the leader, ρ_1, governs the overall movement, and the followers behave with respect to the leader in the predefined formation. In the event of obstacles, the whole formation splits and rejoins at a safer location, regaining the desired formation and converging towards the target. Figure 3 shows the front view of Fig. 2. The Lyapunov function (red) and its derivative (blue) are shown in Fig. 4 as they evolve. This gets closer to zero as the formation gets closer to the target, indicating that the energy of the system is waning and will reach zero at the target, allowing the formation to come to a stop there. Table 1 provides the configurations for the point mass robots, ρ_i, as well as additional convergence parameters needed for the simulation of Fig. 2, assuming that all units used have been taken into account.

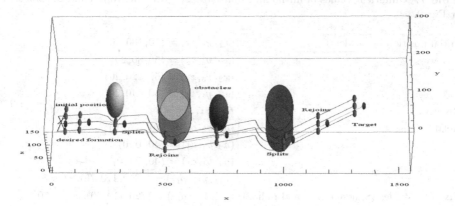

Fig. 2. Positions of ρ_i in arrowhead formation. Red denotes the following, while blue denotes the leader. The brown and black lines depict the system's trajectory. The formation splits in case of obstacles and rejoins later at a safer distance. (Color figure online)

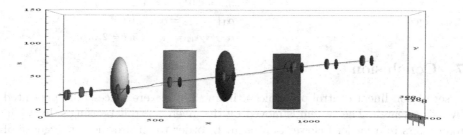

Fig. 3. Front view of Fig. 2

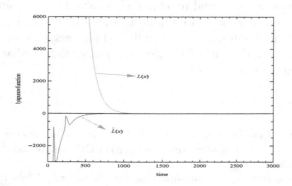

Fig. 4. Evolution of $L(\mathbf{x})$ in red and $\dot{L}_{(}\mathbf{x})$ in blue

Table 1. Numerical values of initial and final states, with constraints and parameters for Fig. 2

Initial position of Leader	$(x_1, y_1, z_1) = (50, 100, 20)$
Followers	$(x_2, y_2, z_2) = (50, 80, 20)$
	$(x_3, y_3, z_3) = (50, 120, 20)$
	$(x_4, y_4, z_4) = (50, 140, 20)$
Radius	$r_{pi}, i, 1, ...n = 8$
Relative Distance	$(a_2, b_2, c_2) = (40, -20, 0)$
	$(a_3, b_3, c_3) = (40, 0, 0)$
	$(a_4, b_4, c_4) = (40, 20, 0)$
Leader's target	$(p_{11}, p_{12}, p_{13}) = (1350, 110, 75), rt = 5$
Fixed Obstacles (Sphere center and radius)	$(o_{11}, o_{12}, o_{13}) = (720, 110, 50), ro_1 = 50$
	$(o_{21}, o_{22}, o_{23}) = (270, 150, 40), ro_2 = 40$
(Cylinder, (center, radius and height))	$(a_1, b_1, c_{11}) = (530, 130, 0), rc_1 = 70, c_{12} = 90$
	$(a_2, b_2, c_{21}) = (980, 100, 0), rc_2 = 60, c_{22} = 85$
Collision avoidance (Sphere)	$\alpha_{il} = 1$, for $i = 1, ..., n, l = 1, ..., q$
Collision avoidance (Cylinder)	$\beta_{ik} = 1$, for $i = 1, ...n, k = 1, ..., m$
	$\kappa_{ip} = 0.001$, for $i = 1, ..., n, p = 1, ..., 6$
	$\eta_{ij} = 0.01, i, j = 1, ..., n, j \neq i$
Convergence	$\alpha_{11} = \alpha_{12} = \alpha_{13} = 0.005$,
	$\alpha_{i1} = \alpha_{i2} = \alpha_{i3} = 5, i = 2, ..., n$

7   Conclusion

A set of non-linear control principles utilizing LbCS were successfully presented by this research. The system is moved by the given controllers using split-rejoin maneuvers in a leader-follower approach. In order to ensure the convergence of the entire system to its equilibrium state while avoiding obstacles and providing feasible routes, acceleration-based controllers have been developed. The follower vehicle followed and maintained the position of the predetermined leader, splitting in the event of obstacles and rejoining afterward. Finally, computer simulations of a virtual scenario have been done to show the effectiveness of the approach and controllers. Future research will include rectangle-shaped obstacles and examine stability dynamically utilizing a leader-follower-based low-degree formation technique in other UAVs.

References

1. Arrichiello, F.: Coordination control of multiple mobile robots. Dipartimento di Automazione, Elettromagnetismo, Ingegneria Dell'informazione e Matematica Industriale (2006)
2. Balch, T., Hybinette, M.: Social potentials for scalable multi-robot formations. In: Proceedings 2000 ICRA. Millennium Conference. IEEE International Conference on Robotics and Automation. Symposia Proceedings (Cat. No. 00CH37065), vol. 1, pp. 73–80. IEEE (2000)

3. Chand, R., Raghuwaiya, K., Vanualailai, J.: Leader-follower strategy of fixed-wing unmanned aerial vehicles via split rejoin maneuvers. In: Babichev, S., Lytvynenko, V. (eds.) ISDMCI 2022, vol. 149, pp. 231–245. Springer, Cham (2023). https://doi.org/10.1007/978-3-031-16203-9_14

4. Chand, R., Raghuwaiya, K., Vanualailai, J., Raj, J.: Leader-follower based control of fixed-wing multi-robot system (MRS) via split-rejoin maneuvers in 3d. In: Reddy, A.B., Nagini, S., Balas, V.E., Raju, K.S. (eds.) ICACECS 2022. LNNS, vol. 612, pp. 195–209. Springer, Singapore (2023). https://doi.org/10.1007/978-981-19-9228-5_18

5. Chand, R., Raghuwaiya, K., Vanualailai, J., Raj, J.: Leader-follower based low-degree formation control of fixed-wing unmanned aerial vehicles in 3d. In: Reddy, A.B., Nagini, S., Balas, V.E., Raju, K.S. (eds.) ICACECS 2022. LNNS, vol. 612, pp. 101–118. Springer, Singapore (2023). https://doi.org/10.1007/978-981-19-9228-5_10

6. De La Cruz, C., Carelli, R.: Dynamic model based formation control and obstacle avoidance of multi-robot systems. Robotica 26(3), 345–356 (2008)

7. Ebert, J.T., Gauci, M., Nagpal, R.: Multi-feature collective decision making in robot swarms. In: Proceedings of the 17th International Conference on Autonomous Agents and MultiAgent Systems, pp. 1711–1719 (2018)

8. Ho, F., Goncalves, A., Salta, A., Cavazza, M., Geraldes, R., Prendinger, H.: Multi-agent path finding for UAV traffic management: robotics track (2019)

9. Liu, M., Ma, H., Li, J., Koenig, S.: Task and path planning for multi-agent pickup and delivery. In: Proceedings of the International Joint Conference on Autonomous Agents and Multiagent Systems (AAMAS) (2019)

10. Mamino, M., Viglietta, G.: Square formation by asynchronous oblivious robots. arXiv preprint arXiv:1605.06093 (2016). https://doi.org/10.48550/arXiv.1605.06093

11. Raghuwaiya, K., Chand, R.: 3D motion planning of a fixed-wing unmanned aerial vehicle. In: 2018 5th Asia-Pacific World Congress on Computer Science and Engineering (APWC on CSE), pp. 241–245 (2018). https://doi.org/10.1109/APWConCSE.2018.00046

12. Raghuwaiya, K., Sharma, B., Vanualailai, J.: Leader-follower based locally rigid formation control. J. Adv. Transp. 2018 (2018)

13. Raghuwaiya, K., Vanualailai, J., Raj, J.: 3D cylindrical obstacle avoidance using the minimum distance technique. In: Bhatia, S.K., Tiwari, S., Ruidan, S., Trivedi, M.C., Mishra, K.K. (eds.) Advances in Computer, Communication and Computational Sciences. AISC, vol. 1158, pp. 199–208. Springer, Singapore (2021). https://doi.org/10.1007/978-981-15-4409-5_18

14. Raj, J., Raghuwaiya, K., Vanualailai, J.: Collision avoidance of 3D rectangular planes by multiple cooperating autonomous agents. J. Adv. Transp. 2020, 1–13 (2020). https://doi.org/10.1155/2020/4723687

15. Raj, J., Raghuwaiya, K., Sharma, B., Vanualailai, J.: Motion control of a flock of 1-trailer robots with swarm avoidance. Robotica, 1–26 (2021). https://doi.org/10.1017/S0263574721000060

16. Raj, J., Raghuwaiya, K., Vanualailai, J.: Collision avoidance of 3d rectangular planes by multiple cooperating autonomous agents. J. Adv. Transp. 2020, 1–13 (2020)

17. Sharma, B.: New directions in the applications of the Lyapunov-based control scheme to the findpath problem. Ph.D. thesis, University of the South Pacific, Suva, Fiji Islands, Ph.D. dissertation, July 2008

18. Sharma, B., Vanualailai, J., Prasad, A.: Formation control of a swarm of mobile manipulators. Rocky Mountain J. Math., 909–940 (2011)
19. Sharma, B., Vanualailai, J., Prasad, A.: A dø-strategy: facilitating dual-formation control of a virtually connected team. J. Adv. Transp. **2017** (2017)
20. Sharma, B.N., Raj, J., Vanualailai, J.: Navigation of carlike robots in an extended dynamic environment with swarm avoidance. Int. J. Robust Nonlinear Control **28**(2), 678–698 (2018)
21. Shojaei, K.: Neural adaptive output feedback formation control of type (m, s) wheeled mobile robots. IET Control Theory Appl. **11**(4), 504–515 (2017). https://doi.org/10.1049/iet-cta.2016.0952
22. Vanualailai, J., Sharan, A., Sharma, B.: A swarm model for planar formations of multiple autonomous unmanned aerial vehicles. In: 2013 IEEE International Symposium on Intelligent Control (ISIC), pp. 206–211. IEEE (2013)
23. Wong, C., Yang, E., Yan, X.T., Gu, D.: An overview of robotics and autonomous systems for harsh environments. In: 2017 23rd International Conference on Automation and Computing (ICAC), pp. 1–6. IEEE (2017)

LAPRNet: Lightweight Airborne Particle Removal Network for LiDAR Point Clouds

Yanqi Ma, Ziyu Yue, Youwei Wang, Risheng Liu, Zhixun Su,
and Junjie Cao[✉]

Dalian University of Technology, 2 Linggong Road, Dalian 116024, Liaoning, China
jjcao@dlut.edu.cn

Abstract. Autonomous vehicles and mobile robotics usually rely on
LiDAR sensors for outdoor environment perception. Airborne particles,
such as fog, rain, and snow, introduce undesired measurement points
resulting in missing detection and false positives. Hence LiDAR-based
perception systems must contend with inclement weather to avoid a significant drop in performance. This paper introduces a lightweight network to infer these undesired measurement points. It mainly consists of
three Wide Multi-Level Residual modules (WMLR). WMLR is delicately
designed to integrate wide activation, multi-level shortcuts, and shuffle
attention seamlessly, to make it an effective and efficient pre-processing
tool for subsequent tasks. We also introduce an enhanced LiDAR data
representation to boost the performance further. It integrates point cloud
spatial distribution with the standard intensity and distance inputs.
Thus, two models following the same network architecture but with the
standard and enhanced input representation, namely $LAPRNet_2$ and
$LAPRNet_3$, are proposed. They are trained and tested in controlled and
natural weather environments. Experiments on the WADS and Chamber datasets show that they outperform state-of-the-art deep learning
and traditional filtering methods by a significant margin. Considering
the limited computing resources on edge devices, both $LAPRNet_2$ and
$LAPRNet_3$ provide an optimal balance between quality and computation to ensure successful deployment. $LAPRNet_2$ is more efficient, and
the parameters and computations of it against WeatherNet are 1.53M
vs. 0.39M and 18.4 GFLOPs vs. 4.9 GFLOPs, respectively. The source
code will be available on GitHub soon.

Keywords: LiDAR Point Clouds · Airborne Particle Removal ·
Lightweight · Inclement Weather

1 Introduction

Point clouds, as one of the most common representations for 3D objects and
scenes, have been widely used in many scenarios, such as geometric analysis,
autonomous driving and robotics applications. However, the scanned raw points
are inevitably contaminated by noise and outliers. A large amount of point cloud

© The Author(s), under exclusive license to Springer Nature Singapore Pte Ltd. 2024
W. Q. Yan et al. (Eds.): PSIVT 2023, LNCS 14403, pp. 287–301, 2024.
https://doi.org/10.1007/978-981-97-0376-0_22

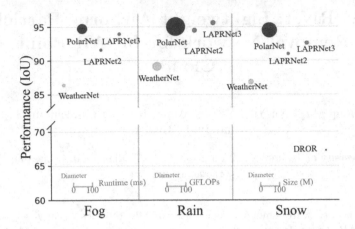

Fig. 1. Airborne particle removal results for the traditional method (DSOR [9]), previous deep learning methods (WeatherNet [6] and PolarNet [25]), and our LAPRNet2 and LAPRNet3. The left and middle columns show the results for fog and rain on the Chamber Dataset, and the right column shows the results for snow on the WADS dataset. From the left to right column, each bubble's area is proportional to runtime, FLOPs, and model size respectively. The proposed LAPRNet2 and LAPRNet3 are more suitable for deployment on constrained edge devices to provide effective pre-processing for subsequent tasks. Note[1]: PolarNet is re-trained on the same datasets to focus on airborne particle removal. Note[2]: The IoU of DSOR on fog and rain are 6.94 and 7.37 which can be found in Table 2.

denoise methods [11,12,16] are proposed to restore high-quality points, which is crucial for downstream missions. But these methods are not suitable for denoise LiDAR point clouds polluted by undesirable measurements of airborne particles, such as fog, rain, snow, and dust. Therefore, environment perception based on LiDAR sensors under inclement weather conditions has received increasing attention [1,3–6,22], since it is inevitable to encounter these inclement weather outdoors (Fig. 2).

Both classical and deep learning perception methods are employed in practice. The perception neural networks might better cope with such issues without the need for explicit handling of these noisy measurements if the networks are re-trained in inclement weather conditions. Compared with collecting and labeling enough data manually for various tasks under inclement weather, it is relatively easier to label a small dataset with airborne particles and clear classes, as done in [9] to train a shared airborne particle removal method for various subsequent applications. Still, many classical LiDAR perception algorithms, which usually are implemented on devices with minimal computational resources, depend on denoising the noisy point cloud measurements in a pre-processing step. This sparks much research on airborne particle removal for LiDAR point clouds [3,6,9,19,21].

These LiDAR airborne particle removal methods can be further divided into 3D filtering [3,9,21] methods and deep learning based methods [6,19]. 3D filter-

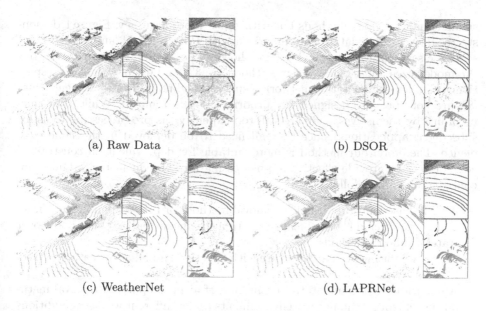

(a) Raw Data   (b) DSOR

(c) WeatherNet   (d) LAPRNet

Fig. 2. Snow removal results of DSOR (b), WeatherNet (c), and the proposed LAPR-Net (d). The LiDAR point cloud corrupted by snow (grey points) is shown in (a). The proposed LAPRNet removes more snow compared to both the DSOR [9] and WeatherNet [6]. (Color figure online)

ing methods are based on statistical analyses of point intensity and density. It is hard to handle airborne particles near the device and sparse environment points at medium or large distances at the same time. They may be falsely-marked as environment points or noisy points respectively. Besides that, [3,9,21] focus on desnowing and their performance usually drops dramatically on fog and rain data, see Table 2. Supervised deep learning approaches are far more accurate for identifying fog, rain, and snow particles [6,13]. But their model size and inference time should be further reduced to boost their deployment on edge devices with limited inference budgets, see Fig. 1.

The paper addresses this issue by proposing a lightweight airborne particle removal network for LiDAR in inclement weather. The network mainly consists of three delicately designed WMLR modules integrating wide activation, multi-level shortcuts, and shuffle attention. It is an effective and efficient network architecture. An enhanced LiDAR data representation utilizing point cloud spatial distribution is also explored to boost the performance further. We introduce two models following the same network architecture but with the standard and enhanced input representation, namely $LAPRNet_2$ and $LAPRNet_3$. Both of them surpass state-of-the-art deep learning and traditional filtering methods by a significant margin. At the same time, they have the right quality-computation trade-off for deployment on edge devices with limited computational resources. $LAPRNet_2$ is more efficient, and its model size and FLOPs are both four times smaller than previous methods but with much more accuracy. Figure 1 demonstrates these on two datasets. Comparison with PolarNet [25], an online LiDAR semantic segmentation method, is also shown. The results are comparable, but the model sizes and FLOPs of our methods are 3% and 6% of PolarNet, respectively. Similar segmentation networks, such as Cylinder3D [27], RangeFormer [8], are not specially designed for airborne particle removal. While they may be online by themselves, they are still too expensive as pre-processing tools for subsequent applications, since they all need to be deployed in the same edge device. Therefore, our method is more suitable for deployment on constrained edge devices to provide effective pre-processing for subsequent tasks. Our main contributions are as follows:

- A CNN-based airborne particle removal method for LiDAR point clouds integrating point cloud spatial features with a significant performance boost over state-of-the-art methods.
- A lightweight network architecture with effective and efficient feature extraction ability.
- A quantitative and qualitative evaluation of airborne particle removal methods in controlled and natural environments under different weather conditions with different types of LiDAR devices.

2   Related Work

2.1   Environment Perception in Inclement Weather

LiDARs are susceptible to weather-related scattering and absorption effects, which are observed in natural environments and well studied in climate Chambers [2,6,10,22]. Water drops or arbitrary airborne particles (e.g. rain, fog, snow, or dust) cause undesirable noise in the point cloud. Therefore, environment perception methods either have to handle these influences or require pre-processing by denoise algorithms.

There are two kinds of approaches to handle these influences directly: multi-modal perception [1,15] and inclement weather simulation [4,5]. The former utilizes multiple sensors, such as a camera, LiDAR , and Radar. The latter avoids the time, labor, and cost-intensive data collection and annotation for retraining deep perception models. This paper present a lightweight airborne particle removal network. It is a denoise method for the sparse LiDAR point cloud. Until now, only a few denoise algorithms for this issue have been developed [6,9].

2.2   Dense Image and Point Cloud Denoise

Denoise or filtering is a basic and important topic in computer graphics and computer vision [11,16,20]. But these denoise methods handle dense information. They usually assume that noises are caused by devices, materials, and lighting conditions, and locate near the underlying ground truth surface. There is no physical substance at the position of the noise measurement.

LiDAR point clouds are far sparser than camera images and point clouds scanned for surface reconstruction. Furthermore, the noise points are undesired measurements of fog, rain, or snow, which can be observed at any position instead of around the object's surface. Hence, as shown by Charron *et al.* [3], the direct application of previous image denoise algorithms not only fails to effectively remove snow but also blurs edges in key regions.

2.3   Sparse LiDAR Point Cloud Denoise

Traditional filters, such as Statistical Outlier Removal (SOR) filter and Radius Outlier Removal (ROR) filter provided by the Point Cloud Library (PCL) [17] can be used to denoise the point cloud. The SOR defines the vicinity of a point based on its mean distance to all k neighbors. It is then compared with a global threshold derived by the global mean distance and standard deviation of all points. The ROR filter counts the number of neighbor points within a fixed radius to decide whether a point is filtered or not. However, Charron *et al.* [3] has shown that these general purpose filters are not suitable for the sparse and non-uniformly distributed LiDAR point cloud corrupted by snow. LiDAR point cloud is less dense at far distances. Hence they propose the enhanced dynamic radius outlier removal (DROR) filter, which is an extension of the ROR filter. The filter changes the search radius for neighboring points with range dynamically to remove snow. More recently, Kurup and Bos [9] introduce a dynamic extension of the SOR filter, denoted as DSOR. They derive a dynamic threshold from the SOR's global threshold and the distance of the point to the device. DSOR achieves higher recall and comparable precision on Winter Adverse Driving dataSet (WADS) than DROR. Both of them are state-of-the-art traditional filters for LiDAR point cloud de-snowing.

Point-Wise Semantic Segmentation Approaches. Point-wise semantic segmentation has been applied to label airborne particles to handle various distance, intensity, and clutter distribution. Stanislas *et al.* [19] compared voxel-wise segmentation network based on [26] and pixel-wise classification networks based on U-Net. They also study the impact of different combinations of input data (geometry position, intensity, and multi-echo returns) for fog and dust removal. Heinzler *et al.* [6] propose WeatherNet for LiDAR point cloud denoise inspired by a 2D CNN segmentation network - LiLaNet [14]. They demonstrate a performance improvement and less runtime over the traditional filter DROR [3] and two LiDAR semantic segmentation networks (LiLaNet and RangeNet [13]) on filtering rain and fog. This paper also proposes a CNN-based LiDAR denoise method. It is a far more lightweight network but demonstrates higher IOU for rain, fog, and snow on different devices and datasets.

3   Proposed Method

The proposed LAPRNet adopts a fully convolutional architecture for semantic segmentation to filter the airborne particles out. It consists of three WMLR

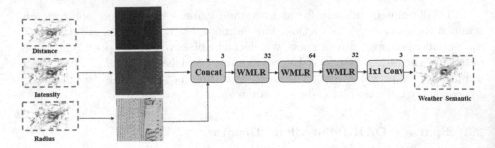

Fig. 3. Our fully convolutional semantic segmentation architecture for airborne particle removal. Channel numbers after each operation are marked at the top right corner of the module. WMLR is illustrated in Fig. 5.

(Wide Multi-Level Residual) modules and a 1×1 convolutional classifier Fig. 3. The classifier infers 2 or 3 semantic classes provided by the dataset, such as clear, fog, and rain. The width and height of feature images are kept untouched throughout the network for accurate point-wise classification.

Considering that our method mainly is used as a pre-processing step for classical perception algorithms implemented on edge devices with limited inference budgets, we design a lightweight WMLR module for the task and explore enhanced input representation to boost its performance.

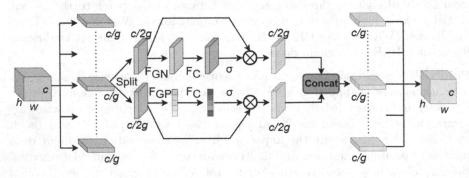

Fig. 4. The structure of SA block. F_{GP} means global pooling, F_{GN} group normalization, F_C fully connected layer, $\otimes$ multiplication, and σ sigmoid function.

3.1 Enhanced LiDAR Point Cloud Representation

Rotating LiDAR sensors commonly provide raw point clouds with an estimated intensity. The point cloud is stored in spherical coordinates with the radius r, azimuth angle ϕ, and elevation angle θ. Similarly to [6], we transfer the row point cloud into two cylindrical depth images: the distance matrix $D \in \mathbb{R}^{H \times W}$

and intensity image $I \in \mathbb{R}^{H \times W}$, where $H = 32$ or 64 for LiDAR sensors with 32 or 64 vertically stacked send/receive modules. Each column represents one of the segments over the full $360°$. The input image $X^0 = Concat < D, I >$ with the distance and intensity channels is a kind of standard LiDAR point cloud representation.

The distribution of point to neighbors distances is an important characteristic for airborne particle removal in traditional unsupervised filters. To fully explore the features embedded in the raw point cloud, we compute the mean distance of points to their $k = 30$ neighbors and record them in a matrix $R \in \mathbb{R}^{H \times W}$. We find that concatenation of the three matrices, $X^0 = Concat < D, I, R >$, is superior to only using D and I. The enhanced representation boosts the network's ability for inferring airborne particles. We denote LAPRNet as $LAPRNet_2$ when D and I are fed into the network and as $LAPRNet_3$ if all the three matrices are fed into the network.

3.2 Wide Multi-level Residual Module

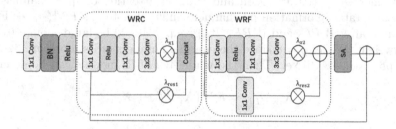

Fig. 5. The structure of the proposed Wide Multi-Level Residual (WMLR) module. Table 1 lists the steps of the first WMLR.

A wide multi-Level residual module (WMLR) is the most important component of LAPRNet. The network consists of three WMLR modules $WMLR_i, i = 1, 2, 3$. The input features of them are denoted as $X^{i-1}, i = 1, 2, 3$. As shown in Fig. 5, The first operation of $WMLR_i$ is to double or halve input feature channels and it is defined as

$$X_i^1 = Relu(BN(Conv_{1 \times 1} X^{i-1})). \tag{1}$$

Then a wide residual concatenation block (WRC) and a wide residual fusion block (WRF) follow. Both of them adopt the wide activation mechanism [23], which can extract richer features with fewer parameters [7,18,23]. After them, we append an efficient yet effective shuffle attention block (SA) [24] into our WMLR module. SA is a combination of spatial attention and channel attention but with less computational overhead. It further enhances WMLR's feature extraction abilities. Last but not the least, WMLR also has another skip connection to facilitate the preservation of low-level features besides the two residual shortcuts in WRC and WRF. By these, we find LAPRNet with a good quality-computation trade-off for deployment on edge devices with limited computational resources.

WRC and WRF are two wide activation residual blocks. WRC_i doubles the feature channels by the concatenation of X_i^1 and the features after wide activation. Its output is

$$X_i^{WRC} = Concat < \lambda_i^{x1} F_i^W(X_i^1), \lambda_i^{res1}[X_i^1] >, \tag{2}$$

where $F_i^W(\cdot) = Conv_{3\times3}(Conv_{1\times1}(Relu(Conv_{1\times1}(\cdot))))$, λ_i^{x1} and λ_i^{res1} are learnable parameters determined by training. Compared with WRC_i, a 1×1 convolution is added to the shortcut path of WRF_i to halve the number of output channels so that it matches X_i^1 and achieves the interaction between different levels of features (SA_i block does not change channel numbers). The operation can be expressed as follow

$$X_i^{WRF} = \lambda_i^{x2} F_i^W(X_i^{WRC}) + \lambda_i^{res2}[Conv_{1\times1}(X_i^{WRC})], \tag{3}$$

where λ_i^{x2} and λ_i^{res2} are learnable parameters. Note that the expansion factor t of wide activation of WRC_i and WRF_i are both set to 6 experimentally.

SA_i merges spatial attention and channel attention of split channels and further integrates information by channel shuffle, denoted as $F_i^{SA}(\cdot)$, see Fig. 4. It is placed after WRC_i and WRF_i. Its group g should be large enough to keep it lightweight. We let $g = 8$ since the channel numbers of its input are 32 or 64 in the proposed LAPRNet. Then the whole $WMLR_i$ module can be described by

$$X_{WMLR}^i = F_i^{SA}(X_i^{WRF}) + X_i^1. \tag{4}$$

Table 1. The pipeline of the first WMLR module: Each line describes the inputs, outputs, and operations in that step. The SA module is shown Fig. 4.

Step	Input Channel	Operator	Output Channel
1	3	1×1 Conv, BN, Relu	32
2	32	1×1 Conv, Relu	192
3	192	1×1 Conv	32
4	16	3×3 Conv	32
5	32,32	Concat	64
6	64	1×1 Conv, Relu	384
7	32	1×1 Conv	32
8	32	3×3 Conv	32
9	32,32	$\oplus$	32
10	32	SA	32
11	32,32	$\oplus$	32

3.3 Loss Function

During training, this network is optimized end to end using momentum gradient descent and a weighted cross-entropy loss $\mathcal{L}$:

$$\mathcal{L} = -\sum_{c=1}^{C} w_c y_c \log\left(\hat{y}_c\right), where \quad \hat{y}_c = \frac{e^{logit_c}}{\sum_c e^{logit_c}}. \tag{5}$$

where $\hat{y}_c$ gives a probability distribution per pixel in the input image and $logit_c$ is the unbounded output corresponding to class c. $w_c = \frac{1}{\log(f_c + \epsilon)}$ penalizes the class c according to the inverse of its frequency f_c. It handles imbalanced data, as is the case for most datasets in our task, e.g. the class "clear" represents a significantly larger number of points in the dataset than the class "rain" or "fog".

4 Experiment

We evaluate the proposed method through extensive experiments. In addition to evaluating results on two publicly available datasets in inclement weather, we also demonstrate the lightweight characteristics and excellent generalization performance of the proposed LAPRNet. Eventually, the principle components of LAPRNet are analyzed in the ablation experiment.

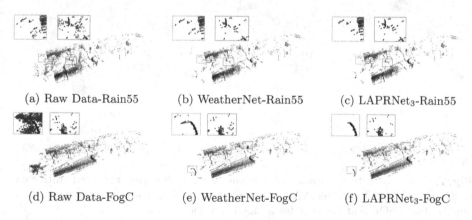

(a) Raw Data-Rain55   (b) WeatherNet-Rain55   (c) LAPRNet$_3$-Rain55

(d) Raw Data-FogC   (e) WeatherNet-FogC   (f) LAPRNet$_3$-FogC

Fig. 6. Comparison for rain (top row) and fog (bottom row) removal on the Chamber dataset. Our method removes rain and fog more thoroughly than WeatherNet at both the regions near the device and the regions at medium distances, which are zoomed in by green boxes and pink boxes respectively. Clear points are in black, rain points in red and fog points in blue. (Color figure online)

4.1 Dataset

Collecting a large-scale data set for training weather segmentation models is very challenging, due to the fact that weather conditions are very unique and manual annotations are very difficult and complex. There are few LiDAR datasets in extreme weather conditions. Among them, only Climate Chamber Scenarios Dataset (Chamber) [6] and Winter Adverse Driving dataSet (WADS) [9] have point-wise ground truth labels for fog, rain, and snow as far as we know. WADS dataset is collected in winter outdoor and the Chamber dataset is collected in indoor with controlled weather environments. We conduct a series of experiments on the two publicly available datasets.

4.2 Evaluation Metrics

We assess the LiDAR denoise performance using Intersection-over-Union (IoU) and Precision/Recall (PR), following WeatherNet and DSOR. IoU is widely used in semantic segmentation and many other tasks to measure the agreement between detected labels w.r.t the ground truth. TP_{noise}, FP_{noise} and FN_{noise} correspond to the number of true positive, false positive, and false negative predictions for all kinds of airborne particles in the dataset.

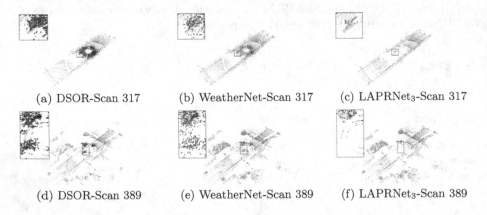

| (a) DSOR-Scan 317 | (b) WeatherNet-Scan 317 | (c) LAPRNet$_3$-Scan 317 |

| (d) DSOR-Scan 389 | (e) WeatherNet-Scan 389 | (f) LAPRNet$_3$-Scan 389 |

Fig. 7. Comparison for snow removal of scenes with moving (top row) and stationary (bottom row) vehicles of the WADS dataset. Our method removes snow more thoroughly than DSOR and WeatherNet in both scenarios.

4.3 Comparisons with State-of-the-Art Methods

As illustrated in Table 2, the proposed methods, LAPRNet$_2$ and LAPRNet$_3$, achieve 61.58 mIoU higher than the unsupervised method DROR [3]. The potential reason could be that the minimum number of points within the specified search radius assumed by DROR is proper for snow but not for rain and fog.

Table 2. Comparison on the Chamber Dataset. The best method is highlighted in **bold** and the second best in blue.

Model	IoU			mIoU	PR	
	Clear	Fog	Rain		Precision	Recall
DROR [3]	88.13	6.94	7.37	34.15	-	-
LiLanet [14]	82.72	79.57	88.16	83.48	-	-
WeatherNet [6]	91.65	86.40	89.29	89.11	89.87	92.23
PolarNet [25]	**99.08**	**94.75**	91.35	95.06	**96.33**	97.00
LAPRNet$_2$	97.17	91.58	94.80	94.51	95.46	97.99
LAPRNet$_3$	97.83	93.93	**95.13**	**95.63**	93.04	**98.13**

Table 3. Comparison on the WADS Dataset. The best method is highlighted in **bold** and the second best in blue.

Model	IoU		mIoU	PR	
	Clear	Snow		Precision	Recall
DROR [3]	-	67.26	-	71.51	91.89
DSOR [9]	-	63.18	-	65.07	**95.60**
WeatherNet [6]	92.29	81.39	86.84	94.88	85.13
PolarNet [25]	**98.72**	**90.34**	**94.53**	**98.74**	91.41
LAPRNet$_2$	94.73	87.31	91.02	95.42	91.13
LAPRNet$_3$	95.65	89.53	92.59	95.95	93.04

Many fog and rain are inferred as "clear". Our methods also surpass the state-of-the-art supervised LiDAR segmentation network (LiLanet [14]) and LiDAR denoising network (WeatherNet) by a 5 to 12 mIoU approximately. We also compare with PolarNet [25], an online LiDAR semantic segmentation network. We re-trained it for point-wise airborne particle classification. PolarNet achieves the highest precision and IoU for clear and fog points. While LAPRNet$_3$ obtains the highest recall, IoU for rain points and the mIoU for all the three types. LAPRNet$_2$ also attains some second-best performance. Given the larger model size and FLOPS of PolarNet, see Table 4, our lightweight networks might be more suitable for real-time processing on constrained edge devices. Visual comparisons between WeatherNet and LAPRNet$_3$ are shown in Fig. 6.

Table 3 compares the traditional unsupervised snow removal method DROR [3], DSOR [9] with the CNN-based WeatherNet, PolarNet and our LAPRNet$_2$ and LAPRNet$_3$. The comparison of the denoise effect between our LAPRNet$_3$ and WeatherNet on the Chamber dataset for rain and fog is shown in Fig. 7. Although traditional filters have high recall values, their precision is very low. A large number of clear points will be mistakenly removed, thus affecting the segmentation or detection tasks. WeatherNet has higher precision against them by 94.88 vs. 71.51. But it fails to maintain a high recall. Thus a large number of snow points will remain in the scene after denoising, which will also interfere with the subsequent tasks. Although PolarNet achieves 1.94 mIoU higher than LAPRNet$_3$ on the WADS dataset, LAPRNet$_3$ demonstrates 0.57 mIoU higher than PolarNet on the Chamber dataset, see Table 2. Hence they are comparable, but the model sizes and FLOPs of our methods are 3% and 6% of PolarNet, respectively, which can be found in Table 4. Note that mIoU of DROR and DSOR can not be evaluated since there are some unlabelled points in the WADS dataset.

4.4   Runtime and Model Complexity

In order to verify the efficiency and the lightweight design of the proposed LAPR-Net, we compare the parameters of the model, model sizes, FLOPs and runtime with other methods in Table 4. The experiment is conducted on the test set of the Chamber dataset with a total of 19787 samples. Each sample represents one frame of LiDAR point cloud, and the runtime in the table represents the inference time of one frame. As shown in Table 4, our LAPRNet$_2$ is 26% faster than WeatherNet and 72% faster than Lilanet on average. The parameter amount and GFLOPs are both reduced by nearly four times and both LAPRNet$_2$ and LAPRNet$_3$ have almost the same parameter amount and GFLOPs. Although LAPRNet$_3$ uses the K-D tree to generate the radius channel, it runs 53% faster than PolarNet. According to Fig. 11 of [3], the runtime of DROR is 100.0 ms. Hence the proposed LAPRNet$_3$ is much faster than the traditional filter DROR, since K-D tree is used.

Table 4. Comparison of runtime and model complexity. The best method is highlighted in **bold** and the second best in blue.

Model	Params (Mio)	GFLOPs	Runtime (ms)	Size (M)
DROR [3]	$4e^{-6}$	-	100.00	$4e^{-6}$
LilaNet [14]	9.31	447.67	5.9417	37.34
WeatherNet [6]	1.5313	18.2267	2.22	6.044
PolarNet [25]	13.6091	87.9441	22.11	54.523
LAPRNet$_2$(ours)	**0.3884**	**4.9119**	**1.64**	**1.568**
LAPRNet$_3$(ours)	**0.3884**	4.9919	10.32	**1.568**

4.5   Generalizability

The input image size used in the paper is 32×400 or 64×400 according to the number of receiving and transmitting modules of LiDAR and the horizontal FOV we cared. In Table 5, we also compare the proposed LAPRNet$_3$ with WeatherNet for different input image heights and widths to show the generalizability of our method. The experiment is conducted on the WADS dataset with models trained with 64×400 input images. We see that LAPRNet$_3$ surpasses WeatherNet on all conditions and with less IoU drop in most cases. For example, the accuracy of the proposed LAPRNet$_3$ only degrades 8.4 IoU, and that of WeatherNet degrades 16.5 IoU, when the image width is 400 and its height is reduced from 64 to 16.

Table 5. IoU of snow detection on WADS with different input image sizes.

	Model	H = 64	H = 32	H = 16
W = 400	LAPRNet$_3$	**89.5**	**87.3** ($-$**2.2**)	**81.1** ($-$**8.4**)
	WeatherNet	81.4	74.1 ($-$7.3)	64.9 ($-$16.5)
W = 200	LAPRNet$_3$	**86.2** ($-$3.3)	**84.0** ($-$**5.5**)	**78.6** ($-$**10.9**)
	WeatherNet	81.0 ($-$**0.4**)	73.8 ($-$7.6)	64.6 ($-$16.8)
W = 100	LAPRNet$_3$	**83.8** ($-$5.7)	**81.9** ($-$**7.6**)	**76.5** ($-$**13.0**)
	WeatherNet	80.1 ($-$**1.3**)	73.0 ($-$8.4)	63.9 ($-$17.5)
W = 50	LAPRNet$_3$	**81.9** ($-$7.6)	**80.1** ($-$**9.4**)	**74.7**($-$**14.8**)
	WeatherNet	78.4 ($-$**3.0**)	71.5 ($-$9.9)	62.5 ($-$18.9)

4.6 Ablation Study

We have shown that LAPRNet$_3$ has better performance and LAPRNet$_2$ is a trade-off between accuracy, runtime, and model parameters. The rest of the ablation study is about the network architecture design.

SA Module and Residual Structure. To evaluate the benefits of introducing the SA module and residual structure across WRC and WRF, we trim the proposed network by removing the SA module (denoted as w/o SA) or the shortcut across WRC and WRF (denoted as w/o Res) or both of them (denoted as w/o

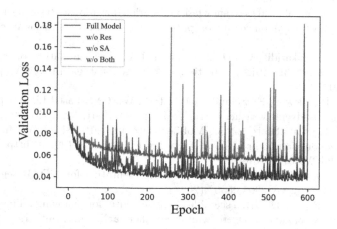

Fig. 8. Comparison of validation losses of our four network variants.

Both). As shown in Fig. 8, the SA module is very effective. From the two curves with lower validation loss, it can be seen that although they finally converge to a similar position, adding the residual structure can increase the stability. Thus we adopt the combination of the two mechanisms to improve the stability of the training process and the accuracy of the model.

5 Conclusion

We present a CNN-based architecture for removing airborne particles from LiDAR point cloud data in inclement weather. As an essential pre-processing tool for the subsequent LiDAR-based perception tasks, it has to be effective and efficient. LAPRNetoutperforms state-of-the-art geometry filters and methods based on deep learning by a large margin. They also demonstrate better generalizability over two LiDAR types and various input sizes. They are designed to offer an optimal trade-off between accuracy, runtime, and model size, which makes them more suitable for successful deployment on constrained edge devices to provide efficient and effective pre-processing for subsequent tasks. An interesting further work may be how to boost the methods' performance on unseen data. So it can be more easily adapted for different kinds of LiDAR devices.

References

1. Bijelic, M., et al.: Seeing through fog without seeing fog: deep multimodal sensor fusion in unseen adverse weather. In: CVPR (2020)
2. Bijelic, M., Gruber, T., Ritter, W.: A benchmark for lidar sensors in fog: is detection breaking down? 2018 IEEE Intelligent Vehicles Symposium (IV), pp. 760–767 (2018)
3. Charron, N., Phillips, S., Waslander, S.L.: De-noising of lidar point clouds corrupted by snowfall. In: 2018 15th Conference on Computer and Robot Vision (CRV), pp. 254–261 (2018)
4. Hahner, M., et al.: LiDAR snowfall simulation for robust 3D object detection. In: IEEE/CVF Conference on Computer Vision and Pattern Recognition (CVPR) (2022)
5. Hahner, M., Sakaridis, C., Dai, D., Gool, L.V.: Fog simulation on real LiDAR point clouds for 3D object detection in adverse weather. In: ICCV, pp. 15263–15272 (2021)
6. Heinzler, R., Piewak, F., Schindler, P., Stork, W.: CNN-based LiDAR point cloud de-noising in adverse weather. IEEE Rob. Autom. Lett. 5(2), 2514–2521 (2020)
7. Howard, A., et al.: Searching for MobileNetV3. In: 2019 IEEE/CVF International Conference on Computer Vision (ICCV), pp. 1314–1324 (2019). https://doi.org/10.1109/ICCV.2019.00140
8. Kong, L., et al.: Rethinking range view representation for LiDAR segmentation. arXiv preprint arXiv:2303.05367 (2023)
9. Kurup, A., Bos, J.: DSOR: a scalable statistical filter for removing falling snow from LiDAR point clouds in severe winter weather. arXiv preprint arXiv:2109.07078 (2021)

10. Kutila, M., Pyykonen, P., Holzhuter, H., Colomb, M., Duthon, P.: Automotive LiDAR performance verification in fog and rain. In: 2018 21st International Conference on Intelligent Transportation Systems (ITSC), pp. 1695–1701 (2018)

11. Luo, S., Hu, W.: Score-based point cloud denoising. In: ICCV, pp. 4563–4572 (2021)

12. Luo, S., Hu, W.: Differentiable manifold reconstruction for point cloud denoising. In: ACMMM (2020)

13. Milioto, A., Vizzo, I., Behley, J., Stachniss, C.: RangeNet++: fast and accurate LiDAR semantic segmentation. In: 2019 IEEE/RSJ International Conference on Intelligent Robots and Systems (IROS), pp. 4213–4220. IEEE (2019)

14. Piewak, F., et al.: Boosting LiDAR-based semantic labeling by cross-modal training data generation. In: Leal-Taixé, L., Roth, S. (eds.) ECCV 2018. LNCS, vol. 11134, pp. 497–513. Springer, Cham (2019). https://doi.org/10.1007/978-3-030-11024-6_39

15. Qian, K., Zhu, S., Zhang, X., Li, L.E.: Robust multimodal vehicle detection in foggy weather using complementary lidar and radar signals. In: CVPR, pp. 444–453 (2021)

16. Rakotosaona, M.J., La Barbera, V., Guerrero, P., Mitra, N.J., Ovsjanikov, M.: PointCleanNet: learning to denoise and remove outliers from dense point clouds. Comput. Graph. Forum **39**, 185–203 (2020)

17. Rusu, R.B., Cousins, S.: 3D is here: point cloud library (pcl). In: 2011 IEEE International Conference on Robotics and Automation, pp. 1–4 (2011)

18. Sandler, M., Howard, A., Zhu, M., Zhmoginov, A., Chen, L.C.: MobileNetV2: inverted residuals and linear bottlenecks. In: Proceedings of the IEEE Conference on Computer Vision and Pattern Recognition (CVPR), June 2018

19. Stanislas, L., et al.: Airborne particle classification in LiDAR point clouds using deep learning. In: Ishigami, G., Yoshida, K. (eds.) Field and Service Robotics. SPAR, vol. 16, pp. 395–410. Springer, Singapore (2021). https://doi.org/10.1007/978-981-15-9460-1_28

20. Tian, C., Fei, L., Zheng, W., Xu, Y., Zuo, W., Lin, C.W.: Deep learning on image denoising: an overview. Neural Netw. **131**, 251–275 (2020)

21. Wang, W., You, X., Chen, L., Tian, J., Tang, F., Zhang, L.: A scalable and accurate de-snowing algorithm for LiDAR point clouds in winter. Remote. Sens. **14**, 1468 (2022)

22. Yang, T., Li, Y., Ruichek, Y., Yan, Z.: Performance modeling a near-infrared ToF LiDAR under fog: a data-driven approach. TITS, 1–10 (2021)

23. Yu, J., Fan, Y., Huang, T.: Wide activation for efficient image and video super-resolution. In: BMVC (2019)

24. Zhang, Q.L., Yang, Y.B.: SA-Net: shuffle attention for deep convolutional neural networks. In: ICASSP 2021–2021 IEEE International Conference on Acoustics, Speech and Signal Processing (ICASSP), pp. 2235–2239. IEEE (2021)

25. Zhang, Y., et al.: PolarNet: an improved grid representation for online LiDAR point clouds semantic segmentation. In: CVPR, pp. 9598–9607 (2020)

26. Zhou, Y., Tuzel, O.: VoxelNet: end-to-end learning for point cloud based 3D object detection. In: Proceedings of the IEEE Conference on Computer Vision and Pattern Recognition, pp. 4490–4499 (2018)

27. Zhu, X., et al.: Cylindrical and asymmetrical 3D convolution networks for lidar segmentation. In: Proceedings of the IEEE/CVF Conference on Computer Vision and Pattern Recognition (CVPR), pp. 9939–9948, June 2021

REAL-NET: A Monochromatic Depth Estimation Using REgional Attention and Local Feature Mapping

Harsh Bhandari and Sarbani Palit[✉]

Indian Statistical Institute, Kolkata, India
sarbanip@isical.ac.in

Abstract. Estimating the depth of a scene from a color image is an arduous task as it requires prior depth information to remove any uncertainty in the 3D interpretation. In recent works, many supervised depth estimation methods gave promising results, learning the priors based on end-to-end training. Unfortunately, inadequate addressing of actual physical constraints leads to inaccurate estimation. In this paper, we present **REAL-Net**, a supervised depth estimation encoder-decoder net by incorporating **RE**gional constraints in the encoder through the **A**ttention mechanism, and neighborhood feature constraints in the decoder taking care of the **L**ocal mapping. These make the output significantly clear and robust to the structural and color information. Results obtained upon conducting extensive experiments on benchmark datasets namely KITTI, Foggy Zurich, and Cityscapes establish the proposed method's capability to outperform results obtained with the existing approaches.

Keywords: Regional constraint · Attention Encoded · Feature Attention

1 Introduction

Multiple computer vision applications such as 3D modeling, autonomous vehicle driving, virtual and augmented reality, etc. have a fundamental need for appropriate depth estimation using given a color image. The conventional method deploys lidar sensors to capture the structure information gathered from multiple view geometries. Advancement in deep learning has provided an alternative to conventional methods, leading to the development of many depth estimation methods [1–4].

The fundamental concept behind developing deep learning-based models is to make the models learn features using a pair of color images and the corresponding depth map, such that the model is able to generate the depth map of any arbitrary color image. Such learning is based on large and diverse benchmark datasets covering large variations in color images and their corresponding depth maps.

© The Author(s), under exclusive license to Springer Nature Singapore Pte Ltd. 2024
W. Q. Yan et al. (Eds.): PSIVT 2023, LNCS 14403, pp. 302–311, 2024.
https://doi.org/10.1007/978-981-97-0376-0_23

In the case of the supervised approach, the model tries to minimize the loss between the estimated and the reference depth value from the pixel-by-pixel end. However, such methods often lead to unsatisfactory local depth estimation, chiefly due to the absence of the inclusion of physical considerations, adding undesired noise to the results.

In the paper, we provide a supervised monocular depth estimation by introducing regional constraints that capture the homogeneity among the neighboring pixels with similar features in the encoder. The decoder part in the proposed model utilizes both the regionally encoded features as well as the local feature values as a form factor to make the local depth estimation satisfactory, thus making the process both spatially shared and locally adaptive. This makes the resultant outputs more robust and aesthetic to our eyes.

2   Related Work

2.1   Supervised Monocular Depth Estimation

The supervised monocular depth estimation technique uses a pixel-by-pixel continuous depth estimation to generate the map. Previous works [1,5–8] used a convolution neural network to estimate the weights and parameters to generate a depth map by optimizing a loss function of predicted and actual depth maps. In [2], a spacing-increasing discretization approach was used to estimate the depth map. Adabins [9] proposed a strategy of fragmenting the depth range into various bins and using a transformer to produce a depth map. In [10,11], the multimodel approach of learning depth estimation has been used.

2.2   Self-supervised Monocular Depth Estimation

Self-supervised methods transform the domain of the monocular depth estimation into an image reconstruction. The methods deploy monocular sequences to supervise and train the neural networks. The first work to produce a depth map from a color image under this framework was proposed by Garg et al. [12]. In 3Net [13], a trinocular stereo strategy was proposed to solve the problem of occlusion between stereo pairs. In Monodepth [14], a novel training loss was proposed to enforce consistency between the disparities relative to the left and right stereo images. In Monodepth2 [15], the authors proposed a new auto-masking and reprojection loss to get rid of the problem of moving objects and occlusion. Depth Hints [16] used Semi-Global Matching (SGM) techniques to generate depth priors helping the network to learn accurate weights. In EPCDepth [17], the model focuses on horizontal image positions through data grafting techniques to generate an accurate depth map. Zhou in [18] proposed an efficient neural network to accomplish the task of monocular depth estimation.

The performances of all the above-mentioned methods still leave much to be desired, paving the way for the development of superior approaches.

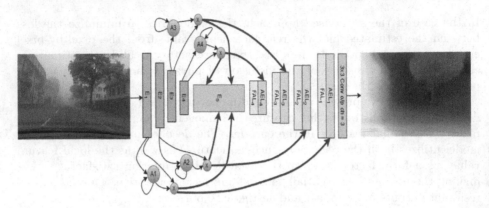

Fig. 1. Architecture of Monochromatic Depth Estimation module extracting the depth-based regional information from the encoder. The model utilizes the extracted attention-encoded features and spatial-feature value attention layer in the decoder to produce the estimated depth map. The deep blue arrows represent the flow of attention-guided information and 'x' denotes product between the encoded layer and its respective attention layer. (Color figure online)

3 Proposed Approach

3.1 Overview

The challenge of estimating the depth map of a color image can be considered as a non-linear mapping f between the color image I and the real-valued depth map D defined in (1). Our objective is to formulate f based on a set of trained data $T = \{I_i, D_i\}_{i=1}^{M}$, such that the function is able to learn the weights and parameters used to compute the depth map D_i from input color image I_i.

$$f : I \to D \tag{1}$$

We propose a neural network-based method to generate a depth map of an outdoor image as shown in Fig. 1. An encoder-decoder network has been used to retrieve the depth map of an image. The objective of estimating the depth map corresponding to the color image is achieved by utilizing features at the last encoded layer E_L. E_L is obtained through a set of intermediate multi-scale features $\{E_l\}_{l=1}^{L}$. Here, $E = \{E_l\}_{l=1}^{L}$, $E_l = \{e_l^i\}_{i=1}^{N}$ and $e_l^i \in R^{Cin}$ with L set to 5 and Cin being the input number of channels. We associate attention maps A_l to each intermediate encoded layer E_l that helps in self-regulating the information from intermediate encoded layers relevant for depth estimation. Here, $A = \{A_l\}_{l=1}^{L-1}$, $A_l = \{a_l^i\}_{i=1}^{N}$ and $a_l^i \in R^{Cin}$. In order to appropriately extract region-based information, a regional constraint is imposed forcing the neighboring pixel attention variables to be related.

We formulate an energy function by associating the intermediate encoded layers and their corresponding attention maps as in (2).

$$\Gamma(\mathbf{E}, \mathbf{A}) = \phi(\mathbf{E}, \mathbf{A}) + \psi(\mathbf{A}) \tag{2}$$

In the first term, we try to establish the relationship between the intermediate and the final encoded layers involving the attention maps. This assists in regulating the features that are vital in producing the depth map. We define the term $\phi(\mathbf{E}, \mathbf{A})$ as:

$$\phi(\mathbf{E}, \mathbf{A}) = \sum_{l=1}^{L-1} \xi(\mathbf{A}_l, \mathbf{E}_l) \tag{3}$$

$$\xi(\mathbf{A}_l, \mathbf{E}_l) = \sum_{i,j} a_l^i \beta_{i,j}^l e_l^j \tag{4}$$

where a_l^i is the attention variables and $\beta_{i,j}^l \in R^{C_l \times C_l}$ with C_l refers to channel dimension of the intermediate layer E_l. The last term $\psi(\mathbf{A})$ adds a regional constraint to the energy function such that the relation between the neighboring pixels of the attention map is appropriately captured. We define $\psi(\mathbf{A})$ as follows:

$$\psi(\mathbf{A}) = \sum_{l=1}^{L-1} \sum_{i,j} \kappa_{i,j}^l a_l^i a_l^j \tag{5}$$

where $\kappa_{i,j}^l$ is the relation parameter to be trained.

3.2 Attention Approximation

Given the energy function as defined in (2), finding its optimized solution is intractable as the distribution of the function is not known to us. To solve such a problem we take the help of Mean Approximation, whereby a new distribution q is estimated such that the KL divergence of distribution of Γ is minimum.

Encoding Strategy: We utilize the concept of mean-field approximation to derive the updates of the final encoded layer and attention variables of each intermediate encoded layers. We denote $\mathbf{E}_q$ as the expectation with respect to distribution q, and we get

$$\log\{q(e_L^i)\} \propto \sum_{l \neq L} \mathbf{E}_{q(a_l^i)}\{a_l^i\} \sum_j \mathbf{E}_{q(e_l^j)}\{\xi(a_l^i, e_l^j)\}$$

$$\log\{q(a_i^l)\} \propto a_i^l \sum_j \mathbf{E}_{q(e_L^j)}\{\xi(a_i^l, e_L^j)\} + \sum_l \sum_j \mathbf{E}_{q(a_l^j)}\{\kappa_{i,j}^l a_l^i a_l^j\} \tag{6}$$

By considering the distributions $q(e_L^i)$ and $q(a_l^i)$, we denote $\mathbf{E}_{q(a_l^i)}\{a_l^i\}$, $\mathbf{E}_{q(e_l^i)}\{e_l^i\}$ and $\mathbf{E}_{q(e_L^i)}\{e_L^i\}$ as $\mathbf{a_l^i}$, $\mathbf{e_l^i}$ and $\mathbf{e_L^i}$ respectively, we get.
Considering the potential defined in (3) we write:

$$\mathbf{e_L^i} = \sum_{l \neq L} \sum_{i,j} \mathbf{a_l^i} \beta_{i,j}^l \mathbf{e_l^j} \tag{7}$$

Considering the potential defined in (5) and (7), we compute the attention variables employing the sigmoid function as shown in (8) below making the variable normalized:

$$\mathbf{a_i^j} = \sigma(\sum_j \beta_{i,j}^l \mathbf{e_L^j} + \sum_j \kappa_{i,j}^l \mathbf{a_i^j}) \tag{8}$$

Hence we show that our framework computes attention variables by putting in a sigmoid function on the extracted features and also considering the relations among different a_l^i helping in maintaining the regional constraint. This way we achieve simultaneous learning of the feature and attention vectors as well as the parameters κ and β helpful in maintaining constraints. Necessary downsampling operations are performed on intermediate encoded resulting in Attention Encoded Layer (AEL) that are finally used to generate the final encoded layer E_5.

Decoding Strategy: Our decoder follows a simple up-scaling operation by increasing the spatial dimension to its original shape with the help of four decoder blocks. Each decoder block consists of an attention-mapped encoded layer denoted as Attention Encoded Layer (AEL) and Feature Attention Layer (FAL). AEL stores the encoded feature maps generated by the product of encoded layer E_l and A_l preserving the fine and semantic details of the image.

In the case of a normal convolution layer, a single kernel is used throughout the feature map, thus making the weights of the kernel global in nature. Considering $I = (i_1, i_2, \cdots, i_N)$, $i_v \in R^{c_{in}}$ being a decoded feature vector with N pixels and c_{in} channels, the spatial convolution with filter weight $W \in R^{c_{out} \times c_{in} \times p \times p}$ is computed as per (9). The weights are spatially shared and are not in synchronicity with the feature values.

$$i_u' = \sum_{v \in N(u)} W[s_u - s_v]i_v + b \tag{9}$$

where $\mathcal{N}(u)$ denotes the pixels in the neighborhood of u with patch size $p \times p$, $s_u = (x_u, y_u)$ are pixel coordinates, $b \in R^{c_{out}}$ refers to the biases, $(s_u - s_v)$ points to the spatial indexing of an array with 2D spatial offsets, $i_u' \in R^{c_{out}}$ is the output of the convolution operation for each pixel u.

In our decoding strategy, to overcome this shortcoming, we multiply the weight with a factor incorporating the feature values of the corresponding pixel coordinates as in (10). Our Feature Attention Layer (FAL) uses a local weight factor computed on the basis of the feature f_u and f_v where $v \in \mathcal{N}(u)$, referred to as the neighboring pixels of pixel u.

$$i_u' = \sum_{v \in \mathcal{N}(u)} \chi(f_u, f_v)W[s_u - s_v]i_v + b \tag{10}$$

$$\chi(f_u, f_v) = e^{-\frac{1}{2}(f_u - f_v)^T(f_u - f_v)} \tag{11}$$

where χ is a fixed-parametric function in the form of a Gaussian curve, taking $f_u, f_v \in R^{c_{in}}$ as feature values at index u and v respectively. We perform this filtering on each of the c_{out} 2D matrices. We refer to such convolution as the Feature Attention layer (FAL). Thus, the FAL not only considers, the spatial variation but also incorporates the variations in feature values around the neighboring pixels. Thus features with similar values tend to have higher weights corroborating with our task of maintaining regional constraint in the resultant image.

Thus, each decoder block l consists of FAL applied to its previous layer followed by the concatenation of the AEL of encoded layer l as displayed in Fig. 1. Finally, we perform a convolution operation using a 3×3 kernel to get the depth map.

4   Experiment and Evaluation

This section focuses on the experimental settings used in developing the method. This includes the datasets used for training and testing the model, evaluation metrics to judge the performance, implementation details, and the ablation study. Finally, in the end, we collate the performance of our proposed model with some latest methods.

4.1   Datasets

We perform extensive testing and validation of our proposed method using various benchmark datasets. We have used KITTI [19], Cityscape [20], and Foggy Zurich [21] datasets for training, validation, and testing of our model. We have followed the strategy used in [1] with 22K images taken from KITTI dataset as training data and 700 images for test purposes.

4.2   Implementation Details

We have implemented our proposed method using the Pytorch platform with the input image size fixed at 640×480 for training purposes. Our model has been optimized using Adam optimizer with an initial learning rate set to 10^{-4}, $\beta_1 = 0.9$, $\beta_2 = 0.999$, $\epsilon = 10^{-7}$. We have used NVIDIA GeForce RTX 2060-8GB GPU to train our model with the batch size and the number of epochs set to 16 and 100 respectively.

4.3   Comparison Methods

This section emphasizes the comparison of our proposed method with recent works as shown in Fig. 2 and 3 with quantitative evaluation provided in Table 2, 3 and 4 with respect to KITTI, Cityscape and Foggy Zurich dataset respectively with results obtained by our proposed method in bold letters. We compute Accuracy (δ), the Mean Relative Error (REL), and Root Mean Squared Error (RMS) as detailed. Given a test data, $\hat{d}_i$ and d_i refers to the estimated and the ground-truth depth for pixel i respectively, we compute: (i) δ (% of d_i)

$= \max(\frac{d_i}{\hat{d}_i}, \frac{\hat{d}_i}{d_i}) < t$ where $t \in [1.25, 1.25^2]$; (ii) REL $= \frac{1}{N}\sum_{i=1}^{N}\frac{\|\hat{d}_i - d_i\|}{d_i}$; (iii) RMS $= \sqrt{\frac{1}{N}\sum_{i=1}^{N}(\hat{d}_i - d_i)^2}$.

4.4 Ablation Study

To prove the potency of the developed method, an ablation study has been conducted on the KITTI dataset with the quantitative results shown in Table 1. We have considered the following three cases in our ablation study: (a) without attention mapping in the encoder and local mapping in the decoder, (b) without attention mapping in the encoder, and (c) without local mapping in the decoder.

Table 1. Ablation Study on the KITTI dataset.

Method	REL	RMS	$\delta < 1.25$	$\delta < 1.25^2$
(a)	0.217	5.917	0.611	0.632
(b)	0.197	4.988	0.683	0.695
(c)	0.152	4.712	0.750	0.797

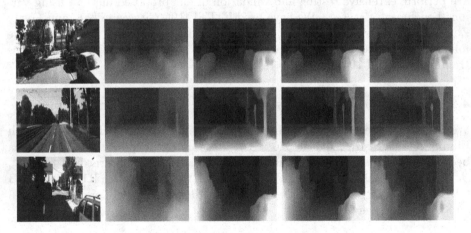

Fig. 2. Visual comparison of depth estimation on images from KITTI [19] dataset. The first to the fifth column refers to the color image with the results obtained from [8,15,18], and our proposed method respectively.

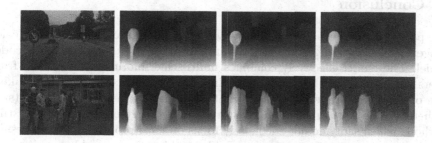

Fig. 3. Visual comparison of depth estimation on images from Cityscapes [20] dataset. The first to the fourth column refers to the color image with the results obtained from [15,18], and our proposed method respectively.

Table 2. Quantitative comparison of Visual Quality performance on KITTI dataset.

Method	REL	RMS	$\delta < 1.25$	$\delta < 1.25^2$
Xu et al. [8]	0.143	4.691	0.872	0.887
Monodepth2 [15]	0.115	4.865	0.877	0.959
DIFFNet [18]	0.102	4.483	0.896	0.965
Ours	**0.097**	**4.131**	**0.901**	**0.971**

Table 3. Quantitative comparison of Visual Quality performance on Cityscapes dataset.

Method	REL	RMS	$\delta < 1.25$	$\delta < 1.25^2$
Xu et al. [8]	0.158	4.013	0.755	0.793
Monodepth2 [15]	0.127	3.502	0.811	0.874
DIFFNet [18]	0.104	3.195	0.836	0.891
Ours	**0.098**	**2.787**	**0.910**	**0.933**

Table 4. Quantitative comparison of Visual Quality performance on Foggy Zurich dataset.

Method	REL	RMS	$\delta < 1.25$	$\delta < 1.25^2$
Xu et al. [8]	0.147	1.980	0.891	0.903
Monodepth2 [15]	0.131	1.964	0.916	0.928
DIFFNet [18]	0.124	1.955	0.922	0.931
Ours	**0.112**	**1.936**	**0.936**	**0.952**

5   Conclusion

The paper proposes a supervised approach to estimate the depth map of a color image by incorporating regional structural constraints in the encoder-decoder model. The model effectively combines multi-scale information extracted from layers at different resolutions by adapting the regional constraints and taking care of local features whereby significantly enhancing the resultant outputs. It is thereby able to very successfully overcome the shortcomings of the existing methods which sadly do not adequately focus on local properties. As the results clearly demonstrate, our proposed model has achieved appreciably superior performance in comparison to that of the state-of-the-art approaches on multiple benchmark datasets.

References

1. Eigen, D., Puhrsch, C., Fergus, R.: Depth map prediction from a single image using a multi-scale deep network. In: Proceedings of the 27th International Conference on Neural Information Processing Systems - Volume 2 (NIPS 2014), pp. 2366–2374. MIT Press, Cambridge, MA, USA (2014)
2. Fu, H., Gong, M., Wang, C., Batmanghelich, K., Tao, D.: Deep ordinal regression network for monocular depth estimation. In: 2018 IEEE/CVF Conference on Computer Vision and Pattern Recognition (CVPR), Salt Lake City, UT, USA, pp. 2002–2011 (2018)
3. Laina, I., Rupprecht, C., Belagiannis, V., Tombari, F., Navab, N.: Deeper depth prediction with fully convolutional residual networks (2016). https://doi.org/10.1109/3DV.2016.32
4. Liu, F., Shen, C., Lin, G., Reid, I.: Learning depth from single monocular images using deep convolutional neural fields. IEEE Trans. Pattern Anal. Mach. Intell. **38**(10), 2024–2039 (2016)
5. Liu, F., Shen, C., Lin, G.: Deep convolutional neural fields for depth estimation from a single image (2014)
6. Yu, Z., Jin, L., Gao, S.: P^2Net: patch-match and plane-regularization for unsupervised indoor depth estimation. In: Vedaldi, A., Bischof, H., Brox, T., Frahm, J.-M. (eds.) ECCV 2020. LNCS, vol. 12369, pp. 206–222. Springer, Cham (2020). https://doi.org/10.1007/978-3-030-58586-0_13
7. Hu, J., Ozay, M., Zhang, Y., Okatani, T.: Revisiting single image depth estimation: toward higher resolution maps with accurate object boundaries. In: 2019 IEEE Winter Conference on Applications of Computer Vision (WACV), Waikoloa Village, HI, USA, pp. 1043–1051 (2019)
8. Xu, D., et al.: Structured attention guided convolutional neural fields for monocular depth estimation. In: 2018 IEEE/CVF Conference on Computer Vision and Pattern Recognition (CVPR), Salt Lake City, UT, USA, pp. 3917–3925 (2018)
9. Farooq Bhat, S., Alhashim, I., Wonka, P.: AdaBins: depth estimation using adaptive bins. In: 2021 IEEE/CVF Conference on Computer Vision and Pattern Recognition (CVPR), Nashville, TN, USA, pp. 4008–4017 (2021)
10. Parida, K., Srivastava, S., Sharma, G.: Beyond image to depth: improving depth prediction using echoes. In: 2021 IEEE/CVF Conference on Computer Vision and Pattern Recognition (CVPR), Nashville, TN, USA, pp. 8264–8273 (2021)

11. Leistner, T., Mackowiak, R., Ardizzone, L., Kuthe, U., Rother, C.: Towards multimodal depth estimation from light fields. In: 2022 IEEE/CVF Conference on Computer Vision and Pattern Recognition (CVPR), New Orleans, LA, USA, pp. 12943–12951 (2022)

12. Garg, R., Vijay Kumar, B.G., Carneiro, G., Reid, I.: Unsupervised CNN for single view depth estimation: geometry to the rescue. In: Leibe, B., Matas, J., Sebe, N., Welling, M. (eds.) ECCV 2016. LNCS, vol. 9912, pp. 740–756. Springer, Cham (2016). https://doi.org/10.1007/978-3-319-46484-8_45

13. Poggi, M., Tosi, F., Mattoccia, S.: Learning monocular depth estimation with unsupervised trinocular assumptions. In: 2018 International Conference on 3D Vision (3DV), Verona, Italy, pp. 324–333 (2018)

14. Godard, C., Mac Aodha, O., Brostow, G.J.: Unsupervised monocular depth estimation with left-right consistency. In: CVPR (2017)

15. Godard, C., Aodha, O., Firman, M., Brostow, G.: Digging into self-supervised monocular depth estimation (2019). https://doi.org/10.1109/ICCV.2019.00393

16. Watson, J., Firman, M., Brostow, G., Turmukhambetov, D.: Self-supervised monocular depth hints. In: 2019 IEEE/CVF International Conference on Computer Vision (ICCV), Seoul, Korea (South), pp. 2162–2171 (2019)

17. Peng, R., Wang, R., Lai, Y., Tang, L., Cai, Y.: Excavating the potential capacity of self-supervised monocular depth estimation. In: 2021 IEEE/CVF International Conference on Computer Vision (ICCV), Montreal, QC, Canada, pp. 15540–15549 (2021)

18. Zhao, C., et al.: MonoViT: self-supervised monocular depth estimation with a vision transformer (2022). https://doi.org/10.48550/arXiv.2208.03543

19. Geiger, A., Lenz, P., Stiller, C., Urtasun, R.: Vision meets robotics: the KITTI dataset. Int. J. Rob. Res. **32**, 1231–1237 (2013). https://doi.org/10.1177/0278364913491297

20. Cordts, M., et al.: The cityscapes dataset for semantic urban scene understanding. In: 2016 IEEE Conference on Computer Vision and Pattern Recognition (CVPR), Las Vegas, NV, USA, pp. 3213–3223 (2016)

21. Sakaridis, C., Dai, D., Hecker, S., Van Gool, L.: Model adaptation with synthetic and real data for semantic dense foggy scene understanding. In: Ferrari, V., Hebert, M., Sminchisescu, C., Weiss, Y. (eds.) ECCV 2018. LNCS, vol. 11217, pp. 707–724. Springer, Cham (2018). https://doi.org/10.1007/978-3-030-01261-8_42

Spike-EFI: Spiking Neural Network for Event-Based Video Frame Interpolation

Dong-Sheng Wu [ID] and De Ma [✉]

Zhejiang University, Hangzhou 310027, People's Republic of China
{wuds,made}@zju.edu.cn

Abstract. In order to model complex motions between video frames more accurately, many video frame interpolation methods have introduced event cameras to obtain additional high speed motion information. These methods use deep artificial neural networks (ANN) to process RGB images and event streams. However, traditional ANN-based methods are unable to effectively utilize the sparse and asynchronous nature of event streams, leading to unnecessary computations and increased energy consumption. As an alternative to ANN, spiking neural networks (SNN) can naturally process asynchronous and sparse event streams, reduce computational complexity and achieve lower energy consumption when combined with neuromorphic hardware. In this paper, we propose Spike-EFI, a lightweight fully spiking neural network for event-based video frame interpolation task. A spiking neural network with Leaky-Integrate and Fire (LIF) neuron is utilized to learn from a sensor fusion of RGB frames and event streams. This is also the first attempt to achieve video frame interpolation with neuromorphic computing paradigm. We trained and evaluated our network on public dataset, and the experimental results demonstrated that the proposed method has comparable performance to prior ANN-based methods. Benefitting from the event triggered computing paradigm of SNN, our method also achieves lower computational power consumption compared to ANN-based method.

Keywords: Event camera · Video frame interpolation · Spiking neural network · Neuromorphic computing

1 Introduction

Due to hardware limitations, ordinary RGB cameras are unable to record high frame rate videos, making it difficult to capture high speed and complex motions. One of the solutions is using expensive high-speed photography equipment to record high frame rate videos, and the other is using the video interpolation frame (VFI) algorithm to synthesis a video frame between two consecutive frames, which will be able to scale up original frame rate. With the development of deep learning, the performance of video frame interpolation algorithms has reached a new level. With VFI, high frame rate video can be synthesised from low frame rate video. However, there are still many problems remained. Complex motions are still difficult to be modeled because most methods assume linear motions only.

© The Author(s), under exclusive license to Springer Nature Singapore Pte Ltd. 2024
W. Q. Yan et al. (Eds.): PSIVT 2023, LNCS 14403, pp. 312–325, 2024.
https://doi.org/10.1007/978-981-97-0376-0_24

Event cameras [14] are neuromorphic visual sensors that can sensitively respond to changes in scene brightness. Ordinary frame-based cameras output RGB images with a certain frame rate, while event cameras output brightness change events of the scene continuously as asynchronous and sparse event streams, which are represented by Address-Event-Representation (AER). Sparse information usually requires less memory and energy consumption to process, which offers a energy efficient approach to record high time resolution information. Event camera can be used on edge computing device where low power and low latency feature is required.

With it's advantage of low latency, some studies [5,17,23,24,26] proposed video frame interpolation algorithms which combines image frames and event streams to obtain more motion information. These studies shown the advantages of using event camera in video frame interpolation task, and more and more researchers turn to explore methods to make better use of event information. Most of these studies utilized artificial neural networks to process event streams and image frames. However, ANN-based models are usually unable to effectively leverage the sparsity of event stream. Large ANN models also incur substantial computational and energy consumption.

Spiking neural network (SNN) is more suitable for processing the asynchronous and sparse data. Previous studies have shown the great potential of SNN in various vision tasks including object detection [9], optical flow estimation [4,11], depth estimation [20], etc. Thus the event-based video frame interpolation task could be a new application area for SNN. Moreover, SNN could bring great improvement on energy efficiency with unique neuromorphic computing paradigm.

In this work, we propose Spike-EFI, which is a lightweight fully spiking neural network for event-based video frame interpolation task. To the best of our knowledge, this is also the first attempt to achieve video frame interpolation with SNN. The main contributions of our work can be summarized as follows:

- We explore a SNN-based architecture (Spike-EFI) for event-based video frame interpolation, which utilizes SNN with LIF neurons to simultaneously process images and event streams for video interpolation, combining the unique characteristics of both sensors.
- We propose event-guided attention (EA) module to more effectively fuse the image and event sensor information when jointly processing images and event streams. This approach has shown promising results in improved performance while maintaining computational efficiency.
- The evaluation results on public dataset indicate that our method has comparable performance compared to ANN-based methods, and has a significant advantage on computational efficiency.

2 Related Works

2.1 Video Frame Interpolation

Video frame Interpolation technology usually uses the information of low frame rate video to generate intermediate frames, which makes the motion in the video smoother. The research of video frame interpolation technology has gone a long way. Nowadays, mainstream video frame interpolation algorithms are mainly divided into warping-based algorithm, kernel-based algorithm and phase-based algorithm.

Warping-based methods use the feature of optical flow map, which indices the motion of every pixel on the image. Warping-based video frame interpolation can be regarded as a downstream application of optical flow estimation task. The entire process can be divided into three phase: optical flow estimation, image warping and refine stage. In the prior stage, optical flow map is estimated. In the image warping stage, the most commonly used method is image backward warping, which warps destination image to generate former image according to the optical flow map between them. Warped images usually contain some noises and artifacts, thus a refine stage is designed to refine the interpolated frame.

Many state-of-the-art video frame interpolation algorithms are warping-based [7,8]. Warping-based methods usually assume linear motion and brightness consistency in scenes, thus they are not work perfectly on complex motions and significant brightness changes. Some approaches like [1] attempted to introduce more complex motion assumptions to overcome these problems.

Kernel-based methods [12,16,22] regard video frame interpolation task as a convolution progress. The intermediate frames are generated by apply adaptive convolution on consecutive frames. In these methods, the key stage is prediction of adaptive convolution kernels. Without linear motion and brightness consistency assumptions, kernel-based VFI methods are more robust to complex motions.

Phase-base methods [15] use phase-shift to describe motion in the video frames. Deep learning models used in these methods are to estimate phase-shift of input frames. Images need to be decomposed to get phases of images. Theoretical analysis support the validity of phase-based algorithms. But in practice, when the motion is too large, phase-based algorithms can't estimate the phase-shift accurately.

Fusion with Other Sensors. VFI from only frames is a ill-posed task because the information between the frames are unknown, complex motions are difficult to be modeled with certain algorithms. Some researchers attempt to get more motion information from additional sensors. In [17,23,24,26], event cameras are introduced to get more motion information. With additional inter-frame information, event-based video frame interpolation methods achieve better performance than frame-only approaches.

2.2   Spiking Neural Network

Spiking neural network (SNN) is bio-inspired neural network. It is known that the computation of artificial neural network (ANN) is based on large scale matrix operations, which could require massive computing resources and energy consumption. SNN differs greatly in this regard because all the calculations of spiking neurons are triggered by sparse and discrete spikes. Combining with neuromorphic computing hardware [2], SNN has a significant advantage over ANN on energy efficiency. However, due to the non-differentiability of spiking signal and complex temporal behavior, SNN suffered from the lacking of effective training algorithm and usually has a poor performance compared to ANN. Recently years, methods using surrogate gradients [13] have been proposed to train SNN directly. These methods utilized surrogate gradient functions to replace the gradient of non differentiable spike step function, enabling SNN to be trained with back propagation like ANN and requires fewer time steps, which makes it possible for SNN's application in more tasks.

SNN have been designed to be applied in many tasks, including optical flow estimation [4,11], object detection [9], depth estimation [20], etc. In [19], a spiking U-Net architecture is utilized for image segmentation tasks. Moreover, authors of [27] proposed a fully spiking neural network as a new method for reconstructing video frames from event streams, it demonstrated SNN's potential in image synthesis tasks. There are still more application areas of SNN to be explored.

In this work, we utilize SNN for event based video frame interpolation task, which achieves energy efficient video frame interpolation with the nature of SNNs and further broadens the application scenarios of SNN.

3 Method

3.1 Problem Statement

Given consecutive video frames and the event stream between them, the goal of our proposed framework is to predict a intermediate frame. The input sensor information includes consecutive key frames I_0, I_1 and corresponding event stream E_{01}. The predicted intermediate frame I_t could be at any time $t \in [0,1]$. According to intermediate time t, the event stream is divided into E_{0t} and E_{t1}. Raw event stream is represented by Address-Event-Representation(AER), which includes event coordinate, event polarity and event timestamp. Like previous methods [23,24], we convert the AER event steams to event voxel representation, which will be easier for further processing.

3.2 Spiking Neuron Model

One of the key characteristics that sets SNN apart from ANN is that SNN is composed of biologically inspired spiking neuron models. In this work, We utilize leaky-integrated and fire (LIF) [3] model as SNN's basic element. For a LIF neuron at the l_{th} layer, it's behavior could be described by following equations:

$$\begin{cases} I_t^l = W^l S_t^{l-1} \\ V_t^l = (1 - \frac{1}{\tau})V_{t-1}^l + \frac{1}{\tau}I_t^l \\ S_t^l = \hat{H}(V_t^l, V_{th}) \\ V_t^l = V_t^l - S_t^l V_{th} \end{cases} \tag{1}$$

where S_t^{l-1} denotes the input spikes from previous layer at time t, τ denotes the membrane time constant, V_t^l denotes the membrane potential of the neuron and V_{th} denotes firing threshold. The function $\hat{H}(\cdot)$ is the Heaviside step function. At every time step, the input spikes are first weighted by the synaptic weights W^l, the weighted sum represents the input current I_t^l, which will be accumulated on the membrane potential. If the membrane potential exceeds the firing threshold, the LIF neuron will firing a output spike and reset the membrane potential. With these neuron update mechanisms, LIF neuron is able to extract temporal features from input spikes.

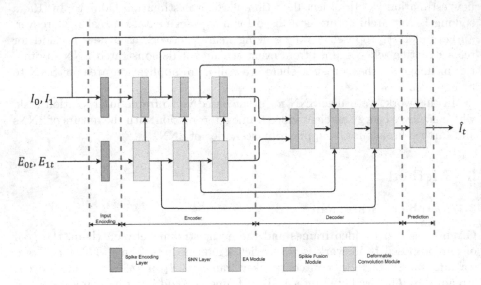

Fig. 1. The Architecture of Spike-EFI

3.3 Architecture of Spike-EFI

As shown in Fig. 1, the proposed network has four stages, including input encoding, encoder, decoder and prediction. In the input encoding stage, the spike encoding layer will encode the input information as binary spikes. These layers are also LIF neurons, the only difference is that they receive non-spike information. The encoder is responsible for processing and extracting multi-scale spike features. It includes image processing branch and event stream processing branch for separately processing images and events. In the decoder stage, the spike features of images and events are first fused, and then the multi-scale spike features are gradually upsampled and fused. As for prediction, we utilize deformable convolution block to predict the final image. The deformable convolution block first predicts convolution kernels from the output spike features of decoder and then perform convolution on key frames to obtain the predicted intermediate frame. The whole network is based on LIF spiking neuron, except the deformable convolution block. We utilized convolution for neuron synapse connection, which means the input current is calculated by convolution of input spikes.

The input of the network is image-event pairs. For one prediction, We have two input image-event pairs: $\{I_0, E_{0t}\}$ and $\{I_1, E_{t1}\}$. In ordered to make the network reusable for both image-event pairs, we reverse E_{t1} to E_{1t}. As mentioned before, we convert the event stream to event voxel. The shape of input images is $3 \times H \times W$. The shape of input event voxel is $N_T \times H \times W$, where N_T is the number of time bins, we set $N_T = 32$. The running time steps of the proposed SNN is 4, and we directly input the images and event voxels, which means they are first encoded to spikes by the spike encoding layers.

To predict the intermediate frame $\hat{I}_t$, the network separately processes image-event pairs. The input images and event voxels are processed by corresponding branch in the decoder. Then their spike features are fused by spike fusion module to obtain fused spike features. The decoder upsamples the low resolution features with spiking transposed convolution layers and then fuses them with higher resolution features through skip connections, which is similar to the decoder in UNet [21]. We collect the output spike features of the decoder at every timestep. Let S_{0t} denotes the output spike features of pair $\{I_0, E_{0t}\}$, S_{1t} denotes the output spike features of pair $\{I_1, E_{1t}\}$. In the next stage, the deformable convolution block will predict convolution kernels from these spike features. Similar to [12], the predicted convolution kernels include weights W_k and coordinate offsets $\{\Delta x, \Delta y\}$. We also introduce bias parameter b in the predicted convolution kernel. The bias parameter could be regard as brightness change compensation in the scene.

For a better understanding, the above pipeline could be written as following equations:

$$S_{0t} = F(I_0, E_{0t}) \tag{2}$$

$$S_{1t} = F(I_1, E_{1t}) \tag{3}$$

$$K_{0t} = F_k(S_{0t}) \tag{4}$$

$$K_{1t} = F_k(S_{1t}) \tag{5}$$

where $F(\cdot)$ denotes to feature extract part of the network, $F_k(\cdot)$ denotes the convolution kernel prediction module. The kernel K_{0t} is the convolution kernel for I_0, and K_{1t} is the convolution kernel for I_1.

With predicted convolution kernels, the convolution on the key frames are calculated by:

$$I'(x,y) = [\sum_{i=0}^{n} W_i(x,y)I(x + \Delta x_i(x,y), y + \Delta y_i(x,y)] + b(x,y) \tag{6}$$

where n equals to the element count of convolution kernel, and $b(x,y)$ denotes the predicted bias value at pixel coordinate (x,y).

Let $\hat{I}_{0t}$ and $\hat{I}_{1t}$ denotes the convolution results of I_{0t} and I_{1t}. To fuse them, blend weights are predicted by both S_{0t} and S_{1t}, which could be formulated as follows:

$$\begin{cases} B_0 = \sigma(F_b(S_{0t}, S_{1t})) \\ B_1 = 1 - B_0 \end{cases} \tag{7}$$

where B_0 and B_1 are the predicted blend weights, $\sigma(\cdot)$ is sigmoid function, F_b denotes the convolution block which predicts the blend weights. With blend weights, the final predicted intermediate frame is obtained by:

$$\hat{I}_t = B_0\hat{I}_{0t} + B_1\hat{I}_{1t} \tag{8}$$

3.4 Event-Guided Attention Module

We propose event-guided Attention (EA) module for the image processing branch. The module calculates attention score from event features, and applies the attention on the input current of image processing neurons. The event information naturally indicates the brightness change area on the image, thus the guidance of the event information could help image processing neurons to focus on the area where the event occurred meanwhile reducing activity on areas where there are no events. For neuron with EA module, the membrane potential is updated by:

$$V_{t+1} = (1 - \frac{1}{\tau})V_t + \frac{1}{\tau}\sigma(W_e S_e)I_{in} \tag{9}$$

where $\sigma(\cdot)$ is sigmoid function, S_e denotes spikes from event processing neurons and W_e is trainable weight matrix to calculate attention score.

3.5 SNN Training with Back-Propagation

We trained our SNN with Back Propagation Through Time (BPTT) [25]. We use L1 loss as the network's loss function. As mentioned before, the spike firing in neuron based on Heaviside step function, which is non-differentiable. Thus we utilized surrogate gradient mechanism [13] to calculate the gradient of spike firing module. The surrogate gradient we used could be written as follows:

$$\hat{H}'_{surrogate}(x) = \frac{1}{\alpha x^2 + 1} \tag{10}$$

where α is a hyper parameter, and we set $\alpha = 10.0$. As for the firing threshold V_{th} and the membrane time constant τ, we also regard them as trainable parameters, which means their values are updated through gradient back propagation during the training.

4 Experiments

4.1 Experimental Setup

We trained and tested our network on BS-ERGB dataset [23], which contains continuous event streams between high-frame-rate video images and video image frames. The original spatial resolution of both images and event streams is 720p and we unified the resolution to 256×256 for experiments.

We implemented the proposed spiking neural network with Pytorch [18] framework. We train the network for 200 epochs, and the batch size is 4 during the train. We utilized Adam optimizer [10] in training, the initial learning rate is 0.0003 and decrease for half every 60 epochs. The data augmentation is performed using random horizontal and vertical flipping, random time inversion and random rotation during training. The simulation time steps for SNN is 4 and we set the initial τ 2.0 and the initial threshold 0.5 for spiking neurons.

4.2 Results

The comparison of quantitative results are listed in Table 1. We use Peak Signal-to-Noise Ratio (PSNR) and Structural Similarity Index Measure (SSIM) to metric the performance of algorithms. We compare the quantitative results with recently event-based video frame interpolation methods, which are based on ANN models. Figure 2 shows qualitative comparison with state-of-the-art ANN-based methods. The results show that SNN-based method could also handle well on the video processing task, the proposed method has a comparable performance to the ANN-based methods.

Table 1. Comparison of quantitative results with state-of-the-art ANN-based methods.

Methods	PSNR/dB	SSIM
Time-lens [24]	28.36	0.932
Time-lens++ [23]	28.56	—
Spike-EFI(Ours)	29.12	0.889

4.3 Computational and Energy Efficiency

In order to quantify the compute energy consumption benefit from SNN-based architecture, we analysed the computational and energy consumption of our SNN-based method and listed ANN-based methods.

We first analyzed the differences in computational operations between SNN and ANN. For SNN, the basic computational operation is accumulation (AC) of synaptic weights, and these operations are triggered by input spikes. With the event triggered computing paradigm, the computation in SNN is sparse and asynchronous. For SNN and ANN with the same topology structure, they have same operation count when all synapse connections in the SNN are triggered. For ANN, the basic computational operation is multiply and accumulate (MAC) of activation values and weights, which is more expensive than SNN's.

More specifically, for SNN layers based on the LIF model, the overall computation includes two stages: synaptic weight accumulation and membrane potential update. In the membrane potential update stage, each neuron requires an additional complete MAC operation for leaky-integral on membrane potential. Thus, the computational operation count for LIF-based SNN includes:

$$\begin{cases} \#OP_{SNN\_AC} = \#OP_{AC} \times R \times T \\ \#OP_{SNN\_MAC} = N \times T \end{cases} \tag{11}$$

where R is average spike firing rate, T is number of time steps, N is the number of spiking neurons. $\#OP_{AC}$ denotes the AC count of the SNN layer when all synapses are activated.

The AC count of SNN layer is equal to the MAC count of ANN layer which has the same topological structure. For convolutional ANN layers, the MACs can be written as:

$$\#OP_{MAC} = K_W \times K_H \times C_{in} \times C_{out} \times W_{out} \times H_{out} \qquad (12)$$

where K_w and K_H denotes the kernel size, C_{in} and C_{out} denotes the input channels and output channels, W_{out} and H_{out} denotes the output tensor size. It should be noted that for the beginning layers of our proposed SNN, they process non-spike information, thus their computational operation should be counted for MAC. For EA module, one more MAC is required for each neuron, which means it brings additional operation count: $\Delta\#OP_{EA\_MAC} = N \times T$.

As for energy consumption, it is known that under the 45 nm CMOS technology, the energy consumption of a multiply-accumulate operation for a 32-bit floating-point number is 4.6 pJ [6], and the energy consumption of an accu-

Fig. 2. Qualitative comparison with state-of-the-art ANN-based methods.

mulation operation is 0.9 pJ. Thus SNN could reduce energy consumption by 5.1× compared to ANN. With a cheaper basic operation and event-triggered computing paradigm, SNN has a natural advantage in computational energy consumption.

Table 2. Average spiking firing rate in Spike-EFI

Module Name	SNN Layer	Number of Spiking Neurons	Average Spike Firing Rate/%
Input Encoding Layer	Ev-LIF	32×H×W	6.10
	Img-LIF	32×H×W	29.92
Encoder (Event Branch)	LIF1	32×H×W	7.39
	LIF2	32×H×W	5.81
	LIF3	64×(H/2)×(W/2)	5.19
	LIF4	64×(H/2)×(W/2)	7.54
	LIF5	128×(H/4)×(W/4)	8.10
	LIF6	128×(H/4)×(W/4)	8.85
Encoder (Image Branch)	LIF1	32×H×W	31.08
	EA1	32×H×W	23.51
	LIF2	64×(H/2)×(W/2)	17.86
	EA2	64×(H/2)×(W/2)	13.02
	LIF3	128×(H/4)×(W/4)	11.87
	EA3	128×(H/4)×(W/4)	9.85
Spike Fusion	LIF1	32×H×W	17.38
	LIF2	64×(H/2)×(W/2)	10.38
	LIF3	128×(H/4)×(W/4)	16.8
Decoder	Up-LIF1	64×(H/2)×(W/2)	11.93
	LIF1	64×(H/2)×(W/2)	20.58
	Up-LIF2	32×H×W	13.58
	LIF2	32×H×W	23.88
	LIF3	32×H×W	4.56
Overall			13.87

Table 3. Energy consumption of Spike-EFI

Average $\#OP_{AC}$	20.3 G/frame
Average $\#OP_{MAC}$	5.6 G/frame
Average Energy Consumption of SNN	44.2 mJ/frame
Energy Consumption of ANN[a]	144.2 mJ/frame
Energy Consumption Benefit	3.3×

[a]This is the energy consumption of ANN with the same topological structure as Spike-EFI.

Based on the discussion above, we first measured the average spike firing rate of the network on the whole test dataset, as shown in Table 2. And In Table 3, we analyse the energy consumption of Spike-EFI. The overall spike firing rate of the proposed method is 13.87%, and the energy efficiency improvement compare to the ANN with the same topology structure is up to 3.3×.

We also compared the energy consumption between previous ANN-based methods and Spike-EFI. It should be noted that we measure the energy consumption required to interpolation of a intermediate frame, and in the process there are network reuse, therefore the energy consumption is larger than the single network inference requires. The results in Table 4 demonstrate that Spike-EFI has a significant advantage on energy efficiency compare to other ANN-based methods. Moreover, the proposed method is also much more lightweight than other ANN-based methods.

Table 4. Comparison compute energy consumption with other methods

Method Name	#Parameters	#OP	Energy Consumption
Time-lens	72.2M	103.4 G/frame	475.6 mJ/frame
Time-lens++	53.9M	85.8 G/frame	395.9 mJ/frame
Spike-EFI(Ours)	**1.35M**	**25.9** G/frame	**44.2** mJ/frame

From results above, the proposed method maintains performance while being lightweight and low energy consumption. It will be quite suitable for applications on resource limited edge devices.

4.4   Ablation Study

We conducted ablation experiment on the proposed EA module. For comparison, we replace EA module with regular LIF neuron in image processing branch. The results in Tables 5 the PSNR by 0.3 dB and increases the SSIM by 0.002. It indicates that the event-guided attention could help the network more effectively learn from the fusion of image and event stream. In terms of energy consumption, the results in Table 6 show that EA module increases energy consumption by 0.1 mJ, which means that it almost has no impact on energy efficiency. We could conclude that EA module can bring positive effects on performance, and maintains computational efficiency.

Table 5. Ablation study of EA module (Comparison on performance)

Method	PSNR/dB	SSIM
Spike-EFI	**29.1**	**0.889**
Spike-EFI(w/o EA)	28.8	0.887

Table 6. Ablation study of EA module (Comparison on energy consumption)

Method	Average Spike Firing Rate	$\#OP_{AC}$	$\#OP_{MAC}$	Energy Consumption
Spike-EFI	13.87%	20.3 G	5.63 G	44.2 mJ
Spike-EFI(w/o EA)	13.97%	20.3 G	5.60 G	44.1 mJ

5 Conclusion

In this paper, we present Spike-EFI, a lightweight fully spiking neural network for event-based video frame interpolation that fuses event streams and RGB images. The experimental results indicate that our method has significant energy efficiency advantages over previous ANN-based methods while maintaining comparable performance levels. We show that SNN could effectively extract motion feature from the fusion of event stream and video frame. With the natural advantage of SNN on energy efficiency, the proposed Spike-EFI has 3.3× less energy consumption than the ANN-version one. These findings demonstrate the great potential of SNN for energy-efficient video processing tasks.

References

1. Chi, Z., Mohammadi Nasiri, R., Liu, Z., Lu, J., Tang, J., Plataniotis, K.N.: All at once: temporally adaptive multi-frame interpolation with advanced motion modeling. In: Vedaldi, A., Bischof, H., Brox, T., Frahm, J.-M. (eds.) ECCV 2020. LNCS, vol. 12372, pp. 107–123. Springer, Cham (2020). https://doi.org/10.1007/978-3-030-58583-9_7
2. Davies, M., et al.: Loihi: a neuromorphic manycore processor with on-chip learning. IEEE Micro **38**(1), 82–99 (2018)
3. Gerstner, W., Kistler, W.M., Naud, R., Paninski, L.: Neuronal Dynamics: From Single Neurons to Networks and Models of Cognition. Cambridge University Press (2014)
4. Hagenaars, J., Paredes-Vallés, F., De Croon, G.: Self-supervised learning of event-based optical flow with spiking neural networks. Adv. Neural. Inf. Process. Syst. **34**, 7167–7179 (2021)
5. He, W., et al.: TimeReplayer: unlocking the potential of event cameras for video interpolation. In: Proceedings of the IEEE/CVF Conference on Computer Vision and Pattern Recognition, pp. 17804–17813 (2022)
6. Horowitz, M.: 1.1 computing's energy problem (and what we can do about it). In: 2014 IEEE International Solid-State Circuits Conference Digest of Technical Papers (ISSCC), pp. 10–14. IEEE (2014)
7. Huang, Z., Zhang, T., Heng, W., Shi, B., Zhou, S.: RIFE: real-time intermediate flow estimation for video frame interpolation. arXiv preprint arXiv:2011.06294 (2020)
8. Jiang, H., Sun, D., Jampani, V., Yang, M.H., Learned-Miller, E., Kautz, J.: Super SloMo: high quality estimation of multiple intermediate frames for video interpolation. In: Proceedings of the IEEE Conference on Computer Vision and Pattern Recognition, pp. 9000–9008 (2018)

9. Kim, S., Park, S., Na, B., Yoon, S.: Spiking-YOLO: spiking neural network for energy-efficient object detection. In: Proceedings of the AAAI Conference on Artificial Intelligence, vol. 34, pp. 11270–11277 (2020)

10. Kingma, D.P., Ba, J.: Adam: a method for stochastic optimization. arXiv preprint arXiv:1412.6980 (2014)

11. Lee, C., Kosta, A.K., Zhu, A.Z., Chaney, K., Daniilidis, K., Roy, K.: Spike-FlowNet: event-based optical flow estimation with energy-efficient hybrid neural networks. In: Vedaldi, A., Bischof, H., Brox, T., Frahm, J.-M. (eds.) ECCV 2020. LNCS, vol. 12374, pp. 366–382. Springer, Cham (2020). https://doi.org/10.1007/978-3-030-58526-6_22

12. Lee, H., Kim, T., Chung, T.Y., Pak, D., Ban, Y., Lee, S.: AdaCoF: adaptive collaboration of flows for video frame interpolation. In: Proceedings of the IEEE/CVF Conference on Computer Vision and Pattern Recognition, pp. 5316–5325 (2020)

13. Lee, J.H., Delbruck, T., Pfeiffer, M.: Training deep spiking neural networks using backpropagation. Front. Neurosci. **10**, 508 (2016)

14. Lichtsteiner, P., Posch, C., Delbruck, T.: A 128 × 128 120 db 15 μs latency asynchronous temporal contrast vision sensor. IEEE J. Solid-State Circuits **43**(2), 566–576 (2008)

15. Meyer, S., Wang, O., Zimmer, H., Grosse, M., Sorkinehornung, A.: Phase-based frame interpolation for video. IEEE (2015)

16. Niklaus, S., Mai, L., Liu, F.: Video frame interpolation via adaptive convolution. In: Proceedings of the IEEE Conference on Computer Vision and Pattern Recognition, pp. 670–679 (2017)

17. Paikin, G., Ater, Y., Shaul, R., Soloveichik, E.: EFI-Net: video frame interpolation from fusion of events and frames. In: Proceedings of the IEEE/CVF Conference on Computer Vision and Pattern Recognition, pp. 1291–1301 (2021)

18. Paszke, A., et al.: PyTorch: an imperative style, high-performance deep learning library. In: Advances in Neural Information Processing Systems, vol. 32 (2019)

19. Patel, K., Hunsberger, E., Batir, S., Eliasmith, C.: A spiking neural network for image segmentation. arXiv preprint arXiv:2106.08921 (2021)

20. Rançon, U., Cuadrado-Anibarro, J., Cottereau, B.R., Masquelier, T.: StereoSpike: depth learning with a spiking neural network. IEEE Access **10**, 127428–127439 (2022)

21. Ronneberger, O., Fischer, P., Brox, T.: U-Net: convolutional networks for biomedical image segmentation. In: Navab, N., Hornegger, J., Wells, W.M., Frangi, A.F. (eds.) MICCAI 2015. LNCS, vol. 9351, pp. 234–241. Springer, Cham (2015). https://doi.org/10.1007/978-3-319-24574-4_28

22. Shi, Z., Xu, X., Liu, X., Chen, J., Yang, M.H.: Video frame interpolation transformer. In: Proceedings of the IEEE/CVF Conference on Computer Vision and Pattern Recognition, pp. 17482–17491 (2022)

23. Tulyakov, S., Bochicchio, A., Gehrig, D., Georgoulis, S., Li, Y., Scaramuzza, D.: Time Lens++: event-based frame interpolation with parametric non-linear flow and multi-scale fusion. In: Proceedings of the IEEE/CVF Conference on Computer Vision and Pattern Recognition, pp. 17755–17764 (2022)

24. Tulyakov, S., et al.: Time Lens: event-based video frame interpolation. In: Proceedings of the IEEE/CVF Conference on Computer Vision and Pattern Recognition, pp. 16155–16164 (2021)

25. Werbos, P.J.: Backpropagation through time: what it does and how to do it. Proc. IEEE **78**(10), 1550–1560 (1990)

26. Zhang, X., Yu, L.: Unifying motion deblurring and frame interpolation with events. In: Proceedings of the IEEE/CVF Conference on Computer Vision and Pattern Recognition, pp. 17765–17774 (2022)
27. Zhu, L., Wang, X., Chang, Y., Li, J., Huang, T., Tian, Y.: Event-based video reconstruction via potential-assisted spiking neural network. In: Proceedings of the IEEE/CVF Conference on Computer Vision and Pattern Recognition, pp. 3594–3604 (2022)

ScrambleMix: A Privacy-Preserving Image Processing for Edge-Cloud Machine Learning

Koki Madono[1](✉), Masayuki Tanaka[2,3], and Masaki Onishi[3]

[1] Department of Communications and Computer Engineering, Waseda University, Tokyo, Japan
madonomadonorunning@gmail.com
[2] National Institute of Advanced Industrial Science and Technology (AIST), Tokyo, Japan
[3] Tokyo Institute of Technology, Tokyo, Japan

Abstract. This paper proposes ScrambleMix, a novel privacy-preserving image processing for edge-cloud machine learning. ScrambleMix combines image scrambling and AugMix to improve visual information hiding. Specifically, to make two scrambled images from a single input image, each copy of the input image is scrambled using a different key every time. Then, the scrambled images are mixed with a randomly sampled mixing ratio. A self-teaching loss is introduced to improve the classification performance of ScrambleMix. In this study, we first evaluate the visual information hiding quantitatively using Learned Perceptual Image Patch Similarity (LPIPS). Then, the experiments with different settings demonstrate the proposed ScrambleMix outperforms the existing approaches for edge-cloud machine learning in terms of both classification accuracy and visual information hiding.

Keywords: Image Processing · Cloud-based Machine Learning · Privacy-Preserving Machine Learning

1 Introduction

Machine learning has been recently developed more powerful and suitable for a mobile application. A variety of people want to use machine learning on their own mobile devices; however, machine learning needs a large number of hardware resources that cannot be physically available to mobile devices. As a solution for these resource-constrained edge devices, an edge-cloud system is used for the training and inference of machine learning. By using the computationally rich resources of the cloud system, people can make a machine learning-based model using their own dataset. However, the use of personal datasets raises privacy issues because the cloud servers might be involved in malicious transactions. Therefore, both privacy-preserving training and inference are highly demanded for edge-cloud machine learning.

Recently, privacy-preserving image processing has been applied to edge-cloud machine learning. In this paper, we focus on an image classification task which is a typical problem of machine learning. For those approaches, a homomorphic encryption [18,25] has been proposed to ensure security against arbitrary attack by third parties; it, however, needs very high computational power and memory during both the training and inference phases. A federated learning [8,15] is another method that

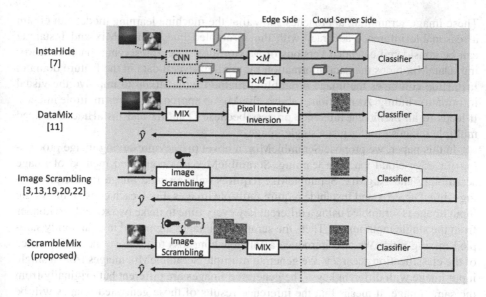

Fig. 1. Inference phase of privacy-Preserving image processing for edge-cloud machine learning: DataMix [11], InstaHide [7] Scrambling [3,13,19,20,22], and ScrambleMix (proposed).

enables the model to train itself on the edge side. This method is used by sharing the gradient of the training model with the cloud server. This method is not secure because a recent attacking approach [32] would recover the training data. A differential privacy [1] has been proposed to deal with the weakness of federated learning by adding noise on a gradient before sending it to the cloud server. This can be applied only to the training phase because noise addition decreases the classification performance in the inference phase. Due to the aforementioned disadvantages, we focus on privacy-preserving image processing because this method requires less computational power and memory with a high classification performance.

In general, we can consider that privacy-preserving image processing is a kind of data augmentation [5,12,14,21,24,27,31]. Data augmentation include geometrical transformation [4,23], Mixup [29], and AugMix [6]. In the geometrical transformation, an image is geometrically transformed with parameters such as a scaling ratio and a rotation angle. Mixup mixes a pair of images and the labels by linear interpolation, where the labels are represented in the form of one-hot encoding. In AugMix, first, several images are generated by applying the data augmentation to a single image. The augmented image is obtained by mixing those images. Then, the original image and the augmented image are mixed. Note that the Mixup requires multiple images in the process of visual information hiding while the geometrical transformation and AugMix require only a single image.

While showing a relationship with data augmentation, we overview the existing methods of privacy-preserving image processing: image scrambling [3,13,19,20,22], DataMix [11], and InstaHide [7]. In these images scrambling approaches [3,13,19, 20,22], an input image is first scrambled with parameters, called a key, to hide the visual information. Then, the machine learning model is trained with scrambled images.

These image scrambling approaches show that the machine learning model can obtain a reasonable inference accuracy with the scrambled images. DataMix and Instahide can be considered extended versions of Mixup for privacy-preserving machine learning. DataMix hides the data information by mixing several data in the feature domain. InstaHide combines the image scrambling method with Mixup to improve the visual information hiding. As mentioned above, the Mixup approach requires multiple images. It leads to an inefficient inference process because DataMix and InstaHide also need multiple images to infer just a single image.

In this paper, we propose ScrambleMix, a novel privacy-preserving image processing for edge-cloud machine learning. ScrambleMix is a combined method of image scrambling and AugMix. ScrambleMix requires only a single image for the processing while DataMix and Instahide require multiple images. First, each copy of the single input image is scrambled using a different key every time to make two scrambled images from the single input image. Then, the scrambled images are mixed in a randomly sampled mixing ratio. We also introduce a self-teaching loss to improve the performance of the classification accuracy. We generate multiple ScrambleMix images from a single input image with different keys. The generated images are different but originally from the same image. It means that the inference results of those generated images will be consistent. We evaluate this consistency by the KL divergence, which we define as a self-teaching loss.

In many privacy-preserving image processing methods for machine learning, the performance of the visual information hiding is only qualitatively evaluated. In this study, we use Learned Perceptual Image Patch Similarity (LPIPS) [30] for the quantitative evaluation of the visual information hiding. The experiments with different settings demonstrate the proposed ScrambleMix outperforms the existing privacy-preserving edge-cloud machine learning approaches in terms of both classification accuracy and visual information hiding.

This work mainly contributes to:

- Introduction of a simple and efficient method, ScrambleMix to implement privacy-preserving image processing for edge-cloud machine learning,
- Efficient data training with the self-teaching loss,
- Qualitative comparisons of the visual information hiding with LPIPS.

2 Related Work

2.1 Privacy-Preserving Image Processing

Figure 1 summarizes the inference phase of three existing privacy-preserving image processing methods and the proposed ScrambleMix for edge-cloud machine learning. The privacy-preserving image processing can be classified into two categories; multiple-image processing and single-image processing. DataMix [11] and InstaHide [7] are in the multiple-image processing group which requires multiple images for the processing. Those algorithms need multiple images even if they infer only a single image. Image scrambling [3, 13, 19, 20, 22] and the proposed ScarmbleMix are single-image processing which requires only a single image for the processing. Due

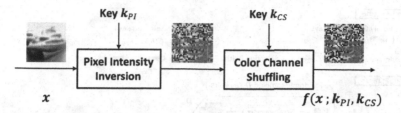

Fig. 2. Processing pipeline of pixel-based image scrambling [20]. First, pixel intensities of an input image are inverted according to a scramble key k_{PI}. Then, the color channels of each pixel are shuffled according to a scramble key k_{CS}.

to efficiency in both communication and computation, single-image processing is better than multiple-image processing.

Multiple-image processing can be considered an extension of the Mixup data augmentation algorithm for privacy-preserving processing. DataMix conducts a Mixup in a feature space. Specifically, DataMix multiplies a pre-processed feature in the edge side by a randomly generated orthogonal matrix M and a post-processed feature on the cloud server by a corresponding inverse matrix M^{-1}. When Mixup is conducted in a feature space, they use a group size S_G (i.e. 8, 16)). DataMix needs to prepare a GPU on the edge side to train the first N convolutional neural networks (CNNs) and the last fully-connected (FC) layer in the classifier. InstaHide is a combined method of Mixup and pixel intensity inversion. This method mixes a private image and a public image and conducts pixel intensity inversion for privacy preservation. InstaHide has a low classification accuracy because it uses a public image that affects to classification. For this reason, test-time augment (i.e. with 10 tests for a single image inference) is necessary for an inference phase although it further makes the process computationally expensive.

As a typical method of single-image processing, Fig. 2 shows the image scrambling pipeline of a pixel-based image encryption [20]. An image is scrambled with a scramble key $k = (k_{PI}, k_{CS})$. First, the pixel intensities of each channel specified by a key k_{PI} are inverted. Then, RGB pixel intensities are shuffled according to a key k_{CS}. The scrambled image can be expressed by $f(x; k)$, where f represents the image scrambling operation, x is an input image, and k is a scramble key. This method is very simple and computationally efficient. However, a third party easily restores the plain images from the scramble images if they obtain the scramble key. In order to overcome this drawback, randomization of the scramble key has been proposed [19]. However, randomization of the scramble key leads to the degradation of the classification performance.

2.2 Data Augmentation

The data augmentation approaches [5, 12, 14, 21, 24, 27, 31] have been proposed to improve the robustness of a training model. Here, we review Mixup [29] and AugMix [6] which are related to privacy-preserving image processing. Mixup synthesizes an image and an associated label from two different images and labels as follows:

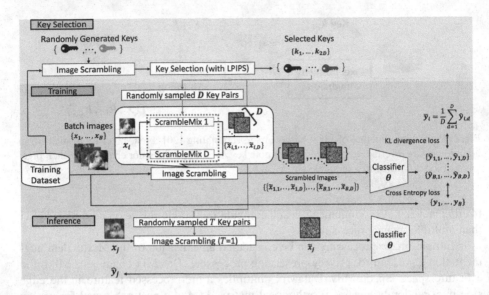

Fig. 3. Overview of the proposed privacy-preserving image processing consisting of three phases: key selection (top), training (middle), and inference (bottom). Each phase of training and inference describes processing on both the edge side and the cloud server side.

$$\widetilde{\boldsymbol{x}} = m\boldsymbol{x}_i + (1-m)\boldsymbol{x}_j, \tag{1}$$

$$\widetilde{\boldsymbol{y}} = m\boldsymbol{y}_i + (1-m)\boldsymbol{y}_j, \tag{2}$$

where $\boldsymbol{x}_i$ and $\boldsymbol{x}_j$ are i- and j-th training image, $\boldsymbol{y}_i$ and $\boldsymbol{y}_j$ are associated training label, $(\widetilde{\boldsymbol{x}}, \widetilde{\boldsymbol{y}})$ is a synthesized training image and associated label, and $m \in [0,1]$ is a mixing ratio. The label is represented by the one-hot encoding. The mixing ratio is sampled from the Beta distribution with parameter α, Beta(α, α) where $\alpha \in (0, \infty)$. The parameter α in Mixup is typically 0.1 to 0.4. Mixup extends the training distribution by incorporating the prior knowledge that linear interpolations of feature vectors should lead to linear interpolations of the associated targets. Mixup has little computational overhead to train a classifier.

AugMix makes a synthesized training image from one training image as follows:

$$\widetilde{\boldsymbol{x}} = m\boldsymbol{x} + (1-m) \sum_{k=1}^{K} \eta_k \boldsymbol{g}(\boldsymbol{x}_i; \boldsymbol{\phi}_k), \tag{3}$$

where $\boldsymbol{x}$ is a training image, $\widetilde{\boldsymbol{x}}$ is a synthesized image, m is the mixing ratio sampled from the Beta distribution, K is the number of data augmentation sets, η_k is a weight ratio sampled from the Dirichlet distribution, $\boldsymbol{g}$ is an image processing operation for the data augmentation, $\boldsymbol{\phi}_k$ is k-th parameters of the data augmentation. The parameters $\boldsymbol{\phi}$ are randomly sampled from several data augmentation operations. AugMix extends the training distribution by making a high diversity of augmented image $\sum_{k=1}^{K} \eta_k \boldsymbol{g}(\boldsymbol{x}; \boldsymbol{\phi}_k)$. AugMix, then, enforces a consistent embedding by the classifier across diverse augmentation of the same input image through the use of Jensen-Shannon divergence as a consistency loss.

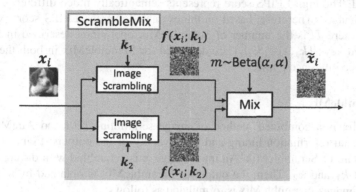

Fig. 4. Overview of ScrambleMix. An input image x is first scrambled with different scramble keys, k_1 and k_2. Using two scrambled images $f(x_i, k_1)$ and $f(x, k_2)$, mixed images are calculated as $\tilde{x}_i = m f(x_i, k_1) + (1 - m) f(x_i, k_2)$ where $m \in [0,1]$ from Beta distribution.

3 Proposed Privacy-Preserving Image Processing

Figure 3 shows an overview of the proposed privacy-preserving image processing. This framework consists of three phases; key selection, training, and inference.

In the key selection phase, training images are first scrambled with randomly generated scramble keys. The performance of the visual information hiding the image scrambling depends on the keys. Therefore, we select keys that are suitable for image scrambling based on LPIPS score. The selected keys are used for ScrambleMix in both the training and inference phases. In the training phase, the user applies ScrambleMix with D pair of keys to the plain images. Then, the scrambled images are sent to the cloud server. On the cloud server, the deep learning model is trained with scrambled images. In the inference phase, an image to be inferred is scrambled by ScrambleMix. Then, the scrambled image is sent to the cloud server. The result inferred by the trained model on the cloud server is sent back to the edge side. For the inference, the test time augmentation (TTA) can be optionally applied because the output of the ScrambleMix depends on the key pair and the mixing ratio.

3.1 Key Selection

The first phase in Fig. 3 indicates the key selection phase of the proposed image processing. The visual information hiding performance of the image scrambling depends on the keys. We select keys to ensure the visual information hiding performance of the image scrambling.

Here, we evaluate the visual information hiding performance by LPIPS scores [30] between original plain images and scrambled images. We scramble images in the training dataset with a randomly generated scramble key. Then, the average LPIPS score is evaluated. The high LPIPS score represents semantically much difference between compared images. Therefore, based on the evaluated average LPIPS score, we select $2D$ keys, where D is the number of ScrambleMix operations described in Sect. 3.2. The selected keys $\{k_1, \cdots, k_{2D}\}$ are deployed for ScrambleMix in both the training phase and the inference phase.

3.2 ScrambleMix

ScrambleMix is a combined method of image scrambling [20] and AugMix [6] to improve visual information hiding and the diversity of the outputs. Figure 4 shows a block diagram of ScrambleMix. An input image x is scrambled with different scramble keys of k_1 and k_2. Then, the output of ScrambleMix is obtained by mixing two scrambled images. ScrambleMix is formulated as follows:

$$\widetilde{x} = m f(x; k_1) + (1 - m) f(x; k_2), \tag{4}$$

where $\widetilde{x}$ is a scrambled image or an output of ScrambleMix, x is an input image, f represents the image scrambling process, m is a mixing ratio, and (k_1, k_2) is a pair of scramble keys. The mixing ratio m is randomly sampled from Beta distribution, $beta(\alpha, \alpha)$. In the proposed ScrambleMix, we typically set 0.005 to 0.01 to the parameter α of the Beta distribution. The key pair of (k_1, k_2) is randomly sampled from the keys selected in the previous subsection. In ScrambleMix, we pick up the key from the finite number of key pools. Although we select a certain number of keys, the diversity of the output is guaranteed by mixing two scrambled images with a randomly sampled mixing ratio.

3.3 Training

The second phase in Fig. 3 indicates the training phase of the proposed privacy-preseving image processing. We follow a very popular mini-batch training manner. Each image in the mini-batch is applied ScrambleMix D times. The i-th image of the processed images is referred as $\{\widetilde{x}_{i,1}, .., \widetilde{x}_{i,D}\}$. In the key selection phase, we prepare $2D$ scramble keys because each ScrambleMix requires two scramble keys. ScrambleMix processes the mini-batch D-times before sending it to the cloud server. On the cloud server, the network model is updated with the processed mini-batch. For training, we introduce a self-teaching loss to improve classification performance. The loss function L is written as

$$L = L_{CE} + \lambda L_{ST}, \tag{5}$$

where L_{CE} denotes a mean cross-entropy loss for classification, L_{ST} denotes a self-teaching loss, and λ is a hyper-parameter. The mean Cross-Entropy loss L_{CE} for the processed mini-batch is formulated as

$$L_{CE} = \frac{1}{BD} \sum_{i=1}^{B} \sum_{d=1}^{D} \mathrm{CE}(h(\widetilde{x}_{i,d}; \theta), y_i), \tag{6}$$

where CE represents a Cross-Entropy, $h(\cdot; \theta)$ represents a network model with a parameter θ, $\widetilde{x}_{i,d}$ is i-image processed by d-th ScrambleMix, y_i is i-th label, D is the number of ScrambleMix operations, and B is a mini-bach size.

We define the self-teaching loss L_{ST} as

$$L_{ST} = \frac{1}{BD} \sum_{i=1}^{B} \sum_{d=1}^{D} \mathrm{KL}(h(\widetilde{x}_{i,d}; \theta) \| \bar{y}_i), \tag{7}$$

$$\bar{y}_i = \mathrm{StopGrad} \left[\frac{1}{D} \sum_{d=1}^{D} h(\widetilde{x}_{i,d}; \theta) \right], \tag{8}$$

where KL represents Kullback-Leibler divergence [10], $\bar{y}_i$ is the average of the network inference and StopGrad means that we did not the back propagation.

Even if the processed images are different in terms of ScrambleMix parameters of the scramble keys and the mixing ratio, the inference by the network model should be consistent because the processed input image and the original plain image are identical in classification. Considering this property, we introduce the self-teaching loss. To adjust the strength of the loss, we empirically set the parameter λ.

Note that the cloud server always receives scrambled images whose visual information is hidden.

3.4 Inference

The third and final phase in Fig. 3 indicates the inference phase of ScrambleMix. When the edge side receives an image to be inferred, the image is scrambled by ScrambleMix, where the key pair and the mixing ratio are randomly sampled. Then, the scrambled images are sent to the cloud server. On the cloud server, the trained network model directly infers the scrambled images. Then, the inference result is sent back to the edge side. Note that the proposed framework requires only a single image to obtain the inference result. The outputs of the proposed ScrambleMix with different parameters of the scramble key pair and the mixing ratio.

The resultant inference can be expressed as

$$\hat{y}_j = h(\widetilde{x}_j; \theta), \tag{9}$$

where $\widetilde{x}_j$ is the image scrambled by the ScrambleMix.

At this time, we can optionally apply a test-time augmentation (TTA). The resultant inference can be expressed as

$$\hat{y}_j = \frac{1}{T} \sum_{t=1}^{T} h(\widetilde{x}_{j,t}; \theta), \tag{10}$$

where T denotes the number of TTA, and $\widetilde{x}_{j,t}$ is the image scrambled by t-th ScrambleMix. Since the different key pairs, we can augment the same image in a secure way.

4 Experiment

We performed an experimental comparison to validate the proposed privacy-preserving image processing with ScrambleMix. For fair comparisons, we performed the experiments using multiple methods, models, and evaluation indices. The reproduction code is available online[1].

4.1 Evaluation

We evaluated the proposed and existing privacy-preserving image processing methods with two aspects: the classification performance and the visual information hiding performance. For the classification performance, we simply evaluated the classification accuracy. In many studies on the privacy-preserving image processing [3,7,11,13,19, 20,22], the performance of the visual information hiding is just qualitatively evaluated. In this paper, we quantitatively evaluated the visual information hiding by the LPIPS score [30]. For the image quality assessment, metrics of Mean Square Error (MSE) and Structural Similarity Index (SSIM) are usually used to evaluate the similarity between two images. However, MSE and SSIM are not suitable to evaluate the performance of the visual information hiding because those metrics are very sensitive to small geometrical and photometrical perturbations. Even if the target image includes such small geometrical and photometrical perturbations, a human can easily obtain visual information from the target image. For this reason, the metrics for the image quality assessment are not suitable to evaluate the performance of the visual information hiding. Recently, the LPIPS score has been proposed to evaluate the semantic difference between the two images [30]. We assumed that the privacy-preserving image processing has a high performance of the visual information hiding if the scrambled image is semantically different from the original plain image. Based on that assumption, we quantitatively evaluated the performance of the visual information hiding by the average LPIPS score between the processed images and the original plain images. The high LPIPS score means having a large semantical difference so the higher LPIPS score is better for the visual information hiding.

4.2 Experimental Setups

We evaluated the image classification accuracy using two models: WideResNet 40×10 [28], and Shakedrop [26]. All models were trained by using SGD for 200 epochs. The initial learning rate was set to 0.1 and divided the learning rate by 10 at the epoch in $\{60, 120, 180\}$. In the training, we used a weight decay of 0.0005, a momentum of 0.9, and a batch size of 256 using 4 GPUs. The data augmentation of random cropping and horizontal flipping is conducted on a real image before applying privacy-preserving image processing. We evaluated three datasets: CIFAR-10 [9], CIFAR-100 [9] and SVHN [16]. We used proposed ScrambleMix with four existing methods to compare both classification performance and visual information hiding;

---

[1] The reproduction code will be available when the paper is accepted.

DataMix [11], InstaHide [7], Learnable Encryption (LE) [22], and random pixel-based image encryption (Random PE) [19].

In DataMix [11], the preprocessed model contains the first 1 convolution block in each model, the post-processed model contains the final layer in each model, and the rest of the layers in each model is deployed on the cloud. We used a group size S_G=8 for mixing images in a feature space.

In InstaHide [7], we considered the cross-dataset setting to hide private images by public image. We mixed one private image and one public image. The hyper-parameters of InstaHide are the same as the original paper [7]. For CIFAR-10 and SVHN, we used CIFAR-100 as the public dataset; For CIFAR-100, we used CIFAR-10 as the public dataset. We used the author's publicly available code in this experiment[2] The number of TTAs is one of the critical parameters for the InstaHide. We evaluated two numbers of TTA which are 1 and 10. The authors of InstaHide [7] recommend TTA=10 in their paper.

LE [22] is an image scrambling method with a single key. We used the block size 4 × 4 of the scrambling key. We used the author's publicly available code in this experiment[3]

Random PE [19] is the randomized key version of the pixel-based image scramble as shown in Fig. 2. For every sample, we randomly drew a scramble key.

In the proposed ScrambleMix, we used pixel-based image encryption (PE) [20]. In key selection, we first randomly generated 20 keys. Then, the average LPIPS scores were evaluated between the original plain images and the scrambled images with each key. Based on those average LPIPS scores, we selected $2D$ keys, where D is the number of ScrambleMix operations. In this paper, we set 4 for the parameter D. The hyper-parameter of the loss function, λ, is set as 1. The parameter α of the Beta distribution for the mixing ratio was set to 0.005. In the proposed ScrambleMix, TTA is optional. We evaluated two settings: without the TTA which is the same as the number of TTA is 1 and with the TTA which is 4 iterations.

4.3   Experimental Results

Classification Performance. Table 1 summarizes the classification accuracy of compared methods with three models and with three datasets. The proposed ScrambleMix (TTA=4) shows the best or the second-best accuracy for all settings. In terms of classification accuracy, the proposed ScrambleMix (TTA=4) with the Shakedrop model archived the best classification accuracy for every dataset.

The TTA application requires additional computation and communication costs for the inference. The proposed ScrambleMix without TTA (TTA=1) still has reasonably good performance, while InstaHide without TTA (TTA=1) shows very low classification accuracy. It implies that InstaHide should be applied with TTA while the proposed ScrambleMix still works well without TTA.

---

[2] https://github.com/Hazelsuko07/InstaHide.
[3] https://github.com/mastnk/ICCE-TW2018.

Visual Information Hiding Performance. First, we quantitatively evaluated the visual information hiding performance by the average LPIPS scores. Table 2 shows the average LPIPS scores for three datasets. The proposed ScrambleMix achieved the highest scores of all datasets. That quantitative comparison demonstrates that the proposed ScrambleMix has the highest performance of visual information hiding.

4.4 Security Evaluation of ScrambleMix

In this section, we investigate the security of Scramblemix. To evaluate the security, we use the attack on InstaHide [2] using publicly available code[4] InstaHide [2] does not provide the original image of encrypted images. To conduct the same setting as a challenge for InstaHide[5] we sample 100 test images from CIFAR-10 and prepare the Scram-

Table 1. Accuracy of image classification. For each model, the best score is in bold and the second best is underlined per dataset.

Model	Method	CIFAR-10	CIFAR-100	SVHN
WideResNet 40×10 [28]	Plain	95.71	79.65	96.98
	DataMix [11]	66.89	38.31	19.60
	InstaHide [7], # of TTA = 1	53.58	39.06	52.47
	InstaHide [7], # of TTA = 10	**94.92**	**78.32**	94.97
	LE [22]	91.34	70.62	96.50
	Random PE [19]	92.23	70.82	96.83
	ScrambleMix (proposed), # of TTA = 1	93.08	71.71	<u>96.96</u>
	ScrambleMix (proposed), # of TTA = 4	<u>93.12</u>	<u>71.87</u>	**97.01**
Shakedrop [26]	Plain	96.56	83.31	97.41
	DataMix [11]	80.10	50.97	93.42
	InstaHide [7], # of TTA = 1	52.93	39.95	52.87
	InstaHide [7], # of TTA = 10	92.91	74.06	93.38
	LE [22]	94.02	77.59	97.26
	Random PE [19]	93.51	77.10	97.26
	ScrambleMix (proposed), # of TTA = 1	<u>95.02</u>	<u>79.39</u>	<u>97.47</u>
	ScrambleMix (proposed), # of TTA = 4	**95.31**	**79.41**	**97.54**

Table 2. Comparison of average LPIPS scores. The higher LPIPS is the better. The best score is in bold per dataset.

	InstaHide [7]	LE [22]	Random PE [19]	ScrambleMix (proposed)
CIFAR-10	0.4007	0.3035	0.4225	**0.4478**
CIFAR-100	0.4026	0.3252	0.4408	**0.4690**
SVHN	0.6263	0.4703	0.6242	**0.6577**

---

[4] https://github.com/carlini/privacy/tree/instahide/research/instahide_attack_2020.
[5] https://github.com/Hazelsuko07/InstaHide_Challenge,.

bleMix's output. Then, we use the inception score [17] to measure the quantitative score of attacking. The inception score [17] has a high value if the input image is more recognizable from the model perspective. Therefore, a high value of inception score indicates that restoration was successful and vice versa. Since the inception score [17] can measure the score without the original image, we can measure the score of both InstaHide and ScrambleMix. By the attack on InstaHide to ScrambleMix, ScrambleMix can not be recovered since it fails to construct the clustering with 100 clusters. For this reason, we visualize midway results after we take the absolute value against ScrambleMix. As a reference, we also visualize the reconstruction result of compared InstaHide.

Table 3, 4 shows the inception score of attacked privacy-preserving images. Since InstaHide Attack fails to attack the way, we show the resultant inception score of "Remove instance hiding" [2]. ScrambleMix changes inception scores a little while InstaHide changes over 1 point. It indicates that the proposed approach is more secure than the previous approach.

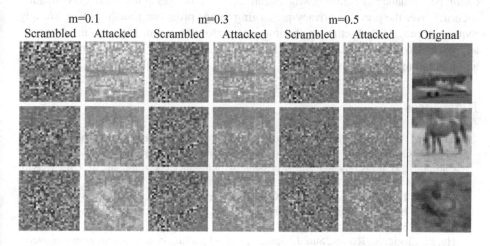

Fig. 5. Qualitative results of InstaHide Attack [2] to ScrambleMix with different mixing rates: Proposed method consistently shows consistently protect the visual information over the attacking.

Table 3. Inception score [17] over the attacked privacy-preserving images

	InstaHide [7]	ScrambleMix (proposed)
InstaHide Attack [2]	2.777	**1.177**

Table 4. Inception score [17] over the original privacy-preserving images

	InstaHide [7]	ScrambleMix (proposed)
InstaHide Attack [2]	1.394	**1.012**

Figure 5 visualizes the several reconstruction results of ScrambleMix with different mixing parameters. Although the content is partially recognizable, we find that image mixing increases security strength. From this result, the proposed ScrambleMix improved the security of the previous method. However, further security improvement should be considered in future work.

5 Conclusion

The present paper proposed ScrambleMix, a novel privacy-preserving image processing for edge-cloud machine learning. ScrambleMix combines image scrambling and AugMix to improve visual information hiding. Specifically, to make two scrambled images from a single input image, each copy of the input image is scrambled using a different key every time. Then, the scrambled images are mixed with a randomly sampled mixing ratio. A self-teaching loss is introduced further to improve the classification performance of ScrambleMix. ScrambleMix produces competitive classification accuracy over the previous privacy-preserving image processing methods that strongly require more restricted setups to obtain better performance. Furthermore, the proposed approach also has a high LPIPS score than compared methods. This result indicates that an output image is the most dissimilar to the input image visually.

References

1. Abadi, M., et al.: Deep learning with differential privacy. In: Proceedings of the 2016 ACM SIGSAC Conference on Computer and Communications Security (SIGSAC), October 2016
2. Carlini, N., et al.: Is private learning possible with instance encoding? In: 2021 IEEE Symposium on Security and Privacy (SP), pp. 410–427. IEEE (2021)
3. Chuman, T., Sirichotedumrong, W., Kiya, H.: Encryption-then-compression systems using grayscale-based image encryption for jpeg images. IEEE Trans. Inf. Forensics Secur. **14**, 1515–1525 (2019)
4. He, K., Zhang, X., Ren, S., Sun, J.: Spatial pyramid pooling in deep convolutional networks for visual recognition. IEEE Trans. Pattern Anal. Mach. Intell. **37**, 1904–1916 (2015)
5. He, K., Zhang, X., Ren, S., Sun, J.: Deep residual learning for image recognition. In: Proceedings of the IEEE/CVF Conference on Computer Vision and Pattern Recognition (CVPR), pp. 770–778 (2016)
6. Hendrycks, D., Mu, N., Cubuk, E.D., Zoph, B., Gilmer, J., Lakshminarayanan, B.: AugMix: a simple data processing method to improve robustness and uncertainty. In: Proceedings of the International Conference on Learning Representations (ICLR) (2020)
7. Huang, Y., Song, Z., Li, K., Arora, S.: InstaHide: instance-hiding schemes for private distributed learning. In: Daumé III, H., Singh, A., (eds.) Proceedings of the 37th International Conference on Machine Learning (ICML), vol. 119, Proceedings of Machine Learning Research, pp. 4507–4518. PMLR, 13–18 July 2020
8. Konečný, J., Brendan McMahan, H., Yu, F.X., Richtarik, P., Suresh, A.T., Bacon, D.: Federated learning: strategies for improving communication efficiency. In: NIPS Workshop on Private Multi-Party Machine Learning (2016)
9. Krizhevsky, A.: Learning multiple layers of features from tiny images. Master's thesis, University of Tront (2009)

10. Kullback, S., Leibler, R.A.: On information and sufficiency. Ann. Math. Statist. **22**(1), 79–86 (1951)
11. Liu, Z., Wu, Z., Gan, C., Zhu, L., Han, S.: Datamix: efficient privacy-preserving edge-cloud inference. In: Proceedings of the IEEE/CVF Conference on Computer Vision and Pattern Recognition (CVPR) (2020)
12. Gontijo Lopes, R., Yin, D., Poole, B., Gilmer, J., Cubuk, E.D.: Improving robustness without sacrificing accuracy with patch gaussian augmentation. arXiv preprint arXiv:1906.02611 (2019)
13. Madono, K., Tanaka, M., Onishi, M., Ogawa, T.: Block-wise scrambled image recognition using adaptation network. In: Workshop on AAAI conference Artificial Intellignece (AAAI-WS), abs/2001.07761 (2020)
14. Madry, A., Makelov, A., Schmidt, L., Tsipras, D., Vladu, A.: Towards deep learning models resistant to adversarial attacks. In Proceedings of the International Conference on Learning Representations (ICLR). OpenReview.net (2018)
15. McMahan, B., Moore, E., Ramage, D., Hampson, S., Arcas, B.A.: Communication-efficient learning of deep networks from decentralized data. In: Artificial Intelligence and Statistics, pp. 1273–1282. PMLR (2017)
16. Yuval Netzer, Tao Wang, Adam Coates, Alessandro Bissacco, Bo Wu, and Andrew Y. Ng. Reading digits in natural images with unsupervised feature learning. In NIPS Workshop on Deep Learning and Unsupervised Feature Learning 2011, 2011
17. Salimans, T., et al.: Improved techniques for training GANs. In: Lee, D., Sugiyama, M., Luxburg, U., Guyon, I., Garnett, R., (eds.) Advances in Neural Information Processing Systems (NIPS), vol. 29. Curran Associates Inc. (2016)
18. Singh, S., Jeong, Y.-S., Park, J.H.: A survey on cloud computing security: issues, threats, and solutions. J. Netw. Comput. Appl. **75**, 200–222 (2016)
19. Sirichotedumrong, W., Kinoshita, Y., Kiya, H.: Pixel-based image encryption without key management for privacy-preserving deep neural networks. IEEE Access **7**, 177844–177855 (2019)
20. Sirichotedumrong, W., Maekawa, T., Kinoshita, Y., Kiya, H.: Privacy-preserving deep neural networks with pixel-based image encryption considering data augmentation in the encrypted domain. In: 2019 IEEE International Conference on Image Processing (ICIP), pp. 674–678. IEEE (2019)
21. Takahashi, R., Matsubara, T., Uehara, K.: Data augmentation using random image cropping and patching for deep CNNs. IEEE Trans. Circuits Syst. Video Technol. **30**, 2917–2931 (2019)
22. Tanaka, M.: Learnable image encryption. In: 2018 IEEE International Conference on Consumer Electronics-Taiwan (ICCE-TW), pp. 1–2. IEEE (2018)
23. Taylor, L., Nitschke, G.S.: Improving deep learning with generic data augmentation. In: 2018 IEEE Symposium Series on Computational Intelligence (SSCI), pp. 1542–1547 (2018)
24. Tokozume, Y., Ushiku, Y., Harada, T.: Between-class learning for image classification. In: Proceedings of the IEEE/CVF Conference on Computer Vision and Pattern Recognition (CVPR), pp. 5486–5494 (2018)
25. van Elsloo, T., Patrini, G., Ivey-Law, H.: Sealion: a framework for neural network inference on encrypted data (2019). arXiv:1904.12840
26. Yamada, Y., Iwamura, M., Akiba, T., Kise, K.: Shakedrop regularization for deep residual learning. IEEE Access **7**, 186126–186136 (2019)
27. Yun, et al.: Cutmix: regularization strategy to train strong classifiers with localizable features. In: Proceedings of the IEEE/CVF Conference on Computer Vision and Pattern Recognition (CVPR), pp. 6023–6032 (2019)

28. Zagoruyko, S., Komodakis, N.: Wide residual networks. In: Hancock, E.R., Wilson, R.C., Smith, W.A.P., (eds.) Proceedings of the British Machine Vision Conference (BMVC), pp. 87.1–87.12. BMVA Press, September 2016

29. Zhang, H., Cissé, M., Dauphin, Y.N., Lopez-Paz, D.: mixup: beyond empirical risk minimization. In: Proceedings of the International Conference on Learning Representations (ICLR). OpenReview.net (2018)

30. Zhang, R., Isola, P., Efros, A.A., Shechtman, E., Wang, O.: The unreasonable effectiveness of deep features as a perceptual metric. In: Proceedings of the IEEE/CVF Conference on Computer Vision and Pattern Recognition (CVPR), pp. 586–595 (2018)

31. Zhong, Z., Zheng, L., Kang, G., Li, S., Yang, Y.: Random erasing data augmentation. In: Association for the Advancement of Artificial Intelligence (AAAI), pp. 13001–13008 (2020)

32. Zhu, L., Liu, Z., Han, S.: Deep leakage from gradients. In: Wallach, H., Larochelle, H., Beygelzimer, A., d'Alché-Buc, F., Fox, E., Garnett, R., (eds.), Advances in Neural Information Processing Systems, vol. 32. Curran Associates Inc. (2019)

Comparison of Simplified SE-ResNet and SE-DenseNet for Micro-Expression Classification

Xiangbo Chen, Masashi Nishiyama[iD], and Yoshio Iwai[✉][iD]

Tottori University, Tottori, Japan
{nishiyama,iwai}@tottori-u.ac.jp

Abstract. Micro-expressions are rapid and subtle facial movements that can reflect the most real emotional state hidden in the human heart. Classifying different micro-expressions is still challenging because of their short duration and low intensity. This paper proposes new neural network models, Simplified SE-DenseNet-cc and SE-ResNet-cc, incorporating Eulerian video magnification (EVM) to enlarge micro-expression movements. Important features can be selectively enhanced, and unimportant features can be compressed using SE-block. The experimental results show that our proposed methods perform better than most of the algorithms in CASME-II and SMIC.

Keywords: Micro-expression classification · EVM · deep learning · SE-DenseNet-cc · SE-ResNet-cc

1 Introduction

Emotions are different combinations of facial muscle movements that eventually represent specific types of emotions. Human facial expressions are the main means of conveying emotions in daily communications [1].

Micro-expression is a short-lived spontaneous expression usually lasting between $1/25$ s–$1/5$ s, it is essentially an unconscious action of a person, with characteristics that cannot be hidden and cannot be changed so that it can be true reflect people's emotional state [2]. Studies in psychology also show that it is feasible to identify people's real emotions through micro-expressions [3]. Thus, micro-expression recognition is valuable for many applications in emotion interfaces [4], medical treatment, lie detection and security [5], and so on.

Because the time of micro-expression lasts very short, it is challenging for humans to detect and recognize micro-expressions with the naked eye. For verifying the effectiveness of the methods, several micro-expression video databases have been collected, such as CASME II [6], SMIC [7], MMEW [8] and SAMM [9]. Since then, many methods have been proposed and verified on these databases, and the performances on these databases have improved gradually. Some proposed an Enriched Long-term Recurrent Convolutional Network (ELRCN); the network first applied the CNN module to encode each micro-expression frame

© The Author(s), under exclusive license to Springer Nature Singapore Pte Ltd. 2024
W. Q. Yan et al. (Eds.): PSIVT 2023, LNCS 14403, pp. 341–352, 2024.
https://doi.org/10.1007/978-981-97-0376-0_26

into a feature vector, then used the long short-term memory network (LSTM) to perform predictions. The method achieves 60.98% on the CASME dataset with leave-one-subject-out cross-validation (LOSOCV) protocol [10].

Some researchers used apex frames for micro-expression recognitions. The facial muscles in apex frames have the most extensive range of motion and distinct features. 3D Fast Fourier Transform (FFT) is used to convert micro-expression clips in apex frames in [12,13]. This method has been tested on the SMIC, CASME, and CASME-II datasets, and the results show that the feature extraction using Apex frames is superior to the feature extraction of the entire original video. Meanwhile, some researchers utilize Eulerian video magnification (EVM) to magnify motion features.

In this paper, we are focused on a different method to deal with the problems: the limitations of datasets, overfitting problems, redundant parameters, and computations. We choose SE-DenseNet and SE-Resnet to propose a new, robust, and simplified feature learning model with Eulerian video magnification, which can efficiently represent the subtle facial muscle movement in the micro-expression process. The main contributions of this paper are summarized as follows:

1. Use simplified SE-DenseNet and SE-ResNet to build a better and lighter model to extract deeper and better facial muscle features.
2. Investigation of the effects of the recognition accuracy of Eulerian video magnification varying the magnification parameters and finding the best parameter for recognition,

2   Related Work

The former researchers always selected specific operating points, related action units (AUs), or regions of interest (ROI), which are easier to detect and track. In these conditions, the frames in the images are divided into several areas, and the Hough forest will test the facial regions, and the lip contour will be located for drawing. The tracking learning detection algorithm receives the position of the edge of the lips, eyes, and some other range of a face and autonomously learns and tracks the feature points. These methods are suitable for emotion recognition when the specific field is the focal point and provides a subtle description of the micro-expression. However, this operation will provide less information for the model to learn, which may make the feature extraction incomplete and limited [11].

Some researchers used apex frames for micro-expression recognition [12,13]. During the feature extraction process, facial expressions are roughly divided into three time points, called onset frame, apex frame, and offset frame, representing the moments when facial expressions appear, peak, and disappear, respectively. Among them, the method can accurately find the position of the peak frame without relying on complex optical flow calculations. Using apex frames is superior to feature extraction of the entire original video. Meanwhile, utilizing Eulerian video magnification (EVM) to magnify motion features is also superior to feature extraction.

2.1   Apex Frame Extraction

We use 3D fast Fourier transform (3D-FFT) to extract apex frames for SMIC [13]. The micro-expression videos f are transformed into frequency domain signals F. The apex frames are extracted by locating the maximum frequency amplitude. We mask a sliding window of length N in the current frame and exploit 3D-FFT for the i-th interval to calculate the frequency value of 36 small regions. We denote these small regions as $b_{i,1}, b_{i,2}, \ldots, b_{i,36}$. For the j-th region in the i-th interval, its frequency value is:

$$F_{b_{ij}}(u,v,q) = \int_{-\frac{N}{2}}^{\frac{N}{2}} \int_{-\frac{L_b}{2}}^{\frac{L_b}{2}} \int_{-\frac{W_b}{2}}^{\frac{W_b}{2}} f_{b_{i,j}}(x,y,z)e^{j2\pi(ux+vy+qz)}dxdydz, \qquad (1)$$

where (u,v,q) represents the position in the frequency domain, L_b and W_b represent the height and width of the j-th region $b_{i,j}, j = \{1,2,\ldots,36\}$ in the i-th interval, respectively. We exploit a high-frequency band-pass filter to remove low frequencies and reduce the influence of invariant pixels and low-frequency signals in the micro-expression sequence. The high-frequency filter is defined as:

$$H_{b_{ij}}(u,v,q) = \begin{cases} 1 \text{ if } \sqrt{u^2 + v^2 + q^2} \geq D_0 \\ 0 \text{ if } \sqrt{u^2 + v^2 + q^2} < D_0 \end{cases}, \qquad (2)$$

where D_0 is the threshold. The video is filtered in the frequency domain by the following formula:

$$G_{b_{ij}}(u,v,q) = H_{b_{ij}}(u,v,q)F_{b_{ij}}(u,v,q). \qquad (3)$$

Then, the frequency amplitude of 36 blocks in the i-th video interval is accumulated according to the following formula:

$$A_i = \sum_{j=1}^{36} \sum_{x=1}^{N} \sum_{y=1}^{L_b} \sum_{z=1}^{W_b} G_{b_{ij}}(u,v,q), \qquad (4)$$

where A_i is the frequency amplitude in the i-th interval. It represents the range of rapid facial movement in the i-th interval. In this way, the frequency information of all videos is obtained, and the interval with the largest amplitude as the apex frame represents the frame with the most obvious facial motion.

2.2   Eulerian Video Magnification

We briefly explain the Eulerian video magnification proposed in [14]. Euler video magnification is used to enhance facial muscle movement to ensure that computers learn more easily. The enhanced image $\hat{I}(x,t)$ at pixel x at time t is calculated from the original image $I(x,t)$ as follows:

$$\hat{I}(x,t) = f(x + (1+\alpha)\delta(t)), \qquad (5)$$

Table 1. Network structure of SE-ResNet-cc

Layers	Output size	SE-ResNet
Input layer	$3 \times 256 \times 256$	-
Convolution 1	$3 \times 128 \times 128$	$\begin{bmatrix} 3 \times 3,\ 64 \\ 3 \times 3,\ 64 \end{bmatrix}$ $\times 2$
Convolution 2	$3 \times 64 \times 64$	$\begin{bmatrix} 3 \times 3,\ 128 \\ 3 \times 3,\ 128 \end{bmatrix}$ $\times 2$
Convolution 3	$3 \times 32 \times 32$	$\begin{bmatrix} 3 \times 3,\ 256 \\ 3 \times 3,\ 256 \end{bmatrix}$ $\times 2$
Convolution 4	$3 \times 16 \times 16$	$\begin{bmatrix} 3 \times 3,\ 512 \\ 3 \times 3,\ 512 \\ fc,\ [32, 512] \end{bmatrix}$ $\times 2$
Classification layer	$1 \times 1 \times 1$	Global max pooling Fully connected Softmax

where $I(x,t) = f(x+\delta(t))$, and $\delta(t)$ represents the motion displacement function on pixel x. As the above equation, the displacement $\delta(t)$ is magnified by $(1+\alpha)$ times. In this paper, we tried different values of α to judge whether it can improve the accuracy and which parameter is most helpful to improve the classification accuracy.

2.3 Micro-expression Recognition

L. Cai et al. achieves good performance for micro-expression recognition [13]. We propose a new, more simplified network model than the model proposed in [13] and find the best range of parameters of EVM in this paper. The data preprocessing phase is performed after taking out the obtained apex frame image. In this paper, we aligned and cropped the face based on OpenCV and Dlib's 68-point face detection, and we used color images for classification instead of monochrome images.

3   Proposed Method

The process flow of the proposed method is shown in Fig. 1. The image sequences of micro-expressions are pre-processed by means described in the previous sections. Then, the image sequences are applied to the networks as shown in Fig. 1.

We, hereafter, denote our simplified SE-ResNet and SE-DenseNet as SE-ResNet-cc and SE-DenseNet-cc, respectively.

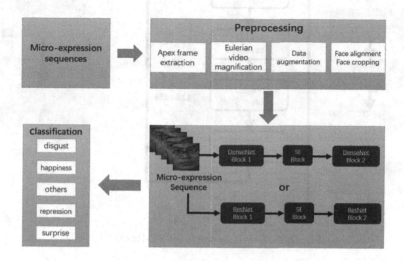

Fig. 1. The process flow of the proposed method

3.1   SE-ResNet-cc

The first is the position of the SE block in SE-ResNet-cc. We refer from MobileNet V3 [15, 16] to place the SE block between 3×3 convolution and 1×1 convolution and uses Standard SE block [17]. The former research shows that it is more effective to add SE modules in the last two stages of the model. [18] The details of the network constructions of the proposed method are shown in Tables 1 and 2.

In the SE-ResNet-cc, The first is to define the downsample structure for the first residual block. The downsampling structure is required when the input and output sizes of the residual block are inconsistent or the number of channels is inconsistent. The downsampling structure consists of a 1×1 convolutional layer and a BatchNorm layer. Afterward, residual blocks are defined, and only the first residual block requires a downsampling layer. In ResNet, the number of input channels and the number of output channels in Stage 1 are the same, and the convolution with a stride of 1 is used, so there is no need for a downsampling layer in Stage 1, and a downsampling layer is required in the rest of the stage. The network construction of this paper refers to ResNet-18. Based on this network, SE Block is added to achieve the purpose of improving accuracy. As shown above, SE-block is placed in the last stage, and the details are shown in Table 1. Furthermore, the simple illustration of the network is shown in Fig 2.

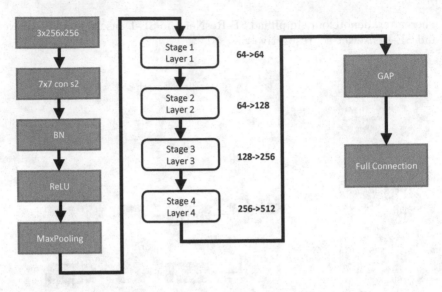

Fig. 2. Network structure of SE-ResNet-cc

3.2   SE-DenseNet-cc

In the DenseNet-cc, we use the non-linear transformation function between Dense and SE blocks. It can filter out some unimportant features and squeeze the effective features of the transition layer. We use global average pooling as the squeeze operation and then apply two fully connected layers to build the correlation between channels and output the same number of weights as the input features. The images are input into a convolution layer with kernel dimensions of $7 \times 7 \times 7$. Then there is a $3 \times 3 \times 3$ maximum pooling layer to decrease the calculation in the training process. The details are shown in Table 2. This network is simpler than that proposed in [13] at the following points:

1. Remove the transition layer and SE block between Dense block 1 and Dense block 2.
2. The number of output channels is totally reduced from the former models.

As a result, our network is smaller and can be trained faster than the former models.

4   Experiments

4.1   Dataset

We used CASME-II and SMIC because they have a large sample size and carry video clips that induce subjects' micro-expressions. CASME-II has a total of 255 micro-expression samples from 26 subjects recorded with a resolution of 640×480 and a sampling rate of up to 200 fps. It has seven tags: Disgust, Fear, Happiness,

Table 2. SE-DenseNet-cc

Layers	Output size	SE-DenseNet
Input layer	$3 \times 256 \times 256$	-
Convolution	$3 \times 128 \times 128$	$7 \times 7 \times 7$ Conv
	$3 \times 64 \times 64$	$3 \times 3 \times 3$ max pooling
Dense block 1	$3 \times 64 \times 64$	$3 \times 3 \times 3$ Conv
Dense block 2	$3 \times 32 \times 32$	$3 \times 3 \times 3$ Conv
Transition layer	$3 \times 32 \times 32$	$1 \times 1 \times 1$ Conv
	$1 \times 8 \times 8$	$3 \times 3 \times 3$ max pooling
SE layer	$1 \times 8 \times 8$	scale $\times 1$
Dense block 3	$1 \times 8 \times 8$	$3 \times 3 \times 3$ Conv
Classification layer		Global max pooling
	$1 \times 1 \times 1$	Fully connected
		Softmax

Repression, Sadness, Surprise, and Others. In this experiment, we only classify the samples into five different classes because there are few samples of Fear and Sadness classes.

SMIC has a total of 164 samples with Positive (51), Negative (70), and Surprise (43), three different classes from CASME-II, and recorded with a resolution of 640×480 rating of up to 100 fps. The LOSOCV protocol is exploited on CASME-II and SMIC databases to conduct the training and testing processes.

4.2 Data and Parameter Settings

In order to ensure the correctness and reliability of the experiment, we randomly take 5% of each class into pre-validation data before data augmentation. After performing data augmentation, we randomly take 50% of the data from it as validation data and the rest as test data. Then, we perform data augmentation on the rest of the 95% data and split the data into 70% for training, 20% for additional test data, and 10% for additional validation data. In total, 66.5% of the data is training data. 24% of the data is test data, and 9.75% of the data is validation data.

In the training process, we set the batch size to 10 and use SGDM as the optimizer whose momentum, learning rate, and weight decays are 0.9, 0.0003, and $1e^{-15}$, respectively. The training process is performed in 120 epochs. Parameter α of EVM is varied from 0 to 30. We also set the bandpass frequency of EVM from 0.05 to 0.5 Hz, and the spatial wavelength of EVM is 0.1.

4.3 Experimental Results

After getting the apex frames, we make these sequences as input to our models with/without data augmentation and Eulerian video magnification. The results

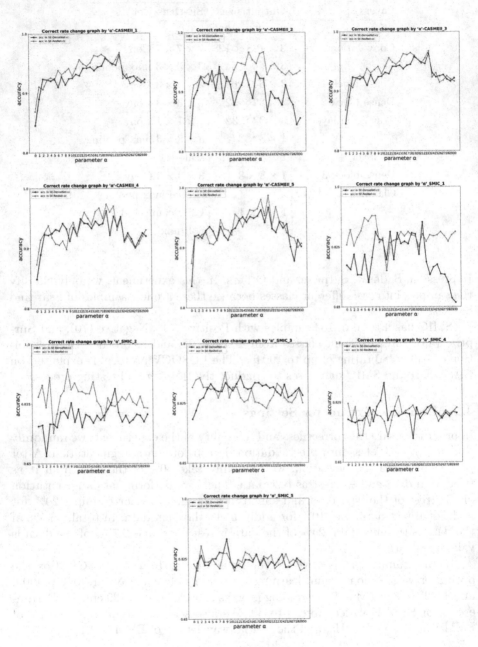

Fig. 3. Accuracy variation of parameter 'α' in EVM

Table 3. Accuracy effects of data augmentation (DA) and Eulerian video magnification (EVM)

	no DA no EVM	+DA	+DA+EVM
SE-DenseNet-cc in CASMEII	67.45%	86.52%	**96.35%**
SE-ResNet-cc in CASMEII	73.62%	86.88%	**97.57%**
SE-DenseNet-cc in SMIC	43.75%	75.94%	**88.41%**
SE-ResNet-cc in SMIC	53.13%	84.56%	**89.25%**

Table 4. Comparison results with the existing models

Methods	Accuracy
CNN [17]	38.00 %
CNN+LBP-TOP [19]	52.16 %
CNN+Apex [12]	59.00 %
CNNs+LSTM + TV-L1 [7]	60.98 %
3D-CNNs [17]	65.90%
3D SE-CNN [17]	66.28%
ResNet [19]	76.30%
3D-DenseNet+EVM [13]	81.18%
3D-DenseNet-T+EVM [13]	82.75%
SE-DenseNet-cc w. a=0	86.52%
SE-ResNet-cc w. a=0	86.88%
SE-DenseNet-cc w. CASMEII	**96.35%**
SE-ResNet-cc w. CASMEII	**97.57%**
SE-DenseNet-cc w. SMIC	**88.41%**
SE-ResNet-cc w. SMIC	**89.25%**

are shown in Table 3. The accuracy of SE-DenseNet-cc and SE-ResNet-cc without data augmentation and Eulerian video magnification is 67.45% and 73.62%, respectively. After we have performed the data augmentation, the accuracy rises to 86.52% in SE-DenseNet-cc and 86.88% in SE-ResNet-cc. After using the EVM, the accuracy increases to 95.74% in SE-DenseNet-cc and 98.75% in SE-ResNet-cc. As shown in Fig. 3, we repeated the experiment 5 times for each dataset. The first is marked as '_1', and the last is marked as '_5'. As parameter 'α' of EVM increases, it tends to increase to a certain peak point, although there are some fluctuations as shown in Fig. 3. We repeated all experiments five times. In CASMEII, the highest accuracy rate in SE-ResNet-cc is 98.75% when $\alpha = 23$. The highest accuracy in SE-ResNet-cc are 98.75% ($\alpha = 23$), 96.67% ($\alpha = 21$), 96.76% ($\alpha = 23$), 98.67% ($\alpha = 21$) and 97.02% ($\alpha = 21$). The average of the results is 97.57%. The variance is 8.742×10^{-5}. In SE-DenseNet-cc, the highest accuracy rate is 97.02% when $\alpha = 18$. The highest accuracy are 97.02%

(α = 21), 95.74% (α = 16and19), 96.32% (α = 23), 96.67% (α = 21), 96.02% (α = 19). The average of results is 96.35%. The variance is 2.066×10^{-5}. In SMIC, the highest accuracy rate in SE-ResNet-cc is 92.69% when α = 8. The highest accuracy in SE-ResNet-cc are 91.56% (α = 7and8), 92.69% (α = 8), 91.56% (α = 9), 84.19% (α = 14) and 86.25% (α = 2). The average is 89.25%. The variance is 1.142×10^{-3}. In SE-DenseNet-cc, the highest accuracy rate is 90.31% when α = 13. The highest accuracy is 90.31% (α = 13), 89.69%(α = 21), 86.94% (α = 21), 88.19% (α = 9), 88.19% (α = 10). The average is 88.41%. The variance is 0.1252.

For comparison, we repeat our experiment on ResNet50. The highest accuracy rate in CASMEII is 97.46% when α = 19. The highest accuracy is 97.46% (α = 19), 97.00% (α = 17), 96.84% (α = 19), 97.14% (α = 21), 96.54% (α = 16). In SMIC, the highest accuracy rate is 94.69% when α = 1. The highest accuracy is 94.69% (α = 1), 93.44% (α = 17), 92.63% (α = 6), 86.56% (α = 12) and 90.63% (α = 19). The results varied widely among databases. When in CASMEII, in the process of the increasing value 'α' in the model SE-ResNet-cc, the trend is on the rise when α < 24 but decreases after. Moreover, in the model SE-DenseNet-cc, the accuracy increases when α < 23 but decreases after that point. Overall, accuracy volatility increases in both models. Furthermore, the highest accuracy is around α = 22 in both models. However, in SMIC, the result is more complicated. The reason may be why the classification of CASMEII is based on AUs, and the classification of SMIC is based on the feelings of the tested volunteers.

We show the comparison results with the existing models in Table 4. As shown in Table 4, the proposed model improved recognition accuracy in comparison to the existing methods. Moreover, after tuning the parameter of EVM, the average recognition rates of the models, SE-DenseNet-cc and SE-ResNet-cc in CASMEII and SMIC, are shown in Table 4, respectively.

5   Conclusion

In this paper, we proposed a novel micro-expression recognition approach based on ResNet and DenseNet. We also changed parameter 'α' in EVM and compared the results to explore the possibility of increasing accuracy by changing 'α.' The proposed SE-ResNet-cc and SE-DenseNet-cc are simplified network models than the conventional ones; however, they achieved better accuracy than the conventional ones. The models use SE-block to assign weights to feature channels to enhance learning adaptively. Utilizing the EVM and the deep network can achieve favorable performance results on the database CASME-II. In the SMIC database, it is possible that an unbalanced distribution of data makes the accuracy high and low and makes parameter α not in a narrow range. Nevertheless, EVM increases the accuracy of both two databases.

References

1. Darwin, C.: The expression of the emotions in man and animals: frontmatter. Portable Darwin. **123**(1), 146–147 (2013)
2. Porter, S., Brinke, L.: Reading between the lies. Psychol. Sci. **19**, 508–514 (2008). https://doi.org/10.1111/j.1467-9280.2008.02116.x
3. Ekman, P., Rosenberg, E., (eds.) What the face reveals: Basic and Applied Studies of Spontaneous Expression Using the Facial Action Coding System (FACS), 2nd ed., Oxford University Press (2012). https://doi.org/10.1093/acprof:oso/9780195179644.001.0001
4. Weinberger, S.: Airport security: intent to deceive? Nature **465**, 412–415 (2010). https://doi.org/10.1038/465412a0
5. Ekman, P.: Telling lies clues to deceit in the marketplace, politics, and marriage. W W Norton & Co. (1991)
6. Yan, W., et al.: CASME II: an improved spontaneous micro-expression database and the baseline evaluation. PLoS ONE **9**(1), 1–8 (2014). https://doi.org/10.1371/journal.pone.0086041
7. Li, X., Pfister, T., Huang, X., Zhao, G., Pietikäinen, M.: A spontaneous microexpression database: inducement, collection and baseline. In: 2013 10th IEEE International Conference and Workshops on Automatic Face and Gesture Recognition, FG 2013, 2013, pp. 1–6 (2013). https://doi.org/10.1109/FG.2013.6553717
8. Ben, X., et al.: Video-based facial micro-expression analysis: a survey of datasets, features and algorithms. IEEE Trans. Pattern Anal. Mach. Intell. **44**(9), 5826–5846 (2022). https://doi.org/10.1109/TPAMI.2021.3067464
9. Davison, A., Lansley, C., Costen, N., Tan, K., Yap, M.H.: SAMM: a spontaneous micro-facial movement dataset. IEEE Trans. Affect. Comput. **9**(1), 116–129 (2018). https://doi.org/10.1109/TAFFC.2016.2573832
10. Zhao, G., Pietikäinen, M.: Dynamic texture recognition using local binary patterns with an application to facial expressions. IEEE Trans. Pattern Anal. Mach. Intell. **29**(6), 915–928 (2007). https://doi.org/10.1109/TPAMI.2007.1110
11. Yao, S., He, N., Zhang, H., Yoshie, O.: Micro-expression recognition by feature points tracking. In: International Conference on Communications, Bucharest, Romania, pp. 1–4 (2014). https://doi.org/10.1109/ICComm.2014.6866671
12. Li, Y., Huang, X., Zhao, G.: Can micro-expression be recognized based on single apex frame? In: 25th IEEE International Conference on Image Processing (ICIP), Athens, Greece, pp. 3094–3098 (2018). https://doi.org/10.1109/ICIP.2018.8451376
13. Cai, L., Li, H., Dong, W., Fang, H.: Micro-expression recognition using 3D DenseNet fused squeeze-and-excitation networks. Appl. Soft Comput. **119**, 108594 (2022)
14. Wu, H., Rubinstein, M., Shih, E., Durand, F., Freeman, W.: Eulerian video magnification for revealing subtle changes in the world. ACM Trans. Graph. **31**(4), 1–8 (2012). https://doi.org/10.1145/2185520.2185561
15. Howard, A., et al.: Searching for MobileNetV3. In: 2019 IEEE/CVF International Conference on Computer Vision (ICCV), Seoul, Korea (South), pp. 1314–1324 (2019). https://doi.org/10.1109/ICCV.2019.00140
16. Hu, J., Shen, L., Sun, G.: Squeeze-and-excitation networks. In: 2018 IEEE/CVF Conference on Computer Vision and Pattern Recognition, Salt Lake City, UT, USA, pp. 7132–7141 (2018). https://doi.org/10.1109/CVPR.2018.00745

17. Yao, L., Xiao, X., Cao, R., Chen, F., Chen, T.: Three stream 3D CNN with SE block for micro-expression recognition. In: 2020 International Conference on Computer Engineering and Application (ICCEA), Guangzhou, China, pp. 439–443 (2020). https://doi.org/10.1109/ICCEA50009.2020.00101
18. https://doi.org/10.1109/TAFFC.2016.2518162
19. Wang, C.Y., Peng, M., Bi, T., Chen, T.: Micro-attention for micro-expression recognition. Neurocomputing **410**, 354–362 (2020)

Facial Deepfake Detection Using Gaussian Processes

Uzoamaka Ezeakunne$^{(\boxtimes)}$ and Xiuwen Liu

Florida State University, Tallahassee, FL 32306, USA
{ufe18,xliu}@fsu.edu

Abstract. Facial deepfake detection involves detecting images and videos with tampered faces. In this paper, we automatically detect four types of deepfakes: Deepfake, Face2Face, FaceSwap and Neural Textures. From a deepfake video, we extract the faces in its image frames to serve as input. Given a facial image, we preprocessed the image by capturing the different compression levels, extracted features using a feature extraction backbone that focuses on mesoscopic properties, and we make use of Gaussian Processes (GPs) for binary classification because GPs inherently provide more accurate uncertainty estimation which leads to lower prediction error and higher accuracy. To the best of our knowledge, we are the first to apply GPs in deepfake detection. The proposed method was compared with state-of-the-art baseline methods; we performed a cross-dataset evaluation and observed no significant accuracy difference between this approach and the baseline. Also, we experimented on varying dataset sizes and the results show that our method has a competitive accuracy on large datasets and outperforms on small datasets. The implementation is available at: https://github.com/harmz123/FacialDeepfakeDetection

Keywords: deepfake detection · neural networks · image forensic

1 Introduction

Due to the rise in the use of social networks, the propagation of digital images and videos has been made easier and faster. Some of these images and videos have been manipulated using modern techniques. These techniques [14,15,24,27,28] can produce lifelike pictures called deepfakes that can trick users who are not on guard. Deepfake is a term derived from the words "deep learning" and "fake", which is the combination of machine or deep learning with something that is fake. Deepfakes are the combination of artificial images and sounds using machine learning algorithms. A deepfake creator can replace someone's voice, image, or both. It can even create people who do not exist and can also manipulate media to show real people doing and saying things that they never said or did - this can lead to the propagation of false information. The deepfake invention is open to possible misuse; numerous individuals with ulterior motives have used these techniques to produce fake videos of celebrities and various members of the public [6,8,9,13]. Due to the fact that the deepfake technology is prone to misuse, researchers have proposed various approaches to deepfake video detection [2,5,19,21,30,33,35]. The effects of facial deepfakes are especially drastic as they enable impersonation, defamation, fake news, blackmail and fraud [6]. Hence, the need to detect facial deepfakes or deepfakes that contain human faces. Throughout this paper, when we mention deepfake detection, we refer to deepfake images and videos that contain human faces, so deepfake detection and facial deepfake detection are used interchangeably. Neural networks have been used to detect fake contents and deepfakes [10,20,34] but an inherent issue with neural networks is that they struggle to provide uncertainty estimates which affects classification accuracy. Hence, we propose to use gaussian processes (GPs) for classification as they perform uncertainty estimations more reliably [16]. Our research questions are:

(1) Can we propose an alternative method for detecting facial deepfakes which leverages uncertainty estimation?
(2) How accurate are the predictions of the proposed method when compared to the predictions of existing methods?

In this paper we detect deepfakes automatically by extracting facial images from several frames in the videos from the datasets during the image extraction phase, and preprocess them to capture the different compression levels within a face image - a likely indicator of manipulation. Next, we use a feature extraction backbone [1] to extract 1024 features from the preprocessed image and send as input to gaussian process [17] for classification. After classification, we compared this method with some baseline methods. First, we performed a cross-dataset evaluation and observed no significant accuracy difference between this approach and the baseline. Also, we performed experiments by varying dataset sizes, and the results show that the proposed approach has a competitive accuracy on large datasets and outperforms on small datasets. To the best of our knowledge, we are the first to show the gaussian process as an alternative classifier for deepfake detection. Also, in order to respond to the research questions above, this paper makes the following contributions:

(1) We build a facial deepfake detection method that uses gaussian processes for classification in order to leverage uncertainty estimation.
(2) We compare the accuracy of our method to the existing state-of-the-art methods to show that gaussian processes can improve accuracy in facial deepfake detection specifically in smaller datasets.

The rest of this paper is organized as follows. Section 2 summarizes the related works. The proposed method is discussed in Sect. 3, Sect. 4 explains the experiments performed and their results, and Sect. 5 concludes this paper.

2   Related Work

It has been demonstrated some visual cues could be used in deepfake detection, for example, unusual eye blinking [18]. Additionally, image splice detection techniques [3, 12, 25] try to take advantage of the deviation brought on by splicing close to the borders of image manipulations. After the generation of deepfakes using GAN models, there could be some patterns introduced into the images due to passing through GAN models. These patterns are usually leveraged by researchers to detect deepfakes. For example, reference [23] leveraged the presence of unique low-level noise patterns present in deepfakes due to GAN generation to identify deepfakes. We also discuss other existing works in deepfake detection and how they perform data preprocessing, feature extraction, and classification respectively.

In deepfake detection, data preprocessing could be used to reveal patterns in images which could support feature extraction, and classification. Reference [34] preprocessed data by applying gaussian blur to facial region and transformed it into negative data, and reference [32] used a preprocessing module to improve robustness in deepfake detection as performance can reduce in compressed images if the detector is not robust enough.

In order to extract features, reference [31] extracted feature vectors of facial images, and the Euclidean distances among the vectors of different real and fake facial images. Reference [20] extracted co-occurrence matrices on three red, green, and blue (RGB) channels in the pixel domain, and reference [11] used a convolutional neural network (CNN) to extract frame-level features.

In order to classify the extracted features, reference [31] performs binary classification using GBDT (Gradient Boosting Decision Tree), logistic, and SVM. References [20, 34] trained detection models using convolutional neural networks (CNN) and reference [11] used a recurrent neural network (RNN) for deepfake classification.

In addition to the discussions above, we summarize some existing methods in deepfake detection for comparisons. Reference [31] extracts feature vectors of facial images, and the Euclidean distances among the vectors of different real and fake facial images are learned, then binary classification of is performed using GBDT (Gradient Boosting Decision Tree), logistic regression, and SVM. Convolutional neural networks (CNNs) were employed in reference [10] to extract frame-level features. Then, a recurrent neural network (RNN) is trained using these features to determine whether or not a video has been altered. Reference [20] detected GAN generated fake images using a combination of pixel co-occurrence matrices and deep learning. This means that reference [20] extracted co-occurrence matrices on three red, green, and blue (RGB) channels in the pixel domain and trained a model using a deep convolutional neural network (CNN) framework.

3   Proposed Method

In this paper, we propose a new method of deepfake detection called the Meso-GP which focuses on the Mesoscopic properties from preprocessed facial images during the feature extraction phase, and uses Gaussian Processes (GP) for classification. Given the dataset which contains videos, we extracted facial images from the image frames in the videos. Next, we preprocessed the facial image by performing Error Level Analysis (ELA) which captures the different compression levels within a facial image to indicate manipulation, then we extracted 1024 features from each preprocessed facial image, using a feature extraction backbone, and then, we perform binary classification by using gaussian processes (GPs). As illustrated in Fig. 1, the Meso-GP facial deepfake detection method is made up of four main components: (i) face extraction, (ii) preprocessing (iii) feature extraction backbone and (iv) classification. Each component of the proposed Meso-GP method is described in the following subsections.

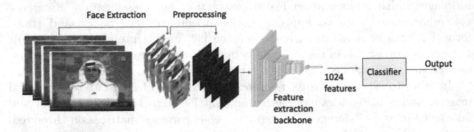

Fig. 1. The proposed Meso-GP method for facial deepfake detection.

3.1 Face Extraction

The dataset used is the FaceForensics++ dataset [24] which contains video sequences from four different types of deepfakes. For each video sequence V, we select N video frames. For each of the video frames, we use the haar cascade algorithm [29] with a scale factor of 1.3, minimum neighbors was set to 5, minimum size was set to 100×100, and maximum size was set to 300×300 to get the face images. The result of this phase is a set of face images which are passed for preprocessing.

3.2 Preprocessing

The preprocessing phase takes the extracted facial images as input. In this phase, we performed Error Level Analysis (ELA) on the facial images. Error Level Analysis (ELA) involves the identification of areas within an image that have different compression levels - this is a likely indication of manipulation. For JPEG images, an entire image should be about the same level. If a part of the image is at a significantly different error level, this is a likely indicator of digital modification. We took a face image and re-saved it at 90% error rate, the resulting ELA image then shows the amount of difference that occurs during the re-save. In Fig. 2, we show ELA samples of three facial images across real and various deepfake types. These ELA facial images are the output of this phase.

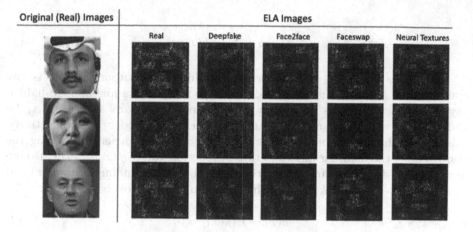

Fig. 2. Samples of ELA preprocessed images across real and deepfakes

3.3   Feature Extraction Backbone

The ELA preprocessed facial images are taken as input for feature extraction. The feature extraction backbone focuses on the mesoscopic properties of the facial images to improve robustness against the different manipulation techniques by leveraging visual cues that lie between microscopic and macroscopic scales. Mesoscopic features capture visual information beyond pixel-level, encompassing texture, patterns, and structure thereby enhancing the ability to detect manipulated regions, as deepfakes often exhibit discrepancies in these mesoscopic characteristics. The feature extraction backbone is inspired by the MesoNet or Meso-4 [1] which specializes in extracting mesoscopic properties. The feature extraction backbone takes in the input image of size $256 \times 256 \times 3$ and passes it through four sequences of convolutions. The first convolution operates on input feature maps of dimensions $256 \times 256 \times 1$ using small filters, extracting local patterns. The second convolution applies filters to feature maps of dimensions $128 \times 128 \times 32$, capturing more complex representations. The third convolution operates on feature maps of dimensions $64 \times 64 \times 64$, extracting higher-level features. The fourth convolution processes feature maps of dimensions $32 \times 32 \times 128$, capturing fine-grained details and spatial inconsistencies. After the fourth convolution, there is a flatten layer which produces 1024 features. These 1024 features are the outputs of the feature extraction phase.

3.4   Classification

The 1024 features extracted were used in this stage to make binary classification using Neural Network Gaussian Process [17] in this phase. Consider the function of a neural network $f(x)$ with one hidden layer, the kernel for the neural network is derived as:

$$f(x) = b + \sum_{i=1}^{J} v_i h(x_i u_i) \tag{1}$$

where b is a bias, v_i are the weights for hidden-to-output layer, h is any unit transfer function that is bounded, u_i are the weights for input-to-hidden layer, and J symbolizes how many hidden units there are. Let b and v_i be independent with a mean of zero and variances of σ_b^2 and σ_v^2/J, respectively. Also, let u_i have distributions that are identical and independent. Using the central limit theorem, for any collection of function values $f(x_i), ..., f(x_n)$ there is a joint multivariate Gaussian distribution. The corresponding mean $m(x)$ and the covariance function $k(x, x')$ of the Gaussian process are shown below:

$$m(x) = E[f(x)] = 0 \tag{2}$$

$$k(x, x') = cov[f(x), f(x')] = E[f(x)f(x')] = \sigma_b^2 + \frac{1}{J} \sum_{i=1}^{J} \sigma_v^2 E[h_i(x; u_i) h_i(x'; u_i)] \tag{3}$$

The GP makes predictions by constructing a kernel matrix based on a neural network architecture, propagating the kernel through the layers to capture covariance information, and calculating the output covariance matrix. After training and calibration, the kernel function is used and hyper parameters are calibrated to compute the mean and variance of the predictive distribution, providing predictions with uncertainty estimates. This phase produces binary prediction as output.

4   Experiments

In this section, the experiments performed to evaluate the performance of our proposed Meso-GP method are discussed. Firstly, we describe the datasets used. Secondly, we describe the baseline methods. Thirdly, we show the accuracy of the predictions recorded for all baselines and the proposed method. Fourthly, we compare the generalization ability of the outperforming networks by performing cross-dataset evaluation. Finally, we compare the performance of the top networks on different training dataset sizes.

4.1   Datasets

We used the diverse FaceForensics++ dataset [24] which is a collection of deepfake and real videos where the deepfake videos are made up of several types of deepfakes. We used the dataset with light compression (where constant rate quantization parameter is 23). The dataset is made up of 5,000 videos from five categories with 1000 real, and 4,000 fake videos from four different types of deepfakes (1000 each) -Deepfake, Face2Face, FaceSwap and Neural Textures. The data extraction algorithm is shown in Fig. 3.

Algorithm 1: Data Collection

---

data_output is a Directory
F is an Image

N = 5
frame_counter=0
frame_sum=0
frames=ϕ
for each video *V:*
      for each video frame *F:*
            if *frame_counter* % 10 == 0:
                frames = frames + F
                if *frame_sum* == *N:*
                      ela_images = ELA_Process*(frames)*
                      Save_Images *(data_output, ela_images)*
                end if
            end if
      end for
end for

return *data_output*

Fig. 3. Data Collection Algorithm

In order to extract the required data, we extracted N frames from each video for the five categories mentioned above with a sequence interval of 10 frames to ensure the diversity of the chosen frames. For the training set, we processed 700 videos and for the test set, we processed 300 videos. For instance, to create a training set for the Face2face experiment, we split the 1000 Face2face videos to 700:300 for train:test and we also split the real videos the same way. Then for each video, we extract N frames where N = 5. We expect 7000 videos (3500 fake and 3500 real) for training set and 3000 videos for test set (1500 fake and 1500 real) but some videos were shorter and couldn't produce up to 5 frames so we end up with about 6.6k frames for training and 2.8k for testing. Then, we extract the faces, performed ELA preprocessing and saved the resulting face images in a directory. Table 1 shows the exact size of data extracted for each binary classification experiment corresponding to the four categories of deepfakes.

Table 1. Datasets Information

	Training set size	Testing set size
Deepfake	6622	2834
Face2face	6614	2832
Faceswap	6613	2833
Neural Textures	6603	2832

4.2 Baseline Methods

The experiments were performed on six baseline models. Each of these baseline models also took ELA-processed face images as input to produce binary predictions.

Inception-V3. The Inception-v3 [26] is a convolutional neural network architecture that was introduced for image classification tasks. The Keras implementation of Inception-V3 was used with Transfer learning and loaded with weights pre-trained on ImageNet [7].

Xception. Xception [4] is a convolutional neural network architecture that relies on depthwise separable convolution layers. The Keras implementation of Xception was used with Transfer learning and loaded with weights pre-trained on ImageNet [7].

Meso-4. The MesoNet also called Meso-4 [1] is a deepfake detection model which uses a traditional neural network for classification. To implement the model, we used the authors' provided code.

Meso-NaiveBayes. The Meso-NaiveBayes baseline refers to the use of the MesoNet feature extraction backbone to obtain 1024 features and using Naive Bayes classifier to make predictions. The scikit-learn library [22] implementation of Naive Bayes was used.

Meso-LogisticRegression. The Meso-LogisticRegression baseline refers to the use of the MesoNet feature extraction backbone to obtain 1024 features and using Logistic Regression classifier to make predictions. The scikit-learn library [22] implementation of Logistic Regression was used.

Meso-SVM. The Meso-SVM baseline refers to the use of the MesoNet feature extraction backbone to obtain 1024 features and using a Support Vector Machine (SVM) classifier to make predictions. The scikit-learn library [22] implementation of SVM was used.

4.3 Classification Accuracy

For each of the four categories of deepfakes, we performed a binary classification experiment and recorded the accuracy obtained in Table 2. For instance, when we performed the Faceswap experiment, using a training set of Faceswap and real faces to train the Xception model, and then tested it on a test set which contains Faceswap and real faces, we obtain an accuracy value of 79.35%. As shown in Table 2. After recording the accuracies for each deepfake category and baseline models, we observed that the Meso-4 had the highest accuracy for the Face2face experiment and the Faceswap experiment with accuracy values of 85.35% and 77.08% respectively. On the other hand, the proposed Meso-GP model had the highest accuracy for the Deepfake and Neural textures experiments with accuracy values of 82.50% and 82.60% respectively. The result obtained could further be explained as the Deepfake and Faceswap fall into the sub-category of identity modification deepfakes due to the way they were produced, while the Face2face and Neural Textures fall into the sub-category of expression modification. Hence, the Meso-4 model outperformed in expression modifying deepfakes while the Meso-GP outperformed in identity modifying deepfakes.

4.4 Cross-Dataset Evaluation

In this experiment, we compare the generalizability of the two outperforming models - Meso-4 and Meso-GP by performing a cross-data evaluation. Here, each of the two models were trained on one dataset, and tested on the other datasets, and the achieved accuracies were recorded. For instance, when the Meso-GP was trained on a combination Faceswap and real data, and tested on a combination of Face2face and real data, the test accuracy obtained was 57%. As shown in Fig. 4, after recording the accuracies of all cross-evaluation experiments for the two models for comparison, the results show no significant difference in the generalization performance between the two models.

Table 2. Classification Accuracy Results

Accuracy(%)	Deepfake	Face2face	Faceswap	Neural Textures
Inception-V3	79.43	78.67	78.93	67.62
Xception	79.29	78.35	79.35	70.20
Meso4	79.40	**85.35**	78.22	**77.08**
Meso-NaiveBayes	71.14	68.36	73.81	50.78
Meso-LogisticRegression	81.86	79.77	77.30	71.50
Meso-SVM	81.65	82.94	80.83	72.03
Meso-GP	**82.50**	83.90	**82.60**	72.10

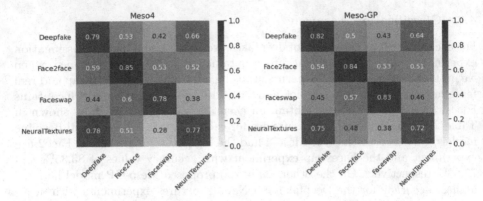

Fig. 4. Cross-dataset Evaluation Results

4.5   Performance on Various Training Dataset Sizes

In order to evaluate the effect of different training data sizes on the performance of the two outperforming models, we extracted datasets using the algorithm in Fig. 3 with different values of N. We used values N = 1, N = 3 and N = 5 which resulted in training sets of sizes 1.3k, 4k and 6.6k respectively. Then, we repeated the binary classification experiment from Subsect. 4.3 and recorded the accuracies obtained for each category of deepfakes. The results of this experiment is shown in Fig. 5. We observe that the Meso-GP performed significantly better than Meso-4 when the training data size is smaller.

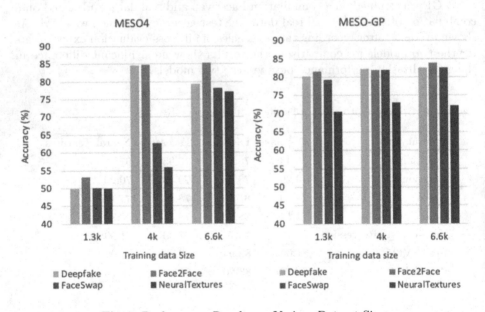

Fig. 5. Performance Results on Various Dataset Sizes

5   Conclusion

The detection of deepfake faces is a crucial problem as the spread of media containing manipulated faces could support scams, defamation and the spread of fake news. Existing methods of facial deepfake detection make predictions using neural networks. These traditional neural networks struggle to provide accurate uncertainty estimates which affects prediction error. However, the use of Gaussian Processes (GPs) which inherently make more accurate uncertainty estimations have lower prediction error. Hence, we proposed a method of detecting deepfake faces called the Meso-GP with a feature extraction process that focuses on mesoscopic properties, and uses Gaussian Processes (GPs) [17] to make predictions. We performed a cross-dataset evaluation, and the results show no significant accuracy difference between this approach and the baseline. We also performed experiments by varying dataset sizes, and the results show that the proposed method performs competitively when compared to other methods, and outperforms on smaller training sets. To the best of our knowledge, we are the first to use GPs to detect deepfakes.

References

1. Afchar, D., Nozick, V., Yamagishi, J., Echizen, I.: Mesonet: a compact facial video forgery detection network. In: 2018 IEEE International Workshop on Information Forensics and Security (WIFS), pp. 1–7. IEEE (2018)
2. Agarwal, S., Farid, H., Gu, Y., He, M., Nagano, K., Li, H.: Protecting world leaders against deep fakes. In: CVPR Workshops, vol. 1, p. 38 (2019)
3. Bappy, J.H., Roy-Chowdhury, A.K., Bunk, J., Nataraj, L., Manjunath, B.: Exploiting spatial structure for localizing manipulated image regions. In: Proceedings of the IEEE International Conference on Computer Vision, pp. 4970–4979 (2017)
4. Chollet, F.: Xception: deep learning with depthwise separable convolutions. In: Proceedings of the IEEE Conference on Computer Vision and Pattern Recognition, pp. 1251–1258 (2017)
5. Cozzolino, D., Pianese, A., Nießner, M., Verdoliva, L.: Audio-visual person-of-interest deepfake detection. In: Proceedings of the IEEE/CVF Conference on Computer Vision and Pattern Recognition, pp. 943–952 (2023)
6. Croft, A.: From porn to scams, deepfakes are becoming a big racket —And that's unnerving business leaders and lawmakers (2019). https://fortune.com/2019/10/07/porn-to-scams-deepfakes-big-racket-unnerving-business-leaders-and-lawmakers. Accessed 11 Jan 2023
7. Deng, J., Dong, W., Socher, R., Li, L.J., Li, K., Fei-Fei, L.: Imagenet: a large-scale hierarchical image database. In: 2009 IEEE Conference on Computer Vision and Pattern Recognition, pp. 248–255. IEEE (2009)
8. Dickson, E.: Deepfake porn is still a threat, particularly for k- pop stars (2019). https://www.rollingstone.com/culture/culture-news/deepfakes-nonconsensual-porn-study-kpop-895605. Accessed 11 Jan 2023
9. Edwards, C.: Making deepfake porn could soon be as easy as using Instagram filters (2019). https://www.thesun.co.uk/tech/9800017/deepfake-porn-soon-easy. Accessed 11 Jan 2023

10. Ezeakunne, U., Ho, S.M., Liu, X.: Sentiment and retweet analysis of user response for early fake news detection. In: The International Conference on Social Computing, Behavioral-Cultural Modeling, & Prediction and Behavior Representation in Modeling and Simulation (SBP-BRiMS 2020), pp. 1–10 (2020)
11. Güera, D., Delp, E.J.: Deepfake video detection using recurrent neural networks. In: 2018 15th IEEE International Conference on Advanced Video and Signal Based Surveillance (AVSS), pp. 1–6. IEEE (2018)
12. Huh, M., Liu, A., Owens, A., Efros, A.A.: Fighting fake news: image splice detection via learned self-consistency. In: Ferrari, V., Hebert, M., Sminchisescu, C., Weiss, Y. (eds.) ECCV 2018. LNCS, vol. 11215, pp. 106–124. Springer, Cham (2018). https://doi.org/10.1007/978-3-030-01252-6_7
13. Kan, M.: Most AI-generated deepfake videos online are porn (2019). https://www.pcmag.com/news/371193/most-ai-generated-deepfake-videos-online-are-porn. Accessed 11 Jan 2023
14. Karras, T., Aila, T., Laine, S., Lehtinen, J.: Progressive growing of GANs for improved quality, stability, and variation. arXiv preprint arXiv:1710.10196 (2017)
15. Kowalski, M.: Faceswap: Github repository (2021). https://github.com/MarekKowalski/FaceSwap. Accessed 11 Jan 2023
16. Kristiadi, A., Hein, M., Hennig, P.: Being Bayesian, even just a bit, fixes overconfidence in Relu networks. In: International Conference on Machine Learning, pp. 5436–5446. PMLR (2020)
17. Lee, J., Bahri, Y., Novak, R., Schoenholz, S.S., Pennington, J., Sohl-Dickstein, J.: Deep neural networks as gaussian processes. arXiv preprint arXiv:1711.00165 (2017)
18. Lee, S., Tariq, S., Shin, Y., Woo, S.S.: Detecting handcrafted facial image manipulations and GAN-generated facial images using shallow-fakefacenet. Appl. Soft Comput. **105**, 107256 (2021)
19. Li, Y., Chang, M.C., Lyu, S.: In ICTU oculi: exposing AI generated fake face videos by detecting eye blinking. arXiv preprint arXiv:1806.02877 (2018)
20. Nataraj, L., et al.: Detecting GAN generated fake images using co-occurrence matrices. arXiv preprint arXiv:1903.06836 (2019)
21. Nguyen, H.H., Yamagishi, J., Echizen, I.: Use of a capsule network to detect fake images and videos. arXiv preprint arXiv:1910.12467 (2019)
22. Pedregosa, F., et al.: Scikit-learn: machine learning in python. J. Mach. Learn. Res. **12**, 2825–2830 (2011)
23. Pu, J., Mangaokar, N., Wang, B., Reddy, C.K., Viswanath, B.: Noisescope: detecting deepfake images in a blind setting. In: Annual Computer Security Applications Conference, pp. 913–927 (2020)
24. Rossler, A., Cozzolino, D., Verdoliva, L., Riess, C., Thies, J., Nießner, M.: Faceforensics++: Learning to detect manipulated facial images. In: Proceedings of the IEEE/CVF International Conference on Computer Vision, pp. 1–11 (2019)
25. Salloum, R., Ren, Y., Kuo, C.C.J.: Image splicing localization using a multi-task fully convolutional network (MFCN). J. Vis. Commun. Image Represent. **51**, 201–209 (2018)
26. Szegedy, C., et al.: Going deeper with convolutions. In: Proceedings of the IEEE Conference on Computer Vision and Pattern Recognition, pp. 1–9 (2015)
27. Thies, J., Zollhöfer, M., Nießner, M.: Deferred neural rendering: image synthesis using neural textures. ACM Trans. Graphics (TOG) **38**(4), 1–12 (2019)
28. Thies, J., Zollhofer, M., Stamminger, M., Theobalt, C., Nießner, M.: Face2face: real-time face capture and reenactment of RGB videos. In: Proceedings of the

IEEE Conference on Computer Vision and Pattern Recognition, pp. 2387–2395 (2016)

29. Viola, P., Jones, M.: Rapid object detection using a boosted cascade of simple features. In: Proceedings of the 2001 IEEE Computer Society Conference on Computer Vision and Pattern Recognition, CVPR 2001. vol. 1, pp. I-I. IEEE (2001)

30. Wang, T., Cheng, H., Chow, K.P., Nie, L.: Deep convolutional pooling transformer for deepfake detection. ACM Trans. Multimed. Comput. Commun. Appl. **19**(6), 1–20 (2023)

31. Wu, J., Feng, K., Chang, X., Yang, T.: A forensic method for deepfake image based on face recognition. In: Proceedings of the 2020 4th High Performance Computing and Cluster Technologies Conference & 2020 3rd International Conference on Big Data and Artificial Intelligence, pp. 104–108 (2020)

32. Xia, Z., Qiao, T., Xu, M., Wu, X., Han, L., Chen, Y.: Deepfake video detection based on mesonet with preprocessing module. Symmetry **14**(5), 939 (2022)

33. Yang, X., Li, Y., Lyu, S.: Exposing deep fakes using inconsistent head poses. In: ICASSP 2019–2019 IEEE International Conference on Acoustics, Speech and Signal Processing (ICASSP), pp. 8261–8265. IEEE (2019)

34. Zhang, W., Zhao, C.: Exposing face-swap images based on deep learning and ELA detection. In: Proceedings, vol. 46, p. 29. MDPI (2019)

35. Zhou, P., Han, X., Morariu, V.I., Davis, L.S.: Two-stream neural networks for tampered face detection. In: 2017 IEEE Conference on Computer Vision and Pattern Recognition Workshops (CVPRW), pp. 1831–1839. IEEE (2017)

A Novel Steganography Scheme Using Logistic Map, BRISK Descriptor, and K-Means Clustering

Hassan Jameel Azooz[1]([✉]), Khawla Ben Salah[4], Monji Kherallah[2], and Mohamed Saber Naceur[3]

[1] University of Almuthanna, Samawah, Iraq
hasanazooz@mu.edu.iq
[2] University of Sfax, Sfax, Tunisia
monji.kherallah@fss.usf.tn
[3] University of Carthage, Carthage, Tunisia
[4] National engineering School, University of Sfax, Sfax, Tunisia
khawla.bensalah@fsgf.u-gafsa.tn

Abstract. This paper introduces a novel steganography method for embedding and extracting a secret message from an image file using three stages. In the first stage, Binary Robust Invariant Scalable Keypoints (BRISK) and Good Features to Track are utilized to identify keypoints in the image. In the second stage, the k-means clustering algorithm is applied to these identified keypoints. The keypoints derived from the good features to track algorithm serve as cluster centers while the keypoints from the BRISK algorithm are distributed around these centers. In the last stage, the logistic map algorithm is employed to add more randomness to the obtained keypoints. This is done by distributing the points using the random list property. The results obtained indicate that the proposed method surpasses comparable techniques in terms of PSNR (Peak Signal-to-Noise Ratio), SSIM (Structural Similarity Index), and BER (Bit Error Rate) values metrics. Thus, the proposed scheme offers a performance advantage over existing methodologies.

Keywords: clustering algorithm · BRISK · embedding · steganography

1 Introduction

The advancement in digital technology has provided the means of copying and transferring sensitive documents over networks such as the Internet and others. Steganography is used to hide data inside documents because the process of transferring documents has become a major issue in some businesses, such as transfering medical images, which is done openly. Moreover, it is considered

Contributing authors—K.B. Salah, M. Kherallah and M.S. Naceur.

a risky process due to the possibility of forging or stealing the entire data [1]. Steganography can be defined as the study of invisible communication, which often focuses on many methods of concealing the existence of the messages that are being sent. The success of this process depends on the amount of information that can be hidden and the robustness of various image-processing attacks. The components of a steganography system are the embedding and the extraction algorithms, as well as the attacks themselves. The data in the images is hidden using the spatial domain or the frequency domain. In the first one, the hidden message is entered directly by changing the pixel value of the cover image, where one of the techniques known as least significant bit (LSB) is used. The frequency domain depends on the transformation of the cover image first, then the secret message is hidden [2,13]. The least significant bit is a method that has been used for a long time in masking operations but it has become common, traditional, and predictable. In our research, we have utilized a hybrid approach combining BRISK and Good features to track for determining the locations for embedding secret message bits. This hybrid mechanism positions the points from BRISK around central points sourced from the Good Features to Track technique, a process termed as clustering. These points are then randomized based on a particular pixel within the cover image, using chaotic sequences to bolster security. The rest of this paper is structured as follows: the next section gives an overview of various past prominent methods of steganography and feature detection. In Sect. 3, the proposed approach is presented. Finally, the findings of the study are discussed in the final section.

2   Related Works

Steganography is a method for concealing information, such as text, sound, or video, within another media. According to supplementary research, however, steganography is insufficient to guarantee the information's security in and of itself. Therefore, it is essential to design a more reliable approach by integrating multiple security measures. Additionally, it's worth noting that the integration of deep learning techniques has significantly enhanced various security tasks, underscoring the invaluable contribution of deep learning in diverse domains [17–19]. A study conducted by Yi et al. is concerned with one-dimensional steganography (audio) [12]. This study proposes a generalized adaptive Huffman code mapping (AHCM) architecture to improve payload security. The authors define a distortion-limited suppressible code space that allows for the use of equal-length entropy codes for data embedding. This is done to counteract the impact of the audio codec and eliminate the frame offset. To further ensure statistical and aural undetectability, a stegonagraphy key is incorporated into the dynamic generation of the Huffman code mapping of each frame. To minimize total distortion, they consider combining the intraframe psychoacoustic model (PAM) and the interframe perceptual distortion model (PDM). Finally, an adaptive embedding strategy that employs syndrome-trellis codes requires the creation of a distortion function based on the PAM and an ideal steganographic frame path. A study by Chowdhury et al. provides a further LSB-based approach to audio steganography [13]. The authors have implemented a two-tier encryption in their technique. Initially, text encryption is based on its positional value through a pattern-matching strategy, ensuring the message's confidentiality. First, they encrypt the text based on its positional value using a pattern-matching approach. This is done to ensure the confidentiality of the message. In the second level, the cover file includes the positional value encoded in the tried-and-true LSB fashion. This type of dual encryption will guarantee that data security is kept effectively. The LSB method makes it possible to obfuscate a sizable secret message within a cover image. Using scanned document pictures, Soleymani and Taherinia [15] present a spatial domain steganography technique. They use a halftoning technique on the scanned documents to generate secret decimal integers. The photos' hidden message is encoded using a 3-LSB methodology, which saves a lot of space but is less robust than compressed distortion. Lin et al. [17] have developed a similar method whereby hidden information is encoded into the value of the ith pixel in a hosted image C. This technique allows the stego-image to be relatively resistant to deformation. As Loc et al. believe, grayscale document images can now be hidden in a special domain thanks to a novel steganographic technique developed by them. The authors break their method down into three parts. At first, they use the Speed Up Robust Feature (SURF) detector to generate embedding regions. Next, the secret message is encoded with Local Binary Pattern (LBP) and Local Ternary Pattern (LTP) and then embedded in the corresponding positions (LTP). This method is robust against image distortion and can locate hidden information. In [14], a Binary Robust Invariant Scalable Keypoints (BRISK) based detection is used to streamline the localization of a flying UAV inside the constraints of a fully autonomous landing on the runway. Ganguly et al. [3] introduce a steganographic technique that can be applied to the spatial realm. The method uses Galois field operations with pixel value differencing (PVD) or singular value decomposition (SVD) to provide double-layer security for secreting message bits. After encrypting the message with the secret key (obtained from MSB) and double XOR operations in binary representation. Ahmed et al. [4] implements a method of hiding the encrypted stream of bits in the cover image. They used LSB technology to include the place value in the Cover file, noting that this double-encryption makes the technique more secure. The distinction between the two mechanisms (PVD) is that the secret data are embedded by comparing the differences involving the intensity value of subsequent non-overlapping pixels, as proposed by Pal and others [5]. In [6]), the authors advocate employing encryption and steganography together to safeguard sensitive data. The first layer uses elliptic curve cryptography (ECC) to encrypt the text, and the second layer uses 1-LSB and 2-LSB picture steganography to conceal the encrypted text within an image. Swain et al. [7] proposed a two-tiered steganographic embedding method. The image is broken up into non-overlapping 3x3 pixel blocks, and the message bits are replaced in the LSBs of each pixel inside a block. The final six bits are subjected to quotient value differencing (QVD), as well. The simulations and performance evaluations conducted by Pak et al. [8], who suggest an enhanced model of a 1D chaotic system, demonstrate that the proposed model is capable of adequately overcoming the existing limitations. Using the enhanced 1D chaotic map, and LSB steganography algorithm has significantly outperformed prior approaches. Many methods for masking a document's picture using a combination of methods are summarized in Table 1.

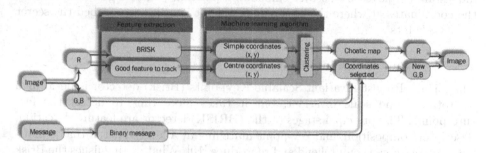

Fig. 1. The proposed embedding process flowchart

3 Proposed Approach

The strategy resulting from our research relies on the ability to hide a secret message within an image of a document. This is achieved by employing a chaotic map combined with the least significant bit, termed Chaotic-LSB. The proposed method centers on determining the positions to embed the secret message bit and then dispersing these positions. After obtaining the secret message data (Binmess), keypoints from the good features to track detector are chosen as the centroids. The selection depends on the Center Key Control Point, and keypoints from the BRISK detector are selected based on the Points Data Key Control Point. This process is termed clustering. We compute the absolute distance for each point from the centroid and observe each cluster of points nearer to the centroid. These steps can be iterated to find a new centroid until the centroid remains constant or the length of the message becomes shorter than the number of keypoints, as outlined in Algorithm (2). Subsequently, the control points, chosen via the unsupervised machine learning algorithm (specifically k-means clustering), are distributed. The logistic map enhances randomness due to its capacity to generate a sequence of random numbers. This step involves creating a matrix with dimensions (for instance, 5×5). Here, keypoints are distributed using the logistic map for its entropy properties, such as randomness in distribution and dispersion. In our study, we design a G-Matrix of size 5×5 and populate it with the one-dimensional locations derived from the previously selected keypoints (control points). This matrix is sequentially filled based on the indexed coordinates of the prior extracted points. In the subsequent phase, to embed the message in the document image, it's converted to binary and segmented into pairs. Each pair is then embedded using the row and column of the matrix (G), as detailed in Fig. 1 and Algorithm 3.

3.1   Embedding Process

Binary Robust Invariant Scalable Keypoints and Good features to track techniques are employed to discover embedding positions; these algorithms identify the coordinates at where the least significant bit is utilized to embed the secret sequence's bits.

3.2   Relevant Keypoints Detection

The Binary Robust Invariant Scalable Keypoints (Brisk) detector is performed by rotation and scale invariant, but it takes more time to detect the feature points. The principal stages of the (BRISK)detector are feature detection, descriptor composition, and key-point matching at a level of detail that a motivated observer can comprehend and reproduce [10]. What distinguishes the Brisk detector is that it allows using another keypoint descriptor along with it and vice versa. This method relies on a good tracking algorithm that expands the previous search methods in the Newton-Raphson method to work under horizontal image transformations. This algorithm tests performance after movements and experiments on real images. To overcome the defects of the two algorithms (BRISK and Good features to track), we propose a combination of two for quicker and more rotationally and scale stable feature detection. The choice of the (good features to track) algorithm is explained by the fact that the key points extracted from it are limited, but they are distributed. The [BRISK] algorithm produces a large number of points, but it chooses the key points sequentially, not scattered or distributed. So, the hybrid algorithm that we produce is based on the projection of the points extracted from (good features to track) on the points of the (BRISK) algorithm. The embedding process is divided into four steps: message acquisition, message preprocessing, detection of embedding positions, and embedding algorithms. The mechanism used in this research hides the message after converting it to binary format, at the specified points for the pixels of the cover document image, and after dividing it into three bands. The suggested scheme's efficiency and simplicity are demonstrated by the fact that neither the embedding nor the extracting processes require significant computational time. In addition, It does not cause distortion or decrease in the quality of the steganography document image. The innovative approach presented here embeds secret message bits utilizing the chaotic LSB, ensuring preservation of the steganographic image's quality.

3.3   Message Acquisition

Confidential information can be taken from the message by typing the letters of the message using the keyboard of a computer or tablet and then converting them into a binary message.

3.4   Message Preprocessing

The algorithm for selecting control points is employed in the process of obtaining embedding locations within the document image. Embedding positions across the three image bands (red, green, and blue) are chosen in which the length of the message is hidden in the green and blue bands. For example, a message with a length of (100) is divided into two where 50 are hidden in blue and 50 in green. These locations are pinpointed using the proposed hybrid algorithm, combining BRISK and Good Features to Track.

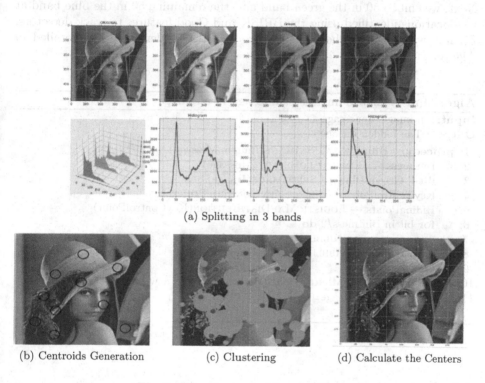

(a) Splitting in 3 bands

(b) Centroids Generation   (c) Clustering   (d) Calculate the Centers

Fig. 2. Detecting embedding positions

3.5   Detection Embedding Positions

To identify embedding positions in the document image with size of 512×512, the K-mean clustering is employed. Initially, centroids are determined based on the Center key Control Point. We then compute the absolute difference between each point and all centroids, subsequently assigning the observation to the cluster with the nearest centroid. Following this, a new centroid for every cluster is recalculated by averaging all observations within that specific cluster. Subsequently, we compute the number of points associated with each centroid. This procedure continues until either the centroids remain unchanged or the message length becomes shorter than the Count, which no longer has additional points, as illustrated in Fig. 2.

3.6   Embedding Algorithm

The first step to embedding the secret message in the cover document image is to convert the message to binary and divide the number of the binary bits by two. Then, we apply the BRISK detector to obtain Point Data key Control Point and apply the Good features to track to obtain Center key Control Point. Next, we embed 50 in the green band and the remaining 50 in the blue band at the locations identified using the BRISK and Good features to track detectors. Finally, we merge all the bands to produce the hidden image as detailed in Algorithm 1.

Algorithm 1. Embedding secret message in an image

Input: An image, a message
Output: The hidden image

1: **procedure** HIDEMESSAGEINIMAGE(Image, Message)
2:      Bin_mess ← CONVERTTOBINARY(Message)
3:      [Red, Green, Blue] ← SPLITIMAGE(Image)
4:      KeyControlPoint ← SELECTKEYCONTROLPOINT()
5:      HidingPoints ← LOGISTICMAPDISTRIBUTION(KeyControlPoint)
6:      **for** bit in Bin_mess/2 **do**
7:           new_green ← NIBBLEBITS(Green, bit)
8:           new_blue ← NIBBLEBITS(Blue, next_bit)
9:      **end for**
10:     HiddenImage ← MERGEBANDS(Red, new_green, new_blue)
11:     **return** HiddenImage
12: **end procedure**

3.7   Logistic Map

The logistic map is a form of chaotic system that is developed by Robert May. It generates chaotic sequences which are very sensitive to the initial values, as in the following equation:

$$X_{n+1} = r \cdot x_n(1 - x_n) \tag{1}$$

where x_n is a number between 0 and 1, and r represents different cases of the logistic map.

Chaos can be defined as systems that show great sensitivity to initial conditions, which is a characteristic of the logistic map for most values of r between 3.57 and 4.

In the above equation, we assume that $r = 3.57995$ or $r \geq 4$ because values of r that exceed 3.57995 show chaotic behavior. This is used to generate random points to hide the secret message bits inside the cover document image.

In the current study, the logistic map is used to determine the locations where the secret message is included in the cover image. Then, it is replaced by the least significant bit of the specified locations where the logistic map exhibits chaotic behavior when r is greater than 3.57 and less than 4. The logistic map gradually approaches periodic movement when r is greater than three and less than 3.45. Moreover, because the iterative sequence with the first value X_0 is chaotic, different sequences can be generated for different initial values in the interval $(0,1)$. They may also contain sub-intervals corresponding to the bits of differently embedded pixels. Interestingly, the sequences are acyclic and are normally distributed within the mentioned interval $(0,1)$.

The question is, "How to generate the random points for long periods when the message size is long?" The answer lies in the fact that the logistic map generates random points by defining special points called fixed points, which are the values of x in the above equation. These points remain invariant if we plug them into the iterated map, as follows:

Algorithm 2. Selection of Key Control Point locations based on k-means

---

Input: an image, length of the message
Output: lists X and Y Coordinates

1: **procedure** SELECTKEYCONTROLPOINT(Image, MessageLength)
2:     [Red, Green, Blue] ← SPLITIMAGE(Image)
3:     PointDataKeyControlPoint ← APPLYBRISKKEYPOINTS(Red)
4:     CenterKeyControlPoint ← APPLYGOODFEATURESTOTRACK(Red)
5:     **while** centroids are changing or MessageLength < CountNumberofPoints **do**
6:         ChooseCentroids(CenterKeyControlPoint)
7:         ChooseData(PointDataKeyControlPoint)
8:         CalculateDifference()
9:         PutObservationInCluster()
10:        CalculateNewCentroids()
11:        CalculateCountNumberofPoints()
12:        **if** Centroids are not changing **then**
13:            **break**
14:        **end if**
15:    **end while**
16:    **return** X and Y Coordinates
17: **end procedure**

$$x_{n+1} = x_n \tag{2}$$

The iterated map can have more than one fixed point, and sometimes it isn't easy to compute the fixed points of the logistic map equation, $x = r \cdot x(1 - x)$, which have the solutions $x^* = 0$ and $x^* = 1 - \frac{1}{r}$.

3.8   Extraction Process

At this stage, we extract the secret message data by determining the embedding positions in the stego document image by tracking the coordinates in the red band. Next, the following steps can be considered reverse steps of the embedding process. In these steps, we use the Brisk equation to extract:

$$K_p = \prod_{i=1}^{n}(x_i, y_i) \tag{3}$$

Here, n denotes the keypoints; accordingly, we get a list arranged in descending order, and after placing the keypoints in the list of descending order comes the step of extracting the first least significant bit for each i-th pixel value by extracting the secret key that is included in the embedding algorithm. In the end, the secret bits we get are represented by binary representation, so we convert them to the original form of the original message as detailed in Algorithm 4.

Algorithm 3. Logistic map distribution of hiding points

Require: A green-band image, lists X and Y Coordinates, $X_0 = 0.4$, $r = 3.0$, Length of the message

Ensure: A list containing index location hiding

1: Create a matrix called G_matrix with dimensions width × height
2: Convert X and Y Coordinates from 2D to index in 1D in a green-band image called XY_1D
3: Fill G_matrix by assigning XY_1D values based on sequence index
4: Convert the red-band image from 2D to 1D matrix
5: **for** $i = 0$ to Length of message **do**
6:     Get Row and Col from the logistic map
7:     $x = r \cdot x \cdot (1 - x) \rightarrow \text{Row} = (x \cdot 10^5)\%\text{width}$
8:     $x = r \cdot x \cdot (1 - x) \rightarrow \text{Col} = (x \cdot 10^5)\%\text{height}$
9:     Save the index location to a list called Select_index
10:    Get the index = G_matrix[Row][Col]
11:    Select_index.append(index)
12:    Update the G_matrix
13:    G_matrix[Row][Col] = index
14: **end for**

---

4   Experimental Results

4.1   Metrics of Evaluation

PSNR (Peak Signal-to-Noise Ratio) is the most objective measure for assessing image quality when it comes to image attacks like distortion and compression attacks. The PSNR value is obtained from the pixel, where it is the difference between the original image and the stegonagraphy image.

$$PSNR = 10 \log_{10} \left(\frac{\max^2}{MSE} \right) \tag{4}$$

$$MSE = \frac{1}{XY} \sum_{y=0}^{Y-1} \sum_{x=0}^{X-1} \epsilon(y,x)^2 \tag{5}$$

4.2 Performance Comparaison Between Different State of the Art Methods

We assessed the robustness of our method across five distinct data sets. They are labeled as Type1, Type2, Type3, Type4, and Type5: Tobacoo800 Document image, archive3 data set, standard grey scale testing images, dataset1-document-images, and L3iDocCopies from L3i Laboratory. Table 2 displays the average values of PSNR for each type of dataset. The proposed approach shows higher values than state of the art methods. This confirms that our proposed system is more efficient than the classic LSB and that of the related works in terms of distortion measurement. A comparative analysis, especially when comparing the same kind of datasets utilized in certain related studies, confirms that our

---

Algorithm 4. Extracting the secret message from a stego document image

---
Require: Stego image
Ensure: Secret message
1: **function** EXTRACTMESSAGE(stego_image)
2:     Initialize an empty list to store the secret bits: secret_bits = []
3:     Get the red band of the stego image: red_band = stego_image[:, :, 0]
4:     Apply the BRISK algorithm to detect keypoints in the red band: brisk = BRISK(), keypoints = brisk.detect(red_band)
5:     Sort the keypoints in descending order of response value: keypoints.sort(key=lambda x: x.response, reverse=True)
6:     **for each** keypoint **in** keypoints **do**
7:         Get the pixel coordinates of the keypoint: $x = $ int(keypoint.pt[0]), $y = $ int(keypoint.pt[1])
8:         Get the pixel value of the red band at that coordinate: pixel_value = red_band[y, x]
9:         Extract the least significant bit of the pixel value and append it to the secret bits list: lsb = pixel_value&1, secret_bits.append(lsb)
10:    **end for**
11:    Convert the secret bits list to a binary string: binary_string = "".join(map(str, secret_bits))
12:    Extract and decode the secret key from the binary string using some method: secret_key = decode_key(binary_string)
13:    Decrypt and decode the secret message from the binary string using some method: secret_message = decrypt_message(binary_string, secret_key)
14:    **return** the secret message: **return** secret_message
15: **end function**

---

376 H. J. Azooz et al.

method excels in image quality, particularly when converting document image bits to binary and leveraging the least significant bit to toggle pixel bit positions. These positions are ascertained by a hybrid algorithm, grounded on PSNR outcome reviews. Furthermore, examining the SSIM metrics detailed in the same table affirms our method's superior performance in document image stego quality relative to alternative approaches.

4.3 Qualitative Study

In the heart of our study, we conduct a qualitative analysis to assess the robustness of our proposed system. This is done by comparing the original images to stego images obtained using three benchmarks from the hiding process We use well-known metrics, NPCR, UACI, BER, and Pixel Difference Histogram, and embed a secret message in each of the three benchmarks. After obtaining stego images, we apply Pixel Difference Histogram analysis to each stego image and compare it with its corresponding cover image. The resulting image is evaluated by the Human Visual System (HVS) based on visual quality. Figure 3 shows that there is no difference between the document images and the original image, and the graphs for both images are similar. NPCR, which measures the pixel difference between the original image and the stego image where we embed the secret message. Our results show that the difference values between the two images are very small and less than what is found in related works. This confirms that our system outperforms other systems. The image quality is not affected, making it difficult to detect the points where the secret message is embedded with the document remains clear.

Table 1. Performance Evaluation between different state of the art methods.

References	Technique used	Secret Data type	Datasets	PSNR
17	SURF, LBP, LTP	Message Bits	Tobacco800, L3iDocCopies, Standard grayscale test images	37.88/103.25/86.74
18	Halftoning	Document image	Standard grayscale test images	37.02
19	algorithm, LSB	pseudo random number	Standard grayscale test images	51.13
11	Spatial domain	Text message	Standard grayscale test images	39.70
12	Spatial domain using LSB	Text message	Standard grayscale test images	40.74
13	Logistic map based secret key	Logo	Standard grayscale test images	38.80

Table 2. Comparison of PSNR and SSIM values with different state of the art methods

Image	Our approach		Soleymani and Taherinia		Ganguly et al.	
	PSNR	SSIM	PSNR	SSIM	PSNR	SSIM
newspaper	85.23	0.9854	-	-	-	-
magazine	92.24	0.691	-	-	-	-
Daily newspaper	92.29	0.948	-	-	-	39.70
Lena	94.53	0.999	93.41	0.999	-	-
Baboon	88.05	1.0	93.00	0.999	35.59	0.996
Man	93.24	0.999	93.15	0.999	-	-
Barbara	94.13	0.999	94.53	0.999	-	-
Cameramen	95.52	0.999	93.95	0.999	-	-
Document 1	87.11	0.999	-	-	-	-
Document 2	86.39	0.999	-	-	-	-
Document 3	86.54	0.529	-	-	-	-
Document 4	86.93	0.653	-	-	-	-

4.4 Robustness Evaluation

To assess the resilience of the extracted secret message, we employ a metric called the Bit Error Ratio (BER), also known as the accuracy ratio. It measures the number of bit errors per unit of time. The Bit Error Ratio is the number of bit errors divided by the total number of transferred bits during a studied time interval.

$$\text{BER} = \frac{\text{number of incorrect bits}}{\text{total number of bits}} \tag{6}$$

And the results are presented in Table 3. The table shows that the proposed system achieves a high accuracy ratio in a noise-free environment.

Table 3. Error rate and Bit errors related to the proposed approach

Benchmark Type	Bit Errors	Bit Error Rate
Type 1	52	0.01%
Type 3	37	0.01%
Type 4	63	0.01%

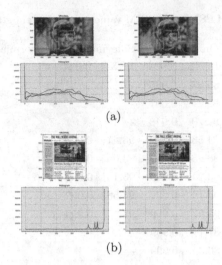

Fig. 3. Histograms of Original images and steganography images embedding the secret key

5   Conclusion

The current study presents a steganography system that uses a combination of Binary Robust Invariant Scalable Keypoints, Good features to track algorithms, clustering algorithms, and the logistic map algorithm to embed and extract a secret file contained in an image file. The proposed approach provides a fast and accurate method for identifying keypoints in a document and it is capable of encoding and decoding secret files within image files. The results obtained indicate that this mechanism is superior to all that of the related works in terms of PSNR, SSIM, and BER values. This underscores steganography's capability as a secure avenue for transmitting confidential files across networks, like the Internet, ensuring the data's privacy.

References

1. Laimeche, L., Meraoumia, A., Bendjenna, H.: Enhancing LSB embedding schemes using chaotic maps systems. Neural Comput. Appl. **32**, 16605–16623 (2020)
2. Jayapandiyan, J.R., Kavitha, C., Sakthivel, K.: Enhanced least significant bit replacement algorithm in spatial domain of steganography using character sequence optimization. IEEE Access **8**, 136537–136545 (2020)
3. Leutenegger, S., Chli, M., Siegwart, R.Y.: BRISK: binary robust invariant scalable keypoints. In: 2011 International Conference on Computer Vision. IEEE (2011)
4. Mukherjee (Ganguly), N., Paul, G., Saha, S.K.: An efficient multi-bit steganography algorithm in spatial domain with two-layer security. Multimedia Tools Appl. **77**(14), 18451–18481 (2018). https://doi.org/10.1007/s11042-018-5720-3
5. Ahmed, A., Ahmed, A.: A secure image steganography using LSB and double XOR operations. Int. J. Comput. Sci. Netw. Secur. **20**(5), 139–144 (2020)

6. Prasad, S., Pal, A.K.: Logistic map-based image steganography scheme using combined LSB and PVD for security enhancement. In: Abraham, A., Dutta, P., Mandal, J., Bhattacharya, A., Dutta, S. (eds.) Emerging Technologies in Data Mining and Information Security, pp. 203–214. Springer, Singapore (2019). https://doi.org/10.1007/978-981-13-1501-5_17

7. Hureib, E.S.B., Gutub, A.A.: Enhancing medical data security via combining elliptic curve cryptography with 1-LSB and 2-LSB image steganography. Int. J. Comput. Sci. Netw. Secur. (IJCSNS) 20(12), 232–241 (2020)

8. Swain, G.: Very high capacity image steganography technique using quotient value differencing and LSB substitution. Arab. J. Sci. Eng. 44(4), 2995–3004 (2019)

9. Pak, C., et al.: A novel color image LSB steganography using improved 1D chaotic map. Multimedia Tools Appl. 79(1), 1409–1425 (2020)

10. Nazari, M., Mehrabian, M.: A novel chaotic IWT-LSB blind watermarking approach with flexible capacity for secure transmission of authenticated medical images. Multimedia Tools and Appl. 80(7), 10615–10655 (2021)

11. Nevriyanto, A., et al.: Image steganography using combine of discrete wavelet transform and singular value decomposition for more robustness and higher peak signal noise ratio. In: 2018 International Conference on Electrical Engineering and Computer Science (ICECOS). IEEE (2018)

12. Yi, X., Yang, K., Zhao, X., Wang, Y., Yu, H.: AHCM: adaptive Huffman code mapping for audio steganography based on psychoacoustic model. IEEE Trans. Inf. Forensics Secur. 14(8), 2217–2231 (2019). https://doi.org/10.1109/TIFS.2019.2895200

13. Bikku, T., Paturi, R.: Frequency domain steganography with reversible texture combination. Traitement du Signal 36(1), 109–117 (2019)

14. Burie, J.-C., Ogier, J.-M., Loc, C.V.: A spatial domain steganography for grayscale documents using pattern recognition techniques. In: 2017 14th IAPR International Conference on Document Analysis and Recognition (ICDAR), vol. 9, p. 100. IEEE (2017)

15. Soleymani, S.H., Taherinia, A.H.: High capacity image steganography on sparse message of scanned document image (SMSDI). Multimedia Tools Appl. 76, 20847–20867 (2017)

16. Lin, I.-C., Lin, Y.-B., Wang, C.-M.: Hiding data in spatial domain images with distortion tolerance. Comput. Stand. Interfaces 31(2), 458–464 (2009)

17. Fourati, J., Othmani, M., Ltifi, H.: A hybrid model based on bidirectional long-short term memory and support vector machine for rest tremor classification. SIViP 16, 2175–2182 (2022). https://doi.org/10.1007/s11760-022-02180-9

18. Ben Salah, K., Othmani, M., Kherallah, M.: Long short-term memory based photoplethysmography biometric authentication. In: Badica, C., Treur, J., Benslimane, D., Hnatkowska, B., Krotkiewicz, M. (eds.) ICCCI 2022. CCIS, vol. 1653, pp. 554–563. Springer, Cham (2022). https://doi.org/10.1007/978-3-031-16210-7_45

19. Ben Salah, K., Othmani, M., Kherallah, M.: Contactless heart rate estimation from facial video using skin detection and multi-resolution analysis. In: WSCG (2021). http://dx.doi.org/10.24132/CSRN.2021.3002.31

A Holistic Approach to Elderly Safety: Sensor Fusion, Fall Detection, and Privacy-Preserving Techniques

Hoa Nguyen, ThuGiang Mai, and Minh Nguyen[✉]

Auckland University of Technology, Auckland, New Zealand
{vxp9792,thugiang.mai}@autuni.ac.nz, minh.nguyen@aut.ac.nz

Abstract. In light of the rising need for elderly care, this paper introduces a comprehensive integrated system centered on ensuring the safety of solitary senior individuals, leveraging the capabilities of the Internet of Things (IoT), deep learning, and sensor technology. We explore both wearable and non-wearable sensors for continuous monitoring. Recognizing the challenges associated with wearable devices - such as battery constraints, user discomfort, and potential inaccuracies - we highlight the benefits of visual object-based fall detection using environmental sensors. These include visual cameras and depth sensors optimally placed within living spaces to bypass the limitations of wearable devices and elevate monitoring precision.

To address potential privacy concerns from ongoing video monitoring, we utilize advanced methods like human skeleton extraction and reversible visual data-hiding schemes. By camouflaging visual data, our proposed method ensures the content remains undetected by conventional means. This data-hiding scheme for videos and images encrypts media in a way that, to the general observer, it appears as random noise, yet it can be securely stored and transferred across platforms. Moreover, our encryption technique draws inspiration from water wave patterns and utilizes circular patterns derived from images, making the chance of brute force decryption nearly impossible. As a result, the system transforms human visuals into anonymous skeletal structures and encrypts visual data, safeguarding both privacy and data integrity.

In essence, our holistic system marries technological advancements with the principles of humane care, striving for a harmonious blend of comfort, precise monitoring, and rigorous privacy preservation.

Keywords: Fall detection · Visual object-based algorithm · Human skeleton extraction · Privacy preservation · Deep learning · Environmental sensors · Data encryption · Reversible data-hiding · Visual camouflage

1 Introduction

In contemporary society, the growing number of elderly individuals living alone presents significant challenges for healthcare professionals, with risks ranging

W. Q. Yan et al. (Eds.): PSIVT 2023, LNCS 14403, pp. 380–393, 2024.
https://doi.org/10.1007/978-981-97-0376-0_29

from medical emergencies to social isolation and mental health concerns. One specific concern is the prevalence of falls among the elderly. Such falls can lead to severe injuries, with long-term consequences, and around 40% to 60% of these incidents may occur without witnesses [31]. The rising global trend of aging populations further complicates these health issues, leading to increases in chronic diseases and healthcare expenditures [5,11,30,32].

With traditional health monitoring models proving time-consuming and inconvenient [17], the demand for efficient healthcare solutions grows. One looming challenge is the projected surge in healthcare spending; for instance, New Zealand's healthcare spending is anticipated to soar, reaching about 11 percent of GDP by 2060 without changes in healthcare service delivery [20].

Emerging technologies, particularly the Internet of Things (IoT), offer promising avenues for developing remote health monitoring systems [2]. Despite the proliferation of tech solutions, there's a dearth of applications specifically tailored for real-time elderly monitoring. Such monitoring presents its set of challenges, from ensuring the privacy and security of sensitive data to addressing storage needs for vast amounts of generated data.

This research delves into the exploration and design of an affordable system that employs IoT technologies to monitor the elderly within their domiciles, ensuring their privacy and security. As we traverse this investigative landscape, we grapple with several pressing research questions. Firstly, we address the issue of identifying technologies that are apt for home-based elderly monitoring while ensuring their privacy (RQ 1). Secondly, we explore the accuracy of wearable IoT devices in classifying activities, notably in fall detection (RQ 2). Our inquiries also extend to discerning potential non-wearable IoT devices that can offer precise activity classification (RQ 3). As we pivot to the realm of surveillance, we scrutinize methodologies to minimize data breaches, especially within RGB/IR surveillance camera systems (RQ 4). In tandem, we delve into avenues to bolster human detection accuracy through the lens of deep learning models (RQ 5). Finally, our research contemplates strategies that can effectively curtail the need for voluminous cloud storage, especially in the context of real-time health monitoring (RQ 6).

Addressing these questions could pave the way for creating comprehensive and privacy-preserving solutions for monitoring the elderly. Our research contributions revolve around designing a low-cost, efficient ecosystem for elderly monitoring, as illustrated in Fig. 1. This system integrates both wearable and non-wearable devices, processes data securely on a Cloud-server, and provides caregivers with real-time insights.

To realize this vision, we contribute to (1) the overall design of a cloud-based system combining wearable and external visual sensors, (2) an AI server-side process using deep learning for human activity detection, and (3) a full-stack process ensuring secured visual content hiding capability.

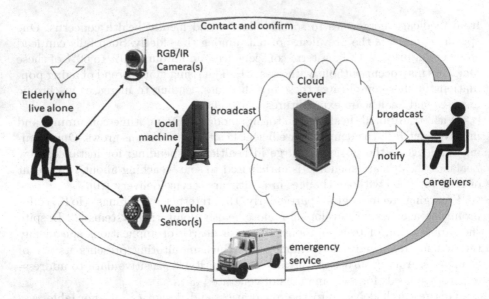

Fig. 1. Overall Architecture of the proposed system.

2   Literature Review

The world has observed a notable rise in ageing populations [11], leading to intricate health concerns and surges in medical service costs [30]. Europe faces a significant burden of Chronic Heart Failure (CHF), Chronic Obstructive Pulmonary Disease (COPD), and Diabetes, affecting 15 million people annually. Efforts to mitigate this challenge have pushed for advanced healthcare solutions, including the usage of fuzzy logic for early diagnostics [3] and the application of deep learning for societal problems since 2010 [8].

Health monitoring is crucial for maintaining the health of individuals, particularly older adults and those with chronic illnesses. Traditional health monitoring models may not meet the growing demand for medical services in our aging society. IoT is promising for developing efficient healthcare solutions to alleviate pressure on hospitals, enhance care quality, and reduce costs by keeping patients out of hospitals for routine needs [23].

IoTTA [23], an architecture fostering IoT-based applications, is an emerging solution. This framework encompasses five key tiers: Sensing, Sending, Processing, Storing, and Mining and Learning. In the healthcare sector, a synergy of accelerometers and gyroscopes helps in data collection to predict fall risks [7]. Other essential considerations include the cost, deployment strategy, and communication capability of sensors [19]. Various communication protocols, such as Bluetooth [7,16] and ZigBee [35], are utilized. Additionally, technologies like 3G, 4G, and LTE are employed in health systems for data transfer [6,7,25]. IoT applications benefit from diverse hardware platforms and operating systems, including Raspberry Pi, Android, and iOS [1]. Cloud platforms, like Amazon and Google Cloud, facilitate IoT data storage [1]. Results from [23] also shows that current IoT healthcare applications can be enhanced by utilizing data mining and machine learning tools for more effective clinical decision support. This may help patients by predicting changes and reducing the need for clinician involvement.

Machine learning techniques are instrumental in healthcare, managing vast databases and learning from data [9]. Monitoring services, diagnosis, and treatment services are significant aspects of the healthcare market [33]. IoT-driven healthcare systems, such as those monitoring vital signs and ensuring medication adherence, have been proposed [3,10,15]. Moreover, IoT applications in healthcare focus on Self Care and Data Mining and Machine Learning. Notably, non-adherence to healthcare guidelines can lead to worsening heart conditions [21].

Furthermore, Convolutional Neural Network architectures like VGG [28], ResNet [12], and EfficientNet [29] are vital for improving human detection in elderly monitoring systems. LSTMs enhance fall detection by understanding human movement dynamics. Data augmentation methods can boost deep learning models' efficacy [27], making healthcare systems more efficient. In summary, innovations like CNNs and the IoTTA framework are paving the way for real-time clinical feedback systems, bridging the gap between sensor data and critical healthcare decisions.

3   Integrated Fall Detection and Monitoring System

As the necessity to protect solitary elderly individuals intensifies, our proposed system, as depicted in Fig. 1, ingeniously integrates wearable and environmental monitoring tools. By capitalizing on IoT and deep learning, our objective is to provide exhaustive surveillance without compromising individual comfort or privacy.

3.1   Recording Sensors

In the intimate living spaces of elderly individuals, an array of sensors is judiciously deployed. This gamut includes wearable devices like smartwatches, which track biometric data, to subtly installed cameras and infrared sensors that furnish a panoramic observational scope. Wearable devices, when donned, are primed to detect falls and, upon detection, relay an alert to a centralized monitoring team. These wearable devices operate based on movement-induced triggers. Concurrently, non-wearable sensors employ advanced computer vision techniques to perform local detection of falls, subsequently triggering alarms. Nevertheless, the ubiquitous challenge of consistent use due to comfort considerations and battery longevity remains an Achilles' heel for wearable devices. Insights into these challenges are delved into in the following subsections Wearable Sensor-based Fall Detection and Centralized Monitoring and Response.

3.2 Wearable Sensor-Based Fall Detection

Wearable sensor-based fall detection systems are designed to discern between actual falls and Activities of Daily Living (ADL) by processing data types like acceleration signals [14]. Several research works have incorporated accelerometers in tandem with gyroscopes to monitor patients' movements [18]. Our novel Acceleration Change-based Fall Detection Algorithm (ACFDA) concentrates on specific features, including the slowly varying waveform of SMV and the pitch, which denotes the angle between the Y-axis and the ground.

Upon detecting a fall, the wearable device immediately triggers an alarm and dispatches a notification to caregivers or a centralized monitoring team. This immediate alert mechanism facilitates rapid assessment, allowing professionals to promptly verify if the detected fall is genuinely perilous or not. For evaluating the precision of our algorithm, we conducted tests encompassing nine varied activities, from standard walking to abrupt falls. These trials utilized devices such as the accelerometer X8M-3 and smartphone applications like Physics Toolbox Accelerometer [22]. The data from these experiments were parsed through machine learning methodologies, including the k-CNN classifier, SVM, and ANNs [24]. The ensuing results elucidate that the algorithm's efficacy is contingent on the chosen thresholds. Selecting the optimal threshold emerges as paramount to curtailing false alarms and ensuring the reliability of the alerts [13].

3.3 Centralized Monitoring and Response

Upon a fall detection, alarms are channeled to a centralized team of professionals. Using the vision-based sensors, this team evaluates the skeletal representations of the elderly to ascertain the veracity and severity of the fall. Local processing ensures promptness in detection and reduces the latency in response times.

Wearable sensors have been extensively explored for fall detection, as seen in systems such as SmartFall and those combined with smartphones. However, these often come with limitations like short battery time, potential discomfort, and inaccurate data recording. To address these concerns, environmental sensor-based systems have been introduced that leverage visual sensors, laser diodes, and radars, although they too have their limitations.

Previous systems have employed depth sensors, like the Microsoft Kinect, to differentiate falls from other activities. There have also been efforts to employ robots equipped with camera vision to identify falls in real-time. FallRisk, a unique context-aware platform, combines sensors, gateways, and cloud platforms to enhance fall detection.

The fall detection approach we propose consists of four primary stages: human detection, tracking, skeleton extraction, action recognition, and post-processing. We've opted for the YOLO v3-tiny model for object detection, complemented by the DeepSORT algorithm for tracking purposes. Action recognition is handled using the Spatial-Temporal Graph Convolutional Network (STGCN).

Fig. 2. Illustration of a detected fall within real-time video footage using our proposed algorithm.

Following this, there's a post-processing phase designed to refine results, differentiating actual falls from other similar activities based on the duration (Fig. 2).

For our research, we have employed multiple public datasets including the Fall Detection Dataset (FDD) and the UR Fall Detection Dataset (URFD).

We evaluate the performance of our algorithm using standard metrics such as accuracy, precision, and recall. A side-by-side comparison with other existing fall detection systems further underscores the superior efficacy of our system.

Our visual object-based fall detection algorithm has demonstrated promising results across diverse scenarios, indicating its potential for deployment in healthcare settings. The inclusion of the CFD dataset provides an impetus to further research in this domain. Additionally, once the optical sensor devices detect a fall using AI, they trigger an alarm and send a notification to caregivers or centralized personnel responsible for validating whether it's a genuine hazardous fall or not.

3.4   Storing and Processing Server

Perched in the cloud, this critical server shoulders the responsibilities of data storage, swift analytics, and emergency alert management. It exemplifies the transformative prowess of IoT in healthcare, emphasizing the synergy between wearables and the intelligence gleaned from passive environmental sensors.

IoT systems connect a large number of physical objects and generate a huge data that needs efficient storage [1]. In IoT-based healthcare systems, the collected data from sensing layer are stored for further analysis. Many cloud platforms are available for data storage from IoT such as ThingWorx, OpenIoT, Google Cloud, Amazon, GENI [1]. Cloud Servers and Physical Servers in storing layer have three functions including storing data, computing data and analyzing data. These functions are performed based on cloud computing technology to extract valuable knowledge and trends [1]. With the emergence of cloud computing technologies, the burden of managing and maintaining the massive and complex medical data is shifted to the cloud, hence the efficiency and effectiveness of the health data storage and management is improved remarkably. Simultaneously, ubiquitous healthcare has been promoted by using cloud computing as a medium for e-health service delivery [34]. For example, medical professionals and patients are allowed to review the health data remotely.

Processing server consists of processing units and software applications that apply computational part of the application [19]. Processing units may be smart phones, microcontrollers, microprocessors, hardware platforms, System On Chip (SOC), Field Programmable Gate Array (FPGA). Hardware platforms such as Arduino, Phidgets, Intel Galileo, Raspberry Pi, Gadgeteer, BeagleBone, Cubieboard as well as operating systems such as Contiki, TinyOS, LiteOS, Android, and iOS have been developed recently for running IoT applications [1]. The collected data is processed for further analysis, decision making, generating notifications and alerts.

3.5   Client Interface

Designed for patients, caregivers and medical practitioners, this interface permits live monitoring. It acts as a vigilant guardian, priming caregivers to initiate rapid response strategies when emergencies surface.

The web part of the application plays a crucial role in facilitating communication between processing server and sensor nodes. It acts as a central hub where data from the sensor nodes is collected and processed, ensuring seamless information flow. When a fall is detected, it generates alert and sends to caregivers or medical practitioners. Additionally, web part for health monitoring applications may serve as a platform for the interested parties to access and analyze the statistical reports derived from the data. These reports provide valuable insights and help in making informed decisions. The web part's ability to handle data exchange and generate comprehensive reports makes it an integral component of the app, contributing to its overall effectiveness and usability.

The mobile application module for health monitoring can be designed to provide users with seamless access to their health records stored on a cloud server. By fetching the data from the cloud, the application ensures that users can view their health records anytime and anywhere. To enhance the user experience, the module offers different registration options for new users. Patients, guardians, and doctors can sign up and create their accounts according to their respective roles. Once registered, users can log in securely to the application and gain access to a patient's comprehensive health records. This application goes beyond just displaying real-time health records; it also allows users to access previous health records. This feature enables doctors and patients to track progress, monitor trends, and make informed decisions based on historical data. By providing a user-friendly interface and secure access to health records, this mobile application module aims to empower individuals to take control of their health and facilitate effective communication between healthcare providers and patients.

4   Preserving Privacy

Privacy is a major concern in IoT due to the lack of user control over shared data. It is crucial for IoT solutions to ensure the protection of personal data. Data breaches can lead to economic losses and pose threats to personal, medical, and national security. These concerns impact IoT in areas like privacy regulations and data management protocols [26].

Maintaining privacy in eldercare is of utmost importance, echoing the non-negotiable tenet of privacy in eldercare:

1. The system transmutes raw visual data into de-identified skeletal graphics, thereby obfuscating personal data.
2. To further bolster privacy, an encryption framework built on a public-private key architecture is integrated. This mechanism ensures that raw visuals remain shielded, accessible only to personnel armed with the requisite decryption key. The nuances of this visual encryption method, and how it dovetails with the skeletal evaluation by the centralized team, are meticulously covered in this section.

In summation, this system manifests as a beacon at the intersection of avant-garde technological prowess and the deep-seated ethos of compassionate elderly care. It heralds a vista where the elderly can cherish their independence, comforted by the unwavering sentinel of monitored security.

4.1   Preserving Privacy Through Skeleton-Based Visual Processing

In the age of advancing digital technology and the ubiquity of surveillance mechanisms, privacy preservation has emerged as a central concern. In the domain of fall detection, the balance between efficient monitoring and safeguarding individual privacy becomes paramount. In this section, we discuss how our approach, leveraging skeleton-based visual processing, strives to maintain this delicate balance. We outline our methodology that ensures efficient fall detection while minimizing privacy intrusions. The following segments detail the techniques employed, their rationale, and their implications on privacy.

Human skeleton extraction is implemented using the AlphaPose network. The skeleton data, representing positions of human body joints, offer crucial information for action recognition. They capture joint movement trajectories vital for assessing human movements. AlphaPose performs exceptionally in human skeleton estimation, identifying a set of 18 key points on the human body, like the nose, shoulders, and neck. Four points-those related to the left and right eyes and ears-are discarded as the primary focus of the algorithm is fall detection, not facial recognition.

AlphaPose Network Overview: AlphaPose is a top-tier network, specifically crafted for human pose estimation. Its high accuracy across various benchmarks makes it apt for our research endeavors.

Key Joint Points and Their Significance: The set of 18 pivotal points pinpointed by the AlphaPose network are essential in action recognition, especially concerning our emphasis on fall detection. This section explores these points' anatomy and their significance.

Pruning Facial Points: We refine the set of points by excluding those that describe facial features. The reasoning behind this choice is discussed here, highlighting the equilibrium between preserving information and maintaining privacy.

(a) Fall detected locally   (b) Skeleton figure posted to reviewers

Fig. 3. Fall detected and skeleton posted to reviewers.

As seen in Fig. 3, the methodology effectively detects a fall and subsequently posts the skeleton to reviewers. The meteoric rise in internet technology, alongside potential benefits in machine learning and big data, brings forth privacy challenges. Sending raw footage for fall detection might infringe on individual privacy. Our solution suggests transmitting only the detected human skeleton or pose. This approach offers multiple advantages: safeguarding individual identity by moving away from recognizable features, reduced data footprint aiding efficient transmission and processing, aligning with strict global privacy standards, enhancing public and stakeholder approval, ensuring seamless integration and analytics focus, and a pinpointed emphasis on fall-related movement patterns. This strategy goes beyond a technical shift-it embodies a profound commitment to user privacy, setting new ethical boundaries for AI applications. We aim to foster trust, ensuring that fall detection progress remains both potent and privacy-centric, creating a model for future ethical and efficient advancements in this arena.

4.2 Reversible Visual Data-Hiding Scheme for Digital Media

To craft a fully functional system, crucial services comprise data cabling, home fiber optimization, and camera setup. Video data typically resides in local recorders for legal substantiation, and transferring it to the cloud can pose privacy risks. Our method retains visual content even after lossy compression and online transmission, ensuring secure transfers across various platforms like Dropbox, YouTube, Vimeo, and others.

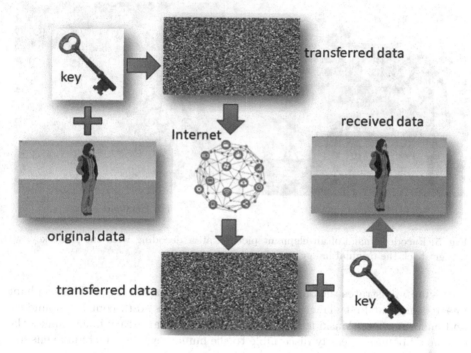

Fig. 4. Diagram of our proposed system with encryption and decryption of videos

Referring to Fig. 4, the system design emphasizes privacy and efficiency. Given YouTube's immense upload frequency, there arises a need to find a balance between compression speed and quality. Our method camouflages visual data, ensuring it remains undetected by filters. Steganography, often preferred over cryptography, effectively conceals messages. Focusing on steganography for images and videos, we evaluate storage and transmission techniques using diverse compressions, including JPEG, and codecs like H.264/MPEG-4.

Encoding of the Circular Pattern with Keys. Drawing inspiration from water wave patterns and based on the formula referenced in Eq. 1, we propose an encoding process to generate a circular pattern from any image. For each pixel, its encoded form is determined by:

$$I'(i,j) = k_1 \times ((k_2 \times i - k_3)^2 + (k_4 \times j - k_5)^2) - I(i,j) \qquad (1)$$

Here, $I(i,j)$ denotes a pixel of the original image, $I'(i,j)$ is its encrypted counterpart, and the set of keys $k_{1..5}$ serve as the encryption and decryption mechanism. Assuming each key is a three-digit number, the correct decryption requires a sequence of $3 \times 5 = 15$ correct digits. The brute force probability for such a setup is a near-impossible $1/10^{15}$.

(a) Original image   (b) Encoded image

Fig. 5. Encoded image of an elephant picture, after decoding with the same key, we will get back the original image

Figure 5 illustrates the output of our encoding using the Eq. 1. This elephant image, simple at first glance, is challenging due to its stark contrast boundary and uniform colors. Masking this image with another arbitrary image makes the elephant's boundary easily discernible to the human eye. Our technique ensures complete obfuscation.

Decoding of the Circular Pattern with Keys. The decoding process is designed to be straightforward. Each pixel is decoded using:

$$I(i,j) = k_1 \times ((k_2 \times i - k_3)^2 + (k_4 \times j - k_5)^2) - I'(i,j) \qquad (2)$$

Rather than employing XOR, our approach harnesses a simple subtraction function using unsigned 8-bit integers. Thanks to Binary Overflow [4], the properties of the unsigned integer ensure that the encoded output is always valid for display.

We further delve into the intricacies of image compression, examining the effects of different compression levels on the decrypted image. Results showcasing the accuracy of our method across various JPEG compression scales are presented. Upon rigorous testing, our system demonstrates its capability to maintain the majority of image quality, proving its suitability for further image processing.

Performance metrics were recorded on a standard machine equipped with Python 3.4. The images used for testing were resized to four distinct dimensions, with results cataloged accordingly.

A significant challenge arises when reviewers need to frequently revisit and verify videos-consisting solely of skeletons-for accuracy. Using a free third-party video storage server like YouTube can minimize costs. However, posting on such a public platform means that anyone can access these videos. To address this privacy concern, we propose encoding the video prior to posting it on a public repository, ensuring that only authorized individuals can decode and view the content. In summary, our reversible visual data-hiding scheme for RGB images or videos ensures that encrypted media, appearing as random noise, remains indistinguishable to the general public but can be stored and transferred securely across platforms.

5 Conclusion

Over the course of this work, we've delved deep into the challenges and solutions surrounding the pressing issue of fall detection, particularly for the vulnerable elderly demographic. In doing so, we've presented an integrated system that combines the potency of both wearable and non-wearable technologies, augmented by the unprecedented capabilities of IoT and deep learning.

Our exploration began with the criticality of recording sensors, which provided continuous monitoring, albeit with associated challenges. We then transitioned into the realm of data storage and processing, emphasizing the immense capabilities of cloud-based solutions. Further, our client-interface brought to light the significance of real-time surveillance and swift intervention during emergencies.

Technologically, our dive into deep learning and various fall detection techniques highlighted not only the current state-of-the-art but also the immense potential lying ahead. Additionally, the challenge of data privacy, a significant concern in today's age of information, was addressed head-on with our novel solution of transmitting skeletal data, eschewing conventional footage. This approach ensures a blend of efficiency and ethical responsibility.

We also cast light upon the idea of reversible visual data-hiding schemes, emphasizing their potential for secure data transfer across popular platforms without compromising on the richness of the data. The introduction of steganography, particularly inspired by natural patterns, showcased a novel approach to image encryption. Our experimental results and evaluations attest to the viability and efficiency of our proposed methods.

In wrapping up, this work has not just been about the integration of technology but more so about redefining the contours of care, safety, and ethical responsibility in the age of AI and IoT. Through the system we propose, we envision a world where the elderly aren't just watched over but are cared for, where technology doesn't intrude but serves, and where innovation doesn't compromise but upholds privacy. As we tread forward, it is our hope that this research serves as a beacon, guiding further endeavors at the intersection of technology, ethics, and care.

References

1. Al-Fuqaha, A., Guizani, M., Mohammadi, M., Aledhari, M., Ayyash, M.: Internet of things: a survey on enabling technologies, protocols, and applications. IEEE Commun. Surv. Tutor. **17**(4), 2347–2376 (2015)
2. Azimi, I., Rahmani, A.M., Liljeberg, P., Tenhunen, H.: Internet of things for remote elderly monitoring: a study from user-centered perspective. J. Ambient Intell. Humaniz. Comput. 1–17 (2016)
3. Baig, M.M., GholamHosseini, H.: A remote monitoring system with early diagnosis of hypertension and hypotension. In: 2013 IEEE Point-of-Care Healthcare Technologies (PHT), pp. 34–37. IEEE (2013)
4. Brown, B.: Binary arithmetic. Computer science department Southern Polytechnic State University, pp. 1–9 (1999). http://www.spsu.edu/cs/faculty/bbrown/papers/arithmetic.pdf
5. Centers for Medicare & Medicaid Services: Nhe-fact-sheet 2015 (2015). https://www.cms.gov/research-statistics-data-and-systems/statistics-trends-and-reports/nationalhealthexpenddata/nhe-fact-sheet.html
6. Cheng, Y., Jiang, C., Shi, J.: A fall detection system based on sensortag and windows 10 IoT core (2015)
7. Chuang, J., et al.: Silverlink: smart home health monitoring for senior care. In: Zheng, X., Zeng, D., Chen, H., Leischow, S. (eds.) ICSH 2015. LNCS, vol. 9545, pp. 3–14. Springer, Cham (2015). https://doi.org/10.1007/978-3-319-29175-8_1
8. Dhande, M.: What is the difference between AI, machine learning and deep learning? Geospatial World (2017)
9. Fang, R., Pouyanfar, S., Yang, Y., Chen, S.C., Iyengar, S.: Computational health informatics in the big data age: a survey. ACM Comput. Surv. (CSUR) **49**(1), 12 (2016)
10. Fanucci, L., et al.: Sensing devices and sensor signal processing for remote monitoring of vital signs in CHF patients. IEEE Trans. Instrum. Meas. **62**(3), 553–569 (2013)
11. Harper, S.: Ageing societies: Myths. Challenges and Opportunities, p. 116 (2006)
12. He, K., Zhang, X., Ren, S., Sun, J.: Deep residual learning for image recognition. In: Proceedings of the IEEE Conference on Computer Vision and Pattern Recognition, pp. 770–778 (2016)
13. Huynh, Q.T., Nguyen, U.D., Irazabal, L.B., Ghassemian, N., Tran, B.Q.: Optimization of an accelerometer and gyroscope-based fall detection algorithm. J. Sens. **2015** (2015)
14. Igual, R., Medrano, C., Plaza, I.: Challenges, issues and trends in fall detection systems. Biomed. Eng. Online **12**(1), 66 (2013)
15. Jeon, B., Lee, J., Choi, J.: Design and implementation of a wearable ECG system. Int. J. Smart Home **7**(2), 61–69 (2013)
16. Jimenez, F., Torres, R.: Building an IoT-aware healthcare monitoring system. In: 2015 34th International Conference of the Chilean Computer Science Society (SCCC), pp. 1–4. IEEE (2015)
17. Karthikeyan, S., Devi, K.V., Valarmathi, K.: Internet of things: hospice appliances monitoring and control system. In: 2015 Online International Conference on Green Engineering and Technologies (IC-GET), pp. 1–6. IEEE (2015)
18. Li, Q., Stankovic, J.A., Hanson, M.A., Barth, A.T., Lach, J., Zhou, G.: Accurate, fast fall detection using gyroscopes and accelerometer-derived posture information. In: Sixth International Workshop on Wearable and Implantable Body Sensor Networks, BSN 2009, pp. 138–143. IEEE (2009)

19. Li, S., Da Xu, L., Zhao, S.: The internet of things: a survey. Inf. Syst. Front. **17**(2), 243–259 (2015)
20. Ministry of Health: New Zealand health strategy: Future direction (2016). http://www.health.govt.nz/publication/new-zealand-health-strategy-2016
21. Moser, D.K., Dickson, V., Jaarsma, T., Lee, C., Stromberg, A., Riegel, B.: Role of self-care in the patient with heart failure. Curr. Cardiol. Rep. **14**(3), 265–275 (2012)
22. Nguyen, H., Mirza, F., Naeem, M.A., Baig, M.M.: Detecting falls using a wearable accelerometer motion sensor. In: Proceedings of the 14th EAI International Conference on Mobile and Ubiquitous Systems: Computing, Networking and Services, pp. 422–431 (2017)
23. Nguyen, H.H., Mirza, F., Naeem, M.A., Nguyen, M.: A review on IoT healthcare monitoring applications and a vision for transforming sensor data into real-time clinical feedback. In: 2017 IEEE 21st International Conference on Computer Supported Cooperative Work in Design (CSCWD), pp. 257–262. IEEE (2017)
24. Özdemir, A.T.: An analysis on sensor locations of the human body for wearable fall detection devices: principles and practice. Sensors **16**(8), 1161 (2016)
25. Parida, M., Yang, H.C., Jheng, S.W., Kuo, C.J.: Application of RFID technology for in-house drug management system. In: 2012 15th International Conference on Network-Based Information Systems (NBiS), pp. 577–581. IEEE (2012)
26. Rodríguez, E., Otero, B., Canal, R.: A survey of machine and deep learning methods for privacy protection in the internet of things. Sensors **23**(3), 1252 (2023)
27. Shorten, C., Khoshgoftaar, T.M.: A survey on image data augmentation for deep learning. J. Big Data **6**(1), 60 (2019)
28. Simonyan, K., Zisserman, A.: Very deep convolutional networks for large-scale image recognition. In: International Conference on Learning Representations (2015)
29. Tan, M., Le, Q.V.: Efficientnet: rethinking model scaling for convolutional neural networks. In: Proceedings of the 36th International Conference on Machine Learning, pp. 6105–6114 (2019)
30. Thom, T., et al.: Heart disease and stroke statistics-2006 update: a report from the American heart association statistics committee and stroke statistics subcommittee. Circulation **113**(6), e85 (2006)
31. Ungar, A., et al.: Fall prevention in the elderly. Clin. Cases Miner. Bone Metab. **10**(2), 91 (2013)
32. United Nation, Department of Economic and Social Affairs, Population Division: World population ageing 2015 (2015). http://www.un.org/en/development/desa/population/.../pdf/ageing/WPA2015_Report.pdf
33. Vishwanath, S., Vaidya, K., Nawal, R., Kumar, A., Parthasarathy, S., Verma, S.: Touching lives through mobile health: assessment of the global market opportunity. Price water house Coopers (2012)
34. Yang, J.J., et al.: Emerging information technologies for enhanced healthcare. Comput. Ind. **69**, 3–11 (2015)
35. Zanjal, S.V., Talmale, G.R.: Medicine reminder and monitoring system for secure health using IoT. Procedia Comput. Sci. **78**, 471–476 (2016)

On Deploying Mobile Deep Learning to Segment COVID-19 PCR Test Tube Images

Ting Xiang[1(✉)], Richard Dean[2], Jiawei Zhao[2], and Ninh Pham[1]

[1] University of Auckland, Auckland, New Zealand
txia202@aucklanduni.ac.nz, ninh.pham@auckland.ac.nz
[2] Institute of Environmental Science and Research Limited (ESR),
Auckland, New Zealand
{Richard.Dean,Jiawei.Zhao}@esr.cri.nz

Abstract. Effective detection of the COVID-19 pandemic is essential for timely disease treatment and prevention. This work studies compact deep-learning models executed on mobile devices for segmenting COVID-19 RT-PCR test tube images, a crucial image-processing step preceding higher-level tasks. Since the device resource constraints and the need for rapid results necessitate compact and streamlined models with reasonable accuracy, we employ the hyperparameter width multiplier α to the trainable components in the two deep learning models based on the U-Net architecture, including MobileNetV2 and Xception. Our new compact models, called α-MobileNetV2 and α-Xception, facilitate the progressive simplification of the U-Net model structures, maintaining high accuracy. By varying the width multiplier α, we explore diverse training conditions for the models, analyzing the model size and its performance. The final model achieves a $3.2\times$ reduction in size and $3\times$ faster inference, with merely a 1.2% loss in accuracy compared to standard MobileNetV2 on segmenting COVID-19 PCR test tube images.

Keywords: U-Net · Image Segmentation · Xception · MobiletNetV2

1 Introduction

The COVID-19 pandemic poses an immense global challenge. Its high transmission rate results in a surge in cases that significantly burden healthcare systems, exacerbated by the prolonged duration required for accurate testing. Two standard methods to conduct COVID-19 tests are Rapid Antigen Tests (RAT) and Reverse Transcription Polymerase Chain Reaction Tests (PCR). RAT provides quicker results within minutes but is generally less sensitive than PCR, resulting in a higher potential for false negatives. PCR is a more sensitive and specific method widely employed for COVID-19 testing; however, its requirements for laboratory processing lead to a turnaround time ranging from a few hours to several days.

Our research team participated in the PCR testing process. Typically, a swab is collected by testing centers or general practitioners and sent to a diagnostic

W. Q. Yan et al. (Eds.): PSIVT 2023, LNCS 14403, pp. 394–407, 2024.
https://doi.org/10.1007/978-981-97-0376-0_30

laboratory for processing. Positive results are conveyed to central surveillance databases, and the samples are forwarded to our team for further analysis. Participating in this process has led our team to recognize the considerable time delay inherent in this complex procedure. Although large-scale diagnostic laboratories have made achievements in automation, transporting tests to these centralized facilities introduces additional logistical challenges and hampers the overall testing process. The reliance on manual labor in handling the large testing workload limits the advantages gained from employing machine-based analytics for laboratory processes.

Recent work [7] proposed to develop a point-of-use diagnostic testing process and support mobile applications to facilitate decision-making. In particular, the tube samples are screened by a custom-built app that uses the smartphone's camera to measure a chemical reaction and determine the test outcome. The approach aims to capture images of the test and assist in result analysis, enhancing detection speed, reducing costs, addressing existing inequalities, and empowering communities to take charge of their health and environmental resources.

Following the recent diagnostic vision process, we employ deep-learning approaches to analyze collected tube sample images to facilitate virus detection. We found that segmenting tube images is a crucial image-processing step preceding higher-level tasks, especially when deploying the approach on the mobile platform. We conducted initial experiments using laboratory-captured images of COVID-19 test tubes. We first utilize recent advanced deep learning models for medical image segmentation [10], including MobileNetV2 [22] and U-Net [21]. Then, we convert the trained model into TensorFlow.js [2] format and integrate it into a web application. While the U-Net architecture and the pre-trained weights of MobileNetV2 guaranteed accurate segmentation results in practical experiments, the model significantly consumed memory resources, resulting in prolonged loading and execution times. In some instances, excessive resource usage caused the model to become unresponsive. This finding motivates us to study image segmentation models with suitable models capable of producing satisfying segmentation results, deployable and executable on mobile devices.

This paper introduces a novel approach that applies a hyperparameter width multiplier $\alpha \leq 1$ introduced in MobiletNet [9] to the two deep learning models based on the U-Net architecture, yielding two new compact models. On the first U-Net-based MobileNetV2 architecture, we leverage recent MobileNetV2 in *transfer learning* as the encoder backbone. The width multiplier is selectively integrated into the trainable decoder part. This strategy progressively simplifies the model's structure while maintaining high accuracy. On the second U-Net-based Xception architecture that leverages the Xception [4] model as its backbone to support *training from scratch*, we adapt the width multiplier to adjust the filter numbers in each convolutional layer. Using a width multiplier gives rise to a diverse range of models with significant adjustments in complexity and size. Throughout the experiments, we explore several training configurations for both sets of models, dissecting the size alterations, accuracy, and computational efficiency. The final model achieves a 3.2× reduction in size and 3× faster inference, with merely a 1.2% loss in accuracy compared to standard MobileNetV2 on segmenting COVID-19 RT-PCR test tube images.

2 Related Work

Since segmenting PCR test tube images is a crucial image-processing step preceding higher-level tasks, we survey recent advanced deep-learning methods for image segmentation.

Image segmentation identifies and classifies objects in images by generating masks for corresponding areas [16,18]. It helps process images before higher-level functions like Object-Based Image Analysis [8,23], facilitating more accessible analysis and interpretation. Image segmentation [16,18] can be classified into two categories, including (1) instance segmentation [24], which identifies individual objects as separate targets, and (2) semantic segmentation [19], which classifies objects with class labels. The first category implements image segmentation based on lower-level image information, which can be classified as pixel-based, contour-based, and region-based segmentation [16]. Recently, neural network-based image segmentation in the second category has gained prominence, leveraging labeled images to improve accuracy and performance [12].

Convolutional Neural Networks (CNN) differ from other neural networks by applying convolutional operations. This feature enables it to perform well in many applications, especially in the field of image processing, such as image classification and image restoration [13,20]. U-Net [21] produces precise segmentation results with few annotated samples as training images. It utilizes a U-shaped encoder-decoder structure involving skip connections. The skip connection concatenates the output feature map produced by each convolutional block in the encoder part with the corresponding convolutional block in the decoder part. It keeps some of the information before the max pooling operations. Based on the U-Net architecture, using different CNN models [5,11,25] as the backbone can lead to different styles of the U-Net models.

MobileNet [9] uses depthwise separable convolutions, enabling a lighter model weight, decreased complexity, and computational cost. Andrew et al. [9] also proposed two hyperparameters, width multiplier and resolution multiplier. To thin the network, a width multiplier performs on each layer to change the number of input channels from M to αM and the output channels from N to αN. Its computational cost is reduced according to the adjustment of α. The width multiplier was applied to create a thinner model that requires to be trained from scratch. According to the summary of experiments with these two hyperparameters, it was claimed that MobileNet architecture with the width multiplier can reduce the computational operations and model sizes with a smooth decrease in accuracy until the value of width multiplier $\alpha = 0.25$.

ResNet [6] introduces residual blocks to CNN architectures, inserting shortcut connections to the network. The Xception model is based on depthwise separable convolutions and inserts residual connections to its linear stack architecture of depthwise separable convolutions. It is easy to combine with U-Net to provide a model architecture to be trained from scratch.

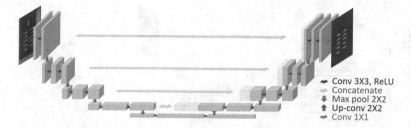

Fig. 1. U-Net architecture consists of the encoder, decoder, and concatenation operation between each level.

Computer vision models trained with large datasets are refined [9,14,15]. However, on some specific occasions, the dataset suffers low quality with incorrect labels, especially for medical images [26]. This raises the need to transfer existing models trained for one scenario to another new scenario. Transfer learning aims to utilize models trained with large image datasets to build new models aiming for a new task.

Deep learning-based mobile applications have become more common in recent years, enabled by advancements in neural networks and mobile device hardware [1,3]. Deployment methods for deep learning-based mobile apps include cloud services and model conversion [2,17] for integration into mobile platforms like Core ML for iOS and TensorFlow-Lite for Android. Open Neural Network Exchange (.ONNX) supports trained models to be converted to serialized versions and stored in compressed files. TensorFlow.js supports deep learning models to be converted and integrated into web applications run in browsers [2].

3 Methodology

This work studies the U-Net architecture shown in Fig. 1 to segment the tube images collected from the PRC test samples. We apply the width multiplier method on investigated U-Net-based models to reduce the model size and enable mobile deployment. We first present a baseline model that uses *transfer learning* with MobileNetV2 as the encoder of the U-Net. Then, we apply the width multiplier $\alpha \leq 1$ to thin the decoder component of the baseline model. Though this thinner MobileNetV2-based model, named α-MobileNetV2, achieves high accuracy, it still demands a relatively large memory to deploy on mobile devices. To provide a smaller model architecture that allows *training from scratch*, we propose to apply the width multiplier α on each convolution layer of the U-Net Xception-Style model. The new compact Xception-based model, named α-Xception, preserves a reasonable accuracy but uses $4\times$ less memory than the compact α-MobileNetV2.

3.1 U-Net Baseline Model

We use U-Net [21] architecture and transfer learning with MobileNetV2 [22] as the encoder as shown in Fig. 2(a). U-Net provides an efficient U-shape CNN

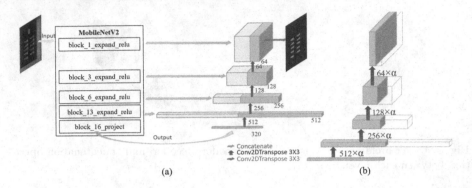

Fig. 2. (a) The baseline U-Net MobileNetV2. (b) The new α-MobileNetV2 applies width multiplier α to the decoder part in the architecture.

architecture that contains skip connections between the encoder and decoder parts to keep some lost information through the operations of layers. It supports using different models as the backbone of the architecture.

Since MobileNetV2 decreases the model's complexity and computational cost by using separable convolutions, we propose to use MobileNetV2 as the encoder in the U-Net architecture with transfer learning to have pre-trained weights suitable for vision tasks on mobile devices.

For each upsampling step, a specific number of 3×3 transposed convolution layer is applied to halve the number of feature channels; here, each is 512, 256, 128, and 64, and a concatenation operation is applied to concatenate the output with the extracted feature map of corresponding layers in the MobileNetV2. Finally, depending on the desired output channels, a corresponding number of 3×3 transposed convolution layers are applied to generate the results. These used corresponding layers in MobileNetV2 are 'block 1 expand relu', 'block 3 expand relu', 'block 6 expand relu', 'block 13 expand relu', and 'block 16 project'.

3.2 α-MobileNetV2

To progressively streamline the model while upholding a high accuracy, we combine the usage of width multiplier with transfer learning. Like the baseline model, we utilize specific layers from the pre-trained MobileNetV2 to form the encoder part in the U-Net architecture and apply a width multiplier $\alpha \leq 1$ to each trainable convolution layer in the decoder part. The filter numbers in the four convolution layers of the decoder part are adjusted from [512, 256, 128, 64] to $[512 \times \alpha, 256 \times \alpha, 128 \times \alpha, 64 \times \alpha]$, as shown in Fig. 2(b).

The width multiplier adjusts the model's trainable parameters and total parameter numbers. Table 1 summarises the models' total and trainable parameter number adjustments with various values of the width multiplier. As we decrease the width multiplier by half from its original value, we observe a gradual deceleration in the reduction of parameters. This trend happens because the

Table 1. The numbers of total and trainable parameters (M) in α-MobileNetV2 and α-Xception models.

Model	α	Total params	Trainable params
α-MobileNetV2	1	6.504	4.660
	1/2	3.787	1.944
	1/4	2.719	0.877
	1/8	2.258	0.415
	1/16	2.045	0.203
	1/32	1.943	0.101
α-Xception	1	2.059	2.055
	1/2	0.521	0.519

MobileNetV2 for the encoder part is locked and not applied with the width multiplier. Moreover, when combined with the reduction in the number of trainable parameters, it is observed that the number is reduced by approximately half of their original value in parallel with the change of the width multiplier.

3.3 α-Xception

To create a smaller model architecture that allows training from scratch, we use U-Net with the Xception model as the backbone to have a U-Net Xception style model [5]. The model architecture uses residual blocks in both the encoder and decoder parts to replace the concatenation operations in the original U-Net architecture to implement the skip connections between information in early and deeper layers. We apply the width multiplier α to each convolution layer, adjusting the filter numbers from D_{filter} to $D_{filter} \times \alpha$, as shown in Fig. 3. We name it as α-Xception.

In the encoder part, each downsampling step is implemented by a downsampling residual block. The residual block contains two groups of operations, each with one ReLU operation followed by a 3×3 depthwise separable convolution. After the two groups of operations, it conducts a 3×3 max pooling layer with

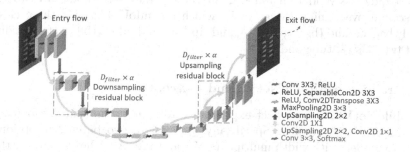

Fig. 3. α-Xception model based on the U-Net architecture.

2×2 strides. The residual connection is implemented by applying a 1×1 convolution operation to the output before the operations of the convolution groups and max pooling, and adding the values to the output of the max pooling layer.

In the decoder part, each upsampling step is correspondingly implemented by an upsampling residual block. Similarly, the upsampling residual block comprises two groups of operations, while in each group, it uses a ReLU followed by a 3×3 transpose convolution. A 2×2 upsampling layer follows after these two convolution groups, and the residual connection here experiences a 2×2 upsampling layer and a 1×1 convolution. Compared with the original U-Net architecture, the Xception style has a different entry and exit flow besides the difference in using residual blocks. The entry flow uses 3×3 convolution filters followed by a ReLU. The exit flow uses 3×3 convolution filters with SoftMax as the activation function.

Table 1 reveals that the numbers of trainable and total parameters of new α-Xception are very close. Each time the width multiplier changes to half of its original value, the total number of parameters in this architecture becomes almost one-quarter of its original number.

4 Experiment

4.1 Dataset and Experiment Settings

Our research partner collects the dataset by taking photos of the test tubes under suitable angles and light conditions. Manual annotation with Label Studio provided boundary boxes or the target regions and corresponding labels ("Tube" for tube bodies and "Tip" for tip regions). The annotations are exported in COCO format and read in to conduct pre-processing. OpenCV is applied to approximate target region contours, merge elliptical boundaries derived from key points, and generate final target masks. The resulting individual tube and tip masks were reassembled to create complete masks for each image. The dataset comprises 628 images, 504 single tube images, and 124 multiple tube images, split into 80% training and 20% test sets. When performing k-fold cross-validation, the data is divided into 64% training, 16% validation, and 20% test sets (Fig. 4).

Training Settings. To explore appropriate training settings for models, we apply 5-fold cross-validation and evaluate the accuracy performance by two Mean Intersection over Union (Mean-IoU), which are mIoU(+bg) for three classes, namely background (bg), tube (tb), and tip (tp), and mIoU(tb+tp) for a reduced set of two classes, tube and tip.

4.2 Training α-MobileNetV2 and α-Xception

α-MobileNetV2. We conduct experiments to identify the suitable batch size for α-MobileNetV2 models. Specifically, we explore two batch size options, 8 and 2, to models with width multipliers of 1 and 1/2. All other training settings remain consistent throughout the experiments, with Cross-Entropy as the loss function, Adam as the optimizer, and 50 epochs for training. Table 2 summarises

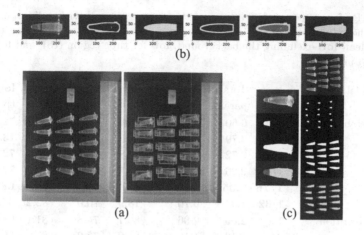

Fig. 4. Dataset sample: (a) The original and annotated images. (b) The process to generate the mask for an individual tube. (c) Original and mask images of a complete image and an individual tube in it.

Table 2. Cross validation results of α-MobileNetV2 performing on 5 folds with two metrics, Mean-IoU (mIoU(+bg)) including the background and Mean-IoU (mIoU(tb+tp)) excluding the background.

Width multiplier	Batch size	mIoU(+bg), %	mIoU(tb+tp), %
1	8	77.2 (75.8 – 80.4)	67.5 (65.6 – 71.9)
	2	81.3 (80.5 – 82.5)	73.1 (71.9 – 74.9)
1/2	2	81.0 (79.7 – 81.9)	72.7 (70.9 – 74.1)
	8	78.2 (77.6 – 78.6)	68.7 (67.9 – 69.1)

Table 3. Cross validation results of α-Xception with and without learning rate (lr) reduction performing on 5 folds with two metrics, Mean-IoU (mIoU(+bg)) including the background and Mean-IoU (mIoU(tb+tp)) excluding the background.

α	Batch size	lr reduction	mIoU(+bg), %	mIoU(tb+tp), %
1	2	Yes	**77.1 (75.0 – 78.5)**	**67.2 (64.1 – 69.2)**
		No	77.1 (74.3 – 78.6)	67.1 (63.3 – 69.3)
	8	Yes	74.2 (71.7 – 77.9)	63.1 (59.5 – 68.2)
		No	74.6 (72.6 – 76.1)	63.7 (60.8 – 65.9)
1/2	2	Yes	**78.3 (76.5 – 79.7)**	**68.9 (66.4 – 70.9)**
		No	77.1 (74.2 – 78.9)	67.2 (63.3 – 69.8)
	8	No	72.6 (70.8 – 74.5)	61.0 (58.3 – 63.5)
		Yes	71.5 (69.5 – 73.6)	59.3 (56.4 – 62.2)

the performance results, showing mean, minimum, and maximum values of the metrics obtained from 5-fold validation. The first row represents the baseline model's performance. We observe that a batch size of 2 yields more favorable results for α-MobileNetV2 with and without the background.

Table 4. Performance on the test set of the models trained with validation set. We measure the total and trainable parameters in millions, Mean-IoU including the background, Mean-IoU excluding the background, IoU for tube region (tb), and IoU for tip region (tp) in %.

Model	α	Total params	Trainable params	mIoU (+bg)	mIoU (tb+tp)	IoU tb	IoU tp
α-MobileNetV2	1	6.50	4.66	85.0	78.8	85.2	72.4
	1/2	3.79	1.94	85.3	79.3	85.6	73.1
	1/4	2.72	0.88	84.8	78.6	85.1	72.0
	1/8	2.26	0.42	84.7	78.5	83.7	73.3
	1/16	**2.05**	**0.20**	**83.2**	**76.3**	**83.8**	**68.7**
	1/32	1.94	0.10	78.9	70.0	82.2	57.6
α-Xception	1	2.06	2.06	82.1	74.8	81.1	68.6
	3/4	1.16	1.16	81.0	73.2	80.3	66.2
	1/2	0.52	0.52	80.8	72.9	80.1	65.7
	1/4	**0.13**	**0.13**	**79.4**	**71.0**	**77.9**	**64.1**

α-Xception. We explore α-Xception's hyperparameters: batch size and learning rate. Regarding the batch size, we investigate two options, 8 and 2, while also exploring the impact of applying a reduced learning rate. The reduced learning rate follows a mechanism that monitors the validation loss improvement with patience of 5 epochs. If no further improvement occurs within this period, the learning rate is reduced to 0.3 of its original value. This process repeats until the learning rate reaches its minimum value, 0.00001. Table 3 summarizes the model performance for various width multiplier values, batch size settings, and learning rate configurations. Our findings indicate that both models perform optimally when using a batch size of 2 and applying a reduced learning rate.

4.3   Accuracy and Model Size

This subsection studies the effects of the width multiplier α on α-MobileNetV2 and α-Xception. During the training process, we employ two methods: (1) training the models with a validation set split from the training set, with a rate of 20%, and using the validation loss to adjust the learning rate, and (2) utilizing the whole training set and employing the training loss to adjust the learning rate. Both provide similar performance.

Table 4 summarises model performance on the test set and model size for models trained with the validation set, employing four metrics (two Mean-IoUs and two individual IoUs, each for tube and tip areas). On the other hand, models trained with the complete training set exhibit similar performance. The accuracy performance of the two compact models using the two training methods mentioned above is visualized in Fig. 5. Notably, both architectures demonstrate a smooth change in accuracy, except for the 1/32-MobileNetV2 model, which experiences a significant decrease in IoU-tp, leading to a substantial drop in two

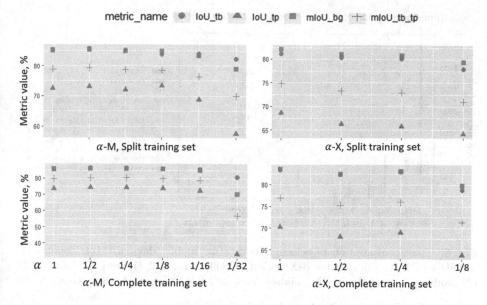

Fig. 5. Accuracy performance of two models on different training sets.

Mean-IoUs. When evaluating the IoU for the tubes, whose average target region size is larger than the tips, both α-MobileNetV2 and α-Xception models consistently maintain higher values. Models with different widths achieve IoU-tb no less than 77%.

4.4 Time Consumption

We select six models to deploy on the web application "GLO" to conduct benchmarking tests. In this application, each selected model is used to perform 294 predictions on a set of 21 images. We calculate the average time consumption of the 294 predictions to represent the time consumption for each test record. Following that, we group these test records based on model index and device type and once again calculate the average time consumption within each group. This approach allows us to assess performance more effectively for different model-device combinations.

Figure 6 illustrates a comparative analysis of the time-consuming performance of the baseline model and the six proposed models. Among the latter four models developed and released later in the project, we will conduct a detailed performance analysis on the same device. Table 5 presents the baseline model's performance in the first row, followed by the relative performance of the five models compared to the baseline. The size and duration are expressed as times shorter than the baseline model. The four accuracy metrics are presented as percentages, indicating the difference between the baseline model's performance and each specific model.

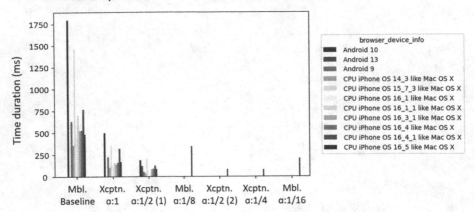

Fig. 6. Time consumption of selected models on mobile devices (Mbl. denotes α-MobileNetV2; Xcptn. denotes α-Xception). Xcptn. $\alpha : 1/2$ (1) and Xcptn.$\alpha : 1/2$ (2) models are trained with the validation set and full training set, respectively.

Table 5. Performance of selected models - The following rows are relative values to the first row. Four accuracy metrics are Mean-IoU including the background, Mean-IoU excluding the background, IoU for tube region, and IoU for tip region (%).

Model	α	Model size Improvement	Time, ms Improvement	mIoU (+bg)	mIoU (tb+tp)	IoU tb	IoU tp
α-MobileNetV2	1	6.5	478.8	85.6	79.7	85.8	73.5
	1/8	2.9×	1.4×	-0.1	-0.1	0.2	-0.3
	1/16	3.2×	1.5×	0.6	0.9	0.5	1.2
α-Xception	1	3.2×	3.0×	2.0	2.8	2.4	3.2
	1/2	12.5×	6.0×	2.6	3.7	2.9	4.5
	1/4	50.0×	6.5×	5.9	8.4	7.1	9.7

Figure 7 visualizes the model performances to observe the patterns better. Both compact models exhibit a smooth decrease in accuracy and a right-skewed reduction in time consumption as the width multiplier progressively simplifies the structure. Notably, the 1/16-MobileNetV2 model, despite having a size similar to the 1-Xception model, requires approximately twice the time consumption of 1-Xception. This observation underscores the impact of the number of operations in the model on the execution time, even when the model size and the number of parameters are comparable.

4.5   An Ablation Study on PCR Tube Images

Several representative images are selected to illustrate observable patterns in Fig. 8. The figure showcases three groups, each containing six images: the original

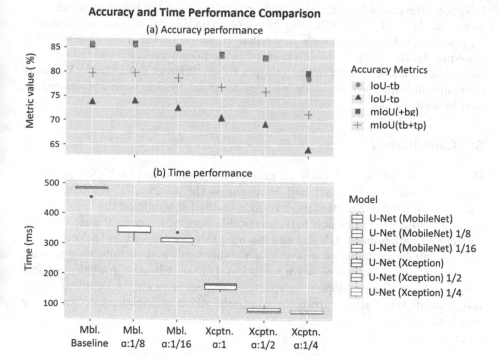

Fig. 7. Accuracy and time performance comparison. (a) Accuracy performance of the six models from Fig. 5 for comparison. (b) The range of time consumption of the six models performed on the same device.

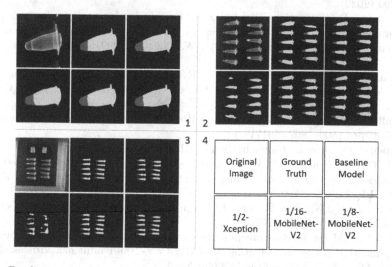

Fig. 8. Prediction image examples. The images are divided into four groups, each containing the original image, ground truth image, prediction of the baseline model, and predictions of four proposed models.

lab photo, the ground truth image, and predictions from the baseline model, 1/2-Xception, 1/16-MobileNetV2, and 1/8-MobileNetV2. All models demonstrate high accuracy for images with individual tubes, with the 1/16-MobileNetV2 revealing distinct patterns of particulates at the boundaries of predicted regions. In contrast, for images containing multiple tubes, different α-MobileNetV2 models maintain impressive accuracy, while α-Xception models have a slight reduction in accuracy.

5   Conclusion

We apply the width multiplier to progressively simplify two U-Net architectures, utilizing MobileNetV2 and Xception as the backbones, resulting in α-MobileNetV2 and α-Xception models. This method streamlined the U-Net structures for improved efficiency with acceptable accuracy. By exploring training settings encompassing batch size and learning rate, we trained and selected suitable models for mobile deployment in a web application, benchmarking metrics across size, accuracy, and time consumption. Our contribution provides a referable framework for developing compact segmentation models tailored to point-of-use diagnostic testing, advancing computer vision applications in healthcare contexts.

References

1. Anisuzzaman, D.M., Patel, Y., Niezgoda, J.A., Gopalakrishnan, S., Yu, Z.: A mobile app for wound localization using deep learning. IEEE Access **10**, 61398–61409 (2022)
2. Castanyer, R.C., Martínez-Fernández, S., Franch, X.: Integration of convolutional neural networks in mobile applications. In: 1st IEEE/ACM Workshop on AI Engineering - Software Engineering for AI, WAIN@ICSE 2021, Madrid, Spain, 30–31 May 2021, pp. 27–34 (2021)
3. Chen, Y., Yang, T., Emer, J.S., Sze, V.: Eyeriss v2: a flexible accelerator for emerging deep neural networks on mobile devices. IEEE J. Emerg. Sel. Topics Circuits Syst. **9**(2), 292–308 (2019)
4. Chollet, F.: Xception: deep learning with depthwise separable convolutions. In: CVPR, pp. 1800–1807 (2017)
5. Gutierrez-Lazcano, L., Camacho-Bello, C.J., Cornejo-Velazquez, E., Arroyo-Nunez, J.H., Clavel-Maqueda, M.: Cuscuta spp. segmentation based on unmanned aerial vehicles (UAVs) and orthomasaics using a U-net xception-style model. Remote Sens. **14**(17), 4315 (2022)
6. He, K., Zhang, X., Ren, S., Sun, J.: Deep residual learning for image recognition. In: CVPR, pp. 770–778 (2016)
7. Heithoff, D.M., et al.: Assessment of a smartphone-based loop-mediated isothermal amplification assay for detection of SARS-CoV-2 and influenza viruses. JAMA Netw. Open **5**(1), e2145669–e2145669 (2022)
8. Hossain, M.D., Chen, D.: Segmentation for object-based image analysis (OBIA): a review of algorithms and challenges from remote sensing perspective. ISPRS J. Photogramm. Remote. Sens. **150**, 115–134 (2019)

9. Howard, A.G., et al.: Mobilenets: efficient convolutional neural networks for mobile vision applications. CoRR abs/1704.04861 (2017)

10. Huang, L., Ruan, S., Denoeux, T.: Application of belief functions to medical image segmentation: a review. Inf. Fusion **91**, 737–756 (2023)

11. Ibtehaz, N., Rahman, M.S.: Multiresunet: rethinking the U-net architecture for multimodal biomedical image segmentation. Neural Netw. **121**, 74–87 (2020)

12. Khan, M.Z., Gajendran, M.K., Lee, Y., Khan, M.A.: Deep neural architectures for medical image semantic segmentation: review. IEEE Access **9**, 83002–83024 (2021)

13. Khan, S.H., Rahmani, H., Shah, S.A.A., Bennamoun, M.: A Guide to Convolutional Neural Networks for Computer Vision. Morgan & Claypool Publishers, San Rafael (2018)

14. Kirillov, A., et al.: Segment anything. CoRR abs/2304.02643 (2023)

15. Krizhevsky, A., Sutskever, I., Hinton, G.E.: Imagenet classification with deep convolutional neural networks. Commun. ACM **60**(6), 84–90 (2017)

16. Lei, T.: Image Segmentation: Principles, Techniques, and Applications. Hoboken, NJ (2023)

17. Lucas, A.M., Ryder, P., Li, B., Cimini, B.A., Eliceiri, K.W., Carpenter, A.E.: Open-source deep-learning software for bioimage segmentation. Mol. Biol. Cell **32**(9), 823–829 (2021)

18. Minaee, S., Boykov, Y., Porikli, F., Plaza, A., Kehtarnavaz, N., Terzopoulos, D.: Image segmentation using deep learning: a survey. IEEE Trans. Pattern Anal. Mach. Intell. **44**(7), 3523–3542 (2022)

19. Mo, Y., Wu, Y., Yang, X., Liu, F., Liao, Y.: Review the state-of-the-art technologies of semantic segmentation based on deep learning. Neurocomputing **493**, 626–646 (2022)

20. Mukherjee, G., Chatterjee, A., Tudu, B.: Identification of the types of disease for tomato plants using a modified gray wolf optimization optimized mobilenetv2 convolutional neural network architecture driven computer vision framework. Concurr. Comput. Pract. Exp. **34**(22) (2022)

21. Ronneberger, O., Fischer, P., Brox, T.: U-net: convolutional networks for biomedical image segmentation. In: Navab, N., Hornegger, J., Wells, W., Frangi, A. (eds.) MICCAI 2015. LNCS, vol. 9351, pp. 234–241. Springer, Cham (2015). https://doi.org/10.1007/978-3-319-24574-4_28

22. Sandler, M., Howard, A.G., Zhu, M., Zhmoginov, A., Chen, L.: Mobilenetv 2: inverted residuals and linear bottlenecks. In: CVPR, pp. 4510–4520 (2018)

23. Summers, G., Lim, A., Wheeler, A.J.: A characterisation of benthic currents from seabed bathymetry: an object-based image analysis of cold-water coral mounds. Remote. Sens. **14**(19), 4731 (2022)

24. Torres, R.N., Fraternali, P., Romero, J.: ODIN: an object detection and instance segmentation diagnosis framework. In: Bartoli, A., Fusiello, A. (eds.) ECCV 2020, Part VI. LNCS, vol. 12540, pp. 19–31. Springer, Cham (2020). https://doi.org/10.1007/978-3-030-65414-6_3

25. Wu, X., Hong, D., Chanussot, J.: UIU-NET: U-net in U-net for infrared small object detection. IEEE Trans. Image Process. **32**, 364–376 (2023)

26. Yang, Q., Zhang, Y., Dai, W., Pan, S.J.: Transfer Learning in Computer Vision, pp. 221–233. Cambridge University Press, Cambridge (2020)

Enhancing Safety During Surgical Procedures with Computer Vision, Artificial Intelligence, and Natural Language Processing

Okeke Stephen(✉) 🆔 and Minh Nguyen 🆔

Department of Computer Science and Software Engineering, Auckland University of Technology (AUT), 6 St. Paul Street, Auckland, New Zealand
{stephen.okeke,minh.nguyen}@aut.ac.nz

Abstract. Administering the incorrect substances during procedures can lead to undesired outcomes. Anesthetists, especially when fatigued, distracted, or under stressful conditions, are at risk of such oversights. The conventional manual method for identifying, verifying, and preparing such substances has inherent challenges. Addressing these issues is paramount for healthcare professionals and those under their care. This study explores the application of computer vision and artificial intelligence techniques to refine the processes of selection, verification, preparation, and dispensing in procedure settings. The advanced method initiates with scene text detection, extraction, and matching models to discern inscriptions on labels. These inscriptions are subsequently matched with a pre-established database of item attributes using the token set ratio, Levenshtein, and Jaccard distance algorithms. These algorithms provide similarity scores, with the item having the top confidence score being identified as the appropriate one. A ground-breaking facet of this approach is the incorporation of a generalized Ukkonen algorithm, upper bound theory, and branch pruning algorithm. These elements offer an enhanced and more accurate adaptation of the traditional Levenshtein algorithm. Utilizing this method has the potential to drastically diminish errors in procedures and elevate safety measures.

Keywords: Surgical Procedures · Computer Vision · Artificial Intelligence · Natural Language Processing

1 Introduction

Erroneous substance administration in the operating rooms is a serious problem in healthcare and can have catastrophic consequences for patients. In surgical rooms, anesthetic drug preparation errors are particularly concerning, as they can lead to serious complications or even death. A study by Wheeler and Wheeler [1] found that the drug administration error rate was 0.75% and having a 'near miss' rate of 0.37%. The most prevalent errors were dose errors of about 20% and drug substitutions of about 20%. About 63% of the errors emanated from intravenous boluses, 20% from infusions, and

15% involved inhalational agents. There are several factors that can contribute to anesthetic drug preparation errors. These include look-alike and sound-alike drugs, confusing or incomplete drug labels, fatigue, and stress. Many anesthetic drugs have very similar names, which can lead to errors when being prepared. For instance, Protamine Sulfate and Glycopyrrolate, Mepivacaine (Polocaine), and Calcium Chloride look very similar in label presentation (see Fig. 1), and they can easily be confused if the labels are not carefully checked [2].

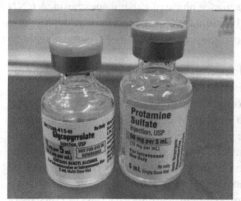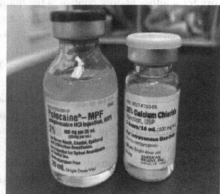

Fig. 1. Protamine Sulfate vs. Glycopyrrolate, Mepivacaine (Polocaine) vs Calcium Chloride

Confusing or incomplete drug labels can also lead to errors. For example, if the label does not include any of the drug's name, strength, or expiration date, it can be challenging to ensure that the correct drug is being used. Also, anesthesiologists often work long hours and under high levels of stress. This can lead to errors, as they may be more likely to make mistakes when tired or stressed. There are existing methods used to prevent anesthetic drug preparation errors. These include using a checklist to ensure that all of the steps in the drug preparation process are followed correctly, color-coding drugs to prevent errors, making it easier to identify the correct drug category, and double-checking drugs to detect any mistake that may have been made. These methods are manually driven and thus prone to mistakes. Therefore, an automated method is needed to identify and verify the drugs correctly and thus forms the motivation of this work.

2 Related Works

In recent times, automatic anesthetic drug detection and recognition for safer surgical procedures have attracted numerous interests. Computer vision, artificial intelligence (AI), and natural language processing methods can potentially improve the safety and accuracy of anesthetic drug administration by automating the detection and recognition of anesthetic drugs process. Hwang, Kim, Kim and Nam [3] proposed a deep learning-driven technique for real-time monitoring of the status of intravenous medication bags in the operating room. The study used a deep learning model for automated camera selection (CNN-1) and CNN-2 for liquid residue monitoring and implemented a drug residue estimation model.

Khalid, Ali, Liu, Qurashi and Ali [4] proposed a machine-learning classifier with photoplethysmography temporal markers for anesthesia drug detection. The study identified that a KNN classifier trained on significant photoplethysmography (PPG) features could be a reliable, non-invasive, and low-cost method for detecting anesthesia drugs and analyzing their depth during surgical operations and postoperative monitoring. Ren, Chen, Liu, Fu, Yao, Chen and Teng [5] investigated using a convolutional neural network for intelligent drug control in the maintenance phase of general anesthesia. A CNN model with a sliding window sampling and residual learning module was deployed to construct an "AI anesthesiologist" model for intraoperative dosing of tailored anesthetic medications (propofol and remifentanil).

To address the shortage of anesthesiologists in recent times, a machine learning model was deployed to predict the decisions made by anesthesiologists during surgery. This was done by formulating the decision-making process as a supervised binary classification problem, where the goal is to predict whether the flow rate of analgesic remifentanil should be increased at each time point [6]. Schamberg, Badgeley, Meschede-Krasa, Kwon and Brown [7] introduced continuous action deep reinforcement learning for propofol dosing during general anesthesia. They expanded their previous work on deep RL for the automation of anesthetic dosing with a continuous-driven model powered by actor-critic RL. The suggested reinforcement learning (RL) agent consists of a policy network responsible for translating observed anesthetic states into a continuous probability distribution representing propofol-infusion rates. Accompanying this is a value network that gauges the desirability of these observed states. They trained and evaluated three iterations of the RL agent, each employing diverse reward functions. To foster resilience towards patient-specific differences, the agent is trained utilizing simulated pharmacokinetic/pharmacodynamic models, deliberately incorporating randomized parameters.

3 Theoretical Background

The proposed method is based on scene text detection, extraction, and matching. In real-time processing, the proposed framework first recognizes the presence of inscriptions on the drug labels; extracts and matches them with precomputed features in a knowledge-base that contains all the existing drug samples using the token set ratio, Levenshtein, and Jaccard distance algorithms. These algorithms were combined in this work to establish layers of verification and reduce to the barest minimum the possibility of making errors during the drug preparation. They ecompute the drugs' similarity scores, and the drug with the highest confidence score is returned as the rightful drug. The Levenshtein Distance, also called Edit Distance, is one of the three anesthetic string-matching algorithms selected for this study. It is defined as a similarity gauge between pairs of strings [8].

Given two strings, $S = s_1 \ldots s_n$ and $Z = z_1 \ldots z_n$, the distance between them is the minimum edit operations required to convert S into Z [9], where likely operations are:

- Insertion operation

  Insert $(s, i, c) = s_1 s_2 \ldots s_i c s_{i+1} \ldots s_n$.
- Deletion operation

  Delete $(s, i) = s_i s_2 \ldots s_{i-1} s_{i+1} \ldots s_n$.
- Substitute operation

  Substitute $(s, i, c) = s_1 s_2 \ldots s_{i-1} c s_{i+1} \ldots s_n$.

For instance, the minimum edit operation required to transform the substance "Bromide" into "Chloride" is 4, as shown in the memorization matrix process table presented in Fig. 2 below:

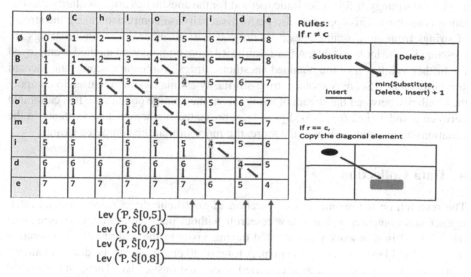

Fig. 2. Memorization matrix process to convert Bromide to Chloride.

To enhance the accuracy and processing speed of the proposed method, an enhanced Levenshtein Distance computation method using a generalized Ukkonen algorithm, upper bound theorem, and branch pruning was introduced.

For the generalized optimization of Ukkonen's algorithm, if the modification or editing of the string matching steps that cost more than Q is not considered, then the compute, at most, the $Z \times (2Q + 1)$. Given two strings U and V that have lengths q and r, respectively, with $q \leq r$. Using the upper bound theorem, it is inevitable that the Levenshtein distance cannot be above q. Thus,

$$LevDist(U, V) \leq q$$

where LevDist is the Levenshtein Distance between U and V. For instance, let $i - th$ character of a given string L be denoted with L_i. Then applying this notation, U and V

can be represented below:

$$U = U_1, U_2, U_3 \ldots U_{q-1}U_q$$

$$V = V_1, V_2, V_3 \ldots V_{r-1}V_r$$

Since $q \leq r$, V can be transformed into

$$U = U_1, U_2, U_3 \ldots U_{q-1}U_q$$

$$V = V_1, V_2, V_3 \ldots V_{q-1}V_q \ldots V_r$$

To reaffirm the confidence score obtained using the Levenshtein similarity score estimation strategy, a Token Set Ratio method for the anesthetics drug similarity computation is adopted. This approach also performs a pairwise comparison using the stream of strings from an incoming anesthetic drug against all other drugs whose strings are pre-stored in the look-up table. A third similarity score computation method is employed for further validation of the obtained anesthetic drugs' confidence score. The Jaccard similarity or Jacc Score is another string-similarity estimation method used to compute the similarity between the stream of strings from the ampule containers. It is calibrated between 0 and 1 (i.e., $0 \leq J(S_1, S_2) \leq 1$), represented mathematically as stated in the equations above, and the higher the score, the more similar the compared strings.

4   Data Collection

The research on the automatic identification of anesthetic drugs using artificial intelligence and computer vision is new research without publicly available datasets. The dataset used in this work was collected during visits to the real anesthetic operating rooms at Auckland University Hospital. A total of 30 empty anesthetic drug containers, which are the actual dataset, were collected in the first onsite visit. Then, on the second operating room visit, the remaining dataset of about 23 used empty anesthetic drugs were received for the experiments. The data comprises different empty drug containers used in the operating rooms. The containers appear in the form of ampoules and vials with different shapes, sizes, structures, and orientations. Of utmost importance are the labels embedded on the drug containers as they are extracted and made use of in this work. The labels on the drug containers appear in different shapes, color, and the text inscriptions on them are of different font colors, curvatures, and sizes.

5   Experimental Setup

The visual acquisition and feeding of data into the proposed framework were handled using the OpenCV-python module and a Logitech 1080p HD camera which can capture the about 180 degrees view of the anesthetic drug containers. The hardware components and their corresponding measurements used in performing this experiment are shown in Fig. 3.

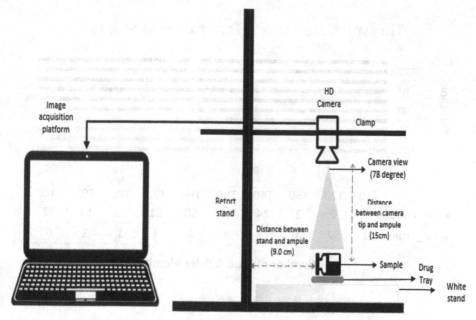

Fig. 3. The experimental setup for the anesthetic drug image acquisition.

The experimental set consists of a personal computer, a retort stand, a 1080p HD camera, and a drug tray, as shown in Fig. 3. The distance between the camera and the anesthetic drug ampoule positioned to be captured is 15cm, and the length between the positioned drug ampoule and the retort stand is 9.0cm. A total of 52 empty anesthetic drug images were captured for the experiments performed throughout the work. During the experiments, a python programming language, the dominant language for computer vision application research, Anaconda jupyter notebook, and a pycharm development environment or editor were used for the frameworks' development process. Google Vision OCR was deployed for the anesthetic drugs text inscription detection and vital information extraction. Also, the Fuzzywuzzy-python module is used to compute the token set ratio for similarity estimation, Python-Levenshtein (a tool for the Levenshtein string similarity measurement), and the Win32printing python module for the experimental physical printing tasks. For the artificial voice feedback generation, the pyttsx3x python module was used to convert the relevant extracted features from text to speech.

6 The Threshold Computation Process

In selecting the appropriate threshold for the proposed framework, the threshold value was split or calibrated between T10 and T100 in the range of ten. Then, tests run iteratively on each drug sample, observations are recorded, and the outcome is analyzed. For the first drug sample, the plot of similarity scores obtained is shown below in Fig. 4. At each threshold, the number of false drug identification is denoted as No_False, and true identification is represented as No_True. The complete and summarized results of the threshold computation experiment are attached in Appendix A and B.

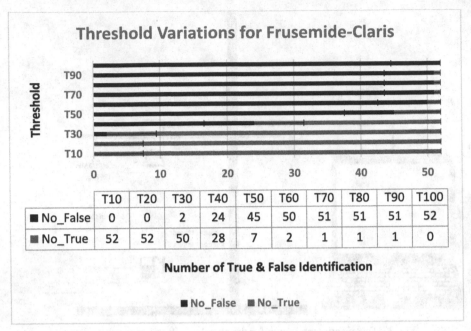

Fig. 4. Threshold variation and observation using Frusemide-Claris drug sample.

From Fig. 4, at thresholds 10 (T10) & 20 (T20), the total number of drugs returned as false by the proposed framework is 0, while the total number of drugs returned as true is 52. This implies that the framework recognized all the drug samples as right at these thresholds, making 10 and 20 unsuitable candidates for the standard threshold. At T30, the overall drug samples returned as false by the framework is 2, while 50 samples were identified as true, knocking T30 out as the potential threshold candidate. Furthermore, a cumulative total of 24 drug samples were identified as false, and 28 were identified as true at T40, giving T40 no hope as the right threshold value. In continuation, a total of 45 and 50 drug samples each were identified as false at T50 and T60; respectively, 7 and 2 samples returned as true, drawing nearer to the right threshold candidate for the sample under analysis. Between T70 and T90, all the drug samples (51) except the right drug (1) were returned as false, while only the Frusemide-Claris drug sample was returned as true. This gives us hope that any value between 70 and 90 can serve as a threshold for the framework depending on the required sensitivity level and the analysis outcome of the remaining drug samples. At T100, all the drug samples were identified as false, making 100 unsuitable for the threshold value. The next drug sample analyzed for the appropriate threshold selection is the Morphine Sulphate injection, as illustrated in Fig. 5.

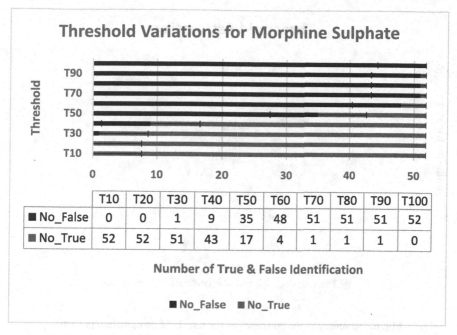

Fig. 5. Threshold variation and observation using Morphine Sulphate drug sample.

Like the previous sample in Fig. 5, at T10 & T20, the total number of drugs returned by the framework as false is 0, while the total number of drugs returned as true is 52. This means that the framework identified all the drug samples as appropriate at these thresholds, making 10 and 20 unsuitable candidates for the standard threshold. In continuation, the framework recognized only one drug sample as false at T30; unlike the immediately analyzed sample, the framework returned two drug samples as false when the threshold value was set at 30. The overall drug samples returned as true were 50, knocking T30 out as the potential threshold candidate. Furthermore, a cumulative total of 9 drug samples were identified as false, and 43 were recognized as true at T40, giving T40 no hope as the right threshold value. Also, at T50 and T60, a total of 35 and 48 drug samples each were identified as false, while 17 and 4 drug samples each returned as true, respectively, drawing closer to the right threshold candidate for the sample under analysis. Similar to the sample in Fig. 5, between T70 and T90, all the drug samples (51) except the right drug (1) were identified as false, while only the Morphine Sulphate drug sample was returned as true. Again, this gives us confidence that any value between 70 and 90 can be selected as a threshold for the framework subject to the sensitivity requirement level of the user and the analysis outcome of the remaining drug samples. At T100, all the drug samples were returned as false, making 100 unsuitable for the threshold value (Fig. 6).

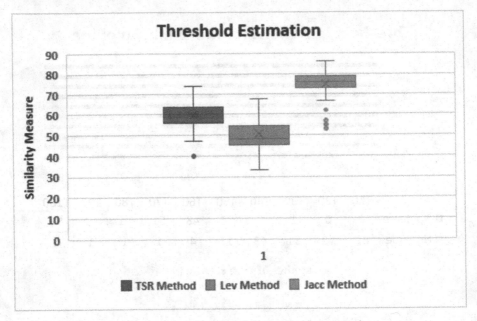

Fig. 6. Summary of the outcomes of the threshold computation process.

Furthermore, the proper threshold search operation continued until all the drug samples were each compared with others until the overall average best threshold was obtained with the proposed framework, as shown in Fig. 5. As can be seen in the summary chat in Fig. 5, the second-highest values extracted from the pool of the computed similarity scores are illustrated, and the chart shows variation because some drug labels are more similar to each other than others. The different anesthetic drugs analyzed returned different minimum threshold values. At T50, a total number of 6 drug samples returned 50 as their minimum threshold, 13 drug samples returned 60 as the minimum threshold, 20 anesthetic medication samples returned 70 as the minimum threshold value, 12 anesthetic drug samples returned 80 as the minimum threshold while no drug sample returned 10 to 40 and 90 to 100 threshold values as the minimum threshold value. Therefore, a threshold value set at 85 can ensure that no drug can be misidentified, no matter how similar they seem to be. The threshold restores confidence in an identified drug and prevents the closely related medication from being identified as another.

7 Experimental Results and Analysis

The outcome of the experimental processes and procedures are presented in this section. This section precedes the earlier established threshold computation strategy required for reliable and rapid anesthetic drug identification tasks. In this result analysis and demonstration, 5 to 6 results from different randomly selected anesthetic medication samples shall be presented in charts. The overall compact outcome of the experimental iterations involving all the used drug samples will be presented in a tabular form. The Rocuronium Bromide Injection is the first randomly selected drug to be analyzed in this section.

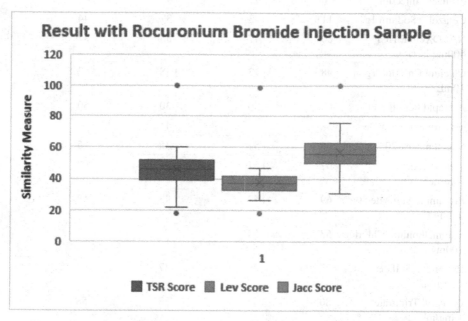

Fig. 7. Result obtained from the Rocuronium Bromide Injection sample iterative test.

During the pairwise comparative iterative process, the Rocuronium Bromide Injection produced a similarity confidence score of about 99% with the Levenshtein similarity estimation algorithm (Lev Score). In contrast, the Token Set Ratio (TSR Score) and Jaccard distances (Jacc Score) returned a 100% score each; these positioned the Rocuronium Bromide Injection as the rightly identified drug shown in Fig. 7. The framework also generated an edit distance of 1 (see Table 1), implying that the algorithm correctly matched all the characters from the test ampule image with its corresponding ampule string in the lookup table and needed only one edit operation to transform both strings.

The Rocuronium Bromide Injection sample score is closely followed by three drug samples with scores ranging from 71% to 76% using the Jaccard confidence computation matric, 44% to 47% using the Lev similarity computation metric, and 56% to 60% with the TSR string estimation method. Then, followed by another six sets of drug samples with a range of scores from 65% to 68% scores with the Jaccard matric, seven samples scoring between 43% to 45% with the Lev similarity computation algorithm, and 53% to 56% scores by the TSR string similarity computation strategy. In continuation, another set of six drug samples scored between 62% and 64% with the Jaccard matric, eight sets of the drug samples scored between 39% and 42% using the Lev method, and the TSR polled 50% to 52% on seven drug samples. Also, another set of nine drug samples scored between 46% and 48% using the TSR method, 37% to 38% by the Lev method, and 57%

Table 1. The extracted results using the Rocuronium Bromide Injection sample.

Drug Name	Edit Distance	TSR Scores (%)	Lev Scores (%)	Jacc Scores (%)
Primacor Injection	70	47	43	47
Cefazolin Sodium 1g	111	43	37	44
NALOXONE HCl 400mg in 1mL	60	47	38	57
Calcium Chloride 1g in 10mL	98	43	38	52
Actrapid Penfill 3ml	65	50	30	50
Vecuronium bromide	58	53	46	60
Sugammadex 200mg/2ml	69	53	35	65
Amiodarone Hydrochloride	67	51	36	60
Protamine Sulphate 50mg in 5ml	69	52	43	57
Summethonium Chloride 100mg in 2mL	53	54	47	68
Protamine Sulfate 10mg/ml	72	50	37	63
Glyceryl Trinitrate 1 mg/ml	80	45	33	58
Tranexamic acid	68	38	32	50
Heparin Injection 25000IU in 5 mL	63	54	45	55
Sterile Potassium Chloride	84	39	40	57
Metaraminol 10mg/ml	62	56	36	65
Cyclizine lactate	72	22	18	31
PITRESSIN argipressin	59	48	37	64
Dexamethasone phosphate 4 mg/ml	59	54	38	56
Ephedrine Hydrochloride	62	46	36	59
Ondansetron Solution	72	36	34	50
FRUSEMIDE	66	32	29	44
DALACINC PHOSPHATE	62	39	33	52
METOPROLOL Mylan	77	51	36	62

(*continued*)

Table 1. (*continued*)

Drug Name	Edit Distance	TSR Scores (%)	Lev Scores (%)	Jacc Scores (%)
WATER FOR INJECTIONS BP	82	43	34	53
MORPHINE SULFATE	52	57	44	67
Glycopyrronium Bromide and Neostigmine	65	6	41	72
Clonidine HCl	59	54	39	76
Rocuronium Bromide Injection	1	100	99	100
Fresofol 1% MCT/LCT	315	52	26	44
Sedative Midazolam 5mg	65	43	33	47
Adrenaline Injection	58	48	43	67
Paracetamol Kabi	522	18	18	40
Provive MCT-LCT 1%	259	46	29	47
Adrenaline Injection 1mg in 10mL	58	48	43	67
Amoxicillin Sodium	121	39	32	44
Lidocain Injection	61	39	35	57
SODIUM CHLORIDE	103	36	37	53
Remifentanil-Act Injection	73	42	39	54
Sterile Dopamine	55	38	43	58
Hypnomida Etomidate 2mg	65	44	38	52
Xylocaine 1%	63	44	33	48
Fentanyl Injection	107	46	39	56
Noradrenaline acid	72	35	34	62
Magnesium Sulfate 2.47g in 5mL	58	56	47	55
Sugammadex Injection	60	55	42	71
Dynastat Powder	75	47	40	63
Hydrocortisone sodium	80	45	39	55
Atracurium Besylate	64	42	37	64
Atropine	62	38	33	54
PancuroInresa	72	51	43	55

to 60% similarity confidence scores with the Jacc estimation method. Returning lower similarity confidence scores are set of about 23 drug samples ranging from 18% to 45% scores using the TSR similarity confidence computation method, 18% to 36% using the Lev method, and finally, 31% to 56% scores using the Jacc similarity confidence score computation algorithm. This whole computation process costs 0.3593s, which is within the desired processing time for the anesthetic workflow (Fig. 8).

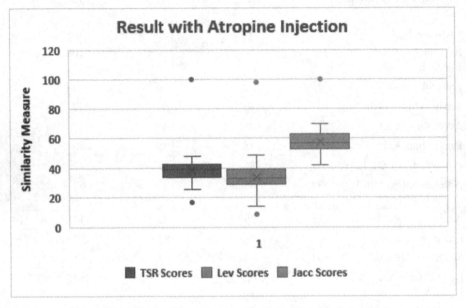

Fig. 8. Results obtained from the Atropine Injection sample iterative test.

On the other hand, another five-set of the drug samples scored against the main sample with scores ranging from 57% to 59% deploying the Jaccard confidence computation algorithm, 39% to 49% using the TRS method, and 33% to 34% with the Lev confidence similarity estimator. Closely followed by the last set of drug samples are another set of 10 drugs that scored between 54% and 56% using the Jaccard method, 36% to 39% with the TSR confidence scoring method, and 31% to 33% using the Lev similarity computation algorithm. However, another set of nine samples was closer to the last sample with a 50% to 53% score range using the Jaccard similarity estimator, a 31% to 35% score range with the TSR algorithm, and 26% to 31% using the Lev strategy.

8   Conclusion

This study introduced a framework to identify and verify the medications used during surgical procedures accurately. The method uses scene text detection, extraction, and matching methods to observe the presence of inscriptions on surgical medication labels and enables rapid and critical decision-making. Each marching algorithm scores a given drug sample, and the drug must meet a set threshold for each matching algorithm before it is permitted for use. The threshold ensures that the introduced framework adheres strictly to set rules and ensures no medication is misidentified and verified. The use of the generalized Ukkonen algorithm, upper and lower bound theorem, and the branch pruning algorithm to optimize the Levenshtein algorithm is our method's major contribution to advancing computational theory. The proposed method can rapidly and accurately identify and verify all the medications used during surgical procedures, thereby ensuring patient safety. However, in the event of an extreem angula positioning or rotation of the drugs, the accuracy of the proposed method can be affected. This could form the basis for futher investigation.

References

1. Wheeler, S., Wheeler, D.: Medication errors in anaesthesia and critical care. Anaesthesia **60**(3), 257–273 (2005)
2. Meyer, T.A.: Medication errors related to look-alike, sound-alike drugs—how big is the problem and what progress is being made? (2023)
3. Hwang, Y.J., Kim, G.H., Kim, M.J., Nam, K.W.: Deep learning-based monitoring technique for real-time intravenous medication bag status. Biomed. Eng. Lett., 1–10 (2023)
4. Khalid, S.G., Ali, S.M., Liu, H., Qurashi, A.G., Ali, U.: Photoplethysmography temporal marker-based machine learning classifier for anesthesia drug detection. Med. Biol. Eng. Comput. **60**(11), 3057–3068 (2022)
5. Ren, W., et al.: Feasibility of intelligent drug control in the maintenance phase of general anesthesia based on convolutional neural network. Heliyon **9**(1) (2023)
6. Miyaguchi, N., Takeuchi, K., Kashima, H., Morita, M., Morimatsu, H.: Predicting anesthetic infusion events using machine learning. Sci. Rep. **11**(1), 23648 (2021)
7. Schamberg, G., Badgeley, M., Meschede-Krasa, B., Kwon, O., Brown, E.N.: Continuous action deep reinforcement learning for propofol dosing during general anesthesia. Artif. Intell. Med. **123**, 102227 (2022)
8. Haldar, R., Mukhopadhyay, D.: Levenshtein distance technique in dictionary lookup methods: an improved approach. arXiv preprint: arXiv:1101.1232 (2011)
9. Trevisan, L.: Notes for Lecture 13–Edit Distance. In: Editor (Ed.)^(Eds.): 'Book Notes for Lecture 13–Edit Distance (United State, 2001, edn.)

Deep Learning Model with Atrous Convolutions for Improving Skin Cancer Classification

Ranpreet Kaur[1](✉) and Hamid GholamHosseini[2]

[1] Media Design School, Department of Software Engineering, 10 Madden Street, CBD, Auckland 1010, New Zealand
ranpreet.kaur@mediadesignschool.com
[2] School of Engineering, Computer and Mathematical Sciences, Auckland University of Technology, Auckland, New Zealand
hamid.gholamhosseini@aut.ac.nz

Abstract. Skin cancer is the most common problem all over the world, and some forms of skin cancer are not as aggressive as melanoma. It is vital to identify the type of skin cancer whether benign or malignant for providing timely treatment to the patients to increase the survival rate. The proposed work aims to address this task by proposing a convolutional neural network (CNN) model by leveraging the architecture of a network named EfficientNetB0. The network is fine-tuned with the optimized selection of hyperparameters and network layers are modified to make it suitable for the given dataset. Moreover, the atrous dilated convolution rate is added to some of the feature extraction layers of the existing network. The outcome of the network is analyzed using the locally interpretable model-agnostic explanation (LIME) technique to verify whether the proposed network learned suitable features from the lesion region in different skin cancer images. The proposed model employed three datasets of skin cancer; International Skin Imaging Challenge (ISIC), PH^2, and MED-NODE. It is concluded from the experimental results that the adopted deep neural model with the proposed modification is effective in classifying forms of cancer.

Keywords: Skin cancer · Melanoma · Convolutional neural network

1 Introduction

The incidence of skin cancer is becoming prevalent across the globe, becoming the reason for the highest number of deaths each year [8]. There are different types of skin cancer known as malignant and benign. Melanoma is classified as a malignant form of cancer which is a serious disease because it causes metastasis. The other known forms of cancer such as nevus, dermatofibroma, actinic keratosis, basal cell carcinoma, and squamous cell carcinoma are benign cancers that are not as deadly as melanoma however, these benign forms may develop into serious cancer. According to the American cancer society, it is reported in 2017 that in the USA, there were 1,688,780 new cancer cases diagnosed, and 600,920 cancer deaths occurred [26]. In 2018, there were 1,735,350 new cancer cases diagnosed, and 609,640 deaths occurred [18], in 2019 1,762,450 new cancer cases and 606,880 cancer deaths [24], and 1,806,590 new cancer cases found and 606,520 cancer deaths happened in 2020 [27]. The number of melanoma deaths is expected to increase by 4.4 percent in 2023 [25]. The mortality rate may be reduced by a significant rate if cancer is diagnosed at an early stage.

Medical experts face great difficulty in identifying melanoma due to its complex nature. Several factors contribute to this complexity: (a) irregular border (b) different shapes (c) intensity variations (d) color illuminations (e) evolution over time. The similarity between different types of skin lesions makes the visual examination process very hard and can lead to wrong identification results. Therefore, the idea of employing computer-aided systems for skin cancer diagnosis is highly significant. The automated classification system is achieved using image processing techniques and artificial intelligence. Many attempts were proposed in the literature by presenting various automated computer vision techniques to overcome these challenges [13]. The earlier techniques suffer from two major issues: First, the availability of an insufficient amount of data to develop an accurate classifier. Second, difficulties in the image acquisition process using special devices such as dermatoscopes, microscopy, and biopsy for acquiring skin cancer images. The main problem that occurs during the acquisition process is the contamination of various noisy elements like unwanted backgrounds and hairlines. The old method of artificial intelligence (AI) requires extensive use of pre-processing techniques to eliminate unwanted elements for increasing classification accuracy.

Recently, deep learning frameworks have been widely used by researchers for classification and object detection tasks. The main advantage of these architectures is that they do not require any external pre-processing or segmentation step, thus automatically learning features to perform visual task recognition. Therefore, in the proposed work, the deep learning technique is adopted for use due to its high performance for classification tasks. In this paper, a classification technique to diagnose melanoma is proposed that helps in making fast and early predictions between melanoma and benign. This automatic detection system will be a significant step towards saving the lives of people by providing an initial assessment of the nature of the lesion. The main contributions of this work are as follows:

- The CNN model, EfficientNetB0 is used as a baseline model, and optimized hyperparameters are finalized after several experiments for training to make the network more suitable for melanoma classification.
- Atrous dilated convolutions are added in the feature extraction layers of the base network to obtain a wider view of the receptive field and an extra fully connected layer is added at the end to regain voting of predictions.
- LIME method is used to deeply understand the modified networks' decision process depending upon the weightage of the features calculated from a particular region.

2   Literature Review

In the literature, the diagnosis process is divided into three categories: manual, automatic detection, and hybrid models. In the first category, the visual inspection of skin lesion tissues and cells is performed manually with the use of histopathological analysis. This process is very time-consuming, labor-intensive, and inaccurate. The second category is proposing automatic techniques with the aid of computer-aided methods which are efficient in giving results within a less time framework. The last category is the combination of both also known as embedded systems. The current research focuses on the second category to investigate the suitable and high-performing network to detect cancer. Due to the varying nature of skin cancer images, automatic diagnosis is a difficult task to achieve. The hairlines, and ruler marks acquired on images during the acquisition process pose a major challenge because these artifacts overlap with the important information. To overcome this problem, color contrast enhancement, transformation to different color spaces, and adjusting the brightness of images were employed in the literature to boost the performance. For the automatic diagnosis process, various neural frameworks have been proposed so far, like a hybrid system with a combination of support vector machine (SVM), and features from a deep learning network to perform classification [6]. Ozkan and Koku [21] employed four different types of machine learning algorithms such as SVM, K- nearest neighbor (KNN), artificial neural network (ANN), and decision trees to identify skin cancer as normal or abnormal, whereas the highest performance was achieved with ANN. This work employed a small dataset which is not enough to decide the efficiency of the network towards the diagnosis process. Another work by Khalid et al. [14] proposed a transfer learning approach with the use of AlexNet by replacing the softmax layer of the original architecture to classify three types of skin cancer on the PH^2 dataset. Additionally, they used data augmentation and performed fine-tuning of parameters to make the network well-suited for the problem. In 2019, Jason et al. [12] proposed a fusion method by utilizing the ResNet50 network's learning knowledge and handcrafted features from the clinical information module. The prediction score of each category from both types of information modules was combined and the final prediction score was identified using logistic regression.

The presence of an insufficient amount of training and testing data also poses another major challenge, as the network suffers from an underfitting problem. Due to this problem, the network is not able to give the expected classification performance. To address this issue, Luis et al. [22] explained the advantages of using a data augmentation technique that improves the classifier. The data augmentation approach comprises different operations such as rotation, flipping, and cropping. It generates multiple copies of the same data with different forms of transformation. Another work by Amirezza et al. [16] presented a hybrid model by employing three deep neural networks such as AlexNet, VGG-16, and ResNet-18 to extract features and fed them into the support vector machine for predicting three types of cancer. M.A.R Ratul et al. [23] given a new network by using the concept of dilated convolutions in the four popular pre-trained networks such as VGG16, VGG19, MobileNet, and InceptionV3 and leveraging the knowledge of these networks through transfer learning for skin cancer prediction. For a detailed study, one can refer to the latest survey articles [1,20] stating the use of various deep learning techniques, explains the availability of datasets, performance measures, challenges, and opportunities that come across skin cancer prediction. The discussed studies based on transfer learning, and hybrid models have given the motivation to design a system for skin cancer classification. The proposed work aims to design an effective modified network to classify melanoma despite the complexities present in the input data by achieving a high trade-off between accuracy and complexities.

3   Methodology

In this work, the baseline model used is the EfficientNetB0 neural network for classifying skin cancer. The network accepts the different types of skin cancer images as input. Generalized preprocessing operations such as oversampling and re-scaling of images were performed to keep the calculations minimum. The neural network extracts feature from images and classify test images into two types; Benign and Malignant. The proposed neural network follows the layered architecture of EfficientNetB0 which is organized among seven blocks. In the proposed network, the atrous convolutions are incorporated as a part of our contribution to expanding the field of view over the feature maps.

3.1   Datasets

In this work, three benchmark datasets having dermoscopic images were used to train, validate and test the network. The overall distribution of data from three sources is given in Table 1. The first dataset was acquired from the open-access repository, ISIC 2016 dermoscopic archives [7,11] having training, validation, and testing sets. This dataset contained 727 benign images and 622 malignant images collected from over 2000 patients. The malignant images have been confirmed via histopathology, and benign types have been confirmed either by experts, or histopathology.

Table 1. Distribution of images across three datasets.

Class Name	Training Set				Validation Set	Test Set
	ISIC 2016	PH^2	MED-NODE	Total		
Melanoma	622	39	70	731	124	86
Benign	727	161	100	988	145	319

The second dataset used was PH^2 [17] acquired at the Dermatology Service of Hospital Pedro Hispano, Matosinhos, Portugal. This dataset contained a total of 200 images distributed among two types i.e., 39 melanoma and 161 non-melanoma. Finally, the third dataset used was MED-NODE [10] have 170 images. A separate dataset containing 269 images (124 melanoma and 145 benign) was used for validation purposes. For testing, a set of 405 images that is unseen by the network was used. The available images were 8-bit with size ranges from 540×722 to 4499×6748 pixels. These images were resized using the nearest neighbor interpolation method into 224 × 224 × 3 dimensions to make them suitable for the EfficientNetB0 network without losing image resolution. A few samples of input images are shown in Fig. 1.

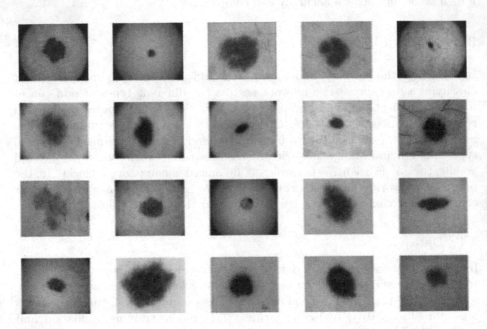

Fig. 1. Few sample images from the datasets.

3.2 Oversampling Technique

The available dataset contains the imbalanced distribution of data among two classes which causes the network to be biased towards a class having large samples. Therefore in the proposed work, a random oversampling technique was implemented to randomly duplicate images from the minority class and add them to the training dataset. This is a process of applying transformations such as flipping, rotation, and translation to increase data many folds. It is a technique to artificially create a new training dataset from the existing data to satisfy the requirements of deep learning models using a large dataset. Therefore, this oversampling method enlarges the training dataset of minority class i.e. melanoma samples become equivalent to benign samples (988 images) after oversampling.

It also helps to overcome the overfitting problem of deep learning networks. In this work, transformation operations such as rotation of $[-20^0, 20^0]$ and translation in X & Y direction by $[-5, 5]$ factors were applied to randomly generate the synthetic data. These random transformations performed on the minority class represent a new set of data to the network while training which is broken into mini-batch sizes over each epoch.

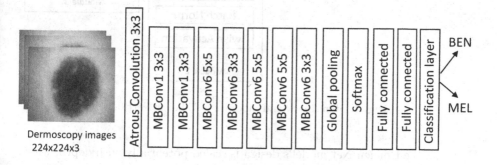

Fig. 2. Network framework.

3.3   Network Model

Many CNN models have been proposed since 2012 for classifying more than 1000 categories on the ImageNet dataset. A few of them are not effective in achieving high performance either in their application on different datasets or sometimes due to their complex architecture not being suitable for the task. From the existing state-of-the-art models, we employed EfficientNetB0 [28] for the given dataset because it is one of the networks that achieved 84% accuracy with 66 million learning parameters on ImageNet data. EfficientNetB0 network is efficient in learning complex image data. The main difference between efficient and other CNN models is that it uses a new activation function, Swish, rather than ReLU (Rectifier Linear Unit). The Swish function seems to perform better than ReLU, as it is a non-parametric smoothing function having mathematical expression as follows:

$$Y = X * sigmoid(X) \quad or \quad \frac{X}{1 + e^{-\beta X}} \tag{1}$$

Depending on the model, the β is either constant or a trainable parameter. When $\beta = 0$, the swish functions turn into the scaled linear function $f(x) = x/2$, whereas, for $\beta = 1$, it becomes equivalent to the sigmoid weighted linear unit. In general, the standard CNN frameworks are designed either too wide, deep, or have high resolution that helps the network to learn initially but it saturates quickly and left with a high number of learnable parameters, thus not efficient.

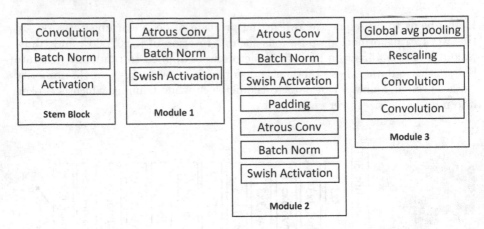

Fig. 3. Stem block and modules of EfficientNetB0.

However, the EfficientNet model's design is scaled potentially with depth, width and has high resolution.

The overall proposed network's architecture is shown in Fig. 2 where the atrous dilation rate is added in the first convolutional layer and into other convolutional layers of various MBConv blocks of the original network. The basic building block in the network is MBConv modules that receive two inputs, the first is the data from the previous layers, and the second is a set of arguments such as input/output filters, squeeze ratio, expansion ratio, and stride. The layers in these blocks first expand and then reduces the number of channels resulting in fewer computations. In the network layout, a stem block is added at the front containing a few sets of layers i.e., convolutional, batch normalization, and activation layer followed by three modules as given in Fig. 3. The core idea introduced in EfficientNetB0 is compound scaling that scales all the three parameters such as depth, input image resolution, and width together to boost the performance of the network. The coefficient ϕ is used in scaling to set three elements according to the following formula:

$$depth : d = \alpha^{\phi}$$
$$width : w = \beta^{\phi}$$
$$resolution : r = \gamma^{\phi} \tag{2}$$
$$w.r.t \quad \alpha.\beta^2.\gamma^2 \approx 2$$
$$where \quad \alpha \geq 1, \ \beta \geq 1, \ \gamma \geq 1$$

The α, β, γ are the scaling elements representing depth, width, and resolution respectively whose values are determined through grid search and these constants decide the allocation of resources to the model's scaling elements. Also, ϕ is a coefficient defined by a user to control the availability of resources for the model scaling. Therefore, the computation cost is less in this network.

3.4 Atrous Convolutions

In this work, the idea of incorporating atrous convolutions is applied to receive a wider view of the field. In the convolutional layers of the network, the convolution operation is performed for extracting features by sliding a template over an image. We used atrous convolutions instead of general convolutions which is a powerful tool to extract more contextual information by expanding the field's view. Standard convolutional operation is described below with the dilation rate as '1'.

$$C[i] = \sum_{s=1}^{S} I[i + s] * K[i] \tag{3}$$

whereas, (4) describes the atrous convolution operation when the dilation rate is more than '1'.

$$C[i] = \sum_{s=1}^{S} I[i + s.r] * K[i], r \geq 2 \tag{4}$$

$C[i]$ is a convolution function at location i with a filter K of size S, and r is the dilation rate. When the dilation rate is above 1, then, we can have a broader view of the receptive field.

3.5 Network's Fine Tuning

Fine-tuning a network is a method to train the given model from scratch on the given dataset for gaining higher performance. In contrast, in the transfer learning approach, the first few layers remain intact and their weights are fixed to use the learned knowledge for other fields. Whereas, in fine-tuning process, the network's layers can be replaced or modified targeting to achieve higher performance. In the proposed work, two types of modifications were applied to the baseline model. Firstly, instead of standard convolutions, dilated atrous convolutions were employed in the feature extraction layers of the MBConv modules. Secondly, two fully connected layers were added to gain a voting score, and finally, a classification layer with two classes is defined to perform the prediction between benign and malignant. Moreover, training parameters were fined tuned to run a smooth training process considering the given skin cancer dataset. The details of the selected hyperparameters for the network's training are given in Table 2.

3.6 Evaluation Metrics

For testing and evaluation purposes, a standard tool known as a confusion matrix is computed that comprises four elements True positive (TP), True negative

Table 2. Optimized hyperparameters for training.

Parameter	Values
Input image size	$224 \times 224 \times 3$
Batch size	6
Learning parameter,α	1×10^{-4}
Epochs	20
Gradient decay factor	0.99
Loss function, $E(\theta)$	Cross entropy loss
Optimizer	ADAM

(TN), False positive (FP), and False negative (FN). Based on these values, a few performance metrics such as accuracy (ACC), recall (REC), and precision (PRE) are computed. Accuracy is defined as the ratio of correctly classified samples and the total number of samples in the dataset. Recall measures the rate of true positives i.e. out of actual classes, how many classes are truly predicted by the model. Out of all positively labeled classes (sum of true positive and false positive, TP+FP), how many are truly predicted (TP) as positive by the model is known as precision.

$$ACC = \frac{TP + TN}{TP + TN + FP + FN} \tag{5}$$

$$REC = \frac{TP}{TP + FN} \tag{6}$$

$$PRE = \frac{TP}{TP + FP} \tag{7}$$

3.7 Results and Experimental Analysis

The proposed network is trained on three datasets ISIC 2016, PH^2, and MED-NODE. The image distribution in each dataset is already described in Table 1 containing different images for melanoma and benign skin cancer. To obtain quantitative results, the network is evaluated using 5-Fold cross-validation to obtain performance metrics such as accuracy, sensitivity, and precision. The analysis of the diagnostic metrics achieved by the proposed model on the validation and test dataset is illustrated in Table 3.

It can be seen in Table 4 that with the given selection of hyperparameters, and modifications to the existing base model, EfficientNetB0 has given higher performance for the adopted datasets as compared to the original EfficientNetB0 tested using the transfer learning approach.

The comparison is shown in Table 5 between the proposed network and other state-of-the-art methods that conducted classification tasks on ISIC challenge, PH^2, and MED-NODE. In the table, the performance of related studies based

Table 3. Diagnostic metrics on validation and test set using the proposed approach.

Diagnostic Category	Validation Set			Test Set		
	ACC	REC	PRE	ACC	REC	PRE
Melanoma vs. Benign	0.922	0.965	0.897	0.867	0.839	0.906

Table 4. Performance impact of the modified network on the given datasets.

Approach (EfficientNetB0)	Validation Set			Test Set		
	ACC	REC	PRE	ACC	REC	PRE
Original architecture	0.835	0.844	0.848	0.749	0.865	0.830
Modified architecture	**0.922**	**0.965**	**0.897**	**0.867**	0.839	**0.906**

on three metrics are given along with the name of the dataset and the number of images used in the test set. It is observed from the tables that the proposed network achieved comparatively higher values of accuracy of 92.2%, recall of 96.6%, and precision of 89.7% on the validation set and accuracy of 86.7%, recall of 83.9%, and precision of 90.6% on test data.

Table 5. Comparison of the proposed model with other state-of-the-art methods on the given dataset.

State-of-the-art models	Approach	Metrics		
		ACC	REC	PRE
S Mukherjee [2]	Multi-Layer Perceptron	0.859	0.862	0.855
MA Al-masni [3]	Inception-ResNet-v2	0.817	0.818	—
SM Alizadeh [4]	VGG-19	0.852	0.52	0.66
SS Chaturvedi [5]	MobileNet	0.831	0.830	0.890
M Fraiwan [9]	DenseNet201	0.758	0.627	0.709
S Jain [15]	MobileNet	0.824	0.82	0.84
S Mukherjee [19]	Multi-Layer Perceptron	0.833	0.867	0.727
Our Model on validation set	EfficientNetB0	**0.922**	**0.965**	**0.897**
Our Model on test set	EfficientNetB0	**0.867**	0.839	**0.906**

* No. of classes predicted are two i.e. melanoma and benign in each study

To visualize the performance of the proposed network on the test set, a graph between accuracy and loss is displayed in Fig. 4(a) for some iterations. It represents the loss is quite low whereas accuracy is high on the given data. The confusion matrix for the given model on the test set is displayed in Fig. 4(b).

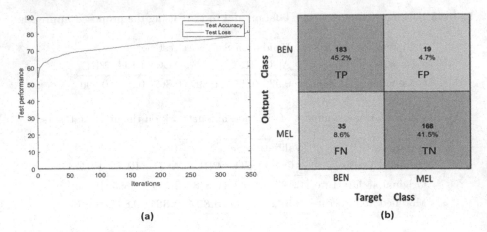

Fig. 4. (a) Accuracy vs Loss and (b) Confusion Matrix on the test set.

shows the prediction rate between melanoma and non-melanoma. In this figure, the diagonal positions show the number and percentage of samples correctly identified by the trained model. Here, in this case, 183 benign samples are truly classified as benign out of a total of 405 samples which corresponds to 45%. Similarly, 168 melanoma cases are correctly determined by the model equivalent to 42% of the total samples. The metric called balanced multi-class accuracy determines the true score of each sample corresponding to the respective class i.e., the sum of diagonal-wise elements divided by true positive samples also known as accuracy which is achieved by the proposed model as 86.7% on the test set.

3.8   Feature Analysis

To analyze which features are highly contributing toward accurate class predictions, we have used the LIME method. The method describes how features affect the performance of a classification process. It finds a set of superpixels belonging to the region having the strongest correlation with the prediction label. It helps to compute the map of predicted features from input images that are important for classifying the category of data. The method accepts input images, then analyzes the feature vector computed by a trained network to produce a visual heat map displaying prominent features.   The advantage of this method is that it helps to understand the behavior of the classification network for the given dataset. The assessment of a model based on performance metrics is not sufficient. The LIME method explains the decisions of the classification network and verifies whether the network has extracted features from the correct region of interest. It works by approximating the local linear behavior of the model.

The visual analysis of classified image features using the LIME method is given in Fig. 5. First, it generates the super-pixel image as given in Fig. 5b from the original image given in Fig. 5a to show the perceptual grouping pixels that

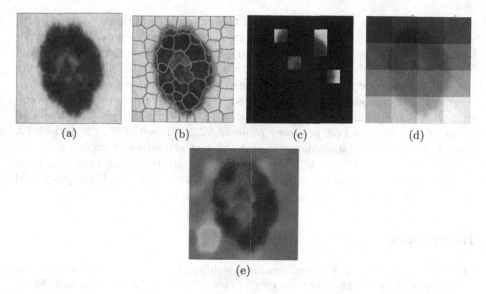

Fig. 5. Visual representation of image features using the LIME method: (a) Original image (b) Superpixel image (c) Masked image (d) Segmentation map (e) Heat map generated using LIME.

carry more information of edges and patches than normal pixels. Next, it predicts the class of each super-pixel and generates the perturbed image as shown in Fig. 5c. This image displays color on the positions having super-pixel value as '1', otherwise displays black color. The third step involves a calculation of each pixel's weight to measure its importance. For weight computation cosine distance metric is employed that finds how far the predicted pixel position lies from the original input point. The distance is normalized in the range of [0,1] using a kernel function. The higher value of weight shows the higher importance of a certain pixel. Figure 5d presents the corresponding segmentation map that explains why the trained model extracted features from the lesion area only. As it can be seen in this map that the only lesion is visible. The positions marked with different colors in Fig. 5d show the important regions whose features contributed more towards the prediction of a given image. Thus, the LIME method helps to understand the process of learning features by the proposed model.

4   Conclusion

In this paper, we proposed a modified network based on EfficientNetB0 trained on three datasets (ISIC, PH^2, and MED-NODE) and tested them on different data. This network addressed the primary challenge of detecting skin cancer as benign or melanoma by extracting features from dermoscopic skin cancer images. The last layers of the baseline model i.e. softmax and classification layers were changed to make it suitable for the given two classes. An extra fully connected layer was added at the end of the network. Additionally, atrous convolutions were employed in the feature extraction layers of modules to have a larger receptive field without involving an extra computation cost or losing resolution. Further, analysis of the most contributing features was determined using the LIME technique which helped to assess the classification task performed by the model. This model has been evaluated based on accuracy, recall, and precision that outperformed the existing studies reported in Table 5. The proposed network achieved the best accuracy score of 92.2%, recall of 96.6%, and 89.7% precision on the validation dataset, and the test set achieved accuracy, recall, and precision of 86.7%, 83.9%, and 90.6% respectively. In the future, a large dataset will be employed to predict more classes and the network's depth would be optimized to reduce the execution time.

References

1. Adegun, A., Viriri, S.: Deep learning techniques for skin lesion analysis and melanoma cancer detection: a survey of state-of-the-art. Artif. Intell. Rev. **54**(2), 811–841 (2021)
2. Adhikari, A., Mukherjee, S., Roy, M.: Malignant melanoma detection using multi layer perceptron with optimized network parameter selection by PSO. In: Mandal, J., Sinha, D., Bandopadhyay, J. (eds.) Contemporary Advances in Innovative and Applicable Information Technology. Advances in Intelligent Systems and Computing, vol. 812, pp. 101–109. Springer, Singapore (2019). https://doi.org/10.1007/978-981-13-1540-4_11
3. Al-Masni, M.A., Kim, D.H., Kim, T.S.: Multiple skin lesions diagnostics via integrated deep convolutional networks for segmentation and classification. Comput. Methods Programs Biomed. **190**, 105351 (2020)
4. Alizadeh, S.M., Mahloojifar, A.: Automatic skin cancer detection in Dermoscopy images by combining convolutional neural networks and texture features. Int. J. Imaging Syst. Technol. **31**(2), 695–707 (2021)
5. Chaturvedi, S.S., Gupta, K., Prasad, P.S.: Skin lesion analyser: an efficient seven-way multi-class skin cancer classification using MobileNet. In: Hassanien, A., Bhatnagar, R., Darwish, A. (eds.) Advanced Machine Learning Technologies and Applications. Advances in Intelligent Systems and Computing, vol. 1141, pp. 165–176. Springer, Singapore (2020). https://doi.org/10.1007/978-981-15-3383-9_15
6. Codella, N., Cai, J., et al.: Deep learning, sparse coding, and SVM for melanoma recognition in Dermoscopy images. In: Zhou, L., Wang, L., Wang, Q., Shi, Y. (eds.) Machine Learning in Medical Imaging. Lecture Notes in Computer Science(), vol. 9352, pp. 118–126. Springer, Cham (2015). https://doi.org/10.1007/978-3-319-24888-2_15
7. Codella, N.C., et al.: Skin lesion analysis toward melanoma detection: a challenge at the 2017 international symposium on biomedical imaging (ISBI), hosted by the international skin imaging collaboration (ISIC). In: IEEE International Symposium on Biomedical Imaging (ISBI 2018), pp. 168–172. IEEE (2018)
8. Fontanillas, P., Alipanahi, B., et al.: Disease risk scores for skin cancers. Nat. Commun. **12**(1), 1–13 (2021)
9. Fraiwan, M., Faouri, E.: On the automatic detection and classification of skin cancer using deep transfer learning. Sensors **22**(13), 4963 (2022)

10. Giotis, I., Molders, N., et al.: Med-node: a computer-assisted melanoma diagnosis system using Non-Dermoscopic images. Expert Syst. Appl. **42**(19), 6578–6585 (2015)

11. Gutman, D., et al.: Skin lesion analysis toward melanoma detection: a challenge at the international symposium on biomedical imaging (ISBI) 2016, hosted by the international skin imaging collaboration (ISIC). arXiv preprint: arXiv:1605.01397 (2016)

12. Hagerty, J.R., Stanley, R.J., et al.: Deep learning and handcrafted method fusion: higher diagnostic accuracy for melanoma Dermoscopy images. IEEE J. Biomed. Health Inform. **23**(4), 1385–1391 (2019)

13. Hameed, N., et al.: A comprehensive survey on image-based computer aided diagnosis systems for skin cancer. In: International Conference on Software, Knowledge, Information Management & Applications (SKIMA), pp. 205–214. IEEE (2016)

14. Hosny, K.M., Kassem, M.A., Foaud, M.M.: Skin cancer classification using deep learning and transfer learning. In: International Biomedical Engineering Conference (CIBEC), pp. 90–93. IEEE (2018)

15. Jain, S., Singhania, U., et al.: Deep learning-based transfer learning for classification of skin cancer. Sensors **21**(23), 8142 (2021)

16. Mahbod, A., et al.: Skin lesion classification using hybrid deep neural networks. In: IEEE International Conference on Acoustics, Speech and Signal Processing (ICASSP), pp. 1229–1233. IEEE (2019)

17. Mendonça, T., et al.: PH 2-a Dermoscopic image database for research and benchmarking. In: 35th Annual International Conference of the IEEE Engineering in Medicine and Biology Society (EMBC), pp. 5437–5440. IEEE (2013)

18. Miller, K.D., et al.: Cancer statistics for Hispanics/Latinos, 2018. CA Cancer J. Clin. **68**(6), 425–445 (2018)

19. Mukherjee, S., Adhikari, A., Roy, M.: Malignant melanoma detection using multi layer preceptron with visually imperceptible features and PCA components from MED-NODE dataset. Int. J. Med. Eng. Inf. **12**(2), 151–168 (2020)

20. Naeem, A., Farooq, M.S., et al.: Malignant melanoma classification using deep learning: datasets, performance measurements, challenges and opportunities. IEEE Access **8**, 110575–110597 (2020)

21. Ozkan, I.A., Koklu, M.: Skin lesion classification using machine learning algorithms. Int. J. Intell. Syst. Appl. Eng. **5**(4), 285–289 (2017)

22. Perez, L., Wang, J.: The effectiveness of data augmentation in image classification using deep learning. arXiv preprint: arXiv:1712.04621 (2017)

23. Ratul, M.A.R., et al.: Skin lesions classification using deep learning based on dilated convolution. BioRxiv., 860700 (2020)

24. Siegel, R.L., Miller, K.D., Jemal, A.: Cancer statistics, 2019. CA Cancer J. Clin. **69**(1), 7–34 (2019)

25. Siegel, R.L., Miller, K.D., Wagle, N.S., Jemal, A.: Cancer statistics, 2023. CA Cancer J. Clin. **73**(1), 17–48 (2023)

26. Siegel, R.L., et al.: Colorectal cancer statistics, 2017. CA Cancer J. Clin. **67**(3), 177–193 (2017)

27. Siegel, R.L., Miller, K.D., et al.: Colorectal cancer statistics, 2020. CA Cancer J. Clin. **70**(3), 145–164 (2020)

28. Tan, M., Le, Q.: EfficientNet: rethinking model scaling for convolutional neural networks. In: International Conference on Machine Learning, pp. 6105–6114. PMLR (2019)

Fusion-Based Approach to Enhance Markerless Motion Capture Accuracy for On-Site Analysis

Abderrahman Ben Abdeljelil[1,2,3]([✉])[ID], Mohamed Hédi Bedoui[3][ID],
and Khalil Ben Mansour[2][ID]

[1] Sfax National Engineering School, Sfax, Tunisia
ibnabdeljelil@gmail.com
[2] UMR CNRS 7338, Biomécanique et Bioingénierie, Université de Technologie de
Compiègne, Sorbonne Université, Compiègne, France
[3] Laboratory of Technologies and Medical Imagery LTIM-LR12ES06,
University of Monastir, Monastir, Tunisia

Abstract. Markerless motion capture systems offer the advantage of
non-intrusive and on-site motion analysis, but they often suffer from
limited accuracy compared to marker-based systems. In this paper, we
propose a novel fusion-based approach to enhance the accuracy of on-site
motion analysis using OpenPose, a popular markerless motion tracking
framework. The proposed method combines data obtained from Open-
Pose with a marker-based Regions of Interest (ROIs) detection method,
aiming to improve the accuracy and reliability of markerless motion capture for on-site applications. Multiple cameras are utilized for 3D reconstruction to refine the joint positions initially provided by OpenPose.
The obtained results exhibit a significant improvement in limb length
and angle measurements, achieving root mean square errors (RMSE) of
less than 32.7mm and 7.61°, respectively, after correction. These findings
outperformed the accuracy achieved by OpenPose prior to employing our
fusion-based approach.

Keywords: Markerless Motion Capture · Fusion-Based MoCap ·
OpenPose · Pose Correction · Motion Analysis

1 Introduction

Motion Capture, often abbreviated as MoCap, is the process of recording and
digitizing the real-life movements of objects or living beings [19]. Its applications
range from creating realistic animations [2] or collect data for analysis [16,25].
Over the last decades, MoCap has made significant advancements in parallel with
major technological progress and increasing demand for faster and more sophisticated methods [6]. Basically, Mocap techniques falls into two major categories:
marker-based and markerless [24]. Marker-based techniques, specifically Opto-
electronic systems, are well-known for their high precision and widespread use.
These systems are crucial in industries that require accurate motion capture,

W. Q. Yan et al. (Eds.): PSIVT 2023, LNCS 14403, pp. 436–450, 2024.
https://doi.org/10.1007/978-981-97-0376-0_33

such as ergonomic risk assessments, clinical research, and biomechanics studies [1,19,25]. They use multiple cameras that emit infrared (IR) light, which is then reflected by passive markers placed on the subject or object being tracked. Given their high quality, they are considered the "gold standard" when it comes to detecting motion parameters, including displacement, speed, and joint angle measurements. However, marker-based MoCap systems have some limitations, including expensive hardware, intricate setup procedures, extensive post-processing requirements, and the need for a controlled environment [10]. Furthermore, the accuracy of joint angle measurements heavily relies on the precise marker placement, demanding a thorough understanding of human anatomy [23].

In recent years, markerless MoCap technologies have made remarkable progress, as substantiated by numerous surveys conducted by experts in the field [8,11,20,31]. Markerless MoCap eliminates the need for physical markers on the subject's body. Instead, it relies on standard video sequences and advanced computer vision techniques, often based on deep learning algorithms, to precisely identify and track the positions and orientations of various body segments [27]. This approach offers a completely non-intrusive method for capturing motion, reducing participant discomfort, and allowing for more natural movement. Furthermore, markerless MoCap presents fewer restrictions regarding equipment requirements, recording rate, and lighting conditions. This makes it particularly well-suited for on-site ergonomic assessments [6]. Prominent examples of markerless MoCap methods include OpenPose [3] and MediaPipe [17], both of which are recognized for their robust performance and applicability in various fields.

Several studies have investigated the accuracy and versatility of such methods across a wide range of applications [4,22,26]. For instance, OpenPose stands out as a widely acclaimed open-source library for precise pose estimation [3], drawing immense attention within the computer vision community. To illustrate the effectiveness of OpenPose in markerless MoCap, Nakano et al [21] developed a 3D markerless MoCap technique using OpenPose, combined with multiple synchronized video cameras. They conducted a comprehensive comparison against commercial optical marker-based MoCap evaluating various tasks, including walking, jumping, and ball throwing. The findings revealed that approximately 47% of the calculated mean absolute errors were less than 20 mm, with 80% falling below the 30 mm. However, there were cases experienced mean absolute errors exceeding 40 mm, though they constituted about 10% of the measurements. Furthermore, OpenPose has been extensively utilized for gait analysis, where its measurements were compared to inertial sensors [7] and marker-based system [29]. In these comparisons, the joint angle measurements using OpenPose exhibited a maximum error of 9.9° compared to inertial sensors [7], and a maximum root mean square error of 60 mm in length measurements when compared to marker-based system [29]. The growing interest in leveraging OpenPose for ergonomic postural assessment is also evident in recent research [15]. In this study, the authors aimed to compare the performance of two low-cost MoCap systems, OpenPose and Kinect. They simultaneously recorded 12 different tasks using the two systems along with VICON as a reference system. The study's findings indicated that OpenPose, when evaluated under three different conditions (with and without occlusions and tracking from non-frontal views), exhibited an overall mean root mean square error of joint angles at 8.4°, 8.2°, and 10.4°.

The existing literature recognizes the limitations of markerless systems in comparison to their marker-based counterparts [6,26,28]. These studies highlight that the current accuracy and precision of markerless systems are yet to be clearly defined when pitted against other well-established motion analysis technologies available on the market. It is evident from previous research that markerless systems may not yet match the level of precision exhibited by marker-based systems for motion analysis. However, Nakano et al. [21] suggested that integrating an algorithm capable of correcting tracking errors could potentially enhance the accuracy of OpenPose for human motion science.

Building upon these insights, we present a novel approach to enhance the accuracy of markerless motion capture by drawing on the benefits of marker-based and markerless approaches. Our proposed fusion process leverages the data obtained from OpenPose while integrating a straightforward yet effective method based on colored spherical markers to define specific regions of interest (ROIs). This integration of cutting-edge markerless MoCap technology and traditional marker-based principles enables us to attain higher level of accuracy in markerless motion tracking, without the need for complex setup, extensive post-processing, or in-depth anatomy knowledge, all while using a minimum of spherical markers. We understand that these studies require careful measurements and kinematic validations, and our fusion process aspires to bridge the gap between marker-based precision and the flexibility of markerless MoCap. In addition, we have made the source code of the proposed approach available on GitHub (GitHub repository: https://github.com/msakni22/Fusion-Based-Mocap).

2   Materials and Methods

Our proposed approach focuses on improving the accuracy of OpenPose, thereby ensuring precise on-site motion analysis. The first step of the proposed workflow entails tracking human body movement from multiple views using OpenPose, while concurrently identifying specific ROIs based on the presence of colored spherical markers strategically placed on the human body. Triangulation was then applied to achieve high-fidelity 3D reconstruction of the detected joints and ROIs. Finally, the ROIs serve as references to refine and correct the 3D reconstructions of joint positions provided by OpenPose. This integration helps to identify and correct the erroneous joints' positions. The proposed approach was evaluated by comparing OpenPose's performance in delivering biomechanical variables pre- and post-correction. This evaluation involved the use of ground truth data concurrently acquired via the VICON system. The following is a detailed description of the proposed approach workflow and the conducted experiments.

2.1 Materials

For image acquisition, two GoPro Hero 8 Black cameras [12] were used due to several essential factors. These cameras stood out for their fixed focus, which made them ideal for our purposes. Furthermore, their portability, affordability, and robustness were crucial features that perfectly suited for on-site motion analysis. Notably, these cameras are capable of capturing high-resolution images at a frame rate of up to 240 frames per second. During the recording session, the settings which were selected were 60 frames per second and 720p resolution, see Table 1. To evaluate the proposed approach, the VICON system at the University of Compiègne was employed. This system comprises 37 IR cameras and served as our reference for capturing the ground truth of the tasks performed. To ensure precise and reliable camera calibration, a checkerboard with 45mm×45mm squares was employed. This allowed the estimation of both intrinsic parameters and distortion coefficients. Additionally, a T-shaped Wand served as an efficient tool to estimate the camera pose parameters in the world coordinate system (WCS).

Table 1. Description of the Vicon system setup and the utilized equipment for the proposed approach

	VICON system	Proposed system
Camera count	37 optoelectronic cameras	2 RGB cameras GoPro
Frame rate	100 FPS	60 FPS
Capture volume w × l × h	2.4 m × 3.8 m × 3 m	1.8 m × 2 m × 2 m
Resolution	1280 × 1024	1080 × 720
Calibration tool	T-shaped Wand	Checkerboard + T-shaped Wand

2.2 Workflow of the Motion Capture System

The workflow of our proposed approach consists of four main steps, namely: (i) Camera calibration, (ii) Joints center estimation and ROIs detection, (iii) Triangulation, (iv) and 3D joints' positions refinement/correction. The overall workflow is depicted in Fig. 1. Below, we provide a brief description of each step.

Camera Calibration. To ensure precise and reliable tracking and to optimize the accuracy of all subsequent measurements, we conducted camera calibration process. This involves estimating the intrinsic and extrinsic parameters, and distortion coefficients.

$$intrinsic\ matrix = K = \begin{bmatrix} \alpha_x & s & x_0 \\ 0 & \alpha_y & y_0 \\ 0 & 0 & 1 \end{bmatrix} \tag{1}$$

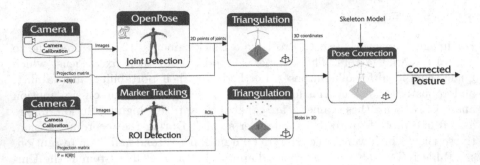

Fig. 1. The workflow of the proposed fusion-based approach including the 4 main steps: camera calibration, detection of joint centroids and ROIs, triangulation and pose correction.

where α_x and α_y represent the focal lengths of the camera in terms of pixel dimensions in the x and y direction, respectively. $(x_0, y_0)^T$ is the principal point's coordinates in terms of pixel dimensions. The parameter s is the skew parameter [14].

$$extrinsic\ matrix = [R|t] \qquad (2)$$

where t represents the coordinates of the camera in the WCS and R is a 3×3 rotation matrix representing the orientation of the camera coordinate system [14].

The calibration was carried out utilizing multiple images of a checkerboard pattern within each camera's field of view. Zhang's method [30] was employed to determine the intrinsic parameters, including focal length, principal point, and image skew, ensuring a robust foundation for camera model. To account for any lens distortion, we utilize Brown's method [9] to estimate distortion coefficients. Additionally, the extrinsic parameters were determined using a calibration wand and applying the Infinitesimal Plane-based Pose Estimation (IPPE) method described in [5].

Joints Center Estimation and ROIs Detection. OpenPose utilizes RGB images to accurately detect and locate anatomical joints in a two-dimensional space. This framework utilizes a sophisticated two-branch multi-stage Convolutional Neural Network (CNN) architecture. The initial stages of the CNN model are dedicated to predicting Part Affinity Fields (PAFs), which encode limb location and orientation represented as precise 2D vector fields. The subsequent stages of the CNN model focus on generating confidence maps for body part locations. These confidence maps serve as a vital component in accurately pinpointing the precise positions of anatomical joints. To extract the 2D positions of anatomical joints, OpenPose employs an inference method that leverages the interplay between the PAFs and confidence maps, enabling the framework to extract precise joint locations. 3D human pose can be estimated via 3D triangulation from multiple views using at least two synchronized and calibrated cameras (see next sub-section for more details).

For ROIs detection, a precise method was applied to distinguish spherical markers from the surrounding scene and to accurately determine their centroid coordinates. This method is based on a color-based segmentation technique that effectively isolates the markers from the background. First, the intensity of the image was normalized, and a Gaussian filter was applied to reduce any noise present. Next, the image was converted from RGB to the HSV color space. A binary image was created using adaptive thresholding techniques that highlights the marker ROIs while suppressing the background. To further refine the binary image, erosion and dilation operations were applied, enhancing the marker shape and structure for more accurate detection. The marker selection process filtered out any potential false positives by identifying markers with circular shapes and a minimum radius. This process was applied to each frame individually, as depicted in Fig. 2. In addition, marker tracking involves both temporal and spatial correspondences, inspired by the work of Guerra-filho et al. [13]. Temporal correspondence involves tracking markers over time within the same camera view, ensuring robustness in tracking within each view. On the other hand, spatial correspondence involves establishing matches between markers from different camera views at the same instant t.

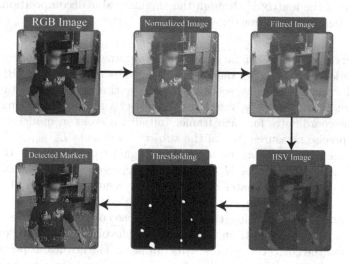

Fig. 2. ROIs detection and tracking process using color-based segmentation and temporal-spatial correspondences

Triangulation. The 3D human pose estimation can be reconstructed from either a monocular image [8] or from multi-view images. Notably, multi-view capture methods have been shown to yield superior accuracy compared to monocular approaches [18]. Triangulation is a fundamental process for determining the 3D coordinates of joints' centroids and ROIs in space based on their 2D projections onto two or more images. The intersection of rays of light passing through the 3D points in space and the camera's centers with two image planes, resulting in 2D image points denoted as $x = (u, v)$ and $x' = (u', v')$. The two rays-back projected from image points x and x' intersect at a point X in the 3D world. The reconstruction of 3D points from multiple perspective views considers the homogeneous coordinates of the observed 2D points and the projection matrices $P = K[R|t]$ (derived from Eqs. 1 and 2) of the respective camera views. The projection equation, expressed as the cross vector product $x \times PX = 0$, allows to derive three equations for each image point. Among these equations, two are linearly independent and can be represented as [14]:

$$u(P_3^T X) - (P_1^T X) = 0$$
$$v(P_3^T X) - (P_2^T X) = 0 \tag{3}$$

The independent equations of all cameras can be written into a homogeneous system as [14]:

$$AX = 0 \tag{4}$$

To obtain an optimal solution for X that satisfies Eq. (4), the linear-Eigen method was employed with the objective of minimizing $\|AX\|$. This involves finding the unit eigenvector corresponding to the smallest eigenvalue of the matrix $A^T A$. The 3D reconstruction of point X can be obtained by extracting it from the last column of the matrix V through the singular value decomposition, denoted as UDV^T, performed on matrix A.

Pose Correction. The primary goal of our approach is to enhance the accuracy of motion capture using data captured by OpenPose and the ROIs detection described in the previous section. To achieve this, a pose correction process was implemented iteratively, refining the subject's pose by adjusting the estimated joint coordinates for each frame. Initially, a skeleton model M was created with precise measurements of the subject's segments $L_{segment}$. The length of each segment $d_{segment}$ was then compared against the target length $L_{segment}$ defined in the skeleton model M. The $d_{segment}$ represents the Euclidean distance between two joints' coordinates of a specific segment, denoted as $j1 = (x, y, z)$ and $j2 = (x', y', z')$. A tolerance threshold ϵt was defined to determine the acceptable error rate for segment length during the pose correction process (Eq. 5). If a segment length deviated from the target, the involved estimated joint j_i was identified and the correction process was initiated. The erroneous position problem was translated into an optimization problem. The pose correction process used optimization techniques to find the optimal coordinates for the joints that required adjustment j_i. The objective function in the optimization method was defined based on the distance between an initial guess and the target length L. Additionally, it calculated the difference between the segment vector and a reference vector. By minimizing Eq. 6, the corrected positions of the joints were obtained.

$$\left| \frac{d_{segment}}{L_{segment}} - 1 \right| <= \epsilon t \tag{5}$$

where $d_{segment}$ represents the Euclidean distance between two joints of a specific segment. $L_{segment}$ represents the target length of the segment defined in the skeletal model M. Threshold ϵt refers to the error threshold or tolerance level used for determining the correctness of segment lengths.

$$\text{minimize} \quad \begin{cases} \left| \sqrt{(x-a)^2 + (x-b)^2 + (z-c)^2} - L_{segment} \right| = 0 \\ \left| \frac{v_r}{\|v_r\|} - \frac{v_s}{\|v_s\|} \right| = 0 \end{cases} \qquad (6)$$

where $(x, y, z)^T$ represents the coordinates of the joint j_i to be corrected or optimized, $(a, b, c)^T$ represents the coordinates of the second joint on the same segment, and $L_{segment}$ represents the target length of the segment. $\|v_s\| = (a - x, b - y, c - z)^T$ is the vector pointing from the joint j_i to the second joint, and $\|v_r\|$ is the reference vector formed by the ROIs that points in the desired direction for the segment.

2.3 Experimental Set-Up

In the present work, we aim to validate the accuracy of the proposed approach through a serie of experiments. The captured pre- and post-rectification data, using OpenPose, were employed to calculate biomechanical variables, and subsequently these results were compared the groundtruth data obtained throught the VICON system. The GoPro cameras were mounted on two-metre-high tripods positioned at the center of the VICON system's field of view (FOV), at a fixed distance of two metres from the subject's performance area. Data were simultaneously collected using both systems and synchronized using a light signal to indicate the start of the recording session. The conducted experiments consisted of two tasks: lifting and leaning. A total of 8 colored spherical markers were placed on ROIs, as depicted in Fig 3. These markers were utilized to identify ROIs and subsequently refine the OpenPose outputs to achieve a more accurate motion capture. During the lifting task, the participants performed an arm elevation task, simulating the action of lifting a box. In the leaning task, the subjects executed a forward movement of the spine, commonly referred to as trunk flexion, starting from a standing position.

3 Results

The results of our experiments reveal the accuracy and reliability of the proposed approach, as validated through a comprehensive analysis and comparison with the data obtained from the commercial VICON system. The proposed approach exhibited a significant improvement in accuracy for segment length measurements, with a maximum root mean square errors of 20.8 mm and 32.7 mm for lifting and leaning tasks respectively (mean absolute errors of 20.1 mm, and 22.5 mm, respectively), as depicted in Fig. 4, and Fig. 5. In contrast, the values obtained from OpenPose prior to employing the proposed approach reached as

444   A. Ben Abdeljelil et al.

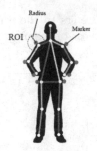

Fig. 3. Colored spherical marker positions for accuracy enhancement.

high as 98.3 mm and 9423 mm for lifting and leaning tasks, respectively (mean absolute error 98.3 mm and 2519 mm), as shown in Table.2 and Table.3. Furthermore, for angle measurements, our proposed approach achieved a RMSE of 3° (MAE of 2.43°) in the leaning tasks, as depicted in Fig. 6 and a RMSE of 3° and 7.61° (MAE of 2.03° and 6.27) for right and left arm elevation task, respectively, as depicted in Fig. 7.

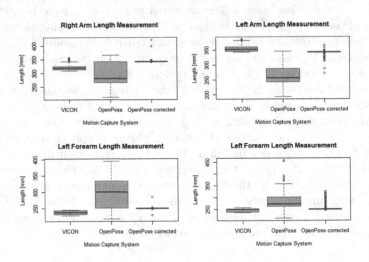

Fig. 4. Lifting Task: Measurements of the length of the left and right arms and forearms before and after pose correction in comparison with the VICON system.

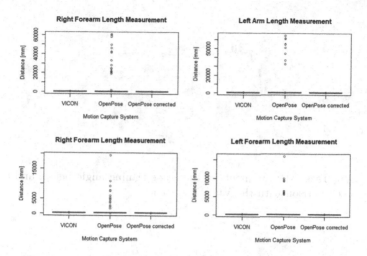

Fig. 5. Leaning Task: Measurements of the length of the left and right arms and forearms before and after pose correction in comparison with the VICON system.

Table 2. Lifting task: the results in comparison of the VICON system in measurement of limbs length. MAE (mean absolute error), SD (standard deviation), and RMSE (root mean square error)

	OpenPose			OpenPose post-correction		
	MAE	SD	RMSE	MAE	SD	RMSE
Right Arm	24.6	35.8	43.4	20.1	9.3	20.8
Left Arm	93.7	29.9	98.3	10.8	9.8	14.6
Right Forearm	62.3	41.4	74.7	12.8	3.53	13.7
Left Forearm	48	48.5	68.2	7.5	6.3	14.8

Table 3. Leaning task: the results in comparison of the VICON system in measurement of limbs length. MAE (mean absolute error), SD (standard deviation), and RMSE (root mean square error)

	OpenPose			OpenPose post-correction		
	MAE	SD	RMSE	MAE	SD	RMSE
Right Arm	2519	9107	9423	22.5	4.06	32.7
Left Arm	4519	5779	6479	12.6	6.25	13.33
Right Forearm	424	1748	1798	4.5	33.3	4.81
Left Forearm	559	1855	1935	6.25	1.83	28.59

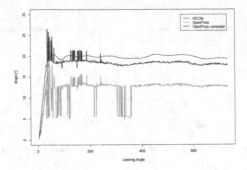

Fig. 6. Leaning Task: Measurements of the angle leaning angle before and after pose correction in comparison with the VICON system.

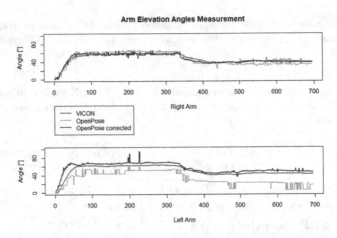

Fig. 7. Lifting Task: Measurements of the angle of the left and right limbs before and after pose correction in comparison with the VICON system.

4   Discussion

In this paper, we proposed a new approach that combines the advantages of marker-based and markerless methods through the integration data obtained using OpenPose and a ROIs detection method. This fusion permit to enhance the accuracy and reliability of markerless motion capture, while offering several notable advantages. The proposed approach involved tracking human body movement using OpenPose and simultaneously tracking colored spherical markers placed on the human body to identify ROIs. Multiple cameras were utilized to achieve 3D reconstruction for even finer precision. Subsequently, the ROIs were employed to refine and correct the 3D joints' positions obtained using Open-Pose. The experimental results demonstrated the effectiveness of this approach in improving the accuracy of MoCap for the previously described tasks.

Markerless MoCap offers the advantage of non-intrusiveness, reducing participant discomfort and enabling natural movement. However, markerless systems have been criticized for their limited accuracy compared to marker-based systems. In our study, we addressed this limitation by leveraging the benefits of both approaches. By integrating the data obtained from OpenPose with the ROIs detection method, we were able to improve the accuracy of motion tracking. This approach eliminates the need for a complex setup, extensive post-processing, or in-depth anatomical knowledge. Additionally, it minimizes the use of markers, in stark contrast to the more extensive marker requirements in commercial marker-based systems. Two experiments targeting the upper limbs were conducted to evaluate the efficacy of the proposed approach, comparing it with the VICON system. The pose correction process based optimization principal helped refine the joint positions and reduce errors, leading to a significant improvement in the accuracy of limb length and angle measurements.

Comparing our approach to previous work, our proposed method yielded promising results. The proposed method accurately measured lengths within a RMSE of less than $32.7mm$ after correction. These results is in line with the findings of Nakano et al. who reported length measurement accuracies of less than 30mm for 80% of cases in their study [21]. Regarding angle measurements, our approach demonstrated considerable success in accurately estimating angles. The proposed method achieved reliable measurements for angles with an RMSE of $7.61°$, compared to the results reported by D'Antonio et al. with an RMSE of $9.9°$. However, it is important to note that while our proposed approach shares similarities with Nakano et al.'s work in length measurement and D'Antonio et al.'s work in angle measurement, there may be differences in the experimental setup, methodology, and data used, which can account for variations in the reported results.

The results obtained using OpenPose pre-correction exhibited a noticeable degree of inaccuracy, particularly evident in the measurement of limb length during the leaning task. This inaccuracy can be primarily attributed to self-occlusion problems that arise when subjects perform more complex movements. Self-occlusion disrupts the accurate estimation of joint positions in two-dimensional space, leading to errors that are subsequently amplified during 3D triangulation reconstruction. It is important to note that these errors have a cumulative effect when considering multiple views, progressively compromising the overall measurement accuracy.

Despite the promising results, our study has several limitations. First, The study was conducted with a small sample of healthy adults performing only two upper limb tasks. Future research should aim to include a larger and more diverse sample, including people with different physical abilities and performing a wider variety of movements and tasks. Second, although our approach demonstrated improvements in accuracy, it still relies on the initial joint positions estimated by OpenPose. Therefore, any errors or limitations in OpenPose's joint estimation could affect the accuracy of our approach. Moreover, our approach requires the use of colored markers, which may not be applicable in all settings and can be affected by environmental factors such as lighting and occlusion. Lastly, it is essential to note that our approach was implemented offline. To fully evaluate its practical applicability, future investigations should assess its real-time processing capabilities. Future research could focus on improving the accuracy of OpenPose or exploring alternative pose estimation methods to further enhance the performance of our approach.

5   Conclusion

This paper presents a new approach that combines the strengths of marker-based and markerless methods to enhance the accuracy and reliability of markerless MoCap. This fusion aim to bridge the gap between marker-based precision and markerless MoCap's flexibility, offering a non-intrusive solution for natural movement analysis. The study significantly improving MoCap accuracy for length and angle measurements, achieving RMSE of under 32.7mm and 7.61° after correction. These findings have broader implications, especially for on-site ergonomic assessments. Moreover, this approach is not restricted to OpenPose but is adaptable to similar pose estimation methods, such as MediaPipe, further extending its relevance to a broader scientific audience.

Acknowledgment. This work was financially supported by the "PHC Utique" program of the French Ministry of Foreign Affairs and Ministry of higher education, research, and innovation and the Tunisian Ministry of higher education and scientific research in the CMCU project number 23G1403.

References

1. Aurand, A.M., Dufour, J.S., Marras, W.S.: Accuracy map of an optical motion capture system with 42 or 21 cameras in a large measurement volume. J. Biomech. **58**, 237–240 (2017)
2. Bregler, C.: Motion capture technology for entertainment [In the spotlight]. IEEE Signal Process. Mag. **24**(6), 160–158 (2007)
3. Cao, Z., Hidalgo, G., Simon, T., Wei, S.E., Sheikh, Y.: OpenPose: realtime multiperson 2D pose estimation using part affinity fields. IEEE Trans. Pattern Anal. Mach. Intell. **43**(1), 172–186 (2021)
4. Clark, R.A., Mentiplay, B.F., Hough, E., Pua, Y.H.: Three-dimensional cameras and skeleton pose tracking for physical function assessment: a review of uses, validity, current developments and Kinect alternatives. Gait Posture **68**, 193–200 (2019)
5. Collins, T., Bartoli, A.: Infinitesimal plane-based pose estimation. Int. J. Comput. Vis. **109**(3), 252–286 (2014)
6. Colyer, S.L., Evans, M., Cosker, D.P., Salo, A.I.: A review of the evolution of vision-based motion analysis and the integration of advanced computer vision methods towards developing a markerless system. Sports Med.-Open **4**(1), 1–15 (2018)

7. D'Antonio, E., Taborri, J., Palermo, E., Rossi, S., Patane, F.: A markerless system for gait analysis based on OpenPose library. In: 2020 IEEE International Instrumentation and Measurement Technology Conference (I2MTC), pp. 1–6. Institute of Electrical and Electronics Engineers Inc. (2020)
8. Desmarais, Y., Mottet, D., Slangen, P., Montesinos, P.: A review of 3D human pose estimation algorithms for markerless motion capture. Comput. Vis. Image Underst. **212**(2016), 1–49 (2021)
9. Duane, C.: Brown: close-range camera calibration. Eng. Remote Sens. **37**(8), 855–866 (1971)
10. Field, M., Pan, Z., Stirling, D., Naghdy, F.: Human motion capture sensors and analysis in robotics. Ind. Robot: Int. J. **38**(2), 163–171 (2011)
11. Gong, W., et al.: Human pose estimation from monocular images: a comprehensive survey. Sensors **16**(12), 1966 (2016)
12. GoPro: world's most versatile action cameras. https://gopro.com/. Accessed 01 May 2023
13. Guerra-Filho, G.: Optical motion capture: theory and implementation. RITA **12**(2), 61–89 (2005)
14. Hartley, R., Zisserman, A.: Multiple View Geometry in Computer Vision. Cambridge University Press, Cambridge (2003)
15. Kim, W., Sung, J., Saakes, D., Huang, C., Xiong, S.: Ergonomic postural assessment using a new open-source human pose estimation technology (openpose). Int. J. Ind. Ergon. **84**, 103164 (2021)
16. van der Kruk, E., Reijne, M.M.: Accuracy of human motion capture systems for sport applications; state-of-the-art review. Eur. J. Sport Sci. **18**(6), 806–819 (2018)
17. Lugaresi, C., et al.: MediaPipe: a framework for building perception pipelines. arXiv preprint arXiv:1906.08172 (2019)
18. Mehta, D., et al.: XNect: real-time multi-person 3D human pose estimation with a single RGB camera. arXiv preprint arXiv:1907.00837 (2019)
19. Menolotto, M., Komaris, D.S., Tedesco, S., O'flynn, B., Walsh, M.: Motion capture technology in industrial applications: a systematic review. Sensors **20**(19), 5687 (2020)
20. Moeslund, T.B., Hilton, A., Krüger, V.: A survey of advances in vision-based human motion capture and analysis. Comput. Vis. Image Underst. **104**(2–3), 90–126 (2006)
21. Nakano, N., et al.: Evaluation of 3D markerless motion capture accuracy using OpenPose with multiple video cameras. Front. Sports Active Living **2**, 50 (2020)
22. Patrizi, A., Pennestrì, E., Valentini, P.P.: Comparison between low-cost markerless and high-end marker-based motion capture systems for the computer-aided assessment of working ergonomics. Ergonomics **59**(1), 155–162 (2016)
23. Sandau, M., Koblauch, H., Moeslund, T.B., Aanæs, H., Alkjær, T., Simonsen, E.B.: Markerless motion capture can provide reliable 3D gait kinematics in the sagittal and frontal plane. Med. Eng. Phys. **36**(9), 1168–1175 (2014)
24. Sharma, S., Verma, S., Kumar, M., Sharma, L.: Use of motion capture in 3D animation: motion capture systems, challenges, and recent trends. In: 2019 International Conference on Machine Learning, Big Data, Cloud and Parallel Computing (comitcon), pp. 289–294. IEEE (2019)
25. Valevicius, A.M., Jun, P.Y., Hebert, J.S., Vette, A.H.: Use of optical motion capture for the analysis of normative upper body kinematics during functional upper limb tasks: a systematic review. J. Electromyogr. Kinesiol. **40**, 1–15 (2018)

26. Van Hooren, B., Pecasse, N., Meijer, K., Essers, J.M.N.: The accuracy of markerless motion capture combined with computer vision techniques for measuring running kinematics. Scandinavian J. Med. Sci. Sports **33**(6), 966–978 (2023)

27. Wade, L., Needham, L., McGuigan, P., Bilzon, J.: Applications and limitations of current markerless motion capture methods for clinical gait biomechanics. PeerJ **10**, e12995 (2022)

28. Yang, S.X., et al.: Markerless motion capture systems for tracking of persons in forensic biomechanics: an overview. Comput. Methods Biomech. Biomed. Eng.: Imaging Vis. **2**(1), 46–65 (2014)

29. Zago, M., Luzzago, M., Marangoni, T., De Cecco, M., Tarabini, M., Galli, M.: 3D tracking of human motion using visual skeletonization and stereoscopic vision. Front. Bioeng. Biotechnol. **8**, 181 (2020)

30. Zhang, Z.: A flexible new technique for camera calibration. IEEE Trans. Pattern Anal. Mach. Intell. **22**(11), 1330–1334 (2000)

31. Zheng, C., et al.: Deep learning-based human pose estimation: a survey. ACM Comput. Surv. **56**(1), 1–37 (2023)

Using an Optimal then Enhanced YOLO Model for Multi-Lingual Scene Text Detection Containing the Arabic Scripts

Houssem Turki[1], Mohamed Elleuch[2]([⊠]), and Monji Kherallah[3]

[1] National Engineering School of Sfax (ENIS), University of Sfax, Sfax, Tunisia
[2] National School of Computer Science (ENSI), University of Manouba, Manouba, Tunisia
elleuch.mohameds@gmail.com
[3] Faculty of Sciences, University of Sfax, Sfax, Tunisia
monji.kherallah@fss.usf.tn

Abstract. In recent years, significant advancements have been made in deep learning and the recognition of text in images of natural scenes, thanks to the advancements in machine learning and artificial intelligence. The limited availability of diverse datasets containing multiple languages and scripts often restricts the effectiveness of deep learning and text detection in the wild, particularly when it comes to Arabic language as an additional challenge. Despite notable progress, this scarcity remains a constraint. The deep learning neural network known as YOLO (You Only Look Once) has become widely popular due to its versatility in addressing a wide range of machine learning tasks, particularly in the domain of computer vision. The YOLO algorithm has gained increasing acknowledgment for its outstanding ability to tackle complex problems in conjunction with complex backgrounds of an image captured from nature, handle noisy data, and overcome various challenges encountered in real-world situations. Our experiments offer a succinct analysis of text detection algorithms that rely on convolutional neural networks (CNNs); In particular, we focus on various iterations of the YOLO models, employing same specific data augmentation techniques on both SYPHAX dataset and ICDAR MLT-2019 dataset, which comprise Arabic scripts in real natural scene images. The aim of this article is to identify the most effective YOLO algorithm for detecting text containing the Arabic scripts in the wild then to enhance this optimal model obtained in addition to explore potential research avenues that can enhance the capabilities of the most robust architecture in this field.

Keywords: Scene text detection · Multi-lingual and Arabic script · YOLO · Optimal model · enhanced architecture · Deep Learning · Computer Vision

1 Introduction

Within the field of computer vision, text detection plays a crucial role, and it is essential to employ diverse machine learning and deep learning models to enhance the efficiency of text detection and related tasks. The task of real-time text detection in the wild introduces several challenges, including the presence of mixed languages, intricate character designs, and a wide range of degradations (such as size, shape, orientation, noise, blur, etc.) within images of natural scenes. These challenges are particularly prominent when dealing with multilingual scripts that include the Arabic language [1, 2]. The challenges mentioned earlier and focusing on Arabic scripts are inherent only in the two datasets: "SYPHAX dataset" [3] and ICDAR MLT-2019 dataset [4], as depicted in Fig. 1. We will extensively leverage these datasets in the experimental section of our study. Moreover, the identification of text within images of natural scenes has become a vital component across various applications, spanning diverse domains such as multilingual text conversion, geo-location, efficient data search, road safety for navigation, and autonomous driving systems for vehicles, among others. Among the numerous algorithms used for object and text detection, the YOLO framework has garnered significant attention [5] due to its notable attributes of high speed, accuracy, and precise recognition of objects within images of natural scenes. Over the course of its evolution in the field of text detection, the YOLO algorithm family has undergone several improvements, with each enhancement of a version it tries to overcome the limitations and achieve improved performance to meet the challenge of localizing scripts in the wild. This progression varies from YOLOv5 to YOLOv7, as the timeline is depicted in Fig. 2. This motivation drives us to employ the choice of the three successive versions of YOLO and to evaluate their detection performance of these diverse neural network architectures when applied to text detection in the wild, utilizing the "SYPHAX dataset" [3] and ICDAR MLT-2019 dataset [4].

Our selection of the three YOLO models is based on their status as state-of-the-art approaches and the promising outcomes they have demonstrated. In this study, we make three key contributions:

To begin with, our first contribution entails the introduction of a novel publicly available dataset from Tunisia [3], which comprises images of natural scenes containing Arabic-Latin scripts. Secondly, we contribute by selecting and implementing specific data augmentation techniques that are specifically tailored for natural scenes images designed for images in the wild containing text and taking into account to preserve the particular details related to the properties of Arabic scripts such as punctuation marks, multi-level baselines, intersection letters, Skewness letters, intra-word space, inter word and line spaces, etc. (see Fig. 3). Lastly, we will perform a comprehensive comparative analysis of the key results obtained by applying different YOLO models and to improve the effective algorithm obtained.

The paper is organized into four sections, which are outlined as follows. Section 2 offers an overview of various related works and their methodologies, emphasizing the commonly utilized techniques. Section 3 introduces the methodology and presents the experimental evaluation. Finally, Sect. 4 provides the conclusion for the paper.

(a)   images from SYPHAX dataset

(b)   images from MLT-2019 dataset

Fig. 1. Samples of images from SYPHAX dataset [3] and MLT-2019 dataset [4] containing the Arabic script

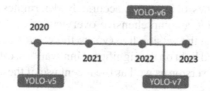

Fig. 2. The YOLO timeline of its three versions

(a) punctuation marks   (b) multi-level baselines   (c) intersection letters

(d) Skewness letters   (e) intra-word space   (f) inter word and line spaces

Fig. 3. Samples of Arabic scripts properties from SYPHAX dataset (top row) and MLT-2019 dataset (down row)

2 Related Work

Numerous applications leverage the capabilities of deep learning and computer vision algorithms to optimize the learning process in text detection [6]. Object detection encompasses the task of identifying specific objects within images, videos, or real-time applications. This includes the detection of text scripts within the wild [7]. YOLO has emerged as a widely adopted technology for various object and text detection applications [8]. By dividing the input image into a grid, YOLO simplifies the detection process by enabling the prediction of bounding boxes and class probabilities for each grid cell. This approach facilitates fast and efficient object detection. Due to its simple architecture, low complexity, ease of implementation, and speed, YOLO has become one of the most widely utilized models for object detection [9]. The overall structure of YOLO consists of three main parts: the Backbone, Neck, and a prediction Head for generating dense predictions (refer to Fig. 4). The pre-trained network known as the backbone is employed to extract comprehensive feature representations from images. This process aids in decreasing the image's spatial resolution while enhancing its feature (channel) resolution. The neck component of the model is utilized to extract feature pyramids, which enhances the model's ability to generalize effectively to objects of various sizes and scales. The model's head is employed for the concluding stage tasks. It places anchor boxes on feature maps and produces the ultimate output, encompassing classes, objectness scores, and bounding boxes.

The acronym YOLO, representing "You Only Look Once," signifies the ability to perform the detection task in a single network pass. Through a single examination of the image, a convolutional neural network predicts the bounding boxes and their respective positions. By utilizing the information encapsulated within the bounding boxes, this algorithm adeptly identifies objects and accurately determines their spatial locations [10]. Our aim is to provide a comprehensive overview of the evolution of the YOLO framework, spanning from the version five (v5) to the version seven (v7) (see Table. 1). This review intends to shed light on the significant innovations, differences, and enhancements introduced in each version as well as the recent use of these three versions for text detection in natural scenes.

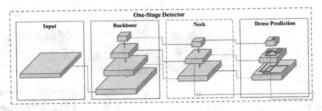

Fig. 4. Stage Detector Architecture of YOLO [11]

2.1 The Development of the YOLO Framework from v5 to v7

- YOLOv5: Shortly after the release of YOLO v4 in 2020, Glenn Jocher introduced this version, known as YOLOv5 [12]. YOLOv5 is an open-source solution that is simple to implement. It offers five different scaled versions, allowing for flexibility in adjusting the model size and applying data enhancement techniques. The architecture of YOLOv5 is trained and evaluated using the MS COCO dataset [12, 13]. The YOLOv5 is used and enhanced in [14–16].
- YOLOv6: The Meituan Vision AI Department released this version on ArXiv in September 2022 [17]. Similar to YOLOv5, it includes various models of different

sizes designed for industrial applications. However, in contrast to its predecessors, YOLOv6 adopts an anchor-free detector approach, aligning with the anchor point-based method trend [18]. The architecture of YOLOv6 is trained and evaluated using the MS COCO dataset [13]. The YOLOv6 is used and enhanced in [19, 20].

- YOLOv7: In July 2022, the publication of YOLOv7 took place on ArXiv [21]. Unlike previous versions, YOLOv7 was exclusively trained on the MS COCO dataset [13], without utilizing pre-trained backbones. This iteration introduced several architectural modifications and incorporated a series of bag-of-freebies (BoF) techniques. These enhancements resulted in improved accuracy without sacrificing inference speed or significantly increasing training time. The YOLOv7 is used and enhanced in [22, 23].

Table 1. Summary of the three YOLO architectures

YOLO version	Date	Anchor	Framework	Backbone
YOLO v5	2020	Yes	Pytorch	Modified CSP v7
YOLO v6	2022	No	Pytorch	EfficientRep
YOLO v7	2022	No	Pytorch	RepConvN

2.2 Datasets Used for Natural Scene Text Detection

Numerous datasets comprising natural scene images are widely utilized in computer vision and image processing research. These datasets encompass images acquired from diverse environments. Here are some popular databases of natural scene images:

- COCO-text [24]: This dataset, created in 2016, is widely acknowledged as one of the largest and most comprehensive collections for text detection. It consists of more than 63000 images and includes approximately 173000 labeled text regions, encompassing a wide range of text orientations.
- ICDAR 2015 [25]: The Incidental Scene Text dataset primarily concentrates on Latin-scripted text. It comprises a collection of 1670 images, encompassing a total of 17548 annotated regions.
- RRC-MLT datasets [4]: These datasets are included as components of the ICDAR 2017 and ICDAR 2019 Robust Reading Challenge, with a specific emphasis on multi-lingual scene text detection and script identification. The images of ICDAR MLT-2019 Dataset of Real Images are natural scene images with embedded text, such as street signs, street advertisement boards, shops names, passing vehicles and users photos in microblogs. This dataset is comprised of 20000 images containing text of 10 different languages (2000 images per language). Most images contain text of more than one language, but each language is represented in at least 2000 images. The ten languages are: Arabic, Bangla, Chinese, Devanagari, English, French, German, Italian, Japanese and Korean.

- SYPHAX dataset [3]: This dataset was gathered in the city of "Sfax" located in Tunisia, which is the second-largest city in the country after the capital. It comprises a total of 2008 images, with 80% of the dataset (1607 images) allocated for training purposes, and the remaining 20% (401 images) dedicated to testing. The dataset comprises 16 different folds, covering a distance of approximately 365 km. The images in the dataset primarily consist of text, encompassing both Arabic and Latin scripts.
- ARASTI [26]: The dataset comprises a collection of 374 Arabic scene text images that were captured in real-life scenarios, without specific consideration of environmental conditions. Moreover, it includes an Arabic word image dataset that contains 1280 cropped word images extracted from scene texts.

These datasets offer labeled images that serve as valuable resources for researchers and developers to train and assess algorithms pertaining to scene text detection and related tasks. However, there are only a limited number of databases in the field that support multiple languages and specifically contain Arabic scripts. Furthermore, as the YOLO framework continues to progress, most researchers primarily concentrate on the concept of "object detection" and not "text detection". In light of this, we made the decision to take on the new challenge and apply YOLO using two datasets: SYPHAX dataset [3], which presents a novel challenge of multilingual text detection, including 100% of total images with Arabic scripts Furthermore, the ICDAR MLT-2019 dataset [4] incorporates Arabic scripts in 10% of the total images.

2.3 YOLO Applications in Various Domains of Text Detection

The YOLO algorithm, renowned for object detection, has extensive applications across a wide range of domains, including text detection. Utilizing YOLO for text detection entails training the algorithm to identify and locate text regions within an image. Here are a few examples of applications where YOLO is applied for text detection tasks in various fields:

- Text Detection in the wild: YOLO has the capability to be used for detecting text in images of natural scenes [10]. This application is particularly valuable in fields like autonomous driving, where the identification and recognition of text on road signs, billboards, and traffic signs are crucial for navigation and decision-making processes.
- Video Surveillance: YOLO can be utilized within video surveillance systems to achieve real-time text detection [27]. This application proves beneficial in identifying text within surveillance videos, including tasks like license plate detection [28], vehicle identification numbers, traffic sign recognition [29], or text present on suspicious objects. By facilitating security and forensic analysis, YOLO contributes to enhancing overall surveillance capabilities.
- Augmented Reality (AR): YOLO can be utilized for text detection in augmented reality (AR) applications [30]. It can accurately identify text in real-time captured frames, enabling seamless integration of virtual content with the detected text regions. This capability proves valuable for various applications, including text translation, information overlay, and interactive experiences, enhancing the interactive experiences.

- Document Analysis: YOLO can be employed for document analysis tasks [31], which involve extracting text from scanned documents, forms, or invoices. By training YOLO using annotated document images, the algorithm becomes capable of identifying and localizing text regions within the document. This facilitates automated text extraction and analysis, streamlining document processing workflows.

Through the utilization of appropriately annotated datasets specifically for text detection, YOLO can by training to proficiently localize and identify text regions within images or videos. This capability paves the way for automating text-related tasks across diverse domains, presenting a wide range of possibilities for efficient text processing.

3 Methodology

This research consists of several experiments aimed at developing an optimal version of YOLO for the best text detection in images of natural scenes containing the Arabic scripts. The study is based on the latest advancements in the field and using SYPHAX dataset [3] and ICDAR MLT-2019 Dataset of Real Images [4]. In the first step, after the application of the specific data augmentation techniques on the two datasets, different versions of the YOLO models, ranging from version 5 to version 7 were subjected to experimentation. In the second step, we will improve the architecture of the optimal version of YOLO detected. This improvement certainly depends on the version selected and the new experimentation tests will be explored again.

3.1 A Specific Data Augmentation Techniques

Employing best data augmentation techniques can be beneficial when training YOLO-based models for text detection in the wild. These techniques enhance the diversity and volume of training data, improving the models' ability to adapt to real-world scenarios. The selection of an appropriate augmentation technique is crucial as it should closely resemble the characteristics of the actual images found in nature and aligns with the properties of the chosen dataset. By applying text detection approaches in this manner, effective results can be achieved. We have selected four data augmentation techniques (see Fig. 5) that involve fundamental image manipulations [32]:

- We opted for geometric transformations using rigid transformations [33] to generate two additional skew angles that closely resemble challenging camera shooting positions, one to the right and one to the left.
- We incorporated a horizontal directional blur effect that simulates the capture of moving images from a camera.
- We employed color space transformations using white balance adjustments. This technique enabled us to generate two different variations in color temperature and brightness, representing distinct times of the day.
- Noise injection drawn from a Gaussian distribution with 20% augmentation of the contrast, Histogram equalization and the Sharpen.

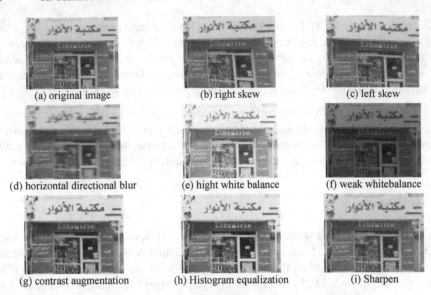

(a) original image   (b) right skew   (c) left skew

(d) horizontal directional blur   (e) hight white balance   (f) weak whitebalance

(g) contrast augmentation   (h) Histogram equalization   (i) Sharpen

Fig. 5. Samples of the specific data augmentation techniques

3.2 Experiments and Results

It is important to emphasize that the performance of text detection algorithms utilizing YOLO can vary depending on the specific version employed, the characteristics of the dataset used, and the training methodology applied. Therefore, in our work, the reported precision, recall, and F-scores differ based on the various architectures of YOLO, the presence of multilingual text containing the Arabic script, and the employed of specific data augmentation techniques. The evaluation metrics are the precision, recall and F-score defined as:

$$Precision = \frac{\sum_i^N \sum_j^{|D^i|} M_D(D_j^i, G^i)}{\sum_i^N |D^i|} \tag{1}$$

$$Recall = \frac{\sum_i^N \sum_j^{|G^i|} M_G(G_j^i, D^i)}{\sum_i^N |G^i|} \tag{2}$$

$$F - score = 2 \times \frac{Precision \times Recall}{Precision + Recall} \tag{3}$$

N represents the complete count of images within a given dataset. $|D^i|$ and $|G^i|$ are the number of detection and ground true rectangles in i^{th} image. $M_D(D_j^i, G^i)$ and $M_G(G_j^i, D^i)$ are the matching scores for detection rectangles D^i and ground true rectangle G^i.

In Table 2 and Table 3 we can note that the YOLOv5 obtains the better result of Precision (74.5%), Recall (68.4%) and F-score (71.3) with SYPHAX dataset also the better result of Precision (70.1%), Recall (62.2%) and F-score (65.9%) with ICDAR

MLT-2019. The YOLOv5 is the optimal model for the two datasets and it is the best for SYPHAX dataset which contains more homogeneous data from the point of view of limiting the number of languages and close characteristics of scripts which was more suitable with the architecture of YOLOv5. We notice that the values of the metrics are not growing following the succession of YOLO versions. Finally, the results of YOLOv5 are encouraging but they need more improvements, which will be achieved in the next step by adding a reinforcement module "The Attention Mechanism".

Table 2. Experimental result on the SYPHAX Dataset

YOLO version	Precision (%)	Recall (%)	F score (%)
YOLOv5	**74.5**	**68.4**	**71.3**
YOLOv6	68.6	62	65.1
YOLOv7	70.2	66	68

Table 3. Experimental result on the ICDAR MLT-2019 Dataset

YOLO version	Precision (%)	Recall (%)	F score (%)
YOLOv5	**70.1**	**62.2**	**65.9**
YOLOv6	61.3	55.4	58.2
YOLOv7	63.5	60.3	61.9

3.3 Enhancement of the Optimal YOLO Model

The YOLOv5 model comprises three main components: a backbone section responsible for extracting features, a neck section for combining these features, and an output section dedicated to text detection. The backbone utilizes a convolutional neural network to derive feature maps of varying scales from the input image through a series of convolution and pooling operations [34]. The backbone network produces four tiers of feature maps with dimensions of: 152×152 pixels, 76×76 pixels, 38×38 pixels, and 19×19 pixels. Using these feature maps of various sizes, the neck section blends the feature maps from different tiers to capture enhanced contextual details and minimize the loss of information. The attention mechanism aims to extract more crucial information by concentrating on significant areas within the input image. In the wild, various implementations of the attention mechanism are utilized across diverse applications. We opt for ECA-Net [35], which is a potent channel attention mechanism capable of capturing cross-channel interactions – that is, the interdependence among channels – leading to a substantial enhancement in performance. Following global average pooling at the channel level without reducing dimensions, ECA-Net captures local interplay among channels by examining each channel alongside its K neighboring channels. For the purpose of identifying multi-scale and small text within images, we enhance the YOLOv5 detection approach by incorporating the attention mechanism ECA-Net [35]. This adaptation aligns more effectively with the characteristics of Arabic scripts, leading to a reduction in model complexity, efficient handling of varying-weighted output feature channels, and successful extraction of real image features. In Table 4 we can see that the final results are improved and still remain encouraging (Fig. 6).

Table 4. Final experimental result using an enhanced YOLOv5

Dataset	Precision (%)	Recall (%)	F score (%)
SYPHAX	**79**	**72.5**	**75.6**
MLT-2019	73	63.3	67.8

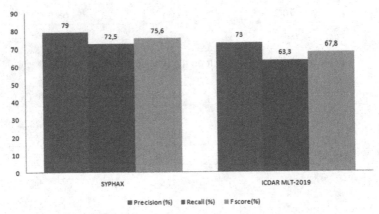

Fig. 6. Metrics of the final experimental results

3.4   Discussion

YOLOv5 has systematically explored various aspects of the algorithm and especially improving and supporting it with attention mechanism, in our work it achieving encouraging detection performance applied to two datasets containing essentially two challenges of images in natural scenes and containing Arabic scripts (Fig. 7). We notice that YOLOv5 offers flexibility in model selection, with its smaller models delivering impressive results. While the overall network architecture of YOLOv5 shares similarities, it also emphasizes the detection of text across different scales, accommodating text of varying sizes. On the other hand YOLOv6, known employs higher levels of parallelism compared to the backbone of YOLOv5, in our case these results are less than the previous version. YOLOv7 use a new classification with fewer losses and obtains encouraging results and reduces the number of box predictions but remains slightly less efficient than version 5.

(a) Successful text detection samples using the enhanced YOLOv5 from SYPHAX dataset (top row) and ICDAR MLT-2019 (down row)

(b) Failed text detection samples using the enhanced YOLOv5 from SYPHAX dataset (right) and ICDAR MLT-2019 (left)

Fig. 7. Text detection samples based on the enhanced YOLOv5

4 Conclusion

This paper offers a succinct summary of the structure and applications of three different YOLO models from version 5 to version 7, emphasizing their utilization in text detection containing the Arabic script from natural scenes images. Furthermore, it places greater emphasis on comparative implementations, specifically exploring text detection using different iterations of YOLO frameworks on multilingual scripts, with a particular focus on the Arabic language within the SYPHAX dataset and ICDAR MLT-2019 dataset. The results indicate that an optimal outcome is achieved with the version 5. Then we made an improvement on the YOLOv5 version by adding the attention mechanism, encouraging results are also achieved.

The YOLO family of algorithms has the potential to evolve further by incorporating targeted improvements for enhancing text detection capabilities. This could entail adjustments to the network architecture, refining training strategies, or integrating novel techniques to address text-specific challenges. Given their relatively recent emergence, the YOLO models still hold substantial promise for future research and exploration. However, they currently face certain limitations; particularly when it comes to the challenges associated with text detection in the wild with multilingual scripts, in comparison to their application in general with the object detection tasks. Subsequent research endeavors can further refine the top-performing architectures for text detection and strive to enhance the overall performance of text detection algorithms especially for the Arabic language, thereby addressing a wide array of challenges more effectively.

References

1. Bai, X., Yang, M., Lyu, P., Xu, Y., Luo, J.: Integrating scene text and visual appearance for fine-grained image classification. IEEE Access **6**, 66322–66335 (2018)
2. Abdelaziz, I., Abdou, S., Al-Barhamtoshy, H.: A large vocabulary system for Arabic online handwriting recognition. Pattern Anal. Appl. **19**, 1129–1141 (2016)
3. Turki, H., Elleuch, M., Kherallah, M.: SYPHAX Dataset. IEEE Dataport (2023). https://doi.org/10.21227/ydqd-2443
4. Nayef, N., et al.: ICDAR2019 robust reading challenge on multi-lingual scene text detection and recognition—RRC-MLT-2019. In: 2019 International Conference on Document Analysis and Recognition (ICDAR), pp. 1582–1587. IEEE (2019)
5. Sultana, F., Sufian, A., Dutta, P.: A review of object detection models based on convolutional neural network. Intell. Comput.: Image Proc. Based Appl., 1–16 (2020)
6. Turki, H., Halima, M.B., Alimi, A.M.: Text detection based on MSER and CNN features. In: 2017 14th IAPR International Conference on Document Analysis and Recognition (ICDAR), vol. 1, pp. 949–954. IEEE (2017)
7. Amrouche, A., Bentrcia, Y., Hezil, N., Abed, A., Boubakeur, K.N., Ghribi, K.: Detection and localization of Arabic text in natural scene images. In: 2022 First International Conference on Computer Communications and Intelligent Systems (I3CIS), pp. 72–76. IEEE (2022)
8. Redmon, J., Divvala, S., Girshick, R., Farhadi, A.: You only look once: unified, real-time object detection. In: Proceedings of the IEEE Conference on Computer Vision and Pattern Recognition, pp. 779–788 (2016)
9. Ravi, N., El-Sharkawy, M.: Real-time embedded implementation of improved object detector for resource-constrained devices. J. Low Power Electron. Appl. **12**(2), 21 (2022)
10. Diwan, T., Anirudh, G., Tembhurne, J.V.: Object detection using YOLO: challenges, architectural successors, datasets and applications. Multimedia Tools Appl. **82**(6), 9243–9275 (2023)
11. Bochkovskiy, A., Wang, C.Y., Liao, H.Y.M.: Yolov4: optimal speed and accuracy of object detection. arXiv preprint: arXiv:2004.10934 (2020)
12. Jocher, G., Nishimura, K., Mineeva, T., Vilarino, R.: Yolov5 by ultralytics. Disponível em: https://github.com/ultralytics/yolov5 (2020)
13. Redmon, J., Farhadi, A.: Yolov3: an incremental improvement. arXiv preprint: arXiv:1804.02767 (2018)
14. Latha, R.S., et al.: Text detection and language identification in natural scene images using YOLOv5. In: 2023 International Conference on Computer Communication and Informatics (ICCCI), pp. 1–7. IEEE (2023)

15. Xu, Q., Zheng, G., Ren, W., Li, X., Yang, Z., Huang, Z.: An efficient and effective text spotter for characters in natural scene images based on an improved YOLOv5 model. In: International Conference on Artificial Intelligence, Virtual Reality, and Visualization (AIVRV 2022), vol. 12588, pp. 64–68. SPIE (2023)
16. Luo, Y., Zhao, C., Zhang, F.: Research on scene text detection algorithm based on modified YOLOv5. In: International Conference on Mechatronics Engineering and Artificial Intelligence (MEAI 2022), vol. 12596, pp. 620–626. SPIE (2023)
17. Li, C., et al.: YOLOv6: a single-stage object detection framework for industrial applications. arXiv preprint: arXiv:2209.02976 (2022)
18. Ge, Z., Liu, S., Wang, F., Li, Z., Sun, J.: Yolox: exceeding YOLO series in 2021. arXiv preprint: arXiv:2107.08430 (2021)
19. Norkobil Saydirasulovich, S., Abdusalomov, A., Jamil, M.K., Nasimov, R., Kozhamzharova, D., Cho, Y.I.: A YOLOv6-based improved fire detection approach for smart city environments. Sensors **23**(6), 3161 (2023)
20. Gupta, C., Gill, N.S., Gulia, P., Chatterjee, J.M.: A novel finetuned YOLOv6 transfer learning model for real-time object detection. J. Real-Time Image Proc. **20**(3), 42 (2023)
21. Wang, C.Y., Bochkovskiy, A., Liao, H.Y.M.: YOLOv7: trainable bag-of-freebies sets new state-of-the-art for real-time object detectors. In: Proceedings of the IEEE/CVF Conference on Computer Vision and Pattern Recognition, pp. 7464–7475 (2023)
22. Negi, A., Kesarwani, Y., Saranya, P.: Text Based Traffic Signboard Detection Using YOLO v7 Architecture. In: Singh, M., Tyagi, V., Gupta, P., Flusser, J., Ören, T. (eds.) Advances in Computing and Data Sciences. Communications in Computer and Information Science, vol. 1848, pp. 1–11. Springer, Cham (2023). https://doi.org/10.1007/978-3-031-37940-6_1
23. Moussaoui, H., El Akkad, N., Benslimane, M.: Arabic and Latin license plate detection and recognition based on YOLOv7 and image processing methods (2023)
24. Veit, A., Matera, T., Neumann, L., Matas, J., Belongie, S.: Coco-text: dataset and benchmark for text detection and recognition in natural images. arXiv preprint: arXiv:1601.07140 (2016)
25. Karatzas, D., et al.: ICDAR 2015 competition on robust reading. In: 2015 13th International Conference on Document Analysis and Recognition (ICDAR), pp. 1156–1160. IEEE (2015)
26. Tounsi, M., Moalla, I., Alimi, A.M.: ARASTI: a database for Arabic scene text recognition. In: 2017 1st International Workshop on Arabic Script Analysis and Recognition (ASAR), pp. 140–144. IEEE (2017)
27. Ashraf, A.H., et al.: Weapons detection for security and video surveillance using CNN and YOLO-v5s. CMC-Comput. Mater. Contin **70**, 2761–2775 (2022)
28. Chen, R.C.: Automatic License Plate Recognition via sliding-window darknet-YOLO deep learning. Image Vis. Comput. **87**, 47–56 (2019)
29. Dewi, C., Chen, R.C., Jiang, X., Yu, H.: Deep convolutional neural network for enhancing traffic sign recognition developed on YOLO v4. Multimedia Tools Appl. **81**(26), 37821–37845 (2022)
30. Zhang, L., Xu, F., Liu, Y., Zhang, D., Gui, L., Zuo, D.: A posture detection method for augmented reality–aided assembly based on YOLO-6D. Int. J. Adv. Manufact. Technol. **125**(7–8), 3385–3399 (2023)
31. Zhang, D., Mao, R., Guo, R., Jiang, Y., Zhu, J.: YOLO-table: disclosure document table detection with involution. Int. J. Doc. Anal. Recogn. (IJDAR) **26**(1), 1–14 (2023)
32. Shorten, C., Khoshgoftaar, T.M.: A survey on image data augmentation for deep learning. J. Big Data **6**(1), 1–48 (2019)
33. Schaefer, S., McPhail, T., Warren, J.: Image deformation using moving least squares. In: ACM SIGGRAPH 2006 Papers, pp. 533–540 (2006)

34. Zeiler, M.D., Taylor, G.W., Fergus, R.: Adaptive deconvolutional networks for mid and high level feature learning. In: Proceedings of the 2011 International Conference on Computer Vision, Barcelona, Spain, 6–13 November 2011, pp. 2018–2025 (2011)
35. Wang, Q., Wu, B., Zhu, P., Li, P., Zuo, W., Hu, Q.: ECA-Net: efficient channel attention for deep convolutional neural networks. In: Proceedings of the Conference on Computer Vision and Pattern Recognition (CVPR), Seattle, WA, USA, 14 June 2020 (2020)

Author Index

Printed in the United States
by Baker & Taylor Publisher Services